A History Of Texas And Texans

A HISTORY

OF

TEXAS and TEXANS

BY

FRANK W. JOHNSON

A LEADER IN THE TEXAS REVOLUTION

Edited and Brought to Date by

EUGENE C. BARKER, Ph. D.

PROFESSOR OF AMERICAN HISTORY

THE UNIVERSITY OF TEXAS

With the Assistance of

ERNEST WILLIAM WINKLER, M. A.

TEXAS STATE LIBRARIAN

To which are added Historical, Statistical and Descriptive Matter pertaining to the important Local Divisions of the State, and biographical accounts of the Leaders and Representative Men of the State in Commerce, Industry and Modern Activities.

VOLUME III

THE AMERICAN HISTORICAL SOCIETY

CHICAGO AND NEW YORK

1916

Very Sincerely yours

Jno. L. Clem

TEXAS AND TEX[illegible]

Brig.-Gen. John L. Clem. After more th[illegible] tical and continuous service as a soldier, Jo[illegible] from the United States Army in 1915 with t[illegible]. Before his retirement he had been sta[illegible] capacity of assistant quartermaster ge[illegible] of being the only active officer of the re[illegible] a soldier in the Civil war. He was thus t[illegible] of the Union who continued their act[illegible] century.

General Clem, who has long been w[illegible] larly at San Antonio where he was fo[illegible] Fort Sam Houston, and where he has a so[illegible] one of the remarkable characters of A[illegible] great historian of the Civil war, says: "[illegible] youngest soldier who ever bore arms i[illegible]

He was born at Newark, Ohio, Augus[illegible] yet sixty-five years of age at retireme[illegible] years of childhood when he was not en[illegible] responsibilities of military life. His fa[illegible] of Alsace. General Clem was not quit[illegible] Lincoln called for volunteers at th[illegible] already shown evidence that he was a [illegible] ambition at the beginning of the war t[illegible] front. He was rejected several time[illegible] he presented himself for enlistment. [illegible] attempts to break into the army as a [illegible] boy were finally accepted by the [illegible] Twenty-second" Michigan Infantry. [illegible] regiment was at Covington, Kentuck[illegible]

He was in the whirl of death at [illegible] "rat-ta-ta-tat" of his drum could [illegible] cannonading and incessant musketr[illegible] that he received his real initiation [illegible] The drum he carried was smashed [illegible] the boy was knocked down by the fo[illegible] from death was regarded by men o[illegible] bravery and coolness on this field [illegible] and shell gained for him his first [illegible] Shiloh." At Chickamauga, where the hornets [illegible] their sting Johnny Clem again demonstrated t[illegible] was made of, and in the face of fiery blasts showed hi[illegible] to be a hero. The attent[illegible] of both General Rosecrans and General Thomas was attracted to [illegible] courageous performances, and these distinguished officers bestowed u[illegible] him the affectionate title of "The Little Drummer Boy of Chickama[illegible]" Throughout the Army of the Cumberland the lad was lauded by [illegible] and enlisted men for his patriotic spunk and devotion to ever[illegible]

yours
J. Clem

TEXAS AND TEXANS

Brig.-Gen. John L. Clem. After more than half a century of practical and continuous service as a soldier, John Lincoln Clem was retired from the United States Army in 1915 with the rank of brigadier-general. Before his retirement he had been stationed at Washington in the capacity of assistant quartermaster general, and enjoyed the distinction of being the only active officer of the regular army who had served as a soldier in the Civil war. He was thus the last of those gallant veterans of the Union who continued their active service for more than half a century.

General Clem, who has long been well known in Texas, and particularly at San Antonio where he was for a number of years stationed at Fort Sam Houston, and where he has a son in business, is without doubt one of the remarkable characters of American history. Lossing, the great historian of the Civil war, says: "Little Johnny Clem was the youngest soldier who ever bore arms in battle."

He was born at Newark, Ohio, August 13, 1851, and as he was not yet sixty-five years of age at retirement there remains only the tender years of childhood when he was not engaging his time in the duties and responsibilities of military life. His father, Roman Clem, was a native of Alsace. General Clem was not quite ten years of age when President Lincoln called for volunteers at the beginning of the war. Having already shown evidence that he was a born soldier, it became his greatest ambition at the beginning of the war to don a suit of blue and go to the front. He was rejected several times by the recruiting sergeant when he presented himself for enlistment, but after five or six unsuccessful attempts to break into the army as a little lad his services as a drummer boy were finally accepted by the colonel commanding the "Fighting Twenty-second" Michigan Infantry. That was in May, 1862, while the regiment was at Covington, Kentucky.

He was in the whirl of death at the awful battle of Shiloh, and the "rat-ta-ta-tat" of his drum could be heard mingling with the furious cannonading and incessant musketry fire. It was in this fearful fight that he received his real initiation into soldier life, his baptism of fire. The drum he carried was smashed to pieces by a Confederate shell, and the boy was knocked down by the force of the explosion, while his escape from death was regarded by men on the firing line as miraculous. His bravery and coolness on this field swept by a veritable cyclone of shot and shell gained for him his first army appellation "Johnny Shiloh." At Chickamauga, where the hornets of death were busy with their sting, Johnny Clem again demonstrated the sort of stuff he was made of, and in the face of fiery blasts showed himself to be a hero. The attention of both General Rosecrans and General Thomas was attracted to his courageous performances, and these distinguished officers bestowed upon him the affectionate title of "The Little Drummer Boy of Chickamauga." Throughout the Army of the Cumberland the lad was lauded by officers and enlisted men for his patriotic spunk and devotion to every duty.

He received his first promotion soon after he had reached the age of twelve years. Appreciating the fact that in Johnny Clem, although diminutive in size, he had a real soldier, the commanding officer of the Twenty-second Michigan detailed him as a "marker," an assignment of much importance in war times. He was provided with a musket, its barrel being shortened to the boy's size, in which he carried his little marker flag. This distinction filled his boyish mind with pride. On occasions when the army was moving to the front he rode on a caisson until it was time for him to take his place in the firing line as marker with his shortened musket, which could "really shoot," but which bore the appearance of a toy gun in the hands of a play soldier. But there was no play about Colonel Clem's boyhood experience in the army. He was always at the front in the harvest of death, and big, brawny soldiers pointed him out as an example to be followed by older ones. It may be said that his early boyhood was entirely spent in the fray of battle.

A war-time incident which may be found on the pages of history will serve in a manner to illustrate the valor and coolness of the little drummer boy of the '60s. After the battle of Chickamauga, when the Union army was retiring toward Chattanooga, the brigade to which Johnny Clem was attached was ordered to hold its position. The brigade gallantly charged, but was repulsed and surrounded by Confederates, yelling like demons and demanding the surrender of the Union forces. Johnny Clem, who had charged with the line, was unable to fall back as rapidly as the others, and was consequently far in the rear when a mounted Confederate colonel rode toward the little "marker" and demanded that he surrender. As the officer approached, Johnny Clem brought his short musket to "order arms," the Confederate officer attempted to seize the boy and drew him to his saddle, but, quickly elevating his gun to the position of "charge bayonets" the wee marker pulled the trigger of his weapon and there was a blinding flash. The boy's aim had been true and the colonel fell from his horse. Johnny then lay upon the ground and pretended to be wounded until darkness came, when he managed to find his command. He afterward learned, with gratification, that he had not killed the officer in gray, but had wounded him severely and that he lived for many years after the war.

Other incidents of the great struggle in which Johnny Clem figured, always as an irrepressible boy patriot, might be given. He participated in nearly every important engagement of the western campaign, and was in service until the war closed. He served at Perryville, Stone River, Resaca, Kenesaw Mountain, Peach Tree Creek, Atlanta and Nashville. At Chickamauga three musket balls passed through his cap, and on other fields of carnage he received two wounds. While carrying a dispatch from General Thomas to General Logan at Atlanta his pony was hit by a ball near the top of its head, killing it instantly and wounding the little rider. At the close of the war he was mustered out with honor.

He then began a course of study and endeavored to qualify himself for a cadetship at West Point, to which he had been appointed by General Grant on recommendation of Generals Thomas and Logan and other officers of the Army of the Cumberland. When examination time came, however, he found that he had been handicapped by serving as a soldier in his tender years while other boys of his age were attending school. The examination problems proved to be too much for his boyish mind and he failed to pass. Bitterly disappointed, but not discouraged, the youth went to Washington and obtained an audience with General Grant, who then had become president. Grant had seen the drummer boy under the fatal fire at Shiloh and had noted his brave bearing in the shambles of death at that battle. When the boy asked the President that further time he granted in which to complete the necessary studies, the great general replied: "We can beat that; I will make you a second lieutenant now." The necessary order was given, and from that time the drummer boy has been a commissioned officer in the regular army, rising to the rank of colonel, and finally retiring with the rank of brigadier-general. He has seen service in many sections of the country and has been around the world. His first assignment after being commissioned second lieutenant was with the Twenty-fourth Infantry, then at Brownsville, Texas. The first ten years of his life as an officer was spent in Texas, where he displayed great activity in preserving order along the Rio Grande in the wild and riotous times of the early '70s, in suppressing the outlawry of cattle thieves and quelling outbreaks among the Indians.

The people of Texas indeed hold General Clem in the warmest affection. Since his first Texas assignment he has been in Porto Rico, and after the Spanish-American war he was returned to Texas and stationed at Fort Sam Houston, San Antonio. He went from San Antonio to Manila, from there to San Francisco, then back to San Antonio again, and then to Chicago, and finally to Washington, District of Columbia, where he was serving at the time of his retirement. He is deservedly popular in military circles and among the Civil war veteran comrades of the Grand Army of the Republic and those of the Spanish-American war.

General Clem married Anita R. French, who died several years ago. She belonged to a Delaware family, and was a daughter of Maj.-Gen. William H. French of the United States regular army, who was stationed at San Antonio before the Civil war. General Clem married, September 23, 1903, Elizabeth Sullivan, daughter of Daniel Sullivan, of San Antonio, and they have one daughter, Elizabeth.

John L. Clem, Jr., a son of General Clem, is one of the energetic young business men of San Antonio, now a partner in the firm of Collins-Clem Company, dealers in Studebaker automobiles.

John L. Clem, Jr., was born at Fort Henry, Maryland, in 1885, and as a boy he lived in San Antonio with his father. He attended the West Texas Military Academy, and spent four years as a student in the University of the South at Sewanee, Tennessee. He is now one of the trustees of that fine old institution.

Mr. Clem was one of the organizers of the company that built the Gunter Hotel at San Antonio, and was secretary of the company for some time. Later he became auditor of the Gunter Hotel, resigning that position in the fall of 1914 to enter the automobile business. He is a member of the Delta Tau Delta fraternity. At San Antonio he married Miss Lillian E. Benton of that city, and they have two children: Lillian Anita and Eileen Clem.

George Daniel Armistead. When, in May, 1914, George Daniel Armistead was appointed postmaster of San Antonio, it was universally agreed by press and public that President Wilson could have made no wiser or happier choice. Known through a long period of years as one of the most brilliant newspaper men in Texas, in a number of ways he had come before the people, and in each instance had displayed his thorough ability to cope with conditions in whatever circumstances he found himself. In his present office, which he assumed July 1, 1914, he has vindicated the faith reposed in him, and his administration has already been marked by achievements which promise, when followed up, to make Mr. Armistead one of the most successful as well as most popular officials the city has known.

Mr. Armistead belongs to the distinguished family of the name which has been known in the Old Dominion state for many years, and was born at Pembroke, Christian County, Kentucky, in 1874. His parents were R. B. and Susan F. (Hutchison) Armistead, natives of Virginia, the father having been born at Appomattox. He was a cousin of Gen. Louis A. Armistead, a Confederate army officer, who led a division and met his death in Pickett's famous charge at Gettysburg. The father has been dead for many years, but the mother still resides at the old southern family home, where the son visits her at least once a year. After attending the public schools of his home town, Mr. Armistead became a student in the University of Kentucky, and almost immediately following his graduation from that institution received his introduction to the newspaper business, a vocation for which, it veritably seems, he was destined. He passed through his journalistic baptism of fire at Fort Worth, in 1894, as a member of the repertorial staff of the Evening Mail, which has since discontinued publication, and from that time the young newspaper man gained steady promotion and served in one or another capacity every prominent newspaper in Texas. For two years he was Washington correspondent for Texas newspapers, and during this time formed acquaintances and connections with men prominent in public life that were to prove of the greatest value to him in later years. Returning to the Lone Star state in 1904, Mr. Armistead became press representative of Texas railroads, but subsequently went to Missouri and for a period of years devoted his talents to writing as a member of the staff of the St. Louis Republic. In 1910 Mr. Armistead returned to Texas to accept a position as staff correspondent of the San Antonio Express, in which work he continued to be actively engaged until assuming the duties of his official position. While thus engaged he handled assignments of the most important character, including the sessions of the Legislature and the state and national conventions of the big political parties.

It is related of Mr. Armistead that when he decided to leave newspaper work in St. Louis and return to Texas, he confided to his city editor, Sam Hellman: "I am going to Texas, but I don't know where I shall stop when I get there. No matter what town I locate in I am going to be its postmaster when the National Administration changes, and that change is coming pretty soon." He had had his finger on the pulse of politics and public sentiment for so long that he felt safe in making the latter prophecy. When his appointment as postmaster came to him in May, 1914, he was not surprised. He had been offered three other appointments by President Wilson, but none of them had suited him, but the postmastership realized for him his highest ambitions. He had the endorsement of the Thirty-third Legislature, was the choice of every member of the Texas delegation at Washington, was endorsed unanimously by the Texas Press Association, had the personal endorsement of a large majority of the Texas delegates to the Baltimore convention, and beyond and above all was a warm personal friend of Woodrow Wilson long before the New Jerseyan was a candidate for the presidency. Mr. Armistead was the first to openly espouse the candidacy of Mr. Wilson, was the first to open the Wilson campaign in the state, and served as secretary of the Wilson committee and was one of the state's electors at large in 1912.

That Mr. Armistead's appointment met with general public favor is shown by an extract taken from a San Antonio newspaper at the time, and which said in part: "The popularity of the selection was made prominently manifest in many ways. No sooner had the news been flashed by wire to San Antonio than the recipient of a high honor at the hands of the president became the object of a gratified host of political and personal friends. The telephones in the editorial department of the Express brought scores of congratulations to Mr. Armistead and congratulatory telegrams by the dozen from newspaper men and other friends in many sections of the state were delivered to him. That was not the extent of the keen interest shown—not by any means. A score or more of intimate friends of Mr. Armistead in San Antonio called at The Express office in person to extend their best wishes and express pleasure over his nomination. So insistent and steady was the inflow of congratulations that Mr. Armistead had to give up for the time writing into news items the grist of his daily assignment. Forsaking the typewriter to become host to his friends, the future postmaster held an informal levee from 4:30 to 6:30. One of the first men to come to the Express office and offer congratulations in person was Postmaster John J. Stevens and every one of his words rang true as steel. No expression of best wishes for his future career pleased Mr. Armistead better or touched a more responsive chord."

The San Antonio Express, of May 15, 1914, speaking editorially, said: "George Daniel Armistead has been appointed postmaster of San Antonio. President Wilson and Postmaster General Burleson have substantially recognized the services of one of Texas' best newspaper men and best citizens in behalf of the campaign that made this Administration, and in behalf of the Administration in the year past. Since 1911, Mr. Armistead has been staff correspondent of The Express. He is known over Texas, liked and respected by all the people of San Antonio. His associates in the publication and management of this newspaper are right glad his honor has come to him; the people of San Antonio will be glad. 'It is not the place that honoreth the man,' said the Ethics of the Fathers, 'but the man that honoreth the place.' Mr. Armistead will honor this important office. He is an educated, courteous gentleman. He has been excellently trained in the ways and needs of this city's residents. In the conscientious, informative exercise of his talents in San Antonio's best interests, he has made the city his debtor to a degree beyond all knowing of her people. With regard to the worth and popularity of the Federal service in San Antonio, The Express sees much to be grateful for in this appointment. That Mr. Armistead will succeed in the postmastership goes without the saying. It is equally certain that the community will be served zealously and well. In this instance, the office has sought the man. Mr. Wilson has appointed not a few newspaper men to responsible posts. No appointment of his will be more cordially greeted throughout the state than that which rewards Mr. Armistead with some measure of his desert."

In 1904 Mr. Armistead was married to Miss Estelle Huvelle, daughter of Mr. and Mrs. C. H. Huvelle, of Dallas. The family is prominent in both the social and business life of the North Texas city. Mr. and Mrs. Armistead have one child, George, Jr., who is now ten years of age.

Nat M. Washer. For thirty years or more the name Washer has been synonymous in Texas with successful and honorable merchandising. In 1882, when Fort Worth was still a frontier town, with less than 10,000 population, Nat M. and the late Jacob Washer established there a stock of merchandise under the firm name of Washer Brothers. Washer Brothers is still the title under which one of the leading department stores of North Texas is conducted at Fort Worth, though Jacob Washer, one of the founders, died on May 9, 1906, and Mr. Nat Washer has since sold his interest, the store being now conducted by a corporation under the old name, which is of itself a valuable asset to the company. Everywhere in Texas Washer business methods are known to harmonize with the highest standards of mercantile integrity, and a reputation such as this is the result of long and painstaking industry, careful management, and an exceptional degree of judgment and skill in the handling of opportunities and resources.

Mr. Nat M. Washer, who is now president of the Washer Brothers Company and head of the splendid department store at San Antonio conducted under that name, is not only a successful merchant but a man well known for his civic work in behalf of San Antonio, prominent for his various connections with commercial and philanthropic institutions, and as past grand master of the Texas Lodge of Masons, one of the best known members of that old and time honored fraternity in the Southwest.

Nat M. Washer was born April 12, 1861, at Somerville, Tennessee, son of Mr. and Mrs. Benjamin Washer. His early education came from the public schools in Memphis and from that city he went to St. Louis in 1879 and lived there three years. The training acquired in school was supplemented by a broad experience beginning with early youth in the lines which have defined his real business accomplishment, and his success has been to a large degree the unfolding of the natural elements in his own character. He came to Texas in 1882, locating at Fort Worth, where he and his brother Jacob established the firm of Washer Brothers. In 1899, after the business had been built up to large proportions, a branch house was opened in San Antonio, and at that time Nat M. Washer moved to the latter city to become active manager of that store and subsequently sold out his business in Fort Worth.

In addition to the large store at San Antonio known to every resident and visitor in that city, Mr. Washer has varied and extensive interests, is a director of the National Bank of Commerce and of the gas and electric and traction companies, a director of the Masonic Widows and Orphans' Home of Texas, of the Associated Charities, is president of the San Antonio Music Festival Association, is one of the directors and most active workers and a former president of the San Antonio Chamber of Commerce, has membership in the San Antonio, the Travis, the Country, the Harmony, the Automobile, the Fort Sam Houston Polo and the San Antonio Press clubs, the Beethoven and Casino Association and the Turn Verein. When a deserving movement needs leadership or practical assistance in San Antonio it never fails to receive the support of Nat Washer. Like many successful merchants, he is charitably inclined, and manifests this trait of character in various ways. For several years it has been his custom to give the newsboys of San Antonio a banquet at one of the leading hotels each Christmas, and this is only one of numerous acts of philanthropy which is associated with his name. He is a finished public speaker, possesses the real art of oratory, and his intellectual and artistic talents are betrayed in some commendable verse which he has written, and he has also assisted in the entertainment of many social gatherings and conventions as a singer. He is an honorary member of the Bohemian Scribblers, and personally is one of the most likable and popular men in San Antonio. Mr. Washer is one of the trustees of the Carnegie Library of San Antonio.

His fraternal record, particularly in Masonry, calls for a paragraph to itself. He was made a Mason in Fort Worth Lodge No. 148, Ancient Free and Accepted Masons in July, 1888, and after filling successively the positions of senior deacon and senior warden was in 1892 elected worshipful master of that lodge. He received the capitular and cryptic degrees in the chapter and the council at Fort Worth in the same year he was "raised" and after filling several subordinate positions in these bodies was elected in 1895 to the offices of high priest in the chapter and thrice illustrious master in the council. Mr. Washer first made his appearance in the Grand Lodge of Texas in 1888, and has been a regular attendant ever since. After having served as district deputy grand master and also as chairman of the committee on petitions he was elected junior grand warden in 1897 and by line of promotion was regularly advanced until 1900, when he was elected grand master of Masons in Texas. In every station he has occupied he has merited the distinguished honors bestowed upon him by his brethren of the craft in Texas. Mr. Washer also ranks high in Scottish Rite Masonry, is past venerable master of Bexar Lodge of Perfection No. 9 and has been crowned by the Supreme Council of the Rite with the thirty-third degree inspector general honorary. He is also a past exalted ruler of the Benevolent and Protective Order Elks and a member of San Antonio Lodge No. 216.

February 17, 1891, Mr. Washer married Miss Belle Schloss of Baltimore. Their two children are: Pauline Eva, now Mrs. Nat Goldsmith, and Jay Burnett Washer, who is associated with his father in the business of Washer Brothers Company.

Herbert Barnard. This distinguished artist, whose genius and skill in transferring to canvas the outward form and expression of the inward spirit of illustrious men, great events and beautiful objects have been an important factor in imprinting upon the material energy characteristic of San Antonio a high aesthetic quality, has been a resident of this city since 1912. Here his greatest success as an artist has been gained, and here the monuments of his genius constitute enduring and conspicuous features of the city's pictured glories. Born at Chicago, Illinois, in 1879, a son of Phillip B. and Hattie (Chapin) Barnard, he is an artist by talent, training, inclination and inheritance. His father is an artist, as are also a number of his near relatives on both his father's and his mother's side, his father now being a commercial artist in Chicago. The Barnards are of German descent, and on his mother's side, the Chapins, Mr. Barnard's family is still more famous in art circles. Mrs. Barnard is the daughter of the late John R. Chapin, an old-time woodcut engraver of note, who was one of the first engravers in the art department of the Harper Company, publishers of Harper's Magazine, New York City. One of her brothers, Will E. Chapin, is a noted cartoonist and was connected in this capacity on the Los Angeles Times for a number of years, and another of her brothers is Harry Chapin, of Providence, Rhode Island, who is an old-time wood engraver, well known to all the art publishers of America.

Mr. Barnard has found a fine field in San Antonio and Texas for the practice of his profession, and it will grow with the increasing wealth and culture of the people of the state, for his work is always original, he never allows himself to sink into a rut, and his mind is active and adaptable, enabling him to design the most beautiful schemes for decorating homes, as well as all kinds of private and public buildings. Mr. Barnard grew up in an atmosphere of art and took to the profession naturally. While he was a youth, studying, the family lived not only in Chicago, but in New York, Boston and other eastern cities, as well as in Cincinnati, and his education, training and experience were therefore broad. He began at a very early age to develop his talent as an artist. One of his first successes was in designing and painting the scenery for the original production of the musical extravaganza, "The Land of Nod," for Kohl & Castle, in Chicago, the producers of that spectacle. While still a young man he had a fine studio in Chicago, where he had particular success in originating scenery for high-class theatrical productions. Mr. Barnard devotes his time and his talents as an artist just as a business man would, and as a result has been financially successful. He is very versatile, and, besides his regular work as a painter, he designs interior decorations and interior furnishings for all sorts of buildings, both private and public.

Mr. Barnard came from Chicago to Texas in 1911, and since 1912 has made his home in San Antonio. His first commission was the interior decorating and furnishing of the Corpus Beach Hotel, at Corpus Christi, Texas, which brought him into much favorable notice in South Texas, and a congenial acquaintance with its leading citizens. For the annual fiesta and battle of flowers at San Antonio, in April, 1914, he designed all the floats from his own original designs; they were the most beautiful ever seen in San Antonio and attracted wide commendation. Three of his paintings, depicting early Southwestern scenes, of a highly historic value, adorn the lobby of the Gunter Hotel in San Antonio. In the summer of 1914 Mr. Barnard completed the remodeling and decoration of the concert room of the Beethoven Hall, in San Antonio, pronounced to be a work of the highest artistic merit. The scenery that he painted for this has attracted especial favor from the members and patrons of Beethoven Hall. One of Mr. Barnard's early achievements in Chicago was the designing, painting and decorating of the various amusement features at Forest Park, Chicago, and he has since had splendid success in this line of work in various cities.

As a result of his work at Corpus Christi, above referred to, he was awarded the honor of doing the interior decorating and designing the interior furnishings for the magnificent new courthouse located at Corpus Christi, this being completed in 1914. Likewise, his work for the Fiesta Association, in San Antonio, has brought him into close personal friendships and association with the leading business and professional men of this city, who are proud to have Mr. Barnard a citizen of San Antonio.

Capt. Duncan C. Ogden. A scion of a family whose name has been one of distinction in American annals since the colonial period of our national history, the character and achievement of the late Capt. Duncan C. Ogden caused him to bring new honors to the name which he bore and to mark for himself a large place on the history of Texas, of which state he may well be termed one of the founders and builders, as he aided gallantly in the preservation of the Republic of Texas and in the development and progress of the Lone Star State after its admission as one of the sovereign commonwealths of the United States. His character was the positive expression of a strong, noble and loyal nature, and his name merits enduring place on the roll of the honored pioneers of Texas. Captain Ogden was born at Ogdensburg, St. Lawrence County, New York, on the 22d of September, 1813, and he died at his home in San Antonio, Texas, on the 22d of March, 1859.

The Ogden family, of sterling English lineage, was founded in America in 1612, and in 1665 John Ogden, a son of the original American progenitor, was a member of the governor's council in New Jersey, holding a commission as such from King Charles II. John Ogden was one of the founders of the historic old City of Elizabethtown, New Jersey. Members of this family took a prominent part in colonial and revolutionary affairs, and were leading characters in the first settlements of the states of New Jersey and New York. Captain Ogden's grandfather was a loyalist in the war of the revolution, as were various other members of the family, and several representatives of this family were prominent figures in both the military and civil operations that led to American independ-

Duncan C. Ogden

ence. Captain Ogden's father was the founder of the now beautiful and populous City of Ogdensburg, New York, which was named for him, and there he had a beautiful home, the same overlooking the St. Lawrence River. He was a distinguished lawyer and jurist of the Empire State, a citizen of much prominence and influence, and at one time he was a law partner of Alexander Hamilton, one of the great characters in American history.

Capt. Duncan C. Ogden received excellent educational advantages in his youth and as a young man he went to the City of New Orleans, Louisiana, where other representatives of the Ogden family had settled, and there he became associated with one of his uncles in the mercantile business. It was his first purpose to practise law in that city. In 1838, impressed by the struggles of the people of the new Republic of Texas to preserve the independence which they had gained at the battle of San Jacinto, Captain Ogden became ardently in sympathy with the citizens of the struggling young republic, and this sympathy was one of characteristically definite action as well as sentiment. In the summer of 1838 he came to Texas and at once joined in the military operations against the Mexicans, with the resolve to give his best service, and his life if necessary, in defense of the cause of the Texans. His first commission was that of second lieutenant of the Second Brigade, and was signed by Gen. Sam Houston. By subsequent promotions he received commission in turn as first lieutenant and captain, and it was in the year 1839 that he became captain of a company in the newly organized First Regiment of Texas Infantry. He served against Santa Anna on his second invasion of Texas, and later was chosen Adjutant General of the Republic. In all his military service during this climacteric period he maintained a splendid reputation for bravery, efficiency and gallantry. In the Cherokee Indian war he commanded his company, which served under General Burleson, and, as a member of the command of Col. William G. Cook, he participated in the expedition by which was laid out the military road extending from the Red River to Austin,—an enterprise that was fraught with much danger and great hardships. Captain Ogden was engaged in a number of sanguinary conflicts with the Indians on the Texas frontier, and suffered greatly from the perils and privations incidental thereto.

The most notable and thrilling event of this period of the career of Captain Ogden was his capture by the Mexicans under General Adrian Woll, in San Antonio, in the year 1842, and the incidents relative to this capture. With a number of other captives from San Antonio he was transported as a prisoner to the Castle of Perote, far in the interior of Mexico. On this journey the captives were beset by the gravest dangers and hardships, which were multiplied manifold by the gross cruelties and indignities which they endured at the hands of their Mexican captors after they had been placed in prison. He was captured September 11, 1842, and escaped July 2, 1843. Most of the Perote prisoners, including Captain Ogden, made their escape by means of an excavation which they had dug at great pains and peril. But it was Captain Ogden's great misfortune on thus gaining his liberty to find that the horse on which he had expected to make his ultimate escape back to Texas had been taken by someone else. As a consequence he was recaptured and again imprisoned in Perote, from which vile duress he was not released until after a long two years of continual suffering and privation, his liberation finally being accomplished through international negotiations carried on by Hon. Henry Clay.

After his release from the terrible dungeon of Perote, Captain Ogden returned to Texas and established his residence in San Antonio, where he continued to be successfully engaged in business until the time of his death. He was a man of extraordinary mental and physical strength and he retained to the last his mental faculties, his death having been caused by a pleuritic affection. His untimely death was uniformly regretted and deplored by all who knew him or were familiar with the great and loyal service which he had rendered to Texas, the City of San Antonio as a whole manifesting a deep sense of personal loss and bereavement. He had been one of the founders of the great State of Texas, to the obtaining of whose liberty he had given devoted and gallant service. He was not alone courageous and efficient in warfare, but strength of intellect and his superior educational advantages had gained for him a high place in the councils of his people and in the public and political affairs of his time. When the wars were over and dangers to Texas no longer called him to the tented field, a grateful people sent him as representative of his district in the Congress of the Republic of Texas. Faithfully and ably he represented his constituents in the national Legislature and, with never a murmer of objective disapproval of any of his official acts, he retired from politics, as he had from war, to follow the peaceful callings of private life. After leaving politics and up to the time of his death he was engaged in extensive mercantile business in San Antonio, in partnership with Maj. George T. Howard, a brother of Dr. H. P. Howard. Both Major Howard and Captain Ogden distinguished themselves as soldiers. He left a devoted wife and three small children to mourn his untimely death, which occurred about six months after he had celebrated his forty-fifth birthday anniversary. His was an exalted character, his was great and worthy achievement, and his place in Texas history is forever established. He was brave, chivalrous, gentle and considerate, and by him was never a trust betrayed or infringed.

On the 30th of May, 1845, was solemnized the marriage of Captain Ogden to Miss Elizabeth Cox, who was born in Scott County, Kentucky, May 8, 1826, and who came with her parents to Texas in 1832, the family settling in what is now Washington County. Texas was then a part of Mexico and the Cox family were among the earliest of the American settlers. It is not generally known, even among students of history, that under the Mexican domination of those days every non-Catholic coming to the Mexican possessions was required to undergo baptism in the Catholic Church. One of the prized documents and heirlooms in the Ogden family is the certificate of baptism issued, in 1832, to James Cox, father of Mrs. Elizabeth (Cox) Ogden, this ancient instrument bearing the signature of Father Michael Muldoon, a well known Catholic priest. The representatives of the Cox family were prominent in the events leading up to and succeeding Texas independence. Mrs. Ogden, who survived the husband of her youth by nearly half a century and who died in San Antonio in November, 1902, recalled with great vividness the battle of San Jacinto, in 1836, when she was a girl of ten years. She was a member of a company of women and children who were camped within a short distance of the battlefield, and she personally conversed with Mrs. Dickinson, who, with her child, were the only survivors of the Alamo. She was one of the founders of the "Battle of Flowers" festival and was a recognized authority on Texas history.

Mrs. Cora Ogden Wilson, of San Antonio, and her brother, Duncan Ogden, a resident of Fort McKavett, Menard County, Texas, are the only surviving members of the immediate family of Capt. Duncan C. and Elizabeth (Cox) Ogden, the parents to whose memory they pay lasting reverence. Mrs. Wilson was born in San Antonio and was an infant at the time of her father's death. She was educated in her native city and prior to her marriage was a teacher in private schools of San Antonio and also a successful and accomplished teacher of music. In this city was solemnized her marriage to Nathan Taylor Wilson, whose death here occurred on the 28th of October, 1907. Mr. Wilson was born in the State of Georgia, in 1847, and when a lad of fourteen years he there entered the Confederate army, as a gallant young soldier of which he fought under the colors of the South until the close of the war between the states. After the war he attended school two years, at the expiration of which he went to New York City, where for some time he held a position in the employ of his uncle, R. T. Wilson, a noted millionaire business man of the national metropolis at that time and a first cousin of Cornelious Vanderbilt. The Wilson family in New York have for several generations been folk of wealth and distinction, and related through marriage with many notable families.

On coming to Texas, in the late '70s, Mr. Wilson assumed charge of important cattle interests in the western part of the state, with headquarters in the City of San Antonio. Later he became prominently concerned in the banking business in this city, as a member of the banking firm of R. E. Stafford & Company, the business of which became the nucleus of the present City National Bank. Mr. Wilson was a successful man of affairs and though he had no desire to bask in the light of publicity or to assume political office, his ability and unqualified civic loyalty marked him as being specially eligible for positions of public trust, and he consented to serve as alderman at large for San Antonio and as a member of the Live Stock Sanitary Commission of Texas, besides being at all times ready to lend his influence and co-operation in the furtherance of all things tending to advance the welfare and progress of his adopted city and state.

Within a comparatively short period after establishing his residence in San Antonio Mr. Wilson here married Miss Cora Ogden, and of the children of this ideal union two survive the honored father: Duncan Campbell Ogden Wilson, a young man of distinctive talent and sterling character, remains at San Antonio, where he is now treasurer of the Prudential Life Insurance Company of Texas; and Mary Elizabeth is the wife of Capt. George Evans Stewart, of the United States Army.

Mrs. Wilson has long been a recognized leader in the representative social activities of her native city, where her circle of friends is coincident with that of her acquaintances. She holds membership in the Colonial Dames of America, the Daughters of the Republic of Texas, and the Daughters of the Confederacy. Her beautiful home, at 303 East Quincy Street, is known for its gracious hospitality, but aside from her prominence in the social life of San Antonio she is a woman of distinctive business and executive ability. She has important capitalistic interests, and it is specially worthy of note that she is the active vice president of the Prudential Life Insurance Company of Texas, of which progressive and successful corporation she is the largest individual stockholder, her executive association with which is marked by her taking active part in the directing and managing of the business.

Albert V. Huth. It is difficult for the general public to realize or appreciate what responsibility lies with the tax assessor, and how much thought and study and experience it requires to bring about justice and equalization in the matter of assessments on property. It requires a trained, experienced man to efficiently handle the affairs of this office, and for this reason the people of Bexar County are to be congratulated upon having as their county tax assessor the present capable and energetic incumbent, Albert V. Huth, who is considered an authority on the subject of taxation and assessment, has made it a lifelong study, and recognizes it as one of the foundation principles of civilized society.

Mr. Huth is a native son of San Antonio, Texas, and was born July 19, 1873, his parents being Louis and Lena (Heiner) Huth. The father was born at Castroville, Medina County, Texas, and was a son of Louis Huth, Sr., a native of Alsace Lorraine, France. The grandfather came from his native country to Texas in 1844 as one of the representatives of the Alsatians in the founding of the Castro's colony of Castroville, in Medina County, and as the years passed successfully conducted mercantile pursuits, first at Castroville, and later at San Antonio, to which city the business was removed. His death occurred at San Antonio, in 1892, and thus passed away a citizen who had been an important factor both as a pioneer citizen and as a stirring man of business. Mr. Huth was not unknown to public affairs in Texas, at all times exerting a helpful and wholesome influence in the promotion of beneficial movements, and in his earlier years served as district clerk of Medina County. His later years were devoted to his business activities and he held no further office, although always being found as a sturdy supporter of good men and worthy enterprises in his community.

Louis Huth, father of Albert V. Huth, was given his introduction to business life in his father's store, and for several years was associated with the elder man in commercial enterprises under the firm style of L. Huth & Son, beginning in 1872. This concern owned and controlled one of the most prominent establishments in the wholesale and retail trade. The store was located on Market Street, which in those days was the principal business thoroughfare of the city. Louis Huth, Jr., also became prominent in the public life of Bexar County, and for ten years served as county assessor, proving a most capable official. He died at his home at San Antonio, where Mrs. Huth still makes her residence. She was the daughter of William Heiner, a pioneer business man of this city, long engaged as an undertaker.

Albert V. Huth was reared in his native county, acquiring the greater part of his education in the old German-English school which was located on South Alamo Street, and in the San Antonio High School. Upon entering business life, he accepted a position as bookkeeper and stenographer for the firm of C. H. Bond & Company, cotton merchants with an office at Cuero, Texas. He remained in this capacity until 1891, when he secured his first experience in public position in the county assessor's office, as clerk under his father, and about the time he became of age was appointed one of the deputies in office, while later he became chief deputy county assessor under the assessorship of his father. After the elder man's retirement, Albert V. Huth continued as chief deputy in the office under the four years' administration of John Wilkins, Jr., so continuing until 1904, when he became a candidate for office and was elected at the regular election in November of that year. Through his education, experience and well known ability he is particularly well qualified for this responsible position, which he has continued to hold to the present time, to the utmost satisfaction of the people of the County of Bexar. The work of the office is conducted on thoroughly business principles, and Mr. Huth is uniformly regarded as a competent and trustworthy official. With Mr. Huth taxation is a profession and a science, and he is a student of modern methods and reforms, such as the single tax, which he recognizes as excellent in theory, but hardly practicable for the present age, at least. He is familiar with the Somers systems, the block book system, and all other methods of taxation and assessment that are in vogue both in America and in Europe. Mr. Huth is ex-president of the Tax Assessors Association of Texas, and has been twice a delegate, appointed by Governor Campbell and Governor Colquitt, to the International Taxation Conference.

Mr. Huth was united in marriage at San Antonio to Miss Theresa O'Farrell, of this city, and to this union there have been born six children, namely: Joseph Albert, who died at the age of five and one-half years; James Leo; Mary Theresa; Elizabeth Mary; John Francis and Patricia Cecelia.

HON. HENRY TERRELL. High on the roll of distinguished lawyers of the Lone Star State stands the name of Henry Terrell, who has lent dignity and honor to his chosen profession both as a private practitioner and as United States district attorney. A resident of San Antonio for a period of forty-nine years, he has steadily arisen in distinction and success in his calling and in the confidence and respect of his fellow-citizens, who have recognized in him one who has been true to each trust, whether private or public.

Hon. Henry Terrell was born on a farm in Floyd County, Indiana, in 1860, and is a son of Gen. Charles M. and Sarah I. (Speake) Terrell, and a member of the well known Terrell family of Colonial Virginia, whose members have achieved distinction in events and affairs relating to Texas history. Gen. Charles M. Terrell was a brother of the late Hon. E. H. Terrell, who was a resident of San Antonio, at one time minister from the United States to Belgium, and for many years a prominent figure in republican politics in Texas. The ancestry of the family is traced back to Henry Terrell, who was a leading and stirring citizen of Hancock County, Virginia, but who moved to Kentucky in 1787, there becoming closely identified with the early history of the Blue Grass State. The son of this progenitor, Capt. John Terrell, was the great-grandfather of Hon. Henry Terrell, and a gallant and conspicuous officer in the campaigns against the Indians shortly following the War of the Revolution, being present at the engagement known in history as Harmer's defeat, in 1790, near the present site of Fort Wayne, Indiana. Subsequently he took an active part in General Wayne's victory over the forces of the Miamis at Maumee Rapids, the present site of Toledo, Ohio. Capt. John Terrell married a sister of Chilton Allan, one of the famous lawyers in the early history of Kentucky, who represented the Ashland district in Congress for many years after the promotion of Henry Clay to the Senate.

The son of Capt. John Terrell, Williamson Terrell, entered the ministry of the Methodist Church as a youth, and in the years that followed became one of the most popular and widely known preachers in the Hoosier State, where he held a number of pastorates.

Gen. Charles M. Terrell, a member of the United States regular army for a period of forty years, the greater part of this time being spent in Texas, entered the army as paymaster, June 30, 1862, and during the Civil war was in the service in the West, being connected with the Army of the Cumberland. Following the close of hostilities he was stationed at New Orleans, from which city he came in 1867 to San Antonio, and here he was stationed for approximately all of the remainder of his military career, although a brief period was passed also at the army posts at Omaha, Nebraska, and Detroit, Michigan. General Terrell was promoted, December 30, 1888, to a lieutenant coloneley and was detailed deputy paymaster general, and on the 6th of January, 1893, was promoted to colonel and assistant paymaster general. In 1896, under the army regulations, he was retired, and later, under the Act of Congress going into effect April 25, 1904, General Terrell was commissioned brigadier general on the retired list. His death occurred at San

Antonio, November 22, 1904. As a result of wise and well-placed investments, General Terrell was enabled to leave to his family a comfortable competency, and during his life was known as one of his city's substantial citizens. He was a man of more than ordinary influence in the community of his residence, was a man of the highest standing in military and social circles, and had the unqualified esteem and regard of the people in whatever community his home was made. As a soldier his record was an admirable one; and in civic life his affairs were conducted on the same well-regulated lines. General Terrell was united in marriage in 1853, at New Albany, Indiana, to Miss Sarah I. Speake, who still survives him and makes her home at San Antonio.

Hon. Henry Terrell was a lad of seven years when he accompanied his parents to San Antonio, in 1867, and in this city he passed his boyhood and youth, receiving excellent educational advantages. When he had graduated from what was old Asbury College, but is now known as DePauw University, at Greencastle, Indiana, he became a student at the University of Michigan, at Ann Arbor. There his literary training was completed, and succeeding his graduation from that institution he entered upon his legal studies at Cumberland University, Lebanon, Tennessee, from which fine old southern college he was graduated with his degree of Bachelor of Laws, as a member of the class of 1886. Returning to his home in San Antonio, Mr. Terrell at once opened an office and embarked in the practice of his chosen profession, and this city has continued to be his field of endeavor and the scene of his success to the present time. Politically a republican, he has never been a partisan or bigoted in his views, and his absolute fairness and impartiality have commended him to all, whether in professional, private or public life. An able and astute lawyer, he was assistant United States district attorney for the western district of Texas from 1889 until 1894, and in 1898 was appointed United States district attorney, a capacity in which he served efficiently until his retirement in the spring of 1905.

Judge Terrell is the author of a work entitled, "Crimes by National Bank Officers," which has enjoyed a large circulation and has attracted favorable mention in various parts of the country. When he had given up his official duties, Judge Terrell resumed the private practice of his profession at San Antonio, in which he has gained an enviable place, his connection with a number of important cases fully demonstrating the breadth and scope of his ability.

Mr. Terrell was married in San Antonio to Miss Kate Rivers Brahan, who belongs to an old and distinguished family of the Old Dominion State, while on the maternal side she is descended from the prominent Haywood family of North Carolina and Tennessee. Her great-grandfather was Judge John Haywood, of the Supreme Court of North Carolina and later of Tennessee, and further back in this line of ancestry was Col. John Haywood, prominent in the affairs of North Carolina, and a brother of Sir Henry Haywood, Englishman, who was governor of Barbadoes Island. Four children have been born to Judge and Mrs. Terrell: Lieut. Frederick Brahan, of the United States army; Nellie, who became the wife of Maj. F. R. Keefer, also of the United States regular army; Robert Weakley, who studied at Philadelphia, and took a law course at Cumberland University under the same preceptors as his father, and is now practicing his profession at San Antonio; and Henry, Jr., who studied at Philadelphia, and subsequently passed a competitive examination and was given a commission in the United States army, being attached to the Twenty-second Infantry.

David S. Combs. One of the surviving veterans of the famous Terry Rangers of the Confederate army, David S. Combs is a Texan whose career deserves more than incidental mention in the history of his state. He is one of the fine characters who still live in these modern days of the twentieth century, but whose early associations and interests were with the exciting events of the frontier and the old cattle range. His own experiences have closely followed the development of Texas from the days of the open range to the modern stock farm, and while his later years have been passed in the enjoyment of leisure in the beautiful City of San Antonio, his interests are still extensive in the western cattle districts and are now under the active management of his son.

David S. Combs came up from comparative poverty into abundance and extended influence. A brief survey of his life indicates that he has never sought the easier paths of least resistance, but has always been willing to face with courage and persistence the difficulties of the rough-and-tumble conflict with chance and circumstance. He was born in Johnson County, Missouri, May 26, 1839, and has already passed the three-quarter century mark of life. His parents were David B. and Rebecca (Burruss) Combs, natives of Kentucky and early-day settlers in Johnson County, Missouri. The father died in Missouri, and when David was seven years of age his mother and stepfather removed to Hempstead County, Arkansas. Eight years later they came to Texas, and in 1854 located on the frontier in Hays County, near San Marcos. At that time and for a number of years following the frontier was held only by constant vigilance and by frequent encounters with Indians, and in these experiences the Combs family had its full share.

Mr. Combs grew up with an education along most practical lines rather than from contact with books, and in early manhood proved his ability to hold his own as a worker on the farm and ranch. At the age of twenty-two the war between the states broke out. In 1861 he enlisted for service in the Confederate army, joining Company D of the Eighth Texas Cavalry at LaGrange, in Fayette County. The Eighth Texas Cavalry was best known to fame as the Terry Rangers, a body of Texas cavalrymen whose services have since been perpetuated in the splendid Terry Ranger monument, now standing in front of the capitol at Austin. Mr. Combs was with the rangers in their service through Kentucky, Tennessee, Mississippi, Alabama and Georgia, and participated at Shiloh, Murfreesboro, Perryville and Chickamauga, and many other minor engagements and campaigns. About a year before the war closed he came on a short furlough, and on re-entering service was assigned to duty in the Trans-Mississippi department in Texas, and the rest of his enlistment was passed with the Confederate army on the lower Rio Grande in the vicinity of Brownsville. Mr. Combs has the distinction of having participated in the last battle of the war, which was fought about two weeks after the surrender of Appomattox, on the Rio Grande, between Brownsville and Santiago de Brazos.

With the close of the war Mr. Combs returned to San Marcos, and entered actively into the cattle industry as then conducted in the Southwest. With the establishment of the great cattle trails that led north from the Texas ranges through the Indian Territory to Kansas and other northern states, he was one of the men who frequently took the Texas herds to northern pastures and markets. He had the courage, the self-reliance and the business instinct which marked him out from many less ambitious cow punchers of the day, and in a few years he was in business for himself. In 1880 Mr. Combs established his ranch on the South Concho River in Tom Green County, near San Angelo, and in 1882 moved his outfit still further west to Brewster County, one of the few districts of Southwest Texas which have been slowest to yield to the encroachments of the agricultural settler. For more than thirty years Mr. Combs has maintained an increased extensive ranch interest in Brewster County, and his holdings have been as high as 100,000 acres.

While Mr. Combs still has large cattle interests in that section, he is now practically retired from active life, and his son, Guy St. Clair Combs, has the executive management. Mr. Combs has lived in San Antonio since 1898, and in 1915 began the erection of a beautiful residence in that city. His son, Guy St. Clair Combs, constructed a beautiful new home in San Antonio in 1913. David S. Combs was married in Missouri to Miss Eleanora Browning. Their three children are: Nora Burruss, Lila Alice and Guy St. Clair Combs.

COL. OTTO WAHRMUND. In the last quarter of a century few citizens of San Antonio have identified themselves so closely and usefully with the substantial welfare of their city as Colonel Wahrmund. His principal business position is as vice president and general manager of the San Antonio Brewing Association, and while that institution is the largest of its kind in the Southwest his responsibilities in its management have not precluded the exercise of a broad public spirit and practical interest in other directions. Colonel Wahrmund has long been unselfishly engaged in promoting the best interests of his home city, and during the past six years his service in the State Legislature has associated with his name a prominence all over the state.

Of that fine German stock that did so much to people and make habitable the wild regions of Southwest Texas during the '40s and '50s, and that is still an active force in many counties, Colonel Wahrmund was born September 19, 1855, in that noted old seat of German colonization, Fredericksburg, Gillespie County. The founder of the family in Texas was his father, Judge William Wahrmund, a native of Wiesbaden who married Amalia Schildknecht, also a native of Wiesbaden. He came to America in 1845, lived at New Braunfels awhile, but soon joined the pioneer colony in the Valley of the Pedernales in Gillespie County. He was long a prominent figure in that district, and was for many years successfully engaged in merchandising at Fredericksburg, and for nearly thirty years gave a capable administration to the office of county judge of Gillespie County. His death occurred at Fredericksburg in 1898.

With a good inheritance of character from his father, and with stimulating surroundings in his youth, Colonel Wahrmund grew up in Fredericksburg. and was well educated, finishing at the old T. M. I. (Texas Military Institute) at Austin. For a number of years he was in business in Fredericksburg. In January, 1887, he became associated as one of the promoters and founders of the San Antonio Brewing Association. This corporation operates the plant known to every San Antonian as the City Brewery, now the largest business of its kind in the state. It has been a feature of the industrial life of the city, and the handsome group of buildings standing alongside the river, at James Street, not far from the site of "the old mill" of the Spanish regime, constitute one of the picturesque and conspicuous landmarks of the city. The plant represents a great aggregate of capital, and the different buildings have been constructed from time to time corresponding with the growth of the business. Every department has been organized and brought up to the highest state of efficiency, and represents the last word in the perfection of the brewer's art. The product now has a standard of excellence recognized everywhere in the Southwest, and none of the brews from other states and countries has greater merit on

districts of [illegible] encroachments [illegible] Mr. [illegible] [illegible]

When Mr. [illegible]

[illegible] to the [illegible] years [illegible] interest in [illegible] as 100,000 acres [illegible] in that section, he is [illegible] son, Guy St. Clair [illegible] has lived in San [illegible] a beautiful residence [illegible] constructed a beautiful [illegible] was married in [illegible] are: Nora [illegible]

[illegible] figure in [illegible] engaged in mercantile [illegible] years gave a capable [illegible] Gillespie County. His [illegible]

[illegible] good inheritance of [illegible] surroundings in his [illegible] and was well [illegible] Military Institute) at Austin [illegible] Fredericksburg. [illegible] of the promoters and four[illegible] This corporation operates [illegible] the City Brewery, [illegible] It has been a feature [illegible] group of buildings [illegible] far from the site of [illegible] of the picturesque [illegible] represents a great [illegible] construction [illegible] business. [illegible]

Eng by E G Williams & Bro NY

The American Historical Society

the basis of purity and quality. One of the largest buildings is the storage house, with a capacity for over 50,000 barrels and most improved facilities for storing and aging. Artesian wells on the grounds furnish pure water, and the refrigeration plant is a big industry in itself, not only supplying ice for the brewing operations but also for the general wholesale trade. As about 250 persons are employed by the industry it is readily seen how important an asset the business is to the prosperity of the city. As a subsidiary organization, the Texas Transportation Company, of which Colonel Wahrmund is an officer, operates the rail lines connecting the brewery with the main railway systems centering at San Antonio.

Colonel Wahrmund in 1908 entered the Texas Legislature as the representative of the Thirty-fifth District, including San Antonio and Bexar County. He has been regularly re-elected each two years since for four consecutive terms without opposition, and has proved one of the most useful members of the body, taking special interest in legislation of a commercial character. Governor Sayres appointed him a member of the governor's staff, and he continued to serve during Governor Lanham's administration. He was appointed to the rank of lieutenant colonel on the staff of Governor Colquitt in 1910 and reappointed at the beginning of the governor's second term in 1912.

For a number of years Colonel Wahrmund has had extensive mining interests in Mexico, and has valuable investments both in San Antonio and elsewhere. His success as a business man has always been accompanied by a thorough public spirit so that his means and practical ability have always been at the disposal of the community. He has long been identified with the International Fair Association of San Antonio, and in February, 1906, was elected president of the body. How highly he was regarded at the time as a helpful citizen, and as a brief estimate of qualities which are even more effective today, a quotation from the local press with reference to his election will illustrate: "Colonel Wahrmund is one of the most substantial as well as one of the most progressive and public spirited citizens of San Antonio. He is thoroughly identified with the business interests of this city and section, and has a personal as well as public interest in the development and prosperity of that portion of the great southwest of which San Antonio is the commercial center. In accepting the office to which he has been chosen Colonel Wahrmund declared his purpose to discharge his duties in the manner which the directors of the association felt quite sure he would do before fixing upon him as their choice. Because of Colonel Wahrmund's intimate connection with other important business enterprises, the giving of his personal attention to the office of president of the fair association will involve some sacrifice of valuable time, but, being a patriotic and public spirited citizen, he makes the sacrifice freely, and without any compensation in the way of salary or emoluments."

In 1879 Colonel Wahrmund married Miss Sophie Nimitz of Fredericksburg, daughter of Hon. Charles H. Nimitz, who was a member of the first band of colonists that settled the Town of Fredericksburg in 1844. This union was blessed by the birth of eight children, seven girls and one boy, and all of these children but one are married.

Henning Bruhn. Among the prominent citizens of San Antonio who have shown the highest type of initiative and constructive ability along business lines and whose civic loyalty has found effective exemplification, a foremost place must be accorded to Mr. Bruhn, who is secretary, treasurer and general manager of the Lone Star Brewing Company, which represents one of the large and substantial industrial enterprises of the city, and whose progressiveness and public spirit have made him a citizen of much influence in the community, the while he has secure vantage-place in popular confidence and esteem. Mr. Bruhn has been a resident of San Antonio since 1903 and came here from Milwaukee, Wisconsin, where he had maintained his residence and been identified with important business interests for a term of years.

Mr. Bruhn was born in the Baltic seaport City of Kiel, in Holstein, Prussia, in the year 1865, and in the same province were born his parents, August and Christine Bruhn. Mr. Bruhn was afforded the advantages of the excellent national schools of his fatherland. In 1886 he came to the United States, going to El Paso, Texas, where he remained for eight years, until 1894, with the firm of Ketelsen & Degetau, a very large concern at the time doing a general wholesale merchandise business all over the Republic of Mexico. From there he associated himself with the Pabst Brewing Company, of Milwaukee, Wisconsin, with which company he remained until 1902, in the capacity of traveling man, auditor and credit manager; he also made a trip for them to all countries of this globe, which lasted about two years. After leaving the employ of the Pabst Brewing Company he accepted the position of manager of the Lone Star Brewing Company, of San Antonio, Texas. He early initiated his association with practical business activities, and his advancement as a business man of large capacity and steadfast purpose has been consecutive and well merited. During the period of his residence in San Antonio he has been closely and prominently identified with the best business and social life of the city, and though he has manifested no predilection for public office he is a staunch advocate of the cause of the democratic party and takes a lively and liberal interest in all that touches the civic and material prosperity and progress of his home city. He is a member of the San Antonio Club, the Travis Club, the Casino Association, the Chamber of Commerce and other representative organizations in San Antonio, where he is affiliated also with the lodge of the Benevolent and Protective Order of Elks.

In the City of Milwaukee, Wisconsin, in 1901, was solemnized the marriage of Mr. Bruhn to Miss Elsie Fischer, who has become a most popular figure in the representative social activities of San Antonio. They have four children: Erich, May, Minnie, and Lottie.

As indicative of the civic loyalty and public spirit of Mr. Bruhn it is but consistent to enter the following extracts from an edition of the San Antonio Express of June, 1914:

"Through the generosity of Henning Bruhn the art exhibition which has been on at the Carnegie Library since March 12, will be free to the public after Friday morning. The San Antonio Art League, under whose auspices this exhibit was brought to San Antonio, has been forced to charge an admission fee to help defray the expenses of the exhibit. Mr. Bruhn has assumed all of the remainder of the expense of the exhibit and made it possible for everyone in San Antonio to see this wonderful collection of paintings by America's foremost artists. In addition to the collection of paintings now on exhibition at the library, which are the masterpieces of America, Mr. Bruhn has made arrangements to add two masterpieces from the other side of the water—'The Immigrant,' by Edward Farazyn, a Belgian artist of renown, and 'The Forest,' by the famous Russian painter, Danisoff Uralsky. These paintings are now the property of the Adolphus Busch estate and it was through the co-operation of E. A. Faust, of St. Louis, that Mr. Bruhn was enabled to bring them to San Antonio. Through his public-spirited generosity Mr. Bruhn is making it possible for everyone in San Antonio to see some of the most striking paintings that have ever been exhibited here. * * * Members of the Art League are deeply grateful to Mr. Bruhn for his generosity in assuming the remainder of the expense. 'This is to be the first large gift in this city to the cause of art,' said Julian Onderdonk, 'and it is appreciated by members of the Art League and will be remembered by the public. The cause for which the people in San Antonio are working is a noble and worthy one, and a great satisfaction is felt in the results so far attained. The aim to establish an art museum is each day drawing nearer to realization.' "

Edward W. Heusinger. He whose name initiates this review has achieved prominence as a scientist, is recognized as the leading and most influential figure in the Scientific Society of San Antonio, and in his native city is prominent also in connection with business affairs, as secretary of the A. E. Staacke Automobile Company. He is essentially and consistently a loyal Texan, within whose border his father established a home more than half a century ago.

Mr. Heusinger was born in San Antonio June 9, 1874, and is a son of Adolph and Anna (Haenal von Krohenthal) Heusinger, the former of whom died at his home in San Antonio on the 8th of November, 1913, after a residence of more than three-score years in Southwestern Texas, and the latter of whom still maintains her home in San Antonio. Adolph Heusinger was born at Nastaetten, a town in the Province of Hesse-Nassau, Prussia, Germany, the date of his nativity having been October 8, 1831, and the full name given him at his christening having been Carl Gottlieb Adolph Theodore Heusinger von Waldegg. His father, August Conrad Heusinger von Waldegg, a man of scholarship and consecrated zeal, long served as pastor of the Lutheran Church at Nastaetten. Young Heusinger received a thorough education in the Real Schule at Mainz on the Rhine, and in the Real Gymnasium at Weisbaden. In 1850, in company with his brother, Dr. Julius Heusinger von Waldegg, he immigrated to America, having been at the time about nineteen years of age. The two brothers had been moved by the accounts that were appearing in the German papers concerning the wonderful opportunities afforded in Texas, then the youngest commonwealth of the United States, its admission to the Union having occurred in 1845. The brothers made their way to Texas immediately after landing in America, their disembarkation having occurred in the City of New Orleans, where they took passage on a sailing vessel and came to Indianola, Texas, from which point they traveled overland to San Antonio, which then had a population of about 4,000. From this city they proceeded to the German colony of New Braunfels, in Comal County, where their elder brother, Gustav Heusinger von Waldegg had previously settled, his death having occurred soon after their arrival. Thereafter they remained for some time in the thriving French settlement or colony at Castroville, Medina County, and after Adolph Heusinger had returned to San Antonio he here engaged in contracting and building.

Shortly after establishing his permanent residence in San Antonio Adolph Heusinger was here united in marriage to Miss Anna Haenal von Krohenthal, the daughter of a piano manufacturer at Halbrest, Germany. In 1858 the young couple removed to Austin, where they maintained their home until after the close of the Civil war, Mr. Heusinger having been ineligible for military service on account of the condition of his eyes. After the war the family returned to San Antonio and here Mr. Heusinger turned his attention to the mercantile business. He became the owner of a dry-goods store near Main Plaza, but though the enterprise prospered it was not long before he met with disaster, his establishment and all of its contents having been destroyed by fire. He carried no insurance indemnity and thus was compelled to begin anew and put forth strenuous efforts to recoup his fortune and make proper provision for his wife and children, to whom his devotion was ever intense and solicitous. He finally became associated with Honore Grenet in the mercantile business, on the site of the present Crockett Hotel, and in 1873 he again engaged in business in an independent or individual way, by opening a hardware store on Commerce Street, whence he later removed to Main Plaza. He continued successful in the hardware and implement business about forty years and was known and honored as one of the representative business men and loyal and influential citizens of San Antonio. In 1865 he became a member of the Casino Association, which then held its meetings in a rented building on Commerce Street, and in 1904 he had the distinction of being made an honorary member of this association, to the upbuilding of which he had contributed greatly. As early as 1856 Mr. Heusinger was an influential member and official of San Antonio Lodge, No. 11, Independent Order of Odd Fellows, with which fraternal organization he continued to be affiliated until his death. He took a vital and helpful interest in the industrial and commercial development and upbuilding of San Antonio and was one of the original stockholders of the San Antonio & Aransas Pass Railroad Company, which was organized in 1885. In the gracious evening of his long and useful life two successful operations restored the eyesight of Mr. Heusinger, which had been greatly impaired for many years, and he was a pioneer whose name and memory shall long be honored in the city and state which represented his home for many years.

Edward W. Heusinger acquired the major part of his early education in the German-English School of San Antonio, and in earlier years he was associated with his father's hardware business, his present business activities being principally in connection with the affairs of the A. E. Staacke Automobile Company, of which he is secretary.

To Mr. Heusinger must be accredited both honor and distinction for the achievement that has been his in the field of science, especially in view of the fact that his scientific attainments represent virtually the result of his many years of self-application and research. He first became interested in geology and mineralogy and accumulated an extensive collection of specimens. He next directed his attention to the study of the geography of the earth and later became an enthusiastic student of ethnology and anthropology. As an ethnologist he has specialized in study and research pertaining to the origin of races in the Southern Pacific and West India Islands. He has prepared and placed in manuscript form a very interesting and valuable work on the mission establishment among the Indian tribes of Texas, and this is recognized as an authoritative work that upon publication will prove of enduring value. For several years he has been foremost in developing and maintaining the work of the Scientific Society of San Antonio, of which he is secretary and which is the leading learned society of the Southwest.

Mr. Heusinger is a fellow of the Royal Geographical Society, and is identified also with the Sociological Society of London, the American Anthropological Society, the American Historical Association, the Texas State Historical Society, the Hawaiian Historical Society, and the Institute of Jamaica,—affiliations that indicate that his fame as a scientist has far transcended local limitations.

In San Antonio was solemnized the marriage of Mr. Heusinger to Miss Teodolinda Bruni, daughter of Antonio and Trinidad (Arocha) Bruni, honored pioneers of San Antonio, and they have three children,—Edward F., Lucille M. and Frederick Waldegg.

Henry S. Groesbeeck. There is much of patrician and romantic interest attaching to the ancestral history of this representative lawyer of the younger generation in San Antonio, which is the place of his nativity, the family name having been long and prominently identified with the history of this city and the lineage being traced back to the fine old Holland Dutch stock that early found representation in the present State of New York. Authentic genealogical data show that the Groesbeecks of America are descended from William of Orange, pre-eminent in the history of Holland and a scion of the nobility of the Netherlands. The original American representatives of the Groesbeeck family settled at New Amsterdam, the nucleus of the present City of New York, about 1620. In later generations members of the family became early settlers of Albany, New York. The spirit that animated the adventurous forebears to leave their native land and found a home in the American wilderness has not been lacking in later generations, and thus it came that John D. Groesbeeck became a resident of Texas in the days of the republic, the while it was his to become a most influential figure in the civic and material development and progress of the Lone Star State. Of so great romantic and historic interest are statements that appeared in the columns of the San Antonio Press of December 27, 1914, that there is all of consistency in making quotations from this source as a consistent preliminary to the sketch of personal order here presented:

"As the work of widening and improving various thoroughfares progresses, old landmarks are being either obliterated or so changed in contour and appearance as to render them unrecognizable. Among them are some snug and luxurious old Southern homes, typical of the last century, that were built in San Antonio to shelter prominent people. When the work of widening Dwyer avenue is done, one such home made memorable by many social functions held there will have a considerable slice from the premises pared off. It is the old Groesbeeck home, at 138 Dwyer avenue, which sits embowered in shrubbery, with borders of flowers fringing its broad walks, and nestles cozily among clusters of shapely trees and evergreen foliage. This lovely old home, when built, was one of the true types of architecture characteristic particularly of San Antonio. Its wide porch ran the full length of the great front. Its massive double doors, fashioned of mahogany, were often flung wide open in warm welcome of the many distinguished guests who were entertained there, or closed behind and held in happy thrall the inmates who enjoyed its shelter and its fare.

"Late in the '40s of the past century it was built for Thomas Howard, who was the United States Indian agent, an officer in the United States Army and a major during the Mexican war. He, after his family had dwelt there several years, sold it to John D. Groesbeeck, whose family have occupied it ever since. John D. Groesbeeck, the head of the family, was a descendant of one of the original Knickerbocker families of Holland Dutch who settled in New York shortly after Hendrick Hudson, the navigator, landed there. John D. Groesbeeck was a surveyor and likewise an artist and painter. He first located at Galveston, and laid out and defined the metes and bounds of that city, where he remained several years. Coming to San Antonio from the Island City, he purchased from the late John James, likewise a surveyor and civil engineer, a tract of land which commenced at Garden and King William streets and went west as far as the San Antonio River, including the old Wulff Castle. He formed a partnership with the late Nat Lewis in a general merchandizing business, and their store was first located on Main Plaza, in front of what is now the Bexar county court house. They did an immense business and were surveyors and sutlers to the United States Government. They owned large wagon trains and huge carts, the former drawn by mules and horses and the latter by stout oxen. These wagons and carts carried freight and supplies for the quartermaster and commissary departments of the Government to the various frontier posts. Besides hauling freight to these forts their trains took many wagons heavily laden with goods of various character to Mexico, with which this firm did an immense business. The firm of Lewis & Groesbeeck also owned and conducted, from 1847 to 1851, one of the early weekly newspapers of Texas and San Antonio.

"The old Groesbeeck home on Dwyer avenue has an attractive interior that takes the visitor back to the olden days. It has every comfort and luxury incident to such time. * * * It has commodious chambers, dining hall, a broad hall in its center connecting with the dining salon and the parlors and bed-chambers. Its fireplaces are all large, and in them even to-day large logs are used to warm by the cheerful blazes that burn there. There are two kitchens, with immense chimneys and broad as well as deep fireplaces in which the cooking was done. The same kind of furniture that the father and the grandfather and grandmother used is still there. It was in this dining room that many famous men and women of from a half to three-fourths of a century ago were feasted as they sat about this table and were guests of the hospitable host. As Mr. Groesbeeck was one who furnished the soldiers and officers of the army with supplies, most of his favored guests were army people of high rank and station, but gathered there frequently were to be seen civilians of prominence and importance and men and women of high social position. Among those who may be incidentally mentioned were Generals Robert E. Lee, Winfield Scott, Hancock, Albert Sidney and Joseph E. Johnston, Hood, Hooker, Magruder, Kirby Smith, Longstreet, Van Dorn Twigges, the two McCulloughs, Bee, Taylor, Harney, John R. and G. W. Baylor, Sibley, Worth, Mason, and colonels and majors, captains and lieutenants almost too numerous to attempt to mention. Two of the presidents of the Texas Republic, Sam Houston and Mirabeau Lamar; one president of the United States, Zachariah Taylor, and many other people of prestige and importance, among them one prince and member of a royal family, Solms-Braunfels, Barons Meusebach, Herff, and foreign or native dignitaries and resident citizens, Major Joseph E. Dwyer, Major Hardin B. Adams, Joseph D. Sayers, who afterward was governor, and a whole host or legion of others.

"On the walls hang many pictures, and among them are the art creations of John D. Groesbeeck, including some landscapes and some paintings of dogs, of which animals the artist was very fond. All of these pictures are very creditable. Two of the paintings are those of the father of General Robert E. Lee and show him fishing.

"One of the very attractive features of the old Groesbeeck home is the series of terraces that rise from the banks of the river behind it to the level of the yard in which the house stands. There are five of them, each terrace being between three and four feet high and between five and six feet broad. In the center are stone steps extending from the river's edge to the top of the terraces, and on all of the terraces are growing fruits, vegetables and flowers. This picturesque terrace has attracted the admiration of numerous artists and it has been sketched by Onderdonk, Lee Cotton and lately by the Danish artist, Sorenson, who made the models for some of the statuary for the Chicago World's Fair groups."

In the historic old homestead mentioned in the foregoing paragraphs Henry Smythe Groesbeeck was born in the year 1888, and he is a son of John Norton Groesbeeck, Sr., and Lydia Horton (Phelps) Groesbeeck. John N. Groesbeeck was born in San Antonio, in 1850, and is still a resident of this city,—a man of remarkable talents and achievements but one of absolute lack of ostentation. He has been an influential figure in the railroad and industrial development of Texas and has eminently upheld the high honors of the family name, he being a son of the late John D. Groesbeeck, previously mentioned, and the maiden name of his mother having been Phoebe Henrietta Tuttle. It may be further stated that John D. Groesbeeck came to the Republic of Texas in 1837 and that he not only laid out the City of Galveston but also engaged in the wholesale drug business there, as did he later at Houston, where he resided for six years, at the expiration of which he established his permanent home in San Antonio, in 1846. He died in 1856 and his widow attained to venerable age, her death having occurred in 1904. She was born in Augusta, Maine, and came to Texas in the regime of the republic, in company with her kinsman, Judge M. P. Norton, a prominent pioneer of the Lone Star commonwealth.

John N. Groesbeeck, Sr., has resided in the old homestead mentioned from the time he was three years of age, save for a period of a few years passed in the western and northwestern parts of the state, in the '70s. He received the best of educational advantages in his youth, having been in turn a student in the military academy at Frankfort, Kentucky; Lafayette College, in Pennsylvania; and historic Washington & Lee University, at Lexington, Virginia, of which institution Gen. Robert E. Lee, who had been a welcome guest in the Groesbeeck home in San Antonio, was then president. At Lafayette College Mr. Groesbeeck became a charter member of its chapter of the Sigma Chi fraternity. He gave special attention to preparing himself for the profession of civil engineer and upon leaving college, in 1870, he returned to Texas, where he was appointed assistant engineer of construction on the Houston & Texas Central Railroad, of which his father's cousin, A. Groesbeeck, was then president. This railroad was then in process of construction northward from Houston to Dallas, and John N. Groesbeeck initiated his work at Calvert, whence he followed the construction until the road was completed to Dallas, in 1872. His surveying corps was then transferred to Waco from which place he completed the branch line of the Houston & Texas Central to Bremond, Robertson County. Incidental to his services with this railroad company Mr. Groesbeeck laid out the towns of Thornton, Palmer, Ennis and Groesbeeck, which last named place, now a thriving municipality, was named in his honor. He also laid out the new part of the City of Corsicana. After his retirement from his activities with the Houston & Texas Central Railroad Mr. Groesbeeck, in 1872, engaged extensively in surveying work and in the real estate business in Western Texas, in the meanwhile establishing his temporary residence at Stephenville, Erath County. He accumulated large tracts of land and did a large amount of important surveying work on railroad lands controlled by the Houston & Texas Central and other railroad companies in the western and northwestern parts of the state, including the famous Panhandle. In 1884 Mr. Groesbeeck returned to San Antonio, where he has since maintained his home and here he is honored as a liberal, progressive and public-spirited citizen, as a man of inviolable integrity in all of the relations of life. In his young manhood he studied law and was admitted to the bar. He became one of the representative lawyers of his native state, was entrusted with legal matters of maximum importance, and in various parts of Texas he is still familiarly known as Judge Groesbeeck.

Mr. Groesbeeck has been closely and influentially identified with the leading interests incidental to the development and progress of San Antonio, where he has been the promoter and mainstay of a number of the city's most important enterprises. He became secretary and engineer of the West End Street Car Company and as such was prominent in the establishing of the first electric street car line in this city. He was also vice president and engineer of the old Alamo Electric Street Railway Company, which built the first electric line to the Bexar County fair grounds. As a capitalist he has in later years been concerned with the development of the oil industry in Texas, with large interests in the various oil fields of the state, including those of Batson, Humble, Sour Lake and Beaumont.

Mrs. Lydia Horton (Phelps) Groesbeeck, a woman of most gracious personality and one prominent in the leading social activities of San Antonio, was summoned to the life eternal in 1903. She was born at Weatherford, Parker County, Texas, at the period when that section was on the very frontier, and she and her brothers were reared at a time when the Indian troubles in West Texas were of the gravest order, the father, John Horton Phelps, who was a native of Illinois, having been a pioneer settler in Western Texas.

Henry S. Groesbeeck, whose name initiates this article, was graduated in the West Texas Military Academy, in San Antonio, as a member of the class of 1906, and thereafter he was for four years a student in the University of Texas, at Austin, the last three years having been given to pursuing the curriculum of the law department, in which he was graduated as a member of the class of 1910 and with the degree of Bachelor of Laws. In June of the same year he opened a law office in San Antonio, and here his recognized professional ability, sterling character and personal popularity have enabled him to build up a substantial and representative practice. Though his general law business extends into the various courts of the county and state he has found it expedient to devote special attention to matters involving the administration of estates, suits incidental to the defining of land titles, and the legal phases pertaining to the organization and promotion of industrial and business corporations, including the issuing of stocks and bonds. He has given close attention to these lines and his careful study and investigation have made his dictum in the connection one of authoritative order.

In his native city was solemnized the marriage of Mr. Groesbeeck to Miss Yadie Clamp, daughter of Judge C. C. Clamp, a distinguished lawyer and jurist of Southwest Texas and an influential citizen of San Antonio.

OLIVER S. NEWELL. One of the beautiful residences of San Antonio is Newell Place on Avenue A, the home of Oliver S. Newell, a retired business man, who has been identified with Texas nearly forty years, first as a rancher and for a long time superintendent of the Pullman Company.

Oliver S. Newell was born in Oneida County, New York, a son of Albert and Ada M. (Stebbins) Newell. His ancestry was Scotch-Irish, founded in Massachusetts during colonial times, while another branch of the same family was established in Louisiana.

Mr. Newell was reared and educated in the vicinity of Utica, and on finishing his schooling came West and entered the service of the Pullman Company at St. Louis, where he remained four years. Resigning from the service he came to Texas in 1876, and for the following ten years or so was actively engaged in ranching in Kinney County. In 1888 Mr. Newell again became connected with the Pullman Company in the posi-

leading interests [illegible] and progress of San Antonio, where he was [illegible] mainstay of a number of the city's most imp[illegible] secretary and engineer of the West End [illegible] was prominent in the establishing of [illegible] this city. He was also vice president [illegible] Street Railway Company, [illegible] Bexar County fair grounds [illegible] concerned with the develop[illegible] interests in the various [illegible] Humble, Sour Lake and [illegible]

Mrs. Lyon [illegible] greatest personal[illegible] of San Antonio [illegible] at W[illegible] was [illegible] a time [illegible] the [illegible] [illegible]

[illegible] the [illegible]strial [illegible] bonds. [illegible] and [illegible]tative

[illegible] distinguished [illegible] of San

[illegible] Antonio [illegible] a retired [illegible] years, [illegible] Pullman

[illegible] a son of [illegible] Scotch-Irish, [illegible] branch

[illegible] Utica, and [illegible] of the Pullman [illegible] Resigning [illegible] ten years [illegible] in 1888 Mr. [illegible] in the posi-

tion of superintendent with headquarters at San Antonio. He had jurisdiction of the interests of the company in Southwestern Texas and Northern Mexico, and was one of the best known members in the service until retiring in 1911. In the course of his business career in the southwest Mr. Newell acquired some extensive mining interests in Mexico, principally at Jimulco in the State of Coahuila, and also in the states of Durango, and Jalisco. He still retains these interests, but is otherwise retired from active business life.

For many years Mr. Newell was one of the prominent republicans in Texas, but with the organization of the progressive party in Chicago in 1912 became identified with the new movement and has done much to extend the organization in his home state. His political activity has never been accompanied with desire for any political office. He is a broad minded man, well versed on all the questions and issues of the day both political and otherwise, and during his long residence at San Antonio has a public spirited devotion to the general good in an active, helpful co-operation with the many movements which have had a direct bearing on the welfare of the city.

His beautiful and costly home, Newell Place, is located on the corner of Avenue A and Newell Avenue. Both in its architecture and its furnishings it represents the taste and culture of a man of means, and is one of the distinctive homes of a city which so many wealthy Texans have selected as a place of residence. Mr. Newell married Miss Lola Stribling, daughter of the late Judge Thomas H. Stribling, a prominent old citizen of San Antonio and one of the ablest representatives of the legal profession. Mrs. Newell died in June, 1906, leaving a daughter, Ruth, and a son, George S., now a metallurgical engineer and connected with the American Smelting & Refining Company in Mexico. George S. Newell married Miss May Jarvis, a daughter of Geo. N. and Lillis (Mason) Jarvis, of Austin, Texas. They were married at Austin, Texas, 1911, and to them have been born two children, Lillis Mason Newell and Oliver J., named after their respective grandparents.

ALVA C. DAUCHY. No real estate operator in San Antonio is better known than Alva C. Dauchy, of the firm of A. C. Dauchy & Company, who during the period of his connection with large realty interests here has built up a reputation as being one of the best business men in Southwest Texas, a splendid judge of real estate values, and possessed of excellent acumen and executive ability in the transacting of important and extensive deals. The gentlemen who compose the firm are not only well known as business men in Texas, but as capitalists handling their own money, in the Lone Star State as well as in Mexico.

Alva C. Dauchy was born at Prairie Lea, Caldwell County, Texas, November 4, 1871, and is a son of Cary C. and Anna E. (Happle) Dauchy. His father was born in New York State, and came to Texas in 1851, locating at San Antonio, where he taught the first white school of this city. At the outbreak of the war between the South and the North, he entered the Confederate Army in Captain Stevens' Company and was substituted for his brother, Dr. Alva N. Dauchy, who was a prominent early citizen of San Antonio and owned and lived on a plantation near the present Fair Ground, and after whom Dauchy Street, in San Antonio, was named. At the close of the war Cary C. Dauchy was married and located on the San Marcos River, at Prairie Lea, Caldwell County, and there continued to reside until a few years before his death in San Antonio at the age of seventy-six years, while Mrs. Dauchy still survives and makes her home at San Antonio.

Alva C. Dauchy received a good education in the schools of his native place, and as a youth entered the employ of J. A. Graves, a merchant at Luling, as a clerk. At the end of one year he bought a half-interest in the store of L. E. Cartwright, at Prairie Lea, and after four years in that business formed a partnership with Mr. W. B. Walker, at Prairie Lea, the firm dealing in general merchandise and being known as Walker, Dauchy & Company. In 1889 Mr. Dauchy sold his interests to Mr. Walker and removed to Junction, Kimble County, Texas, where he entered the ranch business, but later accepted a position as manager for the mercantile business of Charles Schreiner & Company, at Junction, and continued to be thus engaged for three years. Mr. Dauchy next bought an interest in the business of W. B. Lockett, at Georgetown, and organized the Georgetown Mercantile Company, of which he was president, but after two years of identification therewith sold his interest and accepted the position of manager of the land department for Adams, Kirkpatrick & Company, a large real estate firm of San Antonio, afterwards known as J. H. Kirkpatrick Company, to which city he came at that time. It was while with this firm, for a period of eight years, that Mr. Dauchy became widely known in business circles of Texas and thoroughly established himself as a man of organizing and executive ability. He remained in that important capacity until January, 1915, when, in partnership with H. L. Miller and J. G. Trevino, he organized the new firm of A. C. Dauchy & Company, real estate, and opened offices in elegant and commodious quarters in the new Brady Building. The company is organized and capitalized at $250,000, fully paid, and in addition has resources of $3,000,000. Mr. Dauchy's attention at this time is devoted to transactions in real estate of large magnitude, and his great capability and thorough knowledge of values, coupled with many years of business associations with capitalists and men of affairs, render him a valued medium for the carrying through of successful real estate deals. That he is much sought after in this line of business is attested by the fact that transactions covering many millions of dollars have been negotiated by him.

Mr. Dauchy was married to Miss Ophelia C. Graham, of Caldwell County, Texas, and they have three children: Cary G., Lois and Alva C., Jr.

Rebel L. Robertson. It is not unusual to find the men of a family following the same line of endeavor, and this is particularly true of the law, a profession in which inherited qualities and predilections play a large part. An example of this fact may be found in the Robertson family, than which none has contributed more distinguished members to the bench and bar of Texas. A representative of the name is found in the person of Rebel L. Robertson, of San Antonio, a native son of the Lone Star State, and a leading member of the bar of this city since 1911.

Mr. Robertson was born at Tyler, Smith County, Texas, in 1866, and is a son of Hon. John C. and Sarah (Goodman) Robertson, both of whom are now deceased. Judge John C. Robertson was one of the great and distinguished citizens of early Texas, a maker of the Lone Star State. Born in Alabama, he came to Texas during the early '50s, and was one of the prominent residents of Tyler, Smith County, a little city that furnished three governors to Texas and a large number of its most prominent men of the early days in this state, being especially strong in its members of both bench and bar. Judge Robertson was for many years a judge of the District Court and a lawyer and jurist of the greatest distinction. One of his sons, Judge Sawnie Robertson, was especially distinguished in Texas history, being an eminent lawyer and judge and one of the judges of the Supreme Court of Texas, an office, to which he was appointed in 1884 by Gov. Sull Ross. This position he resigned after some years to engage in the practice of his profession at Dallas, which city continued to be his home until his death. Judge John C. Robertson was not only distinguished as jurist, legist and citizen, but also as a soldier. He was a member of the Committee of Public Safety that was organized at the beginning of hostilities between the North and the South, and a little later joined the active ranks of the Confederacy, in which he arose before the war had ceased to the rank of lieutenant-colonel. Throughout his career he gave of his best abilities to the making, growth and development of the great commonwealth of Texas, and few men have enjoyed in greater degree the general regard and esteem of their fellow-townsmen.

Rebel L. Robertson was reared in the town of his birth and there received his primary education in private schools, succeeding which he entered Southwestern University, at Clarksville, Tennessee, from which institution he was duly graduated. Following this, he studied law in the office of his father and also under the preceptorship of his brother, Judge (Sawnie) Robertson, at Dallas, and in 1887 was admitted to the bar at Dallas, Texas. The beginning of his professional career took place at Tyler where he was associated with his father and Judge John M. Duncan under the firm name of Robertson, Duncan & Robertson, and after some years he accepted the position of assistant general attorney for the Texas Company at Houston, where he was located for four years. Going then to New York, Mr. Robertson became an assistant to the general attorney for the Western Union Telegraph Company, an important position which he held until 1911. Since that year he has resided in this city and has been in the enjoyment of a constantly growing practice. He maintains offices at No. 810 State Bank and Trust Building. Mr. Robertson has a general practice in all the courts, and does not confine himself to any one particular line, being equally at home in all branches and departments of his calling. Among his fellow-practitioners he is regarded as a thoroughly learned lawyer, a worthy opponent, a valuable associate, and at all times a courteous upholder of the best traditions of his honorable and honored profession. Mr. Robertson has also had a military career, having joined the old Douglas Rifles, National Guard of Texas, in his youth, while during the Spanish-American war he served capably as quartermaster of the Second Texas Infantry.

Mr. Robertson is the father of one daughter: Miss Minnie Bruce Robertson, and one son Rebel Lee Robertson, Jr.

Matt Russell. During the first meeting of the Southern States Association of Markets, a conference called by the Texas Commissioner of Agriculture Ed R. Kone at Fort Worth in January, 1914, for the purpose of considering the problems of evolving more satisfactory methods of marketing agricultural products, the chairman introduced Matt Russell as "an expert on the onion proposition."

Not only on the authority of the chairman of that association, but for his many varied and substantial achievements, Mr. Russell well deserves credit for having helped to establish the Bermuda onion industry in Southwest Texas and for having done much to advance progress and conserve prosperity throughout the Nueces Valley, a region formerly dedicated and considered fit only for the range cattle industry. For many years Mr. Russell actively operated the Riverdale Farm in the vicinity of Cotulla. He is considered an authority on the culture of the

Bermuda onion and on general scientific agriculture, and has done much to demonstrate the feasibility of irrigation in that district of Texas.

Born on a farm on the Holston River, near Knoxville, Tennessee, August 15, 1851, Matt Russell is a son of M. H. and Louisa (Matlock) Russell, both of whom were likewise natives of Tennessee. His parents died in Parker County, Texas, whither they removed in the '80s. Mr. Russell is of Scotch-Irish ancestry.

With only meager school advantages he grew up on his father's farm in Tennessee, and in 1874, shortly after his marriage to Jennie Lillard, he came to Texas, settling in Montague County. That county was then on the Red River frontier and even then had hardly recovered equilibrium from the turmoil of Indian and civil strife during the decade of the '60s. In fact, Mr. Russell witnessed and participated in some of the stirring events that are well recalled by the old timers of that section. In his own career he has always stood for law and order and has never been known to shrink from danger or shirk any responsibilities when duty called him.

In the year 1904 Mr. Russell purchased the land for and improved and irrigated the famous Riverdale Farm near Cotulla. This is recognized by experts as one of the finest in the Southwest if not in the entire country, and it will long remain a monument to his foresight and industry. The farm is located on the Nueces River seven miles southeast of Cotulla and comprises 640 acres, 300 of which are under cultivation. The farm is beautifully located and is one of the show places of the South. Mr. Russell although still retaining an interest in this farm, in recent years turned it over to an incorporated company.

Mr. Russell was one of many distinguished experts invited to the first meeting of the Southern States Association of Markets at Fort Worth in 1914. To name only a few of the men who participated in that conference, there were present: W. A. Nabors, Winnsboro, Texas, president Four States Fruit Exchange; James E. Ferguson, now governor of Texas; J. D. Tinsley, Brownwood, Texas, agricultural demonstrator G. C. & S. F. Railway; H. T. Musselman, Dallas, editor Texas School Magazine; Will H. Mays, Brownwood; Charles B. Austin, head Division of Public Welfare, Extension Department University of Texas; George S. Wehrwein, Assistant Division of Public Welfare, Extension Department, University of Texas, besides a number of experts on agricultural subjects representing the Federal and various southern states governments.

Perhaps nowhere can be found a better brief history of the Bermuda onion industry in Southwest Texas than is contained in the speech of Matt Russell before this association. In words flavored with the delightful aroma of hearty Bermuda wit and humor, he said in part: "I am the sole survivor of the onion growing industry; or, at least there are none others here; and I suspect that I am as much of a stranger to most of you as is the industry I represent. I have been expecting to hear some one say something about the onion growers' marketing association, but as you do not seem acquainted with this industry, I will tell you a little of its history.

"Cotulla is the place that made Texas famous. It is the birthplace, the home, of the Bermuda onion. Some years ago Colonel T. C. Nye obtained some Bermuda onion seed and planted them near a windmill seven miles east of Cotulla, as an experiment. To his surprise and to the astonishment of his neighbors he raised the most delicious onion ever produced in the United States. Like experiments had been made in the Carolinas and other southern states, but all were failures.

"Colonel Nye's neighbor, George Copp, installed a pump plant on the

Nueces River at Cotulla and set out a few acres to Bermuda onions. One morning Major Sefeldt, a commission merchant in Milwaukee, while at breakfast read that Bermuda onions were being raised at Cotulla, Texas. He at once consulted a map and bought a ticket for Texas. On arriving at Cotulla he went direct to Mr. Copp's place and gazed on the first field of Bermuda onions ever raised in the United States. He bought the crop, which Mr. Copp later gathered and shipped to Mr. Sefeldt. The I. & G. N. Railway Company put them on a through passenger train and placarded the car with letters three feet long 'Bermuda Onions Raised in Texas.' That was the beginning of the chapter of the infant onion industry of Texas. This year (1913) Texas raised more than five thousand carloads."

Mr. Russell then described how men and women from all walks and vocations of life rushed into Southwest Texas to participate in the onion industry with the same fervor that animated seekers for wealth in the gold or oil districts, and with similar inexperience and with many ludicrous failures. He himself left an oil field and raised a crop of Bermudas on two acres, selling the crop for over $800. He then described how in a few years onions became a drug on the market at Cotulla, and how the fragrance of the onion piles characterized the atmosphere of that locality so that the name Cotulla became practically synonymous with onions. How the Bermuda onion industry of Texas was influenced by changing conditions and hostile organizations may be told in Mr. Russell's own words:

"The Texas Bermuda onion is so much nicer put up, and looks so much better than the original Bermuda onion, that it drove the latter out of the market where it had reigned supreme from time immemorial. In the beginning we got a price too that was entirely satisfactory to the growers.

"Then there appeared another man who wanted to be in on the ground floor of the new proposition, to wit, the commission man; and when he got his hand on the man behind the plow, the business began to pick up. As a rule he took the whole crop, and in one instance actually sued the grower for freight from the shipping point to destination.

"Then was organized the Southern Texas Truck Growers' Association, which for a time was a grand success—until the Retail Grocers' Association reached out and took the onion man by the throat with one hand and with the other grasped the consumer by the throat and said, 'I am master of this situation.'

"In the year 1912 Riverdale Farm dumped and left in the patch more than thirty carloads of as fine onions as ever grew. We were told it was overproduction, but hundreds of men from points in the North said they could not buy such onions for less than five to eight cents per pound. The past season, the same farm shipped to Kansas City nine cars of as fine onions as ever went out of Texas. Not hearing from them within a reasonable time a man was sent there to look after them and learn why returns had not been made. The consignee told him that he had nine cars of the old man's onions there and that he had intended to send him a photograph of them but had not done so. The last I heard of that man he was touring Nebraska and Iowa with his family on his summer vacation; while I could not with the proceeds have bought a tie ticket from the farm to San Antonio. In 1912 I lost six thousand dollars and in 1913 four thousand dollars. My opinion is that something needs to be done to correct such appalling conditions.

"Growers of other kinds of truck and of fruit have had similar experiences and will continue to have them until there is an entire change in the system of marketing."

As a pioneer farmer in the Nueces Valley, it is perhaps needless to say after the preceding, Mr. Russell has shown a grit and determination possessed by few men. To strike out and show the way is a trying experiment but one that develops sterling qualities. The Riverdale Farm mentioned above was his school of practical experience in Southwest Texas, and his successful and practical methods attracted widespread attention. Many times the best agricultural and realty journals have solicited his articles and the State Department of Agriculture printed in pamphlet form and gave wide circulation to his article on the Bermuda onion.

It was in 1908 Mr. Russell became interested in irrigation in that section of the state lying between San Antonio and Laredo, and particularly in LaSalle County in the vicinity of Cotulla. He has done more than any other one man to develop and bring the matter of irrigation in Southwest Texas to the favorable consideration of the public. He has devoted his thought, study and efforts to the science of agriculture under modern irrigation, and in this connection he has been a delegate to and attended all of the great irrigation and agricultural congresses during the past several years, giving freely of his time, means and advice to encourage the work of irrigation. He was elected vice president for Texas of the great irrigation congress held in Salt Lake City in 1913. He has constantly exerted every effort in his power to further agricultural conditions in the Lone Star state, and from the foregoing it will be seen that his labor has carried with it a stimulating success.

At Benton, Tennessee, in 1874, Mr. Russell married Miss Jennie Lillard, and to them have been born six children, as follows: Avery M., Jasper L., Walter C., Mary Lou (Mrs. H. E. Plummer), Hamilton and George H. All of them are upright, industrious citizens, showing that they were the recipients of proper care and training in childhood.

In politics Mr. Russell is a loyal supporter of the democratic principles, but has never sought public office of any kind. Fraternally he is a Knight Templar Mason and a Shriner, and is a consistent and earnest member of the Christian Science Church. He enjoys the respect and confidence of all who have the good fortune to know him, and his unflinching honesty and rectitude form one of the greatest assets in his business.

Frank Paschal, M. D. During the closing days of the Mexican regime in Texas, and a short time before the fall of the Alamo, a young Georgian, Frank L. Paschal, a native of Athens, then twenty-one years old, joined a party from the same state and started for Texas with the purpose of avenging or assisting to avenge the Goliad massacre. He was elected a lieutenant of the company, which arrived at San Antonio or in that vicinity in June, 1836, not long after the massacre in the Alamo on March 6, 1836, and saw some of the active fighting which took place in that year of Texas independence. While on a scouting expedition about fifteen miles from San Antonio with the company commanded by the noted Jack Hays, he was wounded, and the wound was so serious that he was taken back to Georgia to the comforts of the old homestead and the care of his family. Not long after independence was an accomplished fact in Texas, his former devotion caused him to return and take up permanent residence at San Antonio, where he lived an honored and useful citizen until his death in 1881. Among other ways in which he was distinguished he had the honor of serving as the first sheriff of Bexar County under the Republic.

Practically ever since the year of revolution, San Antonio has been the home of some one or other of the Paschal family, and both father

and sons have contributed to the honorable associations of the name. Frank L. Paschal married Frances K. Roach, of South Carolina, whose mother was a Miss MacGregor, a direct lineal descendant of the famous MacGregor family of Scotland. Both represented old colonial stock. One of their sons was the late George Paschal, prominent as lawyer, citizen and former mayor of San Antonio, who died in 1894. The city owes the greater gratitude to his memory from the fact that his death was partly a sacrifice to the public cause and came during his term of office as mayor. Mayor Paschal went into office as the leader of a movement for the establishment of an adequate sewer system, and before his unfortunate death had already put under way that improvement which in many ways may be considered as the most beneficent ever undertaken in that city and was the making of San Antonio. He led the campaign, waged against heavy odds and powerful antagonism, that brought about the bond issue to cover the improvement, and it was the hard work and exposure incidental to this campaign that imposed too severe a burden on his somewhat delicate constitution and hastened his death. Before his service as mayor he had been district attorney at San Antonio for about ten years.

It is through his unusual attainments and service as a physician and surgeon that Dr. Frank Paschal, another son of Frank L. Paschal, has lived up to and raised the standards of his family name. Doctor Paschal was born in San Antonio October 22, 1849, was educated in the city schools, and after graduating with the highest honors of his class from the Louisville Medical College in Kentucky in 1873, was appointed and served a year as resident physician of the Louisville City Hospital. In 1875 he located for practice in the City of Chihuahua in Mexico. Doctor Paschal spent nineteen years in Mexico, most of the time in general practice, but for seven years was chief surgeon of the Mexican Central Railway. When this railway was built in 1881 he organized the medical department, and was its chief surgeon until 1892.

Since his return to San Antonio in 1894 Doctor Paschal has become widely known as a skilled surgeon, and now stands at the head of his profession in the state. It was his attainments in the field of surgery that led to his election as a Fellow of the American College of Surgeons in 1914, an honor that was well bestowed and is a specific distinction of recognized ability in surgery made possible through the recent organization of the American College, which fulfills in this country a function similar to the Royal College of Surgeons in Great Britain.

When Doctor Paschal began his studies in medicine, he enjoyed the association and counsel, as preceptor, of the eminent Doctor Cupples of San Antonio, who was one of the organizers of the Texas Medical Association in 1853, and recognized as one of the great physicians and scientists of the Southwest in his time. Just half a century after the Texas Association was organized, Doctor Paschal was honored, in 1903, by election to the office of president, which he held two years. Some years before Doctor Paschal had served as president of the West Texas Association, and subsequently was chosen medical examiner and member of the first state board of medical examiners under the new law. His service on the board of examiners was during the administration of Governor Sayers, beginning in 1901. Doctor Paschal is a recognized authority on the history of medicine in Texas. He has also given much attention to the subject of social economics. It was largely through his efforts that the State Tuberculosis Sanitarium was established. He served four years as health officer, of San Antonio, and for several years was president of the San Antonio charities. When the Southwestern

Casualty Company was organized in 1911 he was the unanimous choice of the directors for the office of medical director of the company.

In 1878 Doctor Paschal was married at San Antonio to Miss Ladie Napier. Their five children are: Edwin G., Mrs. Walter Walthall, Miss Bettie, Frank L. and George.

Not only in Texas but in many parts of the South the Paschal family has a distinguished record covering several generations. The Paschals were originally French Hugenots, who during the era of persecution which followed the revocation of the Edict of Nantes in 1685 fled from their native country and sought protection in Protestant lands. Representatives of the Paschals thus came to America, and William Paschal, the great-grandfather of Doctor Paschal, was born and spent his entire life in North Carolina. The grandfather, George W. Paschal, who was born in Granville, North Carolina, in 1760 and died in Augusta, Georgia, in 1832, was one of the patriotic Americans who fought for independence during the Revolution. George W. Paschal married Agnes Brewer, who died in Georgia in 1869 at the extreme age of ninety-four. She was of Scotch-Irish lineage. Among the sons of George and Agnes Paschal was Judge George W. Paschal, who was a member of the Supreme Court of Arkansas and in 1846 removed to Texas, where he gained distinction as a lawyer and author, crowning his career by a compilation of a voluminous digest of the laws of Texas, known to every lawyer as Paschal's Annotated Digest of Supreme Court Decisions. He died at Washington, District of Columbia, about 1877, while extending his labors in legal literature. Another son, Isaiah Addison Paschal, was born in Georgia in 1807, and for many years was a distinguished member of the bar in Louisiana, and served as state senator and probate judge. From 1846 until his death in 1869 he was prominent as a lawyer at San Antonio.

Leo C. Neutzler. The leading mercantile and banking establishment of the Village of Nordheim, Dewitt County, is that of the firm of Osterloh & Neutzler, of which the junior member is the progressive and popular citizen whose name introduces this article and who claims the Lone Star State as the place of his nativity.

Mr. Neutzler was born near the Town of Burton, Washington County, Texas, on the 6th of March, 1875, and in that community he passed the period of his childhood and early youth, in the meanwhile making good use of the advantages afforded in the public schools, a discipline that was supplemented by a higher academic course in Blinn Memorial College, at Brenham, in which institution he was graduated as a member of the class of 1898. For eight years thereafter Mr. Neutzler gave his attention to effective service as a representative of the pedagogic profession, his initial work as a teacher having been achieved in the schools of his native county, and his final service having been given in the position of principal of the schools at Nordheim, where he assumed this office in 1903 and where he taught successfully for two years, within which he did much to advance the standards and general efficiency of the village school. At the expiration of the period noted he retired from the profession of teaching and turned his attention to the mercantile business.

As the above noted point in his career Mr. Neutzler entered into partnership with Gus Osterloh, who was the pioneer merchant of Nordheim and who here continued his successful activities until his death, which occurred in 1911. The original firm name of Osterloh & Neutzler is still retained and since the death of his honored coadjutor Mr. Neutzler has been the executive head of the general merchandise and substantial banking business conducted under the title mentioned. In 1911 the firm erected for the accommodation of its constantly expanding business the substantial brick building now occupied, the same having been the first brick business block built in the town and having a frontage of 66 feet with a deepth of 135 feet. The firm initiated business on the 11th of July, 1906, and all departments of the large and well equipped establishment cater most effectively to an extensive and appreciative patronage, the banking department affording specially valuable facilities in the furtherance of all business transaction in the village and throughout the territory tributary thereto.

Mr. Neutzler can not claim herculean proportions in a physical makeup, but his energy and ability are not to be gauged by this standard, and he is known and valued as the most vigorous and progressive of the excellent coterie of public-spirited citizens of Nordheim. His interest in all local affairs is of a most insistent order and he is a recognized leader in the progressive movements that tend to advance the civic and material welfare of the community. He has erected in Nordheim four good houses, including his own modern and attractive residence, and is the owner of valuable farm property near Nordheim and also in Lynn County. His success as a teacher and as manager of large business interests marks him as a man of distinctive intellectual and executive ability, his character is the positive expression of a strong, true and loyal nature, and he commands the unqualified esteem of those with whom he has come in contact in the varied relations of life.

The political allegiance of Mr. Neutzler is given to the democratic party, but he has not been imbued with ambition for political office. His civic loyalty and continued interest in educational affairs are shown by his incumbency of the position of trustee of the Nordheim public schools, and his past experience as a teacher makes him a specially valuable member of the board. In the time-honored Masonic fraternity he has made advancement in the Scottish Rite to the point of affiliation with Bexar Lodge of Perfection, No. 9, at San Antonio. He was reared in the faith of the Lutheran Church, of which both he and his wife are communicants.

At the home of the bride's parents, near Carmine, Fayette County, Texas, on the 29th of November, 1899, was solemnized the marriage of Mr. Neutzler to Miss Emma Osterloh, daughter of Henry and Louise (Schlabach) Osterloh, the former of whom became a representative farmer in that locality, where he settled upon his immigration to the United States, after the close of the Civil war. Gus Osterloh, eldest brother of Mrs. Neutzler, was the partner of her husband until the time of his death, and besides herself the other surviving children are Emil, Martin and William. Gus Osterloh, whose name and memory are held in lasting honor, married Miss Annie Piehl, who survives him, as did also four children, Norma, Hertha, David and Ervin, all of whom are living. Mr. and Mrs. Neutzler have four children,—Monroe, Helma, Paula, and Melba.

Adverting to the family history of Mr. Neutzler it may be stated that he is a son of John and Fredericka (Zander) Neutzler, both natives of Silesia, Prussia, their place of birth having been near the Austrian border and the picturesque Snowhead Mountains. In his native land John Neutzler followed the trade of butcher, and he was a gallant soldier in the war between Germany and Austria in 1866. In 1869 he and his wife embarked from Bremen for America, their sailing destination being Galveston, Texas, to which point they came in company with a goodly number of other emigrant families from their native land. In the vicinity of Burton, Washington County, Texas, John Neutzler achieved independence and prosperity through his association with the basic industries of agriculture and stock-growing, and there he continued his residence, as a loyal and honored citizen of the state of his adoption, until his death, which occurred in 1900, his widow still maintaining her residence on the old homestead. Of the children Leo C., of this review, is the eldest; Ida is the wife of Ewald Fuchs, of Burton; Emma is the wife of Paul Fuchs, of Buckholtz, Milam County; Otto is a prosperous farmer near Burton and the maiden name of his wife was Hedwig Krause; Clara is the wife of Prof. Thomas G. Wendt, of Brenham, the judicial center of Washington County; Adolph, who married Miss Alma Wickel, is a resident of Burton; and Charles remains on the home farm with his widowed mother.

FRED BRUNKENHOEFER. The only drug store in the vigorous Village of Nordheim is that owned and conducted by Mr. Brunkenhoefer, who here established his residence in 1909 and who succeeded O. G. Eckhart in the ownership of the village drug store, which he has maintained at an excellent standard in both equipment and service and which he has made altogether worthy of the substantial and appreciative patronage accorded to it. He is not only a skilled pharmacist and enterprising business man but is also a loyal and public-spirited citizen. He takes specially deep interest in educational affairs and he has given most valuable service as a member of the board of education of Nordheim. Prior to establishing his home in this town he has been identified with the same line of business at Bastrop for a period of eight years, and to that city, the judicial center of the county of the same name, he had removed from Weimar, Colorado County, in which locality he was reared and educated, as he was a child of about three years at the time when his parents established their home in Texas.

Mr. Brunkenhoefer was born in the Grand Duchy of Oldenburg, Germany, on the 21st of July, 1876, and in 1879 his parents, who were representatives of the sterling working class in their native land, immigrated to the United States, where they felt assured of better opportunities, for the achieving of independence and a fair degree of prosperity. The family embarked in the City of Bremen and in course of time completed the voyage across the Atlantic and landed at Hoboken, New Jersey. Soon afterward they took passage on a coastwise vessel which transported them to Galveston, Texas, whence they proceeded by rail to Weimar, Colorado County. Weimar was at that time a new and obscure frontier hamlet and the father of the subject of this review settled on a tract of land at the old Town of Content, where he developed a productive farm and never lapsed in his stern habit of industry, to which he had been trained in his native land, under virtually the lash of necessity. He found in Texas the sought for opportunity for bettering his worldly condition, always manifesting deep appreciation of America and its institutions and proving a worthy and valued citizen. He still resides in Colorado County and is now venerable in years.

He whose name initiates this article is a son of Fred and Margaret (Oltmann) Brunkenhoefer, the latter of whom passed to the life eternal on the 18th of October, 1914, the thirty-fifth anniversary of the arrival of the family at Galveston, Texas. Of the children the eldest is Henry, who is a resident of Galveston; John maintains his home at Moulton, Lavaca County; Helena is the wife of Rudolph Boeer, of Weimar, which place likewise is the abiding place of William and Emil; and Erich is a resident of Yorktown, Dewitt County. The venerable father, after years of earnest and fruitful toil and endeavor, is now living in well earned retirement and comfort in the Town of Weimar, the development and upbuilding of which has been compassed within the period of his residence in Colorado County. He is a zealous communicant of the Lutheran Church, as was also his devoted wife, and his political support is given to the democratic party.

On the old homestead farm near Weimar, Fred Brunkenhoefer, Jr., subject of this sketch, was reared to adult age, and his early educational advantages were those afforded in the local schools of the period. He continued to be associated with his father in the operations of the home farm until he had attained to the age of seventeen years, when his intrinsic American spirit led him into a new field of endeavor, his ambition having been quickened through the knowledge of his father's experience in Texas, for when the family arrived at Weimar its worldly possessions were summed up in about $30 and a few articles of bed-clothing.

Upon leaving the farm Mr. Brunkenhoefer obtained employment in a drug store at Weimar, where he applied himself diligently to practical work and also to study that would give him advancement in knowledge of pharmacy. His experience as a drug clerk was extended and amplified after his removal to Bastrop, and thus he was well fortified in technical and business knowledge and experience when he finally removed to Nordheim and engaged in the drug trade in an independent way. He has served three years as a member of the Nordheim school board and was the originator of the very consistent and progressive movement which resulted in the erection of the present substantial and modern school building. He has been a staunch supporter of the cause of the democratic party, though never an aspirant for political office, and he and his family hold membership in the Methodist Church at Nordheim. He is a Master Mason affiliated at Yorktown.

The loyalty of Mr. Brunkenhoefer was significantly shown at the inception of the Spanish-American war. He was at the time employed in the drug store at Weimar and forthwith proceeded to LaGrange, the county seat, where he became the first man from Weimar to enlist. He became a member of Troop H, First Texas Volunteer Cavalry, and was made trumpeter of his troop. The command went to San Antonio, where it remained in reserve camp during the greater part of its period of service, though it was for a period stationed at Brownsville, on the Mexican border. It was not called to the stage of active military operations in Cuba and its members were mustered out in October, 1898.

At Alleyton, Colorado County, on the 5th of December, 1899, was solemnized the marriage of Mr. Brunkenhoefer to Miss Mary Peikert, who was born in that county, on the 11th of May, 1883. She is a daughter of Joseph and Francesca (Schiller) Peikert, and of the other children it may be recorded that Joseph resides at Bonus, Wharton County; Emil died at Alleyton; Julius still maintains his home at that place; Tillie is the wife of A. H. Moore, of Kerrville, Kerr County; Annie is the wife of Virgil Ward and they reside in the City of Waco; and Fannie died in childhood. Of the children Mrs. Brunkenhoefer was next to the youngest. Mr. and Mrs. Brunkenhoefer have two children, Lunes and Roy.

August Teiwes. Coming to Texas upon his immigration to America from his German fatherland, when a young man of about twenty-five years, Mr. Teiwes has imbibed fully of the American spirit of progressiveness and that he has shown marked constructive and initiative ability needs no further voucher than the large and worthy success he has achieved,—largely in connection with real-estate operations. He has been one of the foremost in the material upbuilding of his fine little home town of Nordheim, Dewitt County and has been a resident of the Lone Star State since 1884, when he came from the Grand Duchy of Brunswick, Germany, to seek his fortune in America. He was born on his father's farm, near the Town of Holzminden, Duchy of Brunswick, Germany, on the 20th of November, 1859, and is a son of Conrad and Wilhelmina (Schueniman) Teiwes, both of whom passed their entire lives in that section of the German Empire, where the active career of the father was one of close identification with agricultural pursuits and the butchering business. Of the children the subject of this review is the eldest; Wilhelmina is the wife of Carl Brandt and they reside at Bordenwerder, on the Weser River, in Brunswick, Germany; and Lena, who became the wife of Conrad Schueniman, of New Braunfels, Texas, was a resident of Yorktown, this state, at the time of her death and is survived by two children.

August Teiwes acquired his early education in the excellent schools of his native land and on each of his four visitations to Germany since establishing his home in Texas it has been his privilege and pleasure to greet and renew friendly intercourse with his old and honored schoolmaster, Professor Griiss. Under the direction of his father Mr. Teiwes learned the trade of butcher, and later he acquired facility as a skilled workman in German rolling mills in which were manufactured railroad rails and other steel and iron equipment for railways. In the City of Essen he was employed for some time in the great Krupp firearms factories, and later he was similarly engaged four years in the City of Bockom, Germany, where he remained until 1884, when he set forth for the United States, the fact that he had kinsfolk in this country having further influenced him in his decision to cast in his lot in America.

Sailing from the City of Bremen on the steamship General Werder, he landed in due time in the port of New York City, whence he set forth at once by railroad for Texas. He made New Braunfels, Comal County, his destination, and there his first employment was in the cotton compress operated by his uncle. During the next year he found demand for his services in the digging of wells, and later was employed in his uncle's cotton gin. In September, 1885, he took unto himself a wife, and he then turned his attention to farming, a line of industry with which he had familiarized himself in early youth, through association with the work of his father's farm. In thus initiating his independent career he had but limited financial resources, and his first work as a farmer was done on land which he rented, near New Braunfels. In connection with his agricultural enterprise he resumed operations at his trade of butcher, and within four years he had added materially to his available capital, so that he was then able to make his first purchase of land in Texas,—though he bought at the time only six acres, which he obtained from his uncle who has been previously mentioned. He soon sold this land at a profit and he then removed to Dewitt County and established his residence on a farm near Yorktown, where he continued his operations as a farmer and butcher for the ensuing seven years. He then, in 1897, removed to Nordheim, this county, and purchased some of the cheap land then on the market in this new section of the county. He now found a field of endeavor in which he could show his best powers, for he made rapid progress toward the goal of success through his judicious speculating in such lands and through the erection and sale of houses in the new and thriving Village of Nordheim. He also became a buyer and shipper of cattle, and his activities, vigorous and well ordered, left to him little leisure. He purchased large tracts of land and sold the same to actual settlers, and became influential and aggressive in the platting and developing of additions to the Village of Nordheim, as well as that of Orange Grove. His Nordheim addition is known as the Teiwes-Osterloh Addition, and contains twelve blocks. To Orange Grove he aided in platting and exploiting the Teiwes, Metz & Pfundt Addition,

C A Keeran

containing six blocks and some additional tracts not yet divided into lots. Mr. Teiwes has been concerned with the erection of numerous houses in Nordheim, is a director of the Nordheim State Bank, and has served his district as a member of the school board.

In 1887, at New Braunfels, Mr. Teiwes applied for naturalization papers, and in the following year he cast his first presidential vote in the land of his adoption, his allegiance having since been given unreservedly to the democratic party. For many years he was vice president of the local organization of the fraternity known as Hermann Sohns, and he is affiliated also with the Woodmen of the World and the Praetorians, of the Nordheim lodge of which latter he is president in 1916, besides which he has represented each of these fraternities in their supreme Texas bodies. He and his family hold to the faith of the Lutheran Church. Mr. Teiwes is a man of keen observative powers and of unfailing enthusiasm in the broadening of his mental horizon through travel, study and investigation. Thus he has visited the various sections of his home state, besides which he has made four trips to his native land, which he visited in 1902, 1907, 1911 and 1913, on the last occasion remaining a year and traveling extensively through Germany, thus acquiring a broader knowledge of his native land, which he left on his return voyage to the United States shortly before the inception of the great war that is now bringing devastation and sorrow throughout so many countries in Europe.

At New Braunfels, Texas, in September, 1885, was solemnized the marriage of Mr. Teiwes to Miss Lena Schueniman, a daughter of Henry and Justina (Runne) Schueniman, who came to Texas from Brunswick, Germany, as did Mr. Teiwes himself. Of the Schueniman children three accompanied the parents on the immigration to America,—Mrs. Teiwes; Fritz, a resident of Nordheim; and August, who maintains his home at Lockhart, Caldwell County. Two children died in Germany and one daughter, Mrs. Fred Timmermann, still remains in her native land.

Of the children of Mr. and Mrs. Teiwes Miss Frieda remains at the parental home; Meta is the wife of Fred Schueniman, of Nordheim, and they have one child, Mabel; Alvin, who married Miss Hilda Treude, is a prosperous farmer near Nordheim; William is a student in Seguin College, in 1915; and Ella, Lena and Emma remain at the parental home.

Claude A. Keeran. The popular and progressive owner of the celebrated California Ranch, in Victoria County, Texas, is one of the prominent and successful representatives of the cattle industry in the state that has been his home from the time of his early childhood, and though he continues to give his general supervision to his extensive ranch he maintains his residence and business headquarters in the City of San Antonio. In a preliminary way it may be stated that the California Ranch comprises what was originally the Martin DeLeon Grant, dating back to the time of the Spanish occupation of Texas.

Claude A. Keeran was born at Stockton, California, April 10, 1861, a representative of one of the pioneer families of that state and by nativity eligible for membership in the organization known as the Sons of the Golden West. He is a son of Capt. John N. and Mary (Tyner) Keeran. Captain Keeran was born January 27, 1823, in the beautiful Shenandoah Valley of Virginia, of Irish lineage, and was there reared to maturity. He was a member of one of the first bands of argonauts who made the weary journey across the plains to California in 1849, shortly after the discovery of gold in that state. He set forth for the Pacific Coast in 1848 and arrived in the Sacramento Valley in 1849. He was successful in his quest for gold and became one of the prosperous cattle dealers and business men of California and was the first man to plant wheat in the San Joaquin Valley. He maintained his residence at Stockton for a number of years.

Early in 1871 Captain Keeran set forth with his family for Texas. In company with his wife and their two children, Claude A. and Birdie K., the latter of whom is now the wife of Tom Coleman, of San Antonio, he made the voyage down the coast to the Isthmus of Panama, and after crossing the isthmus the family embarked for New York City. From the national metropolis began a return journey to the West, and from the City of St. Louis the family proceeded by packet steamer down the Mississippi River to New Orleans, from which point the journey was continued to Galveston and Indianola, Texas, and thence overland to Victoria County. In that county Captain Keeran effected the purchase of what has ever since been known as the California Ranch, this name having been applied by him in recognition of the great state in which he had been a pioneer and laid the foundation of his fortune. He was the first man to build wire fences in Victoria County. The California Ranch is an estate of great historic interest and has continued in the possession of the Keeran family from the time it was purchased by Captain Keeran. The ranch is situated on Garcitas Creek, twenty miles east of the City of Victoria, the judicial center of the county. On the place are the ruins of old Fort San Luis, known as the stopping place and headquarters of the great explorer, La Salle, when he made his way down the Mississippi and into the wilds of Texas, so that the ranch figures as the place of first discovery in Texas by white men and must ever constitute a landmark in the history of the Lone Star commonwealth.

Captain Keeran and his family continued their residence on this historic estate until about 1897, when removal was made to the City of San Antonio. Here Captain Keeran passed the residue of his life, a man of sterling character, of fine mentality and of large and worthy achievement. He was large of physique, of mind and of heart, generous and tolerant, and one who gained and retained the confidence and affectionate regard of all with whom he came in contact, both the high and the lowly, the person of affluence and power, the humble negro and others in lowly station. His heart was attuned to sympathy and a dominating trait in his character was his abiding spirit of kindliness and helpfulness. Although living in both California and Texas during the most turbulent periods of frontier history, such was his personality and such the esteem which he commanded, that neither he nor his property ever suffered depredations from desperadoes or Indians. He never carried a weapon of any kind and never had a serious conflict with any human being. He was a man of noble character, strong in the courage of personal rectitude and confidence in his fellow men, and his name merits high place on the roll of the honored pioneers of the great West. The captain was eighty years of age at the time of his death January 25, 1903, and his venerable widow, revered by all who have come within the compass of her gracious influence, still resides in the fine family homestead in San Antonio. She was born at Fayetteville, Arkansas, and was a child at the time of the family removal to California, her mother having been a member of the well known Gunter family and a kinswoman of the late Jot Gunter, of San Antonio, who was one of the wealthiest and best known capitalists and cattlemen of Texas.

Claude A. Keeran was about three years of age at the time of the family removal to Texas, and his early education was received in the public schools of San Antonio, and the high school at Bellevue, Virginia. Thereafter he continued his studies in the historic old University of Virginia, at Charlottesville, and after leaving this institution he received about one year's business education in Poughkeepsie, New York. In his boyhood he became familiar with the various details of the cattle industry, with which he has continued to be identified during his entire active career and in which he succeeded his father as the owner of the magnificent California Ranch. This estate, known as one of the finest in Texas, comprises about 25,000 acres, has the best of modern improvements and is given over principally to the raising of high-grade Short-horn cattle. Mr. Keeran is essentially and exclusively a breeder of live stock, and in the market his cattle command the highest prices.

Mr. Keeran wedded Miss Gertrude Raubold, who was born at Glasgow, Kentucky, and they have three children,—Mary Armel, John N., and Emily. Mr. Keeran is prominently affiliated with the Masonic fraternity. His blue lodge affiliation is at Victoria, Texas, and he is a member of Fannin Commandery, Knights Templar, at Goliad. He also ranks high in Scottish Rite Masonry, at San Antonio being a thirty-second degree Knight Templar, Commandery Court of Honor, also a member of Ben Hur Temple, A. A. O. N. M. S.

JOHN N. PACE. A scion of the third generation of a family whose name has been worthily linked with the history of Texas for virtually three-fourths of a century, Mr. Pace was born near the Town of Kenedy, Karnes County, this state, on the 21st of November, 1866, and from his youth he has been closely concerned with the cattle industry, of which he is at the present time a prominent representative in Dewitt County, where he has maintained his home in the Nordheim community since 1901. He is a son of James N. and Sarah (Liles) Pace.

James N. Pace, father of him whose name introduces this article, was born in the State of Arkansas, and was a child at the time of the family removal to Texas, about the year 1841. His father, Gideon Pace, settled in Karnes County and became one of the pioneer cattle men of that section of the state, where both he and his wife passed the remainder of their active lives. He was a resident of Waco at the time of his death and attained to the patriarchal age of nearly ninety years. He had seen military service and was familiarly known by the title of colonel, it being even probable that he had seen active service as a commanding officer with this title. The maiden name of his first wife was Dixon, and she died in Arkansas, having born to him three children,—J. Daniel, who owns and resides upon the old Pace homestead in Karnes County; James N., who was the father of the subject of this review; and Maggie, who became the wife of Thomas Leggett and was a resident of Lavaca County at the time of her death. For his second wife Gideon Pace married a widow, Mrs. Zipper, and the two children of this union are William, and Miss Mollie, both of whom reside in the City of Waco.

James N. Pace was reared to manhood under the conditions and influences of the frontier and consequently his early educational advantages were limited and somewhat primitive. He went a distance of five miles to attend the little rural school that was the only one in the vicinity of the pioneer homestead, and he had scarcely attained to years of maturity when the Civil war was precipitated and he subordinated all personal interests to tender his aid in defense of the cause of the Confederacy. He enlisted as a private and served in the same gallant Texas regiment as did William Eckhardt and Ferdinand Zeler, of Yorktown, Dewitt County. He was captured at Arkansas Post, and after his release he returned to his home, the long journey having been made on the back of a mule. After the war he conducted a modest but duly successful business as a farmer and cattle-grower, and though he was loyal to all civic duties and responsibilities and was a staunch democrat, he was not active in political affairs and never sought public office. He met a tragic death, in August, 1889, when he was drowned in the San Antonio River, and his widow survived him by a number of years. He wedded Miss Sarah Liles, daughter of Charles Liles, who came to Texas in the pioneer days and who here followed farming and stock-raising as a vocation. He was a Scotch-Irishman and was of the sturdy, robust and self-reliant type of men who were well equipped for the meeting of the obstacles of frontier life. He served as Confederate soldier in the Civil war, and one of his sons sacrificed his life in the same cause. Of the children of Mr. and Mrs. Pace John N., of this review, is the eldest; Lizzie is the wife of J. R. Jones, of Kenedy, Karnes County; Daniel died in 1890, a bachelor; Lulu is the wife of George W. Schrier, of Del Rio, Valverde County; and James, who is still a bachelor, maintains his home in the City of Los Angeles, California.

John N. Pace passed the days of his childhood and early youth on his father's farm, near Kenedy, Karnes County, and in the immediate vicinity he acquired his youthful education in a little rural school that was somewhat precariously maintained, his broader education having been that gained under the preceptorship of that wisest of all headmasters, experience. From his boyhood onward his practical service was in connection with the cattle business, and it was his portion to gain in this line broad and varied experience, his allegiance to the live-stock industry having continued to the present day. More than thirty years ago he became actively concerned with the shipping of live stock, and in 1882, after he had returned from a trip in driving cattle over the trail to Dodge City, Kansas, in the employ of W. G. Butler, of Kenedy, he initiated his work as a cowboy, though he was only sixteen years of age at the time. He followed the free and open life on the range for a period of twelve years, and became adept in all of the activities and mysteries that are commonly associated with the records of the cowboys of earlier days.

As a cowboy Mr. Pace finally went into old Mexico, his employer having been in control of an extensive ranch in the State of Chihuahua, and it having been his assigned duty to make numerous, in fact annual, trips in driving cattle in or out of Mexico and across the Rio Grande, the return trips to the ranch usually demanding the transporting of supplies for the same. This passing to and fro with valuable property exposed the outfit, as the term is commonly applied, to the predatory demands of corrupt or vicious Mexicans who were nominally guards along the border, and numerous unpleasant encounters with these marked the various overland journeyings of the cowboys, who soon learned to place low estimate upon the courage of their adversaries and came to a realization of the fact that one white man equipped with a trusty six-shot revolver could put ten Mexicans to flight. As a result, the ranch force paid little respect or attention to the demands of Mexicans of this type, and both sides resorted to all manner of tricks and subterfuges in order to gain the advantage, and frequently a too vigorous demonstration with a cowboy pistol would place the owner of the firearm in bad odor with officials of the Mexican Republic, the result being that the venturesome American was at times made the subject of arrest and imprisonment on the part of the Mexican authorities, though at other times he was able to buy his freedom by subsidizing his guards and then escaping across the river into the United States, where he would remain until the storm blew over. In many such escapades Mr. Pace came to the front, and he made slight attempt to curb his youthful impetuosity and love of adventure and hazard. On one occasion he and some of his companions were arrested and incarcerated in the jail at Chihuahua, their release having been effected after the expiration of twenty-nine days, by the simple means of paying to the supposedly loyal and upright Mexican officials the American money which they had in their belts. It may thus be readily understood that Mr. Pace acquired as great facility in the use of his pistol as he did in prowess with the lariat, the while he acquired a familiarity with the Spanish language as spoken by the Mexicans,—a knowledge that has since been of much value to him in connection with his independent business activities.

Mr. Pace continued to maintain his residence in Karnes County until 1901, when he removed to Dewitt County and settled in the Nordheim community, the village of this name having had at that time but two stores, and he having driven cattle across this section when it was all unbroken grazing land. He is now the owner of a well improved farm about four miles distant from Nordheim and is one of the prosperous and enterprising agriculturists and stockgrowers of the county. He accords unwavering allegiance to the democratic party and has taken an active interest in public affairs in his community and the county in general. He has served twelve years as constable of his precinct and during much of this interval has also held the office of deputy sheriff of the county, of both of which positions he is the incumbent at the time of this writing, in 1915. He is a Master Mason in the Yorktown Lodge of Ancient Free and Accepted Masons.

At Yorktown, Dewitt County, on the 6th of September, 1906, Mr. Pace married Miss Wilhelmina Zuch, daughter of Robert Zuch, a sterling German pioneer of this section of Texas. Mr. and Mrs. Pace have one daughter, June Iris.

William C. Metz. Among the prominent German families that have found American homes and American prosperity in Texas is the Metz family, established here by Anton Metz in 1853. He was engaged in the saddlery business in Yorktown almost from the date of his arrival, and success attended his efforts. He married Elizabeth Gerhardt in Yorktown on October 14, 1856, and died there on January 16, 1894. Mr. Metz was born on June 2, 1822, in Katznelbogen, Nassau, Germany, and had four brothers and two sisters. The children of Anton and Elizabeth Metz were eight in number. Emily, the first born, is the wife of Wm. Thuem of Yorktown; Adolph lives in this city. William is the father of William C. of this notice. Caroline married Henry Thuem, and both died in Goliad, Texas. Ottomar died unmarried in Yorktown. Reinhardt is a resident of Yorktown, as are also the Misses Nettie and Ida.

William Metz was born in Yorktown on June 25, 1863, and he gained his education in the public schools. He spent some time in the saddlery business with his father, but early turned his attention to stock raising. He was one of the plains riders of the early days, and knew many of the most prominent cattle men of that time. He took up the stock business as a dealer later on, and was always known as a reliable classifier of stock. He was well informed on the various brands of the plains, and the knowledge gained on the ranges before he reached his majority stood him in excellent stead when he became a dealer. He retired from the business in middle life, after sustaining injuries as the result of a horse falling on him. Mr. Metz is a republican and has served Yorktown as a member of its board of aldermen. He is not a member of any fraternal societies.

On November 6, 1883, Mr. Metz married Louise Gohmert, a daughter of Rudolph Gohmert, a tinner of Yorktown who came to America in 1857 from Germany. He served in the Confederate Army during the Civil war and died late in life. He married Justine Menn, who still lives, and their children are Mrs. Metz, born June 2, 1867; Charles W., of Nordheim; Helen, the wife of J. W. Hoff, of Yorktown; Mary, the wife of Charles L. Strieber, of Yorktown; Henry, of this city and Ida, the wife of A. M. Harper, also of Yorktown.

To William and Louise Metz were born William C. of this review, Rudolph and Caesar.

William C. Metz was born on July 1, 1884, in Yorktown, and had his education in the public schools of his native town, and in the Byrne Business College at Tyler, Texas. When he finished school he went into his father's furniture store in Yorktown and managed the business until he left the store to enter the First State Bank as assistant cashier. In 1909 he was promoted to the post of cashier, to succeed R. C. Fechner. This bank, it may be said here, was established in 1907 with a capital of $25,000. Its officers were S. E. Weldon, president; Fritz Kraege, first vice president; Wm. Metz, second vice president; R. C. Fechner, cashier and Wm. C. Metz, assistant cashier. That post is now filled by B. E. Thuem. Mr. Metz and his son are stockholders in the Yorktown Lumber Company and directors in the company, F. Kraege being president, Wm. Metz vice president, F. M. Braunig secretary and manager, and William C. Metz, treasurer.

William C Metz was married in Yorktown to Miss Lena Eckhardt, a daughter of Otto L. and Inez (Blackwell) Eckhardt, of Goliad. She is one of the six children of her parents. To Mr. and Mrs. Metz one son has been born, Winston Charles.

Mr. Metz has a handsome bungalow home in Yorktown and he and his wife are popular and prominent in their city. He is a member of the Knights of Pythias and the Praetorians. He is independent in politics, and a citizen of a fine type.

JOHN M. TAYLOR. The late John Milam Taylor was a native son of the Lone Star State, within whose gracious borders he passed his entire life, and here he marked the passing years with large and worthy achievement as well as undeviating integrity of purpose and steadfast rectitude. There was naught of the spectacular in his career, but he made his life count for good in all its relation, gained through his own ability and efforts substantial success and prosperity, and though he never had any desire for notoriety or for the honors of public office he so lived as to account well for himself and to the world as one of its productive workers. Such are the sons of Texas who specially merit memorial recognition in this publication.

On the present site of Cuero, the judicial center of Dewitt County, Texas, John Milam Taylor was born on the 11th of September, 1835, a date that in itself affords significant evidence of the fact that his parents were very early pioneers of Texas, the year of his birth having been that in which a provisional government was formed and Gen. Sam Houston was chosen commander in chief of the revolutionary forces that won independence for Texas and made it a republic in 1836. He to whom this memoir is dedicated was a son of William Riley Taylor and Elizabeth (Tomlinson) Taylor, who came to Texas while the present state was still under the dominion of Mexico and who himself was one of the gallant frontier soldiers who served under General

Houston in the war for independence and who participated in the ever memorable battle of San Jacinto.

William R. Taylor came to Texas from Louisiana, and in the earlier period of his residence here he maintained his pioneer home at Taylor Lake, which was named in his honor. Thence he removed to Dewitt County prior to the establishing of the Republic of Texas and long before the county had been organized under its present name. He was one of the earliest settlers in the county and here he gave his attention to the cattle industry, of which he was one of the early representatives in Texas, his death having occurred about the year 1846,—probably within a short time after the admission of the state to the Union. There are extant no data to indicate that he was active in governmental or other public affairs in what is now Dewitt County, but it is known that he was a man of strong mentality, good judgment and sterling integrity,—one of the sturdy pioneers who aided in gaining Texas independence and assisted in the initial stages of her industrial and civic development. His wife survived him by several years and her remains rest in the old-time cemetery at Junction City. Concerning their children the following brief information is available: Creed, who passed his life in the vicinity of the old Town of Clinton, Dewitt County, as a farmer and stock-grower, was survived by two children. He was named in honor of his father's brother, Creed Taylor, who likewise was a Texas pioneer and a participant in the Battle of San Jacinto. Joseph, the second child, was a resident of Goliad, Texas, at the time of his death. William Riley, Jr., who was familiarly known as "Buck," died at old Clinton and left one son. John Milam, whose name initiates this article, was the next in order of birth. Elizabeth is the wife of Thomas Bailey, of Junction City, and Delaney is the wife of Joseph McCartney, of Eldorado.

On the old homestead ranch in Dewitt County and on the banks of the Guadalupe River, John Milam Taylor was reared to manhood under the conditions and influences of the pioneer days, and his educational advantages in his youth were those afforded in the primitive schools of the locality and period. When he left the parental home he initiated his independent career in the cattle business, in the vicinity of Yorktown, where he purchased land when the same was sold at the rate of 25 cents, or the colloquial "two bits," an acre. He acquired about 6,000 acres and engaged in the cattle business upon an extensive scale. At a point about eight miles from Yorktown he erected on his ranch the original headquarters house, and the same continued to be his place of abode until the close of his life. He became one of the most extensive cattle-growers of this section of his native state, his brand being "7-J-V," a design that is still utilized by his widow, who continues the industrial enterprise that so long felt the vigorous touch of her honored husband.

At the time of the Civil war Mr. Taylor loyally tendered his aid in defense of the cause of the Confederate States, but by reason of a minor physical affliction he was rejected when he appeared for enlistment in the Confederate ranks. As a citizen he was liberal and public-spirited, but aside from voting the democratic ticket and giving his influence in furtherance of the party cause, he had no predilection for political activity and never consented to become a candidate for or to serve in public office of any description. He earnestly made the best possible provision for the education of his children, two of them having attended the Texas State Normal School at San Marcos; one son having been given the advantages of the Peacock School for Boys, in San Antonio; while the daughter, Myra, attended St. Mary's Hall, another of the excellent educational institutions in San Antonio. Mr. Taylor had unbounded appreciation of the spiritual verities of the Christian faith but never formally allied himself with any church organization. He was a student of the history and teachings of the time-honored Masonic fraternity, in which his original affiliation was with the Lodge of Ancient Free and Accepted Masons at Goliad, and his final association was with the lodge at Yorktown, an organization under the auspices and according to the ritual of which his funeral services were conducted. Mr. Taylor lived a normal, industrious and worthy life, his character was the positive expression of a strong and loyal nature, and he merited and received the confidence and good will of his fellow men. He won substantial financial prosperity and was one of the organizers of the First National Bank of Yorktown, of which he was a director at the time of his death. He passed to eternal rest shortly prior to his seventieth birthday anniversary, his death having occurred on the 5th of March, 1905.

The first marriage of Mr. Taylor was celebrated near Columbus, Colorado County, where he wedded Miss Josephine Adams, whose parents were early settlers in that vicinity. Mrs. Taylor's death occurred in the year 1879, and concerning the children of this union the following brief record is given: Preston, who continued his residence in Dewitt County until the time of his death, married Miss Bettie Weldon, who survives him, as does also one son, Preston, Jr. Nannie is the wife of John C. Busby, of Weesatche, Goliad County, and they have one son, Douglas. Charles married Miss Hepsy Doolin and they now reside at Geary, Blaine County, Oklahoma, their children being Agnes, Joseph, Nannie, Mildred and Louise.

On the 30th of April, 1882, was solemnized the marriage of Mr. Taylor to Miss Virginia Harrington, who survives him, as do also their eight children: Elizabeth is the wife of Columbus Taylor, of Kerrville, Kerr County, and they have two daughters, Lucile and Thelma. John Fletcher Taylor, who is a progressive and representative farmer and cattle-raiser at Charco, Goliad County, married Miss Willie King, of Goliad, and they have three children,—John Milam, Fay and Eloise. Mae is the wife of John G. Kerlick, of Yorktown, and their one child is John G., Jr.; Grane is deceased; and Myra, Fannie, Annie and Leona are all at home.

Mrs. Virginia (Harrington) Taylor, widow of him to whom this tribute is dedicated, is a daughter of Edward and Fannie (Alexander) Harrington, who came from the City of Jackson, Mississippi, to Texas in the early '40s and settled at Manor, Travis County, in which locality Harrington passed the residue of his life as a farmer and stock-grower. He was born in Mississippi, in the year 1804, and was about sixty-one years of age at the time of his death. His wife was born in Louisiana, in 1814, and died in 1882. Of their children the eldest is Ximena, who is the wife of John Secrist, of Smithville, Texas; Allie is the wife of William Gardner and they reside at Crews, Runnels County; Charles K. is a resident of Yorktown, Dewitt County; Mrs. Taylor, the next in order of birth, was born in Travis County, May 6, 1861; and Guy, the youngest of the children, has displayed much of the wanderlust, with the result that it is impossible to designate his residence with any assurance of its being one of permanent order.

Mrs. Taylor, as the above statements indicate, is a representative of sterling old southern stock on both the paternal and maternal sides, and in her gracious personality she exemplifies many of the traits that marked the fine old regime in the fair Southland. She is a member of the Methodist Episcopal Church, South, her fine home, of pleasing

and modern architectural design and of imposing [illegible] is situated contiguous to the corporate limits of Yorktown [illegible] is a center of generous hospitality, she being a popular factor [illegible] representative social activities of the community.

JAMES T. SLUDER. In the attractive [illegible] in regard to matters pertaining to muni[illegible] and correlated subjects, in connection [illegible] development of the towns and cities of [illegible] sistant attorney general of Texas, and [illegible] lawyers, has been successfully engaged [illegible] yer at the San Antonio bar is generally [illegible] ready and sound judgment in these broad [illegible] Mr. Sluder. His knowledge of the law is [illegible] prehensiveness and accuracy, while his [illegible] played themselves in several works, now [illegible] account in large manner for the high and [illegible] fessional standing.

Mr. Sluder was born at Pik[illegible] Bledsoe [illegible] 1864, and is a son of J. A. and Eli[illegible] Frasier [illegible] is of Holland Dutch extraction, an[illegible] founded [illegible] paternal grandfather of James T. Sl[illegible] who moved [illegible] lina to Georgia and from that state [illegible] was born. Elizabeth (Frasier) Sluder [illegible] B. Frasier, who was at one time govern[illegible] States Senator from the Big Bend State, [illegible] He was a son of Judge Tom Frasier, who [illegible] Court at Nashville, Tennessee.

When James T. Sluder was about tw[illegible] removed to the famous little City of McMi[illegible] center of culture and intellectuality, and the [illegible] training, the greater part of which was sub[illegible] College, at Spencer, Tennessee, in the adj[illegible] Sluder came to Texas and, locating in M[illegible] t[illegible] for about two years. He spent two years [illegible] the law department of Cumberland Uni[illegible] Sou[illegible]'s most famous law school, and [illegible] degree of Bachelor of Laws, in the class [illegible] to Texas Mr. Sluder located at Waco [illegible] practice at that thriving city of Centra[illegible] ber of the lower house of the Texas Leg[illegible] in that capacity as a representative of M[illegible] fifth session, 1897. In 1900-1902 he was [illegible] mary of McLennan County as a cand[illegible] State Se[illegible] declined to make the race. He conti[illegible] in the [illegible] practice of the law at Waco until 190[illegible] appointed [illegible] position of assistant attorney-general [illegible] Atty. Gen. [illegible] Davidson, and served in that capacity [illegible] part of 1910, wh[illegible] he resigned. At that time he came [illegible] where he became a member of the bar, and this city has [illegible] to be his home to the present.

As assistant attorney general, Mr. S[illegible] was in charge, especially, of the laws and litigation relating to [illegible] and the bond issues of the counties and municipalities. He has made thorough study [illegible] investigation of the laws relating thereto, and is widely known [illegible] state as an authority on municipal corporations, bond issues, etc. [illegible] the author of the only text-book on this subject in Texas, entitled [illegible]

and modern architectural design and of imposing dimensions, is situated contiguous to the corporate limits of Yorktown and is a center of generous hospitality, she being a popular factor in the representative social activities of the community.

James T. Sluder. In the attractive and profitable field of practice in regard to matters pertaining to municipalities, municipal bond issues and correlated subjects, in connection with the continued growth and development of the towns and cities of Texas, James T. Sluder, ex-assistant attorney general of Texas, and one of San Antonio's leading lawyers, has been successfully engaged here since March, 1910. No lawyer at the San Antonio bar is generally acknowledged to have a more ready and sound judgment in these broad and intricate matters than has Mr. Sluder. His knowledge of the law is remarkable both for its comprehensiveness and accuracy, while his scholarly attainments have displayed themselves in several works, now accepted as authorities, which account in large manner for the high and substantial nature of his professional standing.

Mr. Sluder was born at Pikeville, Bledsoe County, Tennessee, in 1864, and is a son of J. A. and Elizabeth (Frasier) Sluder. The family is of Holland Dutch extraction, and was founded in Tennessee by the paternal grandfather of James T. Sluder, who moved from North Carolina to Georgia and from that state to Tennessee, where J. A. Sluder was born. Elizabeth (Frasier) Sluder was a first cousin of Hon. James B. Frasier, who was at one time governor of Tennessee, later a United States Senator from the Big Bend State, and a very distinguished citizen. He was a son of Judge Tom Frasier, who was chancellor of the Chancery Court at Nashville, Tennessee.

When James T. Sluder was about twelve years of age, his parent removed to the famous little City of McMinnville, Tennessee, noted as a center of culture and intellectuality, and there he prepared for his higher training, the greater part of which was subsequently secured in Burritt College, at Spencer, Tennessee, in the adjoining county. In 1887 Mr. Sluder came to Texas and, locating in McLennan County, taught school there for about two years. He spent two years also as a law student in the law department of Cumberland University, Lebanon, Tennessee, the South's most famous law school, and graduated therefrom, with the degree of Bachelor of Laws, in the class of 1891. Returning at that time to Texas, Mr. Sluder located at Waco and engaged in a general law practice at that thriving city of Central Texas. He was elected a member of the lower house of the Texas Legislature, serving with credit in that capacity as a representative of McLennan County in the Twenty-fifth session, 1897. In 1900-1902 he was endorsed by the democratic primary of McLennan County as a candidate for the State Senate, but declined to make the race. He continued successfully in the general practice of the law at Waco until 1907, when he was appointed to the position of assistant attorney-general of Texas, under Atty. Gen. R. V. Davidson, and served in that capacity until the early part of 1910, when he resigned. At that time he came to San Antonio, where he became a member of the bar, and this city has continued to be his home to the present.

As assistant attorney general, Mr. Sluder was in charge, especially, of the laws and litigation relating to municipalities and the bond issues of the counties and municipalities. He has made thorough study and investigation of the laws relating thereto, and is widely known over the state as an authority on municipal corporations, bond issues, etc. He is the author of the only text-book on this subject in Texas, entitled "Texas

Municipal Corporation Laws," annotated, including forms for the issuance of bonds. This work, in the compilation and authorship of which, he spent several months of the most arduous labor, was published in 1909, and is used as the authority for all municipalities in the state. Mr. Sluder maintains offices at No. 808 Gunter Building.

Mr. Sluder was united in marriage with Miss Lillian Alberta Dewey, who was born in Texas and reared at Waco, and they have two children: James T., Jr., and Chester Lee.

FREDERICK WILLIAM HEINRICH. Of the men of Dewitt County who have combined agricultural and stockraising activities with usefulness in civic capacities, none are better or more favorably known than is Frederick William Heinrich, a substantial farmer and cattleman who has served as mayor of Yorktown since 1913. Through intelligent direction of his operations he has become one of the leading stockraisers of his locality, while in his official capacity he has handled the affairs of his administration in a manner that has been materially beneficial to Yorktown, of which city he became a permanent resident December 30, 1910.

This branch of the Heinrich family was introduced into Texas in November, 1869, by the father of Frederick William Heinrich, Ludwig Heinrich, who was born September 13, 1835, in the Village of Banfe, Westphalia, Germany, a son of Alexander and Catherine Louisa (Fischbach) Heinrich. There were five sons in the family: Ludwig; Carl, who was a man of splendid education, but a rover in disposition, came to Texas with his brother, later went as a miner to Colorado and was lost to view; and Alexander, August and Reinhardt, who all remained in Germany. The son of a farmer, Ludwig Heinrich acquired a common school education in his native land and when he entered upon his career it was as a laborer. Deciding that better opportunities for advancement were offered in America, in 1865 he took passage to this country and landed at New York just a few days after the assassination of President Lincoln. His capital had been insufficient to pay his passage, and at New York he was held by the ship company until he could find employment and pay off the balance of his ticket price. This accomplished, he made his way to Pittsburgh, where he secured work in the iron foundries as a laborer, and there secured his real start. With native thrift he carefully saved his earnings, and after four years decided to make a visit to Texas, having some relatives at Yorktown. Accordingly he went to Galveston and then to Yorktown, where he met his wife, and soon decided that here was to be found a good opening for a poor man, and accordingly established himself in a modest way in stockraising. As the years passed and his capital increased, he bought and sold land, his first home being within three miles of Yorktown, where he cultivated a farm and acquired considerable property. Later he went to Goliad County and improved another farm near Fannin, and was identified with that community for more than twenty years, but in 1904 left that estate to his heirs, returned to Yorktown, and here, in 1909, his death occurred. While still a resident of Pennsylvania, Mr. Heinrich began naturalization, but did not secure his final citizenship papers until coming to Texas. He never failed to vote as a democrat, but cared nothing for public office. Although somewhat deaf, Mr. Heinrich learned to speak good English and to readily understand and make himself understood. He and the members of his family belonged to the Lutheran Church.

Ludwig Heinrich married Miss Anna Rogozus, a daughter of Michael and Julia (Loup) Rogozus, Lithuanian people who came to the United States prior to the Civil war. They landed at New Orleans in November, 1852, and reached Yorktown, Texas, February 5, 1853, and Mr. Rogozus, who had followed fishing and farming in the old country, here became an agriculturist and cattleman. There were three children in the family, but only two lived to years of maturity: Anna, who married Mr. Heinrich; and Catherine, who married Henry Mertens and died near Yorktown. Mr. and Mrs. Heinrich had only one child to grow to maturity: Frederick William of this review.

Frederick William Heinrich was born October 6, 1872, and passed his childhood and early manhood in Goliad and Dewitt counties, his education coming from the public schools and Hill's Business College, at Waco. His schooling completed, he associated himself with his father in the elder man's operations, and when Ludwig Heinrich died the son succeeded to his interests. He is principally engaged in raising stock, and through intelligent experiment he has found that the Hereford and Sacred cattle are the breeds best suited, according to his views, to this climate, the latter being rather a tick-proof cattle. On December 30, 1910, Mr. Heinrich came to Yorktown to make his permanent home, and improved his property with a splendid cottage. Here he soon entered actively into civic and political life, and in April, 1913, was elected mayor of Yorktown to succeed J. W. Hoff. His first term of office was so satisfactory to the people that he was re-elected to succeed himself in April, 1915. Under his administration bonds have been issued and a city hall erected at a cost of $8,000, and claying or surfacing of the city's streets has been carried on to an extent of over $1,000 more than the city street tax. He has surrounded himself with men capable and faithful in the performance of duty and is working energetically to make this the leading city of Dewitt County. Mr. Heinrich is an enthusiastic member of the Yorktown Business Men's Club and chairman of its agricultural committee.

Mr. Heinrich was married April 23, 1895, at Victoria, Texas, to Miss Ida Diegel, a daughter of Martin and Catherine (Kranich) Diegel, who came to Texas from Hesse-Darmstadt, Germany. Mr. Diegel was a farmer and a man of property at Victoria, where both he and his wife died. Five of their children grew to maturity and are living at this time: Mrs. Christine Gossman, of Victoria; Mrs. Annie Fey, of that city; Charles, also a resident of Victoria; Mrs. Ida Heinrich; and Louis, who lives at Leeville, Texas. Two children have been born to Mr. and Mrs. Heinrich: Annie, who is the wife of Dr. W. D. Poindter, of Yorktown, with a child,—Ione Sibyl; and Louis Martin.

Mr. Heinrich is a Blue Lodge Mason and a member of the Knights of Pythias, the Woodmen of the World and the Sons of Hermann.

Charles L. Strieber. The Strieber family came direct to Texas from its native habitat, Germany, and the first of the immediate family to seek American shores was Andrew, grandsire of the subject, a cabinet-maker, or *tischler,* as it is known in the German. He came in 1848, bringing his family with him, and Charles G., father of Charles L. of this review, was then but five years of age. Since that time the family fortunes have been identified with the progress of Texas and they have contributed in a creditable manner to the upbuilding of those communities wherein they have made their homes.

Andrew Strieber, after coming to Texas, settled in Dewitt County and there engaged in carpentering. He was an able builder and much of the early building in the county was carried on through him. He was too old to serve in the Civil war, but two of his sons, Adolph and Charles, participated,—Adolph going into the Union army and Charles going with the Confederacy, according as their consciences dictated. The father died at the age of eighty-four, and his wife passed on a year or more before him. Their children were three sons and three daughters.

Charles G. Strieber was not highly educated, for he had only such advantages as the public schools of Texas afforded in the '40s. The family lived in Yorktown, and there was little opportunity of any sort. The family fortunes then were not at their height, and the boy Charles went into the shop of a wagon manufacturer in Yorktown to learn what he might. He was ambitious and in time he mastered the machinist's trade, continuing in the work for six or seven years thereafter. He was fairly prosperous, but thought it best to make a move, so he sold out and went to Rancho, in Gonzales County, bought a farm and there erected a cotton gin. He continued there for twenty years, successful and prosperous, after which he returned to Yorktown and resumed ginning operations in the old home. He built two gins in this city and was active in the business to the end of his days.

Mr. Strieber was a soldier in the Confederacy, as has already been stated, and he passed through the war unscathed. He married in Dewitt County, June 19, 1867, Marie Zodler becoming his bride. She was a daughter of Ferdinand and Lena (Schultz) Zodler, who came to Texas in 1849, when their daughter Marie was three years old. Their three sons, Gus, Fritz and Ferdinand served in the Confederate army throughout the war.

To Charles G. and Marie Strieber were born seven children. Their first born was Charles L. of this review. William is superintendent of the Yorktown Oil Mill; Lena lives at the family home in this city; Ida is the wife of B. C. Gohmert of Yorktown; Andrew A., is a resident of the home town; Ferdinand F. also lives here; and Marie, the youngest, is the wife of E. O. Kunitz of Cuero.

Mr. Strieber was a man of quiet and homelike instincts. He never took part in the political activities of his home town, and voted as a republican on national matters. He had no church affiliations and was never a member of any secret order. He lived a clean and wholesome life, reared his family in an upright manner, giving them such advantages as his station permitted, and died in Yorktown in March, 1896, when he was fifty-three years old. Mrs. Strieber lives in Yorktown, at the age of seventy years.

Charles L. Strieber attended the public schools of Yorktown and other cities in quest of an education, and learned the gin business under the instruction of his father. When yet a youth he went to the Town of Luling and worked for some time in a mill, and when his father returned to Yorktown he accompanied him and went to work in the gin mills which the senior Strieber installed there. Some six years ago the milling interests of Charles G. Strieber were bought by the subject and his brothers, and Charles L. became the manager of their extensive interests in this line. They have since then added grist milling and grain departments to their gins, thereby adding considerably to the importance of Yorktown as a factory point.

Mr. Strieber was married on January 4, 1894, to Miss Marie Gohmert, a daughter of Rudolph and Justina (Menn) Gohmert. The father was a tinner by trade and the mother came from a well known German family in this county. Mrs. Strieber is one of a family of four daughters and two sons.

To Mr. and Mrs. Strieber have been born three children. Jesse F. is a student in the Agriculture and Mining College, class of 1917, while Carl G. and Carmen Marie are still in school in Yorktown.

Robert P. Korth comes of a German family that established itself in Dewitt County as early as 1849. The founder of the family was Hermann Korth, a farmer and stockman of Yorktown, who came to this country in 1860 as a young man, in company with a party of German settlers from the Fatherland.

Hermann Korth was born in New Karbe, Germany, in 1839. He was given a fair education in the German schools, and when opportunity offered to come to America with his brother-in-law, Charles Hoff, and others, he was not slow to make up his mind. For several years after his arrival Mr. Korth worked for Mr. Hoff as a stage driver in old Mexico from Pedras Negras to Matamoras, and in the early days he also hauled cotton from Indianola to old Mexico. When the Civil war came he enlisted for service in the Confederacy and served in Captain Taylor's Company of the Thirty-third Texas Cavalry under Colonel Wood. He passed through the war without injury or imprisonment, and after the war he became a freighter to the Rio Grande. When he abandoned the hazardous business of a freighter he settled in Dewitt County and engaged in farming and stockraising. A half mile north of Yorktown Mr. Korth established himself, and here he continued to live and prosper for fifty years. He improved the farm he settled on there, and lives today in the house he built half a century ago, his land being in what is known as the Stephen Best League. Mr. Korth has never taken an active part in political matters, has consistently voted the democratic ticket, and has never been a member of a fraternal society. He has had no ambition for public prominence or popularity of any sort, and has applied his natural mental vigor to his own affairs through life.

In Yorktown Mr. Korth married Miss Louisa Menn, a daughter of John Henry Menn, who came here from Westphalia, Germany, in 1849. The Menn family landed first at Indianola, and then settled in Upper Yorktown. Their children are Fritz, a stockman and banker of Karnes County, Texas; Mrs. H. von Roeder, of Dewitt County; Mrs. C. W. Fechner, also of this county; Robert P. of this review; Mrs. Louise Westhoff of Yorktown; Mrs. Tilda Schwab of Yoakum, Texas; Herman H. of Yorktown; Mrs. C. R. F. Randow of Yorktown.

Robert P. Korth was born on the farm home near Yorktown on October 7, 1874, and had his schooling in Yorktown. Among his instructors were Professor Eicholz, of Cuero; Professor Schumacher and Judge Pleasants, the latter now identified with the Galveston court. When he left school he went to work on local ranches and for perhaps ten years he lived the life of a cowboy. He then went to Arizona and was in that state a year. While there he was identified with a large commission house in Tucson, and when he came back to Texas he went direct to Taylor, and there spent two years as clerk and bookkeeper for a merchant in that place. Returning home young Korth went into the cattle business and so continued until the Spanish-American war broke out, when he promptly enlisted as a private in Company D of the First Texas Infantry, Colonel Mabry in command. The regiment went to Miami, Florida, then Savannah, then Jacksonville, and then into Cuba with the General Miles Expedition. The troops landed at Havana and were stationed some thirty miles from that city until peace was assured. The regiment then was returned to Texas and mustered out at Galveston in 1899. His experiences made no apparent effect on him physically, and he returned to his home as sound as the day he left, though many of his comrades were not so fortunate.

Resuming civil life once more, Mr. Korth returned to the stock business, for which he was best fitted by training and inclination. He became a shipper and dealer and is still thus occupied. He has sent as much stock out of this section to the markets as any man who has engaged in the shipping business, and his shipments go to St. Louis, Fort Worth, Kansas City, Galveston and Houston, as well as to the southwest country in the vicinity of Refugio. He is a member of the firm of Eckhardt & Korth, his partner being M. G. Eckhardt. They feed and fatten for the market, and turn off in the neighborhood of 2,000 head yearly.

Other enterprises with which Mr. Korth is connected include the First National Bank of Yorktown, of which he is vice president, and the Yorktown Cotton Oil Manufacturing Company, in which he holds a similar office. He is a farming enthusiast, and he has improved his own farm with comfortable tenant houses. Corn and cotton are the favored crops on his acres.

On June 29, 1905, Mr. Korth was married in Dewitt County to Miss Homer Harper, a daughter of M. A. Harper and his wife, Martha (Odom) Harper. To them have been born Melvyl and Robert P., Jr.

HOMER EADS. A remarkable career, one replete with experience and achievement and the constant following of high ideals in both private and public service was that of the late Homer Eads, who died at his home in San Antonio December 19, 1915. For more than a quarter of a century he had been identified with that city in such relations that he well deserved all the encomiums and public and private tributes paid to his memory when he passed away.

Trained in the rigorous school of railroad discipline he was not only a master of detail but possessed the broad comprehension of the higher executive. As a railroad man he attained the responsible position of superintendent of the International and Great Northern Railway, but resigned that office and for the last four years of his life gave most of his time to the insurance field as president of the Southwestern Casualty Insurance Company of San Antonio.

Both during his lifetime and since his death it has been recognized that San Antonio had no more enthuisastic or persistent worker for the city's welfare. In his position as a railway official he had many opportunities to favor San Antonio and never neglected one. Many times he originated plans which would further advertise the city to the world and would be the means of bringing about improvement commercially and municipally. He was instrumental in getting two conventions of the Texas Cattle Growers Association held in San Antonio. He was one of the organizers and a prominent official of the San Antonio Fair Association. For some time he had charge of the Mexican features of the Fair and in 1905 went to the City of Mexico as chairman of a committee to extend an invitation to President Diaz to participate in the Fair and make an exhibit. He was also a prominent member of the Carnival Association, of the Casino Association and of many other civic and social bodies. It was Mr. Eads who helped to bring the hot sulphur wells south of San Antonio into notice as a resort and sanitarium. For eight years he was member of the board of managers of the Southwest Insane Asylum near San Antonio, and gave much of his time to making that institution a model public philanthropy. In 1906 he was one of the executive committee in charge of the Chapel and Library building presented to Fort Sam Houston by the residents of San Antonio and one of the leaders in the campaign for raising $35,000 to complete the enterprise. He was also active in the associated charities, was chairman of the finance committee two years, and on January 1, 1914, succeeded Dr. Frank Paschal as president of that body.

A son of Thomas and Clementine (Hight) Eads, Homer Eads was born in Sumter County, Alabama, and came with his parents to Texas

Homer Eads

in 1861, when three months of age. The family first located at the old Brazos River town of Port Sullivan in Milam County, and afterwards at Caldwell in Burleson County. Thomas Eads was a teacher by profession, and died at Bryan, Texas, when his son Homer was still a boy.

Homer Eads began his railway career as a messenger at Hearne in the office of H. M. Hoxie, who for many years had charge of the Gould railway interests in the Southwest. At that time Hearne was the southern terminus of the International and Great Northern. In addition to running errands and performing the various duties of office boy Homer quickly learned the art of telegraphy and was given his first responsible work as station agent at Riverside, and subsequently promoted to the dispatcher's office in Palestine. As the construction of the road was pushed south toward the border he became operator and ticket agent at Rockdale, and later was also freight agent at that place.

His superiors quickly found that Homer Eads was to be depended upon and possessed not only the ability to obey without question, but in a case where orders were vague had the courage to go ahead on his own responsibility and do the work or get the business.

It was in 1887 that Mr. Eads first became a resident of San Antonio, having been transferred to that city as commercial agent, with the later addition of general livestock agent. With the exception of two years when he was called to Palestine to assume charge of the car service department with the title of assistant to the general manager and superintendent of car service he remained a resident of San Antonio continuously until his death. He went back to San Antonio from Palestine and was given the title of assistant general freight agent in charge of commercial freight and livestock. This position brought him very closely in touch with the livestock interests of Southwestern Texas and he exerted every effort to perfect conditions for the transportation of livestock. He is said to have been as important a factor in the livestock interests of Southwestern Texas as any other one man. Under his management the International and Great Northern originated more livestock shipments than any other road in the state.

In February, 1907, Mr. Eads was promoted from assistant general freight agent and general livestock agent to the office of superintendent of the San Antonio Division of the International & Great Northern. This gave him charge of the 425 miles of track from Palestine to Laredo, one of the heaviest and most important divisions of the Texas railroad. During the following four years Mr. Eads occupied a correspondingly increased place of influence in Southwest Texas affairs.

It is said to have been the hardest task of his life to quit railroading, with which he had been connected for more than thirty years. In that time he had filled many positions, telegraph operator, station agent, train dispatcher, commercial agent, assistant general freight agent and superintendent of car service, assistant to the general manager, and later as superintendent of the longest division of the road. It was a capacity for hard work and a determination to succeed that took him through these various grades, and he not only mastered the art of running a railroad and managing men, but was always successful in winning the admiration of his subordinates through his business ability and their friendship through the charm of his personality. At the time of his resignation he received letters from all officials and ex-officials of the company, all of them warm personal friends, many of them of long years standing. These letters expressed the sincere regret of the writers at Mr. Eads' resignation and contained words of the highest commendation for his ability and the unswerving fidelity and rectitude of his career as a railroad official. For the two years immediately preceding his resignation there had not been a main line derailment on his division, a record practically unheard of in the history of railroad operation. It should also be stated that Mr. Eads never asked for a promotion or an increase in salary, these favors coming to him voluntarily from the higher officials. There was every reason why Mr. Eads could have gone much higher in railroad circles, but he had achieved the highest position possible that would permit him to live in his home city, San Antonio. He did not care to leave that city on account of the long years of association, both on the part of himself and his family, with the business and social affairs of the community, the numerous and lasting friendships formed, to saying nothing of his extensive property interests.

In 1911 the Southwestern Casualty and Insurance Company of San Antonio was organized, and Mr. Eads offered the presidency and general management of the company. Mr. Eads was also president of the Home Insurance Association of San Antonio, and was vice president of the Southern Surety Casualty Conference. He was also secretary-treasurer of the Russell-Coleman Cotton Oil Company; treasurer of the Encival Mercantile Company; and treasurer of the Winter Garden Irrigation Company.

He was long prominent in Masonic circles, being a Knight Templar and thirty-second degree Scottish Rite Mason and was also a member of the Woodmen of the World, the Independent Order of Odd Fellows, and belonged to the Travis Club and the San Antonio Chamber of Commerce. With all these varied affairs and outside interests he took his greatest delight in his home, and in the companionship of his devoted wife, who survives him, and his two sons and daughter.

While his life was in many ways peculiarly identified with San Antonio, he was a figure of prominence in the entire state. He was one of the builders of modern Texas commerce and for that reason the memory of his fruitful career will not soon be forgotten.

COL. THOMAS ATLEE COLEMAN, of San Antonio, Texas, a native of the Lone Star State, comes of one of the oldest and most influential families of Southwest Texas. His father, the late Judge T. M. Coleman, was a pioneer ranchman in Goliad and San Patricio counties, and stood high in the estimation of all that knew him. Judge Coleman trailed several herds of cattle from the Texas Coast country to Chicago in the '50s. On one of these trips he met Miss Maragret Atlee, of Lancaster, Pennsylvania, whom he married. Of this union there were two children, Thomas Atlee, the subject of this sketch, and a daughter, Anna M., who is now Mrs. E. A. Born, of Corpus Christi. Judge Coleman erected a magnificent home for his bride on his ranch in San Patricio County. A hospitality that was lavish and house parties that were continuous, made it one of the most popular gathering places in the Southwest. Judge Coleman died many years ago, the home was sold, the son and his family taking up their residence in San Antonio.

Mr. Coleman was born in Goliad County, in 1861, received a college education, having attended the University of Virginia. As a stockman, he received a thorough training under the guidance of his father. The early years of his young manhood were spent in trailing cattle to Montana and the Northwestern ranges. As the quarantine line prevented him from going direct from South Texas to the Northern ranges Mr. Coleman secured a pasture just on the line, near what is now Childress, Texas, where he wintered his stock and moved them north the following year. It is estimated that ten thousand cattle were trailed north annually on these drives.

Many of the largest ranches in the counties of Dimmit, LaSalle and in other sections of the state are controlled by Mr. Coleman. He is not only a stockman, but a scientific farmer. He has devoted a great deal of his time to the cultivation of Bermuda onions, and it was mainly through his initiative and intelligent observation that Southwest Texas became one of the greatest truck-growing sections of America. During the last few years Mr. Coleman has disposed of much of his Texas land to truck growers. He recently purchased the famous Milmo Ranch in Mexico, composed of more than one million acres, for which he paid $3,500.00.

Mr. Coleman is prominent in commercial and business circles in San Antonio and Southwest Texas. He is one of the largest stockholders of the Southwestern Casualty Insurance Company, serving a number of years as its President. There his executive ability and his attention to details resulted in his making a brilliant record.

For a number of years Mr. Coleman has served as general live stock agent of the International & Great Northern Railroad, where his superior knowledge of livestock and his honesty of purpose makes him universally popular, not only with the officials of his line, but with the shippers as well.

Mr. Coleman is a member of all Masonic organizations, including the Order of the Mystic Shrine, is an Elk, and is a member of all the social and commercial clubs of San Antonio.

His wife was formerly Miss Birdie Keeran, daughter of Captain and Mrs. J. N. Keeran, of Victoria County. Captain Keeran, who is dead now, was a pioneer ranchman, and was universally loved and honored by all that knew him.

Mrs. Coleman is an accomplished and charming woman, being a graduate from the Conservatory of Music in Boston. Of this union there are four children, Mrs. Capt. John N. Hodges, Marguerite, Birdie, and Thomas Atlee, Jr.

Herman C. Eckhardt, M. D. In his native place, Yorktown, Dewitt County, Dr. Herman Charles Eckhardt holds prestige as one of the able and representative physicians and surgeons of the county, with a substantial and important clientage that indicates alike his thorough preparation for and facility in the work of his exacting vocation and also his personal popularity in a community in which the family name has been long known and honored, the doctor's father, the late Herman P. Eckhardt, having been one of the sterling pioneers of Dewitt County, where he became a prominent and influential citizen.

Doctor Eckhardt was born at Yorktown on the 11th of August, 1878, and is a son of Herman P. and Pauline (Heissig) Eckhardt, the latter having died in 1885. Of the children the doctor was the fourth in order of birth, and concerning the others the following brief record is given: Jane became the wife of W. F. Strieber and her death occurred in the year 1901; Emma is the wife of J. L. Boal, of Yorktown; Frances is the wife of Andrew A. Strieber, of Yorktown; and Pauline is the wife of Gustav Sasse, of the same place. After the death of his first wife Herman P. Eckhardt wedded Miss Jane Heissig, a sister of his first wife, and the two children born of this union are Robert and Hilda.

Herman P. Eckhardt was born in Germany, the family home having been maintained for numerous generations in the Province of Westphalia for many generations, and he was a child when he accompanied his parents and other sterling German families on their immigration to America, with Texas as their destination, further data concerning this noteworthy German colony being given on other pages, in the sketch dedicated to J. von Roeder. Herman P. Eckhardt was born in Westphalia, Germany, on the 13th of December, 1847, and it was within the next year that the family came to the United States and numbered themselves among the pioneers of the present County of Dewitt, Texas. Here Herman P. was reared to manhood under the conditions and influences of the frontier, and in addition to receiving the advantages of the schools maintained in the Yorktown community he completed a course of higher studies in St. Mary's College, at San Antonio. As a youth he began to assist in the work and management of his father's general store in Yorktown and he continued thus engaged until impaired health led him to seek less sedentary occupation and he assumed charge of the cattle department of the business of C. Eckhardt & Sons, in which he was one of the interested principals. With this line of enterprise, which kept him in the open and brought to him robust health, he continued to be actively identified during the remainder of his active career, and he was one of the representative cattle men of this section of the state at the time of his death, which occurred on the 17th of February, 1896, his second wife having survived him.

Herman P. Eckhardt was too young to enter military service at the time of the Civil war, but his father was a supporter of the cause of the Confederacy during that great conflict. Though Mr. Eckhardt had no desire to enter the arena of practical politics and had no ambition for public office, he was a staunch advocate of the principles of the democratic party and through appointment consented to serve in only the one office of cattle inspector, a position for which his broad experience and accurate knowledge specially fitted him. He rendered cooperation in the furtherance of church activities and inclined to the Protestant faith in religious matters. Henry Heissig, father of both of the wives of Mr. Eckhardt, came to Texas from Germany about the same time as did the Eckhardt family, and he became a prosperous merchant and innkeeper in Upper Yorktown. The maiden name of his wife was Henrietta Fry and both continued residents of Dewitt County until their death, their children having been nine in number.

In the schools of Yorktown Dr. Herman C. Eckhardt acquired his early educational discipline, and as a boy and youth he gained a modicum of experience as a worker in a local blacksmith shop. Later he was for a few months an assistant teacher in the Yorktown schools, and from 1895 to 1897 he was employed as a clerk for the pioneer firm of C. Eckhardt & Company. In January, 1898, he entered the Austin Academy, in the Capital City of Texas, and in this institution he was graduated in the same year, having been the only member of his class to complete the required work and to receive this distinction. After the completion of this academic course Doctor Eckhardt went to Kansas City, Missouri, where he was matriculated in the Western Dental College, in which he was graduated as a member of the class of 1901, and from which he received the degree of Doctor of Dental Surgery. Thereafter he was engaged in the successful practice of dentistry at Yorktown until 1903, his ambition having in the meanwhile prompted him to action in reference to preparing himself for the more exacting profession of medicine. In consonance with his ambition he entered, in the autumn of 1903, the medical department of the University of Tennessee, in the City of Nashville, where he applied himself with characteristic diligence and earnestness, completed the prescribed curriculum and was graduated in the spring of 1906, with the well earned degree of Doctor of Medicine. He won first honors in his class, and the interneship in the Nashville City Hospital, but circumstances were such that he did not feel justified in availing himself of the clinical and general experience thus offered, and he returned to Texas soon after his graduation. He initiated the active practice of his profession at Nordheim, Dewitt County, where he continued his effective labors until February, 1909, after which he was engaged in practice at Gonzales, judicial center of the county of the same name, until March, 1910, when he removed to Yorktown, his native place, where he has built up and controls a large and representative general practice and has materially advanced his reputation as an able and progressive physician and surgeon who keeps in close touch with the developments made in the dual science of which he is a devotee.

Doctor Eckhardt is actively identified with the American Medical Association, the Texas State Medical Society, and the Dewitt County Medical Society. While a resident of Gonzales he served as president of the Gonzales County Medical Society and thus became an ex officio vice president of the Fifth District Medical Society. He is loyal and public-spirited as a citizen, has served since May, 1914, as a member of Yorktown Board of Education and is an active member of the Yorktown Business Men's Club. He is affiliated with the Masonic fraternity, the Independent Order of Odd Fellows and the Woodmen of the World, in which last mentioned order he is past consul. The doctor is an enthusiast in his chosen profession, is an exponent of its best ideals and ethics and is appreciative alike of its dignity and of the responsibilities it imposes. He is vitally interested in all that tends to advance the intellectual, moral and civic standards of this community and he has added his quota to the material upbuilding of his native town by the erection of his fine modern residence, which is one of the most attractive in the western section of Yorktown and which is known for its unostentatious hospitality.

At Yoakum, on the 17th of September, 1900, was solemnized the marriage of Doctor Eckhardt to Miss Laura Hudson, adopted daughter of Dr. and Mrs. H. H. Brown, of Yoakum, and the five children of this union are Orland, Hazel Brown, Herman Hudson, Laura Katherine, and Howard Paul.

Col. Joseph Andrew Robertson is a man of international reputation as a capitalist, business man, and a great financial and industrial organizer. For thirty years his interests have been largely in Old Mexico, and his operations have brought him distinctions as probably the most prominent promoter of industrial and commercial enterprises in the Southern Republic.

Colonel Robertson has long had his permanent residence in the City of Monterey, but during the revolutionary troubles has lived in San Antonio, and has extensive business relations with that city and with Texas in general. At San Antonio Colonel Robertson is connected with the A. C. Dauchy Company, engaged in real estate and in capitalistic enterprises. As told on other pages, Colonel Robertson promoted this organization by bringing to San Antonio young Mr. Trevino, and by the association of the almost unlimited financial resources of this young man with the brains, ability and financial judgment of other associates, there has been formed a house of the highest financial strength and responsibility. Colonel Robertson was for many years the close personal friend and financial adviser of Gen. Geronimo Trevino, father of the young Mr. Trevino already mentioned. The two were closely associated in many extensive enterprises in Mexico. One of General Trevino's last requests before his death was that Colonel Robertson should look after his young son, see that he got a good start in life and become associated with the right kind of people. The organization of the San Antonio firm was the result of this request. Thus Colonel Robertson has had an important share in conserving the great fortune left by General Trevino to his son as well as the additional fortune which the son's wife inherits from her grandfather.

Joseph Andrew Robertson was born in Robertson County, Tennessee, December 31, 1849, a son of Hugh and Martha Ann (White) Robertson. His youth was spent in conditions little short of poverty, and he is an entirely self educated man, his remarkable rise to prominence having been viewed through an extraordinary degree of energy and ambition. As the result of his hard work and study he was admitted to the bar at Memphis, Tennessee, May 1, 1873, at the age of twenty-three. In 1874 he removed to St. Louis, and was engaged in the practice of law in that city until January 1, 1887.

At that time Colonel Robertson removed to Monterey, Mexico, where he took charge of the construction and operation of the Monterey & Mexican Gulf Railroad, and was its general manager until October 8, 1895, when he resigned to engage in manufacturing. The most important of Colonel Robertson's large financial interests are still located at Monterey and vicinity. He is generally given credit for having started the great smelting industries in Mexico. He did this by interesting the Guggenheims in the establishment of a smelter at Monterey, assuring them that the modern methods of turning ore into bullion would be a profitable industry in Mexico. The Monterey plant proved to be so profitable to the Guggenheims that they subsequently established similar plants in a number of other cities in Mexico, with the result that their present investments in that country, in mines and smelters, aggregate at least $100,000,000.

Colonel Robertson organized and was president of the Monterey Foundry & Machine Company, of the Monterey Wire & Nail Company, and the Roller Process Flour Mill Company. He established the La Eugenia Orange Grove at Montemorlos and demonstrated that Mexico was capable of producing high grade citrus fruits. He also established the Hacienda La Carlota and erected the largest sugar mill of the kind in the republic. He established and still owns the Monterey Brick Manufacturing Company, the largest in Mexico. Colonel Robertson founded and is still the owner of the Monterey News, a daily newspaper of great influence and circulation, printed in both Spanish and English, and with private wire and Associated Press dispatches.

Colonel Robertson promoted all the great public utilities of Monterey, such as waterworks, sewerage system, electric street car lines, street pavings, the foundries and iron works, the brewery, and many other industries. The concession which he obtained for establishing a system of waterworks and drainage was carried out at a cost of $3,000,000 in gold. With other capitalists he purchased and converted the street railway system into an electric line. He took part in the construction of the jetties at the mouth of the Panuca River, and in the harbor improvements at Tampico. He also constructed and owned the Mineral Railway & Terminal Company at Monterey, and undertook the building of a railway line into the mineral regions of Sierra Madre Mountains. Colonel Robertson established the Colony Bella Vista, a beautiful and artistocratic residence suburb at Monterey. Through the medium of this capitalist hundreds of thousands of dollars of American capital were brought into Mexico, and he supervised its profitable investment. Colonel Robertson has shown a rare genius for organization and the bringing together of large interests for mutual financial profit, and also for the initiation of great enterprises.

Colonel Robertson was married June 10, 1873, to Miss Ida Wells.

Some years ago he was delegate from the Republic of Mexico to the International Congress. Aside from his prominence in business he has taken an active part in religious, charitable and educational work in the Republic of Mexico, and particularly at Monterey.

STEPHEN MUNSON MEEKS. Special inspector for the insurance department of the State of Texas, Stephen M. Meeks has been a well known Texan for many years. He is prominent in railway circles, having been identified with the operating department of the Santa Fe Railway for a number of years. He has had an active and influential part in politics, served the various local offices and was a member of the Legislature for one term. Since 1909 Mr. Meeks has had his home in San Antonio.

Stephen Munson Meeks was born near Tracy City, Grundy County, Tennessee, in 1868, a son of Elijah and Belle (Griswold) Meeks, both of whom were natives of Tennessee. Reared on a farm and educated in local schools, Mr. Meeks soon found his way into railroading, serving as a fireman and later as a locomotive engineer. He came to Texas in 1891, locating at Temple, the division headquarters of the Santa Fe. While living there he became prominent in political affairs, and was elected and served as county assessor of Bell County four years, and was otherwise prominent in the public life of Central Texas. His home was in Bell County fifteen years, after which he lived at Somerville in Burleson County four years. While in Burleson County Mr. Meeks was elected a member of the Texas Legislature, serving during the thirty-first session. He was chairman of the committee on mines, chairman of the committee on military affairs, and a member of several other important committees. An important measure which he introduced and had passed was known as the "Four Years Experience Bill," providing that a man should serve four years as fireman before becoming a locomotive engineer, also as a brakeman four years before being given charge of a train. He was also instrumental in having passed the bill prohibiting toy pistols, cannon crackers, etc., in the celebration of holidays, a beneficent reform which has almost eliminated the great waste in life and property which previously was the chief feature of commemorative occasions. However, his best work in the Legislature was in suppressing useless bills and proposed laws of no practical benefit. He has always taken a deep interest in behalf of union labor and all matters concerning the welfare of the great world of labor and the toilers. During his residence at Temple Mr. Meeks served as an alderman of the city.

When Mr. Meeks left the Legislature in 1909 he removed to San Antonio. For the two years ending January 1, 1915, he was a special assistant in the office of the district attorney. In January he was appointed to and accepted the position of special instructor for the department of insurance of the State of Texas, with headquarters at San Antonio, and in charge of a large section of territory in South and Southwest Texas. This honor came at the hands of his old friend, Governor James E. Ferguson, their friendship having been cemented while both were residents of Temple. Mr. Meeks took a prominent part in starting Governor Ferguson's campaign in the spring of 1914, which came to a triumphant conclusion in the July primaries of that year.

Mr. Meeks occupies one of the most unique homes in San Antonio. It was originally the Idaho Building of the World's Fair in St. Louis in 1904. This beautiful structure was purchased by a citizen of San Antonio at the close of the fair, and was re-established on Beacon Hill as a residence. It occupies a commanding site overlooking the city, and is in the center of nearly a block of ground. It is not only an attractive piece of architecture but a beautiful and comfortable home. Mr. Meeks is still a member in good standing of Lodge No. 147 of the Brotherhood of Locomotive Firemen and Enginemen. He is affiliated with Knob Creek Lodge No. 401, Ancient Free and Accepted Masons of Temple.

Mr. Meeks married Miss Anna Glover, who was born and reared at Moody in McLennan County, Texas. Their children are: Miss Levy Meeks, Curtis Bickett Meeks, Stephen Munson Meeks, Jr., and Loraine Belle, born March 11, 1915.

JOHN M. STEINFELDT. A distinguished representative of his profession, John M. Steinfeldt is not only known in his home City of San Antonio, but because of the rare beauty and merit of his musical compositions has attained almost a national reputation. It is doubtful if any other teacher of music has brought out more prominent musicians than Professor Steinfeldt; certainly none has in Texas. True to the highest ideals of his art he has honored it by his labors, and his reputation rests upon no happy chance or circumstance, but is the legitimate reward of a life's devotion to exalted principles.

Professor Steinfeldt was born at Osnabruck, Hanover, Germany, in 1864, a son of the late Henry Steinfeldt, a native of Germany, who came to America in the early '70s and located at Cincinnati, Ohio. He was a student and a scholar, a teacher of mathematics of note, and was a musician as well, and a man of high artistic attainments. He came to Texas in his late years, and died at Houston at the advanced age of eighty-four. He had lived for a long number of years at Cincinnati. In that city John M. Steinfeldt grew up and was educated. His musical training began at an early age, and has continued almost uninterruptedly. His natural aptitude and love for music led him to pursue his studies with great diligence, and he was reared in the fine artistic atmosphere that has always characterized the musical circles of Cincinnati, coming in touch at an early age with Theodore Thomas and other great artists who came there to the famous May festivals. He studied piano in the Cincinnati College of Music and privately under individual teachers of note, and when still a youth began making trips to Europe, which have continued until later years, these trips being for the purpose of study in Paris and Berlin and other artistic centers of Europe. He has studied under a number of the great masters, both in Europe and America, among whom should be mentioned Rafael Joseffy, Isidor Phillipp, of the National Conservatory of Paris, Maurice Moszkowski, and Bruno Oscar Klein.

Professor Steinfeldt has made his home at San Antonio since 1887, coming to this city at that time on account of his health, which he later fully regained. Notwithstanding this apparent remoteness from the established musical centers of the eastern cities, he has achieved notable distinction as a teacher of piano and voice, and as a composer. He has been organist of St. Mary's Catholic Church continuously since 1894, and has been the teacher of music in the Mulholland School of San Antonio since 1900. He has frequently worked eighteen hours a day at work and in study, being indefatigable in following his art. Nearly every young musician of note in this section of the country has been a pupil of Professor Steinfeldt and he has won a splendid reputation for the thoroughness and efficiency of his teaching and for the success of his pupils.

Professor Steinfeldt has composed a large number of piano studies and piano pieces, a number of which have achieved wide renown among

John M. Steinfeldt

musicians. Many of these are educational pieces which he composed largely for his own work among his pupils. While a large amount of his compositions are in manuscript form and remain unpublished, many of them, especially since 1911, have been published, principally by the Oliver Ditson Company, of Boston, and have met with extended favor. A series of his compositions for the piano especially of note are included in opus 40, opus 41, opus 43, opus 44, opus 45 and opus 47, published by the Ditson house. These include such well known favorites as "A Forest Violet," "La Petite Fileuse," "Toccatina in G," "Chanson d'Amour," and "The Fountain." The last-named, a particularly charming piece, was composed by Professor Steinfeldt in Paris. Much of his composition has been done at his summer home at Morgan's Point, on the Gulf Coast of Texas. While his compositions are of a varied nature, his work is particularly pleasing in lyric and poetic compositions which, although classic, charm the ear with their pure melody.

Professor Steinfeldt was married at San Antonio to Miss Vivia M. Ripley, daughter of a well known lawyer of this city. Their daughter, Cecile, is a young lady of conspicuous merit as a musician.

LEMUEL T. SHAW. He whose name initiates this article has been a resident of the Lone Star State from his boyhood and is a representative of a family whose name has been most prominently and successfully identified with the cattle and general live-stock industry in this state from the period of the extensive operations on the great open ranges of the early days to the present time, which gives evidence that there is little to regret in the passing of the old regime, for the march of progress has brought wonderful advancement in the grades of live stock in Texas and in the successful prosecution of the important industry under improved modern conditions and influences. Mr. Shaw has been concerned with the cattle business from early youth to the present time and is now the owner of one of the finest and most extensive ranch properties within the borders of the Lone Star State, this valuable property, with the best of improvements, comprising 32,000 acres and being situated in Edwards County, about fifty miles north of Del Rio, the judicial center and metropolis of Valverde County. Fortified by long and intimate experience in the cattle industry and with thorough knowledge of land values in the various sections of Texas, Mr. Shaw yet considered it expedient to make a careful investigation throughout the state before purchasing his present ranch property, which came into his possession in September, 1913. After this careful survey he decided that his present extensive landed estate, known as Cedar Springs Ranch, constituted the best investment he could find in the entire state, and he showed his confidence and good judgment by purchasing the fine property. The ranch is exceptionally well supplied with water, derived from never failing wells and springs, and storage capacity is afforded through the provision of three mammoth reservoirs or tanks, each with a capacity of 150,000 gallons. The ranch has throughout the best of modern improvements and facilities, including a large and substantial ranch house with telephone connections and other excellent buildings and a thorough system of barbed and mesh wire fencing. On the ranch Mr. Shaw maintains the best of graded and registered live stock, and he is sparing neither effort nor expense in bringing his stock up to the highest possible standard and thus advancing the general advancement of this line of industrial enterprise in the state. In this connection he is simply upholding his long established and well maintained reputation for handling only the best grades of stock, as he had previously been one of the foremost and most successful breeders of Jersey cattle in Texas, an enterprise in which he was associated with his sons, as a tribute to whom he conducted operations under the firm name of Shaw Brothers, thus bringing the younger generation to the front and personally resting to a certain extent upon his own well earned honors. On the Cedar Springs Ranch are to be found the best grades of registered stock, with an average herd of about 1,000 steers, 500 cows, 5,100 head of goats and sheep, 100 head of mares and other registered horses, and about 300 head of pure-bred, registered swine. All stock from the ranch commands the highest market prices and the estate is widely known throughout the Southwest as of the most reliable sources from which to obtain the best live stock the country affords. In the carrying forward of this important ranch enterprise Mr. Shaw still continued to be associated with his sons, who are vigorous and progressive young business men, and the title of Shaw Brothers is still retained. In September, 1913, Mr. Shaw and his sons disposed of their famous dairy herd of Jersey cattle and farm and the scope and importance of the business which they had developed in that connection is indicated by their having received in consideration of this transaction the sum of $130,000.

Lemuel T. Shaw was born in St. Landry Parish, Louisiana, October 13, 1849, and is a son of Lemuel J. B. and Adelle (Guillory) Shaw, the latter having been a member of a prominent old French family of Louisiana and having there passed her entire life, her death having occurred in 1860, at the Shaw homestead in St. Landry Parish. There the father owned and operated a large plantation, though he was by profession a teacher, having been a man of fine scholastic attainments and having for many years conducted a successful boarding school in his home parish, besides having otherwise been prominent in educational affairs in that state, as was he later in Texas. In the opening year of the Civil war his plantation was overrun and devastated by the contending military forces, and he consequently removed with his family to Texas, bringing also his negro slaves and as much of his material effects as could be transported in wagons. He established his home at Columbus, Colorado County, this state, where he was revenue assessor, superintendent of public schools, and United States cotton weigher, a position he held until his death, and there passed the residue of his kindly, generous and useful life, his death having occurred in 1872 and his name meriting enduring place on the roll of the honored pioneers of the Lone Star commonwealth.

Upon coming to Texas, when Lemuel T. Shaw, of this review, was a lad of about twelve years he and other members of the family became identified with the cattle industry, to which he has continued to pay allegiance during the long intervening period of more than half a century and in connection with which there has been no interruption in his career of success. From a previously published sketch are taken the following pertinent and interesting statements concerning this sterling and popular citizen: "He began to run cattle in Colorado county as soon as he was old enough to take charge of a bunch. He later moved his outfit to the free range further west, and for several years he was located and ran cattle in Burnet, San Saba and McCulloch counties. He engaged also in the sheep business, and by wise management and the acquiring of a thorough knowledge of the live-stock industry he entered upon a successful career that has not been marred by any financial reverses. In 1889 Mr. Shaw located in San Antonio, where he engaged in the dairy business on a modest scale, with headquarters on South Flores Street. There he conducted his enterprise six years, at the expiration of which he removed to more eligible location in the west end of the city. There he had 700 acres under effective cultivation for feed crops for his dairy stock and of the entire tract of land had only five acres in the city.'' In view of his change in the field of operations it is sufficient to say that Mr. Shaw and his sons developed one of the extensive and model dairy enterprises of the state, with the most approved and modern facilities, and that the fine Jersey herd, kept up to full numerical strength through the breeding of the finest registered grades, became known as one of the best in the Southwest, the stock and business having been sold in 1913, as previously noted in this context.

Mr. Shaw and his sons are progressive and public-spirited in their civic attitude and have shown their appreciation of the responsibilities which success imposes. All are unwavering supporters of the cause of the democratic party and all of the sons are worthily upholding the prestige of the family names, both as loyal citizens and successful business men.

In Colorado County, this state, in the year 1869, was solemnized the marriage of Lemuel T. Shaw to Miss Kate Ferguson, who likewise was born and reared in Louisiana, and of the twelve children of this union all are living except one son, Percy, who met an accidental death in 1907, November 26th, when on a hunting expedition, this constituting the only break in this interesting family circle. The eldest of the children is Mrs. Florence Maud Armstrong; Lottie is the wife of Louis Brooks, who is a prominent and influential citizen of McCulloch County, with extensive capitalistic and industrial interests in that section of the state; Mrs. Lucy Carothers was the next in order of birth and after her came Claudius, the eldest of the sons; Percy met a tragic death, as already noted; Thomas, Mrs. Pearl Lacey, Mrs. Della Riley, Essie, Katie and Grover complete the family circle. Claudius E. Shaw, the eldest son, who is now acting as electrical engineer with the traction company of this city, received the best of technical education and in 1906 completed a four years' term of enlistment in the United States Navy, his special skill and knowledge having gained to him prominent preferment in the electrical service of the navy and his concluding Government service having been that rendered while he was in charge of the naval wireless-telegraph station at Portsmouth, New Hampshire, where he was stationed at the time of his resignation from the navy.

The two sons associated in business with their father are Ransom and Thomas Shaw. Grover, the youngest son, is carrying on a successful business known as The Central Vulcanizing Company of this city.

Hamilton G. Blumberg. While many Texas men, with genius for finance, business or industry, have attained eminence both in and out of the state, it has so far been unusual to find inventive talent satisfied to remain at home and attempt to realize the possibilities of the Texas field in manufacturing. A notable exception is the case of the young San Antonio automobile manufacturer, Hamilton G. Blumberg, who has individually financed and begun the manufacture of motor cars with a factory which promises within a short time to rank with the leading industries of the city and later to compete with the great automobile plants of the North and East.

A brief description of the Blumberg plant and its product cannot but prove interesting. The factory is located at the corner of North Mesquite and Burnet streets, with ground sufficient to afford room for the expansion that will follow the growth of the business. Mr. Blumberg will make three different chassis: a 16-horsepower four-cylinder, a

28-horsepower four cylinder, and a 60-horsepower eight cylinder—three types of car that will compete with the best in the United States. They are entirely of his own design. Everything made in the largest automobile factories will be made in this San Antonio plant. He constructs his own steam hammers, die presses, etc. The principal feature of the car is the engine, which is a distinctly Blumberg invention, and competent judges say it is superior to nearly every engine made in this country or abroad. It has a special interest as being the only motor made in Texas. A feature which commends it even to the unexpert mind is that it contains from 170 to 200 less parts than the average standard motor.

After the first Blumberg motor was turned out at the plant early in June, 1914, it was put through a long series of very severe tests, with results in efficiency and endurance that met every expectation. Every part is manufactured from raw material in San Antonio. The motor is cast entire, and many parts, separate in other motors, are integral in this. The intake and exhaust valve ports are cast in the cylinder head. The perfected cooling system and the extended valve jackets make it impossible for the valves to warp. The cooling system is a specially noteworthy feature. The construction of the water jacket permits the circulation of water to practically every portion of the motor where combustion takes place, and thus the possibility of overheating has been eliminated. One of the secrets of the cooling system is that the water is kept in circulation at all times, the current starting from the radiator cap and dividing between the middle two cylinders and passing to either side in equal volume, so as to insure uniform cooling.

The valve area of the new motor is the largest of any motor manufactured with a 3¼ inch bore and a stroke of the same figure. The valve measures 1$\frac{1}{16}$ inches. The engine is rated at 28-horsepower, but will develop an excess of that amount. A higher compression than the average is noted in the operation of the motor, and its weight is about 100 pounds less than other motors of the same power.

Another feature is the removable cam case, one of the most noteworthy conveniences in its make-up. In the Blumberg car a unit power plant is arranged with the transmission abutting the motor at the rear. The drive is three speed, selective, with sliding-gear transmission. A Bosch high-tension magneto and a Stromberg carburetor form a part of the equipment. A low gasoline and oil consumption feature the four and eight cylinder cars. The main bearing adjustment is accomplished from the outside of the motor, thus simplifying its operation and doing away with the necessity of taking down the motor to get at its bearings. This is a patented arrangement of Mr. Blumberg's, and adds to the popularity of the car.

Expert opinion would be convinced from the above brief description that to accomplish so much is a great work for a man still under thirty. Hamilton G. Blumberg was born in Comal County, Texas, in 1886. His parents, E. H. and Frances (Day) Blumberg, are now living on the fine Blumberg farm, on the Guadalupe River in Guadalupe County, six miles from Seguin. His father was born in Comal County, son of one of the colonists who came from Germany with Prince Solms-Braunfels in 1845 and founded the Town of New Braunfels. The Blumbergs are among the highly honored German pioneer families in Southwest Texas. In the late '80s the family moved to its present seat in Guadalupe County.

Hamilton G. Blumberg was reared on a farm. From the age of twelve he manifested the extraordinary interest and knack in practical mechanics which have been the impelling force of his life. Technical education might refine, but could add nothing to such native talent. His attention was turned to automobiles when the industry was at its beginning, and when they were known only as "horseless carriages." There is probably no man so young with so thorough and expert knowledge of the construction and operation of motor driven vehicles. He came to San Antonio in 1908, and after working quietly at the perfecting of his inventions launched the factory in 1914. He has been at work on his motor for fourteen years, in the intervals of other occupations, and concentrated his time on it almost steadily for four years before beginning its manufacture.

Mr. Blumberg resides in San Antonio. He married Miss Hildegard Fischer October 20, 1913, who was born in Gillespie County, Texas, a daughter of Albert D. and Minnie (Willmann) Fischer, the former a native of Gillespie County, Texas, and the latter of Mason County, Texas. Her father, for sixteen years a teacher in the public schools of Gillespie County and for six years in Gaudalupe County, is now associated with Mr. Blumberg in the automobile business.

JOHN S. LANKFORD, M. D. While Doctor Lankford has for many years been one of the leading physicians and surgeons of San Antonio and is medical director of the San Antonio Life Insurance Company, his activities and service have been so concentrated as to give him the highest reputation as a specialist in the public health movement. It is in the public health movement that the physician has had his highest opportunity for public leadership and service. While this movement is in no unimportant sense directly opposed to the financial interests of the profession, it is true beyond question that every notable advance in the conservation of public health has had its initial impulse in the organized and individual activities of the medical profession. Doctor Lankford began his useful service while an official member of the San Antonio school board, and was a prime factor in the campaign which effected such notable results in the education of a younger generation in the essentials of public health, while in later years his scope of activity has been greatly enlarged and he is now making it effective through the great agencies of life insurance organizations.

Dr. John S. Lankford is a native of Mississippi, came to Texas in 1876 when a boy, and was reared and educated in this state. His early years were spent in Milam and Grayson counties, where he attended the local schools, and in 1882 was graduated with honor from the medical department of the University of Louisville, Kentucky. Doctor Lankford began practice at Atoka in the Choctaw Nation of Indian Territory, practiced there until 1892, and has since suited his talent to the broader field of labor at San Antonio. For thirty years Doctor Lankford has been a painstaking student and observer, and is one of the best informed men in his profession in the Southwest. In 1891 he pursued post-graduate studies in the New York Polyclinic. He has served as director and treasurer of the Physicians and Surgeons Hospital of San Antonio, and is one of the five trustees of the Texas State Journal of Medicine, the official organ of the State Medical Association. He has membership in both the County and State and the American Medical Associations, and both through his practical work and his contributions to scientific literature his name is associated with a splendid reputation not only in his home state but elsewhere.

While Doctor Lankford has been a student of public health and hygiene for a number of years, his first important opportunity for practical work along that line was given when he became a member of the San Antonio school board, of which he was elected president in

May, 1906. He came to this public office with a mature reputation and standing as a physician, and soon put himself on record as an active advocate for the plan of teaching preventive medicine to the public school children. He worked to formulate and secure the adoption of the plans whereby children should receive instruction in the essentials of individual and public hygiene, and in a few years his work had brought some splendid results in San Antonio, and had attracted attention from many of the prominent members of the medical fraternity and educators throughout the country.

The public health movement as a vital factor in community affairs is comparatively new, and Doctor Lankford's activities in that line constitute him one of the pioneer leaders, at least in the Southwest. In recent years there has come a somewhat general recognition of the fact that the requirements and conditions of public school life constitute a great strain upon the student, and it was his keen insight into and understanding of such facts that led Doctor Lankford to take so decided a stand when he became a member of the San Antonio school board. In an address read before the Texas State Medical Association in May, 1902, and subsequently printed in the Medical News of New York, on the subject of School Life and Insanity, Doctor Lankford called attention to "the high pressure in the school life of our children." "The constant and terrific strain," he said "upon the brain of the growing child without any attention to the development of the body and with but little care for the general health cannot be otherwise than disastrous." Elaborating on this theme, he came to the conclusion that the burden laid upon children was far beyond the limits of safety, and was a potent factor in the causation of insanity. At that time he outlined some general recommendations for the reduction of these burdens. including a lightening of the course of study, a development of body co-equally with the mind, a better classification of pupils and study of individual tendencies and requirements, the use of object lessons rather than books and the introduction of industrial training as rapidly as possible. The ideals upon which much of his own professional work has been based, especially in later years, were well stated in two sentences taken from another part of this address, as follows: "Every human creature is responsible to his fellow man in the exact measure of his influence and opportunity, but the doctor has a double responsibility in matters of education, for he follows the child from infancy throughout the period of development and he is expected to advise wisely in all things. The physician's greatest responsibility, as well as opportunity, is in preventing disease, and there has never been in human history a danger that called louder for his beneficent aid than is found in the school life of our children today."

It was with these convictions of responsibility that Doctor Lankford undertook his duties as a member of the San Antonio school board. His experience there led to a greater elaboration of reform, and he summed up his ideas and outlined a broad course of principles which should govern the administration of public schools in an address before the Eighth District Medical Society of Texas, which was afterwards reprinted in two Eastern medical journals. In this address, among the things which should engage the attention of school board and health officers, he placed as first the physical training, the providing of ample play grounds and encouragement of outdoor sport, adjustment of courses to the individual requirements of pupils, the introduction of practical training one department of which should be manual training, the study of sanitation and personal and public hygiene, pure food and proper dress, and also attention on the part of school authorities to the con-

Joe L. Hill

struction, lighting, ventilation and heating of buildings, and also the treatment by public school physicians of physical defectiveness and curable diseases. In one of the mild yellow fever epidemics experienced in San Antonio, resulting in several deaths and the interruption of business that cost millions of dollars, Doctor Lankford read a practical lesson which caused him to concentrate his efforts for the proper education of the younger generation, as more important than a campaign against heavy obstacles for reforming a generation that was almost too old to learn. Doctor Lankford was the real author and the motive power behind the plan which introduced into San Antonio public schools a campaign of education that resulted in the instruction of children on the causes and methods of prevention of various epidemics and an effective work that in a short time tended to reduce throughout the city such diseases as malaria, typhoid fever and at the same time improve sanitation both in homes and in the municipality at large. Throughout his connection with the school board Doctor Lankford continued his work along the same line, lectured all over the state on the subject, and no other individual has done more to promote practical education in sanitation and public health in San Antonio than Doctor Lankford.

In later years his efforts have been extended in a systematic and painstaking manner to a still broader field for the conservation of the human race. In his position as medical director of the San Antonio Life Insurance Company he is not only stressing these principles with the policy holders of his own company, but is using his position as a means to enlist the support of all life insurance companies in the United States in a great movement for preventing disease and improving the condition of humanity from infancy upwards. Through the splendid and influential organizations of life insurance companies he hopes to reach 10,000,000 families with instruction and definite methods. His first move in this direction for the improvement of public health as a national measure, he took at a meeting of the medical section of the American Life Insurance Convention which met in San Antonio in 1911. His address on the subject at that meeting was a notable effort, and one of the most impressive papers read before the members. He has continued to write articles along the same line for various professional and general publications, the most notable of which was a contribution to the Popular Science Monthly of September, 1913, under the title "The Lesson of Canal Zone Sanitation." In that Doctor Lankford brought out in his usual illuminating manner the great work of sanitation conducted in Panama by the military authorities and the remarkable reduction in disease and death, and showed how the application of these methods or something suitably similar could effect an even greater change in the United States. Another article that attracted wide attention was on "Life Insurance and the Conservation of Human Life." contributed to the Medical Record of April 13, 1912.

Doctor Lankford has made a thorough study and investigation of public health measures the world over. While he enjoys a large general practice as a physician and surgeon in his home city, his chief interest is in the cause of public health, and it is his greatest ambition to see the results which must inevitably flow to civilization after the movement has been effectively organized and applied systematically in every community of the country.

Joe L. Hill. Among the distinctively prominent and brilliant lawyers of the State of Texas none is more versatile, talented or well equipped for the work of his profession than Joe L. Hill, who maintains his home and business headquarters at San Antonio. Throughout his career as an able attorney and well fortified counselor he has, by reason of unimpeachable conduct and close observance of the unwritten code of professional ethics, gained the admiration and respect of his fellow members of the bar, in addition to which he commands a high place in the confidence and esteem of his fellow citizens.

September 2, 1861, at Caldwell, Burleson County, Texas, occurred the birth of Joe L. Hill, who is a son of William J. and Sarah Elizabeth (Coleman) Hill. The father was an early pioneer in the Lone Star state. He was born in North Carolina, was married in Mississippi, and came to Texas in 1839, during the days of the Texas republic, locating first at Chapel Hill, in Washington County. Subsequently he removed to Burleson County, where he was elected first district and county clerk, in which capacity he served for several years. Having in the meantime studied law and been admitted to the bar, he engaged in the practice of law at Caldwell, eventually becoming a partner in that profession of Judge A. S. Broadus, widely known as one of the greatest lawyers of Texas. Later he was a law partner of W. K. Holman, another distinguished member of the Texas bar. William J. Hill was summoned to the life eternal October 15, 1874, after a most interesting and useful career.

The youngest in order of birth in a family of ten children, Joe L. Hill grew up at Caldwell, Texas, and there received a good common-school education. He was graduated in the Sam Houston Normal School, at Huntsville, in 1881, and for the ensuing three years he taught school at Caldwell, studying law in the meantime and being admitted to the bar in 1884. He initiated the active practice of his profession in his home town and removed thence, in 1886, to Victoria, remaining in the latter place for a period of twenty years, during which time he built up a large and lucrative law practice. Seeking a larger field for his life work, however, he located in San Antonio in 1906 and here he has since maintained his home. He is now a member of the well known law firm of Bullitt, Hill & Fly, a combination of legal lights hard to beat in any community. In his private life Mr. Hill is distinguished by all that marks the true gentleman. His is a noble character—one that subordinates personal ambition to public good and seeks rather the benefit of others than the aggrandizement of self. He is affiliated with a number of representative local organizations and in religious matters is a staunch Methodist.

At Gonzales, Texas, was solemnized the marriage of Mr. Hill to Miss Georgia Fly, a member of the distinguished Texas family of that name. Mrs. Hill is a daughter of Maj. G. W. L. Fly, formerly a law partner of Judge Davidson and now one of the judges of the Supreme Court of Texas. Mrs. Hill is first cousin of Judge Davidson and of Judge W. S. Fly, chief justice of the court of civil appeals in San Antonio, Texas. Mr. and Mrs. Hill have three sons: Rev. Milton Fly Hill is a minister of the Methodist Episcopal Church, South, and is connected with the West Texas Conference: he was graduated in the University of Texas and subsequently attended Vanderbilt University, at Nashville, Tennessee, and was also a student in Harvard University, having been enrolled in the Divinity School at Cambridge; Joe L., Jr., also splendidly educated, is now engaged in the telephone business at Dallas; and William Madden, youngest son, is mentioned more particularly below.

A native of Victoria, Texas, where his birth occurred in 1900, William Madden Hill is already making a name for himself. In June, 1915, he was adjudged the winner in the Agricultural & Mechanical College oratorical contest, for which there were five local entrants, all of whom had excellent orations. His oration, however, was adjudged best by the judges and he was invited to go to College Station and deliver same, all his expenses being paid. In the contest which ensued Mr. Hill won first place over all competitors in the state, gaining thereby a gold medal and a four-years' scholarship in the Agricultural & Mechanical College for himself and much honor for his alma mater, the San Antonio High School. His oration, entitled "The One War and the Common People" follows:

"In one of the largest art galleries of America there hangs a picture entitled 'The Conquerors.' Down a broad highway advances a triumphal parade of the greatest warriors of history. Rameses the Second may be seen at the head of the procession, borne in a gilded chariot, surrounded by all the magnificence of an eastern emperor. By his side rides the youthful Alexander, worthy of being called 'the Great.'

"Imperial Caesar advances fresh from his victories over Pompey. In the middle of the group comes Napoleon, 'grand, gloomy and silent.' We can almost hear the silver notes of bugles proclaiming their glory; we can almost hear the voices of the ages shouting their praises; we can almost see them rise from the storm and turbulence of the battle-field victorious. The world reads of their lives in the pages of history; and poets still stir the hearts of mankind by the recital of their deeds. But there is another part to the picture. On each side of this proudly advancing procession lie row after row of dead, naked men; and stamped on every countenance of these men, and portrayed in every feature is an appeal, which silent as it may seem, rises to the heavens in protest against the injustice and the inequality of war.

"It is a peculiar fact that historians are prone to devote chapter after chapter of history to the recounting of the wars of some bloody conqueror, and briefly mention the efforts of the Legislature, the jurists and the scholars of the world in advancing and preserving civilization. We erect statues to the memory of men who have killed thousands of their fellow creatures, and forget the scientist who is battling in the laboratory against disease, misery and death. It must also be noticed that the makers of the present European struggle, the rulers, politicians and diplomats, are surrounded with all the pleasures of life while hundreds of thousands of common soldiers are being starved and killed in the trenches. After nearly every home in Europe had been left desolate by his war, Napoleon whined at his quarter on St. Helena.

"The idea that war can be destroyed by the power of money or by the force of treaties is a mistake. Carnegie built The Hague Peace Palace, where the kings and emperors of Europe gathered to pledge eternal friendship to each other. To-day the sounds of German guns are reverberating through the empty halls of Carnegie's Palace of Peace. A few years ago the neutrality of Belgium was solemnly sworn to by the crowned heads of Europe. To-day the people of Belgium are wanderers on the face of the earth. To dethrone the Titian war we must forever dethrone kings.

"The beginning of democracy will be the end of war.

"There is no more justification for a Briton hating a German or an Austrian hating a Russian than there is for a man who lives in Texas to hate a man who lives in Ohio, or for a man who lives on one street to hate a man who lives on another. The human race should rise above the narrow limits of nationalism. It is the world for which God gave His Son. 'God must have loved the common people. He made so many of them.' The common people are those who have most served civilization. By them the indestructible monuments of the Nile Valley were erected; by them was created the unsurpassed art of Greece; from them came a Cicero; from them came a Robespierre; and by the struggling masses of this country is the wealth created, the taxes paid and the honor of the country defended.

"The common people are the foundation of society. Upon this foundation our government lies. You cannot destroy the foundation without destroying the entire structure. Goldsmith expressed this fact when he said:

"'Princes and lords may flourish or may fade,
A breath can make them as a breath has made,
But a bold peasantry, a nation's pride,
When once destroyed can never be supplied.'

"Our own Edgar Nye says: 'There is not a crowned head on the Continent of Europe that does not recognize the great truth that God, speaking through the united voices of the common people, declares the rulings of the Supreme Court of the Universe.

"If you would know what Europe thinks of war do not ask the king seated upon his gilded throne; do not ask the general in the full regalia of battle, but go into the homes of the people, and ask the mother who has lost her son; ask the wife whose husband lies sacrificed on some unknown battlefield; ask the father whose silver head is bowed down with his last grief. They are the sole witnesses of war; the sole jurors and the sole judges. And from a million throats comes the verdict; war must be abolished; it must be thrown into the scrap heap with feudalism and serfdom, and a new sun, in comparison with which the sun of Austerlitz will lose its luster, will open the day of universal democracy."

Hon. Robert Hamilton Ward. For many years Robert Hamilton Ward has been one of the prominent lawyers of Texas. He has known most of the prominent characters of Texas history during the past forty years, and when a young man personally participated in the final act which overthrew military and carpet bag government in Texas and brought about the restoration of home rule. Most of his service has been in the line of his profession, he is a former assistant attorney-general, has served at different times on the bench, and has acquitted himself with honor and credit in every relation. His home for the past fifteen years has been in San Antonio.

Robert Hamilton Ward was born in the historic Town of Warrenton, Fauquier County, Virginia, December 27, 1852, a son of Dr. John and Mary Grace (Hamilton) Ward. Both the Ward and Hamilton families were prominent and of long standing in old Virginia. Dr. John Ward was a surgeon in the United States Navy before the war, and during that conflict served with the same rank in the Confederate Army and Navy.

Judge Ward was reared and educated in Warrenton. He came to Texas in 1872 at the age of twenty, and after landing at Galveston took up the study of law in that city. About a year later he went to Austin, finished his legal studies and was admitted to the bar February 4, 1874. His membership in the Texas bar has thus been continuous for a little more than forty years. His first law partnership was with Will P. Gaines, and an association which continued for many years was as partner with George F. Pendexter. It was in 1874, about the time he began practice as a lawyer, that Judge Ward was a member of the old Travis Rifles at Austin, and this body of troops was called into service to occupy the old state capitol in behalf of the regularly elected Governor Coke, whose inauguration was being resisted by the faction of the previous military governor, Edmund J. Davis.

Judge Ward represented his home County of Travis in the State

R. H. Ward

Legislature in 1895 and again in 1897. His two terms as a legislator brought him credit, and resulted in some important and effective influence in behalf of wise and beneficent law making. In 1899, Attorney General T. S. Smith appointed him to the position of assistant attorney general of Texas. That office he resigned after a year, and at the close of February, 1900, came to San Antonio, which city has since been his home, and where he enjoys a large and successful law practice. In his private practice Judge Ward does not confine himself to any one branch of the law. Although not specializing as a criminal lawyer, he is widely known as one of the most successful attorneys in the handling of criminal cases in the state, and has led the defense in a large number of the most prominent murder trials in Southwest Texas.

In December, 1912, Judge Ward was appointed by Governor Colquitt to the position of judge of the Seventy-third District Court at San Antonio, to succeed Judge Claud Birkhead. He resigned this office in October, 1913, in order to resume his private practice, at which time he formed a partnership with P. H. Swearingen under the firm name of Swearingen & Ward. The offices of the firm are in the Swearingen-McCraw Building. Judge Ward's talent and capacity for judicial position has been recognized on many occasions. By appointment he has also served many times as special judge, not only in the district courts but in the courts of civil appeals and criminal appeals, and in the Supreme Court. His decisions were almost invariably sustained when appealed to higher courts, and his many friends assert that no lawyer in the state would lend greater dignity to the judicial office than Judge Ward.

Judge Ward has four children: Mrs. Louise Clarkson of Houston; Mrs. Grace Ransom of San Antonio; Mrs. Addie Robins of Lubbock; and Robert H. Ward, Jr., of San Antonio, Texas.

Alexander M. Courtney. Enjoying the distinction of being now the oldest official, in point of number of years of service, connected with the street railway system of San Antonio, Alexander ("Doc") M. Courtney, superintendent of maintenance of way of the San Antonio Street Railway System, is a man of wide and varied experience in the West. Coming to this city in 1890, shortly previous to the electrification of the system, he began his connection with the company as a driver of a mule car, and from that time to the present his promotion has been consistent and consecutive.

Mr. Courtney was born near Liberty, Clay County, Missouri, in March, 1857, and is a son of A. C. and Ella Anna (Estes) Courtney. His father was born in Kentucky, of Virginia ancestry, and descended from Josephus and Elizabeth Courtney, an Irish family, who sailed from Gravesend, England, for Virginia some time during the sixteenth century, and subsequently located as a pioneer family in Kentucky. The Estes family also was identified with the early colonial history of the Old Dominion State. Mr. Courtney was born on a farm, but was reared in the Town of Liberty, the county seat of Clay County. Two of his elder brothers were soldiers in the Confederate army; the family were of strong Southern sentiment during the war between the states, and in the terrible border warfare that existed on the Missouri-Kansas line during that struggle.

At the age of sixteen years, in 1873, Mr. Courtney first came to the West, and during the following twelve or fourteen years took a prominent part in the making of frontier history as cowboy, Indian fighter, railroad builder, miner, etc. Early in 1874 he landed at Las Animas, Colorado, where he became a driver of ox-teams for a freighting outfit, which hauled goods to Mexico. On that trip he went no further than Las Vegas, New Mexico, where he went to work for the well known old firm of Barlow & Sanderson, operators of stage lines in New Mexico and Colorado. Later he went into railroad construction work as a contractor on the building of the Santa Fe westward into Colorado and New Mexico, and subsequently did railroad contract work in the building of the Denver & Rio Grande at and leading into Glenwood Springs, Colorado, and the Fort Worth & Denver building into Trinidad. Still later he built ten miles of the latter road in the Texas Panhandle as a sub-contractor under the famous western character, "Missouri Bill" Metcalfe, in whose company Mr. Courtney enjoyed many interesting experiences. He also worked as a contractor for the Denver Loan & Trust Company on the irrigation ditch in the San Luis country, one of the largest in the state. During the twelve or fourteen years referred to his life ranged all over the Rocky Mountain frontier, from the Canadian to the Mexican border, and brought him into contact with and participation in all the picturesque phases of frontier life, some of them dangerous and adventurous, including a brush or two with the Apaches in New Mexico and Arizona. One of his prized mementoes is an Indian blanket that he obtained from the late Geronimo, the noted Apache Indian leader.

As before related, Mr. Courtney came to San Antonio in 1890 and accepted a position driving a mule car, but when the system was electrified he became a motorman on the San Pedro line, later on the South Heights line, and then back again on the San Pedro line. He also held a like position on the South Flores line, and when he discontinued being motorman was appointed timekeeper for the construction department. From that position he was promoted to track foreman, and since 1909 has been superintendent of maintenance of way for the entire system, which is operated by the San Antonio Gas & Electric Light Company.

While a resident of Floresville, Texas, Mr. Courtney was united in marriage with Miss Lulu Pagles, who was born at St. Louis, Missouri.

C. W. Hafer. An excellent type of the hardy stock which has built up the western portion of Texas, which has grown and developed with its growth and development, and which has prospered with its prosperity, is found in the person of C. W. Hafer, of San Antonio, who has watched the transformation of this part of the country and taken an active part therein from the days of the open range. At the present time he is the owner of extensive interests in San Antonio, to the direction of which he devotes his attention.

Mr. Hafer was born at Keokuk, Lee County, Iowa, September 8, 1868, and is a son of J. A. Hafer. His father, born in Germany, came to the United States at the age of twenty-one years and for several years resided at Keokuk, Iowa, but in 1871 removed with his family to Texas, locating at Luling, Caldwell County. In his late years he engaged with his sons in the cattle business in West Texas, and his death occurred in 1885, in Hamilton County, Texas, while he was on a visit there to one of his children. C. W. Hafer lived at Luling, where he received an ordinary country school education, until he was fifteen years of age, at which time he began his career in the cattle business as a cowboy, spending some years on the open range. He was engaged in the cattle business for several years in West Texas, living for most of that period at Colorado City, in Mitchell County, and for about two years at Roscoe, in Nolan County. He went through all the varied experiences and hardships incidental to the dangerous life of the cowman in the early days

JEROME B. HATCH

of the open range, and handled successfully large herds of cattle both on the range and on the trail. For several years he was connected with the outfit of Col. C. C. Slaughter, who at that time had headquarters at Colorado City.

In 1902 Mr. Hafer left West Texas and located at Corpus Christi, where he lived for about ten years, then spending nearly two years in Southern California, having property at Riverside. Early in 1914 he returned to Texas and established his permanent home at San Antonio, his residence being on the Corpus Christi Road, adjoining the city on the south, where he owns valuable property in a section that is in the path of the progress and growth of the city southward. He also owns a ranch of 8,000 acres in Terrell County, where he continues to be engaged in the cattle business, with large holdings.

Mr. Hafer was married at Roscoe, Texas, to Miss Leona Lagow, daughter of the late William Lagow, who was a pioneer settler and large land owner of Dallas, Texas. Two children have been born to this union, a son, Charles Augustus, and a daughter, Rosa Lee Hafer.

HARRY J. HATCH. Now president of the Hatch Sand and Gravel Company and one of the leading business men of San Antonio, Harry J. Hatch was for many years engaged in the railway business and had connections with the higher circles of railway men in Texas and the Southwest. The name Hatch is of particular significance in the City of Dallas, where Mr. Hatch himself was located for a number of years, and where his father, the late Jerome B. Hatch was one of the pioneer business men and most useful citizens.

Jerome B. Hatch was born in Winfield, Herkimer County, New York, January 8, 1839, a son of Jerome L. and Pamelia K. Hatch, who afterwards moved out to Illinois and died at Decatur. When Jerome B. Hatch was sixteen years of age he and an older brother came West, locating at Beloit, Wisconsin, for a time and afterwards moving to Decatur, Illinois. While there he served in the Union army with an Illinois regiment for two years. In 1872 he came to Texas to represent the Champion Machine Company of Springfield, Ohio. His journey to the Southwest was made by railroad as far as then completed, to Vinita in Indian Territory, and thence by stage coach to Denison and Dallas. In the course of his business duties he traveled over large sections of the state by horse and wagon or by stage before railway development had fairly begun. In 1874 he became Dallas representative for the D. M. Osborne & Company, implement manufacturers, and continued with that firm until his death. He managed the extensive business of this concern in the territory of Texas, Louisiana, Indian Territory and Mexico. With the exception of Colonel Leeper, Jerome B. Hatch was the first to engage in the implement business at Dallas. He became identified with that city about the time the first railroads reached there and his push and enterprise were extremely useful in giving to Dallas its present distinction as the largest wholesale implement distributing point in the United States with the exception of Kansas City. He never missed an opportunity to help Dallas in its growth by every means in his power. While successful himself, his distinguishing trait was his public spirit. He was one of the founders of the great Texas State Fair at Dallas, and one of his hobbies, which he continually emphasized as a means to procure the continued extension of Dallas, was the introduction of factories, and for about fifteen years he advocated and used his influence at every opportunity to secure new industries. He had an extensive stock farm in Denton County, and took great delight in raising fine grades of live stock, especially Holstein cattle. The old Hatch homestead occupied by Jerome B. Hatch and his family altogether for thirty-five years, was located on South Ervay Street in Dallas. Jerome B. Hatch died suddenly at Boerne, Texas, March 24, 1890, having gone to Southwest Texas for the benefit of his health. In 1865 at Mishawaka, Indiana, Mr. Hatch married Miss Mary Alger, who for several years has had her home in San Antonio. She was born in Brooklyn, New York, but at the age of six years went with her parents to Mishawaka, Indiana, where she was reared. She came to Dallas from Decatur, Illinois, soon after her husband became established in business in the former city.

Harry J. Hatch was born in Decatur, Illinois, in 1863, was about ten years of age when he came to Dallas, where he was reared and finished his education. Before reaching manhood he took service in the employ of the Texas & Pacific Railway as ticket agent at Dallas, and remained with that transportation corporation altogether for about eighteen years, eventually becoming city passenger and ticket agent in Dallas. His genial qualities and popularity were a splendid asset to him in the position of passenger and ticket agent, and when he left the service of the road he had accomplished a record of unusual faithfulness and efficiency. Mr. Hatch was also in the hotel business for a few years, located at San Marcos, Sutherland Springs and one or two other places. He enjoyed the confidence and esteem of many of the higher officials in the railroad world, and for a time was closely associated in railway matters with Judge Freeman, the general attorney of the Texas & Pacific. His first business experience had been in the implement business at Dallas under his father and later with his uncle. At one time Mr. Hatch was sent to San Antonio as passenger representative for the International & Great Northern and the Texas & Pacific railroads, and remained there about four years in that capacity. While his duties required his location at different points in the state, he considered Dallas his permanent home until 1911, in which year he removed to San Antonio and has since been permanently established in business. He was the organizer and is now president and manager of the Hatch Sand & Gravel Company, a corporation owning valuable sand and gravel pits and supplying many large contracts for sand and gravel for municipal and general construction work.

Mr. Hatch is a popular member of the Benevolent and Protective Order of Elks, and has hundreds of friends throughout the state. He was married in Dallas to Miss Willie May Crow who was born at Minden, Louisiana.

BENJAMIN S. CLEMENTS. A native of the City of Antonio and a representative of a family whose name has been identified with the history of the Lone Star State for nearly seventy years, Mr. Clements is one of the well known and highly esteemed citizens of San Antonio, is a civil engineer by profession but is now associated with the old established firm of Staacke Brothers, dealers in automobiles and other vehicles.

Benjamin Sappington Clements was born in the old family homestead, on Oakland Street, San Antonio, in the year, 1854, and is a member of one of the pioneer American families of this fair Texas city. He is a son of Reuben E. and Mary (Frank) Clements, the former of whom was born in Tennessee and the latter in Mississippi, though she was reared and educated in San Antonio, Texas, to which state her parents removed when she was a child. Reuben E. Clements came to Texas in 1848 and established his residence in San Antonio, where he engaged in the work of his profession, that of civil engineer, and where he served several years as city engineer. He became a citizen of prominence and influence in the community and was called upon to serve as a member of the State Legislature. On coming to San Antonio he purchased a home on Oakland Street, and this fine old place continued as the family domicile for more than half a century. Mr. Clements passed to the life eternal in 1868 and his name merits high place on the roll of the honored pioneers of Texas. His widow was in the City of Monterey, Mexico, at the time of her death, and in that republic her venerable sister, Mrs. Esther R. Glass, died in the year 1914. Reuben E. and Mary (Frank) Clements became the parents of four children, of whom two daughters are living as well as the subject of this review.

Benjamin S. Clements is indebted to the public and private schools of San Antonio for his early education, and as a youth he gained a practical knowledge of civil engineering, to the study of which he early turned his attention under the direction of his father, though he was but fourteen years old at the time of the latter's death. As a surveyor and civil engineer he found employment for a number of years, and in this conection he was identified with important engineering work, including service as a member of the surveying staff that defined the route and assisted in the construction of the San Antonio & Aransas Pass Railroad, in the early '80s. He has otherwise been prominently identified with business and civic affairs in his native city, where he is now associated in an executive way with the firm of Staacke Brothers, as previously noted. He is a staunch supporter of the cause of the democratic party, is loyal and public-spirited as a citizen, but has manifested no ambition for the honors or emoluments of political office.

In San Antonio was solemnized the marriage of Mr. Clements to Miss Sallie Bennett, a niece of John M. Bennett, Sr., who was long numbered among the most prominent and successful representatives of the cattle industry in Texas, his landed estate having been in Lavaca County, and who has for several years past been living virtually retired in the City of San Antonio. Mr. and Mrs. Clements have four children, Frank L., Wesley, Esther and Sarah.

HOMER JONES has gained prestige as one of the representative younger members of the bar of his native state and is engaged in the practice of his profession in the City of San Antonio, with offices in the Brady Building, and he is also vice president of the Stewart Title Guaranty Company, an important corporation that effectively exercises most benignant and valuable functions and that has been specially influential in the furtherance of civic and material progress in Texas. The headquarters of the company are in the City of Galveston and it has branches in each of the other four leading cities of the state. The company was organized, at Galveston, in 1907, by Maco Stewart, who is still its president, and it is the strongest and oldest corporation of its kind in Texas. Its records and system are of the highest type and through its interposition in the investigation and guaranteeing of real estate titles it has been a potent influence in bringing about the investment of large amounts of capital in Texas, for industrial and other purposes, its guaranties having done much to overcome the prevalent skepticism of the surety of Texas investments that had previously prevailed in the financial circles of the East. The Stewart Title Guaranty Company is recognized as one of the most important institutions in the state, as the conservator of stable financial conditions and of civic and material progress and prosperity.

Homer Jones was born in Cherokee County, Texas, on the 27th of February, 1885, and is a son of John C. and Susan (Kennedy) Jones, the former of whom was born in Arkansas, whence he came to Texas shortly after the close of the Civil war, and the latter of whom was born in Cherokee County, Texas, a member of one of the honored pioneer families of that section of the state. John C. Jones became a representative agriculturist and stock-grower of Cherokee County and he and his wife now reside at Jacksonville, that county, where he is actively engaged in business and is an honored and influential citizen.

The homestead farm was the place where Homer Jones passed the period of his childhood and early youth and there he gained his initial experience in connection with the practical duties and responsibilities of life. He was afforded the advantages of the public schools of his native county and through his own efforts he largely defrayed the expenses of his higher academic education as well as of his professional education. While attending college he found employment as a stenographer and also as a salesman, and he has not abated in the least his energy and ambition in his independent career as a lawyer and business man. Mr. Jones was for two years a student in the literary or academic department of the University of Texas and thereafter continued his studies for three years in the law department of the university, in which he was graduated as a member of the class of 1907 and from which he received the degree of Bachelor of Laws, with virtually concomitant admission to the bar of his native state. In the City of Galveston he became associated with the prominent Stewart law firm, which now maintains offices also in Houston, San Antonio, Dallas and El Paso, and he is still a member of this representative firm. In 1909 Mr. Jones went to Houston to assume charge of the legal department of the Houston Title Guaranty Company, of which position he continued the incumbent until 1911. Early in the latter year he accepted the position of vice president of the Stewart Title Guaranty Company, as a representative of which he finally removed to San Antonio, where he has since maintained his home and where he has achieved an important work for this admirable company. When he came to San Antonio title guaranty was an innovation in this section of the state, but through his efforts the people have come to a realization of the definite value of this line of enterprise and have given to the company a substantial and representative support, as by its interposition the real estate investor and lienholder are given absolute protection against defective land titles, besides which the services of the company greatly simplify and facilitate real estate transactions and bring about economy in the effecting of such transfers. Within the comparatively short period during which the San Antonio office of the Stewart Title Guaranty Company has been under the able management of Mr. Jones it has shown a remarkable advancement in the scope and importance of the business transacted and it has brought about in this section an appreciative public sentiment in favor of title guaranties.

In politics Mr. Jones accords unfaltering allegiance to the democratic party, but he has manifested naught of ambition for political office. He is a member of the Travis Club in his home city and also of the San Antonio Country Club. His name is enrolled on the list of the eligible young bachelors of the Lone Star State and he is popular in the professional, business and social circles of San Antonio.

William L. Rockwell. Government irrigation engineer for the State of Texas, with headquarters at San Antonio, William L. Rockwell has for several years been the expert in examination and supervision of the various extensive enterprises undertaken in Texas under the auspices of the Federal Government for the irrigation of the vast tracts in the southern and western portions of the state, particularly in the Valley of the Rio Grande and its tributaries. While his work has brought him a special reputation as an irrigation expert, in the practice of his pro-

Caroline E. Rhoads

Died 1913

R. C. Eckhardt
Died 1887

fession of civil and hydraulic engineer his experience covers nearly all the Northwestern and Southwestern states, and he is one of the very able men in his chosen field.

William L. Rockwell was born in Oswego County, New York, in 1860, a son of William S. and Harriet J. (Porter) Rockwell. When he was a child his parents moved to Mount Vernon in Lynn County, Iowa, where he was reared and educated. He spent four years in Cornell College at Mount Vernon, and graduated from the course in civil engineering in 1887.

Practically all his active career has been spent in those portions of the West where the most extensive enterprises in hydraulic and irrigation engineering have been undertaken. In the year of his graduation he located at Spokane, Washington, where he was employed two years as assistant city engineer. After that his headquarters were in Yakima, Washington, until 1895, and while there he was connected with the big irrigation project which has made Yakima the center of one of the most famous fruit-growing sections of the United States. For two years after 1895 Mr. Rockwell was employed on irrigation works in the central and southern sections of California. With an established reputation for thorough and reliable service, his practice as engineer for a number of years kept him busily engaged in irrigation surveys and construction in Washington, Oregon, Arizona and New Mexico.

In 1907 Mr. Rockwell came to Texas, and has since made his home at San Antonio, which is also his official headquarters. As Government irrigation engineer for the state, he has charge of all the experimental irrigation work conducted by the Government in Texas except in the rice district in the eastern part of the state. In this position he is attached to the office of public roads and rural engineering, United States Department of Agriculture, of which Dr. Samuel Fortier at Washington is chief.

As a widely known expert on irrigation and hydraulic engineering his work takes him to all parts of Texas, and he co-operates with land owners and local authorities in making tests and experiments in irrigation and examination of soils. His activities have made him familiar with the irrigation possibilities both from artesian sources and flowing streams, and in his reports he has covered a large portion of the vast area from the Panhandle to the lower Rio Grande Valley. From what has already been done by individuals and corporations and by state and Federal authorities, it is clear that a source of the greatest future wealth in Texas lies in the proper development of irrigation. It is in his work of planning and advising and giving scientfic direction to this work, and enabling private capital in Texas to utilize the wealth of experience and data possessed by the Federal Government, that Mr. Rockwell stands in the relation of an invaluable aid and coadjutor to thousands of farmers, truck growers and fruit raisers in the state. His profession has been his life work, and his study has been enriched by varied practical experience so that he is now at the height of his career of usefulness.

Mr. Rockwell was married at Walla Walla, Washington, in 1890, to Miss Emma Pease. She was born in Springfield, Massachusetts. They are the parents of three children, Clair P., Paul O. and Helen. The two sons are now students in the University of Texas.

ROBERT C. ECKHARDT. **Men make a nation and "states are not great** except as men may make them." It is largely by individual biography that the real history of Texas is best illustrated. Of the fine strong men of the past whose careers furnish suggestive data and the story of individual effort and the really important accomplishments one that deserves careful study and special presentation through these pages is the late Robert C. Eckhardt, whose life work was best exemplified in the Yorktown District of Dewitt County, where his splendid estate is still kept intact, with his son Victor C. Eckhardt as its responsible manager.

At the very zenith of his strong and useful manhood Robert C. Eckhardt passed from the stage of life's action in February, 1887, at the age of fifty-four. He had come to Texas in the early '40s and was one of the pioneer farmers and merchants of Dewitt County, and long had executive charge of the office affairs of the prominent and important corporation of C. Eckhardt & Sons of Yorktown. He was a son of Caesar Eckhardt, who was the founder of the family in Texas and also established the extensive business subsequently known as C. Eckhardt & Sons. Some further interesting details with particular reference to Caesar Eckhardt will be found on other pages under the name Joachim Von Roeder.

The late Robert C. Eckhardt had the distinction of being chosen the first mayor of Yorktown, and filled that office during the administration of Governor Edmund J. Davis. Some years earlier, with the outbreak of the Civil war, he volunteered to support the Confederate cause and became a member of one of the volunteer regiments of Texas and with the rank of lieutenant served with his command in Texas, Louisiana and Mississippi. Though in many engagements he was fortunate in never having been wounded or captured, and besides his loyal and efficient field service he also handled much of the clerical work in his command, being an expert bookkeeper and accountant. He was a citizen of the highest civic ideals, with marked ability in business, and distinctly progressive. He supported every measure and enterprise tending to advance the general welfare of the community and a dominant characteristic was his expert judgment in divining and taking advantage of increasing land values in that part of the state which represented his home. Much of the land which he acquired cost him only 25 cents an acre, and he expanded his landed estates so that his sons frequently referred to him by the familiar phrase "land poor." Along with energy and versatility he combined a faith and confidence and he made his holdings productive by stocking them with excellent grades of horses, cattle and sheep. He should be particularly remembered for having imported some fine bulls of the Shorthorn and Hereford type, and was one of the first and most influential Texans to attempt to breed out the old time Texas longhorn. In his time he was also identified with the sheep industry, grazed his flocks on an extensive scale, and marketed them when the sheep and wool industry were at the high tide of prosperity in Southern Texas. Another feature of his stock industry was a number of jacks of thoroughbred strains which he introduced and from which he bred many splendid mules. His cattle brand was composed of the letters E K with a heart below, signifying his own name Eckhardt, and this brand is still retained on his old ranch.

The late Robert C. Eckhardt was a man admirably qualified for leadership and in many ways his influence was potent in furthering the best interests of the community and section. He was a stalwart democrat and he and his wife were communicants of the Lutheran Church. He was a member of Cameron Lodge No. 76, Ancient Free and Accepted Masons, and it should be mentioned that each of his five sons is affiliated with this lodge at the present time.

In Dewitt County Robert C. Eckhardt married Miss Caroline Kleberg, daughter of Robert J. and Rosa Kleberg, who likewise were sterling pioneers of Dewitt County. In their marriage were united the fortunes of two of the foremost families in Southern Texas. Mrs. Eckhardt was a sister of former Congressman Kleberg of Austin.

Important as were his material accomplishments, the elements of his mind and character were even more important. Robert C. Eckhardt had great foresight, a keen intellect and was usually in advance of his time whether in his ideas of politics and social justice or in such material interests as stock raising. He exhibited the finest of the domestic virtues. While he was in the war he was as faithful as that great Confederate general, Stonewall Jackson, in keeping up daily correspondence with his wife. He was wrapped up heart and soul in his family, and he possessed and exemplified such character as to deserve the tributes of their homage. Some years after the war, in 1879, he built the home occupied by his son Victor C., and that was the family residence for many years. This home in the country was four miles from town. Almost daily he made the trip to town and although he invariably returned at evening, yet whenever it happened that a friend or neighbor was going from town toward the Eckhardt place Mr. Eckhardt would write a little affectionate message to his wife and send it by the bearer. One of his finer personal characteristics was his habit of emitting a peculiarly shrill whistle as a means of signal for announcing his arrival at home. After his service in the army and when returning home, this whistle was the signal which was first caught by his waiting wife and children, who heard it from a considerable distance down the road. Whenever returning home after his day's work he would give this single shrill whistle, and children and family would hasten out to meet and greet him.

After his death the great burden of rearing a large family fell on the shoulders of Mrs. Eckhardt his wife, and a special paragraph should be devoted to this fine pioneer woman, who represented one of the best known names in Texas, and who had a marvelous development of all the virtues and graces associated with Texas motherhood. Equalling her ability in directing the government of her own household was a remarkable acumen in larger business affairs. She reared a family of eleven, seven sons and four daughters, and all of them were given the best of educational advantages. The boys attended a university and they were also well trained in business, and Mrs. Eckhardt lived to see them all married and each one with children of his own. After the death of her husband she assumed the full charge of the great business enterprises and the estate, and with the assistance of her sons she not only maintained the property but did much to improve and increase its value and use. All her children she taught to practice the Golden Rule and she was a living exemplification of the essential beauties of the Christian religion. The last three years of her life she spent in Austin with her youngest son, Dr. Joseph Eckhardt. Whether in Austin or at the old homestead she always maintained an open house, and children and relatives and friends were greeted with such hospitality as is not often exemplified in the complex life of the moderns.

Mrs. Eckhardt died very suddenly September 21, 1913. She is buried on ground that she and her husband had selected many years before, a family plat on the extensive Eckhardt ranch, where both now sleep side by side awaiting the final call of the resurrection. In her will was the request that one acre of ground be set aside and taken care of by the following generations, and this request has been dutifully followed by her children and grandchildren, and on the plat are now stately trees of pecan, palm and lacustrines. Mrs. Eckhardt's father and mother, Robert J. and Rosa Kleberg, are also buried there, her father having been ninety-four and her mother eighty-four years old at the time of their death. Mr. and Mrs. Kleberg had spent the closing years of their life within 300 yards of the present Eckhardt home.

A brief mention of the children of Robert C. Eckhardt and wife is as follows: Jane is the widow of J. J. Atkinson and still maintains her home in Dewitt County; Otto is a successful stock grower in Goliad County; Dr. William is a physician and surgeon in the City of Houston. Helen is the wife of Charles F. Hoff of Yorktown. Robert J. is president of the First State Bank & Trust Company at Taylor, Williamson County. Lena is the wife of R. D. Forqurean of San Marcos, Hays County. Marcellus G. is prominently identified with the livestock industry at Yorktown. Hedwig is the wife of Dr. Edward H. Schwab of Yoakum, Dewitt County. Oscar G. is a druggist in the City of Austin, being a member of the Griffith Drug Company. Victor C. is next in age. Dr. Joseph C. A. has a successful practice as a physician at Austin.

The late Robert C. Eckhardt made the first substantial improvements on the great Eckhardt ranch, which comprised 8,000 acres at the time of his death, and which is still held undivided in the possession of the family. All of this extensive estate is substantially fenced and cross-fenced and about 1,500 acres of the tract are under cultivation. The agricultural development has been largely carried on by the successors of Robert C. Eckhardt, his sons, and they have also made many admirable improvements including the erection of numerous tenant houses and the construction of three large concrete silos, with a total capacity of 500 tons. The ranch is stocked with Aberdeen-Angus cattle, and for the Christmas market in the year 1914 it turned off the best bunch of polled cattle sold to the Houston Packing Company. These cattle were two years old, averaged 1,196 pounds each, and sold at $8.65 per hundred. This stock was produced and placed on the market by Victor C. Eckhardt, and his stock of Aberdeen-Angus steers captured a prize when exhibited at the Fort Worth Fat Stock Show in 1915.

On the old homestead ranch Victor C. Eckhardt was born December 1, 1881, and was the first of the children born on the old homestead. As a boy he attended the public schools of Yorktown, then went to the City of Galveston, and was graduated from the Ball High School there. He continued his higher education in the University of Texas, and completed a part of the work of the junior year. His vital energy and his desire to make himself a productive factor in the world convinced him that he was losing time by continuing his university course and he at once withdrew and took up with characteristic enterprise the breeding and raising of livestock on the old homestead. His success since then has fully justified the decision which he made when he withdrew from the university. For more than a decade he has had charge of the family estate and is one of the most vigorous, liberal and progressive young men of his native county.

In politics he is a democrat, is past master of Cameron Lodge No. 76, Ancient Free and Accepted Masons at Yorktown, and he and his wife are members of the Presbyterian Church at Yorktown, in which he is an elder.

At San Antonio July 16, 1907, Victor C. Eckhardt married Miss Julia Ives. She was the fourth of the five children of Capt. John T. and Catherine (Mitchell) Ives. The Ives family was established in Texas in pioneer times, and in his earlier years Captain Ives was captain of vessels plying Texan rivers and the Gulf of Mexico. He made a gallant record as a soldier of the Confederacy. Of the Ives children the oldest was Charles, who died at Beaumont, Texas; and after him came Norma, now deceased, who was the wife of Doctor King; Bertha, wife of Morris Jackson of Chickasha, Oklahoma; Mrs. Eckhardt; and Miss Gladys, who lives at San Antonio. Mr. and Mrs. Eckhardt have two children: Victor C. Jr., and Julia Damaris.

E. ALLEN MAYOR. No city is greater and better than its ablest and most progressive citizens. The ideals and activities of such a man as E. Allen Mayor would do credit to any urban community and San Antonio ranks him in the group of those most effectively and intimately identified with its commercial welfare. He is executive head of the Mayor Piano Company, whose efficient service and honorable methods have recommended themselves to a very large and exclusive trade. He is also proprietor of the Mayor Temple of Music and Art, a metropolitan establishment almost unique in the facilities it has contributed to the art activities and the civic and material attractiveness of San Antonio. Mr. Mayor is indeed a master of the piano business, not only as a dealer but as an inventor and manufacturer, and in the latter field he is known to the piano world at large as the inventor of a number of improvements of greatest value in producing piano mechanism of a more improved type.

It will furnish a brief chapter on one of San Antonio's most conspicuous institutions to describe briefly the Mayor Temple of Music and Art, which was formally dedicated September 1, 1914. The building is one of the most beautiful of the kind in the United States, and its equipment has been introduced to serve the highest artistic ideals. It is the only institution of its kind in the Southwest entirely devoted to music, painting and dramatic art. It is conveniently situated on the northwest corner of West Travis and Soledad streets and architecturally the design of the building is one that would attract attention anywhere. The first floor is utilized for sales and display rooms for the Mayor Piano Company, and the upper stories are fitted with studios for teachers of music, painting and dramatic art. The building, which has ground dimensions of 38 by 60 feet, is architecturally of the Spanish renaissance order and all the details have been carried out with an admirable consistency as to architectural beauty and utilitarian purposes. The basement is finished in the same manner as the upper floors, and is so well lighted as to be available for both studio purposes and salesrooms. It is of the re-enforced concrete type of construction with exterior facings of stone and tapestry brick, the overlapping eaves being covered with Spanish tile, the porte-awnings and the transoms of prism glass, and the two entrances fitted in marble and art tiling. The steam and electric lighting system and all other appointments are of the most modern design. This Temple of Music and Art as an entirety constitutes a valuable civic and material asset to the city.

Mr. Mayor has been identified with the music business during his entire mature life. Those well acquainted with his business record explain his success as an accompaniment of and result of integrity, progressiveness and careful attention to the demands of an appreciative patronage. His music establishment is now the oldest in San Antonio under one continuous ownership and management. His trade comes from over a radius of 500 miles, the territory of which San Antonio is the normal commercial center.

Born in the City of Glasgow, Scotland, he was a child when his parents came to America. With the sterling characteristics of the Scotch people, he is himself essentially an American, particularly in the spirit of progress which has animated him in all his business affairs. When sixteen years of age he began an apprenticeship in one of the leading piano manufactories of the City of Chicago. He remained until he was pronounced a skilled master workman in the piano maker's trade. Having served his apprenticeship he went to Kansas City and was employed by Conover Brothers, manufacturers and retail dealers. On leaving this concern he subsequently gained a thorough knowledge of modern piano merchandising. With such experience and attainments he decided to locate in Texas and after a short period in business at Waco he established a permanent residence at San Antonio. Here he has since continued as a dealer in pianos and player-pianos, and as a result of the most fair and honorable methods built up a remarkably large and substantial business. Besides giving San Antonio the splendid Temple of Music and Art of which he is the owner, he has accumulated a large amount of valuable real estate and other properties. As an investor his discrimination and judgment have been remarkably keen, and he is often called one of the capitalists of San Antonio as well as a representative business man and loyal and public spirited citizen.

As already noted, in the world of piano makers the name of Mr. Mayor is well known for his work as an inventor. He has become known as an inventor of devices that have proved of inestimable value to piano makers. He invented and patented the "No Rattle Flange Spring," which was purchased and is being exploited by the Staib-Abendschein Company, a large firm of piano action manufacturers of New York City. He also invented a spring-balance key-pin, used in piano manufacturing. But his latest and undoubtedly most important invention is "The Mayor Patent Hammer-Hook" which eliminates the ordinary bridle-strap long used in pianos and so frequently destroyed by mice or by gradual disintegration. This new device is made of metal and produces a repetition that cannot be obtained in the ordinary bridle-strap action. The importance of this invention may well be understood when it is stated that for more than half a century the genius of the piano trade has taxed itself in an effort to find an efficient substitute for the ordinary bridle-strap mechanism. Therefore Mr. Mayor's invention is universally considered in the trade to supply a long-felt want and to be a device that will aid materially in bringing the modern pianoforte one step nearer to ideal perfection.

While the years of his own life have been devoted to successful piano merchandising, and kindred lines, Mr. Mayor's family has been actuated by similar ideals in the lines of music and other arts. Mrs. Mayor has taken much interest in club duties and in the care of her home and is well known in charity work. Miss Rheta Mayor, the only daughter, has devoted her young life with such singleness of aim and purpose to music that she has now become very proficient and has frequently appeared in public recitals. E. Allen Mayor, Jr., the son, has gained favorable distinction in his school work as a young orator of unusual powers and talent.

ALEXANDER MCRAE DECHMAN. The late Alexander McRae Dechman came to Texas more than sixty years ago and he left upon the history of this commonwealth the impress of his strong and noble character,—a man of prominence in business activities, in the furtherance of civic and material development and progress and in public affairs. He was widely known in the state and was one of its honored pioneer citizens at the time of his death, which occurred in the City of Dallas, April 10, 1915. He was major in Parsons brigade of a Texas regiment of the Confederate service in the war between the states of the North and the South and was in all things loyal to Texas and to the United States, though he was born and reared in the Dominion of

Canada and was of staunch Scotch lineage on both the paternal and maternal sides.

Major Dechman was born at Halifax, Nova Scotia, in the year 1831, and thus was eighty-four years of age when he was summoned to the life eternal, in the fullness and symmetry of a nature that had been signally true to itself and that had brought out its best during the long years of a signally active and useful career. The major was reared and educated in his native province and in 1851, when twenty years of age, he indulged his spirit of adventure by making his way to Texas, the voyage having been made down the Atlantic coast and across the Gulf of Mexico to Port Lavaca, Texas, from which point he soon made his way to San Antonio, where he entered the employ of the firm of James R. Sweet & Company, which then conducted a large mercantile establishment in that city. While in San Antonio he became a close friend and associate of "Bigfoot" Wallace, the noted Indian fighter, and he accompanied this historic character on several of his expeditions.

About the year 1855 Major Dechman went from San Antonio to the frontier of Northwestern Texas and located in Young County. Soon afterward he established himself in the general merchandise business at old Fort Belknap, and he lived up to the full tension of the strenuous life on the frontier. There were no railroad facilities in those days and his merchandise was transported by means of wagons and ox teams from Houston, a trip requiring three months. On the return trip of the freighters to Houston he would ship hides and certain other frontier products to that city. While he was a resident of Fort Belknap his eldest son, Alexander F., who was then a baby, was stolen by the Indians, but within a short time thereafter he was recaptured and was returned to his home. Major Dechman witnessed and participated in many of the stirring events of the frontier and in later years he had a fund of graphic and interesting reminiscences and thrilling tales concerning the early days when Northwestern Texas was over run with Indians and border desperadoes.

About the year 1859 Major Dechman removed with his family from Fort Belknap to Tarrant County, where he was soon elected county tax assessor, an office which he filled with characteristic ability. While at Fort Belknap he had served as chief justice of Young County, an office now designated as county judge. In 1861, at the inception of the Civil war, Major Dechman enlisted, in Tarrant County, as a soldier of the Confederacy, and he served until the close of the war, in Parsons' brigade, in which he rose to the rank of major. In later years he found much satisfaction in vitalizing his interest in his old comrades through his affiliation with the United Confederate Veterans.

After the close of the war Major Dechman returned to Tarrant County, and in 1867 he removed with his family to Houston, with the intention of there engaging in the mercantile business, but he soon departed from that place, on account of the epidemic of yellow fever that was there raging in that year. He then made settlement at Bryan, the judicial center of Brazos County, where he was engaged in the mercantile business from 1867 until 1878. For the ensuing two years he was engaged in business at Dallas, and he then removed to Waxahachie, Ellis County, where he continued his operations as a successful and representative merchant about ten years. He then returned to Dallas, where he passed the residue of his life in well earned retirement and in the enjoyment of the merited rewards of former years of earnest and fruitful endeavor. The following appreciative estimate of the character and services of Major Dechman was written by one familiar with his life history and is eminently worthy of perpetuation in this connection:

"Major Dechman was born of Scotch parents and possessed in marked degree the strong mental vigor and balance and the rugged physical powers of the race from which he was sprung. He retained all of his mental faculties until the very hour of his death. He was known and greatly esteemed and beloved as a man of the highest character, his entire life having been ordered on a lofty plane of integrity and honor. He was a faithful and zealous member of the Methodist Episcopal Church and was a prominent and influential layman of this denomination. He was twice a lay delegate to the General Conference of the Church, was many times a delegate to its State Conferences in Texas, and was an active worker in the Sunday school. The Major was a prominent member of the Independent Order of Odd Fellows and in 1881-82 he had the distinction of serving as grand master of the Texas Grand Lodge of this fraternal order. Sincere, generous and kindly, he placed true values upon men and things and had naught of intolerance or bigotry, though he never lacked the courage of his convictions, which were invariably well fortified."

The maiden name of the first wife of Major Dechman was Annie Mills, and she preceded him to the life eternal by several years. She was born in Alabama and was a representative of the same family line as was the late Hon. Roger Q. Mills, the eminent Texas statesman. Major and Mrs. Dechman became the parents of seven children, all of whom are living, namely: Alexander F., Thomas M., James, Edward S., Mrs. Lillian Margraves, Mrs. Annie Warren, and Mrs. E. B. Ward.

Samuel Walter Scott. Now one of San Antonio's prominent capitalists, Samuel W. Scott has had an active career of more than thirty years. He was first a cowboy and rancher on the western frontier, and eventually, as a lawyer, was one of the leading men at Haskell from the beginning of that little city. A few years ago he removed to San Antonio, from which city he directs his financial and real estate operations.

His is one of the oldest and most prominent families in Texas. It is of Southern stock and of colonial antecedents. His great-grandfather, James Scott, was a Virginia gentleman and a soldier from that colony in the revolutionary struggle for independence. Some time after the close of that war the family went across the mountains into Tennessee and took a pioneer part in the development and settlement of Maury County. Joseph Scott, grandfather of Samuel W., enlisted from that county in Captain Looney's Company of volunteers during the War of 1812 and participated in the battle of New Orleans under General Jackson in January, 1815.

The history of the family in Texas begins with the year 1831, five years before Texas gained its independence from Mexico. In that year Joseph Scott brought his family on board a boat from New Orleans to the mouth of the Brazos River, where the ship was wrecked, leaving the passengers stranded with nothing but the clothes they wore. On account of this, they were compelled to remain close to the scene of the disaster, and for a year or two made crops in the Brazos Valley in what is now Fort Bend County. From there they moved into Burleson County. Joseph Scott was accompanied to Texas by his family, consisting of his wife, eleven sons and two daughters. One of the younger of the sons was Samuel A., father of Samuel W. Four of the other sons, Phillip, Euclid, Robert and James, were all soldiers in the Texas army during the war for independence in 1835-36.

In many respects the most notable character in this notable family was Phillip Scott, the oldest of the four brothers above mentioned, and one of the uncles of Samuel W. Scott. His record of achievement justifies the position of his name among the greatest of Texas fighters and frontiersmen. He took part in three wars, the War for Texan Independence, the war between the United States and Mexico and the war between the North and the South. In 1835 he enlisted in the Texas cause, and went with the army at first under the command of Stephen Austin in the expedition against San Antonio in the fall of 1835. Arriving in the vicinity of San Antonio he took part in those historic engagements known as the Grass Fight, the capture of the Mission Concepcion, the assault on Bexar, and the fight at the Veramendi Palace where Ben Milam was killed and was near Milam when he fell. He served with distinction in that war and also in the war against Mexico during 1845-46. During the Civil war he was present in a number of campaigns, with an especial record in the battle of Shiloh. During the '50s he served as sheriff of Burleson County. His achievements as a fighter seem more remarkable in view of his physical size, since he never weighed over 100 pounds. He was a devout Methodist, filled with old fashioned zeal. He was greatly inspired by his mother, Elizabeth Scott, who, when he went into the Texas war for independence, told him never to come back a coward. She was a woman of especially strong character, well fitted for the duties of raising up a generation of strong sons.

Samuel Walter Scott was born one mile south of Granger in Williamson County, Texas, September 25, 1864, a son of Samuel A. and Elizabeth (Posey) Scott. His father was born near Florence, Alabama, in 1824, and was about seven years of age when the family came to Texas. He was a man of splendid education and high intellectual attainments. Most of his education came from the old Gay Hill Seminary near Independence in Washington County. His greatest love was for teaching, and though he reared and provided for his children in the most comfortable circumstances, it was not his nature to accumulate wealth for its own sake. From Burleson County he first went into Williamson County in 1848-49, and had the distinction of teaching the first school in that county, on the San Gabriel River just below the little Town of Circleville. Later he went back to Burleson County, but returned to Williamson County to locate permanently in 1857. His settlement was on a farm near Granger, a place still owned by Samuel W. and his sister, Mrs. W. M. Key, of Austin. Samuel A. Scott subsequently gave a faithful account of himself as a soldier in the Confederate army during the war between the states. He was first lieutenant in Capt. Sam A. Easly's company, and saw most of his service at Galveston and along the coast. Before the close of the war he was commissioned captain of his company. During most of his life after the war he was a farmer and stock raiser and died in 1908 at the age of eighty-four in Austin. His wife was the daughter of James C. Posey, who was born in South Carolina, was an early settler in Texas, first locating in Burleson County, and afterwards in Williamson County.

When Samuel W. Scott was three years of age the family removed to Georgetown, in which fine old city he grew up and received his education. In 1882, at the age of eighteen, he was graduated A. B. from the Southwestern University. His father was one of the founders of that splendid institution, having donated his headright of 320 acres in Comanche County to aid in securing the location of the Southwestern University at Georgetown. Samuel W. Scott is now a member of the board of trustees of Southwestern University, and has also made liberal donations to its endowments. Though still a young man Mr. Scott has witnessed many remarkable changes in Texas. While he now rides in an expensive automobile, the chief means of locomotion when he was a boy was the ox team, and he has himself followed behind the plow drawn by oxen during many a weary day of his youth. He possessed the same courage and enterprise which was displayed by his forefathers in different generations, and in 1884 went out to Haskell County, then on the extreme western frontier, and engaged in the live stock business with headquarters on Paint Creek, about twelve miles south of Rice's Springs, afterwards called Haskell. At that time only three houses marked the town site of the present city. His nearest neighbors were the Tucker family, living on the old California ranch, five miles away, while his postoffice was Albany, thirty-five miles distant. He had all the hardships and interesting experiences of the cowboy. For several years he was almost constantly in the saddle, and there was no duty connected with ranching on the old open range which he has not performed with unflinching courage. However, this was only a phase of Mr. Scott's early career, since his ambition was early directed toward larger things. He returned from the range to Georgetown, and continued the study of law with the firm of Fisher & Key until admitted to the bar in January, 1889. In the following spring, equipped with his law license, he returned to Haskell and took up the active practice of law. As a lawyer he engaged almost altogether in civil practice, and the bulk of his business was in handling land matters.

Mr. Scott continued to live in Haskell until 1913, since which year his permanent home has been in San Antonio. Since retiring from the practice of law he has devoted his time to his extensive land and financial interests. He is a stockholder and a director in the Haskell Telephone Company, a corporation with $100,000 capital. He owns about 9,000 acres of fine ranching and farm lands in Haskell County, and as already mentioned he and his sister own the old homestead in Williamson County. Many other resources give him a high place in general business and financial circles of San Antonio. A great many men who have followed his career are willing to place most implicit confidence in his judgment as to financial and investment matters. Since removing to San Antonio Mr. Scott has taken a very active part in civic and social reform movements, and is one of the most valuable men to the community in its development as something more than a mere business center. Mr. Scott is a member of the Laurel Heights Methodist Church, and has been actively identified as a layman of that denomination for more than thirty years. In 1905 he was elected a lay delegate to the general conference. He has been affiliated with the Masonic Order since 1889, has served as district deputy, and in 1914 was elected worshipful master of San Antonio Lodge No. 1079, Ancient Free and Accepted Masons.

Mr. Scott was married in Haskell in 1896 to Miss Fannie Tandy, daughter of A. H. Tandy, a pioneer ranchman of Haskell County, but now living near Canadian in the Texas Panhandle. Mr. and Mrs. Scott have four children: Samuel Archibald Scott, Walter Tandy Scott, and Misses Elsie and Marion Lacy Scott.

HON. GEORGE J. SCHLEICHER. A son of Hon. Gustave Schleicher, George J. Schleicher has always had before him the example of a distinguished father. His own career has not been unworthy of his noble parents. He has attained a position among the foremost lawyers of Texas, and as a leader in affairs his reputation promises to extend into a national influence. Another fact that deserves to be emphasized is

G. Schleicher

Truly Yours
Geo. J. Schleicher

Truly Yours
Geo. J. Schleicher

that early in life he exemplified the principle of self-help and helpfulness to others, and to a large degree has been the architect of his own destiny.

He was born while his parents resided at San Antonio, and in 1874 he went to Cuero and assisted his father, who in company with Colonel E. H. Cunningham of Sugarland, Texas, had taken a contract for the construction of the railroad from the coast toward San Antonio. In the following year, on his election to Congress, Gustave Schleicher took his family with him to Washington, where George J. Schleicher enjoyed the advantages of the public schools and prepared for college. A few years later, in 1879, the death of Gustave Schleicher completely changed the aspect of things for his young son. The latter then became a wrapping clerk in a grocery store at Cuero, subsequently was a regular salesman and general outside man, and bought cotton, wool and hides, and engaged in classing and shipping to Havre, Liverpool, Boston, Fall River and New York markets. Later he became cashier of a bank and a partner in the institution. During all this time he had been studying for college, and when his brothers and sisters were educated he laid aside moneymaking for what he considered the better things of life, entering Columbia University at New York, where he took the regular college course as well as the university degree of Bachelor of Laws and was graduated as president of his law class.

With such a preparation, gained largely as a result of his own determination and endeavor, Mr. Schleicher returned to Cuero and began the practice of law with Judge R. A. Pleasants, now chief justice of the Court of Appeals at Galveston. Two years later he was nominated and elected county attorney of Dewitt County, an office which he held for six years and from which he voluntarily resigned. After two more years in private practice he made the race for district attorney of the Twenty-fourth Judicial District, comprising Dewitt, Victoria, Karnes, Bee, Goliad, Refugio, Calhoun and Jackson counties. He was elected and reelected, made a splendid record during his four years in office and then voluntarily retired.

As a result of his long experience Mr. Schleicher is now one of the dominant figures in the public life of South Texas and is attracting state wide attention by his campaign for Congress as successor to Congressman Burgess. This campaign will be decided by the primaries to be held in the summer of 1916. Mr. Schleicher has a fluent command of the English, German and Spanish languages, and has been an extensive traveler both in his own country and Mexico, and he has also more than a passing acquaintance with Europe, having visited Italy, Switzerland, Germany, Holland, France, Belgium, England and Scotland.

Mr. Schleicher married Miss Lulu Lane, a daughter of Sam W. and Ann Mary (Puckett) Lane. Mrs. Schleicher is well known in social and club circles of Texas, being a member of the Daughters of the American Revolution and the Society of Colonial Dames.

HON. GUSTAVE SCHLEICHER. A county in Southwest Texas perpetuates the name of one of the most distinguished citizens of Texas beginning with the German colonization era and continuing until his death while a member of the United States Congress more than thirty years later. Gustave Schleicher was one of the Germans of fine family, university training, and high hopes and ideals, who became leaders in the movement to establish colonies for the people of the fatherland in the wilds of Texas during the decade of the '40s. He was closely associated with the prominent men of New Braunfels, with those who attempted settlements in Gillespie County and in the country west of San

Antonio, and eventually was the leading spirit in founding the Town of Cuero, where the family fortunes and home have had their seat for over forty years.

He was born at Darmstadt, Germany, November 19, 1823, was educated at the University of Giessen, Grand Duchy of Hesse-Darmstadt, where he chose the profession of engineering and was drafted by the government into its service in the construction of two railroads, then being built in Germany.

Coming to Texas in 1847 he first settled at New Braunfels, then far out on the frontier, being one of about twenty-five university men of the colony of thirty-nine Germans who received a financial inducement from the state to become settlers of Texas. The colony engaged in agricultural pursuits and stock raising, but the predominance of the professional farmer over the practical one, and the Indian and Mexican depredations committed against them, rendered their enterprise a failure and Mr. Schleicher, with a number of his associates, removed in 1850 to San Antonio.

By close study he became a master of the English and Spanish languages, and soon entered the newspaper field at San Antonio, founding a German paper. His semi-public service as a dispenser of news and as an expounder of the gospel of American citizenship and American settlement brought him prominently before the people, and in 1853 he was elected to the lower house of the Legislature. At the end of his term he was elected surveyor of Bexar Land District, an office in line with his professional training, and his district embraced a territory greater in extent than all New England. His work comprised the dividing up of that domain into counties and he was assisted by a committee appointed for that purpose. This work opened up to him a field for private enterprise subsequently in the settlement of some of these lands, for he planned and carried out a scheme for the locating of actual settlers from his native land, the fee for which and for surveying the various tracts being paid in land at 10 cents an acre. In this manner he acquired a million acres of those lands for himself.

In 1859 Mr. Schleicher was elected senator from Bexar County, and served in that capacity until 1861, when he entered the Confederate service in the engineering corps with the rank of major. Throughout the period of the war he served in that capacity in charge of General Magruder's engineers.

His early training had made him thoroughly competent for planning and carrying out engineering projects involving railroad work. In 1852 he became interested, associated with Gen. Joseph E. Johnston, in establishing the line of the San Antonio and Gulf Railroad from Indianola to San Antonio. Twenty years later in 1872 he built this road as a representative of the Morgan interests, extending it as far as Cuero, and it was afterwards continued to San Antonio as originally planned. It was on the route of this railroad line that he founded the Town of Cuero, of which he became one of the first citizens in point of time and prominence, and he lived there until his death. His name is borne by Schleicher Lodge of the Sons of Hermann at Cuero.

When he left the Texas State Senate Mr. Schleicher did so with the intention of engaging in private enterprises, having assured his wife that he would not again enter politics for himself; but circumstances decreed otherwise. As a democrat he was in harmony politically with his congressional district, the old Sixth, and in 1874 he took a warm interest in the aspirations of Governor Stockdale, later his son-in-law for Congress. He went to the Goliad convention where the candidate was to be nominated, and tried to bring about the nomination of his friend. But the convention was deadlocked for several days and it would seem that neither of the prominent candidates could win. When a dark horse was sought in the interests of party harmony the name of Gustave Schleicher was suggested and he was induced to accept the nomination. He was elected to the Forty-fourth, Forty-fifth and Forty-sixth Congresses. His last campaign was especially strenuous, for he had as his opponent Hon. John Ireland, and the work and worry in the winning of the nomination and election made such inroads on his physical vigor as to impair it permanently, and he died before his last term of office began on the 10th day of January, 1879.

In Congress Mr. Schleicher was appointed a member and after six months service became chairman of the Committee on Indian Affairs. That was during his first term, and in the second term he was chairman of the House Foreign Affairs Committee, these posts being among the most responsible in the Federal Government. While on his sick bed Speaker Randall assured him that he wished to make him chairman of the Ways and Means Committee of the next House. Incidentally it may be stated that he was one of the largest men physically who ever went to Congress, weighing 290 pounds and a special chair was made for him in the House of Representatives.

To sum up the life work of Gustave Schleicher would be difficult, since it would require specific mention of a great number of interests, enterprises and communities in Texas. Everything he touched he vitalized, and it is important that in addition to the county which serves as a permanent memorial to his name there should also be something like an adequate portraiture of his life and character. This is best drawn perhaps from an address by one of his colleagues before the House of Representatives after the death of Congressman Schleicher. From this address the following is quoted:

"Gustave Schleicher was no ordinary man. Possessed of great energy of body and mind, and endowed with a thorough education, he could not be confined within the narrow limits marked out for him in the old world. At the early age of twenty-four he left his native land and sought a home in the then unexplored portion of Western Texas, and by his indomitable will and perseverance, met and overcame as only brave men can, the hardships, privations and dangers of frontier life. He soon became master of two foreign languages, and by his learning, industry, integrity and sound practical common sense so established himself in the confidence and affection of the people of Western Texas as to be chosen to represent them in the legislature, composed of bold and adventurous spirits like himself, and at a time when the legislature of Texas, in point of general intelligence, as well as ability, could compare favorably with any deliberative assembly in any country. He served with credit to himself and his constituency with such associates as Culberson, Mills, Hancock, Reagan, Giddings, Throckmorton, Coke, Wigfall, Potter, Ochiltree, Jennings, Tarver, Willie and Wilson.

"He was eminently practical and thorough in everything he undertook. He made no effort at display but was an earnest seeker after truth, and was one of the most patient investigators it was ever my fortune to know. He went to the bottom of every subject and became fully conversant with it before called on to act or vote. He was a close and logical reasoner, a profound thinker, and was never satisfied with a superficial knowledge of anything. He acquired that accurate knowledge of our language which is possessed only by those who learn it from the best authors. By patient and careful study he acquired a thorough knowledge and understanding of our system of government, differing so widely from that under which he had been reared, and though cherishing a praiseworthy fondness for the Fatherland and home of his childhood, he was nevertheless thoroughly Americanized, fully identified with our people, devoted to the principles of our free institutions and constitutional government, and in all the positions to which he was called by the people he discharged the high trust imposed in him with strict fidelity and a desire to promote the best interests of the whole country.

"In all the relations of life, public and private, as husband, father, neighbor, citizen and legislator, he came up to the full measure of a noble manhood, and in his death the people of Texas, and particularly of the Sixth District, feel that they have sustained irreparable loss. He had devoted the best years of his busy life to their service, and to his efforts, more than to those of any other one man, is attributable the present peaceful and satisfactory condition of the Mexican border."

Gustave Schleicher was married in Texas in 1854 to Miss Elizabeth P. Howard, a daughter of Thomas T. Howard and a representative of an old American family and of the distinguished Howards of England. The Howards of Virginia were Revolutionary soldiers and patriots, and they were also close family connections with the Garret and Tinsley families. Mrs. Schleicher was born in the State of Mississippi, and from there the family came to Texas. The children born to Gustave Schleicher and wife were: Gustave, a resident of Queretaro, Mexico; George J. Schleicher, whose career is taken up in following paragraph; Elizabeth, who is the wife of Governor Stockdale and a resident of Colorado; William Y., died unmarried at Cuero where he had been engaged in practice as a lawyer; Eleanor, a teacher in the Cuero schools; Miss Mary of Cuero; and Fletcher S., a prominent lawyer at Cuero.

William H. Furlong, Jr. Secretary of the San Antonio Automobile Club, good roads enthusiast and promoter and a noted breeder of thoroughbred horses and dogs, there is probably no better known sportsman in Texas than William H. Furlong, Jr., who, because of his genial qualities and his popularity with all with whom he comes in contact, is familiarly and affectionately known as "Colonel Bill." He is a product of the East, having been born at Springfield, Massachusetts, in 1874, but by training and inclination is a true westerner. His father, William H. Furlong, who is now (1915) eighty years of age, lives at Springfield. He was born in Maine and the family is of sturdy Scotch-Irish stock, and since 1886 he has lived in quiet retirement at his Springfield home. In addition to his manifold business affairs, Mr. Furlong has all his life taken a keen interest in horses, which he still maintains. For many years he was one of the best known race-horse men in the United States and raised many noted horses. As a "gentleman driver" he took part in numerous contests of harness horses on the race-tracks of the eastern cities, as well as at Cleveland, Ohio, and at the old Washington Park racetrack, at Chicago.

William H. Furlong, Jr., was reared in the atmosphere of the horse business, and, like his father, has since his youth taken an interest and a delight in horses. However, unlike the elder man, whose choice has always been for harness horses, the son's tastes have always been for the thoroughbred. He is a great out-of-doors man, fond of the life of the ranch and the wide spaces of the desert and mountain country and of the adventures to be found there. He first came to Texas from his then home in the suburbs of Boston, in 1900, and worked as a cow-puncher in Ballinger County, in the Pecos country, and at other places in the cattle districts of Texas. Later, he established a horse-breeding farm on the Sutton place, near Berg's Mill, seven miles south of San Antonio, in Bexar County. After a year or two Mr. Furlong moved his stock from this place to his present ranch, consisting of about 10,000 acres, in Webb County, forty miles northeast of Laredo. Here he has continued to raise thoroughbred horses. His stud has produced many noted animals, one of the most famous being "Furlong," who is now owned in Kentucky, but was raised by Mr. Furlong in Texas. "Furlong" is a stallion of notable stock, being sired by "Ben Howard," who was retired from the race-track several years ago. His grandsire was the great "Ben Dor," who won the English Derby and who was the sire of "Ormonde," a horse that was sold for $150,000. "Furlong" is noted all over the country. He won every event at the San Antonio fair, being given the blue ribbon in each.

Mr. Furlong is also a breeder of English bulldogs and Boston terriers, making a specialty of the latter. One of his dogs, "Daisy," a Dalmatian, has never been beaten, having taken first prize at kennel club shows in New York, Boston, Dallas and other cities. In the latter city she not only took first prize for dogs in the Dalmatian class, but won in the winners' class as well. Mr. Furlong has a large collection of blue ribbons that have been won both by his horses and his dogs.

Mr. Furlong has made his home permanently in San Antonio since 1912, and during this time has occupied the position of secretary of the San Antonio Automobile Club. This organization is noted for its enterprise and progressiveness and for the great things it has done for the good roads movement in San Antonio, Bexar County and the vicinity. In this work Mr. Furlong has been a leading and directing spirit and through his enthusiasm and boosting abilities has been enabled to have the club accomplish some notable achievements. Probably the most helpful of these was the building of a modern toll road from the western suburbs of San Antonio to Medina Lake, in Medina County, shortening the distance between the two points to less than thirty miles and affording quick and easy access to the beautiful lake. The San Antonio Automobile Club has a clubhouse at the lake, and this and the toll road referred to are conducted by what is known as the San Antonio Automobile Club Branch. The San Antonio Club proper has a very fine clubhouse on the North Loop, eleven miles north of the city, on a site of twenty acres of ground, having its own electric light plant, water works and sewerage, and other modern improvements. The good work for the country in general that is being accomplished by this organization can hardly be estimated, and to Mr. Furlong must be given much credit.

Both at Laredo and San Antonio Mr. Furlong has held the position of deputy sheriff, in a special capacity, engaged principally on cases involving smuggling from Mexico into the United States.

J. M. McCormack. On October 8, 1914, when J. M. McCormack was retired by the Southern Pacific, there closed a railroad career remarkable in many ways. For thirty-three years in the service of that company, and for the last twenty-four years of that time a passenger conductor, "Colonel Mack," as he was known to thousands, was perhaps the best-liked conductor in the entire service, his easy-going, pleasant manner and genial personality winning him friends wherever he went.

J. M. McCormack was born at Greenwich, England, October 1, 1844, while his mother was on a visit to her native city. Her home was in New York City, and her maiden name was Anna Taylor, while Mr. McCormack's father was John McCormack, a native of Glasgow, Scotland, who had lived in New York since his early youth and was there married. J. M. McCormack grew up as a boy in New York City, and was intended by his parents to be a physician, and, in 1861, at the breaking out of the Civil war, he had entered as a student in Bellevue Hospital Medical College. Responding to the spirit of adventure, he left the college, and, going to Peoria, Illinois, enlisted in the Forty-fourth Regiment, Illinois Volunteer Infantry. He served throughout the war in various of the southern states, mostly on detached duty as a sharpshooter, and as such his bravery and efficiency were brought frequently to the attention of Gen. John A. Logan, under whom he served. At the close of the war he was recommended by General Logan for appointment to West Point. He preferred not to accept this honor, however, and went into railroad service instead, commencing his career as a railroad man on the Illinois Central Railroad, in train service, in 1868. In 1880 he came to the West and went to work on the Atchison, Topeka & Santa Fe, and in 1881 came to El Paso and went to work in charge of a construction train on the Galveston, Harrisburg & San Antonio Railroad, which is the original name of that part of the Southern Pacific System extending from Houston to El Paso. At that time the Atlantic and Pacific branches were not connected, and construction work was in progress out of San Antonio and out of El Paso. Mr. McCormack took charge of a construction train and continued with the road in that capacity until the connection was made near the mouth of the Pecos River, in 1883. In 1884 Mr. McCormack left the construction work and took the conductorship of a train running from El Paso to Sanderson, but was later transferred to the Eagle Pass branch. Then the greater part of the town was across the river at Ciudad Porfirio Diaz, where the shops for the Mexican National Railway were located. Ciudad Porfirio Diaz grew to be a city of some 25,000 people before the shops were moved away. There is but one other conductor, Lock Campbell, who was in the service of the Southern Pacific that was in the service when Mr. McCormack began. The country was pretty wild at that time and hold-ups were not infrequent, but Mr. McCormack never had that experience, although the trains directly in front and behind him were held up on several occasions. The Indians were hostile, and Mr. McCormack often saw scattering bands of Apaches going across the prairie toward Mexico, where they remained the greater part of the time, only crossing to Texas when they were in need of horses or supplies, then raiding a ranch and again crossing the border. The capture of old Geronimo, however, practically put a stop to this lawlessness.

Mr. McCormack has seen the western country develop from a wilderness into one of the best sections of Texas. When he entered the train service there was hardly a farm between San Antonio and El Paso, and now some of the most beautiful farms in the Lone Star State are to be found between San Antonio and Uvalde. For miles and miles the train would run along between sage brush, cactus, longhorn steers, bronchos and jackrabbits, but these have given way to the well-cultivated farm, fat, thoroughbred Shorthorn cattle, steam plows, silos and automobiles. This progress has been parallelled by the progress of the railroad. Mr. McCormack remembers the time when the wood-burners were discarded and the dinky little coal-burners placed in the service. That was considered a great step forward. At that time sixteen cars furnished a large load for a freight engine. Now the average engine pulls forty or fifty cars. In those days passenger trains were the only ones equipped with airbrakes, the brakeman on freight trains riding the tops of their train and working the old-fashioned handbrakes. One brakeman could handle eight or ten cars, but it was necessary that they be out in all kinds of weather, while at the present time the brakeman rides in the caboose and the engineer handles the brakes with the air. The little engines gave way to the great oil-burners of modern times, and the wooden passenger coaches were replaced by the modern steel cars, while

adobe and shed depots have given way to the modern brick and concrete structures.

"Colonel Mack" has seen generations come and go, and there is hardly a man, woman or child on the Spofford division of the Southern Pacific who does not know and esteem the veteran conductor. Perhaps he knows more traveling men than any one conductor who has ever been in the service, and every one is his warm and admiring friend. While seventy-one years of age, he retains his youth to a remarkable degree. He has taken good care of himself, is straight as an arrow, and has the bearing that marked him as a military man during the days of the great war between the states, while his step is light and springy and his face is unmarked by a wrinkle. This he attributes to the fact that he has been regular in his habits. He now has a 12-acre pecan grove near Lakeview, on which he has recently secured an artesian well, and is devoting himself to the improvement of his land, while his home is located at No. 909 North Pine Street. To display their esteem and friendship for the veteran conductor, the people of Eagle Pass, at the time of his retirement, presented him with a beautiful loving cup, in addition to other appropriate remembrances.

Mr. McCormack was married at San Antonio to Mrs. Sarah E. Riley, and their three daughters are Laura, Emma and Lela.

Erasmus R. Jenson. A retired cattleman, ex-state ranger, old-time trail driver and one of the pioneers who blazed the way for settlement and civilization, Erasmus R. Jenson's history is eminently worthy of a place in the annals of the Lone Star State. Born at Funen, near Odense, Denmark, September 16, 1853, Mr. Jenson was eighteen years of age when he came to the United States, making the journey direct to Austin, by way of Hamburg, Havre, Havana, New Orleans and Galveston, thence to Houston and from that point to Hempstead by railroad, and from the latter place to Austin by stage.

When he landed at Austin, Mr. Jenson had only $11 as capital and was unable to speak a word of the English language, but this latter was soon acquired, as was also Spanish, and at this time he speaks both fluently. He first went to work with two young Danes, his only acquaintances in America, on a small place near Austin, living in a little hut which was entirely lacking in even the crudest comforts and conveniences of civilization. A short time later he secured employment with a Mr. Chambers, who was then managing the George Hancock farm, near Austin, and remained on that property as a farm hand for two years. Subsequently he entered the employ of Doctor Wallace, of Austin, with whom he remained until 1874, in that year joining the Texas State Rangers in the company commanded by the famous Captain McNelly. He served in this company for three years, or until 1877.

During this period Mr. Jenson participated in some of the most dangerous and thrilling expeditions against desperadoes known in the frontier history of Texas. With the two Hall brothers and a number of other Rangers, he helped to capture the Brassel murderers, about six in number, in Dewitt County. A notable exploit was when he rode 1,100 miles in a chase after Sam Bass, the noted desperado who was afterward killed at Round Rock. His experiences in desperado-hunting included also King Fisher, Ben Thompson and numbers of others of lesser note whose operations constituted a reign of terror in Southwest Texas during the '70s. In the history of this country there has probably never been brought together a group of men who for sheer bravery, dogged persistence and ability to cope with discouraging conditions and constant hardships, have been better than the equals of the little band known as the Texas State Rangers. Courageous to the point of recklessness, they were constantly called upon to face men of the most desperate character, who had absolutely no regard for human life, their own or that of another. The work the Rangers accomplished in ridding the Southwest of these criminals and bad men cannot be overestimated; it will always have a part in the history of the commonwealth. In such an organization, it was difficult for any individual to win distinction, but Mr. Jenson constantly had the admiration of his comrades and the esteem of his officers. A hard-riding, hard-fighting, sure-shooting officer, time and again he proved that fear and fatigue did not enter into his make-up, and his record still stands as one of the best made by any of the members of that famous body.

On retiring from the ranger service, in 1877, Mr. Jenson went to work with cattle for the famous cattleman, Capt. Richard King, whose domains extended over a vast extent of territory lying between Corpus Christi and Brownsville. He remained with Captain King for eight years, during which time he drove a herd of 500 horses from Southwest Texas to Caldwell, Kansas, and two herds of cattle of 3,500 head each from Southwest Texas to Wichita, Kansas. When he left the service of Captain King he was employed as a buyer and herd manager for the Dickey Brothers Cattle Company, of Wichita Falls, Texas, for whom he purchased in Southwest Texas thousands of head of cattle which he drove over the trail to the North. One of these herds he took all the way from Cameron County, in the extreme southwest corner of Texas, to Montana, this drive requiring two seasons to finish, the last season of which they were five months on the trail.

Following his connection with the Dickey Brothers, Mr. Jenson took charge of the Seeligson Ranch, in what is now Jim Wells County, of which he was manager for four years. He then purchased a ranch of his own, the Alta Vista Ranch, near what is now the Town of Premont, in Jim Wells County, but this he later sold to Mrs. King and then acquired in partnership with J. H. Howton, of Austin, the Jesus Maria Ranch, in what is now Jim Hogg County. After three years of this connection he sold out and bought his present property, the Casa Verde Ranch, a fine place of 23,000 acres, lying in Starr and Jim Hogg counties, and now has the pasture land of this ranch leased to Mr. Tom East, while Mr. Jenson retains for his own use the farm section of the property, consisting of 640 acres, upon which he has substantial buildings and improvements. This place is about forty miles from Hebronville.

Mr. Jenson was married in September, 1885, to Miss Mary E. Evans, who was born at San Antonio, Texas, a daughter of C. P. and Sinai Elizabeth (Lawler) Evans. Her maternal grandfather was the famous Gen. Michael Lawler, of Gallatin County, Illinois, a graduate of West Point, a participant in two wars, the Mexican and the Civil, achieving especial distinction in the latter, and for bravery and gallantry at the battle of Fort Donelson was promoted from colonel to general. For some time after the war he was stationed at San Antonio, Texas, in charge of the United States troops at this point, but some time later retired from the army and returned to his old home in Gallatin County, where he passed the remainder of his life, and where a beautiful monument has been erected to his memory. Mrs. Jenson's father has been dead for several years, but her mother is still living. Mrs. Jenson lived at San Antonio with her parents until she was ten years old, the family then returning to Illinois with General Lawler, where she resided for a few years. Returning then to Texas, her father engaged in the cattle business. She was reared among the active scenes of the old time cattle days and has herself ridden with the herds with her husband. Early in 1915

Emil Reiffert

Mr. [illegible] Mrs. Jenson [illegible] from the ranch to San Antonio where they have a [illegible]tiful home at No. 3016 West Comm[illegible] Street.

Emil R[illegible]. In the general commercial [illegible]lopment of several towns and comm[illegible]ities in Southern Texas [illegible] has such broad significance as that [illegible] H. Runge & Company [illegible] which has been promin[illegible] activities and enterprise [illegible] Runge, who fo[illegible] was the [illegible] constituents of [illegible] have bee[illegible] ing the late Em[illegible] Reiffert.

Emil Reiff[illegible] was the first [illegible] lived in the [illegible] and bore a conspic[illegible] century. He w[illegible] born at Hersfeld, Hess[illegible] and died Ja[illegible] 10, 1910, within two w[illegible] day. When fourteen years old he landed [illegible] Galveston [illegible] ultimate destination w[illegible] alone so far [illegible] own family was concerned, and [illegible] tion as the v[illegible] of his native country had [illegible] dering w[illegible] curiosity about the wharf [illegible] boat weighed anchor for its next port, and thus [illegible] Runge [illegible] time, 1854, one of the merchant[illegible] Texas. Mr. R[illegible] among other accomplishments was [illegible] of men, and [illegible] a liking to the friendless lad, [illegible] the s[illegible] his employ.

Thus [illegible] had the inestimable advantage of [illegible] tutelage of this wise and kindly business man and [illegible] in the Runge home on Curanchua Bay, where [illegible] the family and soon justified their confidence [illegible] Before reaching his majority he was taken [illegible] Indianola, and was one of its aggressive young[illegible] came on. Leaving the counting room, he was soon [illegible] federate soldier in Captain Reuss' Company. [illegible] the limits of the state, and he escaped without [illegible] rifice save of that of time from business. [illegible] back to the Runge establishment.

His association with William [illegible] about the formation of H. Runge & [illegible] business was conducted at Indianola [illegible] war, Mr. Runge removed to Galveston and [illegible] to the young partners. The two then took in Ed[illegible] established the Cuero branch of H. Runge & [illegible] with the founding of that town. Messrs. Frobese and [illegible] active management of the house at Cuero, while Mr. [illegible] after their interests at Indianola through and after [illegible] 1875 until 1886, when all the firm's interests were [illegible].

As long as he lived Emil Reiffert kept a st[illegible] and steady hand on the varied activities of the firm. While [illegible] business of this widely known and popular house was [illegible] transportation service, it gradually acquired mercantile [illegible] of its own, also banking, cotton manufacturing, then ranching and [illegible], and eventually became identified with the upbuilding of towns and localities. The town of Runge was started as a nucleus in the development of the Runge ran[illegible] and later the town of Nordheim was established on the same [illegible]. Since the older members of the firm have passed out the new [illegible] purchased a tract of land in Live Oak County and has started [illegible] of Whitsett, named for the original owners of the land. Th[illegible]

Mr. and Mrs. Jenson came from the ranch to San Antonio, where they have a beautiful home at No. 3016 West Commerce Street.

Emil Reiffert. In the general commercial development of several towns and communities in Southern Texas no one phrase has such broad significance as that of H. Runge & Company. It is a corporate title which has been prominent for half a century, but behind it are hid the activities and enterprise of a number of men besides the venerable Henry Runge, who for long was the leading spirit in its affairs. Among the constituents of this firm have been several of the Reiffert family, including the late Emil Reiffert.

Emil Reiffert was the first of the family to come to Texas and he lived in the state and bore a conspicuous part in affairs for fully half a century. He was born at Hersfeld, Hesse, Germany, January 27, 1839, and died January 10, 1910, within two weeks of his seventy-first birthday. When fourteen years old he landed from an immigrant boat at Galveston, though his ultimate destination was Port Lavaca. He was alone so far as his own family was concerned, and had only such education as the volkschulen of his native country had provided. He was wandering with wide-eyed curiosity about the wharf at Galveston before his boat weighed anchor for its next port, and thus was discovered by Henry Runge, even at that time, 1854, one of the merchant princes of South Texas. Mr. Runge among other accomplishments was an excellent judge of men, and taking a liking to the friendless lad, induced him to leave the ship and enter his employ.

Thus he had the inestimable advantage of growing up under the tutelage of this wise and kindly business man and for some years lived in the Runge home on Curanchua Bay, where he was treated as one of the family and soon justified their confidence by his own solid ability. Before reaching his majority he was taken into Mr. Runge's business at Indianola, and was one of its aggressive younger workers when the war came on. Leaving the counting room, he was soon transformed to a Confederate soldier in Captain Reuss' Company. All his service was within the limits of the state, and he escaped without injury and no other sacrifice save of that of time from business. With peace restored he came back to the Runge establishment.

His association with William Frobese and Henry Runge brought about the formation of H. Runge & Company, and under that title the business was conducted at Indianola until, a short time after the war, Mr. Runge removed to Galveston and disposed of his interest to the young partners. The two then took in Edward Mügge and in 1874 established the Cuero branch of H. Runge & Company, coincident with the founding of that town. Messrs. Frobese and Mügge had the active management of the house at Cuero, while Mr. Reiffert looked after their interests at Indianola through and after the great storm of 1875 until 1886, when all the firm's interests were concentrated at Cuero.

As long as he lived Emil Reiffert kept a strong and steady hand on the varied activities of the firm. While the original business of this widely known and popular house was "forwarding" or transportation service, it gradually acquired mercantile stocks of its own, also banking, cotton manufacturing, then ranching and cattle, and eventually became identified with the upbuilding of towns and localities. The town of Runge was started as a nucleus in the development of the Runge ranch, and later the town of Nordheim was established on the same ranch. Since the older members of the firm have passed out the new management purchased a tract of land in Live Oak County and has started the town of Whitsett, named for the original owners of the land. The company has subdivided the three ranches into farms, have deeded roads to the county, laid off towns, and sold the property to actual settlers.

While never accepting official position, Emil Reiffert did much to vitalize community affairs, lending his financial aid as well as his business acumen in organizing such institutions as the oil mill, compress, building and loan association, cotton factory, electric light plant, cotton gins, and being a director in these institutions from their inception until his death. He was also an important factor in effecting the construction of the San Antonio & Aransas Pass Railroad Company, not only to Cuero, but in having the same built through the Runge ranch, and thus enabling and furthering the development thereafter of the towns of Runge and Nordheim. He was a lifelong democrat, though his work was only as a voter. He was noted as a reader and traveler, had his home library well stocked with books, chiefly historical novels, and several times revisited his old home in Germany. Socially he was on the conservative and quiet order, but gracious and cordial in his personal relations, but seldom let pleasure interfere with business. Though a member of the Lutheran Church, he was not active in its affairs, and only late in life joined a fraternity, the Knights of Pythias.

Emil Reiffert was married at New Braunfels February 25, 1869, to Miss Helene Tips. She was born at Elberfeld, Germany, June 14, 1844, one of a numerous family among whom was Hon. Walter Tips of Austin, Texas. Her parents were Conrad and Caroline Braun Tips, who brought their family to Texas in 1849, landing at old Powderhorn and going by wagon to New Braunfels. Mr. Tips died at Seguin in 1850. Mrs. Emil Reiffert is still living at Cuero, in her seventy-second year. Her children were: Emil, of Cuero; Walter, of Cuero; Mrs. Dr. J. H. Reuss, of Cuero; Mrs. W. A. Blackwell, Jr., and Mrs. Fred T. Mügge.

Few names reflect so much of the wholesome enterprise and the integrity and dignity that go with commercial and civic upbuilding as that of the late Emil Reiffert.

WALTER REIFFERT. Of the younger generation of South Texas business men, combining the vitality and progressiveness of the new century with the solid and imperishable virtues of the old, Walter Reiffert has succeeded to many of the interests directed by his father, the late Emil Reiffert, and has also acquired many of his own, and has done much to maintain the traditions associated with the family name.

He was born at old Indianola, Texas, January 17, 1874, and spent his early years in that old sea coast town, where he had the advantages of the local schools. At the age of eleven he was sent abroad to Germany, spending five years in the Real Gymnasium at Darmstadt and acquiring a large stock of old world culture. On his return to Texas he attended the State University and subsequently completed a commercial course in St. Edward's College at Austin.

His business career began as office man with J. Moeller & Company at Galveston, and he spent five years in clerical relations with that firm. Coming to Cuero, he was in the cotton business with H. Runge & Company until 1900, when, at the age of twenty-six, he succeeded his uncle, Henry Reiffert, in charge of the mercantile interests of the house. In 1907 he took another step higher when he went into the bank of H. Runge & Company, with general oversight of the affairs of the concern. Then in 1910 he became a partner in the firm, and was associated with Mr. Frobese in the management until the latter's death.

Outside of this old and honorable business house he has various other interests, and is identified with all the varied enterprises which were promoted by his father. He is president of the three townsite companies which in recent years have done so much for the development of certain sections of South Texas, principally in Live Oak County, reference to which development work has been made in the sketch of Emil Reiffert. He is a director of the oil mill, cotton mill, the State Bank of Runge, the Breeden-Runge Wholesale Grocery Company of Cuero, the Cuero Creamery, and the local compress.

Mr. Reiffert has been an especial factor in the development of the modern city of Cuero. He has never been in the official class, but in the ranks has supported all public improvements, good roads in particular, and is chairman of the drainage board of Dewitt District. Fraternally he is a past chancellor of the Knights of Pythias and his accepted religious faith is that of the Lutheran.

At Cuero on February 20, 1901, Mr. Reiffert married Miss Anna Mügge, a daughter of Edward Mügge, his father's old business partner. Their children are Walter, Jr., Mildred, Ralph and James Marion.

Capt. William M. Hanson. Of the men who have assisted in making Texas history during the past several decades few have taken a more active part than has Capt. William M. Hanson. Railroad official, ex-United States marshal, extensive agriculturist, oil producer, rancher and friend of progress, in each line of his labors he has attained distinction and success, and his record in public and private life is one that marks him as one of the truly strong men of San Antonio. Captain Hanson was born in Gonzales County, Texas, in 1866, and is a son of Cornelius J. and Susan L. (Mangum) Hanson, both of whom are deceased. His father was an Englishman by birth, and came to Texas as a young man in 1848, being a pioneer settler, rancher and merchant of Gonzales County, where he fought Indians during the days of the frontier. He fought through the Civil war and was a member of General Waul's staff (Waul's Legion), Southern Confederacy. Mrs. Susan L. Hanson was born in Alabama and came to Texas when a child.

Captain Hanson was reared in Gonzales County, and was brought up amid surroundings that developed a naturally strong body and an inherent spirit of courage. He was but eighteen years of age when appointed deputy sheriff of Gonzales County by Capt. Dan Price, and served as such until the latter's term as sheriff expired. He next served as deputy under the succeeding incumbent, Capt. W. E. Jones, and after retiring from official life in Gonzales County went into railroad construction and assisted in the building of the San Antonio & Gulf Shore Railroad from San Antonio to Cuero, now a part of the Southern Pacific system. After finishing this work, Captain Hanson was appointed, in 1898, deputy United States marshal for the Western District of Texas, under Capt. George L. Siebricht, and held this position until 1902 on the Mexican border, when he was appointed by President Roosevelt to the position of United States marshal, with headquarters at Galveston, for the Southern District of Texas. Captain Hanson at all times showed himself to be a brave and efficient officer, conscientious in his performance of duty, and with high ideals of the responsibilities of public service. He was always capable of coping with the situations which arose, and was determined in bringing criminals to the bar of justice.

In 1906 Captain Hanson resigned his office as United States marshal and went to Mexico, locating in the State of Tamaulipas, where he engaged in the ranching and oil business, and where he has been successfully engaged ever since, having acquired extensive additions to his holdings since his first investment there. He is part owner and general manager of the Mexico Land Company, of St. Paul, Minnesota, owners of the Hacienda El Conejo, consisting of 30,000 acres. On this ranch they have

600 acres of grape fruit and a large nursery of citrus fruits, besides livestock and general agricultural interests. Captain Hanson is the sole owner of the Hacienda Guadaloupe, an irrigated citrus fruit proposition, consisting of 3,000 acres, all under irrigation, and is president of the Buena Vista Land and Irrigation Company, which owns the Hacienda San Procopio, embracing 8,000 acres of irrigated land, is secretary and general manager of the Tamesi Petroleum and Asphalt Company and secretary and general manager of the Standard Petroleum Company, these two latter being oil and asphalt propositions of great wealth and magnitude. The first-named company has about 5,000 acres of land, containing hundreds of springs, from which oil flows from the top of the ground. One of these gushers has been flowing seventy-five barrels of oil per day, consisting of 93 per cent pure asphalt, which is used just as it comes from the well without any treatment. The Standard Petroleum Company owns 6,000 acres of land that up to the time of the revolutionary troubles in Mexico produced 900 barrels of oil per day from shallow wells. Captain Hanson was one of the pioneer oil developers in the State of Tamaulipas, including the famous Tampico field.

As will be noted, Captain Hanson has gone extensively into the citrus fruit industry. He is president of the Mexico Gulf Coast Citrus Fruit Association, that embraces the states of Tamaulipas, Vera Cruz, San Luis Potosi and Nueva Leon. This association has been finding a fine market for its fruit in various countries of Europe, and will have a still better market in the United States when the present quarantine laws are abolished. The association can get citrus fruits into the United States six weeks earlier than from any other section, the fruit is superior to many and equally to any, and Mr. Hanson and his associates are the largest citrus fruit growers in the Republic of Mexico.

On account of the menace from revolutionary factions, operations were temporarily suspended on Captain Hanson's properties during a part of 1914. He then came to San Antonio, where he maintains his home. At that time he was appointed by Duval West, receiver of the San Antonio, Uvalde & Gulf Railroad, to the position of special agent for that company in September, 1914, an office which he will continue to fill until settled conditions allow him to resume his operations in Mexico. Captain Hanson's Mexican postoffice address is Osorio, Tamaulipas, a station on the Monterey and Tampico branch of the Mexican Central Railroad, fifty-six miles below Ciudad Victoria, the capital of the state, and 100 miles northwest of Tampico. It is in the vicinity of this station that the above mentioned properties are located.

While a resident of Gonzales County, Texas, Captain Hanson was married to Miss Malda C. Knowles, and they have four children: Mortimer M., C. J., Dr. W. S. and W. K. The two latter have been educated especially for association with their father's interests in Mexico. Dr. W. S. is a graduate in 1915 from the Memphis Hospital Medical College and is a practicing physician in San Antonio, and W. K. is a graduate of the agricultural course, Agricultural and Mechanical College of Texas.

BAILEY P. TERRY. For a great many years one of the community centers of Dewitt County has been Cheapside, and the Terry family probably more than any other has exercised its influence and enterprise to give that locality its development and its advantages. Bailey P. Terry was a pioneer in land improvement there, and from hard labor and progressive methods finally effected a prosperity which has kept him a man of high standing for many years.

The Terrys are pioneer people in Dewitt County. The family was introduced to this section in 1857 by Weldon Terry, who spent many years in the Cheapside locality. Weldon Terry was born in North Carolina September 26, 1826, but grew up in DeKalb County, Tennessee, from which section he came to Texas. The Terrys are of Irish stock, and grandfather Roland Terry, came to Texas with his son Weldon and died in 1858. Roland Terry spent his life as a farmer, and was twice married. His first children were John and Bounds, both of whom remained in the East, John in Tennessee and Bounds in North Carolina. By his second wife, Polly Terry, Roland Terry had the following children: Weldon; Martha, who married Shelby Rackley and died in Dewitt County, where she left children; James, who was accidentally killed somewhere in West Texas; Amanda, who married W. H. Hester and died in Dewitt County. The second wife of Roland Terry died after the Civil war, and both are buried in Hester Cemetery on the Guadaloupe River.

Weldon Terry grew up at a time and in a community where school facilities were not available to him, and as he lived in a time when manual skill and proficiency in handling practical problems were more desirable than mental accomplishment he was under little handicap for the fact that he could not write his own name. His people were poor, but of the industrious rural class. His brother-in-law, Shelby Rackley, had preceded him to Texas, and it was his presence in this state that led Weldon Terry to bring his family here. He was accompanied on the migration by his parents, a young man named Hasson, and his brother James. The party took a boat at Nashville, came by water to Indianola, Texas, and to that point Mr. Rackley had sent a wagon which conveyed the Terrys to their first home on the Little Creek, which runs by the locality of Cheapside.

The first efforts of Weldon Terry toward the improvement of the new country were the erection of a log cabin of one room, with an adjoining shed, and this rude home accommodated the family until increasing financial means enabled them to substitute a better structure of plank boards. The first year Weldon Terry lived in Texas the field crops were ruined by grasshoppers, and under such discouragement he would have returned to his old Tennessee home had he possessed the money, but conditions were such that he was forced to remain. He lived to bless the day when he came to Texas, since he had a great love for the state itself, helped to defend its borders from incursion of enemies, and contributed modestly toward the building up of a community and at his death left a family of industrious home builders. Some time after the war between the states had started Weldon Terry entered the Confederate service, joining Capt. Josiah Taylor's company and Colonel Wood's regiment. All his service was within the limits of Texas, and a few months before the war closed he left the army, came home and located on his farm at Cheapside. Throughout his career he voted the democratic ticket regularly, but on account of lack of qualifications never filled an office. In his later years he joined the Presbyterian Church. Like many of the pioneers he had a natural love for and skill in the pursuits of the fisherman and hunter, and those avocations furnished him his chief enjoyment. He died December 4, 1904, about ten years after the death of his wife.

Weldon Terry married Emily Isbell. She had been preceded to Texas by her brother Ammon, but he was swallowed up in this country and the family knew nothing of him afterwards. To Weldon Terry and wife were born the following children: Bailey Payton; Caroline, who married Jacob Cordon and they moved from Texas to Roseburg, Oregon; Madison M., who died in Karnes County, Texas, married Katie Wilson and left two children; Polly, who died unmarried; Curt, who spent his life in Dewitt County, married first Ophelia McCullough, and, second, Julia York, of the prominent York family of Yorktown, and he was survived by four children; Lucy married Sid McFarland and lives in Cuero, Texas; Weldon, of Alpine, Texas, married Lula McFarland and has four children.

Bailey Payton Terry, whose home has been in the vicinity of Cheapside nearly sixty years, was born March 4, 1850, in DeKalb County, Tennessee. He was only seven years old at the time but has many recollections of the journey from Tennessee to the Lone Star State. When one recalls what the conditions were in Texas during the late '50s and the Civil war decade, it is not surprising that Mr. Terry gained little information by attending school. His best education he dug out himself from his own experience and by constant observation and study. After the war his labor was required for the support of the family and the management of the farm, and he helped his father improve the old homestead of 500 acres. After his marriage he moved to his present location, buying a tract of 200 acres on which not a spear of grass had been disturbed, located on the Winn League. He was the first man to buy a piece of this league. His equipment and capital at the time comprised two horses and a few household goods, and several cows. The purchase price of the land which he secured in the Winn League was $2.50 an acre. That was $2 more than anybody had ever paid before for land in that section, and he undertook a heavy contract when he agreed to pay $2.50. It required six years of constant economy and hard labor to relieve his land of debt, and he then started the slow process of building up and improving. In order to sharpen his own tools he set up a little blacksmith shop, learned the trade without help from anyone, and soon began serving the community as a regular blacksmith. For several years he spent his spare time in this vocation, but as soon as able to live from the proceeds of his farm he willingly abandoned the drudgery of the shop. As the years went by he steadily prospered, added other lines to his possessions, and bought 200 acres in Gonzales County in the Wilson Simpson One-third League. All the improvements on his place are the result of the labors of his own hands, and all the money that he has made and invested was the proceeds of his intelligent management and hard labor. In recent years Mr. Terry has used his land exclusively for the raising of sheep.

In spite of his exceedingly busy career Mr. Terry has been more or less interested in politics for many years. The elections in his precinct were for thirty years or more held in his old shop. Until recent years he was a regular attendant at both county and state conventions. He helped to nominate Governor Hogg in 1892, and was one of the strongest local supporters of that Texas statesman. He also helped nominate Governor Culberson, Governor Lanham and Governor Colquitt. The old postoffice of Cheapside was for a number of years located at Mr. Terry's home, and nearby was established a cotton gin. It was thus the Terry place came to be the center of considerable domestic trade, but the postoffice is now located over the county line in Gonzales County, half a mile from Mr. Terry's home. Mr. Terry has no affiliations, fraternity or churches, though he is by no means opposed to their work and influence.

On February 10, 1875, in this section of Dewitt County Mr. Terry married Miss Elizabeth Placker. Her parents were John and Mary (Alexander) Placker. Her father was a German by birth, first settled in North Carolina, later moved to Arkansas, and from there came to Dewitt County, Texas, where he spent his career as a farmer. Mrs. Terry, who was the second in a family of seven children, died June 18,

1909. A brief record of the children is as follows: Bailey Payton, Jr., grew up in Dewitt County and died there two months after his marriage to Maggie Carson; Belle is the wife of Fletcher Elder, of the Cheapside locality, and they have children: J. F., Jr., Clifford, Jo Bailey and Harry; Katie married Dr. Nathan Elder of Nixon, Texas, and their children are Florine and Joyce; James M. of Madrid, New Mexico, married Etta Wood, and they have a child named Fay; Sarah married Keyes Carson, and they live at the old homestead and have a child named Birdie; Charles E. is a merchant at Gillette, Texas, and by his marriage to Velasco Riedel has a daughter, Eunice Adele; Miss Jonnie, who graduated at Belton, Texas, in 1914, is now a teacher; Ruth is a member of the class of 1916 in the school at Belton. Other members of the family have taught school, all are well educated, and the sons attended a business college in San Antonio.

Samuel W. Lane, of Cuero, who lives on the Cheapside-Cuero highway, represents a family that has been identified with Dewitt County for more than sixty years.

It was his father, Samuel W. Lane, Sr., who came to this locality about 1854, bringing his young wife from Rankin County, Mississippi, where they had married and where Mrs. Lane was born. The senior Mr. Lane was a native of Tennessee, and as a youth had accompanied the troops in the service of the United States, and in which Jefferson Davis was at that time a colonel, on their passage through Texas to the Mexican war and participated in the battles of Monterey and Buena Vista. On leaving the army Mr. Lane returned to Mississippi and there met and married his wife. On settling in Dewitt County while not one of the first arrivals, he found a country very sparsely inhabited and with only a minimum of real development. He engaged in the stock business, and also handled a large amount of land in trading transactions. His first farm is now the property of his son Samuel W. on the Wentworth League. There he built a log cabin with a stick and branch arbor in front, and with his young wife spent several years with mingled happiness and hardships. The principal town in the settlement of which he was a part was Old Clinton, then the county seat of Dewitt County, and an obsolete community which is mentioned for its historical associations on other pages. That Samuel W. Lane, Sr., was a man of education and business attainment is evidenced by the records of the '50s wherein his name appears in connection with numerous transactions in land. Samuel W. Lane, Sr., died in 1864 when about forty years of age, and had not actively participated in the Rebellion. However, he was a slave holder, took part in the local movement for secession, though his father-in-law in Mississippi had been opposed to that movement, in spite of the fact that he went with his home state when it joined the Confederacy. A sister of the senior Mr. Lane married into the prominent Thomas family of Dewitt County. Mr. Lane had two brothers, James and Nathaniel, who remained in Tennessee. Samuel W. Lane, Sr., married Ann Mary Puckett, a daughter of Dr. S. H. Puckett. She lived to be eighty-four years of age and passed away in 1911. Their children were: Cora, who married Judge Grimes of Cuero; Mary, who married Will Atkinson of Gonzales; Lou, who married George J. Schleicher of Cuero; Samuel W., Jr.; and James, who died in childhood.

It was in the Old Clinton community that Samuel W. Lane, Jr., was born August 1, 1862. After Cuero became the county seat instead of Old Clinton, he identified himself with the newer and more progressive locality. His education came from the public schools and from the Nash

School of Guadaloupe Academy at Cuero. He finally ran away from the school, and accompanied a bunch of Dr. Burnett's cattle on the cattle trail north to the railway shipping point at Caldwell, Kansas. This was an eventful experience of his young life. The cattle trail which he followed crossed the Red River at Doane's store and went on to the wild Indian Territory of that time to Southern Kansas. Later Mr. Lane made several of these journeys along the old-time cattle trails, and subsequent to that took up trading. His beginning was made with a tract of land at Burns Station, which had come to him as a part of his father's estate. His trading was done both in lands and cattle. In 1890 Mr. Lane came to his present locality and his home is now on the Elihu Moss League. He is both a rancher and farmer and his property supports about ten families engaged in the cultivation of his farm lands. For a number of years Mr. Lane has been a well known figure on the Fort Worth cattle market, to which city he has shipped many bunches of fat cattle.

Politically he is a democrat, but his only public service was given when a boy of nineteen to several months as a member of Captain Sealey's ranger company for protection against the "heel flies" who were cutting fences and interfering with the movement of the land owners to enclose their big pastures and thus cut up the open range. This fence building enraged the original settlers and farmers and they replied with numerous cases of fence cutting. The trouble was finally settled by compromise.

On September 30, 1886, Mr. Lane married Miss Eliza Nichols, whose father, Lazarus Nichols, was a pioneer and widely known cattle man in Dewitt County. He came to this part of Texas from Mississippi. Mrs. Lane's mother was Louisa Means. Mrs. Lane was the fourth in a family numbering the other children: Morgan O.; Lee, who married Bud McFadden; Orrel; Elisha; Letitia, who married George Clegg; Mrs. Della McGill of Burnett County. Mr. and Mrs. Lane have only one son, Samuel W., who is also a farmer at Cuero. He married Miss Lee Williams, and their children are Samuel W., who is the fourth in succession to bear that name in the Lane family in Texas; and Thrula May.

William Frobese, Sr. It was a remarkable career that came to a close in the death of William Frobese at Cuero on August 9, 1911. In the full maturity of years and accomplishment this lifetime of seventy-three years reached the hour of bodily dissolution, but the character remained and its influence continues to affect the purposes and acts of many individuals. The forces of his personality were not those which vanish quickly with the mortal presence. In his sphere—and that a large one—William Frobese enacted with care and success those roles of human endeavor which longest deserve the admiration and homage of succeeding generations.

He was one of the three men most closely associated with the larger development and enterprise of the H. Runge & Company in South Texas. He was born February 17, 1838, at Alfeld, Hanover, Germany, where he received a splendid and practical business education, being a product of the Volks-shule of his native land and trained in a store in his youth for a career in merchandising. His father was Ernst Frobese, who was in good circumstances, spent his life in an official and clerical capacity about the courthouse at Alfeld, and died when still in middle age.

Coming to the United States about the time he reached his majority, William Frobese located at Indianola, where his brother-in-law, Hermann Runge, was at that time associated with the latter's brother, Henry

School of Guadalupe Academy at Cuero. He finally [illegible] season and accompanied a bunch of Dr. Burnett's [illegible] trail north to the railway shipping point at [illegible] was an eventful experience of his young life. [illegible] traveled crossed the Red River at Doane's store [illegible] wild Indian Territory of that time to Southern [illegible] Lane made several of these journeys along the old [illegible] and subsequent to that took up trading. His beginning [illegible] a tract of land at Burns Station, which had come to him [illegible] his father's estate. His trading was done both in lands [illegible] In 1890 Mr. Lane came to his present locality and his home [illegible] the Elihu Moss League. He is both a rancher and farmer [illegible] erty supports about ten families engaged in the cultivation [illegible] lands. For a number of years Mr. Lane has been a well kn[illegible] on the Fort Worth cattle market, to which city he has shi[illegible] bunches of fat cattle.

Politically he is a democrat, but his only public service [illegible] when a boy of nineteen to several months as a member [illegible] Sealey's ranger company for protection against [illegible] were cutting fences and interfering with [illegible] ers to enclose their big pastures and [illegible] fence building enraged the original [illegible] plied with numerous cases of [illegible] settled by compromise.

On September 30, 1886, [illegible] Nichols [illegible] father, Lazarus Nichols, was [illegible] widely known cattle [illegible] DeWitt County. He came to [illegible] part of Texas from Mississippi. [illegible] Lane's mother was [illegible] Mrs. Lane was the fourth in a [illegible] numbering the other children: Morgan O.; Lee, who married [illegible] McFadden, Orrel [illegible] Elisha, Letitia, who married George Clegg, [illegible] Della McGill of Burnett County. Mr. and Mrs. Lane have only [illegible] son, Samuel W., who is also a farmer at Cuero. He married Miss [illegible] Williams, and their children are [illegible] Samuel W., who is the fourth in [illegible] son to bear that name in the Lane family in Texas; and [illegible]

WILLIAM FROBESE, SR. It was a remarkable career that [illegible] on the death of William Frobese at Cuero on August [illegible] [illegible] maturity of years and accomplishment this lifetime [illegible] three years reached the hour of bodily dissolution, but [illegible] removed and its influence continues to affect the purposes [illegible] [illegible] The forces of his personality were not [illegible] [illegible] with the mortal presence. In his sphere—and [illegible] [illegible] conducted with care and success those [illegible] [illegible] biggest deserve the admiration and [illegible]

[illegible] men most closely associated w[illegible] [illegible] of the H. Runge & Company, [illegible] born February 17, 1838, at Alfeld, Hanover [illegible] a splendid and practical business educa[illegible] [illegible] schule of his native land and trained [illegible] his [illegible] in merchandising. His father was [illegible] who [illegible] circumstances, spent his life in an official [illegible] capacity [illegible] courthouse at Alfeld, and died when st[illegible] age.

[illegible] United States [illegible] Wil[illegible] [illegible] at Indianola [illegible] [illegible] associate [illegible]

Runge, in business. This business was the nucleus around which grew up the great and permanent corporation of H. Runge & Company. A few years after William Frobese came his brother, Alexander (who died of yellow fever a few months later) and his brother, Ferdinand, who spent his life as a farmer in the vicinity of Clinton, Texas, and was drowned in the Guadaloupe River in 1883, leaving six children. Mr. Frobese left three sisters in Germany: Alma, who became the wife of Julius Rolff; Annie, who married Hermann Runge; and Marie, who remained single.

Not long after Mr. Frobese's arrival in this country the Civil war came on, and he enlisted as a private in the army of the Confederacy, joining Captain Dr. Reuss' Company, with which he served throughout the war without wound or capture. Returning to civil life he rejoined the business of H. Runge & Company, with which he had previously become identified as an employe. The original firm was composed of Hermann and Henry Runge, but later Hermann returned to Europe and Henry Runge took in as his younger associate Emil Reiffert and William Frobese. It was his early associations with Henry Runge that gave William Frobese the best opportunities of his early life and he continued with that veteran South Texas merchant without interruption save during the war between the states, until he and Mr. Reiffert and Mr. Edward Mugge bought the business at Indianola. About the time of the great storm of 1875, which destroyed Indianola, William Frobese moved to Cuero, where he helped to establish the business of the firm and remained one of its leading spirits the rest of his life.

He was connected with the Cuero Cotton Mill and Cuero Compress and Cuero Cotton Oil Mill as a stockholder, and while a most potent factor as a town builder he was never officially a part of the government. He had that interest in politics that caused him to endeavor to select the best man for public office and when all other things were equal favored the democratic nominee. He was a particular friend of Congressmen Schleicher and Crain, who went out from Cuero, and also of Rudolph Kleberg. Mr. Frobese never essayed to be a speech maker. He had a fine mind, was widely read and thoroughly conversant with a wealth of subjects, but his lack of a comprehensive English vocabulary caused him embarrassment when he was called upon for remarks at public gatherings.

Mr. Frobese moved his Indianola home to Cuero by taking it down, numbering its parts, and hauling it to the young city which grew up along the recently constructed line of the Southern Pacific, and there erected it on his extensive grounds on South Line Street, where it still stands, the home of his widow. Mr. Frobese was sociable by nature and loved the companionship of his fellows, but was conspicuously a home man. He belonged to no lodge save the Sons of Hermann. A liberal contributing member to the Cuero Fire Department, he likewise gave freely to everything material which depended upon public support for its success, particularly in the line of education. He educated his brother's children besides his own, and gave liberally to friends and relatives in a degree which will never be known. In fact, his entire life was passed in doing good deeds. He was brought up a Lutheran, but while not opposed to churches, he neglected to identify himself actively with that faith and seldom attended services.

William Frobese was married at Indianola, Texas, to Miss Charlotte Rolle, who was born in Germany and died at Cuero in April, 1882. She was the mother of the following children: Miss Alma, of Cuero; William, Jr.; Charles, a stockman of Dewitt County; Herman, who died unmarried at Cuero; and Henry, connected with the banking firm of

H. Runge & Company. On September 6, 1883, Mr. William Frobese married Miss Alfreda Reuss, a daughter of Dr. J. M. Reuss and a sister of Dr. J. H. Reuss of Cuero. Five children were born to this union: Doctor Joseph of Cuero; Miss Bertha, now Mrs. F. H. Schmidt of Eagle Pass, Texas; Miss Marion; Alfred, a stockman of Dewitt County; and Miss Annie. Mrs. William Frobese has continued to live at the old home in Cuero since the death of her husband, and around her center many of the associations and memories of the previous generation.

William Frobese, Jr. Son of the late William Frobese, Sr., his namesake, is actively engaged in carrying forward many of the extensive enterprises with which his father was associated, and is a member of the firm of H. Runge & Company at Cuero.

Born March 31, 1873, at Indianola, William Frobese, Jr., was only an infant when his parents moved to Cuero. There he attended the public schools until the age of twelve. At that time he was sent by his father to Germany, where he remained five years at the Bremervörde School near Stade, and on his return at the age of seventeen entered St. Edward's College at Austin and later attended Hill's Business College at Waco.

With this excellent training, the result of acquaintance with old world ideals and with the practical life and enterprise of the Southwest, he started his business career as a clerk in a grocery store at Cuero. That gave him several years of experience and he then went to Galveston, where he became a clerk in the office of George B. Dobson & Company, a cotton firm, with which he was connected for two years. He was next with the Texas Star Flour Mills at Galveston as bookkeeper. It was during that time that he experienced all the dangers and hardships incident to the great flood of 1900 which devastated Galveston. Going then to Austin, he became identified with the wholesale grocery firm of W. B. Walker & Son of Austin, and when he left them came to Cuero and took the position of bookkeeper in the grocery establishment of H. Runge & Company, which he held until his father's death. At that time he was admitted to partnership in his father's place.

Mr. Frobese is well known and highly regarded in business circles, and in an official way has been three years in the Cuero City Council, during which time the city sewer plant was installed. He is a member of the Knights of Pythias.

At Victoria, Texas, October 16, 1907, Mr. Frobese married Miss Sophie Gramann, a daughter of Henry C. and Alfreda (Wissing) Gramann. Mr. Gramann, of German parentage, was for some years a prosperous merchant at Victoria. He was the father of six children. Mr. and Mrs. Frobese have had no children.

Louis Burns. When the roll is called of representatives now living of the pioneer colonists who first settled the prairies and woodlands of Texas when it was still a domain of wild Indians and under the jurisdiction of Mexico, hardly one in a hundred of the present population of the Lone Star State could answer with a claim that would justify recognition. One such is Louis Burns of Cuero, who was born on the old headright in Dewitt County where his father, Columbus Burns, lived for many years and which his grandfather, Arthur Burns, secured as one of the old Dewitt Colony that made settlement along the valley of the Guadalupe about 1828.

Arthur Burns took his headright in Dewitt County five miles below Cuero, at what is now Burns Station, and while it was his own home for many years it was also the scene of the bringing up of many of his posterity. Of Irish stock but a native of one of the western states, Arthur Burns before coming to Texas was a resident of old Pike County, Missouri, and many years later in 1856 while on a business trip to that vicinity died there and was buried there. He was a man of little education, and his activities in Texas were devoted to a mill, farm and stock. He had one of the early grist mills whose wheels were turned by the waters of Guadalupe River. He was present as a citizen at the organization of Dewitt County, but was never a factor in public life save as he made himself a useful worker in the community, and was a member of no church. His manner was quiet but firm, and though friendly and gracious, he had little to say. He was three times married. but the names of his first wives cannot be given record. The child of his first marriage was Permelia. who married William Simpson and spent her life in Austin, Texas. The children of the second wife were: Cynthia, who married Lige Williams and lived in Lavaca County; Mrs. John Buchanan, mother of the venerable county clerk and old soldier at Halletsville; and Squire, who was killed when still single, in the Linville raid. Arthur Burns married for his third wife Sarah Moore, who survived her husband until January, 1861. One of her two children was Columbus and the other, Adelia, spent her life in Dewitt County and was the wife of Thomas Cook, a minister of the Methodist Church.

The first white child born at the settlement of Gonzales, Texas, was Columbus Burns. His birthday was in November, 1829. When still a child the family moved from Gonzales to Victoria, and when he assumed the mantle of manhood he identified himself with the family headright in Dewitt County, and there spent his active career. He did much toward clearing up the tract and making of it farms and pastures, building houses and otherwise keeping up with the march of progress in that section. The few slaves he owned were lost by the war, and in that struggle he himself became a soldier. For one year he was on the frontier in Captain Dick's company. but later got an appointment from the Government to haul freight to the Rio Grande, and still later was a member of a "minute" company which was called out at intervals and participated in the capture of a small federal boat at Salura on the coast. In the closing operations of the war he joined Captain Bill Weisiger's company in Colonel Benavides' regiment in the Rio Grande Valley, and was in the very last fight of the war.

With the return of peace he devoted himself to the care of his plantation. His only public service was as cattle inspector in Dewitt County, and he resigned because "he couldn't please everybody." He was somewhat different in character from his father, being more assured and outspoken in his convictions, and always defended himself and his attitude. He was active in church and one of the pillars of the Baptist congregation at Concrete, and he himself erected a little chapel on the Squire Burns headright. He was not a lodge man, and voted the straight democratic ticket. He married Mary Ann DeMoss. Her father, Louis DeMoss, came from Missouri to Texas with the Austin colonists, so that Mr. Louis Burns is descended from two of the very old American families in this state. Mr. DeMoss was a farmer and stockman, his chief activities being in Matagorda County, though he died in Dewitt County. His children by his marriage to Catherine Tomblinson were: Elizabeth, who married Perry Davis; Mrs. Burns; Catherine, who married William Tomblinson; Laura, whose first husband was a Hanks and second a Cox; Jane, whose first husband was a Chamblin and second a Mr. Roberson; Joseph, who died in Dewitt County; and Isabel, who married Blufe Hunter. The children of Columbus Burns were: Louis; Arthur, who died in Cuero; Martha, who married Jesse Agee, and died at San

Marcos; Ardelia, who married John Shanks, and also died in this community; Mary Ann, who married H. C. Pace and died at Cuero; Julia, who became Mrs. W. N. Bonner and died in Dewitt County; James C., who is a lawyer and banker at Goliad; Dr. J. W. of Cuero; Ella, who married Robert Partin of Tres Palacios; and Wade, who died in young manhood.

Louis Burns was born on the old Burns headright May 21, 1851, and spent his boyhood and youth in that locality. The troubles through which the entire nation was passing when he was a boy naturally interfered with his early schooling, but after the war his parents removed to Concrete where instead of the country schools he attended one of the best schools in that part of Texas, Concrete College. With the close of his last term in that institution he became identified with practical affairs as cowboy on the home ranch. His activities were on the old headright until 1875, in which year he moved to his present location, and now owns land in the Lockhart League and the Bibbs third of a league. He started here with 105 acres, bought on credit, and gathered a small nucleus of stock. He continued to be identified with stock raising until fifty years of age, when he took up farming in earnest. His surplus has been invested from time to time in more land, until his possessions now comprise 880 acres in one body, and all its improvements are the direct result of his enterprise. There are seven sets of building improvements, and ten men are kept busy with his agricultural operations. Four hundred acres are in cultivation, and while crop raising is the essential feature of his business, a sort of echo of his former activity as a stockman is found in a small bunch of sheep and he also raises a few colts.

His life has not been inclined toward politics, and he only votes his political sentiments, using no influence even with his own employes. He was reared a Baptist and has been a member of that church while his fraternal affiliations are with the Knights of Pythias and the Woodmen of the World.

December 22, 1874, Mr. Burns married for his first wife Miss Annie White, daughter of Thomas and Jane (Houston) White. At her death in 1888 Mrs. Burns left the following children: Thomas, a stockman near Yoakum, married Myra Booth, and their children are Anna Lee and Louis Thomas; Dr. J. Columbus, who died soon after beginning the practice of medicine, married Pearl Boothe and left one child named Leslie; Mamie is the wife of S. J. Law and has a daughter Dorothy; Frank W., of Cuero, married Fannie Hardy and their two children are Frank and Evelyn.

Mr. Burns for his second wife married Anna Wright, who is one of seven children, five of them living. Her father, John P. Wright, came to Texas from Mississippi, was a farmer, and married a Miss Lockhart. There are two children of Mr. and Mrs. Burns. Nellie, who is a graduate of the Cuero High School and the San Marcos Normal, is now a teacher. Patton is attending the high school at Cuero.

Charles Lenz. The career of Charles Lenz, who is now residing on his farm of eighty acres on the Guadalupe River, not far from Cuero, has been characterized by the vicissitudes which occur in the life of a man willing to take a chance and courageous enough to try his fortune in strange places and untried fields. He has tasted the bitter as well as the sweet, but has enjoyed experiences such as come to but few men, and in every community and every line of endeavor in which he has been engaged, has so conducted himself as to win and hold the respect and esteem of those among whom he has lived and labored.

Mr. Lenz was born at Yorktown, Dewitt County, Texas, June 16,

1856, and is a son of Louis Lenz, who came to America in 1848 or 1849 and located at New Braunfels, Texas. There he spent his funds in seeing the new country and when forced to seek employment went to the community of Yorktown, where, unable to find work at his trade of baker, he engaged in various occupations, including well-digging and rail-splitting. There he was married to Miss Augusta Zedler, the daughter of a German farmer, and after his marriage engaged in freighting from San Antonio to Indianola. In 1860 he removed to Yorktown, where he opened a hotel and bakery and also conducted a liquor store, and when the Civil war came on went to Mexico, but, not finding employment, returned to Texas and joined the Confederate army. He served through the war, at the close of which he returned to Yorktown and resumed his old business, and there died in 1903, at the age of seventy-three years, three months. He and his wife were the parents of the following children: Charles, of this notice; Louis, of Cuero; Gus, a resident of Yorktown; Mary and Agnes, who passed their lives at Cape Girardeau, Missouri; Matilda, who is the wife of Alfred Tips, of Runge, Texas; and Miss Julia, of Yorktown.

Charles Lenz received his schooling at a country school at Yorktown, but the greater part of his education has come from his experience as a traveler and wanderer, in which he early found that he could not only make his own way, but that he could find pleasure and make money as well. He had early learned the confectioner's trade, and was only sixteen years of age when he left the parental roof, determined to pay for his way as he went. His first stop was at New Orleans, but the presence of the dreaded yellow fever precluded the idea of obtaining employment and he went on to Cairo, Illinois, where he was employed as a section hand on the Illinois Central Railroad. He remained only five weeks, however, until he received his first pay check and then went to St. Louis, where he was given a position with a baker. He worked thus for six weeks and then became a bootblack in the Tivoli Hotel, at the corner of Fourth and Elm streets, and within four months worked up to the position of clerk of the house. After about one year he again felt the wanderlust and started out to spend his accumulations, going to Cincinnati, Ohio, and down through Kentucky to visit the famous Mammoth Cave, then on to Niagara Falls, and to New York City. In the metropolis he secured work as a confectioner with Henry Heide, a well known man of the craft in the East, and although he received but $6.50 a week remained for nine months. Next he went to a wholesale paper house as a porter, and here again, by doing more than was expected of him and refraining from the usual habit of the other employes of closely watching the clock, won promotion rapidly and worked his way up to head porter and then to bookkeeper, remaining with the house for two years. During another year he was with the wholesale paper house of J. J. McCloskey, and, having received word from his father to return to Texas and take charge of the family affairs, he prepared to do so. First, however, he visited his father's Lenz relatives in Germany, leaving New York for Hamburg, and while in the Fatherland journeyed all over the country. He visited the old family home at Landsberg, Province of Brandenburg, Prussia, and was in Europe three months, returning to Galveston from Bremen and reaching home after eleven years of absence.

Taking up life anew in the Southwest, Mr. Lenz bought a liquor business from August Kobitz, at Cuero, and in partnership with George Letsch conducted it for three years, then selling out to his partner. He next purchased the Burghardt Restaurant, which he conducted for twenty-three and one quarter years as the Lenz Restaurant, and in August, 1910, retired from business and moved out to his eighty-acre farm, where in that year he erected a splendid country mansion, and where he and his wife have been recuperating.

While living at Cuero Mr. Lenz was for seventeen years continuously an alderman, resigning only when he moved to the country. While a member of the council he was chairman much of the time of the street committee and the streets of the city give eloquent evidence of his capable and faithful performance of duty. The city hall was erected during this time, the artesian water was contracted for, and the efficiency of the fire department was greatly advanced. Mr. Lenz was elected county commissioner in 1912 and represents Precinct No. 1, succeeding J. F. Card, and being re-elected in 1914. This re-election refutes Mr. Lenz's good-natured statement that, whereas he gets kicks by the retail as alderman, he gets them by wholesale as a commissioner. Road improvement and small bridge-building have occupied the board, as well as marketing road bonds and marking off the system of good roads for the county. Mr. Lenz has no church connection and his only fraternal affliation is with the Sons of Hermann.

In October, 1883, Mr. Lenz was married at Yorktown, to Miss Emma Mueller, a daughter of William Mueller, of Magdeburg, Germany. Mrs. Lenz came to America alone to an uncle in Texas, being the only one of her family to come to this state except her brother, William, of Yorktown. Mr. and Mrs. Lenz went to housekeeping at Cuero, and to her much credit is due for the success which they made in the confection and restaurant business. They have been the parents of the following children: Louis, a graduate of the Agricultural and Mechanical College of Texas, and since 1907 a civil engineer with the Southern Pacific Railway; Lottie, who is now Mrs. Hugo Boldt, of Cuero, and the mother of two children,—Helen and Charles Hugo; Elsie, who was married June 29, 1915, to August C. Hartman, a well known lawyer and member of the lower house of the Texas Legislature; and Estella and Margarita, who reside with their parents in the beautiful two-story home, standing above the public highway, just behind a growth of live oaks.

David Hubert Heaton, head of the thriving drug business of Heaton Brothers, at Cuero, is a member of one of the antebellum families of Texas, and a son of the founder, David Henry Heaton, who came to Texas in 1858. He was born in 1846, at Potsdam, St. Lawrence County, New York, a son of an English father and a Scotch mother, the latter from Jedborough, Scotland. The grandparents of David Hubert Heaton after coming to the United States passed the remainder of their lives at Potsdam, New York, and were the parents of five sons: Aaron and Charles, who passed their lives at the old New York home; and Jack C., Laurie and David Henry, who came to Texas.

David Henry Heaton received a fair education in the public schools of his native state, and in 1858 came to Texas, having been preceded hither a year or two by his brothers, Jack C. and Laurie, making the journey on the old Morgan line of boats from New York to Indianola. They entered business at that point as well as Port Lavaca and Victoria, and continued in the management and ownership of a pharmacy at Indianola until the first great storm, in 1875, when they moved to Port Lavaca, and finally came to Cuero. Each brother had a drug store, but all were conducted under the name of Heaton Brothers. David Henry Heaton erected one of the first frame buildings at Cuero, on the lot where the present drug business of Heaton Brothers now stands. It was subsequently destroyed by fire, and in 1884 a new brick store took its place. Mr. Heaton continued in business on that site while he lived, his death occurring June 17, 1911. During the Civil war Mr. Heaton did no service on either side, but remained as near neutral as it was possible to do throughout the period of the conflict. He showed his sincere interest in the welfare of Cuero as well as his executive ability as a member of the board of aldermen, on which he served at different times, but remained a plain, unvarnished citizen, with no fraternal or church affiliations. His life can be said to have been a home one, and at no time was he inclined to thrust himself forward for preferment.

Mr. Heaton married Miss Ellen Hill, at Victoria, Texas, she being a daughter of Col. Benjamin Hill, a United States army officer during the Mexican war under General Scott, who married Mary Hubert, of French-Huguenot ancestors who came to the Carolinas at an early day and from there to Texas. Colonel Hill was a prominent planter along the coast of Texas, at Alligator Head, where he had a big stock ranch. He died at Victoria, and his children were Mrs. Heaton, who now resides in New York City; Annie, who died as the wife of T. A. Graves, one of Cuero's most prominent men; and Benjamin Hill, a resident of St. Louis, Missouri. To David Henry and Ellen Heaton there were born three children: Estelle, who is the wife of Dr. J. L. Smith, of Victoria, Texas; Miss Frances, of New York City; and David Hubert, the proprietor of the business of Heaton Brothers at Cuero, and successor of this firm's enterprises at the other points, his uncles having left no issue at their deaths.

David Hubert Heaton was born at Cuero, February 26, 1891. His early education secured in the public school, he later attended the Vanderbilt preparatory school of Vanderbilt University, Nashville, Tennessee, and a business college at Birmingham, Alabama, and after a year in the latter institution came into the store with his father. He was practically brought up in the establishment and his hand has been on the throttle from the start. Still a young man, he has so far made no history of importance, but is proving a live, energetic young man of business, who is following the lines of honesty and integrity that brought the founders of the business success and respect. Mr. Heaton was married at Cuero, June 18, 1910, to Miss Jennie Alexander, a daughter of W. J. Alexander, and to this union there has come one son; David Henry, born July 24, 1911.

Mrs. Heaton's father, William J. Alexander, belongs to one of the pioneer families of Dewitt County. He was born April 2, 1852, in Yalobusha County, Mississippi, a son of Robert Franklin Alexander, a grandson of Benjamin Alexander, born in Mecklenburg County, North Carolina, where almost a third of the population bore the name, and a descendant of five brothers of Irish stock who fought on the American side during the Revolutionary war. William Alexander was two years old when brought to Texas and grew up at old Terryville. There, after a university education, he embarked in life in the cattle business and with the exception of three years as a merchant has passed his entire life as a farmer and stockraiser. He now owns 450 acres in the Belcher League, where he raises cotton and corn, and breeds Hereford and Red Polled cattle, while his mules are noted in the community and his horse stock is of racing strain, from "Cotton Eye Joe." His experiences during his residence in Texas have included narrow escapes at the hands of murderous Indians, road building with convict labor and participation in all that has gone to develop his community, where he is respected alike as a citizen and a business man. He married Miss Malinda Pearson, the only daughter of William Sherwood and Malinda (Benbow) Pearson. To Mr. and Mrs. Alexander there were born the following children: Willie, who married Frank A. Taylor, a merchant at Cuero, and both are deceased, leaving a daughter,—Corinne; May, who married Irvin Anderson, a farmer on the Guadaloupe, near Burns Station; Maudie, who married Raymond Schrimsher, chief clerk and cashier of the Aransas Pass Railway at Corpus Christi; Jennie, the wife of David Hubert Heaton; Irvin J., and Barue.

JOSEPH H. REUSS, M. D., F. A. C. S. For nearly seventy years one of the foremost names in the medical profession of South Texas has been Reuss. The first of the name was one of the scholarly scientists and polished gentlemen who came out of the fatherland at the beginning of the revolutionary difficulties of the '40s and gave to a new country in the new world the benefit of their distinguished attainments. The present Doctor Reuss of Cuero, though living in a country town, has attainments and associations that permit him to move in fellowship with the ablest of his profession in any state or country. He is strong and robust in body as in mind, and his bearing suggests education, culture and constant kinship with the best minds of the age.

His father, the late Dr. Joseph M. Reuss, was one of the pioneer German physicians in South Texas, and made a name which deserves to live in the professional history of the state. Born in Bavaria, November 12, 1824, he was liberally educated both in literature and science, and graduated in medicine from Heidelberg. He soon found himself out of sympathy with the political and social rules and customs of his native country, and emigrated a short time prior to the actual outbreak of the Revolution of 1848, which caused eventually so many men of education and high ideals to cast their fortunes with the United States. He was the only one of his family to come to America, and therefore must be regarded as the founder of the Reuss family in Texas.

He was already a well-rounded scholarly man when he left Bavaria in 1846. Landing at Galveston, where he married, he soon afterward took his bride to Indianola, where he became established in business and his profession and remained until the town was destroyed by the storm of 1875, when he removed to Cuero. In the early days, probably in the '50s, he was identified with the Government in suppressing an epidemic of cholera, and during the different epidemics of yellow fever along the coast did a prominent work in treating the victims of the scourge. He was noted for the studious pursuits, especially in scientific branches, which he kept up all his life, and was an original thinker on many phases of human activities. He took an active part in the business and social life of the community. During the Civil war he was captain of a company in Shay's battalion, all his service being within the state boundaries. He was in sympathy with the Southern cause and approved secession, and afterwards was in harmony with the policies of the democratic party except in the free silver movement. Though reared as a Catholic he seems never to have participated actively in the affairs of the church in this country. He was never a member of fraternal orders. His friendship with Texas public men included such figures as Governor Ireland, Gustav Schleicher, Ashbel Smith, and others, and intellectually he was on a level with the best of them. His command of language and ideas would have made him a public leader had he desired such distinctions, and in all relations he was virile, earnest and capable. As a business man he established a stock of drugs in a tent at Indianola in the early days, not primarily for the purpose of engaging in the drug business, but in order to have those needed in his own practice and to accommodate the public. In 1872 he started a drug store at Cuero, and this business was continued through his son and is now owned by a grandson, Theodore Reuss.

The senior Doctor Reuss was married in Galveston to Miss Gesene

ried Irvin Anderson, a farmer on the Guadalupe [illegible] Station; Maudie, who married Raymond Schrimsher [illegible] cashier of the Aransas Pass Railway at Corpus Christi; [illegible] the wife of David Hubert Heaton; Irvin J., and Barnie.

JOSEPH H. REUSS, M. D., F. A. C. S. For nearly seventy years one of the foremost names in the medical profession of South Texas has been Reuss. The first of the name was one of the scholarly scientists and polished gentlemen who came out of the Fatherland at the beginning of the revolutionary difficulties of the '40s and gave to a new country in the new world the benefit of their distinguished attainments. The present Doctor Reuss of Cuero, though living in a country town, has attainments and associations that permit him to move in fellowship with the ablest of his profession in any state or country. He is strong and robust in body as in mind, and his bearing suggests education, culture and [illegible] with the best [illegible] of the age.

His [illegible], the late Dr. Joseph M. Reuss, was one of the pioneer [illegible] Texas [illegible] a name which deserves to [illegible] born in Bavaria, Novem- [illegible] literature and science, [illegible] soon found himself [illegible] and customs of his [illegible] actual outbreak [illegible] so many men of [illegible] the United States. [illegible] America, and therefore [illegible] Texas.

[illegible] left Bavaria [illegible] soon afterward [illegible]

[illegible] the drug business [illegible] and to accommodate [illegible] Cuero, and this business [illegible] by a grandson. [illegible]

The senior [illegible] to Miss Gesene [illegible]

Stubemann, who was a native of Germany and died in Cuero. Their children were: Dr. August J., who was sent abroad by his father to get the best of clinical opportunities, served as assistant surgeon during the Franco-Prussian war, continued his medical studies in Germany after that war, but following his return to Texas died when about thirty years old and unmarried; the daughter Alfreda married William Frobese, a member of H. Runge & Company, one of the old established firms of South Texas, and she resides at Cuero, the mother of five children; Miss Bertha, of Cuero, has reared the orphan children of her brother, Oscar J., who was graduated in pharmacy and succeeded his father in the drug business, and at his death left six children by his marriage to Lillie Muegge; and Dr. Joseph H., the youngest.

At the old lost Town of Indianola on the Texas coast Joseph H. Reuss was born January 16, 1867, and eight years later about the time of the storm and flood was brought to Cuero. After attending local schools there he was one of the first to be enrolled as a student at the newly opened University of Texas, where he finished a three year course. In 1889 he was graduated M. D. from Columbia College, New York City. While in the University of Texas he was closely and intimately associated as a student with Albert S. Burleson, now postmaster general, Judge T. W. Gregory, now attorney general of the United States, and Judge Yancey Lewis, who attained great prominence in the law in Texas. Among those whom he knew quite intimately in Columbia were Dr. George B. Deaver, one of the most prominent surgeons of New York City, and George B. Coley, of New York, another man of high standing in the profession.

His training at Columbia was given the edge of practical experience in hospital work at St. Luke's and the city hospitals of New York, after which he returned to Cuero and entered practice. At intervals since he has done post-graduate work in New York, and in 1911 went abroad and spent a year in the royal hospitals of Berlin and for a short time was also a student in the Allgemeine Krankenhaus of Vienna.

When Doctor Reuss opened a hospital at Cuero in 1892 it was the first institution of the kind in all this section of Texas. As the Salome Hospital he conducted it until 1904, when he removed to Dallas, the Cuero Hospital being conducted by Doctors Kirkham and Burns, during his several years' absence. His father in the meantime had retired from active practice, but went along with the son to Dallas, and was associated with the latter after he had established the Marsalis Sanitarium on Marsalis Avenue in Oak Cliff. Dr. J. H. Reuss had another reason for going to Dallas, and that was as one of the original stockholders and incorporators of the Southwestern Life Insurance Company, the first Texas life company on the old-line basis. He became its first medical director, and remained in Dallas looking after his various interests there until 1911. Both his father and brother having died about that time, and the affairs left to his charge compelled him to return to Cuero, where he has resumed practice and has also resumed the Salome Hospital, which is now under his direction.

Doctor Reuss was one of the members of the first board of medical examiners of Texas, having been appointed by Governor Sayres in 1900 and serving four years. He is medical director of the San Antonio & Aransas Pass Railroad, and the Salome Hospital treats its railroad cases of surgery and illness. For years he has been a member of the local and state medical societies, is a former president of the South Texas Medical Association, and his distinctive attainments as a surgeon have recently brought him fellowship in the American College of Surgeons. He was instrumental in organizing and is a member of the Texas Surgical Society.

Though the broad demands of his professional life kept him pretty well out of the activities of politics, he has recently been made president of the Cuero Commercial Club. He has led this organization in its campaign for good roads, and the club was the most important single factor in securing the issue of $54,000 at one time and again of $125,000 in bonds, the proceeds of which are being used in the construction of modern highways radiating from the county seat. He has also given to Cuero one of its most generous and architecturally rich residences, situated at the east end of Esplanade Street.

He was married at Cuero, April 30, 1896, to Miss Meta Reiffert, daughter of Emil Reiffert, who was associated with the old firm of H. Runge & Company of South Texas. They have three children, Gaillard Thomas, Helen and Anita. Doctor Reuss has filled all the chairs except chancellor commander in the Knights of Pythias, and with his family is a member of the Episcopal Church.

VICTOR J. GRUNDER. The manager, secretary and treasurer of the Cuero Compress and Warehouse Company, and president of the Victoria Compress and Warehouse Company, Victor J. Grunder has been a resident of Cuero since 1890, in which year he came to this city from San Antonio. Since that time he has become identified with a variety of commercial and industrial interests, has been well known to the amusement-loving public, and in public life has occupied positions of importance in which he has been instrumental in securing many benefits for his adopted city. He was born January 20, 1863, in the Town of Hagenau, Alsace, and is a son of Florentin and Elizabeth (Hildenbrand) Grunder.

Florentin Grunder was born in the same town in Alsace, in June, 1834, and was a soldier during the Crimean war, subsequently being in the service of the French government when the Franco-Prussian war was fought. In 1873, after the close of that struggle, he brought his family to the United States and, landing at New York City, made his way to St. Louis, through Kansas City, and on to San Antonio. He was a machinist by trade, and in the Texas city opened a repair shop, of which he continued as the proprietor until his death, in 1903. Mrs. Grunder, who still resides at San Antonio, was also born in Alsace, and bore her husband seven children, of whom the following grew to maturity; Victor J., of this review; Mary, who is the widow of a Mr. Prendergast, of San Antonio; Louisa, who is the widow of Herman Doebler and resides at Los Angeles, California; Florentine, who is now Mrs. Tracy Jones, of San Antonio; Elizabeth, who is the wife of T. Z. Barry, of that city; and Louis, who served four years as an electrician in the submarine service of the United States Navy and is now associated with his brother at Cuero.

Victor J. Grunder is thoroughly a self-made, and practically a self-educated man. He was ten years of age when taken by his parents to San Antonio, where he finished his public school education, and while still a schoolboy entered upon his career as a cash boy in a San Antonio department store. There he grew up in the merchandise business and when he left that line was in the employ of L. Wolfson, with whom he had been associated for nine years. Mr. Grunder came to Cuero in 1890 and entered the crockery and house furnishing business, the firm being Keller & Company at the outset, and after several years succeeded to the ownership of the entire store, but sold it in 1910 to identify himself with the compress business. He at once became secretary and treasurer of the Cuero Compress and Warehouse Company, and in 1914 succeeded to the management of the plant. The Cuero compress was built in 1895 by local interests, the heads of the movement being Louis Keller, Emil Reiffert, William Frobese, John Stratton and D. C. Proctor. It is a corporation capitalized at $75,000, and its president is Mr. Keller, who came originally from Indianola. In 1914 the corporate name was changed from the Cuero Cotton Compress Company to the Cuero Compress and Warehouse Company and a warehouse was built, as well as a storage plant for housing cotton to the capacity of 10,000 bales for caring for the possible cotton crop desired to be held in this section. Since he has resided at Cuero he has acquired other interests, being proprietor of the Dreamland Theatre which, under his management, has proven a decided success. He has also managed the Opera House here for a number of years and has given the theatre-going public a high grade of first-class attractions. As a citizen, working for the best interests of the city, he has served several times as alderman and during his incumbency of that office was instrumental in building the city hall, in bringing into existence the present waterworks system and in helping to place the finances of Cuero as a municipality on a sound basis. He resigned as alderman to make the race for mayor under a commission form, the commission charter being submitted at the same election, but the platform he represented met with defeat. However, he is still a strong believer in, and advocate of the commission form of government, as placing responsibility for the public business where it belongs.

As a fraternity man, Mr. Grunder belongs to the Knights of Columbus, having helped to organize the Cuero Lodge of which he is grand knight, and has sat in state meetings as a delegate. He is also a member of the Catholic Knights of America. Mr. Grunder is widely read and an accomplished linguist, being familiar with the English, German, French and Spanish languages. His home, on Morgan Avenue, is one of the attractive and substantial residences in the city.

While working in the Wolfson mercantile house at San Antonio, Mr. Grunder became acquainted with Miss Augusta Keller, who was also employed there, and they were married at Cuero May 4, 1887. She is a daughter of Antone Keller, who came from Germany to America and settled at Indianola, Texas, prior to the war between the states, in which he served as a Confederate soldier, and later became a baker and finally a merchant at Cuero, where he died in 1900. He married Miss Charlotte Kuester, and they had six children, namely: Charles (1), Henry, Louis, Lizzie, Mrs. Grunder and Charles (2). To Mr. and Mrs. Grunder there have been born the following children: Gertrude, who is the wife of John Y. Bell, of Cuero, manager of the Dreamland Theatre, and has two children,—John Y., Jr., and Carlos; Charles L., secretary-treasurer and manager of the Victoria Compress and Warehouse Company, who married Wilhelmina Schmidt, a Cuero lady by birth, and has a daughter,—Armine; and Geneva, who is the wife of L. B. Cole, of Cuero.

Elisha L. Nichols, a successful stock farmer of Cuero, Texas, represents a family that has been located in Dewitt County since before the Civil war. He is a son of Morgan Oliver Nichols, who was born in this county on December 25, 1847, in a community on the Guadaloupe known there as the Nichols Settlement. Morgan Nichols grew up there, gained a little schooling one way and another, and passed his life there engaged in stock raising. He was not of an age to permit him to enter the ranks as a soldier in the Civil war, and he was never a man who wanted a prominent place in the public eye. He was a plain, everyday citizen, a democrat and a life-long member of the Methodist Church. Mr. Nichols in early manhood married Fannie Hardy, the daughter of Covington Hardy, who came to Texas from Hinds County, Mississippi. He spent his life engaged in the stock raising industry, and gave service to the South during the Civil war period.

To Morgan O. and Fanny Nichols were born six children, brief mention of each of them following here: Elisha L. of this review was the first born. Don Covington is occupying the old home place and carrying on a stock business, having taken charge of his father's affairs on the death of the latter. He married Irene Peavy. Beulah is the widow of Murray Kibbie, of Fordtran, Texas. Vallie married Clyde Wofford and lives in the Nichols Settlement. Morgan Oliver, Jr., is also engaged in the stock business in the Nichols Settlement, and is married to Alma Carpenter. Ona is the wife of Trigg Peebles, and also lives in the community named for the family.

The father of Morgan O. Nichols and the grandsire of the subject was Lazarus Nichols, who came to Texas in young manhood, and here married. Jackson, Mississippi, had been his home, and it is believed that city was his birthplace, though there is some doubt as to the actual fact. However that may be, it is established that he was the actual founder of the family in the State of Texas, and it is said that he made the trip here from his native state in one of the typical overland conveyances of that time. He settled near Guadaloupe River, applied himself to the stock business and became widely known in this part of the state as a pioneer stockman and a highly successful one. He acquired an immense tract of land which he used largely as pasture, and his "N. I. C." brand and later the "Diamond P" are well remembered by the people of his day. He was ever a good citizen, and in politics he gained some prominence through his evident sincerity and his talent for leadership. He was a democrat and a church member. He did not serve in any capacity during the Civil war, and what his sentiments might have been are not known. Lazarus Nichols was a man of striking personal appearance. Six feet two in height, he was well built, wore a VanDyke beard, looked squarely through you, and possessed a degree of energy that placed him far beyond the average man in physical endurance. He married Louise Means, daughter of one of the early families of Texas, and she bore him seven children. They were Morgan O., father of the subject; Lee, who married Nathan McFadden and lives in Lakey, Texas; Betty married a Mr. Orrel of Lakey, Texas; Eliza married Sam Lane, of Dewitt County; Elisha, the twin brother of Eliza, died unmarried in Cuero; Lettia married George Clogg, of Alice, Texas; Della married Otis Drake for her first husband; later she married a Mr. Cook and still later became the wife of Will McGill, of Burnett, Texas.

Lazarus Nichols died in about 1888, being then sixty-six years old. His widow survived him for some years and was seventy-five when she passed away.

Elisha L. Nichols of this review, and grandson of Lazarus, was born in the Nichols Settlement on March 28, 1878. He got his education in the Cuero schools, and was brought up to know the details of the stock business from boyhood. His native community held him until recent years, when he settled on the Thomas League east of the Town of Cuero, and there he owns 275 acres of excellent land which he devotes to stock raising. The place was well improved, and Mr. Nichols is making an excellent success of the enterprise, as might be expected. His brand is the quarter circle above the letter "e," and the strains he favors most are the Red Polled and the White Faces.

Mr. Nichols is a family man. He was married in Dewitt County on December 18, 1898, to Miss Jessie Shults, a daughter of Cornelius Shults and his wife, Alice (Moss) Shults, the latter a daughter of William Thomas, holder of the Thomas League and one of the pioneers of this county, coming here from Mississippi. William Thomas' first wife was a Miss Lacey, and there were no children from that marriage. He later married again; of this marriage there were several children. Cornelius Shults came to Texas from Mississippi and engaged in the merchandise business in Cuero. He discontinued that line and went into the stock raising business. He died in 1893 and his widow followed him in 1910. Their children were: Cornelius, wife of Charles Peavy, of Dewitt County; Robert, who passed away in this county, leaving a family; Mrs. Nichols, wife of Elisha Nichols of this review; Ivy, who lives in Amarillo, Texas; Thomas, a farmer in the vicinity of Cuero. Mrs. Shults, it may be said, was the widow of Jody Moss when she married Mr. Shults, and by her first marriage was the mother of a daughter, Josie, who died in young womanhood, unmarried.

Mr. and Mrs. Nichols have no children. They are prominent in social circles of their community, and have a great many staunch friends in and about the county. They are members of the Baptist Church, and Mr. Nichols is fraternally identified with the Woodmen of the World and the Knights of Pythias.

HERMANN CURRLIN. Coming to the United States as a youth of seventeen years, Herman Currlin began his career at Cuero in 1886, as a baker, and since that time had steadily advanced in business circles, until today he occupies a substantial position among the men who are contributing through their energies and talents to the commercial prestige of this thriving City of Dewitt County. Mr. Currlin was born May 11, 1870, at Lorch, Wurttemburg, Germany, and is a son of Karl and Caroline (Brantley) Currlin.

Karl Currlin was a son of a native of Alsace, although himself born in Wurttemburg, and for a number of years was a hotel keeper at Lorch, but subsequently became a quarryman and owned and operated several stone quarries. Both he and his wife passed away at Lorch. Their children were as follows: Gustav, who died single at Vienna, Austria; William, who came to America and is now a resident of Guadalajara, Mexico; Paulina, who married Charles Keller, of Indianola, Texas; Eugene, a mechanical engineer of Zurich, Switzerland; Bertha, who married Traugott Mestling, of Esslingen, Germany; Theodore, a saddler and decorator of Zurich, Switzerland; Hermann, of this review; and Frieda, who is the wife of Max Oberbueller, of Stuttgart, Germany.

Hermann Currlin received his education in the "Folks" and public schools of his native place, and when still a lad became apprenticed to the trade of baker at Stuttgart, his master being Christian Ansel, who conducted one of the leading establishments of the kingdom and who supplied the royal kitchen of Wurttemburg with its culinary supplies. It took Mr. Currlin two years and three months to complete his apprenticeship, following which he continued with Mr. Ansel for several months, and at the end of that time decided to try his fortunes in America, whence he had been preceded by his sister. Sailing from Bremen on the ship Weser, he arrived duly at Galveston and joined his sister subsequently at Cuero, but later retraced his steps to Houston and on back to New Orleans, working in both cities at his trade and remaining at the latter place until 1888, when he came back to Cuero to make his permanent home.

Here Mr. Currlin began to work for a baker, Charles Lenz, and remained in his employ for five years, conducting his shop. In the meantime he had made many business acquaintances, who became impressed with the young man's ability and enterprise, and in July, 1893, he gave up baking to accept the position of agent for the San Antonio Brewing

Association, to represent them at Cuero, and has continued in that capacity to the present time. For the past twelve years, during the cotton season, he has been engaged in buying cotton for the firm of H. Runge & Company, and for some five years has represented the Meyersville, Arneckeville and Mission Valley Truck Growers' Association, as shipping and sales agent at Cuero. While public life has held out no attractions for him, he has been sensible of his duties as a citizen, and has been a member of the Merchants Protective Hose Company No. 1, and was chief of the Cuero Fire Department until 1912. When he attained his majority, he took out his citizenship papers, through Senator John H. Bailey, and in 1892 cast his first presidential vote for Grover Cleveland. He has continued to act with the democratic party as a voter ever since. Fraternally, he is affiliated with the Sons of Hermann, while his religious connection is with the Lutheran Church.

Mr. Currlin was married May 10, 1894, to Miss Lena Dietze, a daughter of the late Gustav Dietze, a German citizen of Cuero and a public official of the town for twenty years. He was a pioneer of the town, and one of his daughters, now Mrs. Julius Wilton, of El Campo, was the first white child born here. Mr. Dietze came from Saxony, married Henrietta Harsdorff, at Meyersville, Texas, and died in 1895, while his widow still survives and makes her home at Cuero. Their family comprised nine children. Mr. and Mrs. Currlin have one child: Jewell, born in October, 1904.

Mr. Currlin made a trip to his native land in 1907, accompanied by his wife and child, and visited various points of interest in Europe, covering Germany thoroughly, through Northern Italy, into Switzerland and the Rhine country, and paying visits to Berlin and other large cities, finally going back to Bremen from whence they returned to the United States. While in the Swiss Alps their attention was attracted to the beautiful bungalow cottages of the mountaineers, and Mr. Currlin decided then to accede to his wife's wishes and to build one for them at Cuero. This was accomplished in 1912, and the Currlin house and grounds are among the most beautiful in this part of the state. The home is spacious, modern and airy, and the grounds, with their generous and picture-like lawns and broad and palm-burdened galleries, contribute greatly to the attractiveness of Cuero's architecture and landscape.

EDWARD MUGGE. The late Edward Mugge was one of the three men most prominently associated with the great South Texas business house of H. Runge & Company, and for a number of years was closely indentified with the growth and extension of that mercantile concern in radiating its influence and business over the vast territory between the main line of the Southern Pacific and the Rio Grande. He continued to be indentified with the business as long as he lived, and his two chief colleagues were Emil Reiffert and William Frobese.

He was born November 7, 1839, and was a member of one of the early German families in Texas. He settled in South Texas and became a factor in its commercial and social development prior to the Civil war. He was at that time a young man and had finished his education in a German gymnasium. Edward Mugge came to Texas to join his brother, Julius, who had become a Texan several years before and who after spending some years in Dewitt County finally removed to San Antonio and is still living there. Later, Edward was joined by a younger brother, Carl Mugge, who became a Dewitt County farmer and died unmarried. Julius Mugge reared a family and has many descendants in Texas.

The first employment to which Edward Mugge turned on coming to

Edward Mügge

[illegible] and has continued in that capac- [illegible] years, during the cotton sea- [illegible] for the firm of H. Runge & [illegible] represented the Meyersville [illegible] Association, as shipping [illegible] has held out no attractions [illegible] as a citizen, and has been a [illegible] Company No. 1, and was chief [illegible] 1912. When he attained his [illegible] papers, through Senator John H. [illegible] presidential vote for Grover Cleveland. [illegible] the democratic party as a voter ever since. [illegible] with the Sons of Hermann, while his religious [illegible] Lutheran Church.

[illegible] May 16, 1894, to Miss Lena Dietze, a daugh- [illegible] a German citizen of Cuero and a public [illegible] twenty years. He was a pioneer of the town, and [illegible] Mrs. Julius Wilton, of El Campo, was the first [illegible] Mr. Dietze came from Saxony, married Henri- [illegible] sville, Texas, and died in 1895, while his widow [illegible] makes her home at Cuero. Their family comprised [illegible] Mr. and Mrs. Currlin have one child: Jewell, born in [illegible]

[illegible] Currlin made a trip to his native land in 1907, accompanied by [illegible] points of interest in Europe, cover- [illegible] Northern Italy, into Switzerland and [illegible] to Berlin and other large cities, [illegible] whence they returned to the United [illegible] their attention was attracted to the [illegible] of the mountaineers, and Mr. Currlin [illegible] wishes and to build one for them [illegible] in 1912, and the Currlin house and [illegible] beautiful in this part of the state. The [illegible] airy, and the grounds, with their generous [illegible] and broad and [illegible] galleries, con- [illegible] attractiveness of [illegible] architecture and land-

[illegible] The late Edward Mugge was one of the three men [illegible] associated with the great South Texas business house [illegible] and for a number of years was closely indenti- [illegible] extension of that mercantile concern in radiating [illegible] over the vast territory between the main line [illegible] the Rio Grande. He continued to be indenti- [illegible] long as he lived, and his two chief colleagues [illegible] William Frobese.

[illegible] 7, 1839, and was a member of one of the early [illegible] He settled in South Texas and became a [illegible] and social development prior to the Civil war. [illegible] young man and had finished his education in a [illegible] Mugge came to Texas to join his brother, [illegible] several years before and who after [illegible] County finally removed to San Antonio and [illegible] Edward was joined by a younger brother, Carl [illegible] Dewitt County farmer and died unmarried. Julius [illegible] and has many descendants in Texas.

[illegible] which Edward Mugge turned on coming to

Edward Mügge

Texas was as a farm hand in Dewitt County, but from this humble employment he rose to a position of commercial prominence second to none. Later he traveled in the interest of an Indianola firm, and subsequently in 1868 became associated with the firm of H. Runge & Company at Indianola. In 1874 he moved to Cuero and with Mr. Frobese conducted the affairs of the firm in that city. In 1886 Mr. Reiffert joined them, and all three were actively associated in extending the interests of their house to merchandising, stock ranching and into various other avenues.

Edward Mugge died May 16, 1897, at the age of fifty-seven years, six months, nine days, and was laid to rest in the cemetery at Cuero. There were many qualities which made him a useful citizen. He took out naturalization papers soon after coming to Texas, and as a staunch democrat was always a factor in politics and local affairs. He was a member of the Lutheran Church, but had no fraternal affiliations. While he did much to build up the interests of his community his only offices were as trustee of public schools at Cuero and as town alderman. He had considerable ability as a speaker, and his opinions on matters of consequence were listened to with respect. Physically he stood six feet, weighed 225 pounds, was deliberate in his movements, and his versatile nature and friendliness proved a valuable factor in the popularity of the great mercantile house of which he was a member. By his kindness of heart and his many charitable deeds, Edward Mugge did much to build up his entire section of country, and many a man now living in Southwest Texas is indebted to Mr. Mugge for the start whereby he acquired his home. Because of the universal knowledge of his generous kindness Mr. Mugge endeared himself in the hearts of all.

The late Edward Mugge was married in New York June 17, 1867, to Miss Pauline Blumenthal. She was born in the Town of Schnackenburg on the River Elbe in the Kingdom of Hanover, and came alone to the United States the same year she was married. She is still living, a venerable and loved woman in Cuero. Her children are: Edward Jr., who died in 1900 and by his marriage to Mildred Hutchenson left a daughter, Pauline; Lillie, who married Oscar Reuss and at her death in Cuero left children named Edward, Joseph, Theodore, John, Pauline and Bertha; Henry A.; Anna who is the wife of Walter Reiffert of Cuero; Dr. Oscar J. of Cuero; and Fred Theodore of Cuero, who married Miss Hilda Reiffert.

Henry A. Mugge. One of the most efficient and popular mayors among all the cities of Southwest Texas is Henry A. Mugge, who since 1912 has been chief executive of Cuero. Mr. Mugge as a business man had long and broad experience; he represents one of the notable names in the business life of Southwest Texas during the last half century, and his experience has been most valuable in directing municipal improvement at Cuero during the past three or four years.

A son of the late Edward Mugge, he was born at the old Town of Indianola, Texas, October 8, 1871. Most of his life has been spent in Cuero, where he attended the public schools, was also a student for a time in Bedford County, Virginia, and passed one year within the halls of the State University at Austin. At the conclusion of his education he started business with the firm of Reiffert & Tips at Runge, but a year later became an employe of H. Runge & Company at Cuero. He was with that great and prosperous firm until 1907, first as clerk, then as bookkeeper, and later became entrusted with various responsibilities of the firm's details. On leaving Cuero he became assistant cashier of the First State Bank at Hamlin, Jones County, in West Texas, and for four years was a resident of that section of the state.

Since returning from Jones County to Cuero Mr. Mugge has, in addition to his public responsibilities, looked after an office business as a real estate man and is also the local representative for the Southwestern Life Insurance Company at Dallas. In 1911 he was elected secretary of the Cuero Commercial Club. In 1912 came his election as mayor to succeed J. C. Woodworth, and he was re-elected to the office in 1914. Under his regime as mayor the city has installed a sewer plant, paid for by the proceeds of a $25,000 bond issue, has made extensive street improvements, including various bridges and culverts, purchased a steam roller, and has carried on other work in the line of progressiveness. The city is particularly proud of its modern and efficient fire department, which has been organized under Mayor Mugge's administration. The equipment comprises auto trucks and chemical engine, and Cuero now has fire protection equal to that of any city of its size and class.

Fraternally Mr. Mugge is affiliated with the Knights of Pythias, the Independent Order of Odd Fellows, the Sons of Hermann, has passed the various chairs in the Knights of Pythias Lodge and has been a representative to the Grand Lodge, and is vice president of the Deutsch-Americanischen Natiönalbundes.

At Cuero, on April 17, 1900, Mr. Mugge married Miss Mayne Wofford. Her father, the late John T. Wofford, who died at Cuero in 1911, was a pioneer citizen, long prominent in Dewitt County, was known both as a farmer and banker, and at one time was Grand Chancellor of the Knights of Pythias in Texas. The children of Mr. and Mrs. Mugge are named Margaret, Edward, Katherine, Henry Jr. and John Tyler Wofford.

HECTOR MCLEAN TIPPETT. The present mayor of the City of Hallettsville has been a valuable citizen. He has held his present office for the past five years, and during the course of his lifetime in Halletsville, while engaged in various occupations, has always performed his duties with a faithfulness and diligence which have done him credit and have made the aggregate of his accomplishment a valuable service to the community. Mr. Tippett represents an old family in Southern Texas, one that has been identified with this state through three generations, covering a period of seventy years, since the last year of the Texas Republic.

Hector McLean Tippett was born in Hallettsville June 8, 1869. Taking his ancestry back to his great-grandfather, we find that Erasmus Tippett served as a soldier in the American Revolution, and with his twin brother Erastus moved into North Carolina and subsequently to Eastern Tennessee, and died in the latter state. Mr. Tippett's grandfather, Benjamin Foreman Tippett, was born in Halifax County, North Carolina, in July, 1785, and spent his early life on a farm. He was married in Blount County, Tennessee, in 1818 to Miss Emma Morris, a daughter of Isaac Morris, a farmer who was born near the James River in old Virginia. Benjamin F. Tippett lived as a slave holding planter in Noxubee County, Mississippi, and also for a time was a resident in Perry County, Alabama, where some of his older children were born. On January 1, 1844, he landed at Matagorda, Texas, having brought his family out from Tennessee, by boat from the Tennessee River to New Orleans and thence by ship across the gulf to the Texas coast. In coming to Texas it was his intention to settle at Eagle Lake on the Colorado River, but the rainy season forced him to abandon this idea, and he reshipped his goods from Matagorda to Port Lavaca and settled in the country back from the coast near Victoria. He brought his negroes with him and permitted them to take charge of his estate under his supervision. Benjamin F. Tippett was not disposed to politics, though voting the democratic ticket, and back in 1832 had supported the "nullification measures." He was a Methodist. Benjamin F. Tippett died in 1867 and his wife passed away in 1886. He was a pensioner from the War of 1812, and had also seen service as a soldier along with Sam Houston in the battle with the Indians at Horseshoe in Capt. McClellan's Company. Benjamin F. and Emma Tippett were the parents of the following children: Homer Milton, who died leaving a family at Abiline, Texas; Miss Sarah, who lives with her nephew at Hallettsville; James, who died unmarried at Victoria; and Robert D.

Robert D. Tippett, father of Mayor Tippett of Halletsville, had only a brief career. He was born at Matagorda, Texas, February 14, 1844, only a few weeks after the family had landed on the Texas coast, and died in Hallettsville in 1871. He was a boy soldier of the Confederacy, serving as a private in General Greene's brigade of Confederate troops in the New Mexico campaign, and later was with his company in General Sibley's command on the Red River and along the Mississippi. He was wounded at Donaldsonville, Louisiana, and before recovering the war had closed. After the war he took up the study of law under Major McClain and General Bagby of Hallettsville, but had only a brief period of practice before taken away by death. Robert D. Tippett married Miss McLean, daughter of Hector R. McLean, who also came from North Carolina and was a commissary quartermaster with the title of major in the Confederate army.

Hector McLean Tippett never knew his father, and has been making his own way in the world since childhood. He grew up in Hallettsville, and at the early age of twelve years had his last schooling in the Moulton Institute. The more practical and valuable part of his education came from the old Herald and Planter printing office in Hallettsville. He worked in every capacity around that office, and can still classify as an old time printer. The training was invaluable in many ways, and after learning the trade he followed it for about five years. Mr. Tippett then left the printing office and became clerk in the mercantile house of Leo Kroschel at Hallettsville. His next position was as assistant cashier for five years with the Lavaca County National Bank. Leaving the bank he spent four years in the life insurance field, representing the New York Life Company as solicitor. From insurance he changed his course to railroad work, and was clerk and later agent for the Aransas Pass Railway Company at Hallettsville Station until 1906. In the latter year Mr. Tippett became manager of the horse and mule market for Rheinstrom & Greenbaum of Hallettsville.

In April, 1909, Mr. Tippett was elected mayor to succeed Mayor T. A. Hester. He has been twice reelected to the office and the last time without opposition. Under his administration Hallettsville has made some splendid strides in the direction of municipal improvements, particularly in the way of better streets, permanent sidewalks and the increase of those facilities and conveniences which characterize the progressive small cities of Texas. Citizens and strangers alike remark the fact that Hallettsville is in a more prosperous condition, municipally considered, today than ever before. Mr. Tippett makes a slogan of continued advancement, and is urging the matter of further pavement of streets and several other measures which will bring Hallettsville to the front as a thriving center of population and trade. Mr. Tippett is a democrat in politics, is affiliated with the lodge and with Boyce Chapter, Royal Arch Masons, of the Masonic Order at Hallettsville, and also with the Knights of Honor and the Sons of Hermann.

At Yoakum, Texas, June 20, 1900, Mr. Tippett married Miss Lillie Dodd. Her father, Capt. Thomas M. Dodd, was a Confederate soldier, came from Tennessee to Texas after the war, and for a number of years has been a Yoakum merchant. Captain Dodd married Miss Irene Beason, and both are still living. The children in the Dodd family are: Mrs. Tippett, Thomas M. Jr., Miss Susie, Jacob E., and Mrs. T. C. Spencer. Mr. Tippett and wife have no children.

George A. Moody. A native son of the Lone Star state who has here achieved distinctive success through his own well ordered endeavors and who has gained secure place as one of the representative contractors and builders in the City of San Antonio, is he whose name initiates this paragraph. Mr. Moody was born in Sutherland Springs, Wilson County, Texas, May 6, 1871, and is a son of Logan L. and Missouri (Wallace) Moody, the former of whom was born in Franklin County, Kentucky, in 1849, and the latter of whom was born at Panola, Panola County, Texas, their home being now at Stockdale, Wilson County, where the father is known as a substantial citizen of sterling character and as a successful contractor and builder. He is a son of George W. Moody, who, in the '50s, came from Kentucky to Texas and established the family home at San Antonio, where he became one of the early merchants on Commerce Street and where he remained until after the close of the Civil war. He then removed with his family to Sutherland Springs, Wilson County, where he and his wife passed the remainder of their lives. The father of the subject of this sketch remained in Wilson County until the '80s, when he returned to San Antonio, where he engaged in contracting and building and contributed not a little to the material advancement of the city. In later years he returned to Wilson County and established his home at Stockdale, where he and his wife have since maintained their home. Mrs. Moody's father was one of the sterling pioneers of Eastern Texas and was a kinsman of "Bigfoot" Wallace, the celebrated Indian fighter whose name was prominent in the frontier history of Texas.

George A. Moody acquired his early education in the public schools of San Antonio and supplemented this by a course of study in the Alamo City Business College. He served a thorough apprenticeship to the carpenter's trade, under the direction of his father, and for several years he found employment as a journeyman carpenter, his compensation at the initiative of his service having been but $1 a day. He finally left San Antonio and for thirteen years was engaged in the work of his trade in other places in Texas, but in 1902 he returned to San Antonio, where his energy, technical skill and progressive policies have enabled him to establish and develop a large and representative business as a contractor and builder. For several years past he has given special attention to the reconstruction and modernizing of buildings, particularly in the installing of high-grade store fronts, his service in this line having done much to add to the attractiveness of the business districts of his home city. He was prominently identified with the improvements incidental to the widening of Commerce Street and reconstructed a number of the business blocks on that historic thoroughfare of San Antonio. The widening of this street, with the incidental improving of the buildings on its south side, was a notable achievement and one of the best municipal improvements that has been made in this fine city. The city government and the property owners were in effective co-operation in the furtherance of the important enterprise, the city having issued special bonds for the carrying forward of the work, and all of the buildings on the south side of the street from Alamo Plaza to Main Plaza were set back sixteen feet. This gave ample room for the installing of the street railway lines on Commerce Street, which previously had entirely lacked this important public service. The entire street was repaved and a new and artistic bridge of reinforced concrete construction was built over the San Antonio River. The most attractive feature of the remodeled thoroughfare, however, is comprised in the attractive new fronts placed in all of the buildings that were removed back on the south side of the street, the varied and effective architectural designs making this one of the handsome metropolitan streets of the United States. In this connection Mr. Moody held the contracts for the installing of artistic new fronts in five buildings—two owned by Henry Rilling, that occupied by the Critzer Brothers jewelry establishment, the building of the San Antonio Music Company, and that occupied by the G. A. Duerler Manufacturing Company, the work throughout being of the highest grade and having done much to add to his reputation in his chosen vocation. Mr. Moody erected the block of store buildings just north of Houston Street on North Flores Street, this contract having been completed by him in 1914. He is essentially loyal and public-spirited as a citizen and his political allegiance is given unreservedly to the democratic party, though he has never manifested any ambition for public office.

Mr. Moody wedded Miss Antonia Rice, who was born and reared at Sweet Home, Lavaca County, this state, and they have one son, Waldo Leslie, who was born in the year 1901.

WILLIAM H. WALKER, M. D. The vigorous and progressive little City of Yoakum, Dewitt County, claims as one of its representative physicians and surgeons and loyal citizens, Dr. William H. Walker, who was born at LaGrange, Fayette County, Texas, on the 16th of October, 1868, and who is well upholding the professional prestige of the family name, his father, the late William Wallace Walker, M. D., having been recognized and honored as one of the leading physicians of Southern Texas and having continued in the active work of his humane profession for many years, the closing period of his life having been passed at Schulenburg, one of the important towns of Fayette County.

Dr. William Wallace Walker was born in Tensas Parish, Louisiana, on the 12th of August, 1844, and was still a young man at the time when he established his residence in Texas. At the inception of the Civil war he was a student in Emory College, at Oxford, Georgia, and he promptly manifested his youthful loyalty to the Confederacy by leaving college, returning to his native state and enlisting in the Third Louisiana Cavalry, with which gallant command he served four years and nineteen days—virtually the entire period of the war. He distinguished himself for gallantry at the Battle of Shiloh and also that of Manassas, and in the second battle of the last title he was wounded. He lived up to the full tension of the great fratricidal conflict and gave of his best to defending the cause which he believed to be righteous and just, his continued interest in his old comrades having in later years been manifested through his affiliation with the United Confederate Veterans. That his patriotism and loyalty were intrinsic elements of his character was significantly shown when his native land became involved in war with Spain, in 1898. He promptly put forth vigorous efforts and raised a company for service in the Spanish-American war, this company becoming Troop G, First Texas Cavalry, and he was made captain of his company or troop, the regiment having been mobilized at Fort Sam Houston but having not been called out of the state to participate in the polemic activities in Cuba. The doctor himself, however, was assigned to duty in Cuba as a military surgeon, and at Santiago de Cuba he was placed in charge of a transport vessel on which sick and wounded soldiers were transferred to Montauk Point, New York. While voyaging to this destination he accidentally discovered among the troops on board his own soldier son, who was lieutenant in command of his regiment. After remaining for some time at Montauk Point, Doctor Walker returned to his regiment, with which he was mustered out, in the City of San Antonio.

After the close of the Civil war Dr. William W. Walker completed the prescribed curriculum in the medical department of Tulane University, in the City of New Orleans, in which institution he was graduated as a member of the class of 1871 and from which he received his well earned degree of Doctor of Medicine. He had previously established his residence in Texas, and after his graduation he engaged in active general practice at LaGrange, Fayette County, in company with Doctor Renfrow. From that place he finally removed to Cistern, in the same county, and later he continued in practice for some time at High Hill, that county, where he remained until the extension of the line of the Southern Pacific Railroad through Schulenburg, in the same county, when, with other residents of High Hill, he removed to the new railroad town, where he continued in successful practice until virtually the time of his death. He was alert in keeping abreast with the advances made in medical and surgical science, had a high sense of his professional stewardship and labored with ability and self-abnegation in the alleviation of human suffering and distress, his name and memory being revered by the many families to which he ministered during the course of his long and loyal service as a physician.

Though Doctor Walker was essentially progressive and public-spirited as a citizen and was a staunch advocate of the principles of the democratic party, he considered his profession worthy of his unqualified attention and would never consent to become a candidate for public office. He was a Master Mason, and from 1869 until the time of his death held membership in the Baptist Church. He was a prominent and honored comrade of Camp Timmons, United Confederate Veterans, at Schulenburg, at the time when his life came to its close, his death having occurred on the 5th of May, 1901—just two years after the date of his departure with his troop for the Fort Sam Houston rendezvous, to make ready for active service, if demanded, in the Spanish-American war.

On the 29th of January, 1865, Doctor Walker wedded Miss Emma Alice Routh, daughter of the late Dr. Kenzie Routh, who was widely known and honored as a successful physician in the Pinoak or Tuttle Store section of Fayette County, he having been a native of the State of Tennessee and a pioneer of Texas. He married Miss Amanda M. Murrell, and both continued their residence in Fayette County until their death. Their children were Zachariah, Joseph, William and Emma Alice. Mrs. Emma Alice Walker died in the year 1874, and of her children four are now living. Dr. Edwin R., who is a representative physician at Ballinger, Runnels County, married Miss Sarah Gussman; Dr. William Hayden, of this review, was the next in order of birth; Kenzie Wallace, who served as captain in the Fifteenth Cavalry, United States Army, is now assigned to the army commissary department in the City of Washington, D. C., the maiden name of his wife having been Helen Hobart Whitman; and Mary is the wife of Dr. Arthur L. Fuller, of Colorado City, Texas.

The second marriage of Dr. William W. Walker was solemnized February 23, 1876, when Miss Eudocia Agnes Henderson became his wife. She is a daughter of Colonel Alfred Henderson, of Schulenburg, who was one of the prominent and distinguished pioneers of Southern Texas, his wife, whose maiden name was Callaway, having been a representative of the famous Kentucky pioneer family of that name. Mrs. Walker now resides in the home of her youngest surviving daughter, in the City of Texarkana, Texas. Of her three children the first born was Kittie, who

was a student in the Sam Houston Normal School at the time of her death, on the 17th of November, 1894; Emma is the wife of L. G. Stark, of San Antonio; and Felton is the wife of A. L. Burford, a prominent railroad lawyer whose home is at Texarkana, while his office is in Kansas City, Missouri.

Dr. William H. Walker, to whom this sketch is dedicated, acquired his early education principally in the public schools of Schulenburg, Fayette County, and at the age of nineteen years he began the study of medicine, his preliminary reading having been pursued under the able preceptorship of his father. He finally entered the latter's alma mater, the medical department of Tulane University, in 1886, and in this institution he received his degree of Doctor of Medicine on the 3d of April, 1889. For two years thereafter he was engaged in practice at Shiner, Lavaca County, and he then removed to Ledbetter, Fayette County, where likewise he practiced two years. The following eighteen years found him engaged in the work of his profession at Oakland, Colorado County, a place originally known as Prairie Point, where he built up a large and widely disseminated practice and where he continued his earnest and effective labors until November, 1910, since which time he has been engaged in successful practice as one of the leading physicians at Yoakum, Dewitt County. The doctor is identified with the American Medical Association and the Texas State Medical Society, besides which he has held membership in the local medical societies of each county in which he has practiced his profession.

With well fortified opinions concerning economic and governmental policies, Doctor Walker has maintained an independent attitude in politics and has exercised his franchise in support of men and measures meeting the approval of his judgment. He has been affiliated with the Knights of Pythias since 1889 and was a charter member of the lodge at Shiner, his present membership being in the lodge at Yoakum. As a member of the Masonic fraternity he is past master of Oakland Lodge, No. 258, Ancient Free and Accepted Masons, at Oakland, Colorado County.

At Ledbetter, Fayette County, on the 20th of December, 1892, was solemnized the marriage of Doctor Walker to Miss Julia Gillespie, who was born in the State of Arkansas and who was a child at the time of her parents' removal to Texas, where she was reared and educated in Fayette County. Doctor and Mrs. Walker have two children, Laurie Douglas and Frances Katherine, both of whom remain at the parental home and the latter of whom was graduated in the Yoakum high school as a member of the class of 1915, and is now attending the College of Industrial Art at Denton, Texas.

That Doctor Walker is a scion of one of the staunch old families of the fair Southland is indicated when it is stated that his grandfather, William Wallace Walker, was born in Fauquier County, Virginia, on the 6th of June, 1814, his ancestors having immigrated to America from England and having settled in the Old Dominion commonwealth prior to the war of the Revolution. The grandfather of the doctor passed the closing years of his life at Schulenburg, Texas, where his death occurred in January, 1884.

Hon. David A. Paulus. Before and after the Civil war for many years Dr. Augustus Paulus made a record of no little distinction in Texas as a physician of thorough training and sound ability and also as a leading and influential citizen. For something over thirty years the son of that old physician, David A. Paulus, has filled a sphere of service as a teacher, lawyer, and in public office. For the past quarter century he has been a resident of Lavaca County, and is now filling the office of postmaster at Hallettsville.

David A. Paulus was born on the frontier in Coryell county, Texas, December 6, 1862. His grandfather, Dr. Christian Paulus, spent all his life at Kiel, Germany, and his only two sons, Augustus David and Henry, were likewise physicians, Henry going to South America. Dr. Augustus David, who was born at Kiel in 1817, was liberally educated, finishing in the universities at Kiel and Heidelberg. In 1839, at the age of twenty-two, he came to the United States and for several years served as assistant surgeon in the United States navy, and had traveled pretty much all over the world before he left the navy. During the ante-bellum period he came to Texas, and joined the vanguard of settlers who were pushing the frontier into what is now west central Texas. He was one of the early comers in Coryell County, conducted a cattle and horse ranch there and also carried on an extensive practice in medicine all over that section. During the Civil war he was a surgeon in Major Erath's company of rangers, and spent several years in active service on the frontier. Soon after the war he moved to Fayette County, and died at Flatonia in 1895. He was a strong southern man in sympathies, and one of the few democratic German settlers. During the reconstruction period he took much share in politics, though never sought an office. His work was done chiefly as a private citizen and by correspondence, and he never attempted a public address. While reared a Lutheran, he took little interest in church affairs in this state. His chief work and service were as a physician, and he was one of the comparatively few university trained men during his generation who practiced in this state. He was prominent in the ranks of Masons and Odd Fellows, and occasionally delivered addresses on Masonry. Dr. Paulus was married in Hickman County, Tennessee, to Mary Mayberry, deceased. Her father was John W. Mayberry, a native of Tennessee, and whose father, a native of Holland, never became proficient in the English language. The children of Dr. Paulus and wife are: Henry, of Flatonia; D. A. Paulus; and Mrs. J. D. Mahoney, of Denver, Colorado.

David A. Paulus was one of the first white children born in Coryell County, the distinction of being the first being held by George W. Tyler. His education began in the private school of Henry Heyer at High Hill in Fayette County, and in 1881 he graduated from the Sam Houston Normal. He began teaching at Bellville, the first town incorporated under the present Texas school law. In 1883 he organized the public school system at Terrell, and remained as superintendent two years. Then followed his election as superintendent of schools at Cleburne, but after a year he resigned to take up the law. In 1884 he conducted the summer normal school at Flatonia, and was selected to take charge of the summer normal at Comanche in 1886, but declined owing to his decision to abandon teaching.

His law studies were pursued at Bellville under Bell & Shelburne, and he was admitted to the bar there before Judge H. Teichmueller. It was in that town he tried his first case by appointment of the court. It was a criminal case, defending a white man charged of killing a negro. In January, 1890, he moved to Lavaca County, and in the following November was elected and succeeded P. H. Green in the office of county attorney, a position he held one term. The duties of the office were not altogether agreeable, and he declined another nomination. On coming to the county he formed a partnership with J. P. Ellis; and in 1895 became senior member of Paulus & Ragsdale, which continued successfully nearly nineteen years, and was dissolved by mutual consent in 1913. Mr. Paulus had suffered the loss of hearing to such an extent as to be unable to take part in court proceedings.

His law firm had a large volume of litigation, including some noteworthy cases. They represented Mrs. Annie Williams and daughter in a suit for damages against the Aransas Pass Railroad for the death of Mr. Williams, and won the largest judgment ever awarded in Lavaca County. The case went to the Supreme Court, was litigated several years, but the sum was finally paid to the plaintiffs. Their principal criminal case was that of Joseph Stefka, charged with killing his wife and child near Shiner. After three trials they secured an acquittal for the defendant. It was a case attracting much public attention, especially among the Bohemians. Another case was one wherein three negroes murdered a white man; one turned state's evidence, but the others stood trial, and Paulus & Ragsdale acquitted them after one had made a confession and then repudiated it at his trial.

In 1896 Mr. Paulus was elected county judge, leaving the office to enter the Senate. As executive head of the county he built the court house, and the construction bonds still outstanding are costing the county only three per cent interest. He was elected to the senate from the Eighteenth District in 1900, succeeding A. B. Kerr, and by re-election continued in that office until his resignation in May, 1913. His consecutive term of service was longer than that of any other member of the Senate, and he was a valuable and serviceable working member of the body. He entered the Senate during the administration of Governor Sayers. He was a member of the Committee on Education, Judiciary No. 1 and No. 2, Finance, and Penitentiary Affairs, and was chairman of Judiciary No. 2, Education and other committees. Much of his service was in behalf of eleemosynary institutions, and he was a member of the committee to investigate the penitentiary during Governor Campbell's term. With Senator Weinert he was author of the "parole law" of Texas. He stood with the opposition to state-wide prohibition, and voted against the prohibition amendment because the people of his district opposed it. He twice voted for the election of Senator Bailey, twice for Senator Culberson, and voted for Senator Morris Sheppard after the primary election had chosen him for the democratic candidate, but voted for Col. R. M. Johnston for the short term.

Senator Paulus attended his first state convention in 1884 at Houston, and has missed only two state conventions since. He supported Sayers for governor, also Tom Campbell, and in the recent gubernatorial campaign voted for Tom Ball. He became acquainted with General Burleson when he was a young lawyer in Travis County, and they have been close friends. This acquaintance led to Mr. Paulus' appointment as postmaster at Hallettsville, though he was not an original Wilson man in the presidential primaries. He took the office of postmaster in May, 1913, as the successor of W. J. Miller.

Senator Paulus is a former city attorney of Hallettsville. He has some valuable interests as a business man and farmer. On his several farms he grows the Essex hog, the Clark horse and the Jersey cattle, though somewhat as a pastime, and has some stock in banks at Houston and Dallas. Mr. Paulus served as a member of the Board of Directors of Agricultural and Mechanical College, under appointment of both Governors Culberson and Sayers, resigning when elected to Senate. For many years he has affiliated with and filled chairs in the Independent Order of Odd Fellows, the Knights of Pythias and the Sons of Hermann.

Senator Paulus married at Bellville, Texas, November 2, 1882, Miss Annie Wilson. Her parents, E. B. and Elizabeth (Averitt) Wilson, both came to Texas from Cadiz, Kentucky, where Mrs. Paulus was born. Mr. Wilson was a farmer and still lives in Bellville. Besides Mrs. Paulus the children are: Mrs. J. J. Kern of San Antonio, and Jesse O. Wilson of

Bellville. Mr. and Mrs. Paulus are the parents of six children: Henry, a lawyer practicing at Yoakum; David and James of Floresville; Julia, wife of B. B. Hale, of Eagle Lake; Roscoe and Claude, both in school.

CHARLES A. PETERSON. The excellent intellectual attainments and marked executive ability of Charles Allen Peterson made him specially eligible for the important office of superintendent of the public schools of the thriving City of Yoakum, where he initiated his work in connection with the schools in the year 1905 and where he achieved splendid results in raising their standard and making the work specially efficient in all departments. After eleven years as superintendent Professor Peterson resigned, and having been elected superintendent of the Kingsville public schools, he will continue his service in that district. His ambition and enthusiasm in his chosen profession are on a parity with his technical and administrative ability, and he has become a prominent and influential factor in connection with educational affairs in the state of his adoption. He has devoted more than a score of years to school work in Texas, where he established his residence and initiated his active pedagogic career in 1894.

Mr. Peterson claims the fine old Buckeye State as the place of his nativity and is a scion of one of its pioneer families. He was born on his father's farm, near Peebles, Adams County, Ohio, on the 24th of August, 1867, and is a son of Joseph J. and Evaline (Smittle) Peterson, who still reside in Adams County, their homestead place being that on which Cornelius Peterson, father of Joseph J., settled upon his removal from Virginia to Ohio, about the year 1830. Cornelius Peterson became a prosperous farmer and rural merchant in the pioneer community and continued his residence in Adams County until his death. He was twice married but all of his children were born of his union with Miss Delilah Scott, namely: Cornelius, Jr.; John Scott; Edward G. and Harvey, twins; Joseph Jasper, father of him whose name introduced this article; Susan, who became the wife of Joshua Florea, and who was a resident of Hopkins, Missouri, at the time of her death; Elen, who married Josiah Florea and resides at Lawshe, Ohio; Maria, who married S. B. Montgomery, with whom she removed to Edgar, Nebraska, where they passed the residue of their lives. None of the sons left the old home district of Adams County, Ohio.

Prof. Charles A. Peterson was reared to the sturdy discipline of the home farm and after fully availing himself of the advantages of the public schools he completed a thorough course in the celebrated National Normal University, at Lebanon, Ohio, where he was fortunate in having as his preceptor the distinguished educator, Prof. Alfred Holbrook. In this institution he was graduated as a member of the class of 1893, and received the degree of Bachelor of Science.

Mr. Peterson has not, like many other ambitious men, utilized his profession only as a means to an end, but, on the contrary, he has given to it his unbounded allegiance and enthusiasm and has held that it is altogether worthy of his continuous and unfaltering allegiance. He served his pedagogic novitiate by becoming principal of the village schools of Point Pleasant, West Virginia, where he passed one year. He then came to Texas, where he has continued his services in his profession with all of zeal and ability during the long intervening years, which have brought to him distinction in educational circles and marked success in practical work. For seven years he held the position of superintendent of the public schools of Hallettsville, the judicial center of Lavaca County, and within his regime at that place the independent school district was established, and bonds were voted for the erection of a new school building. The election, however, proved irregular and was declared null and void. Under these conditions a tax levy was made to accomplish the desired end, and thus was created the building fund necessary for the erection of the new building, which was completed a few years later.

From Hallettsville Mr. Peterson went to Moulton in the same county, where he assumed charge of the Sam and Will Morre Institute, which constituted the public school of the town. As head of this popular school he continued in effective service four years, within which he aided greatly in effecting the proper furnishing and equipping of the school building and in the beautifying of its grounds. He succeeded also in the consolidating of a number of small schools around Moulton, by taking into the district a wide scope of territory, and the standard of the school was so raised under his administration that it was granted affiliation with the Texas Agricultural & Mechanical College.

Upon leaving Moulton, in 1905, Mr. Peterson removed to Yoakum, where he succeeeded T. L. Toland as superintendent of the public schools. Indefatigable in the furtherance of all departments of the school work in this city, Mr. Peterson has had the satisfaction of seeing within his administration a wonderful advancement in the educational provisions and facilities in the important local field. Within his regime has been erected the central school building, at a cost of $3,200, this being a substantial and essentially modern brick structure; two ward school buildings also have been erected, at a cost of $1,500 each; and a building, affording accommodations for two more sparsely settled wards, has been completed at a cost of $2,500. The grading of the schools has been changed by adding the eleventh grade to the high school, and Superintendent Peterson has justified and increased the affiliation credits of the high school from eight to seventeen points with the University of Texas, besides which there have been added departments of domestic science and vocal music. The Yoakum schools have more than doubled their corps of instructors, and at the present time thirty-one white teachers and four colored teachers are employed, six of the number being graduates of the Yoakum high school, and other graduates of the local schools having gone forth to hold responsible clerkships and positions in railroad and other offices.

In the second year of his residence in Texas Mr. Peterson initiated normal work, at Hallettsville, and each succeeding year since that time he has done effective service as an instructor in the summer normal of the state, save for two years when he was retained as a teacher in the State Normal School at San Marcos. He holds a permanent teacher's certificate of the first grade in the State of Texas.

Mr. Peterson is a man of high civic ideals and utmost loyalty, and he has been an earnest worker in the field of religious activity, and he was one of the influential factors in the organization of the Christian Church at Yoakum, having previously maintained the Sunday school which became a part of the church when the latter was organized. He is affiliated with the Knights of Pythias in which order he is past chancellor of Loyal Lodge, No. 97, at Yoakum. He and his wife are prominent and influential members of the Christian Church.

In Missouri City, Harris County, Texas, on the 26th of November, 1896, was solemnized the marriage of Mr. Peterson to Miss Sylvia Daisy Peterson, a daughter of John T. and Drusilla (Florea) Peterson, of Lawshe, Ohio, the former of whom was a distant kinsman of the father of the subject of this review. Mr. and Mrs. Peterson have four children: Melvin, Irene, Allene and Evelyn, and the only son is a member of the class of 1916 in the Yoakum high school.

Henry J. Strunk. A representative of that German nationality that was first and foremost in the settlement and development of many counties in South Central Texas, Henry J. Strunk has had a successful career as farmer, stockman, merchant and banker, and is now in the real estate and insurance business at Hallettsville. He has spent nearly all the sixty years of his life in Texas, and is a sterling citizen as well as a good business man.

His father, Dietrich Strunk, was born December 5, 1830, in the kingdom of Hanover, Germany, at Schwarzen Mohr No. 38, and while growing up learned the bricklayer's trade. In August, 1855, with his wife and oldest child, Henry, he left his native land and landed from a sailing vessel at Galveston in November of the same year. He joined some of his fellow countrymen near Columbus in Colorado County. His old friend Henry Buescher had advanced the funds that brought him to the new world, and while he worked at his trade as a day laborer his wife did most of the farming. The first crop was made near Frelsburg, two bales of cotton, which cost him three dollars a bale for the bagging and baling rope, five dollars a bale for the ginning, and five dollars for transportation to market at Houston, where it sold for six cents a pound. That was in 1856. In 1859 he settled in Lavaca County, and built a log cabin on his 160 acres near the old Town of Sublime. This indicates that he had made some progress in finance, though the cabin home had a dirt floor until 1861, when the laying of a plank floor must have seemed an improvement almost palatial. In May, 1859, the frost hit his corn crop after it was laid by, resulting in a loss that he could ill afford, but this was only one of the experiences in which the early settlers took the bitter with the sweet, and he continued to persevere and press forward.

In 1862 Dietrich Strunk entered the Confederate army; was with Magruder's army at Velasco, until overcome with an illness, and furloughed home. Subsequently he was employed by the Confederate government to do hauling between Alleyton and Brownsville, as part of the transport service by which supplies were brought in through Mexico, and this was his work until the close of the war, and after that he was not in the ranks as a soldier. After the war he established a store which became the nucleus of the old Town of Sublime in Lavaca County, and did a good business until about 1880, when he sold out to his son Charles, and until the advent of the railroad gave his attention to farming and the operation of a gin. In 1887 he was one of the first business men on the ground to take advantage of the opportunities created by the establishment of a railroad station at the new Town of Sublime, and entered the lumber trade, which he followed until his retirement in independent circumstances in 1910. The last two years of his life were spent practically in one room, as a result of a paralytic stroke, and he died December 22, 1914. He was a man of average size, about five feet ten, weighed 160 pounds, and though he lost an eye in childhood seldom used glasses for reading in old age. He made his regular contributions to church and charity, and while not opposed to fraternities had no membership in them. He was almost entirely without partisanship in politics, and voted rather for the man than for any other consideration.

Dietrich Strunk was married in 1852 to Catherine Foltmann, who died January 21, 1891. Both were members of the Lutheran Church, in which faith the children were confirmed. The children were: Henry J.; Ernst R., of Colorado County; Charles H. and Ferdinand A., of Oakland; and Emma, wife of Robert Miller, of Sublime.

Henry J. Strunk was born in Germany April 15, 1855, a few months before his parents started for America. All his education was compressed within about eighteen months of school attendance when a boy.

He had an ambition for independent effort, and at the age of seventeen "ran away from home." Then followed several years of work as farm hand, clerk and teamster in the neighborhood. His employer was August Weller, one of the old-timers and well known German citizens of Lavaca County, whose daughter Charlotte, Mr. Strunk married on January 14, 1875. The following year they spent on the Weller farm, and in January, 1876, Mr. Strunk took charge of the mercantile enterprise of Henry Buck at Oakland, which a year later became the firm of Buck & Strunk. After the business was sold in October, 1882, Mr. Strunk started in May, 1883, in the same town, the general mercantile store of H. J. Strunk & Brother. The brother Ferdinand bought the store in 1891, and Mr. Strunk then engaged in the land and cattle business in that neighborhood, continuing it until December, 1907.

In January, 1908, Mr. Strunk was elected president of the First National Bank of Hallettsville, and was identified with its management two years. Since disposing of that interest he has conducted a good business in real estate and loans at Hallettsville. For a number of years he has been more or less a cotton buyer, and has recently taken it up more definitely as representative of the firm of Tarkington & Stapp at Yoakum. As a resident of Hallettsville since 1908 he has interested himself in local affairs, and is one of the aldermen. He was for fifteen years a justice of the peace at Oakland, and for four years a county commissioner from district No. 4, at a time when the courthouse and jail for Colorado County were erected and provisions were made for the tax levies to pay for that improvement. He is a democrat, a past master of Murchison Lodge, No. 1, Ancient Free and Accepted Masons, at Hallettsville, a member of the Royal Arch chapter, and also of the Independent Order of Odd Fellows, Knights of Pythias, Knights of Honor and the Sons of Hermann.

Mrs. Strunk's father-in-law, Mr. Weller, came from Westphalia, Germany, to America about 1848, and was married in Texas to Annie Schumacher. Their children were: Henry, who died at Yoakum, leaving a family; Mrs. Charlotte Strunk; August, of Harlingen, Texas; Amelia, wife of Hermann Hoffmann of San Antonio; Charles and William of Clodine, Texas; Hermann of Brownsville; Ida, wife of C. F. Laas, of Yorktown; William, of Clodine; Eddie, of Yorktown. The children of Mr. and Mrs. Strunk are: Annie, wife of Dr. Absalom A. Ledbetter of Hallettsville; Alma, wife of C. G. Laas, of the same place; Emma, who is Mrs. Hermann Stuermer of Nordheim and has two children, Henry J. and Cassie; Moritz A., a farmer of Lavaca County, who married Alma Ladwig and has a son Abbie. Mr. Strunk and his family are all members of the Lutheran Church.

Prof. William Eilers. The county superintendent of Lavaca County, now serving his third term of two years in this position. Prof. William Eilers belongs to one of the pioneer German families of Texas, and was born in Fayette County, October 5, 1863. His birth occurred under the "Stars and Bars" and he was one of a trio of neighbors born within six miles of one another and all born under a different flag, one under the emblem of the "Lone Star," in 1843, and the other under the flag of the Union, in 1849.

The father of William Eilers was Henry Eilers, who passed the latter part of his life as a planter and died on the plantation he settled in 1848. He came to Texas in 1845. His native place was Rodenkirchen, Oldenburg, Germany, and his birth occurred in 1823, he being one of two brothers and the only one to come to America. His brother, Gerhard Eilers, remained in Germany and died there, leaving a family, and one of his grandsons is now a prisoner on the Isle of Man, having been captured by the English while he was en route home to join his regiment for participation in the great European war which is now raging. The school education of Henry Eilers was somewhat limited, but he was a great reader and became unusually well informed in history and current events. He grew up in the home of his widowed mother, who had been reduced to modest circumstances. He was twenty-three years of age when he emigrated to America, landing at Galveston, Texas, aboard one of the last immigration vessels to that port. He went on to Houston and finally to Fayette County, and for a few years was a farmer, in 1848 adding freighting and immigrant transportation from Houston to Fayetteville, Austin, San Antonio and Victoria. He and his partner did this with box wagons and it was he who hauled, in 1853, the first Bohemian settler to Cat Spring, Austin County, and placed the first Wendish family into the interior and settled them at Serbin, Lee County, now Northrup, in 1854. Mr. Eilers and his partner brought most of the German and Bohemian settlers into Fayette, Austin and Colorado counties, and they followed the business until the outbreak of the Civil war.

Notwithstanding the frontier character of the country, there was honesty prevailing, and the partners doing this immigration business were never molested in their persons or property, although they frequently had from $1,000 to $2,000 in silver with them in shot sacks. Henry Eilers did not enter the army on either side. His objection to joining the Confederate forces was respected and he was asked by the authorities to care for several families of the neighborhood and this he did, being thus exempt from military duty. He had a brother-in-law in the Confederate service and another in the ranks of the Union. Mr. Eilers believed that the Government should pay for the slaves and emancipate them gradually, although he owned none of them himself. Upon naturalization, he cast his lot with the democratic party and his last vote was cast for William Jennings Bryan for President. He requested his son, William, to do likewise, arguing that the poor man's interests would be best subserved by Mr. Bryan's election, and he left that as a standing admonition for his sons to vote always in favor of the poor man. He never held an office. The editor of the Schulenburg Sticker stated in his obituary that the name of Henry Eilers was a synonym for honesty and veracity. Both Mr. and Mrs. Eilers were devout members of the Lutheran Church.

Henry Eilers married Augusta Frels, a daughter of John Hinrich Frels and his wife Sophie Agnete, nee Ruge. John Hinrich Frels was born at Langwarden, grand duchy of Oldenburg, April 17, 1807. Sophie Agnete Ruge was a member of the noted Wellman family and was born January 6, 1810. They married April 17, 1834, and emigrated to Texas in 1849, settling in La Grange. Henry Eilers died in 1899 and his wife in 1896. Their married life was spent on his farm on Ross Prairie, three miles from Fayetteville, and when he died Mr. Eilers had lived there fifty-one years, and had brought about two-fifths of his farm of 600 acres under cultivation. There were eight children in the family, as follows: Gerhard, of Falfurrias, Texas; Henry, city marshal, of Schulenburg, Texas; William, of this review; August, county commissioner and farmer, and a resident of Hallettsville, Texas; Frederick, of Fayetteville; Ernest, who died at Yoakum, Texas, in 1902, unmarried; Miss Augusta, of Fayetteville; and Anna, who is the wife of Dr. Charles Kaderka, of Fayetteville.

When William Eilers was a boy he worked on the farm, but enjoyed hunting and reading above everything else. He read many trapper stories and stories of pioneer life and until he was sixteen years of age, it was his intention to become a hunter and trapper. Owing to financial losses which his father sustained, he commenced to support himself when he was sixteen years of age although his father offered to continue him at school. Mr. Eilers, Sr., urged all of his children to secure a good education and offered them the means to do this, but William had determined to support himself. He received his father's permission to represent a monthly paper published in Maine and canvassed the rural districts with it. The paper cost only one dollar and the subscriber received six large and six small chromos as premiums. The chromos were worth the money at that time, and he secured ten subscribers a day making thirty cents on each. Board and lodging did not cost him anything among the country people. After canvassing for several months, he went to school again for twelve months and eight days without intermission. After going seven months, he took the teachers' examination at LaGrange, Fayette County, and received a second grade certificate; five months later he took the examination at Hallettsville, Lavaca County, and received a first grade. During his last year at school he paid all of his expenses except board, which he received at home. When he left home to teach he owed a Mr. Henry Forrest $10 for a copy of McCabe's Pictorial History of the World and a watch. He requested Mr. Forrest not to mention this to his father for, in that case, he would pay for them, and he didn't want him to do so. The volume referred to has been much used and is much worn, but it occupies a conspicuous place in his library and is kept as a memento.

William Eilers grew up on the old Eilers homestead, near Fayetteville, and acquired his education in the public schools of Fayetteville. When he was past eighteen years of age, he engaged in teaching in the old Kinkler school of Lavaca County, with a first-grade certificate. He opened his first school in 1882 with thirty-eight children, and at the end of his second year a new schoolhouse was erected and an assistant teacher provided him. At the end of his sixth year, when he resigned from the school, he had eighty-six children under his charge. The fact that the board increased his salary each year, caused him to continue teaching, whereas he had originally intended to do so only for a year or so and then attend the normal school and complete his education. Some of his pupils could not speak English when they entered and four of the same became teachers, one has entered the law, and two have devoted themselves to the medical profession.

On leaving that school, Mr. Eilers entered the Sam Houston Normal School, at Huntsville, and there was graduated in 1891. He was elected superintendent of the Schulenburg schools, was next made principal of the LaGrange High School, then principal of the Burton High School, subsequently teacher at Wardo, Fayette County, and was then appointed to a position in the Department of Education at Austin, by Supt. R. B. Cousins, and stayed there from 1905 until 1909, just four years to a day.

Leaving the state house June 15, 1909, Mr. Eilers matriculated in the summer school of the University of Texas, June 17th, and took three courses, education, history and school supervision, and just before the completion of his term he was appointed a member of the State Summer Normal Board of Examiners by Superintendent Cousins. He spent a year as superintendent of the Sam and Will Moore Institute at Moulton and was elected from there to the county superintendency of Lavaca County, in 1910. The announcement of his candidacy brought his old pupils who had now become voters into line for him and he was nominated over a strong man for the office. He succeeded E. P. Guenther in the office and has been twice re-elected. He has had experience in all phases of school work. He taught in the rural schools and in urban high schools. He was a member of the county board of examiners for many years and twice a member of the state board of summer normal examiners. He taught in two summer normals, conducting one of them. He was always an active participant in teachers' institutes and for many years a member of the South Texas and State Teachers' associations.

As county superintendent, Mr. Eilers has caused twenty-six new districts to vote a local tax for the support of their schools and some fifteen districts have increased their taxes, there being now fifty-three districts levying tax for public education. Many new buildings have been erected and others improved since his advent in office and there has been much new equipment for school work added. The state course of study for rural schools has been substituted for the county course by all the schools of the county, forty-five schools of the county have libraries, totalling 3,114 volumes; fourteen districts own cottages which the teachers occupy free of charge, physical culture was taught in fifty-five schools last year; singing in sixty schools; drawing in fifty-two, and current events find a place in the curriculum of most of the schools of the county. Manners and morals are taught in sixty-three schools, a flag ritual for teaching civic patriotism is used in forty-eight schools; fifty-eight schools have opening exercises; twelve of them have school gardens; seven have organized Audubon societies for the protection of singing and insect-eating birds, and nearly all the teachers of the county are teaching bird protection. One rural school has joined the Boy Scout movement. The teachers all attend the county and local institute, held in six different places in the county, and teachers are expected to attend at least five of them. All teachers take one or more professional papers and read one or more professional books from the county library of 180 professional books during the year.

Mr. Eilers has introduced industrial work into the negro schools of the county, this innovation coming in September, 1914. Upon application to the Anne T. Jeanes Foundation he received $350 for this work. He appointed a colored female of twenty years of experience to take charge of the work and required her to take special training for the work at the Prairie View Normal School. She is required to stay a week at each school and to teach cooking, sewing, rafia and other hand work, and sanitation, and at the end of each week she reports the result of her work to the county superintendent. She also lectures to the colored people of the community and is urged by the superintendent to impress upon their minds the importance of greater care of their school buildings and paraphernalia and the improvement of sanitation at their homes.

Mr. Eilers was married in Fayette County, Texas, October 14, 1906, to Miss Martha Buchschacher, a daughter of Rev. Godfrey Buchschacher, who came to Texas from Berne, Switzerland, and is a Lutheran minister at Warda, Texas. The father of Rev. Godfrey Buchschacher was Dan Buchschacher, who emigrated to New York from Switzerland in the later fifties. He joined a cavalry regiment when the Civil war broke out and participated in eighteen battles. He was in the first battle at Bull Run and the last one which was fought at Brazos Santiago on the coast of Texas after Gen. R. E. Lee had surrendered. Dan Buchschacher was wounded three different times and was blinded in his right eye as the result of a shrapnel striking a cup of boiling coffee which he was holding in his hand. He died at Warda at the age of eighty-two and was laid to rest there in 1913. Mrs. Buchschacher was formerly Amanda Thoensen, and Mrs. Eilers is the second of four children the others being: Rev. Ernest, Emanuel and Miss Irene. Three children have been born to Mr. and Mrs. Eilers: Willie, Ernest and Erwin. Mr. Eilers is a member of the Lutheran Church, is secretary of the congregation at Hallettsville,

a teacher in the Sunday school, and one of the trustees of the church. Mr. Eilers is a Royal Arch Mason and belongs to the Chapter. He also holds membership in the Sons of Hermann, and in both orders has numerous friends.

JUDGE DAN T. PRICE. If there is one achievement more than another in the forty-five years of Judge Price's residence in Texas which deserves something of that lasting credit for which history is responsible, it was his long and efficient administration as mayor of Yoakum, a period in which the town had more substantial growth and assumed more of the functions of a real city than in all the preceding years.

A factor in this civic record was doubtless his long and generally successful career as a lawyer and the faculty for practical and methodical handling of every issue as it comes up. He is a man of education, though partly self-acquired, and has twice served by appointment terms on the bench.

His birthplace was Warrenton, in Warren County, North Carolina, and at least two generations of the name had been identified with that state before him. His forefathers were Scotch-Irishmen, who settled in the Carolinas before the Revolution, and some of them helped in the accomplishment of American independence. Of the same stock came General Sterling Price, of Confederate fame. Judge Price's grandfather was John M. Price, a native of North Carolina, who married Mary Leachman, also of Scotch ancestry. Their only son was John M. Price, Jr. The latter, who was born in Wake County, North Carolina, married Martha Reynolds, a native of Warren County. Prior to the war he followed his trade as tailor in Warrenton, and later became a manufacturer of buggies and wagons there and formed connections with a number of local enterprises. He had held slaves, was a stanch southerner, and furnished two sons to the Confederate Army. His public service was rendered as a business man and good citizen. In politics he was a southern whig and later a democrat. His death occurred in Warrenton in 1890, and his wife died in 1896. Their oldest child was John L. The second is Bettie, the wife of S. W. Dowtin, an ex-Confederate, who lived in Warren County, where they died. Wounds that Thomas received as a soldier in the war hastened his death. Charles, who was one of the youngest captains in the southern armies, entered politics after the war, served first in the senate of his native state and afterwards in the lower house, and was elected speaker. On retiring from politics he devoted himself to the practice of law at Salisbury, gained an eminent position in the North Carolina bar, accumulated a fortune from his profession, and died when fifty-nine years old. The next son, Philip P., is a lawyer and teacher in Jim Wells County, Texas, and following him in age comes Judge Dan T. Henry is a railroad man with home in Fort Worth, while Ed C., the youngest, is a county official at Warren, North Carolina.

Born March 26, 1853, Judge Price grew up on a farm after the war. While his advantage in schools did not extend beyond the academic grades, he made himself proficient largely through his own efforts in the classics and other branches and especially higher mathematics. He has always been a student and lover of the chaste and beautiful in literature, and his friends mention, what he will not confess himself, that he is a master of humorous verse, while his dignified and forceful prose has been widely read in the current press and his ability as a speaker has doubtless been a large factor in his success both in the law and in public life.

His first employment after coming to Texas in 1873 was as teacher in the rural schools of Gonzales County. He was later engaged in similar work in Caldwell County, and was a substitute instructor in Greek and Latin and of higher mathematics at San Marcos, giving special attention to young men who were preparing for admission to the University of Virginia. Though no preceptor directed his studies in the law, he mastered its fundamentals and was admitted to the bar at Lockhart in 1874 by Judge J. P. White, before whom he tried his first case in the same term of court. After some practice at Lockhart and San Marcos he located at old Frio Town, Frio County, then in the heart of the range cattle country, and came into wide repute as a lawyer among the ranchers of that country.

In 1888 Judge Price removed to Yoakum, where his residence covers the development of the town from an outlying hamlet to its present city proportions. For twenty-five years he practiced civil law almost exclusively. He served as district attorney by appointment and for a short period as district judge by special election, and has been several times appointed special district judge, and while in Frio County was county judge. Politics has made little appeal to him, and a sense of duty has been the urgent cause of his service at different times. When first elected mayor of Yoakum, in 1904, the honor was not in any sense a satisfaction of his personal desire, and his continuance in the position for nine years was at great sacrifice to himself. When he became mayor he found himself at the head of a bankrupt town, but in a short time the town became a city and was meeting its obligations in cash, and it continued to do so as long as he remained chief executive. He went out of office in April, 1915, and in the time of his regime can be found record of all the notable improvements of which the local citizens are proud. In that time also individual initiative was stirred and practically all the permanent business houses were erected. Judge Price applied to the conduct of municipal affairs the principle that has always governed his own—"pay as you go." His watchword in public life seems to have been: "Let in the light and respect the virtuous sentiment and will of the people."

Out of his law practice Judge Price has accumulated what he deems sufficient of this world's goods, and to some extent has been a factor in local business affairs. He is one of the directors of the Yoakum National Bank, and erected one of the first large and substantial brick blocks in the business district. Fraternally he has been identified with the Masonic order nearly forty years, and is also a member of the other prominent fraternities of the day. He is a member of the Baptist Church. He has been twice married, and both wives were natives of Texas. He was married in Caldwell County to Miss Sallie Daugherty. Her father, Harrison M. Daugherty, a Texas pioneer, was a native of Tennessee, and a stockman and farmer near Prairie Lea, Texas. The two children of this union were: Carl, who is now a merchant at Berino, New Mexico, and by his marriage to Anna Kilgore has two children, Dorothy and Don. The other son is Dan, a street car man at Houston, and unmarried. Mrs. Price died in Frio County in 1883.

In 1886 Judge Price was married in Lavaca County to Miss Ella V. Morris. By this marriage there is one son, Morris, highly talented, now an expert machinist at Yoakum, who married Miss Norma Everson. They live in Yoakum, to the great satisfaction and comfort of their parents. Mrs. Price is one of the notable women of Texas. She is an accomplished linguist, has the culture of ideal Texas motherhood, and is also distinguished by her unusual business ability. For a number of years she has handled some of the large estates for her brother J. P.

Morris, who is one of the wealthiest ranchers in Western Texas, located at Coleman.

Mrs. Price's parents were August and Adelaide Morris, the former English, the latter German, who came to Texas in the forties and were members of the original colony of forty who constituted the van of German settlement in Southwest Texas. August Morris, like many of his compatriots and fellow colonists, was a man of liberal education and high ideals. In Germany he found himself out of sympathy with the political and social rules and customs of that country, and a short time before the outbreak of the revolution of 1848, which brought so many men of education to the United States, he started with other sons of the fatherland to find homes and freedom in the republic of Texas. He and his wife had been married only a short time when they embarked on this adventurous voyage, and their destination was the Texas port of Galveston. On account of a terrible storm that overtook the vessel en route they landed at old Indianola or Powder Horn Bayou, and not long afterward they established their home as pioneers along the Guadaloupe River. In that community they spent the rest of their years, happy and prosperous, and August Morris was a prosperous farmer and stockman. Thus in Mr. and Mrs. Price are united some of the most stable and vital qualities of American citizenship. Judge Price has behind him a line of American ancestors stretching back before the Revolution, and a commingling of some of the best of the sturdy stock that colonized the New World. Mrs. Price represents an equally sturdy element, and has all the excellencies which have been associated with the early German colonists in America.

REV. ALPHONS MATHIS. Among those earnest workers in the field of church affairs in Texas, a few brief paragraphs should be given to the present pastor of Sacred Heart Church of the Catholic faith in Hallettsville. Father Mathis has been identified with religious work in Texas since 1897. He is a priest who is entirely wrapped up in the performance of the duties to which his life has been dedicated and his earnestness of purpose and his kindliness as a leader and adviser and the ability with which he has administered his various parishes, have brought him a high esteem in the hearts of many people in Southwest Texas.

Born in Schalbach, Lorraine, Germany, July 3, 1874, he was the fifth in a family of four sons and two daughters born to Joseph and Anna (Faust) Mathis. His parents were both natives of the same section of the German Empire and his father was a farmer. Father Mathis and his brother Joseph were the only members of the family to come to America, and his brother is now a business man in Philadelphia.

It was in the atmosphere of a farm that Father Mathis grew to manhood. He attended the common schools of Germany, also a gymnasium, and in 1892 came to America and made his first location at Victoria, Texas. While there he carried on the studies in a seminary in preparation for the priesthood, and finished his course in 1897 and was ordained by Bishop Forrest of the San Antonio diocese. His actual work as a priest began in Hallettsville as assistant to Reverend Netardus. After remaining there a trifle over three years, he was assigned as pastor of Smithville, which was his home a year and during the next thirteen years he was identified with the parish at Schulenburg. He is especially well remembered at Schulenburg, where his efforts resulted in many improvements of a material nature and in the general growth of the congregation and its spiritual welfare. In July, 1914, Father Mathis returned to Hallettsville and has since been the loved pastor of the Sacred Heart Church. On coming to America he became a naturalized citizen as soon as possible, and usually exercises his right of franchise in elections. However, as already stated, the record of his life is that of an earnest, hard-working, straightforward priest, and outside of the church there are no interests that could be said to have vitally affected his career.

Henry Swann Paulus. A son of Senator David A. Paulus of Hallettsville, to whom fitting reference is made on other pages, Henry S. Paulus of Yoakum is a young lawyer of rising reputation and developing powers, who in five or six years has made himself especially successful as attorney for the defense in the numerous cases entrusted to his charge. Mr. Paulus is vigorous in his movements, keen eyed, intellectual, and a hard worker and indefatigable in devotion to the interests of his clients.

Born in Bellville, Austin County, Texas, May 24, 1888, he grew up at Hallettsville, to which city his parents removed in 1890. Attending the city schools there, he was graduated from the Guadaloupe Academy at Cuero, in 1905, from the Sam Houston Normal School in 1906, and during the following year was a teacher in Gonzales County. Mr. Paulus was a student in the State University of Texas from 1907 to 1909, took the bar examinations at Galveston in 1909, and began practice on first of March following. In April, 1909, he was elected city attorney of Hallettsville, but resigned that position on removing to Yoakum on February 1, 1912. For a time he served as city recorder of Yoakum, but a rapidly growing private practice caused him to give up those duties.

On June 9, 1912, Mr. Paulus was married in Yoakum to Miss Lillian Alice Ward. She was the first white child born on the newly established townsite of Alice, Texas, and is a duaghter of the late P. O. Ward, who was a pioneer locomotive engineer on the Aransas Pass Railway and who lost his life in the service of that road. Mr. Ward was born in Ireland, and Mrs. Paulus is the only daughter of his four children.

Mr. and Mrs. Paulus reside in one of the most attractive and comfortable homes in the City of Yoakum. They have one child, a daughter, Rose Cyrene, born December 30, 1915. Fraternally Mr. Paulus is affiliated with the Independent Order of Odd Fellows, the Knights of Pythias, the Benevolent and Protective Order of Elks, the Woodmen of the World and the Sons of Hermann. He is the senior director of the Commercial Club of Yoakum, is attorney for the Yoakum State Bank, and in politics is allied with the democratic interests.

William Lewis Orth. Practically from its beginning as a railroad and commercial center, Yoakum has had one of its most steadfast and active citizens in William L. Orth. For many years he was in the railroad service with the "Sap" lines, and graduated from that service, by reason of a serious injury received while hunting, into his present position as a resident business man. Since starting his own home he has lived at Yoakum save for such intervals as his duties with the railroad called him to other points along its lines.

When only fourteen years old, in 1882, he came to Texas from Kansas. He was born at New Haven, just across the river from Connellsville, Pennsylvania, March 1, 1868, and two years later his father moved to Kansas. His father was a grain elevator man, and with residence at Hiawatha, and had charge of a line of elevators in Eastern Kansas. At Hiawatha the son attended public school up to the eighth grade, and with that amount of education and his experience in the home circle he came to Texas. His coming to Texas was prompted by the desire of his father to get him out of a town where the influence of a set of reckless boys might impress him for the worse and into a country where virtuous nature could train him and inspire him with ideas of industry and an upright life. On coming to the state in the spring of 1882 he was met at San Antonio by his brother Thomas R. T., who is now a prominent capitalist at Wichita Falls. This brother, though older than William, was still young and had been in Texas about a year, being then employed in breaking horses for Ranchman Malley McCowen in Atascosa County. To this ranch the younger brother was taken, and for a time herded horses for his board.

The brothers later went to the Jacobs Brothers ranch in the same locality, Tom as a cowboy and William as a fence rider. With about thirty miles of fence to patrol, he made half the journey each morning, and spent the afternoon in hunting, his wages being fifteen dollars a month and board. It was attractive work, and from it he graduated into a regular cowboy and worked for different ranchmen in that part of the state, among them Ed C. Lassiter, still one of the biggest cattlemen of Texas, and also Dillard R. Fant.

In 1886 another direction was given to his career when, after he and his brother had gained some experience as independent contractors in excavating some ponds or water tanks for ranchmen, they next secured a contract for grading a section of the San Antonio & Aransas Pass Railroad, then in process of construction. After grading a mile near Kennedy and two miles in Dewitt County they sold their outfit at Cuero, Tom entering the railroad train service and William becoming a blacksmith for a year. Then while doing some foundry work at San Antonio he one day heard that the Aransas Pass needed a brakeman, and went right over and got the job.

This was his introduction to a long career of active railroad service. His first run was between Kennedy and Wallis, with headquarters at Yoakum. When he came to the latter town in 1888 there were not more than three or four houses on the site, most of the inhabitants living in tents, and his own boarding house being conducted in the Newsome tent. In 1889 he was promoted from brakeman to freight conductor, and from that grade was made a passenger conductor in 1897. He covered all the lines out of Yoakum, and for several years ran out of San Antonio, but his final headquarters were at Yoakum, and on being given the Waco run in 1908 he built his home in Yoakum.

For a number of years Mr. Orth had recuperated and found a keen enjoyment in hunting, particularly in West Texas, and had a local reputation for his success in getting deer. In December, 1913, while pursuing this diversion near Alice in the coast country, he was accidentally shot, and the injury was of such a nature as to confine him to a hospital for a year. Since then he has not resumed railroading, having already accumulated such business interests as to furnish him permanent occupation in the City of Yoakum.

As a matter of course Mr. Orth became identified with the Order of Railway Conductors, in which he held the office of chief conductor and for a year was chairman of the grievance committee. In 1889 he took his first degree in Masonry at Corpus Christi, and is now affiliated with the lodge and Royal Arch Chapter at Yoakum and also the Eastern Star. He is a member and elder of the Christian Church, and a regular attendant of the men's bible class of the Sunday school.

In business affairs he is the principal owner and president of the Yoakum Ice Company, and is a director and stockholder in the Yoakum State Bank. He also erected the Orth Building, the upper floor of which is the chief lodge hall of the town.

May 5, 1890, Mr. Orth married Miss Sarah Fitzpatrick. She was born October 10, 1870, the only child of Alva and Jane (Farris) Fitzpatrick. Her father, who was born in Pike County, Alabama, came to Texas before the war, served his country as a Confederate soldier, was for many years a farmer in Walker County and for more than thirty years lived in Southwest Texas. He passed away July 10, 1915. He was married in Madison County to Lucy Pettit, and the two children of that union are: Alva, who died unmarried; and Lucy, wife of H. H. Baldwin of San Antonio. He was again married in Walker County to Mrs. Jane Dean, daughter of Edward and Lucy (Boone) Farris, and they now make their home in Yoakum. Mr. and Mrs. Orth have three fine young sons: William Alva, of Yoakum, who married Miss Walter Lee Lander and has a daughter, Sarah Camilla; and Christopher Thomas and Robert Fitzpatrick.

FERDINAND HILLJE. One of the solid Germans of Southwest Texas, a leader among his nationality which more than any other countrymen have developed many of the most prosperous counties of the state, Ferdinand Hillje has spent most of his business career at Hallettsville, is chiefly prominent as a cotton oil mill man, and is also a banker and a factor in public affairs.

Ferdinand Hillje was born at High Hill in Fayette County, Texas, December 12, 1862. He represents the second generation from the Fatherland. His father, John F. Hillje, who died in Colorado County, Texas, in 1893, at the age of seventy-six, was a native of Oldenburg, Germany, the son of a wagon maker, and the son learned the same trade. He came to the United States when a single man, landing at Galveston, and his first location was Frelsburg, where he invested his small capital in the construction of a cotton gin. Although this was to him a new business, he ran it with success for a few years, and then sold the plant to his brother, who had followed him to the United States after two years. John F. Hillje then located in the High Hill country of Fayette County, built there another gin, and also owned and operated a small farm. The ginning business was his principal work during his active career. During war times he was exempt from military service owing to the fact that he was a miller and was more useful in his capacity as grinding the grist for the "war widows" and others than as a soldier in the ranks. In politics he voted as a republican, but held no office. John F. Hillje was married in Colorado County to Miss Mina Fahrenthold, who was born in the town of Pritzwalk, Prussia, and came to America with her father who was a farmer. Mrs. Hillje died at LaGrange, Texas. Aside from Ferdinand her children were Fred, who died while in the oil mill business at Weimar, and left children; Mary, wife of Rudolph Klatt of LaGrange; Louis, an oil mill man in San Antonio; Anna, who married Herman Reissner of Weimar; Bertha, who married Gus Seydler of Wharton; William, who is in the oil mill business at Weimar.

The boyhood of Ferdinand Hillje was spent in the country, where he attended the public schools, learned the arts of farming and the mechanism and operation of a cotton gin, and remained at home in managing these different interests until twenty-seven years of age. At that time Mr. Hillje became interested in and connected with the oil mill business at Weimar and was superintendent of the Hillje Brothers mill one year. In 1893 he removed to Hallettsville, and here purchased the Lavaca Oil Company's plant, which had been built by the Baumgarten interests, and since that time has been secretary and manager of the mill. The Lavaca Cotton Oil Company has a capacity of forty-five tons daily and is the chief manufacturing industry of Hallettsville.

Mr. Hillje has steered as nearly clear of politics as possible for a business man to do, although at the present time he is an alderman

Ferd. Hillje

and is city treasurer of Hallettsville. A business man and manufacturer who has increased the facilities of his home town, and also a capable banker, he succeeded Mr. Henry J. Strunk in the office of president of the First National Bank of Hallettsville. The Hillje home, which he erected some years ago, is one of the best in the city. Mr. Hillje belongs to several fraternities, but is not an ardent lodge man.

Ferdinand Hillje was married at High Hill, Texas, in 1890, to Miss Marguerite Seydler. Her father, Julius Seydler, was a native of Saxony and came to the United States before the war between the states, and followed farming. Julius Seydler married Miss Herder, and they became the parents of a large family. Mr. and Mrs. Hillje have no children.

JOHN J. JARESH. One of the recently elected members of the first city commission of Yoakum is a prominent young business man, enterprising, popular, and in every way qualified for such responsibilities, the bearing of which will make his name honorably associated with the records of the city for all time to come.

A member of the firm of Jaresh Brothers, hardware, groceries and implements, John J. Jaresh is a native of Texas, born at Sweet Home, Lavaca County, July 26, 1883. His father, Lawrence Jaresh, now a farmer at Sweet Home, and his grandfather, Motis Jaresh, were among the early Texas settlers of the Bohemian nationality. Lawrence was born in Austria in 1847, and six years later, in 1853, his father brought the family to America, landing at Galveston and settling in Fayette County. Motis lived many years near Flatonia, but died at Sweet Home in 1885 at the advanced age of eighty-four. He identified himself thoroughly with American life and customs, learned the English language, and after getting citizenship was a regular democratic voter. He accumulated a considerable amount of farming land before his death. He and his wife, who are buried at Yoakum, had the following children: Lawrence; Simon, who died in Flatonia and left children; Motis, of Sweet Home; Frank, a farmer of Lavaca County; Charles, who died at West, Texas, leaving a family there; Mrs. John Boca, of Flatonia; Mrs. Mary Meitsmann, who died near Schulenberg, leaving children; Mrs. Charles Schroeder, of Smithville, Texas; and Mrs. John Ulmann, of Moulton, Texas.

For more than sixty years Lawrence Jaresh has lived in Texas, is a product of its conditions and environment, and has made himself a factor in farming and the establishment of a home and family. His education was limited, and during the war period in his early youth he did some freighting to Mexico. He moved into Lavaca County in 1883, and has since pursued his industrious career in the Sweet Home neighborhood. In politics he has gone no further than casting his vote. The maiden name of his wife was Mary Migel, one of a family of several children born to a German farmer in Texas. The Jaresh children are: Antone W., now one of the firm of Jaresh Brothers at Yoakum: John J.; Tennie, wife of Charles Kananek of Lavaca County; and Thomas, who is a farmer and cotton weigher at Sweet Home.

The public schools of Sweet Home and Yoakum supplied John J. Jaresh with his early advantages, but only until he was seventeen, at which age he became a clerk in Yoakum and for several years was in the employ of several of the leading merchants of the city. With a somewhat matured experience and with a fair amount of capital, in 1910 he engaged in business for himself, under his own name as a grocer. He was prospering up to February 9, 1913, when his store was destroyed by fire. This caused only a temporary interruption, however, and at the beginning of June after the fire and after he had resumed business his brother Antone joined him, making the present firm of Jaresh Brothers. The scope of trade was at that time extended so as to comprise implements and hardware, and they now handle a large volume of business. Mr. Jaresh erected the large building in which the store is located, with a frontage of seventy-five feet and a hundred feet depth.

Reared in democratic atmosphere, Mr. Jaresh has acted rather independently in political matters, as is indicated by the fact that his first presidential vote was given to Roosevelt in 1904. His business record and well known efficiency in handling any issue in his personal affairs furnished the chief recommendation to local citizens when his name was proposed as one to be voted on in April, 1915, for the first board of city commissioners. The commission succeeded the old mayor and council form of government, and so far its chief work has been in selecting a manager and getting the affairs of the municipality shaped on their new course. One result already noted is that the community is getting full value for all money expended upon labor and supplies, and it has also effected a purer moral atmosphere for Yoakum.

Mr. Jaresh was reared a Catholic, and is a member of the S. P. J. S. and the Sons of Herman. His comfortable home, which he erected, is at 702 Grand Avenue, in Dewitt County, while he has erected several other houses in that section of the city which lies in Lavaca County. On November 21, 1904, he married Miss Ida Svoboda, whose parents, John and Theresa (Hollub) Svoboda, were both natives of Bohemia. Her father was brought to the United States in childhood, was reared in Iowa and married in that state, but came to Texas and died at Yoakum. His children were: Mrs. Mary Pustjovsky; Joseph; Mrs. Annie Jilek; Rudolph; Mrs. Jaresh, who was born June 24, 1886; Antone; Miss Katie; and Mrs. Emma Vrazel. Mr. and Mrs. Jaresh have two children: Walter Lawrence and Dorothy Catherine.

Leonard Allen Orth. As the facts hereafter to be set forth show, Mr. Orth has had an exceedingly active and varied experience, from a hard working, poorly paid cowboy, to his present dignity as one of the city commissioners entrusted with the government of the City of Yoakum, and also a very substantial business man, being one of the owners and manager of the Yoakum Ice Company, and also owner of the Orth Milling Company of that city.

All this has been accomplished within a lifetime of forty years. He was born in Denver, Colorado, May 23, 1875, a son of Capt. Christopher Henry Orth, who died in 1884 while living in Hiawatha, Kansas, and is buried in Evanston, Illinois, where his widow now resides. He was a native of Pennsylvania, having been born shortly after his parents' arrival in this country. He graduated from West Point, and, living in Pennsylvania during the war, organized three companies of Union troops for the service and became captain of one of them. In Boston, Massachusetts, Captain Orth married his second wife, Miss Mary Louise Leonard, a native of that city. A brief record of their children: Leonard A.; Mountford S., of Boston, Massachusetts; and Mary Ward, who married H. K. Webster, of Chicago, who is a book and story writer widely read. By his first marriage he had the following children: Thomas Rogers Torrence Orth, of Wichita Falls, Texas; William L., of Yoakum; Luty, who married Chas. De Voe and resides in St. Paul, Minnesota.

Mr. Orth's father was a grain trader and speculator at Hiawatha, Kansas, where the son was reared from the age of two years. He attended the public schools and also the Sunday school of the Episcopal Church, in which ex-Gov. E. N. Morrill was a leading spirit and his teacher. His first practical experience was as cattle herder in Colorado and along the Kansas-Nebraska line. He was also in the Black Hills country, where an uncle and Drell Wood had stock interests and claims, when that country was as new as nature made it. During the three and a half years of contact with that wild and rough country and its denizens, he was getting fifteen dollars a month wages and his board, and this was the total he realized for his labor and hardship. Returning from there to Kansas, he soon came into Texas, following his brothers W. L. and Thomas to this state. The latter brother is now a leading citizen and capitalist of Wichita Falls.

It was in 1891 that he first came to Texas. At Yoakum, he learned the machinist's trade in the shops of the S. A. & A. P. Railroad, and after becoming proficient went to Old Mexico, was employed in the shops of different railways and then took the post of assistant chief engineer in the Monterey brewery. After four years at Monterey he returned to Yoakum in 1900, and has since been a permanent member of that community. Resuming employment in the shops of the S. A. & A. P. Railroad as mechanic, in six months he was made shop foreman, and two years later was promoted to general foreman of the shops, which was his responsible position two and a half years.

Mr. Orth resigned from the railway service to identify himself actively with the newly organized Yoakum Ice Company, in which he was one of the stockholders and has been its manager from the beginning. His brother, W. L. Orth, has been president since incorporation, and the first secretary was C. H. DeVoe and the present one is W. A. Orth. The capital stock at the beginning was $20,000, since increased to $50,000. The plant has a daily capacity of forty-five tons, besides a cold storage department, while another branch of the business is the handling of coal and wood.

At Yorktown, Texas, January 1, 1902, Mr. Orth married Miss Alma Riedel, daughter of Ernest and Louisa (Jacobs) Riedel, German people who settled in Dewitt County just at the close of the Civil war, and after many years as a farmer Mr. Riedel died there. To Mr. and Mrs. Orth have been born two children, Harry and Rosalie.

The political allegiance of Mr. Orth has been given to the republican party, but he has been in politics in no important sense beyond casting his ballot. April 1, 1915, he was chosen one of the first board of city commissioners under the new charter, and party politics had nothing to do with this election, and the honor came to him unsought and was a manifestation of the confidence placed in his ability to perform the service for which the office was created. He gained the largest vote of any member of the board, his support being represented by 351 votes, while the charter itself only polled 307. This board during its first two months in office and in control of city affairs has been looking particularly after the moral welfare of the town, and in a material way its efforts have been directed to the graveling of streets, construction of cement crossings, and has encouraged property owners to build permanent walks. In fraternal matters, Mr. Orth is a Blue Lodge Mason, became a member of the Knights of Pythias in 1901, and is also one of the older local members of the Knights of the Maccabees.

Edwin Thomas Dooley. One of the veteran railroad men of Texas is Edwin Thomas Dooley of Yoakum, who has not only earned the reputation of being a careful and efficient member of the operating force on the San Antonio and Aransas Pass and is one of the oldest conductors of that system, but has also thriftily engaged his earnings by investments in real estate and as a citizen of Yoakum has done much to develop that town by building improvements.

A native of Indiana and of Irish parentage, Edwin T. Dooley was born at Arcola, Allen County, Indiana, October 31, 1857. His parents were John and Joanna (Quinn) Dooley, both natives of Ireland. His mother's people came from County Kerry. When John Dooley came to the United States he first located in East Concord, New Hampshire, where he married. In the '50s he moved from New Hampshire and after a brief stay in Ohio took up his residence in Allen County, Indiana, where the rest of his life was spent. He was a railroad man, a section foreman and track layer. While in New England he laid track on the East Concord & Montreal Railway, later on the Muncie, Jackson & Saginaw Railway, on the Memphis & Charleston Railway, and for a number of years was in the employ of the Pennsylvania Company in Indiana. He became highly regarded as a track man, and continued in the service until too old, after which he retired to a farm. He died in 1890 at the age of seventy, having survived his wife. Their children were: William of Fort Wayne, Indiana; John, who was killed while working as a switchman in Chicago, leaving six children; Jerry, who was also a railroad man and died unmarried; Joanna, who married Mike McLaughlin and died in Allen County, Indiana, leaving three children; Edwin Thomas; Charles, who has been a railroad man all his active career and now lives in San Antonio; Mary, wife of Will Newhouse of Bakersfield, California; and Alice, who died as the wife of James Stack of Plymouth, Indiana.

Reared in the wooded section of Northern Indiana, Edwin T. Dooley gained his education in a little frame schoolhouse at Arcola. On leaving school he found work as a farmer until twenty-two years old, and the beginning of his long service as a railroad man was on March 17, 1879, when he became a freight brakeman on the Pennsylvania Railroad, running between Fort Wayne and Chicago. After about three years as brakeman he was conductor for a year, and then left to come South, spending a short time in Cairo, Illinois, before arriving in Texas.

Mr. Dooley first came to Texas in May, 1883. His first work here was as a switchman in the Eagle Pass yards, where he was employed from September, 1883, to August of the following year. After a few months he was made a fireman on the Mexican International Railway, running south into Mexico from Eagle Pass and Ciudad Porfirio Diaz. In different capacities he worked along that road and in that country for two years, and finally returned to the transportation department and spent two years as yardmaster at Eagle Pass and Ciudad Porfirio Diaz. His next headquarters were at San Antonio, where he continued in the yard service and transportation department, and was then back in Mexico two years in the freight and passenger service of the International. His runs took him through the states of Nuevo Leon, Coahuila and Durango. In the fall of 1893 Mr. Dooley came to Yoakum, and has since been one of the ablest men in the transportation department of the Aransas Pass road. He began as a freight brakeman, five years later was promoted to freight conductor, and in 1905 gained promotion to passenger conductor. He has been running some of the best trains over the Aransas Pass road and out of Yoakum in all directions.

During more than twenty years of residence at Yoakum Mr. Dooley has built five different homes. He was one of the pioneers to locate and start building improvements in the Tucker Addition to that city, and his own home is one of the best in that locality. He also owns a good farm in Dewitt County, and has exercised excellent judgment in the investment of his earnings in local real estate.

G. Mc. Dilworth

Ro. S. Dilworth

As a veteran in railroading service Mr. Dooley is well known among the members of the Order of Railroad Conductors and the Brotherhood of Railway Trainmen, and has filled offices in both orders. He is also affiliated with the Benevolent and Protective Order of Elks, the Knights of Pythias and the Knights of Columbus. At Arcola, Indiana, on October 21, 1888, Mr. Dooley married Miss Rose Steiner. Her parents, Joseph and Mary (Hoerne) Steiner, both came to America from Alsace, which was then a French province. The Steiner children were: Mary, who died unmarried; Fannie, wife of Joseph Champion; Mrs. Dooley, who was born at Columbus, Indiana, October 21, 1859; Susie, who married James Roe; Barbara, wife of Melville Lillich; Josie, wife of Ernest Phillips; and Joseph, who died at Yoakum, leaving a family of five. Mr. and Mrs. Dooley, though without children of their own, have made their home almost an orphanage for the benefit of some of the orphan children of their relatives, and they have done much to rear and contribute to the training of a younger generation.

ROBERT S. DILWORTH. The history of a nation is nothing more than a history of the individuals comprising it, and as they are characterized by loftier or lower ideals, actuated by the spirit of ambition or indifference, so it is with a state, county or town. Success along any line of endeavor would never be properly appreciated if it came with a single effort and unaccompanied by some hardships, for it is the knocks and bruises in life that make success taste so sweet. The failures accentuate the successes, thus making recollections of the former as dear as those of the latter for having been the stepping-stones to achievement. The career of Robert Scott Dilworth emphasizes the fact that success is bound to come to those who join brains with ambition and are willing to work. He is president of the Dilworth Bank and he has done some splendid work as a rancher and in colonizing land in Southern Texas. He is descended from fine old southern stock and following is a brief genealogy of the family.

Capt. John Dilworth, his great-great-grandfather, was probably born in England but he came to America from Dublin, Ireland, landing in this country prior to the Revolution. During that struggle, being a Tory, he became a captain in the English navy. He married a daughter of Governor Peter Aldrich, governor of the Delaware Colony, and both he and his wife died early in life, leaving a young son James Colwell Dilworth. This child was reared in the family of Gen. Nathanael Greene and attended the University of Georgia and Yale College, graduating from both, and subsequently became a prominent planter and slave holder in Georgia and was likewise a ship owner, engaged chiefly in the coasting trade. He was a soldier in the Seminole war. The dirk, with which he killed Indians at that time, is now in the possession of Robert Scott Dilworth. He died in Georgia at the age of thirty-eight and is buried at St. Mary's in Camden County. He married Elizabeth McIntosh Scott, descendant of the Virginia family of Scotts of which Gen. Winfield Scott was a member. To this union were born the following children: James Colwell, William Scott, who enlisted in the Confederate army and attained rank as brigadier general toward the close of the war, was subsequently a lawyer in Florida, and practiced in partnership with Senator Pascoe, who had studied law in General Dilworth's office; George Andrew, who graduated in law but died in young manhood; and Elizabeth, who married a Mr. Mills and passed her entire life in Georgia.

James Colwell Dilworth, Jr., grandfather of Robert S. Dilworth, was born in 1816, grew up on his father's plantation in Georgia, and in 1843 started across the country to Texas, but died en route that year at Vicksburg, Mississippi. His wife, whose maiden name was Frances Elizabeth Norwood, was born in Georgia a daughter of William Norwood, who subsequently came to Texas with his widowed daughter, settling near Gonzales, and is buried at the Botts farm in that locality. After her husband's death in Vicksburg Mrs. Dilworth remained in Yallabusha County, Mississippi, until 1849, in which year she accompanied her family down the Mississippi River to New Orleans, thence by boat across the Gulf to Port Lavaca, and she settled six miles north of Gonzales. She paid $20 per acre for a farm which was in her name until 1912. She was a woman of remarkable mentality and gave her sons a thorough education in Greek, Latin and mathematics. Her death occurred in 1884 at the age of sixty-four, and during her lifetime she was a devout member of the Baptist Church. Her children were George Norwood and James Colwell. The second son James Colwell spent his life in Gonzales County, where he was associated in the cattle business for many years with the prominent Austin capitalist G. W. Littlefield. Subsequently he became interested in banking enterprises in Gonzales, and with his brother founded the Dilworth Bank in 1866. For four years he was a soldier in the Civil war, being a lieutenant in G. W. Littlefield's Company, was wounded at Rogersville, Tennessee, and later was in the campaign from Tennessee to Georgia in Gen. Joe Wheeler's command. He was never interested in politics, was a Baptist in religious matters, and fraternally was a Knight Templar Mason. He married Miss Sallie Broyles, whom he met while he was lying wounded at Rogersville, and their one son George Norwood died at Austin, Texas, being survived by a wife and three children, and one daughter Nola E. Dilworth, married Wm. J. Cocke of Asheville, North Carolina.

George Norwood Dilworth, oldest of the children of James C. and Frances Elizabeth (Norwood) Dilworth, was born in Georgia in 1837. He was educated under the expert tutelage of his mother and in the public schools of Gonzales, and prior to the war was a farmer in Gonzales County. For one year he was in the Confederate army, but that service was of so little consequence that he hardly claimed the distinction of having been a soldier.

At the end of the Civil war, when people were left penniless, George N. and his brother J. C. Dilworth were among the first to create a market for cattle by buying up herds and driving them to Kansas, Utah and other points. Their first drive was made in 1866. G. N. Dilworth was the first to build and erect a steam gin in Gonzales County, this improved plant taking the place of the old horse gin. He was also the first to establish a bank in the county, in 1866. These are incidents that indicate the leadership which was a dominant characteristic of his entire career.

After the war he was for a time in the mercantile business, and then gave most of his attention to the cattle industry and the banking. Prior to 1877 he was in the cattle business with G. W. Littlefield, and from 1877 until 1884 was associated with J. D. Houston as a ranch and stock man. Thereafter he confined his endeavors almost entirely to his banking interests. It was in January, 1866, that he and his brother James C. as partners founded the Dilworth Bank, which is still one of the strong financial institutions of the state and is now conducted by the sons of George N. Dilworth. The original home of the bank was in a two-story red brick building next to the corner of St. George and St. Joseph streets. In 1885 the bank found a new home in a fine stone building on St. Lawrence Street, where it remained until 1912, when headquarters were established in a fine new building on the corner of St. Joseph and St. George streets.

George N. Dilworth was a good judge of human nature, and gave many a young man a start in life. He was a Baptist and one of the financial pillars of the church, and he lived a life of usefulness such as few men know. He lent substantial encouragement to the railroads in his part of the state, and a token of this liberal assistance is found in the fact that the Aransas Pass Railroad Company named one of the stations in Gonzales County Dilworth. God-fearing, law-abiding, his life was as truly that of a Christian gentleman as any man's can well be. Unwaveringly he did the right as he interpreted it. Along honorable and straightforward lines he won the success which crowned his efforts and which made him one of the substantial residents of the state.

He married Martha Ellen Huff, a daughter of Leonard Huff, who in early life was a mining man in Georgia and subsequently an extensive land holder at Luling, Texas, where he settled in 1853. Mr. G. N. Dilworth died in January, 1911, and his devoted wife followed him in 1913. Their children were: Marcus, a cattleman and traveler; Frances, who died in San Antonio, the wife of Gus Witting, by whom she left four children; James Colwell, who at the time of his death left two children by his marriage to Frances Kokernot, was an official in the Dilworth Bank and one of the organizers of the Sour Lake Springs Company, which was sold to the Texas Company; Robert Scott, next in order of birth; Margaret, widow of J. P. Lewis and living with her two children in Gonzales; Coke E., one of the partners in the Dilworth Bank; and Annabel, deceased, who married S. P. Jones.

Robert Scott Dilworth was born on a farm in Gonzales, Texas, September 24, 1868. He received his early education in the public schools of Gonzales, graduated from a high school at Bellevue, Virginia, and also attended the University of Virginia and Eastman's Business College at Poughkeepsie, New York, making a specialty of higher mathematics.

Returning to Gonzales July 3, 1888, on the following day, a holiday, he entered the Dilworth Bank, with which worthy institution he has ever since been identified. Since the death of his father he has been president of the bank.

Mr. Dilworth enjoys the notable distinction of being the first man to colonize land in Southern Texas. Since 1897 he has purchased the following tracts: the Griffith ranch near Floresville, the Miller league near Riedelville, the Tiner near Stockdale, the De Wees near Floresville, the Mitchell ranch in Wilson County, the Ray ranch in Wilson and Karnes counties, the Jo Taylor ranch in Dewitt County, the Butler ranch in Karnes County, the Fant ranch in Live Oak and Bee counties, and the Bennett and Vela ranch in Hidalgo County. This property he sold to actual settlers, and inaugurated the movement for the breaking up of extensive ranch holding and the colonizing of such properties as permanent farmer settlers.

He has also been in the cattle business both in Texas and Indian Territory, is interested in the Gonzales Cotton Oil Mill, and was one of the promoters of the Taylor Oil & Gas Company of Taylor, Texas. In 1912 he was elected to the State Legislature but declined to qualify. He was chosen alternate to the Democratic National Convention at Denver, and was a Harmon delegate to the national convention in 1912. Fraternally he is a Kappa Sigma of the University of Virginia, a member of the Independent Order of Odd Fellows, in which he is past grand, and of the Knights of Pythias.

March 14, 1893, in Gonzales County, Mr. Dilworth married Miss Susan Jones, daughter of Dr. John C. and Mary Kennon (Crisp) Jones, the former a native of Alabama and the latter of Texas. There are four children. Robert Scott, Jr., is president of the Dixie Oil & Refining Company at San Antonio and completed his education in the West Texas Military Academy and in the Culver Military Academy in Indiana. The daughter Annabel is now a student in Gunston Hall at Washington, District of Columbia. The two younger children, Martha Ellen and George Norwood, are still at home. The Dilworth family reside in a beautiful residence on East Avenue in Gonzales and their home is the scene of many attractive social gatherings.

EDMUND HERDER. On other pages of this publication is entered a review of the personal career and family history of William Herder, father of him whose name initiates this article, and thus it were but redundant to repeat in this connection the data there offered. Suffice it to say that Edmund Herder is proud to designate himself a native son of Texas and to know that he is a scion of a sterling pioneer family of this state, in gaining the independence of which his grandfather, George Herder, played a worthy part, as he served as a soldier under the renowned patriot, Gen. Sam Houston and took part in the historic battle of San Jacinto.

On the old homestead farm of his father, just two miles north of the Village of Eagle, Fayette County, Edmund Herder, the present postmaster at Shiner, Lavaca County, was born on the 4th of October, 1882, and thus he was a lad of about five years at the time of the family removal to Lavaca County, in 1887, the family home being established on the famous Half Moon Ranch, where his parents still reside, his father there being the owner of a valuable landed estate of more than 400 acres. To the public schools of Shiner the present postmaster of this town is indebted for his early educational discipline, and he well recalls that as a boy he remembers that the site of the village was marked only by the unbroken prairie, so that he has witnessed personally the inception and rise of this thriving municipality, his home having been in this immediate locality from the time of his boyhood.

At the age of fifteen years Mr. Herder left the parental roof and became a clerk in the Shiner postoffice, under the administration of R. G. Seydler. He continued his service in this capacity of virtual deputy until another postmaster assumed charge of the office, and he then passed the required examination and proved himself eligible for service as a rural mail carrier. He was appointed the first carrier on Rural Route No. 1, from Shiner, and he continued his active and efficient work on this route for ten and one-half years, during which entire period he only once failed to make his regular trip, save for the intervals of his annual vacations. His last official trip over the route was made on the 4th of January, 1915, but he did not find it incumbent upon him to bid farewell to the patrons of the route, for on the 29th of the preceding month he had received his commission as postmaster at Shiner, in which office he succeeded the late G. A. Pannewitz, his commission having been signed on that date by the President of the United States and his assumption of office having occurred on the 14th of January, 1915. His long and practical experience in the local office and as a rural mail carrier makes him a specially able and discriminating incumbent and his administration is giving unqualified satisfaction to the community which he serves and in which his circle of friends virtually is limited only by that of his acquaintances. Since he initiated his service the postoffice has been removed to its present eligible quarters, its equipment and facilities have been much improved and extended, and the office is now headquarters from which are served four rural free-delivery routes. As may naturally be inferred, Mr. Herder is found aligned as a stalwart in the local ranks of the democratic party, and as a loyal citizen he is liberal and progressive, the while he takes specially vital interest in all that touches the welfare of the community that has represented his home since childhood.

At Flatonia, Fayette County, the 23d of September, 1902, recorded the marriage of Mr. Herder to Miss Martha Finkenstein, who was born and reared in that county, daughter of Leopold and Ida (Kuegler) Finkenstein, honored pioneers of the High Hill district of that county. Mr. Finkenstein is deceased and his widow now resides at Flatonia, Mrs. Herder being the fifth in order of birth in a family of six children. Mr. and Mrs. Herder have one child, Elvera, who was born October 19, 1903, and who is a bright and ambitious young student in the public schools of her native Town of Shiner.

WINFIELD S. BUNTON, SR. Education and financial assistance are very important factors in achieving success in the business world of today, where every faculty must be brought into play, but they are not the main elements. Persistency and determination figure much more prominently and a man possessed of these qualities is bound to win a fair amount of success. Winfield Scott Bunton, whose name forms the caption for this article, although handicapped by poor health and bad eyesight, earned his own education and during the latter years of his life has climbed to a high place on the ladder of achievement. He is a prominent citizen in Gonzales, where he was engaged in the grocery business for fifteen years, and he is now a retired property owner, having a couple of farms and considerable residence property in this city.

Alfred Bunton, father of Winfield Scott Bunton, was born in Spencer County, Indiana, in 1822, a son of pioneer settlers in the Hoosier State. His father was Samuel Bunton, a Virginian, who located in Spencer County, Indiana, just after his marriage. The latter lived to the patriarchal age of ninety-three years and most of his active career was devoted to work as a farmer. He was a republican in politics and in religious matters was a Methodist. He married a Miss Young and four of their sons—Thomas, Armistead, James and Franklin—were soldiers in the Union army during the Civil war: all survived that conflict except Franklin. Three other sons were born to Mr. and Mrs. Bunton, namely: Alfred, Robert and one who died in infancy. The Bunton family is of good old English stock. Alfred Bunton was a farmer by occupation and he died in early manhood, in 1857, aged thirty-five years. He married Elizabeth Hahn, of German extraction and a daughter of Michael Hahn, a native of Ohio. The following children were born to Mr. and Mrs. Bunton: Winfield Scott, subject of this sketch; Phoebe, who first married Robert Bedford and, second, A. E. Eaton, of Aurora, Missouri; Retta married, first, Jehoida Crooks and, second, Wm. R. Sorrells, of Gonzales County; Isora married Isaac Shrodes and died in Spencer County, Indiana; and Henry Talbert died in Gonzales County, Texas, leaving four children. After her husband's death Mrs. Bunton married Renssalaer Alexander and to them were born: Richmond, who died in Houston, Texas; Horace, a resident of Houston; Addie, now Mrs. William Aldis, of Gonzales; Amy, twin of Addie, married, first, Thomas Parr and, second, John Stokesberry, of Houston; and Fannie is the wife of Judge Railey, of Houston.

Winfield Scott Bunton was born in Spencer County, Indiana, November 27, 1848. He was reared to maturity on the parental farm and received but meager educational advantages in his youth. His childhood was passed in the community where Abraham Lincoln grew up and he was only seventeen years of age when the Civil war ended. He married in his native county November 7, 1869, went to Louisville, Kentucky, where he worked in a distillery for a time. He was in very poor health, however, and was advised by his physician that only a change of climate could improve his condition. He reached Texas absolutely broke and as it was necessary for him to earn a livelihood he worked for 50 cents a day till spring. Then he bought a yoke of steers on credit and rented a farm on the banks of the Guadalupe River. He remained in that locality for three years and left there with his teams and tools paid for and with $300 in cash. He then rented a farm on Denton Creek for the next three years and there his success was such that he was enabled to buy a farm of 181 acres for which he paid $5 per acre. He remained on the latter farm for two years at the end of which time he was debt free and had some money in the bank. He had recovered his health but his eyes began to trouble him and they gradually grew worse till total blindness set in in 1913. In 1885 Mr. Bunton opened a fruit and candy store in Gonzales and later engaged in the grocery business. He began with $300, a year's rent from his farm, and he remained in business in this city for fifteen years, investing his profits in another farm and in city property. He now has five fine residences in one block facing on the Plaza and he owns ten other residences in different sections of the city. In addition he has other property, including a fine business block and he owns two farms on Denton and Peach creeks. His connection with the Farmers' National Bank in Gonzales began with its organization and he is still one of its stockholders. He votes the democratic ticket but has never been interested in holding office and he and his wife are devout members of the Baptist Church.

In Spencer County, Indiana, November 7, 1869, occurred the marriage of Mr. Bunton to Miss Martha Jane Dempsey, a daughter of Adam H. and Sarah (Smith) Dempsey. Mr. Dempsey was born in County Cork, Ireland, and came to the United States in young manhood, locating in Spencer County, Indiana, where he worked as a brickmason and where he married. He was a soldier under Gen. Winfield Scott and he died at the age of thirty-two years, leaving a widow and the following children: Annie married Daniel Hill, of Spencer County, Indiana; Martha Jane, born October 24, 1852, is Mrs. Bunton, as already noted; Sarah died in childhood; Ella was the wife of Andrew Zumwalt at the time of her demise, in Texas; and Minnie married Jeff Whitehouse, of Spencer County, Indiana. For her second husband Mrs. Dempsey married a Mr. Smallwood and they had two children, one who died in infancy and Grant Smallwood, who died in Texas at the age of twelve. Mrs. Bunton was reared in the family of Herman Verheoff, of Louisville, and received a good common-school education.

Following are brief data concerning the children born to Mr. and Mrs. Bunton: Louis Alfred died as a child in Louisville; William Edward served for three years in the Texas National Guard, at San Antonio, and on the outbreak of the Spanish-American war went to the Philippine Islands with the Tenth Pennsylvania Volunteer Infantry: he was killed in the battle of Malate ten days after reaching the islands and his body was sent home and is buried in Gonzales; Winfield Scott, Jr., is a bookkeeper in the Farmers' National Bank of Gonzales: he married Rhoda Debose and they have a son, James Carroll; and Roy Edgar is a merchant in Gonzales: he married Annie Shuler and they have two daughters: Fay Mildred and Josephine Martha.

William Preston Midkiff. Of the law firms that look after the most important business in Gonzales County, none is spoken of with more commendation of individual ability than that of Rainbolt & Midkiff. Mr. Midkiff is a North Texas man, and had an extensive experience as a lawyer in Gainesville preparatory to his removal to Gonzales.

Born in Cooke County, Texas, March 9, 1876, Mr. Midkiff represents a family that has been identified with Texas for almost fifty years. His father was William Midkiff, who in turn, was a son of Frank Midkiff, and of English ancestry. William Midkiff, who was a retired farmer and stock man living at Gainesville, was born in Lincoln County, Tennessee, January 4, 1833, grew up there as a country boy, and when still in his teens was orphaned by the death of his parents. This threw upon him extraordinary burdens and responsibility, and he had to work as a farm laborer in order to provide for the younger children. Frequently his wages were only "two bits" per day. After he had performed his duty toward his brothers and sisters, he married and brought his young wife to Texas about 1856, making the journey by wagon, and after spending the first year in Grayson County, establishing a permanent home in Cooke County the following year. His settlement was along the Red River at Sivell's Bend. Others of his family also came to Texas. These included his two brothers John and Charles, and his sister Elizabeth, who married J. B. Slaven of Grayson County. Another sister, Ann, married John Hamilton and remained in Tennessee.

William Midkiff spent his active career in the Red River district of Cooke County and has traveled all the way from poverty to independence. As a farmer he has devoted himself to stock and grain, and has improved farms in several different localities. A few years after his settlement in Texas he offered his services to the Confederate government. He joined Captain Taylor's Company and remained in Texas throughout his military service. Following the war the Indians gave him more trouble than he had experienced during the conflict between the states. As students of history know, the Indians were almost constantly engaged in raiding throughout North Texas until the early '70s. In a single raid in 1867 the red men ran off all his fine live stock except one pony, including horses, mules and jack. He pursued the Indians as far as Fort Sill in Indian Territory, but never succeeded in recovering his stock. In later years William Midkiff became indentified with the Confederate Veterans' Association at Gainesville, and was active in that organization until it disbanded. He is a master and chapter Mason, and a member of the Methodist Church and was an officer in the society in earlier years. In politics he is a democrat, and has been an ardent admirer of Joseph W. Bailey, and supported that eminent Texan in all his campaigns. Among other business interests William Midkiff is a director in the First State Bank of Gainesville.

The young woman whom he married back in Tennessee before starting to Texas was Miss Elizabeth Frances Cole. Her father was Mark Cole. Mrs. Midkiff died in 1905. Her children were: Mary, wife of W. M. Finney of Gainesville; George P., a farmer at Sivell's Bend; Sue, wife of H. J. Cole of Gainesville; John H., a former tax collector of Cooke County and a resident of Gainesville; Thomas J. and Robert L., twins, the former a resident of Valley View, Texas, and the latter connected with the Department of Agriculture at Austin; Kate, who married R. L. Dorris of Fort Worth; and William P., the youngest.

When fifteen years of age William Preston Midkiff left the old homestead at Sivell's Bend in order to finish his education. He spent two years in Capt. T. C. Belcher's private school at Gainesville, and then entered the University of Texas, where he spent two and a half years in the academic department, and in 1898 was graduated LL. B. from the law department. Almost immediately after getting his diploma and license as a Texas attorney he took up practice at Gainesville. For a time he was associated with Judge E. P. Hill, and later with H. E. Eldridge under the firm name Eldridge & Midkiff. This firm represented, as attorneys, both the railroads through Gainesville.

With about eight years of successful experience as a lawyer Mr. Midkiff came to Gonzales County January 1, 1906. He was in partnership with Robert F. Nixon as Midkiff & Nixon until the death of the latter in 1912, and has since been associated as a partner of J. W. Rainbolt. While his success in the profession has demanded his energies and time almost completely, Mr. Midkiff has also been quite active in democratic politics, and since 1910 has served as democratic county chairman in Gonzales County. He attends the state conventions regularly, and in the primaries of 1912 helped to carry Gonzales County for Judson Harmon. This was the only county in the entire congressional district that gave a majority for Mr. Harmon in the preferential presidential primaries.

At Gainesville, June 9, 1909, Mr. Midkiff married Miss Elfie Huggins. Her parents were Thomas J. and Frances (Thompson) Huggins, and her father, who came from Tennessee, is a contractor of Gainesville. To their marriage were born two children, William Preston, Jr., and Richard. Throughout his professional career Mr. Midkiff has been noted among his associates and friends for his strict sobriety and cleanly life, and this has been undoubtedly a favorable factor in his success.

W. Emil Appelt. For half a century or more the Appelt family has merited a well deserved reputation in Lavaca and adjoining counties as business men of exceptional acumen, solid and prosperous members of the community, energizers of local industry, and capable citizens and kind neighbors. The name bespeaks a large family relationship, and there are many of the name who might well receive attention. W. Emil Appelt of Hallettsville is a prominent business man and rancher, and represents the third generation of the family since it left Germany.

W. Emil Appelt was born at the county seat of Lavaca County November 14, 1867. He is a son of the late William Appelt, a prominent factor in local affairs who died at Hallettsville in May, 1905. It was the grandfather, Frank Appelt, who brought his family to Texas in 1852, and after a brief stay in Fayette County located at Hallettsville. Frank Appelt improved what is known as the Appelt farm, which is now the property of his son Louis, and was a hard worker and won a commendable degree of prosperity and influence. Frank Appelt came from his native town of Neu Stadtel, Germany, and after a successful business career in America returned to his native land in old age. He had accumulated his property as a farmer and stock man, and during the later years of his residence at Hallettsville was in the retail liquor business. Though a republican, he filled no public office, and was a member of the Catholic Church. Without special education or training, he nevertheless possessed a remarkable business sense, and he seemed to find it an easy matter to make money. He had to come to America with barely enough money to keep his family until he was able to make his industry productive, and after getting started was twice burned out, and lost practically all his accumulation. When he retired from business he was the owner of extensive lands around Hallettsville and in Lavaca County, and at the time of his returning to Germany was one of the largest taxpayers in the county. Frank Appelt married Miss Antonio Appelt, of the same name but not related, and she died in Hallettsville March 10, 1913, at the venerable age of ninety-four. Their children were: William, Antone, who spent his life in Lavaca County as a merchant and farmer and left a family there; August, likewise a farmer and contributing to

FRANK APPELT

MRS. FRANK APPELT

Mr and Mrs W. E. Appelt
and Family

the family reputation for successful efforts; Louis, who lives in Hallettsville, as does his twin sister, Mrs. Annie Kuntz; and Joseph, who spent his life partly as a farmer and partly in the retail liquor business, and left a family at Hallettsville at his death.

The late William Appelt came to Texas in 1852 with his father, and his limited education came largely through his individual efforts. When a young man of twenty-two he took up merchandising in Hallettsville, and for about twenty-five or thirty years was in business under his own name, and was succeeded by his brother, Antone. William Appelt spent about six years on his farm, which he had carried on while an active merchant, and then returned to mercantile lines at his old stand in the building he had erected and which still belongs to his estate. After a few years he was succeeded by his sons, W. E. and J. H. Appelt, and his son-in-law, W. J. Miller. During the war William Appelt, while not a Confederate soldier, did some service by hauling cotton to Mexico, which was then the only open market for that class of merchandise. He also continued as a merchant, and in the aggregate his business success outranked that of his father. He owned a large body of land in Jackson County, used for pasturage, and kept it stocked and was one of the leading cattle men on the coast country. He bred much improved stock, and had his ranch stocked with the Hereford and the Red Poll cattle. It has been said that his life was one continuous span of hustle, and in that characteristic he was perhaps the most conspicuous man in Lavaca County. He did not give up business even in his last hours, and his last act was to pen a letter to his son Emil dealing in detail with business affairs. William Appelt died as the result of a surgical operation at New Orleans. As a voter he was a republican, and his sons followed in his footsteps. He was a member of the Catholic Church, and as a citizen his life was one actuated by human sympathy, and his money was many times used for the relief of distress, not for the advancement of his own interests, and found many channels of practical charity and benevolence. He donated money for the construction of the Aransas Pass Railway, and was one of the committee to secure the right of way for that road. When he died in his sixty-second year there was a tribute in a local paper, and some of its words should be quoted at this point. "He had lived in Lavaca County since a mere lad, and had by his enormous energy, native shrewdness and clear brain amassed a handsome fortune. He made a success in every venture, merchant, cattleman and farmer. He never knew what it was to be tired, for a constitution of iron backed his business career. He was a man of strong traits of character, true to his friends and fearless of his enemies. In his death Lavaca County loses a staunch citizen and a good man."

William Appelt was married in Lavaca County by Rev. C. Eugene Stephen February 25, 1867, to Miss Amelia Pagel. Her father, Gustav Pagel, was another pioneer of Lavaca County, having come to Texas not long after the Appelt family. He was identified with the county as a farmer, was a successful man, and had his home in what is known as the Pagel settlement. Gustav Pagel was twice married and all his children were by his first wife, namely: William of Fayette County; Charley of Lavaca County, one of the most successful farmers of that section; Fritz, who during his rather short life placed his name among the successful agriculturists of Lavaca County; Ernst, who for a number of years has been a farmer at Tivola; Julius, a well to do rancher in Jackson County; the oldest daughter, Mrs. Fischer of Austin County; Fredrica, wife of Fritz Ludwig of Breslau, Texas; and Mrs. Appelt, who was the fifth child and who died in 1913. William Appelt and wife had the following children: Emil; Antonio, wife of Steve Alblinger of Hallettsville;

Julius H. of Hallettsville; Lena, who married C. J. Elstner of Lavaca County; Bertha, who married W. J. Miller of Hallettsville; Oscar, of Sutton County; Frank, of Ector County; Augusta, wife of Robert Ragsdale of Hallettsville; and William, of Hallettsville.

W. Emil Appelt, the oldest of his father's children, grew up in Hallettsville and acquired his early education in the public schools. As soon as he had reached the age of economic usefulness, he divided his time between his father's store and the ranch, and for a short time was associated with his brother and brother-in-law in the merchandise business. But his chief career and his forte as a business man has been in the cattle business. He became identified with the Jackson County ranch, but later sold his interests there and moved his stock and ranch headquarters to Ector County, in West Texas, where he and his brother Frank own and lease 30,000 acres. All of it is under fence, stocked with cattle and horses, and the Herefords are the prevailing cattle they handle. Their business is ranching pure and simple, and after the stock is grown they sell to the feeders from Kansas, Oklahoma and other northern states. In Lavaca County Mr. Appelt has interests as a farmer, and though absent in West Texas during the spring, summer and fall months on his ranch, still maintains his home in Hallettsville.

Like others of the family, Mr. Appelt has taken no active part in politics, and as a voter has cast his ballot usually with the republican party. About ten years ago he took the Master degree in Masonry at the Hallettsville Lodge, and that is his only fraternity.

In Lavaca County on December 5, 1892, Mr. Appelt married Miss Annie Speary, daughter of John Speary. Her father, who came from Switzerland, was a member of an old family in Lavaca County, was for many years identified with the saloon business at Hallettsville, and though coming to this country without means, died in independent circumstances. John Speary married Matilda Frederick. Their children were: Mrs. Appelt; Leona, wife of Herman Schultz of Lavaca County; Miss Elizabeth of Hallettsville; Mrs. Minnie Mollert of Hackberry; John, of Lavaca County; Mrs. Lena Heye of Hallettsville; Albert, of San Antonio; August, of Runge; and Miss Martha of Hallettsville. Mr. and Mrs. Appelt are the parents of two children, Elma and Lillie.

Henry W. Matthews. To Henry W. Matthews has come the attainment of a prominent position in connection with the agricultural and stock-raising business of the state. His life achievements worthily illustrate what may be attained by persistent and painstaking effort. He is a man of progressive ideas and exactness and thoroughness characterize all his attainments. He has cultivated and improved six distinct farms in Gonzales County and at the present time, in 1916, has 2,100 acres, 1,400 under cultivation, devoted to the popular crops of this section.

William A. Matthews, father of the subject of this review, was born in the State of Vermont, in 1800, and he lived there until he had reached his seventeenth year when he went West and joined Col. Green DeWitt in Missouri. They came to Texas in 1824, and Mr. Matthews married a daughter of the colonel. The latter was a great colonizer and did much for the development of Southern Texas. In this work Mr. Matthews joined him and both are remembered with great gratitude by the early settlers of the state. When ready to settle down for himself Mr. Matthews chose a farm on the banks of the Guadalupe River, about two miles from Gonzales. He was a great speculator and dealt largely in slave property and in horses and cattle. His land accumulations were scattered widely over the state and while he was regarded as one of the largest slave owners in Texas, he was also prominent as a farmer, and at that time was the largest land and stock owner in Texas. He was not in the public eye save as the largeness of his affairs attracted public attention. He was specially popular through this immediate section because of the substantial aid he rendered settlers and because of his distinction as a pioneer. By his first marriage to Miss DeWitt he had one son, William, Jr., who died in early youth. Mrs. Matthews died shortly after her marriage and for his second wife Mr. Matthews chose Miss Nancy King, a daughter of John G. King, an early settler in this state. Mr. King married Millie Parchman and they were parents of the following children: Mrs. Matthews; William, who was killed in the Alamo; Polly, wife of Robert Hall, of Gonzales County: she is deceased and is survived by a number of children; Eliza married William Foster and left issue in Gonzales County, as did also Millie, who was the wife of Halsey Miller; John was a ranchman on an island in the Gulf of Mexico and acquired wealth as a stockman; Thomas, a large farmer in Gonzales County, married a Miss Harris and left issue; and James, a wealthy ranchman in Karnes County prior to his demise, married Mattie Morrison and left several children. William A. Matthews passed to the life eternal in 1856 and is interred in the Masonic cemetery in Gonzales. His second wife died in 1890, aged seventy-one years. Their union was prolific of the following children: Almyra, wife of James F. Miller, an attorney in Gonzales and former congressman of this district; Almeda married Newton Hammon and passed her life in Gonzales County; Alvina married, first, Charles Mason and, second, Asa W. Harmon, of Gonzales; Susan is the widow of Whit Ramsey, of Gonzales; Thomas spent many years of his life in the cattle business in Wyoming and died in Spearfish, South Dakota: he married Fannie Walker and is survived by a son, Thomas, Jr., who has a family and lives in South Dakota; William died as a youth; and Henry Walter is the immediate subject of this sketch.

Henry Walter Matthews was born in Gonzales County, Texas, January 21, 1857, and he grew up on the old homestead near Gonzales. He attended school in this city and in Seguin and prior to reaching his majority was identified with the cattle business in Wyoming. In 1881, with his brother, he drove some 1,500 cattle over the trail by way of Dodge City, Kansas, locating on the Bellefourch River, twenty miles south of Gillett, Wyoming. While Mr. Matthews has been interested in the stock business in Wyoming for the past thirty-one years he has always maintained his home in Gonzales and carried on farming in this vicinity. He has been prominently identified with home-building and farm improvement, having purchased and improved six distinct farms. He now has 2,100 acres, 1,400 under cultivation, devoted to the crops peculiar to this section. A great deal of his farm land is in Wilson County and he has some fifty people in his employ. For the past twenty years he has lived in Gonzales and here owns two beautiful residences. His own mansion, of gray brick, was erected in 1912.

Mr. Matthews is not interested in politics except as a voter on the democratic ticket. He is not a lodge man but he has been a member of the Methodist Episcopal Church for a quarter of a century and is one of its board of stewards.

March 10, 1885, in Gonzales County, was solemnized the marriage of Mr. Matthews to Miss Bettie Askey, a daughter of Harrison Askey, who came to Texas from Arkansas prior to the outbreak of the Civil war. Mr. Askey was a farmer and he married Miss Catherine Lloyd. To them were born: Clinton; Lou, wife of John Nixon; Julia, wife of Thomas Morrison; Annie died as a young lady; Mrs. Matthews; Katie married T. B. Fussell, of Gonzales; Hat, John and Otho. Mr. and Mrs.

Matthews have one son, John, who is a direct descendant of William King, who was massacred in the Alamo, is a farmer and stockman and owner of a garage in Gonzales. He married Josie Wright and they have a son, John, Jr.

JAMES D. GRAY, M. D. The thriving Town of Shiner, Lavaca County, is favored in having the interposition of a physician and surgeon of such distinctive ability and sterling character as Doctor Gray, who is one of the representative members of his profession in this section of the state and whose thorough and comprehensive technical training has been supplemented by broad and varied practical experience, his success offering the most effective voucher for his professional ability and his command of popular confidence and esteem. The doctor insistently observes the best ethical ideals of his exacting vocation, has deep appreciation of the responsibilities which it imposes and labors with all of zeal and earnestness in the alleviation of human suffering. His professional loyalty and civic progressiveness were significantly shown by his establishing, on the 1st of May, 1912, the Shiner Surgical Hospital, of which he is the owner and executive head and which proves a most valuable adjunct to the work which he and his confreres are doing in the local field of professional endeavor, the hospital, with excellent modern appointments and facilities, being designed for the reception of patients for both medical and surgical treatment and being open to the patrons of all reputable physicians.

Doctor Gray has been a resident of Texas since he was a lad of thirteen years and here he is well upholding the dignity and usefulness of a profession in which his honored father had likewise achieved marked success and precedence. He was born near Cado Gap, Montgomery County, Arkansas, on the 7th of March, 1871, and in 1884 he accompanied his parents on their removal from that state to Texas. His father, Dr. George W. Gray, was a native of Virginia and was a scion of a family that was founded in the historic Old Dominion in the colonial era of our national history. As a boy he accompanied his parents on their removal to Corinth, Mississippi, where he was reared to adult age and acquired a good common-school education. In preparation for his chosen profession he entered a medical school in the City of Atlanta, Georgia, and after his graduation he came to the West and established his residence in Montgomery County, Arkansas, where he engaged in the practice of his profession, to which he there gave his attention for many years. In 1884 he came with his family to Texas, and he here became one of the prominent and highly esteemed physicians engaged in practice in Comanche and Eastland counties. He passed the gracious evening of his long and useful life at Gorman, Comanche County, where he died in 1908, when nearly eighty-three years of age. He was a staunch adherent of the democratic party but was a man of quiet reserve and had no predilection for the activities of politics or public office, preferring to devote himself without reservation to the work of the humane vocation for which he had fitted himself and in which it was his to give long years of self-abnegating and effective service. He was a Master Mason and was a consistent member of the Baptist Church. Earlier generations of the family were found principally identified with agricultural pursuits, as prosperous Southern planters, but several of his brothers went forth from Corinth, Mississippi, to become prominent and successful in professional and business life. In Montgomery County, Arkansas, Dr. George W. Gray wedded Miss Melissa Freeman, daughter of one of the pioneer physicians of that county, and she died when her youngest child, Doctor Gray of this review, was an infant. The older children are Joseph Gray, M. D., who is engaged in the practice of his profession at Comanche, Texas; Adaline, who is the wife of William Richland, their home being in the State of Oklahoma; Charles J., who is a representative member of the bar of the City of San Antonio; and Alice, who is the wife of William Hollyfield, of Comanche County. For his second wife Dr. George W. Gray wedded Rebecca Gore, who, with several children, survives him and who still resides at Gorman, Comanche County.

The earlier educational discipline of Dr. James D. Gray was obtained in the public schools of his native state, and after the family removal to Texas he continued his studies in the schools of Comanche and Eastland counties. When about seventeen years of age he left the paternal roof and initiated his independent career. After a few months of employment as a farm hand in Comanche County he assumed a position as clerk in a dry-goods store at Gorman, that county, where he remained thus engaged about three years. He was then induced by his brother, Dr. Joseph Gray, to engage in the drug business in an independent way, though at the time he had no practical knowledge of this line of enterprise. While conducting a drug store at Gorman he not only became a practical pharmacist but also gave close study along lines that would aid in his preparation for the medical profession, to enter which his ambition prompted him. He finally entered the Marion Sims Medical College, in the City of St. Louis, Missouri, and while he was there a student his drug store was destroyed by fire. His staunch friends in the wholesale drug trade came to his rescue and enabled him to re-establish his drug business, his brother, Dr. Joseph Gray, kindly giving personal supervision to the store and business while he himself was completing his college course. From Marion Sims Medical College Dr. Gray finally withdrew and he entered Beaumont Medical College, in which institution, which is now the medical department of the University of St. Louis, he was graduated in 1901, duly receiving his well earned degree of Doctor of Medicine.

After his graduation Doctor Gray disposed of his drug store and engaged in the general practice of his profession at Lacasa, Stephens County, Texas, whence, a year later, he removed to Whitney, Hill County, where he likewise practiced one year. He then, in 1897, removed to Lavaca County and established his residence at Moulton, where he continued in successful practice until his removal to Shiner, this county, in 1904. In this community he controls a large and representative practice, with high standing both as a physician and as a surgeon, and it has already been noted that he has amplified the scope of efficacy of his work by the establishing of the Shiner Surgical Hospital, to the supervision of which he gives the closest of personal attention and which he has brought up to high standard.

Doctor Gray continued a close and appreciative student of the best in the standard and periodical literature of his profession and thus keeps in touch with the advances made in both medical and surgical science, this object being further conserved through his active affiliation with the Texas State Medical Society and the American Medical Association. He is a man of fine physical presence, is alert, vigorous and ambitious, broad in mental ken, mature in judgment and thus splendidly qualified by natural predilections as well as excellent technical preparation, for the exacting and responsible duties of his humane profession, which he has considered worthy of his undivided fealty and attention, so that he has had neither desire or time to enter the arena of practical politics or to serve in public office. He was one of the promoters of the cotton-compress industry established at Shiner, and is a stockholder in the company organized for the carrying forward of the enterprise.

On the 31st of December, 1899, at Moulton, Lavaca County, was solemnized the marriage of Doctor Gray to Miss Alma Kubitz, whose father, Doctor Kubitz, was a native of Texas, a graduate of the medical department of Tulane University, in the City of New Orleans, after which he was engaged in the practice of his profession in Fayette County until his untimely death, when he was still a young man. Doctor and Mrs. Gray have two children—Maurine and Willis.

CHARLES L. KOPECKY, M. D. The same ambition and worthy purpose that led Doctor Kopecky to bend his energies to preparing himself thoroughly for the work of his exacting profession have been the dominating forces that have combined with his sterling personal character to insure his distinctive success in his profession, of which he is one of the prominent and honored representatives in Lavaca County, with residence and headquarters in the Village of Shiner. He is a native Texan and is a scion of a family that was founded in the Lone Star State nearly sixty years ago.

Doctor Kopecky was born at Sweet Home, Lavaca County, on the 31st of May, 1882, and is a son of Joseph and Philomena (Janca) Kopecky, who passed the closing years of their lives on their fine homestead farm near Shiner, Lavaca County, the latter having been called to the life eternal on the 3d of November, 1896, and the former having passed away in October, 1906, at a venerable age.

A son of a prosperous farmer and stone mason in the Province of Moravia, Austria, Joseph Kopecky was there born and reared, and he received excellent educational advantages in his youth. The Kopecky family were of the Bohemian district of Moravia, and Joseph Kopecky was not only thoroughly familiar with his native, or Bohemian, language, but learned also to speak with fluency the German language, so that his training aided him greatly in the facile accumulation of the English language after he had come to America. In 1858, when sixteen years of age, he severed the home ties and set forth to seek his fortunes in the United States. His reinforcement consisted of the mental and physical vigor of sturdy youth and an ambition to win for himself independence and prosperity through individual effort. Soon after his arrival in America he made his way to Lavaca County, Texas, and, with virtually no financial resources, he depended upon manual labor to obtain a start in the land of his adoption. As a ranch hand he was employed by Mr. Allen, the well known pioneer of the Sweet Home community, and this initial occupation, though it did not give to him more than nominal compensation in a monetary way, did afford him an opportunity to earn money, the while his good judgment and frugality made him carefully save his earnings from the beginning until he had accumulated a sufficient amount to purchase a small farm in the Sweet Home district. After his marriage he there continued his operations as a farmer for a few years, and after having made good improvements on the place he finally sold the property and removed with his family to the fine Kessler prairie, on which the Town of Shiner was later developed. He was one of the first settlers—and the first Bohemian resident—of this section of Lavaca County, and here he purchased 800 acres of raw prairie land, at the rate of five dollars an acre. After breaking an appreciable acreage of the wild land he engaged in the raising of cotton, and the passing years brought to him large and merited prosperity. As circumstances justified he expanded his land holdings, until he became the owner of one of the extensive and valuable landed estates of Lavaca County, his large domain providing homes and profitable employment for many tenants and his operations as a planter, general agriculturist and minor stock-grower reaching such compass as to make him one of the foremost representatives of these lines of industry in Lavaca County. He was a recognized leader in the civic, business and industrial affairs of the Shiner community, his fine homestead being situated on Rocky Creek, only a quarter of a mile distant from Shiner. He assisted in splendid degree in the development and progress of this now favored section and when the first railroad line was projected he gave for the same the right of way across his farm. Though prominent and influential in local affairs of a public order he had no desire for the activities of politics, but as soon as possible after establishing his home in Texas he became a naturalized citizen and aligned himself as a supporter of the generic cause of the democratic party. Both he and his wife were devout communicants of the Catholic Church, and he was one of the promoters and charter members of the parish organization at Shiner, besides contributing most liberally to the erection of the church edifice. His devoted wife, who was his true helpmeet during the years that he was laboring to establish himself and to win the goal of prosperity, was a daughter of Charles Janca, who immigrated to Texas from Bohemia, in the '60s, and who became a prosperous farmer in Fayette County. Of the children of Joseph and Philomena (Janca) Kopecky the eldest is Agnes, who is the wife of J. J. Kutach, of Yoakum, Dewitt County; Joseph F. is a resident and influential citizen of Hallettsville, the judicial center of Lavaca County, where he is editor and publisher of the Novy Domov, a Bohemian paper; Dr. Charles L., of this review, was the next in order of birth; Lena is the wife of Charles Strauss, of Shiner; Rosa is the wife of Philip Bartosh, of Prague, Oklahoma; Millie is the wife of Frank Merta and they likewise reside at Prague, Lincoln County, Oklahoma; August maintains his residence in the City of Lincoln, Nebraska; and Frances is the wife of Henry Strauss, of Weimar, Texas.

Dr. Charles L. Kopecky was reared to adult age on his father's extensive landed estate near Shiner, and he attended the rural schools until the Village of Shiner was founded, when he was able to continue his studies in the newly established public schools of this town. He finally entered St. Edward's College, in the City of Austin, where he remained as a student until he had attained to the age of sixteen years, when he manifested his independence and patriotic spirit by enlisting in the United States army. He enlisted as a private in Company D, Sixth Regiment of United States Infantry, commanded by Colonel Burns, and his initial service in the ranks was at Fort Sam Houston. He finally accompanied his regiment to San Francisco, from which point the command was sent to the Philippine Islands, where the regiment gained active and varied experience in campaign work and also served on police duty. Doctor Kopecky took part in the battle of the Waterworks at Manila, and thereafter served with his regiment on the more southern islands of the Philippine group, including Panay, Negros, Cebu, Bohol and Leyte. On Panay the regiment had frequent engagements with the insurrectos and captured the towns of Iloilo and Santa Barbara. The command next proceeded to Bohol, to avenge the massacre of the Ninth Infantry, and after successfully achieving the desired end it went to the Island of Leyte, where it took part in a vigorous campaign against the insurgent natives and followed the terse advice of Colonel Smith, to "lick hell out of them." Thereafter the regiment was assigned to police duty on the Island of Negros. Doctor Kopecky lived up to the full tension of the military operations on the Oriental isles and his experiences in jungle warfare with the natives must ever figure as an interesting feature in the history of his career, his fine mentality and alert observative powers having enabled him to gain much and varied information in the Orient, so that his reminiscences concerning his own experiences and incidents and conditions in the Philippines are specially graphic and interesting,—well worthy of perpetuation in published form, to which he should commit them. He remained in the Philippines from March, 1899, until 1902, in the early spring of which year he returned with his regiment to San Francisco, where he received his honorable discharge in April of that year. The regiment crossed the Pacific to the Philippines on the transport Sherman, and returned on the Sheridan. The Doctor made a splendid record as a soldier and he perpetuates the more pleasing memories of his military career through affiliation with the United Spanish-American War Veterans.

In the autumn of 1903 Doctor Kopecky, a youthful military veteran, returned to Texas, and in directing his attention to the pursuits of peace he determined to prepare himself for the profession in which he has since achieved marked success and prestige. His preliminary medical course was taken in the Louisville Medical College, . the metropolis of Kentucky, where he continued his studies two years. His loyalty to his native state and its institutions was then shown by his entering the medical department of the University of Fort Worth, in which he was graduated as a member of the class of 1906 and from which he received the degree of Doctor of Medicine. His professional novitiate was served at Nada, Colorado County, where he remained one year. For the ensuing three years he was engaged in practice at Hallettsville, the county seat of his native county, and since November, 1910, he has been earnestly and effectively engaged in general practice at Shiner, where he controls a substantial and representative individual practice and where he has been closely and pleasantly associated with Drs. James D. Gray and G. Shultze in the Shiner Surgical Hospital. The Doctor is identified with the American Medical Association, the Texas State Medical Society, and the medical societies of his home county and congressional district. He is one of the interested principals in the Shiner Drug Company, of which he is a director; is president of the St. Nicodemus Drug Company, of Shiner, engaged in the manufacturing of various pharmaceutical preparations and proprietary remedies; and at the county seat, Hallettsville, he is president of the Ledbetter-Kopecky Drug Company. Doctor Kopecky holds that his professional and business interests merit his unqualified attention, and thus has had no desire for special activity along either political or religious lines, though he is essentially loyal and public-spirited in his civic attitude. He is affiliated with the Knights of Columbus and with the K. J. T. Bohemian Society, of which he is supreme medical examiner.

At Shiner, on the 29th of August, 1906, was solemnized the marriage of Doctor Kopecky to Miss Amelia Strauss, a daughter of Jacob and Amelia (Chapka) Strauss, the former of whom came from Germany to America prior to the Civil war, in which he served as a valiant soldier of the Confederacy, after which he became one of the prosperous farmers of Texas; his wife was born in Moravia, Austria, and was a child of four years at the time of her parents' immigration to the United States, the family home being established in Texas, where she was reared and educated. Of the children of Doctor and Mrs. Kopecky the first born, Edith, died when one year of age; and the surviving children are Leonard and Leonita.

WILLIAM WATSON

Archie W. Watson. One of the honored ante-bellum families of Texas, founded here in 1859, is that which bears the name of Watson and which is worthily represented at Brenham by Archie Warren Watson, now engaged in the nursery business after a number of years passed in mercantile and kindred lines.

William Watson, the founder of the family in Texas, was born at Drogheda, County Down, Ireland, March 21, 1831, of English parents, his father being William Watson, a native of England, where he secured his education and passed his life as a stockraiser and farmer. The grandfather married Miss Priscilla Reilly, and both passed away in Ireland, their children being: David, who died in Ireland; Elizabeth, who became the wife of Mr. O'Flanagan and came to the United States and settled in Minnesota. William Watson, father of Archie W., was given no college course, but obtained a fair education in the public schools, which he attended until reaching the age of twelve years, this being supplemented by a broad course of reading. He read scientific subjects as well as history and fiction, his knowledge of history and geography being especially comprehensive, and gathered together a library of 4,000 volumes, one of the best libraries to be found in a private home in Texas. As a lad of twelve years he went aboard a sailing vessel and from that time on spent many years on the ocean, crossing the Atlantic no less than twenty-two times, visiting all the important ports of the world, exploring the interior of many of the countries which he visited, and passing two years in merchandising in Africa. He rose to the station of first mate, while his uncle, Captain Jarvis, was first in command of the boat.

Upon coming to America, William Watson passed a few months at Halifax, Nova Scotia, and then moved to the United States and spent a year at Louisville, Kentucky. After the birth of his second child he returned to England, where another child subsequently joined the household, and in 1859 came again to the United States and from his landing point in Galveston, Texas, made his way by rail to Hempstead. When he reached the latter place he counted his cash and found that after he paid some one to bring his family to Brenham he would have just 20 cents left. He told his wife at this time that he was going to reduce his finances so that he would never be able to travel any more.

At Brenham Mr. Watson found employment as a carpenter and the money thus earned was his main support while he was placing his nursery business on a paying basis. Many of the old homes of this locality still stand as monuments to his skill, industry and good workmanship. He was a man of great industry, as well as untiring energy, and his home improvements were made largely during the night and by lantern light after his day's work elsewhere was completed. Mr. Watson started his nursery business at Brenham upon the present site of the Lutheran Church. Beginning with three acres, he added to this tract as his finances would permit and as he could use the land. He established the first nursery in this whole state and an old catalogue shows that trees were sold then for about four times what they would bring now.

In 1869 Mr. Watson moved out to his final home, 2½ miles southeast of Brenham. It was a piece of prairie land with but two trees upon it, and here he opened a 30-acre peach orchard, with as many acres devoted to nursery stock. He grew year by year, shipping peaches, pears and plums to many distant points of the United States and his business ran for some years at more than $100,000 annually, Mr. Watson giving employment to some forty traveling salesmen and from ten to twenty hands. He propagated most of his trees and developed by hybridization the "Rosedale Hybred," known all over the country as a beautiful evergreen. Peaches and plums, new varieties, came from under his developing eye and hand, and his activity and prominence made him nationally known. He was for a number of years president of the Texas Horticultural Association and belonged also to the National Association of Horticulturists, being a regular attendant of its meetings.

Outside of his personal affairs Mr. Watson took a citizen's interest in politics. He had taken part in the Civil war as a member of Colonel Flournoy's regiment, Captain Morole's company, and after serving for a time at Galveston, went on detached duty, remaining actively in the service until the end of the war. He escaped wounds or capture, and after the war always participated in the meetings of the old veterans of the Gray. He went to all democratic conventions, both county and state, and in 1892 was a prominent factor in behalf of Judge George Clark for governor, while his son Archie W. gave his support to Governor James Hogg. Mr. Watson belonged to the Church of England in the mother country, but in Texas was an Episcopalian. He belonged to no order. Although not much of a talker, he was entertaining in conversation and most instructive because of his knowledge of so many practical things and so much about the world from observation. His death occurred in August, 1908.

Mr. Watson married in his native place Miss Sarah Warren, a daughter of Edward Warren, a Presbyterian preacher, who married Priscilla Reilly. The Warren home was at Holly Wood, County Down, Ireland, and the remote ancestor of the family came from Normandy, France, in 920 with William the Conqueror, in the person of William DeWarren. By his first marriage William Watson had seven children, among whom were: William E., of San Antonio; Annie E., who died as Mrs. William Boyle, of Austin; David H., who died at Brenham in 1898, leaving two children: Robert David, and Adele, now of Austin, Texas; Arthur O., an architect of Austin. Mrs. Watson died in 1867, and Mr. Watson was again married to Miss Carrie Thomason, of Alabama, the two surviving children of the eight of this marriage being: John P., secretary and manager of the Perkins-Jones Nursery Company, of Newark, New York; and Stanley H., a well known newspaper man of Texas, associated with the Temple Times. Mrs. Watson lives in New York with her son, John P.

Archie Warren Watson was born November 11, 1859, at Brenham, Texas, beginning life the year the Watson nursery was established. His education was secured in the public school and he was a companion, as it were, of the family's generous library. Save six years his entire life has been passed in Washington County. As a young man he evidenced an independent spirit when he left home to do something for himself, securing employment as a day laborer in the construction of the Erie Telegraph and Telephone Company. That he possessed the ability to "make good" is shown by the fact that within fifteen days he was made foreman of construction in the building of the exchange at Marshall, Texas, and within another month was managing the exchange at Denison. He spent a year in the latter capacity and was then made manager of the telegraph and telephone office at Austin, but in 1887, at the earnest solicitation of his father, returned home and associated himself with the elder man in the nursery business. He was so connected for two years and then embarked in the mercantile business, ginning and general farming, at Stone, now Lusk, Texas. Mr. Watson built the gin and sold goods from 1889 until 1910, when he purchased the old Watson home and since that time has been engaged in the nursery business. Like his father, he is a propagator and is now engaged in restoring the old plant to something of its former prestige.

Mr. Watson has always taken a warm interest in politics. He votes the democratic ticket, has never scratched one, and in the good old days when candidates were chosen from men of capability always attended conventions. He has been precinct chairman, presiding judge of election, and in charge of the box on election day, and comparing the present primary system with the old convention method is convinced that the former is a failure in achieving fair results and in securing the most capable officials. Fraternally, Mr. Watson is a Pythian and is prominent in the Woodmen of the World, being past chancellor, former representative to the grand lodge for ten years, and at present district deputy grand chancellor of the Eighteenth District. A close Bible student, he is active in the work of the Christian Church, being an elder of the Brenham congregation and a Bible School teacher for many years. The Watson home is a large country mansion of the style peculiar to the tastes of its builder, William Watson. Its spacious rooms were provided for the accommodation of a numerous posterity at "home-comings," and the library and reading room, the mental workshop of its owner, occupies a space 16x30 feet.

Mr. Watson was married August 31, 1884, to Miss Katie Roberson, who was born March 10, 1863, daughter of Andrew J. and Martha (Ball) Roberson. Mr. Roberson was a farmer, came from Mississippi in 1848, and was a Confederate soldier of Greene's Brigade. Mr. and Mrs. Watson have no children.

D. Cicero Daniel. Numbered among the representative factors in connection with business activities in his native county, where his popularity is such as to make incongruous any application of the biblical aphorism that a prophet is not without honor save in his own country, David Cicero Daniel is manager of the Shiner Oil Mill & Manufacturing Company, which represents one of the most important industrial enterprises in the thriving Town of Shiner, Lavaca County.

Mr. Daniel was born in Lavaca County on the 29th of October, 1874, and is a son of Joseph R. and Maggie (Dew) Daniel, both natives of Yazoo County, Mississippi, in which state their respective fathers were planters and slaveholders prior to the Civil war, both families having early been founded in the South and Mrs. Daniel having been the daughter of Christian Dew, who was a prosperous planter in Mississippi at the time of his death.

Reared under the conditions and institutions of the old regime in the fair Southland, Joseph R. Daniel, who was born in the year 1846, passed the period of his childhood and early youth on the home plantation and his early educational advantages were those afforded in the field schools of the rural districts of Mississippi. He was not old enough to be eligible for service at the opening of the Civil war, but it is needless to say that he was as a youth signally loyal to the cause of the Confederacy, though circumstances prevented him from entering military service even after he reached an age that made this practicable. He was not yet twenty years old at the close of the war.

In his native commonwealth Joseph R. Daniel initiated his independent career as an agriculturist, and in 1871 he came with his young wife to Texas, the trip having been made by railroad to Columbus, this state, from which point Mr. Daniel continued his journey with team and wagon to Lavaca County. He purchased land near the present Village of Shiner, although the site of the town was at that time an unbroken prairie, and for his land he paid at the rate of $4 an acre. Through industry and good management he developed a productive farm, and here he continued his activities as an agriculturist and stock-grower until 1896, when he removed to Victoria County, where for several years he was engaged in the lumber business, in the Village of Inez. After disposing of this business he resumed operations as a farmer and stock-raiser, and he remains one of the substantial citizens of prominence and influence in Victoria County. His political allegiance has ever been given unequivocally to the democratic party and though he has shown distinctive civic loyalty and public spirit he has had no desire for political preferment, his interest in the cause of education having been such, however, that he consented to serve for a number of terms in the office of school trustee. His religious faith is that of the Baptist Church, of which his wife likewise was a devoted member, her death having occurred at Inez, Victoria County, in January, 1906. Of the children the eldest is Oscar H., who is a prosperous farmer near Richmond, Fort Bend County; D. Cicero, of this review, is the next in order of birth; Joseph B. was a successful agriculturist in Victoria County at the time of his death and is survived by his wife, whose maiden name was Nannie Belle Koontz, and by one son, Barney; Robert T., the youngest of the sons, is a progressive ranchman in Dewitt County.

D. Cicero Daniel is indebted to the rural schools and the public schools of Shiner for his early educational discipline, and that he made good use of the advantages thus afforded him is indicated by the fact that when nineteen years of age he put his scholastic attainments to practical test and use by engaging in teaching. For two years he was thus identified with the pedagogic profession as a successful and popular teacher in the rural schools of this section of his native state.

In 1896 Mr. Daniel assumed the position of bookkeeper in the office of the Shiner cottonseed oil mill, and with the concern he has since continued in active service, his ability as an executive and as a business man of circumspection and mature judgment having led to his advancement, in 1904, to the position of manager of the business and the mill, an office of which he has since continued the valued incumbent. The plant of the Shiner Oil Mill & Manufacturing Company includes a well equipped machine shop, and this auxilliary department of the business is one of important order. Mr. Daniel is a stockholder and director of this company, the Shiner Oil Mill & Manufacturing Company, and also is a director of the adjunct company operating the machine shop and garage. In the West End Addition of Shiner Mr. Daniel erected his attractive and essentially modern house, and this is one of the best residence properties in one of the finest parts of the town.

The democratic party has always enlisted the unqualified allegiance of Mr. Daniel and he is now serving his second term as a member of the board of aldermen of Shiner, in which body he held, in 1915, the chairmanship of the improvement committee that has in charge the drilling of wells and the construction of a reservoir to increase and render more healthful the municipal water supply of the village. He is past chancellor of the local lodge of the Knights of Pythias, and for a number of years was deputy grand chancellor of the grand lodge of Texas. He is affiliated also with the Praetorians, and he and his wife hold membership in the Baptist Church. It may further be stated that Mr. Daniel is a scion of a family that early became one of no little prominence and influence in Georgia, from which historic commonwealth David Daniel, grandfather of the subject of this review, removed to Mississippi, where he became a successful planter and where he passed the remainder of his life. He was too advanced in years to be eligible for service as a soldier in the Civil war. He was twice married and Joseph R., father of him whose name initiates this article, was the only child of the second marriage.

On the 4th of July, 1899, at Pearsall, Frio County, was solemnized the marriage of D. Cicero Daniel to Miss Mamie Cox, a daughter of John Frank Cox and Belle (Smith) Cox, who now maintain their home at Shiner, where Mr. Cox is a carpenter and builder by vocation; he is a native of Texas and in earlier years gave his attention principally to the cattle industry. Mrs. Daniel, who was born May 4, 1880, is the younger of the two children, and her brother, Edward P., is now a resident of Columbus, New Mexico. Mr. and Mrs. Daniel have two children—Margaret Isabel and David Franklin.

Henry Dreyer. Coming with his parents to Texas when he was a lad of seven years, Mr. Dreyer has here maintained his home for more than seventy years and his memory forms an indissoluble link between the remote pioneer era and the latter days of opulent prosperity and progress in the Lone Star State. His life has been one of signal honor and usefulness and he stands today as one of the representative and honored citizens of Lavaca County, his place of residence being the thriving Town of Shiner.

Henry Dreyer was born in the Town of Saltzufel, Prussia, on the 24th of January, 1836, and is a son of A. H. and Charlotte (Potthast) Dreyer, Mrs. Dreyer having been a widow at the time of her marriage to A. H. Dreyer and having had one son by her previous marriage—August Weller, who accompanied the family on the immigration to America and who became a prominent and influential citizen of Colorado County, Texas, where he left a family and where the Town of Wellersburg was named in his honor.

In 1842 A. H. Dreyer and his family embarked at Bremen, Germany, on the sailing vessel Francisco, and this sturdy old-time boat provided them transportation to their destination at Galveston, Texas, the voyage having been thirteen weeks in duration and the only special incident to break its monotony having been when a stop was made at a port in Cuba, to replenish the stock of fresh water. Henry Dreyer, of this review, was a lad of about seven years at the time and recalls vividly the voyage across the Atlantic, the novelty of the same having made due appeal to his boyish imagination and interest. After landing at Galveston the family proceeded by boat to Houston, from which latter point the onward journey to Columbus, Colorado County, was made with a wagon and six yoke of oxen, young Henry having at this time gained his first impressions of frontier freighting, a line of enterprise with which he himself was destined to become identified in later years. Columbus was then a mere village, and that it was the judicial center of Colorado County was indicated by its possession of a dignified courthouse constructed of logs and with dimension about equal to an ordinary living room of the present-day dwelling in this section of the state. Mr. Mallek was at the time the only German citizen in Columbus, and he gave cordial greeting to the family from his Fatherland. A. H. Dreyer found himself in lamentable financial straits upon his arrival in America, as, prior to the sailing from Bremen, a thief had bored holes in the trunk in which the family money was placed and had succeeded in abstracting the funds on which dependence was placed for the establishing of a suitable home after arrival in America. With a few dollars from his small remaining cash capital, Mr. Dreyer purchased a small tract of land on Skull Creek and there initiated farming on a very modest scale,—raising corn and a little cotton. As this section was then overrun with wild hogs he was able to provide meat for the home larder, and the family subsisted principally on corn bread and bacon. Hogs and cattle were so cheap that it hardly paid to handle them on the farms of the locality, and cattle hides were of such little value that they were hung on fences to rot or else made into rawhide ropes.

In his native land A. H. Dreyer had been a manufacturer of tobacco, and finally he removed from his original pioneer farm in Texas to the vicinity of Oakland, in the same county, where he farmed for a time and then turned his attention to the growing and manufacturing of tobacco, being the first in that section to follow these lines of enterprise and one of the first in Colorado County to become a manufacturer of cigars. At Oakland he continued to maintain his home during the residue of his worthy and useful life, and there he died, in 1873, at the age of sixty-eight years. He was an upright, industrious and substantial citizen who made for himself a secure place in popular confidence and good will and he commanded the high regard of all who knew him in the state of his adoption. He seemed fully to appreciate American institutions and advantages, became a naturalized citizen, voted the democratic ticket and at the time of the Civil war was in full sympathy with the cause of the Confederacy, his two sons having served as Confederate soldiers. He acquired the use of the English language and was a man of superior mental force and of mature judgment. Both he and his wife were zealous and consistent communicants of the Lutheran Church, and Mrs. Dreyer passed to the life eternal within a short time after the family home had been established in Texas, her death having occurred at Columbus, in 1845. Of the three children the eldest was Amelia, who became the wife of Henry Bock and who passed the closing years of her life at Weimar, Colorado County; Henry, of this review, was the next in order of birth; and Hermann died in Wharton County, being survived by a number of children.

Henry Dreyer is thus the only surviving representative of this sterling family that came to Texas in the pioneer days, and such were the exigencies and conditions of time and place that he never attended school a day in his life, his education having been gained by self-application and in the school of practical experience. It early became incumbent upon him to assist in the support of the family, as his father had hard work to "make both ends meet." Mr. Dreyer did not learn to read until after he had gone forth as a soldier of the Confederacy. While he was absent from home and doing valiant service as a soldier, his wife would write letters to him in German, also providing him with a copy of the German alphabet, with which he had sufficient familiarity to enable him by its means to decipher the words in her letters, though each letter demanded of him about four hours to accomplish this result. He eventually learned to read a little of both German and English, and though he has never acquired any technical knowledge of mathematics his facility and accuracy in mental calculations have always been a matter of astonishment to those who have been informed that only by this means does he handle his mathematical problems. Those well versed in theoretical knowledge cannot often excell him in rapidity and assurance of calculations incidental to financial transactions, including the purchase and sale of stock and lands, and his ability shows the working out of the natural law of compensation.

Mr. Dreyer recalls that when the family arrived in Colorado County there was but one house between Columbus and Gonzales, this being the home of Mrs. Brocker, on Peach Creek, and about half way between Gonzales and the present town of Shiner. Mr. Dreyer's father was given several leagues of land by the Government of the Republic of Texas, but he considered the land valueless, as at that time any person could settle on any tract which he chose, without fear of molestation. One of his leagues of land the father of Mr. Dreyer traded for a clock, as he believed that the land would never be worth anything. Another of the tracts which he held was that which later became known as the Clements League, a part of which was purchased a few years ago by his son Henry, of this sketch, at a fancy price.

When about sixteen years of age Henry Dreyer considered himself fortunate in being able to enter the ranger service, as a member of Capt. Henry McCullough's company, and as a ranger his service was principally in the country around San Antonio. For a period of about two years he was on active duty as one of the famous Texas Rangers, and he participated in a number of fights with the hostile Comanche Indians. At the expiration of his service as a frontier ranger Mr. Dreyer returned home, and thereafter he was employed as driver of freighting teams and also in the driving of cattle. With these lines of enterprise he was identified in an independent or individual way at the time when the Civil war was precipitated on a divided nation, and in the meanwhile he had brought with his freighting outfit many new German families from Houston to the section of the state in which he himself resided.

In 1861, soon after the inception of the war, Mr. Dreyer enlisted in Company C, commanded by Captain Ford, and this company became a part of Colonel Bates' regiment in General Magruder's command. The regiment first went to the mouth of the Brazos River, and the command continued its service in Texas until 1863, when it was ordered into Louisiana, where many of the men in Colonel Bates' regiment were sacrificed in the battle at Mansfield, in April, 1864. The regiment was in Texas at the close of the war, but Mr. Dreyer had received his honorable discharge some time previously, after being incapacitated by an attack of typhoid fever.

After the war Mr. Dreyer resumed his operations as a farmer and cattleman, and finally he established at the old town of Wellersburg, near Oakland, Colorado County, a mill operated by steam power. Here he not only sawed logs, but also ginned cotton and ground corn, his operations along these lines continuing several years. He hauled his cornmeal to points as far distant as Beeville, Bee County, and found a ready sale for the product among the cattle men. He finally sold his mill and removed with his family to Columbus, where he established a similar manufacturing plant and where he continued his successful business operations several years,—until a severe flood of the river ruined his plant. He sold what was left of appreciable value and then returned to Oakland, where his best efforts were little more fruitful than in permitting him to eke out a living for himself and his family. About this time he gained fame as a rail-maker, with a record for chopping 300 fence rails in a single day, and though he thus emulated the example of the noble Lincoln he has never felt that his prowess added in the least to his eligibility for the presidency of the United States. This arduous labor, his work in plowing among stumps and in doing other pioneer tasks of the hardest kind, sapped his physical energies and he wisely determined to remove to a prairie district, where such formidable odds were not to be overcome. He finally moved with his family to the rich prairie district of Lavaca County, where he purchased 1,000 acres of land, entirely unimproved, and initiated his successful enterprise as a farmer and cattle-grower. For land that is now worth $100 an acre he paid at the rate of only $5.75 an acre, and the appreciation in values, incidental to the development and general progress of the country, has alone tended to bring to him substantial financial independence. On the estate mentioned Mr. Dreyer continued his residence twenty-four years, and the land today gives full evidence of the energy, progressiveness and good judgment which he brought to bear in its reclamation and improvement. He fenced the property, erected good buildings and showed much circumspection in ordering all departments of his farm industry, with the result that large and well merited success attended his efforts. He finally divided the landed estate among his children, who still own and reside upon the property.

A number of years after coming into possession of the property above mentioned, Mr. Dreyer became associated with two other men in the purchase of nearly 7,000 acres of land on the Guadaloupe River, and of this extensive domain he now owns individually about 1,800 acres. Upon the property he had made good improvements, including the erection of twenty-two tenant houses, and the land is well fenced, the major part of its area being under effective cultivation. This land also has been divided among his children, and thus it will be seen that this sterling pioneer has the utmost paternal solicitude, even as his children accord him an equal filial devotion. On the estate last mentioned was formerly established the postoffice designated by the name of Dreyer, and the community is still known as Dreyer.

In 1905 Mr. Dreyer removed to the attractive village of Shiner, where he is the owner of an attractive residence property, upon which he has made numerous improvements, and here he is living virtually retired, in the enjoyment of the well earned rewards of former years of earnest toil and endeavor. He is a liberal and public-spirited citizen and has given support to enterprises that have added much to the civic and business prosperity of Shiner. He is president and chief stockholder of the Garbade Lumber Company and is vice president of the Farmers State Bank of Shiner. While a resident of the town of Charlottenburg he served as school trustee. His political allegiance has always been given unreservedly to the democratic party, and though he is not a communicant he holds to the faith of the Lutheran Church and has been liberal in the support of religious activities. At Charlottenburg he donated to the Lutheran Church the nine acres of land upon which the church edifice and cemetery are established. Mrs. Dreyer is an earnest communicant of the Lutheran Church and her gentle and gracious personality has made her a most devoted wife and mother, besides gaining to her the affectionate regard of all who have come within the sphere of her influence.

Mr. Dreyer has shown himself not lacking in inventive genius, and among the devices invented and patented by him was an arrangement to kill the obnoxious night ants of Texas, this proving successful in operation and bringing to him appreciable financial returns. In company with Mrs. Dreyer he made a trip to California and he has stated that his primary purpose was "to kill ground squirrels." He had patented an invention to work death and destruction to these pestiferous little animals, and while his California trip was not successful from a financial standpoint, his patent was eventually sold by his agent for $20,000, though none of this money ever came into his possession.

Near Oakland, Colorado County, on the 15th of September, 1861, was solemnized the marriage of Mr. Dreyer to Miss Magdalena Anders, a daughter of Joseph Anders, who immigrated to Texas from Austria and who became a prosperous farmer and business man in Colorado County, the other surviving children of the Anders family being: Miss Verona, who resides at Oakland; Amelia, who is the widow of Charles Ling; Bertha, who is the widow of Hermann Pleckner; and Joseph, who is a resident of Flatonia, Fayette County. In the concluding para-

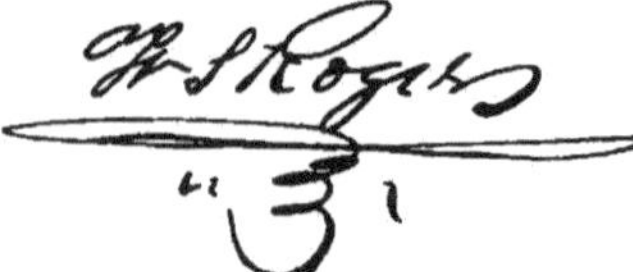

Jos. D. Rogers

graph is entered brief record concerning the children of Mr. and Mrs. Dreyer:

Henry is a successful farmer on the historic staked plains of Texas; Hermann resides at Yoakum, Dewitt County; Frances became the wife of Emil Polar and her death occurred at Shiner; Julius resides at Dreyer, as a farmer and stock-grower, as does also Edward; Charlotte, who died at Charlottenburg, was the wife of John Neizer; Rudolph is a resident of Shiner; Adolph maintains his home at Sweetwater, Nolan County; and Mrs. Emma Schoenvogel resides at Shiner. Adolph, the youngest son, is a civil engineer by profession and vocation. He was graduated in the Massey Business College, in the city of Houston, and thereafter completed a comprehensive correspondence course in civil engineering in a leading correspondence school in the City of Philadelphia. As a practical engineer he assisted in the surveying and laying out of a branch of the Atchison, Topeka & Santa Fe Railroad across the plains of Texas. It is most gratifying to record that Mr. and Mrs. Henry Dreyer can claim as their progeny in the second and third generations forty grandchildren and thirteen great-grandchildren.

Joseph D. Rogers, M. D. The career of Dr. Joseph D. Rogers, of Brenham, has been one of singular and diversified activity and has invaded the fields of professional life, business and agriculture, in each of which he has met with well-merited success. A native of Brazos County, he belongs to a family founded here during the era of the Republic of Texas, the head of the family at that time being his grandfather, John D. Rogers, a native of Tennessee, who as a young man moved to Alabama, and there married in Sumpter County. He lived near Patton's Hill, where William Samuel, his son and father of Doctor Rogers, was born. John D. Rogers was a farmer and slaveholder and came to Texas in 1841, following his son, William S., who had come to this state about the year 1840, John D. Rogers establishing his home about three miles from Anderson, Grimes County, where he died prior to the Civil war. In Alabama he had been a major of militia, was a man of liberal education for his day, a stalwart democrat, and a member of the Presbyterian Church.

John D. Rogers was a son of a Scotchman and his first wife, and had several half-brothers. He married a widow, Mrs. Celia Patton, for whose first husband, Arthur Patton, the town of Patton's Hill, Alabama, had been named. The children of John D., and Celia Rogers were as follows: Thomas died at Anderson, Texas, and left children. Joseph, a lawyer, passed his career at Houston, where he died without issue in 1843 during an epidemic of yellow fever. William S. was the father of Doctor Rogers. Emily married William Atkins and died at Anderson, Texas. Patrick H., who was captain of a Ranger company in Texas during 1854 and 1855, died unmarried. Dr. John D., Jr., who was practicing medicine at Old Washington when the Civil war broke out, and became a lieutenant-colonel in Hood's Brigade, subsequently passing his life at Galveston. He graduated in medicine in 1861 at Tulane University. Dr. Edward W., who in 1854 and 1855 was second lieutenant of Captain Rogers' Company of Texas Rangers, was a practicing physician of Chapel Hill and died there October 16, 1867. Lemuel P. died at Anderson, Texas, just before the outbreak of the Civil war, June 21, 1859, leaving two children, Mary and John D.

William Samuel Rogers, father of Doctor Rogers, was born at Patton's Hill, Alabama, December 22, 1822, and acquired a very good literary education, his medical studies being pursued at the old University of New Orleans, under the Flint-Stone regime, 1843-44. He was eighteen years of age when he came to Texas, and here took part in the defense of Texas against the Mexicans after the battle of San Jacinto, belonging to the command of General Somerville and a member of the troops out of which the Meier expedition was organized. Doctor Rogers attended medical lectures at New Orleans, and began practice before he finished his course, continuing thus until 1858 when he returned and graduated. His regular practice was commenced at old Washington, but after a short period he removed to Boonville, at that time the county seat of Brazos County, and two years later went to Wheelock, the county seat of Robertson County. In 1848 he returned to Washington County and established himself at Jacksonville, remaining there until Chapel Hill began to assume respectable proportions and eclipse Jacksonville, when he moved to the newer community.

Jacksonville was a village three miles north of Chapel Hill and was the outcome of a settlement made by the Jacksons, a numerous family which included several brothers and their families, these being: William Terrell, Joseph and Gilbert Jackson. When Richard Chappell came out from Tennessee in the '40s, these families settled on the old stage road leading from Houston to Austin, which crossed the Brazos at Warren's Ferry, where the Houston & Texas Central Railway crosses the river at this time. Here Jacob Haller, a son-in-law of Major Hargrove, built the first store, the beginning of Chapel Hill, in 1850. As the new community grew, Jacksonville began to diminish, and there is now but one old house left there, this having at one time been occupied by Elisha Little, who was once sheriff of Washington County, and a son-in-law of William Jackson.

Dr. William S. Rogers continued to practice his profession at Chapel Hill uninterrupted until the outbreak of the war between the forces of the South and the North, at which time he was made brigade surgeon of General Carter's Brigade. He served in the Trans-Mississippi Department and was at the surrender of Arkansas Post, but managed to make his escape and returned to Texas, being assigned to the military hospital at Chapel Hill—later the Soule University Building. He was subsequently appointed medical examiner for Washington County, but, owing to rheumatism contracted at Arkansas Post, was unable to perform the duties of this position. After the war Doctor Rogers carried on an office practice and conducted a drug store at Chapel Hill until 1869. He passed through the scourge of yellow fever in 1867, being immune because of having passed through a like epidemic on the Texas frontier at Brownsville in 1864, and rendered invaluable service when his neighbors were falling victims to the dread disease all about him. In 1869 he removed to Galveston, and there continued to engage in practice until his death, which occurred March 16, 1887.

Doctor Rogers was a democrat and took an active part in political affairs. He was appointed by Gen. John Claiborne as surgeon of the state militia and served as such during encampment times. Fraternally he was a Mason and Knight Templar. He was a man of strong likes and dislikes, but while he demonstrated his friendship for those who had won his favor, the other class were always treated courteously and simply passed by. While a resident of Galveston he was appointed by Governor Ireland as a member of the Texas Medical Examining Board.

On July 16, 1844, at Old Washington, Texas, Dr. William S. Rogers was married to Miss Josephine E. George, a daughter of Whitson and Mary (George) George, of Mississippi. Mrs. Rogers passed away in Galveston six weeks before her husband. They were the parents of three children, as follows: Dr. Joseph D., of this review; John D., who fell a victim to yellow fever in 1867; and Whitson, who died in infancy.

Dr. Joseph D. Rogers was born at old Boonsville, Texas, July 4, 1845, and was reared at Chapel Hill, where he secured his literary education at Soule University under presidents Bland, Doctor Halsey and Carter, the last-named of whom served in the Confederate army at the head of Carter's Brigade. Doctor Rogers became a soldier of the South in 1863, when he enlisted in Company B, Capt. Lee Scott's company, Col. Dave Terry's regiment. This regiment saw service in Louisiana, but Doctor Rogers was in no battles and his chief service was as a scout. He was detailed by General Gillespie as one of his staff couriers, and that line of duty closed his service, he being at home on a furlough when the war closed.

On resuming the duties and life of the civilian, Doctor Rogers engaged in farming and raising stock at Chapel Hill. He began reading medicine at this time, but was unable to take a medical course because of lack of funds. However, he felt himself able to take care of a home, and in 1865 was married, continuing to be engaged in farming during the following year. In 1867 he became a merchant at Chapel Hill, in the line of groceries and dry goods and continued in commercial operations for two years, when he again resumed farming and was a tiller of the soil until 1872, that year marking his first course of lectures for the profession for which he had so long cherished an ambition. Doctor Rogers practiced medicine on a certificate in 1873 and 1874 and in the spring of 1876 finished his course. At this time, at the urgent request of his father, he went to Galveston, where he assisted the elder man for nearly a year, then returning to Chapel Hill, which continued to be his field of practice until 1889. In the meantime, in 1882, he took a course in Bellevue Hospital, New York, this being three years before his father took his last course in the New York Polyclinic.

In 1889 Doctor Rogers changed his residence and field of practice to Brenham, where he passed his first years in the drug business, but since his retirement from that line farming has occupied his attention chiefly, and at this time he has large landed interests in the vicinity of Brenham. He has taken an active part in democratic politics, although chiefly in supporting the aspirations of his friends. He is a thirty-second degree Mason, belonging to Brenham Blue Lodge, Chapter and Commandery and Galveston Consistory, has belonged to the Odd Fellows since 1869 and is also a member of the Knights of the Maccabees.

On December 20, 1865, Doctor Rogers was married to Miss Georgie Ann Gayle, who was born and reared in Jackson County, Texas. She died of yellow fever at 4 A. M. on October 13, 1867, and her child, William Alexander, died at 2 P. M., October 14, 1867, both being buried in the same coffin. Doctor Rogers was again married, October 2, 1870, when united with Miss Buelah McClelland, a daughter of George and Margaret (Mayrant) McClelland. Mrs. Rogers is one of a family of several children, and was born, reared and educated in Mobile, Alabama, where her father was a leading commission merchant of Mobile before the Civil war, the firm being McClelland & Rupert. The Doctor and Mrs. Rogers have no children.

Dietrich Garbade. Coming from his German Fatherland to America as a youth of seventeen years, this well known and highly honored citizen of Shiner, Lavaca County, has been a resident of Texas for more than forty years and has here found ample opportunity for the achieving of independence and definite success. He is now living virtually retired, though he finds ample demands upon his time and attention in the supervision of his substantial property interests and to rendering efficient service in behalf of the attractive little city in which he has established his home.

Mr. Garbade was reared and educated in the City of Bremen, Germany, was born on the 19th of July, 1851, and the place of his nativity was his father's farm, near the city mentioned, the family home having been established in that immediate section of the great Empire of Germany for nearly two centuries, and the old ancestral homestead being now occupied by a sister of Mr. Garbade. The lineage of the Garbade family is traced back to remote Italian origin, and many generations ago representatives of the name removed from fair Italy to Germany, the old homestead which was the birthplace of the subject of this review having been in the possession of the family for 170 years. In Germany the family name has been primarily identified with the great basic industry of agriculture, and of the representatives it may be noted that one of the brothers of Dietrich Garbade is a member of the mercantile firm of Garbade, Eiband & Company, in the City of Galveston, and that another brother is engaged in the grocery business in the City of San Antonio.

The presence of certain of his kinfolk in Texas constituted the chief inducement leading to Mr. Garbade's establishing his permanent home in Texas. Prior to coming to America he had not only received good educational advantages in the City of Bremen, but had also gained there excellent practical experience along mercantile lines. At Bremen he embarked for the United States in the winter of 1868, and he arrived in Texas in January of the year 1869, when he joined his kinfolk in Fayette County, the old Town of Flatonia having been made his destination. During the first two years of his residence in Texas he found employment principally in connection with farm operations, his cash capital having been only $28 at the time of his arrival and this money having been expended, with prodigality and pride, in the purchase of a saddle, it having been customary for the farmer employer to provide a horse for his workman, the latter furnishing his own saddle. Mr. Garbade was soon afflicted with illness, however, and for a period of several months he was unable to do work of any kind. His prolonged illness left him badly in debt and he found employment as clerk in a mercantile establishment at Flatonia, some time elapsing ere he was able to free himself from his indebtedness. At old Flatonia he was employed in the store of Gerhard Siems, who paid him $20 a month and provided him with room and board. At the expiration of a year Mr. Garbade went to the northern part of the state and obtained a clerical position in a mercantile establishment at Corsicana, where he remained thus engaged for one year. After his return to Fayette County he devoted two years to farming, and while thus engaged he took unto himself a wife,—a young woman who was destined to be his devoted companion and helpmeet during the years he was working his way forward to the goal of independence and prosperity.

Upon leaving the farm Mr. Garbade went to the new Town of Flatonia, where he was employed four years as a clerk in the general merchandise establishment of H. W. Yeager & Sons. He then engaged in business for himself, by opening a country store at Witting, Lavaca County, where he continued successfully in this line of enterprise for twenty-three years. Witting had at the time a cotton gin and a schoolhouse, the latter being utilized also as a Lutheran church. The place proved a most eligible trading point and as a general merchant Mr. Garbade, by fair and honorable dealings and effective service, built up a singularly large and substantial trade, from the profits of which he eventually found it possible to expand his field of operations and to become successfully identified with farming and cattle raising, with which lines of enterprise he was there successfully concerned for a period of about eight years. As circumstances justified he made investments in land, and he eventually accumulated a valuable landed estate of nearly 800 acres. This property he developed into six individual farms, and when he decided to retire from the mercantile business he disposed of four of his farms also. He continued his residence at Witting for somewhat more than thirty years, and in November, 1911, he and his wife established their residence at Shiner, where they own and occupy one of the commodious and attractive residences of the town, the same being known for its genuine hospitality and the latch-string always being found hanging forth for the accommodation of the many friends of Mr. and Mrs. Garbade. That Mr. Garbade maintains lively interest in local affairs is shown by his having served two years as a member of the board of aldermen of Shiner and two years as street commissioner. In the latter office he did most efficient work, though he did not ask or receive compensation for his services.

In his application for citizenship in the land of his adoption Mr. Garbade took out his first papers of naturalization at LaGrange, Fayette County, and his final papers were given the official sanction at Hallettsville, the judicial center of Lavaca County. He cast his first vote in support of the democratic party's candidate for president, and he continued in the ranks of that party until the panic of 1892, when his honest convictions led him to transfer his allegiance to the republican party, of whose principles and policies he has since continued a supporter. While at Witting he served as postmaster, and at intervals for many years was school trustee.

Dietrich Garbade is a son of Henry and Anna (Brunhsen) Garbade, both of whom passed their entire lives in the immediate vicinity of Bremen, Germany. Of their children it may be recorded that Adelaide, who was born May 22, 1842, became the wife of A. Seggermann and resides in the City of Bremen, Germany; Bernhard, who was born January 24, 1844, continued his residence at Bremen until the time of his death; John, who was born March 17, 1846, married and died at Flatonia, Texas, in September, 1869; Henry, who was born January 23, 1848, is a prosperous merchant in the City of Galveston, Texas, as intimated in an earlier paragraph of this article; John T., who was born October 4, 1852, is a merchant and prominent citizen of San Antonio; Anna, who was born November 2, 1854, is the wife of Frank Harff, of Bremen, Germany, which city likewise is the home of the youngest of the children, Meta, born January 15, 1856, and George, who was born October 28, 1859.

At Flatonia, Fayette County, in December, 1875, was solemnized the marriage of Mr. Garbade to Miss Agnes Muecke, a daughter of Charles and Dora Muecke, the former of whom was born in Holstein, Germany, and the latter in Austria. Mr. Muecke established the family home in Texas prior to the Civil war, during which conflict he was a teamster between this state and Mexico, his vocation thereafter having been that of farmer. Of the children the eldest was Amelia, who became the wife of August Kuenstler and who died near Cuero, Dewitt County; Mrs. Garbade was the next in order of birth and was born in the year 1856; Mrs. Emma Mueller resides at Flatonia; Charles was a resident of Shiner at the time of his death; Emil resides in the City of San Antonio; Mrs. Matilda Stein died at Flatonia; Dora is the wife of Samuel Burkett, of Yoakum, Dewitt County; and Otto resides at Shiner.

In conclusion is given record concerning the children of Mr. and

Mrs. Garbade: Henry, who has become one of the representative business men in the City of Galveston, is there the proprietor of the Galveston Sheet & Metal Works, the maiden name of his wife having been Adele Garbade. Charles J. is made the subject of an individual sketch which follows immeditaely the one here presented. Walter, a young man of fine scientific attainments, completed his academic and professional education in the University of Texas, in the medical department of which he was graduated and he is now demonstrator in chemistry in the medical department of Galveston College. The maiden name of his wife was Helen Smith. Dietrich, Jr., who is bookkeeper for the firm of Arnim & Lane, of Flatonia, married Miss Mollie Laede; Lillie is the wife of August Rogge, of Shiner; Agnes is the wife of Henry Rogge, of this place; William, who resides at Flatonia, married Miss Clara Stein; and Victor remains at the parental home.

The subject of this sketch is loyal and progressive as a citizen, is appreciative of American institutions and advantages and his children have all received excellent educational opportunities, two of his sons having been sent by him to the Texas Agricultural and Mechanical College.

Charles J. Garbade. A son of Dietrich Garbade, the honored pioneer citizen to whom the preceding article is dedicated, Charles J. Garbade, secretary, treasurer and manager of the Garbade Lumber Company, at Shiner, Lavaca County, takes due pride in claiming the Lone Star State as the place of his nativity. He was born at Flatonia, Fayette County, Texas, on the 29th of December, 1878, and his boyhood and youth were passed in the Witting community of Lavaca County, where he duly availed himself of the advantages of the public schools. Thereafter he entered the Texas Agricultural & Mechanical College, at Bryan, in which excellent institution he completed a three years' course in special mechanical engineering, but when he left school he did not take up the work of the profession for which he had thus prepared himself. On the contrary, he found employment in the lumber yard of T. A. Hill & Son at Hallettsville, the judicial center of Lavaca County, where he remained three years and where he acquired a comprehensive and exact knowledge of the various details of the lumber business, both technical and commercial. At the expiration of the period noted he removed to Shiner and became salesman at the Flato lumber yard. When Robert Eschenburg succeeded Mr. Flato in the ownership of the business Mr. Garbade was made manager of the enterprise, and finally he purchased a half interest in the business, under the firm name of Eschenburg & Garbade. The enterprise expanded in scope and importance and it was finally found expedient to organize for its conduct a stock company, Mr. Eschenburg selling his interest at this juncture and Mr. Garbade securing as his coadjutors in the formation of the new organization Messrs. Henry Dreyer, Sr., and J. C. Koerth. These three principals proceeded to the organization and incorporation of the Garbade Lumber Company, which bases its operations on a capital of $20,000, and of which Mr. Dreyer is president; Mr. Koerth, vice president; and Mr. Garbade, secretary, treasurer and manager, the venerable president of the company being individually mentioned on other pages of this work.

Mr. Garbade is known and honored as one of the most progressive business men and liberal and public-spirited citizens of Shiner, and he has contributed to the advancement of the town by the erecting of a number of houses, which he has sold, besides his own residence, which is one of the modern and attractive homes of the village. His political allegiance is given to the democratic party and he is now serving as secretary of the City Council of Shiner, a position of which he has been the only incumbent, his original election having occurred in 1909. He is a member of the volunteer fire department of the village and also a trustee of the public schools. Mr. Garbade is a Master Mason; is affiliated with the Hermann Sohns, and is past chancellor of the Shiner Lodge of the Knights of Pythias, which he has represented as a delegate to the grand lodge of the order in Texas.

At Shiner, on the 18th of February, 1901, was solemnized the marriage of Mr. Garbade to Miss Mollie Gehrels, daughter of Fritz and Johanna (Ummelmann) Gehrels, both of whom likewise were born in Texas, where their respective parents settled in the pioneer days. Mr. Gehrels has been one of the substantial agriculturists of Texas and he and his wife now maintain their home at Shiner, where he is living virtually retired. Their other children are Mrs. Charles Muecke, Mrs. Otto Muecke, and Edward Gehrels. Mr. and Mrs. Garbade have three children,—Rudy C., Walter, and Percy Herbert.

Hugh K. Williams. Having devoted his entire career to the cause of education, Prof. Hugh K. Williams, superintendent of the public schools of Hallettsville, is one of the best known and most popular and efficient teachers in Lavaca County. His preparation for his chosen work was a most thorough and comprehensive one, and at Hallettsville, where he has been located since 1913, he has done much to improve the system and to introduce modern ideas and methods. Professor Williams is a native son of Lavaca County, Texas, born near Yoakum, October 4, 1878, a son of James S. and Ellen (Ridgway) Williams.

Edward W. Williams, the grandfather of Professor Williams, was born in 1813, in New York, and was a member of a company sent south to serve in the war with Mexico, he seeming to have remained here at the close of that struggle, as his advent in Texas dates from about 1848. He was familiarly known as "Uncle Ned" Williams in the old Hope neighborhood, where he settled when his was the only house between Hallettsville and Victoria, and his old homestead, where he died in 1875, is now owned by his son, James S. Williams. Although he was too old for active participation during the Civil war, he drilled several companies of young men for the Confederate service, and sent one of his sons to the front wearing the uniform of the South, Rector Williams, who returned safely home after the close of hostilities. Edward W. Williams married a Miss Owens, and they became the parents of the following children: Rector, who died in Lavaca County and left a family; Katie, who married Edward M. Smith and lives at Beaumont, Texas; Connie, who became Mrs. Samuel C. Thigpen, of Lavaca County; Edward W., Jr., of Dewitt county, Texas; Owen E., a farmer of Lavaca County; Jane, who married Charles E. Power and died in Dewitt County; James S., the father of Hugh K.; and Collatinus B., who is engaged in farming in Victoria County.

James S. Williams was born August 31, 1856, in Lavaca County, Texas, and in that vicinity acquired a smattering of education. His life has been largely spent as a farmer and ranchman near Yoakum and stock-raising has been an important factor in his farming career, although for a short time he also carried on mercantile pursuits at Yoakum. Mr. Williams is a democrat, but has kept aloof from politics. He is a Methodist in his religious belief, but has no fraternal connections. Mr. Williams is a typical Texan, progressive, enterprising, and of good business ability, and his career of industry has been rewarded by the accumulation of a handsome property. Mr. Williams married

Miss Ellen Ridgway, whose father died as a Federal prisoner of war during the struggle between the South and the North. They were the parents of the following children: Alice, who married Ed Weathers, of Gonzales County, Texas; Ellen, who became Mrs. Williams; John, a resident of Yoakum, Texas; Thomas, who resides near Childress, Texas; and Wiley, who passed away unmarried. Mrs. Ridgway had been married first to a Mr. Voss, and had two children by that union: Rhoda, who became the wife of Milton E. Dickinson, of Dewitt County; and Virginia, who married O. F. Williams, brother of James S. Williams. Following the loss of her second husband some years ago, Mrs. Ridgway married a Mr. Madison, and they became the parents of two children, namely: Nannie, who died as a maiden; and George, who makes his home at Yoakum, Texas.

The childhood of Hugh K. Williams was spent largely in the community of his birth and as a youth he moved with his parents to Yoakum, where he completed his high school course. At that time he entered upon his career in the field of education, but after two years passed in teaching in the country schools, realized the necessity for further training, and accordingly, in 1901, entered the State University, where he continued as a student until his graduation with the class of 1905, when he received the degree of Bachelor of Sciences. For three years following his graduation Professor Williams was principal of the school at Benjamin, Knox County, Texas, and then became the incumbent of the same position at the Yoakum High School, a capacity in which he continued for five years. In 1913 he was induced to come to Hallettsville in the capacity of superintendent of schools, and has so remained to the present time, to the general satisfaction of all concerned. Professor Williams is a hard, earnest and zealous worker in his field of endeavor, and through his conscientious labors has done much to advance the cause of education and elevate its standards. He is a general favorite with teachers, pupils and parents, and is justly accounted one of the most capable and popular officials Hallettsville has had. In addition to his work as superintendent, Professor Williams has taught in summer normals at Yoakum and Cuero and has served on the county boards of examiners in Knox and Dewitt Counties. He is a member of the Southern Educational Association, of the South Texas Association and of the Texas State Teachers' Association. Fraternally, he is affiliated with the Knights of Pythias and the Woodmen of the World. He is a Methodist in his religious belief and at various times has been identified with the official life of that religious denomination. As a citizen he has displayed a keen interest in all matters that have affected the welfare of his town and county.

Professor Williams was married in Lavaca County, Texas, June 18, 1907, to Miss Ruth Gephart, daughter of Philip and Susan (Madison) Gephart. Mr. Gephart was born in Indiana, but came to Texas prior to the outbreak of the Civil war, in which he participated as a Confederate soldier. Since the close of the war he has resided in Lavaca County, where he still devotes his attention to the cultivation of the soil. His children are as follows: Miss Annie, who for a number of years was a county school teacher; Susie, who is the wife of T. J. Fitch, of Elmendorf, Texas; Ella, who married R. C. Fitch, of Houston Heights, Houston, Texas; Philip, of Childress County, Texas; Alice, who married J. A. Stroman, of Mineral Wells, Texas; Clara, who is the wife of E. L. Stroman, of San Marcos, Texas; John, of Birmingham, Alabama; Ruth, who is now Mrs. Williams; and Ida, who married Fred Loomis, of Goliad, Texas. Mr. and Mrs. Williams have one child: Orville, who was born November 21, 1913.

T. D. Burton

Travis J. Burton. One of the live towns on the Austin branch of the Houston and Texas Central Railway is named for a representative of a pioneer Texas family. Travis J. Burton died December 29, 1915, venerable in years. He was born in Texas less than a year after the winning of independence at San Jacinto. He did his part as a Texas soldier in the war between the states. His life and activities were largely identified with the community of Burton.

He was born in Burleson County, Texas, February 4, 1837, a son of John M. Burton, who was one of the oldest among the American settlers of Texas, having come in 1829 from the vicinity of Greensboro, Georgia.

A nafive of Georgia, where he was born March 22, 1812, John M. Burton was the son of a farmer and slave holder. When a boy of twelve years he left home and started on a career of wandering which finally brought him up in Texas, before Texas had separated from Mexico. For a number of years in his early boyhood and youth he lived in New Orleans, where he served five years as an apprentice to a cabinet maker. It was with considerable skill in this occupation that he came to Texas. In Burleson County he married Elizabeth Thompson, daughter of Alexander Thompson. In 1839 John M. Burton moved to Washington County, and established his home one mile from the town which bears his name. He had a shop in which he did cabinet work and carpentry, but was best known as a farmer and his generous prosperity came largely from the handling of land and stock. In the early days of the Texas Republic he helped to lay out the townsite of Austin. Still later he was one of the leading men in securing the construction of the Austin branch of the Houston and Texas Central Railroad, and he subscribed stock in that enterprise as did his son. He was in many ways a pioneer leader. He constructed the first frame house in the Burton neighborhood, the lumber being cut with a whipsaw. This house was regarded as a mansion for several years, and people came from a long distance to examine it. That old house is still occupied as a habitation and is perfectly preserved. John M. Burton was also the mechanic whose services were in demand in the construction of all the school houses and churches of pioneer times. He finally moved his home to the hill across the creek from Burton village and sold the railroad company 500 acres of his land on which was started the town of Burton.

So far as school education was concerned John M. Burton had very little. He was a practical man, and everything he did he did well. He hired a substitute to take his place in the ranks in the Mexican war and he himself participated in many excursions against the Indians for the recovery of stolen property. His wife's brother, Max Thompson, was one of Dawson's men in the historic raid into Mexico, drew the black bean and was executed south of the Rio Grande. John M. Burton was a democrat in politics, and had some ability as a speaker, though he seldom exercised it. He spent some money on politics though never with ambition for himself, and he held no political office. For many years he professed no religious belief, but late in life united with the Methodist Church. The last three years of his life were spent as a paralytic and he died in 1879.

His wife's father, Alexander Thompson, brought colonists into Texas from Tennessee, and for his services was granted several leagues of land by the Republic. Alexander Thompson was a large planter in Burleson County and spent his life there. He was a man of religious fervor, did much for the Methodist Church, and steadily upheld all moral standards. Mrs. John M. Burton died in 1873 when about sixty-five years of age. Her children were: Jane, who married Henry Hons; William A., who died from wounds received as a Confederate soldier; Travis J.;

Ann, who died unmarried; Frank, who died in the Confederate army; Jack, who served four years in the Twenty-first Texas Regiment and spent the rest of his career as a farmer; Dora, who married Troup Webb; Laura, who married Thomas Norris; Mary, who married Dr. O. B. Nicholson; Josephine, who died unmarried; and Emma, who became Mrs. Robert Patton.

It was in Washington County that Travis J. Burton was reared to manhood, and in this same locality he spent nearly all the years of his life. As a boy he attended some of the country schools, and otherwise his experiences were bounded by those of a Texas farm until the war came on. From 1862 until the close of hostilities he was a fighting soldier of the Confederacy. He joined Captain's Lusk's Company F of the Twenty-first Texas Cavalry. Colonel Carter, commander of the regiment, was afterwards General Carter, and the Twenty-first Texas was part of his brigade. His service was altogether in the Trans-Mississippi Department. Mr. Burton was in Joe Shelby's Army under General Marmaduke on the Missouri raid towards the close of the war, and fought almost day and night for seven days on the advance and retreat into that territory. He was also in the Arkansas Post region when that post surrendered and was in the battles of Mansfield, Pleasant Hill and Yellow Bayou in Louisiana. He also participated in two small engagements at Shreveport. When the war ended his company was near Navasota and it was disbanded. While not wounded, a bullet pierced his trouser leg, and his gun was marked by the balls of the enemy. One time he captured a sword from a yellow negro soldier, and he kept that as a souvenir of the war. His gun was merely a shotgun which sent "blue whistlers" after the enemy, and this relic as well as his pistol he still possesses. Mr. Burton served as orderly sergeant for a time and was subsequently promoted by Gen. E. Kirby Smith as a second lieutenant, and held that rank at the time he left the army. Mr. Burton was one of the men, who, when the war ended, was through fighting. He accepted the situation, and never actively identified himself with the meetings of veterans and it was very difficult to get him to talk concerning his experiences in war time.

Soon after the war in 1866 Mr. Burton took up a mercantile career, and built the first store building on the Burton townsite. He was engaged in buying cotton and selling general merchandise until 1882, when he resumed his position as a farmer. For a number of years he was associated with the firm of Hons, Burton & Brother. Although the last several years were spent retired, he still owned considerable farm property. In politics he was a democratic voter, but never sought an office. He was a member of the Christian Church.

In 1858 Mr. Burton married Miss Amanda Jones, who died the following year leaving one son, William Alexander, who now lives in San Antonio. His second wife was Miss Mary McGuire. Her father, Col. Frank W. McGuire, was a sawmill man who came to Texas from Tuscaloosa, Alabama, and at one time was a member of the Texas State Legislature. Colonel McGuire married Martha J. Walker, and they were the parents of nine children. Mrs. Mary Burton died in 1867, leaving a daughter Creola Mary, who married Mat Francis and at her death left six children. On November 30, 1868, Mr. Burton married for his third wife Miss Julia McGuire, another daughter of Colonel McGuire. The children of this union are: Milton, who died as a youth of eighteen; Anna, who died in young womanhood; and Scottie the wife of W. M. Aven of Brenham. Mr. W. M. Aven had an unusual career for a man of his years. He was a courier in the Confederate army under General Forrest. He went into the army at the age of fourteen, and saw some of the hardest fighting in the course of that long struggle. He was wounded at Fort Pillow while carrying messages. He escaped capture. Mr. Aven was born in Georgia, the son of a planter, enlisted in the army from Mississippi, and spent his mature years in Texas, where from 1870 he was engaged in the compress and gin business at Brenham associated with the McFaddens, and was manager of a compress at Bowie when he died, on September 1, 1909. Mr. Aven took a prominent part in lodges, was Grand Chancellor of the Knights of Pythias and was an active democrat.

EDGAR U. G. REAGAN. Few families of Texas are better known for achievement in the various activities of life than that bearing the name of Reagan, members of which have attained high distinction in the professions, in business and in national politics. In the field of invention, it has been left to Edgar U. G. Reagan, of San Antonio, to perpetuate the family name, and several products of his skilled hand and brain have served to place him among the eminent members of his family.

Mr. Reagan was born June 17, 1865, in Fayette County, Texas, on the Colorado River, the family home being in that section of the county known as Rabb's Prairie, five miles above LaGrange. His parents were A. R. and Sarah (Rabb) Reagan, and his father was a cousin of John Henninger Reagan, one of the most distinguished citizens and statesmen in the history of Texas. John Henninger Reagan was born in Sevier County, Tennessee, October 8, 1818. At the age of twenty-one years he settled in Texas, where he practiced law and engaged in farming, serving two terms in the State House of Representatives, and in 1856 was elected judge of the District Court for six years, but resigned the judicial office to go to Congress from the First District, in 1867. During the Civil war he served as postmaster-general of the Confederate States, and acting secretary of the Confederate treasury. He subsequently was a member of the Constitutional Convention of Texas in 1875, and a member of Congress in 1875-1887; was United States senator in 1887-1891, and afterwards chairman of the Texas State Railroad Commission. On the maternal side Mr. Reagan is descended from the Rabb family, also famous in the history of Texas.

Edgar U. G. Reagan's father was a miller, and the lad from his earliest boyhood took an interest in mechanics, and has always managed to be connected therewith. He knows machinery most thoroughly, having seemingly an inborn talent for it, and can do anything with any sort of an implement, tool or machine. Although without technical education, he is widely known as an expert draughtsman, with the ability to draw a more accurate line without the use of the gauge than almost anyone else. Mr. Reagan lived at the old home in Fayette County until he was twenty-one years of age, and then went to Flatonia and later became connected with a cotton seed oil mill and became an expert in cotton seed crushing machinery. Mr. Reagan first became known in Texas as an inventor when he perfected the round-bale cotton ginning system. Numbers of these presses were built and installed at gins and much cotton was baled in this manner, but a condition arose which, as stated at the time, had not been foreseen. It was the fact that round-bale cotton could not be loaded into ships' holds with as much compactness as the square bale. The disinclination of ship-owners to handle round-bale cotton, together with an active fight by the square-bale people, caused the collapse of the movement in favor of the square bales. Subsequently Mr. Reagan perfected many other inventions, many of which pertain to the automobile, and came to the front with what is probably his most important and valuable product in 1915. This is an attachment for motor car engines which will save from 30 to 40 per cent in gasoline. The invention allows for the superheating of steam by the wasted heat of the exhaust of the engine. The steam is taken into each cylinder along with the introduction of the gasoline vapor by the vacuum pull of the cylinders, and the steam acts as a propulsive force along with the gas explosion. Much less gasoline is required, for the invention provides for an increase of power in the engine by utilizing the wasted heat from the cylinders, which is returned to the cylinders and compounded. A number of the large automobile manufacturers of the country have already asked the privilege of trying it out. Mr. Reagan has lived at San Antonio since about 1905. He spent three years prior to 1915 at Detroit, Michigan, in the perfection of the above and other devices, one of which the United States Patent Office will soon make known to the world as his latest and most valuable of all. This is a differential for all motor-driven cars, known as the floating pinion device.

Mr. Reagan was married to Miss Orana Callaway, who was born and reared in Wilson County, Texas, and they have eight living children: Emmett, Ivan, Enrique, Bolton, Fay, Marguerite, Edgar and Oralee.

ROBERT MILLER, SR. One of the best known of Lavaca County's citizens, Robert Miller, Sr., who for forty years was engaged in mercantile pursuits at Sublime, is now devoting his attention to his extensive farming and stock-raising interests. He is one of the early settlers of Lavaca County, having come to Texas in 1852 as a youth of seventeen years or less, newly arrived from the Dukedom of Brunswick, then an independent country, but subsequently, under Bismarck, a portion of the German Confederation.

Robert "Mueller," as the name was spelled in the Fatherland, was born in the City of Brunswick, November 22, 1836, and is a son of Theodore Mueller. The latter was also born at Brunswick, and was highly educated, a talented artist with pen and ink, a splendid mathematician, and capable of filling any position the public service might demand in a clerical capacity. A lameness in one of his legs exempted him from military duty. He was, however, a government service man in the employ of the reigning duke, was the private secretary to that personage and had charge of his private seal, and served in that capacity until the use of the seal so crippled his arm that he was incapacitated for further service and was then pensioned and given permission to emigrate and bring his family to the United States. He took sick about a year later and died in Lavaca County in 1853. Theodore Mueller married Annie Premmel, the daughter of a merchant, Theodore Premmel. She died in Lavaca County during the Civil war and is buried at Sublime, while her husband lies in an unmarked grave somewhere on Mixing Creek, where the family first settled and where the father was farming when his death occurred. The children of Theodore and Annie Mueller were as follows: Charles, who is now a resident of Victoria, Texas; August, who died in Travis County, Texas; Robert, of this review; Armina, who was married the first time to August Ziegler, but who died as Mrs. Henry Schott, in Lavaca County; and John, of Great Rock, Texas.

Robert Miller received a good German education, and as a youth began learning the saddler's trade. After more than a year spent thus, he abandoned that vocation to come to America with his parents and the other children, sailing from Bremen aboard the Augusta, a sailing vessel, which was eight weeks on the water. There were no untoward incidents while making the passage and the family landed at New Orleans, from whence they made their way to Lavaca County, Texas, there joining a relative. They rented land at first and Robert worked for his mother and the younger children, his elder brother having set out for himself. His mother subsequently pre-empted a piece of land and to this the family moved, improved it to some extent, cleared up the fields, and later sold.

Robert Miller had just gotten a good start toward a semblance of independence, when the Civil war broke out and in the second year of that struggle he entered the service of the Confederacy. He enlisted in Lavaca County, in Company E, Captain Ford, of Bates' Battalion, made up in Velasco for the protection of the coast. His immediate command served in Texas and in Louisiana, where, at Opaloosas, the army took 1,700 Federal prisoners and was driven back into Texas, where it was situated when the war closed. The company to which he belonged then disbanded and he went on to Old Mexico and was absent from the United States until a semblance of order was restored here.

Mr. Miller's experiences among the Mexicans was something new. He went into the restaurant business opposite Rancher Davis, on the Rio Grande River, and when the chaotic conditions of the United States were settled, he came back to Texas, returned to the farm, picked up his plow and other paraphernalia and resumed industriously the tilling of the soil. When he had straightened up matters to some extent, he decided to become a merchant, and laid in such a stock as a dry goods box would hold, thus starting into business at his home. At that time he owned no land of his own, and his capital came slowly from his modest mercantile venture. He hauled his goods from Columbus with his own team, waited on customers when they came, and returned to his plow while other customers were arriving, thus plowing and farming and selling goods at the same time. When his trade had increased to a volume that made such a move advisable, he built a store at the farm and continued selling goods there until the advent of the Aransas Pass Railway, when he moved his business to New Sublime, and the old town of the name was abandoned. His first location and business place was called "Miller's Store" and the "Sublime" postoffice was located there several years until it was established where it now is situated.

Mr. Miller began buying land soon after he engaged in merchandising, from the E. W. Perry tract, as well as from the Coulter property. He had acquired some 300 acres when it was suggested to him that he take the remainder of the tracts, and this he did, giving his personal notes for the payment and finally paying them off. He acquired in this way some 800 acres and of this property made farms, and when the railroad came through he contracted with the company to let them plat 600 acres of his land for a townsite, he taking the "odd number" lots and they the "evens," the company to pay all the expenses. Mr. Miller moved his store to the new town, it being the third building to be used as a store there. After a period of more than forty years spent successfully in the mercantile business, Mr. Miller retired therefrom and turned his stock over to his son, August Miller, who had been his partner for some time. He has been out of business since 1907 and since then has been raising the popular staples of the region and breeding stock, giving his entire attention to his interests as a stock-raiser and farmer.

As a citizen Mr. Miller has been rather an independent voter. While he has acted with the democrats, he has also voted against them as well as against the republicans when their candidates, according to his judgment have not been men of honor and ability. His only public service has been as postmaster of Sublime and as a trustee of his school district. He has served his church, the Lutheran, as a member of the official board. He is an honorary member of the Sons of Hermann. Mr. Miller has been a man of strong and vigorous constitution, never having called a doctor on his own account. He has been a member of the church all his life, has done his full duty as a citizen as he has seen the light, and was one of the first men in his locality to start an agitation for churches and schools and has been a leading factor in their support to the present. His children, educated at home, have occupied places of honor as citizens of their community. Altogether, Mr. Miller's life has been a very full and useful one, and he is eminently entitled to be accounted one of Lavaca County's foremost citizens.

Mr. Miller was married in 1858 to Miss Louisa Kleibreng, a daughter of a citizen of Minden, Prussia. She came to the United States with her mother and brother, and enjoyed a happy life with her husband for almost fifty years, dying November 10, 1907, at the age of sixty-seven years. The children born to Mr. and Mrs. Miller were as follows: Robert, Jr., who is engaged in business at Sublime; August, who was for some years engaged in business with his father at Sublime, where he died, leaving two children; Henry, a merchant of Altair, Texas; William, of Houston, ex-postmaster of Hallettsville; Charley, railroad agent at Shiner, Texas; and two others who passed away in childhood.

Herman Neumann. Beginning his career as a mechanic, Herman Neumann has for many years been actively identified with Yoakum, where he is now manager of the Yoakum Oil Company, one of the chief local industries outside of the railroad shops.

A member of one of the ante-bellum German families of Texas, he was born at Industry in Austin County, February 28, 1860. His father, Frederick Herman Neumann, was born at Silesigen, Germany, being one of three sons and three daughters, but was the only one to come to America. He learned the trade of blacksmith, lived for several years in Berlin, and was about thirty years old when he sailed from Bremen to Galveston. A few days after landing he arrived a stranger at Industry, but soon found employment at his trade and kept at it actively until 1883. He then bought a farm in Colorado County at Shaws Bend, and upon it spent the rest of his life. He owned 600 acres and produced a number of crops of corn and cotton. His only official service was as school trustee. Soon after he reached Texas in 1858 he took out citizenship papers, but was soon living under the new Confederate government. He intended to enlist in the army under General Magruder, and but it being discovered that he was a mechanic his services were put to better advantage in the government shops at Houston. After the war he voted a republican ticket on national questions, and was a member of the Lutheran Church. He was married in Austin County to Miss Ida Seeliger, whose father, Ernst Seeliger, was a cigarmaker and merchant at Industry. Mrs. Neumann died on the Colorado County farm in 1907 and her husband passed away in 1896. The record of their children in brief is: Herman; Otto, who died on the old farm in Colorado County leaving a wife; Mary, wife of C. L. Buenger, of Yoakum; Charles and Louis, of Yoakum; Henry, of Houston; Annie, who died in Colorado County as Mrs. Henry Kuhn; William, of Houston; Robert, a Yoakum citizen; and Bernhardt, who died unmarried in Colorado County.

Born not long after his father came to Texas, Herman Neumann spent his youth at Industry. During his career in the public schools the teacher from whom he received the greatest inspiration was the soldier educator, Professor Simmons. His father directed his training to proficiency in the blacksmith trade, and with that as a means of livelihood he remained at Industry until 1890. On moving to Yoakum in that year he established a shop, and worked ahead steadily in a rising scale of prosperity until 1911, when he left his shop to become manager of the

Andrew Jackson Blackburn

Yoakum Cotton Oil Mill. He had been one of the original stockholders when the plant was established more than twenty years ago, but became identified with its management only after a reorganization of its affairs. The present officers of the company are: William Green, president; J. B. Harris, vice president; Philip Welhausen, secretary and treasurer; Mr. Neumann, manager; and I. G. Pospisil, mill superintendent.

During the last quarter century Mr. Neumann has been one of the factors in the public life and improvement of his home city. When a young man he did his first public work as a school trustee and was made president of the board. For about ten years he was president of the Yoakum School Board, was an alderman five years, and for four years a commissioner of Dewitt County. He was one of the last members of the city council when its functions were superseded by the new commission, and he can properly take credit during his term for assistance in paving several blocks of the city streets and in erecting the two splendid schoolhouses.

Fraternally he is past master of Yoakum Lodge, Ancient Free and Accepted Masons, is a Royal Arch Mason, is a past chancellor of the Knights of Pythias and has been a delegate to the Texas Grand Lodge, and is also affiliated with the Ancient Order of United Workmen and the Woodmen of the World, and is a member of the Sons of Hermann.

He was first married in Industry to Miss Emma Schmidt, daughter of Fred Schmidt. She left two children: Alice, wife of Walter Jones of Houston, who have two sons; and Emma, who married Leonard Wade. Mr. Neumann was married in Yoakum to a sister of his first wife, Miss Eleanora Schmidt. The children of this marriage are: Annie, who married J. Gus May of Yoakum and has a daughter, Maxine; and Jesse, who is bookkeeper for the Yoakum oil mill.

Wayne Blackburn. Here is a family name that has been identified with Washington County since 1836. It was only a short time after the battle of San Jacinto, and the winning of Texas independence, that Andrew Jackson Blackburn arrived in what is now Washington County. Since then the various members of the family have proved themselves important factors in community upbuilding and development. Andrew Jackson Blackburn was one of the splendid old types of pioneer settlers. His son Wayne Blackburn has lived for a great many years in the Burton community, and from his home in that town have gone forth his influence and activities not only into business affairs as a stock man, but into the public life of his home locality and county.

The founder of this honored family was Andrew Jackson Blackburn, who was born in Mecklenburg County, North Carolina, July 4, 1813, while the second war was in progress with Great Britain. His parents were country people and of Irish blood. His father, Hugh Blackburn, came to Texas about 1845 and spent the rest of his life as a farmer, and died about 1853 at the age of seventy-five. Many years before he had taken part in the War of 1812 as a follower of General Jackson, and his admiration for that great military leader and politician caused him to give his son the name Andrew Jackson. He spent his last years in what is known as the Blackburn settlement of Washington County. Hugh Blackburn married Margaret Boyd, who is buried beside her husband on the old farm. Their children were: Eliza, who married Thomas Reed and spent her last years in Leon County, Texas; Andrew J.; Jerre, who died in Alabama, leaving a family around Broomtown; Franklin, who died in the Blackburn settlement of Washington County; Jane, who married Mr. Black and died in San Saba County, Texas; and Sarah, who married John Henderson and died soon after her marriage in Fayette County.

Andrew J. Blackburn was a vigorous young man at the time he came to Texas. Though the independence of the state had already been won when he arrived, he subsequently participated in defending the settlement from Indians, and also took part in one or two expeditions against the Mexicans along the border. He was a member of Colonel Moore's expedition out to the Red Fork of the Colorado River, where the Indians were routed. He also took part in the Indian battle at San Saba. At various times for a period of years he was again and again called out to perform this militia duty, and he was always ready to serve. Finally the tide of settlement became too strong for the Indians and the forces of barbarism to uphold; and he spent the rest of his years in comparative calm and quiet. After coming to Texas he worked for a number of years in "whipsawing" lumber on Raab's Creek in Raab's pinery. He left that to engage in farming, and in later years he set up a shop for the repair of guns. He had his little gun shop in operation during the Civil war, and it was located about five miles north of Burton in what was known as the Blackburn settlement. He had moved to that locality in 1851, and lived there until his death on June 7, 1899, when at the age of eighty-six years.

He was widely known as "Squire" Blackburn because of his long service as justice of the peace. So far as schools were concerned he was a man of little education, but he was a reader of books, an observer of men and of motives, and proved himself a very useful man in the community. He was especially skilled in the execution of legal documents affecting transfers of real estate, and such other documents as were required in the community. He was also pronounced a fine judge of law, was widely read, and his mind was a storehouse of historic facts. History was indeed his favorite theme, and he knew not only local and state history, but much of the world's affairs, and could discuss intelligently much that went on beyond the horizon of his own life. He had an interesting fund of anecdote and was regarded as a very entertaining conversationalist. He also had a wide acquaintance in a number of counties in South Texas, and always kept in close touch with the old leaders of Texas independence and was a sincere admirer of the early Texas statesmen and leaders. Though opposed to the separation of Texas from the Union, he went with his state into the Confederacy and served as captain of a Home Guard during the war. About twenty years before his death he united with the Christian Church.

The maiden name of his wife was Mary Jane Cottrell, daughter of Caleb Cottrell, who came to Texas from Illinois in 1845. Her death occurred in February, 1901, at the age of seventy-three. Her children were: Martha, who married Thomas Morelock and lives in Lee County, Texas; Wayne; Margaret, who married Henry Struck of Kaufman County; Sarah, who married William Elliott of Somerville, Texas; Mary, wife of Travis D. Garrett of Milan County; Jerome of Lampasas, Texas; and Frank, of Port Arthur.

It was on the old home farm of his father in Washington County, a short time before the latter removed to the Blackburn settlement, that Wayne Blackburn was born October 19, 1850. His boyhood and early manhood was spent in the Blackburn settlement. He was about eleven years of age when the war broke out, and in the unsettled conditions which followed his schooling was much neglected. He had the advantages of such intermittent schools as were maintained during the decade of the '60s. His energies were directed instead into such practical occupations as the farm and ranch presented. He early learned all the details of farming and stock raising, and he made that knowledge of use to himself when he started out on his own account. After his marriage he made his home just west of Burton, but in 1885 he moved his family into the town, and improved his home on a sightly place just across the draw south of the village. Here for thirty years he has lived, has enjoyed the comforts of home and family and friends, and has made his work and influence count for a great deal in the community.

For about twenty years Mr. Blackburn was associated with William Turner in the firm of Blackburn & Turner, ranchers. Their cow brand was "888." Mr. Blackburn's individual brand was "half yoke." In recent years he has not been extensively engaged in feeding and shipping cattle and he now confines his business in that line to the keeping of a number of well graded cattle. His public life is a matter of interest to the community. He served the county as a commissioner for the first term in the early '80s. In 1908 he was petitioned by his fellow citizens to become a candidate for that office and was elected on the democratic ticket as successor to Gus A. Broesche. He served three full terms. While in office the road problem was the one that presented the most important responsibilities. He did all he could to maintain the highways at the least expense consistent with excellent thoroughfares. He had the roads in the three justice precincts to look after and had several steel bridges built. The county was somewhat in debt when he took office, but at the end of his first term the road and bridge fund had $30,000 surplus. He left the board of his own volition and he had the satisfaction of knowing that the county's fiscal affairs were never in a better condition. For several years he served as a trustee of the Burton schools. Mr. Blackburn is a member of the Christian Church, served as an elder for several years and fraternally is affiliated with the Woodmen of the World.

In Washington County on November 9, 1879, he married Miss Mollie Francis. Her father, Cordal B. Francis, married Emily Harris. Mr. Francis came to Texas about 1850 from the vicinity of Davisboro, Georgia. He was a farmer, served in the Confederate army and died at his home near Burton in July, 1882, at the age of fifty-one. Mrs. Blackburn's brothers and sisters were: James; Mat H.; William B.; and Emily, who died as Mrs. Ollie Spencer leaving two children. To the marriage of Mr. and Mrs. Blackburn were born the following children: Miss Mamie; Earl C., who married Georgie Dement and lives in Port Arthur, Texas; Bonham of Port Arthur, a carpenter, who married Alvina Neinstadt; Gus, of Burton; Ross, a student at Blinn College in Brenham; and Florence, still at home.

William E. Pound. While Mr. Pound is not an old Texan, his record shows him to be the leading factor in building construction at Yoakum, where a number of the best permanent business and private structures testify to his skill and management. Coming to the state in 1906, he was for a short time at San Antonio, engaged in contracting of minor nature. Being awarded the contract to build the Creamery Dairy Company's plant at Yoakum, he has since made his home and headquarters in that city.

Among his more notable contracts at Yoakum mention should be made of the following: The Mergenthal brick residence, the finest home of the city: the St. Regis, the only three-story brick hotel; the large ice plant, the Baptist church, the J. S. Hall business house and J. H. Tucker building on Front Street, the block of Mergenthal store and office buildings, the J. B. Harris building, and the remodeling of the J. M. Haller building, where Bass Brothers have their business.

Since early youth he has sought the practical and rugged experiences of life. He was born October 17, 1867, and his father's house at that time was not far from the present center of Chicago's business district, at Twenty-third Street and Wabash Avenue. William and Sarah (Brookland) Pound were both natives of England, the former of Oxfordshire and the latter of Dovershire, and in 1854 after their marriage they came to America and settled in Chicago. Their first home was where the Polk Street Station now stands, but with the growth of the city he moved out close to the city limits, as then, at Twenty-third Street, and lived in that quarter many years. He was likewise a building contractor, and has done work both in the old and the modern Chicago, the high tide of his business activities coming after the great fire of 1871. He became financially independent, and in recent years has enjoyed the leisure of retirement, and now resides at Thirty-ninth Street and Elmwood Avenue in Chicago. His children were: Thomas, a resident of Chicago; Frank, connected with a chemical laboratory in that city; Phebe, wife of Ed Chapman of Chicago; William E.; and Alfred, also of Chicago.

William E. Pound was the restless one in his father's family, his nature calling for satisfaction in frequent change of scene and occupation. He attended public schools, and his first excursion from the parental home came when he was only nine years old, and from that time forward he indulged himself in that boyhood treat of running away from home. He made several scouts about the country, was in the western mining district of Leadville when it was new, and ever since has had a high appreciation for the men engaged in the rough employments, who often exhibit more real tender sympathy for misfortune than some of the professional philanthropists.

When the rambling fever had subsided, he steadied down to work and learned the contracting business under his father, being employed in connection with several of the latter's contracts. On leaving Chicago he went out to Omaha to help build a packing house for Swift & Company, and his next important work was the construction of two blast furnaces at Manistique in the northern peninsula of Michigan. For a number of years his home was in Bloomington, Illinois, to which city he took his wife after their marriage. For twelve years he was general superintendent for J. W. Evans Sons, of Bloomington, among the largest contractors in that section of Illinois. For this firm he had charge of their work in constructing the $140,000 Methodist church at Davenport, Iowa; of the extensive fairground improvements at Springfield, Illinois, including the erection of the cattle building, the big coliseum and part of the exposition building; and of the high school at Lexington, Illinois. On leaving that firm his next service was with the McKinley Traction Company as superintendent of buildings and bridges along its extensive system of interurban lines through Illinois, and he was with them two years. Then followed another two years at Bloomington, after which he came south to Texas. After the Bloomington fire he helped reconstruct the devastated area, and among other evidences of his work there are the Livingstone building, the Odd Fellows' hall and practically all the new schoolhouses.

Fraternally Mr. Pound is a member of the Masons and Elks, and in the former has begun his Scottish Rite work. His wife and he are members of the Episcopal Church. At Bloomington, April 6, 1892, he was married to Miss Caroline N. Pearson, the officiating clergyman being the Rev. Frank Crane, one of America's most brilliant thinkers, whose syndicated articles are now found published in many of the leading newspapers and magazines. Mrs. Pound is a daughter of B. A. and Mary (Newell) Pearson. Her father was born in Louisville, Kentucky, went to Illinois and before settling at Bloomington lived a few years in Fulton County, where Mrs. Pound was born at Vermont.

OTTO WAGENER. The residence of a large family in one state or community for a period of three generations means a great deal for good or evil, and it can be said that the community of Central Texas where the Wageners have lived have always been benefited on the credit side of the account by the presence of this large family. Otto Wagener himself of Yoakum is a representative of the third generation. For the past twenty-five years the Wageners have been identified with Dewitt County, but previously were community upbuilders in Austin County.

It was in Austin County in the vicinity of Shelby that Mr. Wagener's grandfather, Henry Wagener, located on coming to Texas from Germany in 1846. That was about a year after Texas became a state. Landing at Galveston, he brought his family in ox wagons out to Austin County. At Shelby he made his influence count as a miller. He built a mill operated by mule-power, and continued its operation during the period of the Civil war, and on that account was exempt from service in the Confederate army. He died at Shelby at the age of sixty-four, and both he and his wife are buried there. Their children were: Henry, of Dewitt County; Louise, who married Henry Scharnberg and died at Shelby; William; Emily, who married William Wendlandt of Shiner, Texas.

William Wagener, father of Otto, was born at Shelby in Austin County October 18, 1850, only a few years after grandfather Wagener had located there. He had spent his life as a farmer, and since 1890 has been a resident of Dewitt County. As a boy he had limited advantages in the way of schooling, and has always been quietly identified with his own affairs and has never offered himself for public service. He is a democratic voter and a member of the Lutheran Church. William Wagener married Augusta Holzmann. Her father, John Holzmann, came from Germany as a pioneer in Austin County, while her mother was of a Pennsylvania family. Mrs. William Wagener was born at Shelby, and she and her husband became the parents of the following children: Otto; Emily, the wife of E. Gerdes of Dewitt County; Ida, who married Adolph Raetzsch; Norma, who married Eilert Schumacher of Jim Wells County, Texas; Annie, wife of William Menke of Yoakum; Clara, who married H. H. Johnson of Jim Wells County; and Willie and Tellmonth, both of whom are farmers on the old homestead.

That locality in Austin County at Shelby where his grandfather first settled was the birthplace of Otto Wagener, where he first saw the light of day December 1, 1873. He spent the first fifteen years of his life there and gained his education in the local schools. His early experiences and associations were with the rest of the family either in Austin or Dewitt counties, and at the age of twenty-seven he married and established his first home on the Hochheim prairie in Dewitt County. In that locality he improved his land and continued farming until 1912, when he moved to Yoakum. While he has cultivated a large acreage his chief business has been stock farming, and for a number of years he has been a dealer and shipper in fat stock. His cow brand is "OT." It is due to the enterprise of Otto Wagener that three large farm estates have been developed and improved in Dewitt County. His present place embraces 933 acres, situated in the St. Clair and Miskill surveys and including also a part of the G. H. and S. A. railway lands. Five hundred acres of his estate are under cultivation, and six different sets of improvements, with tenant houses and other equipment, and his farm activities furnish labor and livelihood to fifty people. It is located on the Upper Hochheim Road, eight miles from Yoakum.

While these activities have furnished abundant scope for his energies, Mr. Wagener is also a man of affairs and well known in the public life of Dewitt County. In 1912 as a democrat he was elected county commissioner from Precinct No. 2 of that county, succeeding George P. Willis on the board. His present associates as commissioners are R. J. Waldek, county judge, Charles Lenz, Henry Buesing and B. C. Brown. It has been during Mr. Wagener's term as commissioner that the first bond issues for good roads have been voted by Dewitt County, and his home precinct has the honor of leading off in this important improvement. His own precinct voted $100,000 for the two road districts, and the practical work is now under way. Three districts of the county have voted such bonds, and the proceeds are sufficient to provide for the construction of about thirty miles of fine highways. The members of the county board have the responsibilities of disposing of the funds and the planning of these road improvements.

Fraternally Mr. Wagener is affiliated with the lodge of Masonry, with the Sons of Hermann and the Woodmen of the World, while the family have all been reared in the faith of the Lutheran Church. On October 25, 1900, he married Miss Rosena Raetzsch. Her parents were Julius and Matilda (Fell) Raetzsch, all of them German people, and her father was a carpenter by trade. The Raetzsch family comprise the following children: Herman; Gus; Adolph; Mrs. Wagener; Carl; Sophie, wife of Lee Ward; and Alma, who died in young womanhood. Mr. and Mrs. Wagener have four children: Marvin, Matilda, Raetzsch and Otto, Jr.

Charles E. Duve, M. D. One of the leading physicians of Colorado County, with home and office at Weimar, Dr. Charles E. Duve had an ambition when a boy to study medicine and utilize every resource and opportunity to accomplish that end. He is a native Texan, born in Bastrop County January 28, 1873, and it was in that vicinity that he grew up and acquired his early education in the public schools. While he had the comforts of a good home and the ordinary advantages of a Texas boy, his higher education was a matter left to his individual initiative and energy. Therefore being unable to continue his public school training with a college course, he learned the drug business in Bastrop with the firm of C. Erhard & Son, and spent ten years in their employ, acquiring a thorough business training and a practical knowledge of chemistry and pharmacy. From Bastrop he came to Weimar and in 1897 bought the drug business of S. T. Pearson, and was active in the managebent of that business until 1902. Having established his reputation as a business man, he took the surplus of his active efforts and began the study of medicine in real earnest. He entered the Memphis Hospital Medical College, now the medical department of the University of Tennessee, and was graduated M. D. in 1905. He belongs to the regular school of medicine and did his first practice in Madill, Oklahoma. In January, 1908, he returned to Weimar and has since enjoyed a gratifying success as a physician with a large practice both in the village and in the surrounding country.

Doctor Duve's father, Jachin Duve, who was born in Hanover, Germany, in August, 1846, being the youngest of four children, the names of the other three being: Conrad, who was a sea captain, and went down with his vessel in the Bay of Bengal; Fritz, who was a school teacher and died in Austin County, Texas, leaving a family; and one who remained in Germany. Jachin Duve was given a collegiate education in Germany, on a free scholarship granted the family because of his father's services to the state as chief of police in the City of Hanover during the '60s. Duve is a French name, and is said to have originated in one of

A. B. Blackburn

the French provinces of Germany, either Alsace or Lorraine, and in Germany it was pronounced with the accent on the last syllable. Jachin Duve after coming to Texas married Clara Hoppe, a daughter of Fred W. Hoppe. Mr. Hoppe emigrated from Leipzic, Germany, in 1850, and settled in Bastrop, where he was engaged in both sawmill and gristmill work. He died there in 1904, and during the war between the states had been exempt from military duty on account of his occupation as a miller. In the early days the Hoppe family were republicans, but later members of the family voted with the democrats. Both the Hoppe and Duve families are Lutheran Church people. Mrs. Jachin Duve died in 1907 at the age of fifty-seven. Her children were: Mrs. Rosa Stoddard, of New York City; Dr. Charles E.; Mrs. Louisa Zieten, of Wiemar; and Grover C., of Oklahoma City.

Dr. Charles E. Duve was married in Wiemar, December 8, 1896, to Miss Rosalie Brasher, a daughter of Charles and Laura R. (Moore) Brasher. Her father was a Texas by birth and her mother was born in Marshall County, Mississippi. Mrs. Duve was the youngest of four children, her elders being: Henry, of Weimar; Cora Moore, of Bay City, Texas; and Lizzie, who died unmarried. Doctor Duve and wife have two children: Frederick B., born October 5, 1904, and Reginald, born September 22, 1911.

Doctor Duve has interested himself both in and out of his profession. He is president of the Colorado County Medical Society, a member of the Texas State Medical Association, the Southern Medical Association, and is local surgeon of the Southern Pacific Railway. He is also a director and stockholder in the Wiemar Drug Company. In politics his chief interests have been as a democratic voter, and fraternally he is a past master of the lodge of Masons at Weimar.

WAYNE B. BLACKBURN. The entire life of Wayne Blackburn was passed in Washington County, where he achieved worthy success through his well ordered endeavors and where his strong and noble character gained to him inviolable place in the confidence and high regard of all with whom he came in contact. He was one of the loyal and influential citizens of the county at the time of his death, which occurred at his home, in the Village of Burton, on the 22d of March, 1909. His widow still resides at Burton and, as later paragraphs will more definitely show, she is a representative of one of the oldest and most distinguished pioneer families of this section of the Lone Star State.

On the homestead farm of his parents, near Burton, Washington County, Wayne B. Blackburn was born on the 26th of December, 1860, a son of Frank and Elizabeth Blackburn, who here continued their residence until their death, their only other child likewise having been a son and he, too, being deceased. The subject of this memoir initiated a semi-independent career while still but a boy, and through his own exertions he accumulated the funds which enabled him to supplement effectively the meager education which he had acquired in the pioneer schools. As a youth he engaged himself in butchering activities in his home community and was given employment along this line by the neighbors, who appreciated his ambition and his earnest efforts to make a start in life. He finally was able to engage in the cattle business, in connection with which he instituted operations on a very modest scale, and prior to his marriage he maintained a bachelor's home on the Bishop ranch. After he had taken to himself the young wife who continued his cherished and devoted companion and helpmeet until his death, he established his home in the immediate vicinity of the Village of Burton. He became known as a specially fine trader and as a man of much initiative and executive ability, his ever increasing success thus representing the direct results of his own effective efforts, which were always guided and governed by the highest principles of integrity and honor. His buoyant and genial nature and inflexible uprightness gained to him the unqualified esteem of all who knew him and with all consistency can it be said that his circle of loyal friends was limited only by that of his acquaintances. Deception and all other subtle evasions, either in connection with business or social affairs, were utterly foreign to his nature, and it has well been said that he would have sacrificed his property rather than to do an injustice to anyone. Mr. Blackburn became specially prominent and successful in the raising of high-grade horses and cattle and developed a large business as a regular shipper of live stock from Burton. He did much to improve the standards of live stock raised in this section of the state and was a regular and appreciative attendant of the stock shows in the City of Fort Worth.

A man of fine mind and high principles, Mr. Blackburn was essentially loyal, liberal and progressive as a citizen and took lively interest in all that concerned the welfare of his home community. As a general trader he aided much in furthering the business activities of Burton and Washington County, as he was always ready to buy and dispose of the produce and seeds raised by the farmers of this section. He was alert and indefatigable in his business activities and exemplified most fully the true progressive spirit of the West. Politics had no lure for him as a matter of personal exploitation or maneuvering, but he gave a staunch support to the democratic party and was always ready to lend his aid in the furtherance of its cause. He was appreciative of the spiritual verities of the Christian faith and was liberal and generous in the support of religious organizations and movements, with naught of intolerance or denominational bias.

Mr. Blackburn passed to eternal rest in the full vigor of his strong and worthy manhood, exposure while riding over the country in connection with his cattle business having brought about the severe attack of la grippe that finally resulted in his death. While he was lying ill, those who had sold their live stock to him in the final period of his operations held back further disposition of the stock to await his recovery, and finally when death set its seal upon his mortal lips the entire community manifested a sense of personal loss and bereavement, as shown by the great assemblage that met to pay to him a last tribute on the occasion of his funeral.

On the 12th of March, 1902, was solemnized the marriage of Mr. Blackburn to Miss Maggie Armstrong, concerning whose family history due record will be given in appending paragraphs. Mrs. Blackburn was born on the Joel Lakey League in Washington County, and her higher education was acquired in Chapel Hill College, an admirable institution maintained in Washington County for the training of young women. She is a daughter of William T. and Margaret Elizabeth (Francis) Armstrong, and she still resides in the fine homestead provided by her husband and herself. This attractive residence is situated upon a hill a short distance south of Burton, and commands an excellent view of the surrounding country as well as of the village. Mrs. Blackburn entered fully into the confidence of her husband in connection with his business affairs, and thus she has been admirably equipped for continuing the stock business which he had developed. She is an exceptionally efficient and progressive business woman, continues regular shipments of live stock from Burton, as had her husband, and is giving attention most successfully to the breeding and raising of high-grade Durham cattle, her landed estate comprising about 6,000 acres and the same being well improved. This great ranch is situated on the Yegua River and is traversed by Cedar Creek and Nail's Creek, the brand of the cattle on the Blackburn ranch being two Xs barred under, and the stock being shipped principally to the Fort Worth market. The pleasant home of Mrs. Blackburn is pervaded by the atmosphere and accessories of culture and refinement, with a well stocked general library and the best of current literature, and it is known for its generous and gracious hospitality under the régime of its popular chatelaine.

Mr. and Mrs. Blackburn became the parents of five children, all of whom are living except one, their names and respective dates of birth being here entered: Mary Lee, January 21, 1903: Margaret Elizabeth and Nettie May, twins, who were born May 21, 1905, and the latter of whom died at the age of two months; Wayne Bishop, Jr., January 13, 1907; and Lucille Ivy, August 20, 1909. Mrs. Blackburn is a member of the Methodist Episcopal Church, South, and in its faith is carefully rearing her children, one of whom is serving as secretary of the Sunday school of the church of this denomination at Burton.

Mrs. Blackburn may well take pride in being a representative, through the maternal line, of the honored pioneer family that was founded in Texas by Joel Lakey, who came from either Illinois or Iowa and established a home for his family in the Mexican Province of Texas, to which he came with his family in the year that Moses Austin here founded his colony. Mr. Lakey settled on Caney Creek and his original homestead was on the line between the present counties of Austin and Washington. Here he entered claim to a headright of three leagues of land and instituted the development of a frontier farm or ranch. He became one of the influential men of the colony and while the Texas Revolution was in progress he did effective service in caring and providing for the families of soldiers who had gone to the front to fight for Texas independence. He died prior to 1840, at an advanced age, and his name merits high place on the roll of the honored pioneers who played a large part in the initial stages of development and progress on the Texas frontier.

On his removal to the wilds of Texas Joel Lakey was accompanied by his wife and several of their children, and Mrs. Lakey, whose maiden name was Nancy Callaway, survived him by a few years. Of their children who came to Texas the eldest was Elizabeth, and she became the wife of Gibson Kurkendall, who was a gallant soldier in the Texas Revolution, as was also Amos Gates, who married her next younger sister, Lydia. Ruth became the wife of John Hall, another sterling pioneer of Texas. Nancy wedded Miller Francis, who was one of the gallant soldiers who aided in the winning of Texas independence and who took part in the historic battle of San Jacinto; they were the parents of the mother of Mrs. Blackburn, who has kindly furnished the data from which this article is prepared. Thomas Lakey, the only son of Joel and Nancy (Callaway) Lakey, became one of the representative farmers and stock-growers of Texas and was a resident of Walker County at the time of his death. Three other daughters of Joel Lakey remained in Louisiana, where they married and reared their children.

Miller Francis, maternal grandfather of Mrs. Blackburn, came to Texas in 1832, his former home having been near Lexington, Missouri. He settled on Caney Creek and here he eventually married Miss Nancy Lakey, as intimated in the foregoing paragraph. He was a man of superior intellectuality and had been a successful teacher at Nashville, Tennessee, prior to his removal to Missouri, from which state, when a young man, he accompanied the great frontiersman, Kit Carson, on trapping and hunting expeditions on the plains and in the Rocky Mountains. He was in full accord with southern sentiment, was a Methodist in his religious faith, and was the owner of a number of slaves after he had established his residence in Texas. His only son was a gallant soldier of the Confederate service in the Civil war and sacrificed his life in the cause. Mr. Francis died in 1882, at the age of seventy-two years, and his wife, who likewise was an earnest member of the Methodist Church, passed away in 1893, at the age of seventy-seven years. Of their children the eldest is Margaret, who is the widow of William T. Armstrong and who resides in the home of her daughter Maggie, widow of the subject of this memoir, where she is accorded the deepest filial solicitude by her daughter and her grandchildren. James Woodson Francis, the only son, entered the Confederate service early in the Civil war and was still in service at the time of his death, in January, 1865. He never married. Lydia Ann is the wife of Dr. John W. Tottenham, who is engaged in the practice of his profession at Brenham, the county seat of Washington County.

William T. Armstrong, father of Mrs. Blackburn, was born near Montgomery, Alabama, and from Texas he went forth as a soldier in the Mexican war, besides which he took part in various Indian conflicts prior to the Civil war. Prior to his marriage he had established himself in the mercantile business at Chapel Hill, Washington County, and later he became a prosperous agriculturist and stock-grower on the Joel Lakey League, where he continued his successful operations until his death, which occurred on the 7th of March, 1887. He was a stalwart democrat in politics and was a zealous member of the Methodist Episcopal Church, South, as is also his venerable widow, who now resides in the home of their only daughter, Mrs. Blackburn, as has already been stated. Of their children the eldest is William T., who is a successful grain dealer at Mission, Victoria County, where his next younger brother, Miller F., is a representative banker and real-estate dealer and owner. James F. is a prosperous farmer near Orange, the judicial center of the county of the same name. Mrs. Maggie Blackburn, of this review, was the next in order of birth. Robert Lee is a prominent agriculturist and cattle man of Washington County, where he owns property on the ancestral Joel Lakey League. Thomas H. is engaged in the grain business at Mission, where he is associated with his eldest brother.

John Abner Fowlkes. A native of Texas when it was a republic, John Abner Fowlkes owns and operates a fine plantation in Lavaca County, where he is regarded as among the pioneer citizens. Mr. Fowlkes typifies the planter of the older class and generation, and while he has had his share of vicissitudes and hardships possesses a serene optimism which enables him to see the enjoyable side of life. He possesses a large fund of information about people and things of other days, has many entertaining reminiscences, and friends and guests at his hospitable home are never without the entertainment furnished by cultivated talk. At the same time he has made a success in his business affairs, and is one of the ablest representatives of his generation.

John Abner Fowlkes was born near the village of Oakland, at what was known as Prairie Point, only a few miles from his present home, on February 14, 1843. The Fowlkes family is of Scotch-Irish origin, his forefathers going into Ireland following the reign of Cromwell, and a later branch sending its posterity to the shores of America. The name was originally Fawkes, but in America it has taken its present form of orthography.

The grandfather of Mr. Fowlkes was E. B. Fowlkes, a planter and slave holder of Culpeper County, Virginia, who moved to Arkansas in

1839, bringing his retinue of slaves and locating in Hempstead County. There he spent his last years and left a fine estate. He served with the rank of quartermaster in the War of 1812, his official designation being captain, and belonged to the pro-slavery party of the South and acted with the democratic party. He died before the outbreak of the war between the states, but his sons enlisted and served as Confederate soldiers. By his marriage to Miss Bruce he had the following children: Ethelbert B.; Emily, who died at Washington, Arkansas; Eliza, who married J. P. Hervey, and died near Hope, Arkansas; Abner, who served as captain in Price's army, and died near Hope; Louisa, who first married a Mr. Rainey and later a lawyer named Canaday, and lived in Sevier County, Arkansas.

Ethelbert B. Fowlkes, father of John Abner, was born in Culpeper County, Virginia, and in 1839 moved to Texas and located his family at Rutersville, in Fayette County. During the first years spent in the republic he was chiefly occupied in Indian fighting. He taught a session or so of school at LaGrange, being a man of liberal education and a graduate of a college at Georgetown, D. C. He was a man whose ability would have graced any public position, but he possessed that spirit of adventure which kept him in the exciting scenes of the frontier. He had come to Texas for the purpose of aiding Houston in battling with the Mexicans, but the war was over before he arrived, and his service was chiefly as an Indian fighter. He was in the fight at Plum Creek, an engagement frequently mentioned in the historic annals of the time. When he gave up his duties as a soldier he engaged in farming, moved to Colorado County, and settled on Navidad Creek, on what is now the Rabb place. He lived there from 1846 until 1853, and then removed seven miles below Columbus, purchasing a plantation with the inheritance from his father's estate. Some years later his wife died there, and he afterwards married a Mrs. Wooldridge, and spent his remaining years about a mile from Oakland. He is buried in Clear Creek Cemetery. His death occurred March 8, 1880, at the age of sixty-three. He did some service in the Confederate Army as a member of the militia, and was a squire for the Oakland community. A man of thorough and exact information, he had no ability as a public speaker, and his participation in public affairs was always in a modest capacity.

Ethelbert B. Fowlkes first married Mary McClelland, a daughter of Frank McClelland, whose home was at Prescott, Arkansas. Mrs. Fowlkes died below Columbus and is buried in a private cemetery. Her children were: Edward Bruce, who was killed in Georgia just at the close of the war during the Ku Klux troubles of that state, having been a Confederate soldier in the Eleventh Louisiana Infantry; Eliza, who married J. P. Mays, and died near Oakland, Texas; John A.; and Josephine, who became the wife of James W. Carson, and died in 1889 near Oakland.

John Abner Fowlkes grew up on a plantation in Colorado County. It was intended that he should have a liberal education, and he was in the process of carrying out that plan at Sweet Home, in Lavaca County, when the war broke out between the states. He volunteered there in Captain Fred Malone's company, which soon disbanded, and his next enlistment was in Company C, of Willis' Battalion, Wall's Texas Legion. Willis' Battalion left for the front with more than seven hundred men, and its losses were exceedingly heavy during the war. This command made an effort to join the Confederate Army before the battle of Elkhorn, in Northern Arkansas, but failing in effecting a junction with the main body of Confederate troops in October, 1862, it crossed the Mississippi River at Vicksburg and reenforced General Van Dorn's army, and during 1863 took part in the Vicksburg campaign, being in practically all the fighting under General Joseph Johnston in his efforts to relieve that city. After the fall of Vicksburg Mr. Fowlkes and his comrades were placed under General Bedford Forrest for raiding purposes. He participated in the capture of Fort Pillow and was present when General Forrest gave the order to take no negro prisoners, since the South did not recognize them as soldiers. After Fort Pillow the command went into the iron region of Alabama, near Montevallo, then returned into Mississippi, and met Grierson's troops at Guntown, defeated them at Brice's Crossroads and struck A. J. Smith's army at Pontotoc and fought them for four days near Harrisburg, on Town Creek, an engagement which brought heavy losses to Willis' Battalion. After the command had been recruited it was ordered to Mobile to act as pickets for General Maury, and was finally returned into Mississippi, and at Vernon one-half of the Texas troops were furloughed. Mr. Fowlkes was one of the lucky ones who drew a permission to return home, and walked from the army headquarters as far as Beaumont, Texas, then took a train and journeyed by rail to the terminus of the line at Columbus, and from there walked to the home of Mrs. Crenshaw, who urged him to take a horse for the rest of his way home. Mr. Fowlkes had been absent from June, 1862, until April, 1865, and had escaped serious injury and had never become a prisoner in the hands of the Federals. His first captain was Frank Weeks, and his second was John Conn. Maj. T. M. Howard was in command of the battalion at the close of the war. Mr. Fowlkes has been a frequent veteran in the Confederate reunions, and has attended those notable gatherings at Little Rock, Mobile, Houston, Birmingham, and Jacksonville.

As soon as some order had been introduced into industrial and civic life following the chaos of the war Mr. Fowlkes took up farming. In 1865 he planted a crop of cotton and sold his product at fifty cents a pound. The following year misfortune overtook his plantation, and he lost nearly all he had made in previous seasons. Somewhat later he bought a farm from Dr. Bush Wilkins, in Lavaca County, but in the early '70s began buying land included in his present plantation. In 1889 he removed his home to his ranch and built one of the best country residences in the county at that time. His present holdings include over eight hundred acres, and it is all devoted to mixed farming and stock raising. Mr. Fowlkes has been interested in democratic politics, is an anti-prohibitionist, was never a candidate for office, and fraternally is affiliated with the Masonic lodge. In his religious opinions he has a strong leaning toward Universalism.

On March 11, 1869, near his present home, Mr. Fowlkes married Miss Mary Margaret McKinnon. Her father, Laughlin McKinnon, came from McNairy County, Tennessee, to Texas in 1850, and was a carpenter by trade and a farmer by general vocation. His wife was Lizzie Sherman, and among their other children were Mrs. Joseph Simpson, Mrs. Thomas McKay, Mrs. George Brady and Laughlin McKinnon.

Mr. and Mrs. Fowlkes are the parents of the following children: Lizzie, wife of A. W. Turner, of Victoria, Texas; Robert L., of Wichita Falls, Texas; Ed B.; Miss Margaret; McKinnon B.; Abner W., of Caldwell, Texas; and George Clark. McKinnon B. Fowlkes married Miss Katherine Miller, of Sublime, Texas, on November 4, 1914, and they have one son, John Abner Fowlkes, Jr. She is a daughter of Robert and Emma (Strunk) Miller, of Sublime, and a sketch of his father, Robert Miller, Sr., appears elsewhere in this publication.

WILLIAM LAWRENCE. A resident of Lavaca County most of his life, William Lawrence belongs to some of the oldest American stock in Texas, antedating the war for independence in which his father took part. Since the war between the states, in which he was a soldier, he has applied his energies to the staple industry of Lavaca County, farming and stock raising, and has a good estate near Hallettsville.

William Lawrence was born in old Washington County, Texas, December 13, 1839. His grandfather was named William, and among his children are recalled the names of William, Absalom, Jason, Joseph and Mrs. Barbara Beaver.

Joseph Lawrence was the pioneer Texan. Born in North Carolina, he left there at the age of fifteen, spent several years at Nashville, Tennessee, and in 1833 arrived in Texas, then a province of Mexico. He identified himself with the movement for Texan independence during the years of 1835-36, and joined Houston's army in time to participate in the culminating battle at San Jacinto. This service entitled him to a land warrant, which was laid in Ellis County, and which his sons sold at $2.50 per acre, unconscious of the future value of acres now located in one of the richest agricultural sections of the state.

After independence Joseph Lawrence, who first lived in Washington County, moved to Dewitt County, but that locality was so exposed to Indian raids that he found a safer location in LaGrange and spent about five years there. He then moved into Lavaca County, to a place two miles north of where his son William now lives, and there spent his active years in superintending his ranch and stock. When he died, in 1897, at the age of ninety-four, he was one of the oldest residents of Texas, and highly respected both as a soldier of the Revolution and as a man. Though without education, never having signed his name, he possessed the rugged virility of the pioneer, good judgment in business affairs, and had reared and provided home and other advantages for his family of some ten children. Though a Methodist, he was like many of the older settlers rather backward in church matters.

Joseph Lawrence was married at the old town of Washington, on the Brazos, to Mary E. McGary, an Irish lady who died in Lavaca County. Their children were: William; Bettie, who married S. G. McCown, and died in Yoakum, Texas; Cameron, of Goliad, Texas; Margaret, who married Wallace Chrisman, and died in Dallas; Mary, who became the wife of Henry Smith, and died in Floresville, Texas; Ellen, who married James A. Jameson, of Yoakum; Susan, who died in Lavaca County as the wife of Elijah Sewell; Martha, Mrs. James Brown, of Dallas County; Joseph, now deceased; and Jack, who died at Marlin, Texas.

William Lawrence has lived in Lavaca County since 1849. In his youth schools were not held so important factors in training the younger generation as they are now, and his education rather practical than bookish. Just about the time he was getting ready for life on his own responsibilities, the war came on and in August, 1861, his name was enrolled in the Confederate service. Captain Whitfield's company, which he joined, reported for duty to Gen. Ben McCulloch, in Northern Arkansas, and there Whitfield's legion was organized. He fought at the Battle of Elkhorn, armed with a Mississippi rifle, which he had brought from Hallettsville, and after that engagement his command was sent to Des Arc, Arkansas, and there dismounted and sent to Memphis as infantry. It was in the operations about Corinth, fell back to Tupelo, and there rested and recuperated from the epidemic of measles which was making havoc among the soldiers. After the battle at Iuka, in which they participated, the legion was again mounted and resumed rank as cavalry. They went into Tennessee, fought at Thompson's Station, and were in the raid of Gen. Van Dorn against Grant's supply train at Holly Springs and helped capture a number of Federal prisoners there. They were then attached to Johnston's army for the relief of Vicksburg. The fall of Vicksburg Mr. Lawrence regarded as the death blow to the hopes of a victorious Confederacy, and after that he fought only as a soldier's duty and not with the spirit which he had begun. He was always present for any service, and as orderly sergeant called the roll of his company every day, but he realized that it was a loss of time and waste of men to continue the struggle against the overwhelming odds on the side of the North. In April, 1864, an order directed that one man from each company should be furloughed home. When the captain presented him the hat containing the lots of those who should go and those who should remain, he scratched down to the bottom of the hat and pulled out a "furlough." When he left the army for sixty days he bade his comrades farewell, for he had determined never again to engage in the war east of the Mississippi. A month after he reached home he married, and a little later joined a company that was organizing in Horton County for duty on the frontier. Capt. William Townsend was in command of this company, with headquarters near San Patricio, but they patrolled a large part of the Rio Grande district, from San Antonio to Laredo and Eagle Pass, and he had returned from one of these long rounds when the news came of Lee's surrender and the end of the war.

Once more free to take up the duties of civil life, Mr. Lawrence resumed his old vocation, farm and stock. His present estate, containing some 560 acres, is on the Woodard and Fuller leagues, and he and his good wife have labored wisely and well to accumulate and improve this substantial homestead. They have fenced it and have brought 250 acres under cultivation, have set up six sets of buildings, and have directed the work of the tenants chiefly to producing cotton.

Mr. Lawrence was married May 11, 1864, to Miss Henrietta Coffey, who represents another family of early Texas. Her father, William Coffey, was born and reared in Kentucky, but came from Jackson County, Alabama, to Texas in 1844, and settled first in Titus County, and in 1859 came to Lavaca County, where he was a slave-holding farmer until the war. He died in November, 1875, at the age of eighty. He married Elizabeth Schooler, who died in 1871, and their children were as follows: Milton, of Morris County, Texas; Mary J., who married Millis Higginbotham, and died in Titus County; Eliza, who married William Riley, and died in Lavaca County; Emeline, who died unmarried; Catherine, the wife of John Williams, lives near Mrs. Lawrence, who is the next in the family; Margaret, who married Steve Pool, of San Angelo; and John, of Brown County.

To Mr. and Mrs. Lawrence were born five children: Ellen is the wife of Jep Griffith, of Uvalde, Texas; Willie is the wife of Allen English, and they live on the Lawrence farm; Lulu married Laughlin Simpson, a farmer in this neighborhood; Leon died in young manhood, and his twin brother died at the age of eleven years.

Rev. Frederich Neubert. For nearly twenty years Father Neubert has been in the active work of the Catholic ministry in Southern Texas, in and about Fayette County. He is now pastor of St. John's parish at Ammansville, and is regarded as one of the most vigorous leaders and upbuilders of his church in this section of Texas. While his devotion to the ministry has not allowed him to become as well known as men in other walks of life, Father Neubert has the qualities of manhood and

C. T. Sanders

character which, outside the church, would have brought him distinction in any of the professions, or in business or politics. He has spent twenty-two years in Southern Texas, having come to the state and to the United States in 1893, along with his parents and brothers and sisters.

Father Neubert was born in Friedek, an industrial center of Silesia, Austria, January 30, 1872. He grew up in his native city, where his father, Frederich Neubert was a merchant. For generations back the family have lived in that one locality, and had been at different times identified with official life, with the church and with business. Frederich Neubert married Francisco Klisch, whose people were identified with the industries, chiefly in the manufacture of cotton goods. Father Neubert was the oldest of four children, and the only other survivor is Mary, wife of Charles Klimitshek, living near Hallettsville. The family came to the United States in 1893, and the father died at Hallettsville in 1894. The mother is now housekeeper for Father Neubert.

His early education was acquired in his native town. At the age of eight years he entered the gymnasium at Troppau, the capital of Silesia, and was there seven years. He did his classical work in that institution, and after coming to America finished his studies in philosophy and theology at Victoria in St. Joseph's College. At the end of four years he was ordained in 1896 at St. Mary's Church by Bishop Forrest, of the San Antonio diocese. He was ordained with Rev. Father Hefferman, who is now stationed at Bandera, Texas.

Father Neubert's first work was as assistant priest at Hallettsville for two years. He was then assigned to Ammansville, Bluff and Plum, and remained in charge of those localities three years. His next pastorate was at St. John's Church, in Fayette County, near Schulenburg, and he did an important work in maintaining and developing the church activities in that vicinity for ten years. Since then he has resumed his pastorate at Ammansville and Bluff. Soon after coming to the United States Father Neubert took out citizenship papers and has been a voter for eighteen years. While not a politician, and primarily devoted to the interests of his church, he takes some interest in government affairs and has declared himself for democratic principles. Father Neubert, like many men of his profession and class is an excellent linguist, has a mastery over a number of languages both ancient and modern, but his favorite tongues are the Bohemian and Polish.

Rev. Christie T. Sanders. The various activities which have filled the long and useful life of Rev. Christie T. Sanders, of Sealy, have been of a character to make his name one of the best known in Austin County, where he has resided since 1875. Three professions, the law, the clergy and education, have profited by his labors, for a number of years he was engaged in mercantile pursuits, and at the present time he is cashier of the Sealy National Bank. His life has been a full and satisfying one, and in each community in which he has resided he has merited and held the confidence and regard of his fellow-citizens.

Christie T. Sanders was born northwest of Paris, the county seat of Monroe County, Missouri, January 30, 1852, and is a son of Henry Sanders. His grandfather, Wiley Sanders, was a native of Kentucky, where he was engaged as a farmer and worked his land with slave labor. and in his later years moved to Missouri where he died, being buried in the old Sanders family cemetery. He and his wife Sallie were the parents of the following children: William, who passed his life as a farmer in Monroe County, Missouri, and left a large family there; Henry, the father of Christie T.; Pollie, who became the wife of Hartwell

Rigsby and passed her life in Monroe County, Missouri; Wiley, who remained in the same county and at his death left two children; John, who died there unmarried; Thomas, who left a son at his death; Sallie, who became the wife of Jack Herndon and died in Monroe County; and Christie, who passed his life as a farmer and left a large family at the time of his death.

Henry Sanders was born in the vicinity of Lexington, Kentucky, in 1815, and was a youth of eighteen years when he emigrated to Missouri, settling in Monroe County, near Woodlawn. There he passed his entire life in farming and also specialized in mule growing, a branch of agriculture in which he became particularly well known. Through industry, energy and perseverance he was successful in his undertakings, and at the time of his death was considered a man of good property. He died in 1902, in the faith of the Baptist Church, in which he had been an active worker, making a record as a man of God. In political matters he was a democrat.

The childhood and youth of Christie T. Sanders were passed on the homestead farm and his early education was secured in the public schools of Monroe County, this being supplemented by a course in the old Mount Pleasant College, in Randolph County, Missouri. He was inclined to follow the law as a vocation and after some preparation was admitted to the bar and entered practice, but his activities in this direction were confined to his native state and after his arrival in Texas his attention was always turned in other directions. At the age of twenty-four years Mr. Sanders began teaching school in the country districts of Kansas, and remained in that calling for a period of six years, finishing his career as an educator in Austin County, Texas, where from January 1, 1875, until 1880, he was in charge of the city schools of Bellville. At the time that he gave up his career as a teacher, he turned his attention and ambitions to the mercantile business, establishing himself as proprietor of a general store at Bellville. After a short period he admitted a partner, the business style then becoming Langhammer & Sanders, and was subsequently made Sanders & Menke, which firm moved to Sealy in 1889. This almost immediately became recognized as one of the leading firms of the town, and Mr. Sanders remained in business until 1891, when he disposed of his interests to his partner and changed the course of his own career entirely.

In 1891 Mr. Sanders was ordained a minister of the Baptist Church at Sealy by the Presbytery composed of Rev. C. C. Green, Rev. S. A. Poindexter and the deacons of the church. He had been converted while a citizen of Bellville, and at once had commenced taking an active interest in church and congregational work. After his ordination he was assigned to pastoral work of the Sealy Baptist Church, and with the exception of a year spent at Tyler, Texas, was connected with ministerial labors here for ten years. In 1901 Reverend Sanders was forced to abandon active ministerial work because of a nervous breakdown, and has since engaged in but few labors of this character, save when called upon to officiate at baptisms, marriages and funerals. That he was greatly beloved by his parishioners is shown by the fact that they still call upon him on occasions of special importance. In 1902, when he had recuperated from his illness, he entered the Sealy National Bank as assistant cashier, a position which he retained for two years, and in 1904 succeeded J. G. Wessendorf as cashier of this institution, one of the strong banks of this part of Austin County.

Reverend Sanders has always been interested in the effective work of education at Sealy and has served many years in the capacity of trustee of schools, being at the present time president of the board of trustees. He held a like position while a resident of Bellville, at the time when the law providing for independent school districts was passed and the sentiment for such a measure originated among that board and was crystallized into law through the efforts of the representative to the Legislature from Bellville, Hon. A. Chesley. Reverend Sanders was made a Mason at Bellville and is a past master and past high priest of the Bellville Chapter and holds membership also in the Brenham Commandery. He has served as district deputy grand master of his district. Personally, Reverend Sanders' appearance is one of distinction, he being a tall, erect, well-built man, with a very dignified bearing.

At Bellville, Texas, June 20, 1878, Reverend Sanders was united in marriage with Miss Bertha L. Menke, a daughter of Theodore Menke, a merchant at Bellville, a man of prominence, and a native of Germany. Mr. Menke came to America among the early settlers of Texas, became a farmer, and married Amelia Schultz, they becoming the parents of five children, as follows: Henry B., of Sealy; Mrs. Sanders, who was born March 27, 1860; Miss Dora, who died young; Miss Sophie, a resident of Houston; and Emma, who is the wife of F. Roensch, of Bellville. Six children have been born to Reverend and Mrs. Sanders: Harry Oliver, who died at the age of nineteen years; Mahala, who married Paul Hackbarth, of San Antonio; Theodore, who died in childhood; Charles H., assistant cashier of the Texas City National Bank; Juanita, who died in infancy and Miss Christie.

Gus Russek. Cashier of the First National Bank of Schulenburg and mayor of that city, Gus Russek is an active representative in the present vigorous generation of a family which has been identified with Schulenburg and vicinity from early days, and is a son of the late Ignaz Russek, whose career with that of other members of the family will be found sketched on other pages.

Gus Russek was born in Schulenburg November 9, 1879, and grew up in that locality. His education came first from the public schools, and after leaving high school he entered St. Louis College, at San Antonio, spent two years there, and was also in the Agricultural and Mechanical College at Bryan. The first eighteen years of his life sufficed for his training and education and he then took up the serious business of his career in his father's banking house at Schulenburg. His principal forte is finance, and it needed little training to make him proficient in the handling of banking affairs. In 1906 he became associated with some of the local business men in the organization of the First National Bank of Schulenburg, which started out on January 1, 1906, with a capital of $25,000, and Mr. Russek as cashier and director. To a large extent he had helped to popularize this institution in its service, and has occupied his post as cashier from the beginning.

His name is also associated with other business enterprises which are largely in the nature of public utilities. He established the Schulenburg Light & Ice Company, also the Schulenburg Creamery Company. He represents many of the strong insurance companies doing business in the United States, and has one of the leading insurance offices in South Texas. Politically a democrat, he has been interested in politics largely from a local standpoint. His first and only office was that of mayor, to which he was elected in April, 1912, and again in April, 1913, without opposition. He is the successor of Mayor Theo. Wolters, and his administrative duties have been discharged with care and fidelity.

Fraternally Mr. Russek is a Master Mason, is past master of Schulenburg Lodge No. 179, Ancient Free and Accepted Masons, is a past grand in the Independent Order of Odd Fellows, and a member of the Woodmen of the World. April 14, 1904, Mr. Russek was married in Schulenburg to Miss Cora Kessler, daughter of E. B. Kessler, representing an old established family and a prominent business man of Schulenburg. They have two children: Victor Bernard and Evelyn Cora.

In 1911 Mr. Russek built the most attractive home in Schulenburg, a spacious one-story cottage, with generous galleries, attractive architecture, and the product of the best skill of house building, with an environment in the grounds that suggests at once the excellent taste of its owners. Personally Mr. Russek is a man whose aggressive character is at once suggested in the vigorous and positive movements of his body and the expression of his face. He is well described as a force in causing things to happen, and is the logical successor of his father as a financier. His fellow townsmen gave honor where honor was due in making him a mayor of the city.

William Hillje. That section of Colorado County of which Weimar is the metropolis has for many years been influenced in its general development and commercial life by the presence and activities of the Hillje family, of which William Hillje is one of several representatives. Concerning the early ancestry, the first settlement and the fortunes of the different generations of this family in Texas, a more complete sketch will be found on other pages of this publication. William Hillje is one of the younger members of the family, and has gained prominence as an oil mill operator at Weimar, being manager of the large industry of Hillje Brothers, the chief industrial asset of the little city.

William Hillje was born in Fayette County December 24, 1872, and is a son of the late John F. Hillje. His early education came from country schools at his birthplace, and he also attended the LaGrange High School. Practically all his active career has been identified with some phase of the cotton industry, either as a ginner or as an oil mill operator. When he left home he went to San Antonio and took a position in the machinery department of the San Antonio Oil Mill as a foreman, his previous experience at home having well qualified him for the responsibilities of that place. After about six months he returned to Weimar and became foreman of the machinery department of the oil mill there. At the death of his brother Fred, in 1896, he assumed the latter's duties as one of the owners and the manager of the mill.

The Weimar oil works of Hillje Brothers was erected in 1880 by that firm, then comprising Fred and Lewis Hillje, who were especially prominent as oil mill operators. Lewis Hillje is still active in the business in San Antonio. The capacity of the Weimar plant is forty tons daily, and its operations extend over a period embracing about one-half of each year. During the active crushing season its working force embraces about thirty-five employes. Naturally the presence of such a business means much to community prosperity, and the Hillje Brothers Oil Mill is always mentioned as foremost among Weimar's resources. William Hillje is also a stockholder and director in the T. A. Hill State Bank of Weimar and a stockholder and director of the Brady Cotton Oil Company of Brady. For several years he served as an alderman of Weimar, and was a member of the municipal government when the water mains were extended and the new school building erected, in addition to the routine business of the little city. Politically his affiliations are as a democrat, but the only convention service he has performed was in 1914, when Ferguson was indorsed for governor and when the county convention gave its seal of approval to both state and national administration and instructed delegates in their attitude on the candidate for governor at the state convention.

Mr. Hillje was married in Lavaca County, Texas, in July, 1903, near Shiner to Miss Emma Busch. Her father was a German settler, a blacksmith, and the only two children in the family were Mrs. Hillje and her brother, Ed Busch, now of Shiner. Mr. and Mrs. Hillje have become the parents of three children, but the only one still living is Wilma, who was born in January, 1912. Mr. Hillje affiliates with the Sons of Hermann and is a Lutheran in religion. He and his family reside in a new home, erected in 1915, one of the modest but comfortable places of Weimar. Personally Mr. Hillje is an able and successful business man, and physically is typical of the robust and vigorous German family to which he belongs.

Louis W. Wehe. Since the early years of Texas statehood the Wehe family has been identified with the mechanic trades, the agricultural enterprise, and the civic life of Dewitt County. All the influences and sturdy manhood, long continued industry, and upright conduct, have been exercised by members of this family and have entered into the whole life of that community.

The well known farmer citizen near Yorktown mentioned at the beginning of the above paragraph has lived in Texas nearly all his life, though he was born in Magdeburg, Germany, February 15, 1847. His father, Fritz Wehe, was born in the Village of Schweinitz in 1819, and was a son of a physician, Dr. Fritz Wehe, one of the leading members of the profession in that country. Fritz, Jr., was one of thirteen children, several of whom later were soldiers in the Franco-Prussian war, and some were killed. Fritz was the only one of the thirteen to come to America, though his father's brother, Frederick Wehe, had previously left Germany at the time of the revolution of 1848, in order to evade service, and established himself in Texas as a farmer and sheep and goat raiser. He lived at New Braunfels for several years, and died in Comar County, leaving a family.

Fritz Wehe married Minn Hohn. They brought their family to America in 1851. Sailing from Bremen, they landed at the old Texas port of Indianola, and thence continued their journey to New Braunfels, spending eight years on a farm in that locality. Then returning to Indianola Fritz engaged in his trade as a carpenter, living there three years, afterwards spent a year in Victoria County, and finally moved to Yorktown. He had learned his trade in the old country, and after locating in Yorktown in December, 1858, continued this work until the outbreak of the war. He then joined the Confederate service and throughout the period of his enlistment was employed as a wagoner in the commissary department for the Confederate Government. His service never took him outside the state and for several years he hauled supplies back and forth from one camp to another. In Comal County he took out citizenship papers, and was always very much interested in politics as a voter, though he never filled an office. He learned to speak the English language fluently, and he belonged to no church and no fraternity. In time he owned considerable land in Yorktown, and improved it as a home and died there in 1896 when past seventy-seven years of age. Fritz Wehe married the daughter of the chief forester at Schweinitz, Germany. Her father was a man of considerable possessions and was influential in official affairs. Mrs. Fritz Wehe died in 1899. Her children were: Louis W.; Minna, now Mrs. Philip Trenk, of Bexar County, Texas; Gustav, of Arizona; Alvina, wife of Henry Breihan, of Cuero; Mary, who married Fred Metting, of Yorktown;

Ida, widow of Albert Vogelpohl, of Victoria; and Rudolph, who lives in the vicinity of Yorktown.

Louis W. Wehe was four years old when the family came to Texas. Most of his education was acquired at Indianola, in the town schools there. Though only a boy at the time, he saw six months of service in the Confederate cause, enlisting at San Antonio, and went as a teamster in hauling ammunition and provisions between San Antonio and Fort Worth. He learned the trade of butcher, and on leaving the army took up that work at Yorktown, but two years later bought a tract of land and turned his attention to farming. That tract which he bought nearly half a century ago is still part of his extensive land possessions, and he now owns eight hundred acres practically in one body in the vicinity of Yorktown. Two hundred acres of this have been brought under cultivation under his management, and he has erected two comfortable homes and four tenant houses. As a stock man he has handled, has pastured and raised on his own land, a large number of horses and mules, Hereford cattle, and for a time was interested in sheep and goat raising. For several years Mr. Wehe was one of the leading dealers and shippers in this part of the country, shipping his stock to St. Louis, New Orleans, Fort Worth, Houston, and San Antonio markets. His business effort has been clean and has brought him increasing prosperity from year to year, so that he is now regarded as one of the most substantial citizens of the Yorktown community. In later years he has chiefly voted the republican ticket in national affairs. His family are members of the Lutheran Church and he has never formed any fraternal relations.

On July 31, 1871, Mr. Wehe married Miss Caroline Dahlmann. Her parents were Charles and Eva (Stolz) Dahlmann, and a record of the Dahlmann family is found on other pages. Mr. and Mrs. Wehe have the following children: Helen, who died at the age of twelve years; Max, who died at the age of twenty-seven, left a widow whose maiden name was Emma Sauermilch, and children named Adelaide, Ervin and Max; Herman, a farmer in Karnes County, married Jane Wagner, and their children are Herbert, Herman and Louise; Henry is a farmer on the old homestead, and by his marriage to Mary Sauermilch has children named Martha, Ulrina and Amanda; Hedwig married Rudolph Gras of San Antonio; Louise is the wife of Herman Metting of Yorktown, and their daughter is named Olga; Charles is a farmer near Yorktown, and married Rosa Mueller; the youngest of the family is Miss Lottie.

William Owens. After years of active and successful identification with the agricultural and livestock industries in Texas, William Owens, who has passed the psalmist's allotted span of three score years and ten, is now living virtually retired in the pleasant little City of Elgin, Bastrop County, and his worthy achievement and sterling character have gained and retained to him the confidence and good will of all who know him. He has maintained his home in the Lone Star State for more than sixty years and was a lad of thirteen years when he accompanied his parents on their removal from Mississippi to Texas, in 1854. Through his well ordered endeavors he has achieved substantial success and is now one of the wealthy men of Bastrop County.

Mr. Owens was born at Talladega, Alabama, on the 12th of February, 1841, and is a scion of a sterling family that was early founded in Virginia. His father, Thomas Owens, was reared and educated in Virginia and as a youth he participated in the Indian war in Alabama, in the early part of the nineteenth century. He established his home in that state but years later removed with his family to Mississippi, where

[illegible] of Albert Vogelpohl, of Victoria; and [illegible] in the vicinity of Yorktown.

[illegible] was four years old when the [illegible] at Indianola, [illegible] only a boy at the time, he saw six mon[illegible] cause, enlisting at San Antonio, and [illegible] ammunition and provisions between San [illegible] the trade of butcher, and on lea[illegible] work at Yorktown, but two years later bought [illegible] turned his attention to farming. That tract which he [illegible] is still part of his extensive land poss[illegible] eight hundred acres practically in one body [illegible] Two hundred acres of this have been brought [illegible] his management, and he has erected two [illegible] tenant houses. As a stock man he has [illegible] on his own land a large number of hors[illegible] for a time was interested in sheep and [illegible] years Mr. Weise was one of the leading [illegible] of the country, shipping his stock to St. [illegible] and San Antonio markets. [illegible] brought him increasing pros[illegible] regarded as one of the most [illegible] In later years he has [illegible] affairs. His family [illegible] never formed any [illegible] married Miss Caro[illegible] Stolze Dahlmann [illegible] pages. [illegible] died at the age of [illegible] left a widow [illegible] Emma [illegible] Adel[illegible] a farmer in Karnes County [illegible] are Herbert, Herman and [illegible] Henry is [illegible] homestead, and by his marriage to Mary Sauer[illegible] Martha, Ulrina and [illegible] Hedwig married [illegible] of San Antonio. Louise is the wife of Herman Mett[illegible] and their daughter is named Olga; Charles is a farmer [illegible] married Rosa Mueller; the youngest of the fam[illegible]

WILLIAM OWENS. After years of active and suc[illegible] the agricultural and livestock industries in Te[illegible] has passed the psalmist's allotted span of [illegible] virtually retired in the pleasant [illegible] and his worthy achievement and [illegible] to him the confidence and goo[illegible] maintained his home in the Lo[illegible] was a lad of thirteen years [illegible] removal from Mississippi to Te[illegible] endeavors he has achieved [illegible] men of Bastrop County [illegible] was born at Talladega, [illegible] a scion of a sterling [illegible] His father, Thomas [illegible] youth he part[illegible]

he engaged in farming in Kemper County. There he remained until his removal to Texas, in 1854, when he established the family home near old Springfield, Limestone County, where he engaged in farming and stock-growing and where he passed the remainder of his life. He never wavered in his allegiance to the democratic party, though never a seeker of public office, and both he and his wife were members of the Methodist Episcopal Church South, he having been of Irish and his wife of German lineage and both families having been founded in America prior to the war of the Revolution, in which representatives of both were valiant soldiers of the Continental Line. In Alabama was solemnized the marriage of Thomas Owens to Miss Martha Sproul, and they became the parents of eleven children, their first born, William, having died when young; Bird died prior to the Civil war; Hayden was a resident of Jones County at the time of his death and left a family; Robert died, unmarried, in Limestone County, prior to the Civil war; Thomas, Jr., was a resident of Bastrop County at the time of his death and is survived by one son; and William, of this review, is the youngest of the children. Of the daughters, Elizabeth is the wife of John Vincent, of Alabama; Eliza is the wife of Thomas Cooper, of Bastrop County, Texas; Catherine, who died in Limestone County, this state, was the wife of Jefferson Rogers; and Miss Mattie maintains her home at Elgin with her brother William, and she is now in her eighty-fourth year.

William Owens was reared to manhood in Limestone County, Texas, and such were the conditions in that pioneer period that his educational advantages were of most meager order. He was but twenty years of age at the inception of the Civil war but promptly tendered his services in defense of the cause of the Confederate States. He enlisted as a member of Company C, Eighth Texas Cavalry, a command that became known as the Terry Rangers, and with his regiment he proceeded to Bowling Green, Kentucky, where it became a part of the Army of Tennessee. In its first engagement, at Woodsonville, Kentucky, the regiment lost its gallant commander, General Terry, and John A. Horton became colonel of the regiment, as the successor of the slain hero. With his command Mr. Owens took part in the historic battle of Shiloh and thereafter participated in the battles of Perryville, Murfreesboro, Chickamauga and Missionary Ridge, the Atlanta campaign and the opposing of Sherman's army through the Carolinas. The regiment took part in the last battle of the army, at Bentonville, North Carolina, and was disbanded at Greenville, South Carolina, after the surrender of General Lee. For 100 consecutive days the Eighth Texas Cavalry was continuously fighting, and though Mr. Owens had several horses shot from under him and frequently had his clothing pierced by bullets, he was signally fortunate in never having been wounded or having even endured a break of the flesh by a hostile shot. He continued as a "high private" during the entire course of the great fratricidal conflict and his military career was marked by fidelity and valor. Under Captain Shannon, commander of his company, Mr. Owens was one of a squad of twenty men that were selected by Gen. Joe Wheeler to act as his bodyguard and scouts and that served in this capacity all the way from Atlanta until the final capitulation of the regiment, at Greenville, South Carolina. Captain Shannon, who recently died in the City of Galveston, was said to have been the best scout in the entire Confederate service. Mr. Owens was fortunate in leaving the Tennessee Army without enduring the ordeal of formal surrender, and the last horse which he had utilized as his mount in battle afforded him his transportation to his home in Texas. A youthful but weary, jaded and tattered soldier, he made the long overland trip on horseback and girded himself for the winning of the victories which peace ever has in store.

After his return to Texas Mr. Owens engaged in farming in Washington County, with residence at Chapel Hill, and he has stated, with reminiscent appreciation, that he had as his equipment when he thus resumed the arts of peace, a "very fine horse and two six-shooters." He continued his activities as a farmer in Washington County for three years, and in the meanwhile played a modest part in the drama of so-called "reconstruction." At the expiration of the period mentioned he removed to Bastrop county, where he purchased a tract of land at the rate of 50 cents an acre. He improved and effectively developed this landed estate of 200 acres, and on the fine homestead he continued to reside until his removal to the Village of Elgin, in order to afford better educational advantages to his younger children. In connection with his agricultural activities Mr. Owens became somewhat extensively identified also with the live-stock business, and as a raiser of horses he achieved special success, as shown by the fact that he drove many horses to the markets in Kansas, Colorado, Nebraska and Wyoming. He handled the native Spanish horses of Texas, which he crossed with good thoroughbred blood and thus developed a remarkably fine stock. He assisted also in making up herds of cattle that were driven to points in Kansas, and his individual cattle brand was "W O." Mr. Owens' more extensive activities as a representative of the cattle industry began to dwindle about the year 1889, but since that time he has been an active feeder of cattle which he has shipped to the markets of Chicago, Kansas City and St. Louis, though he is gradually retiring from the various industrial activities that so long engrossed his time and attention. He is the owner of a valuable landed estate of 1,400 acres, of which about 700 acres have been brought under effective cultivation. His land is principally situated in the Isaac Castner and the Jameson leagues, in Bastrop and Williamson counties.

In association with Capt. Frederick S. Wade, of whom individual mention is made on other pages of this work, Mr. Owens purchased 100 acres of land adjacent to Elgin, and they platted the same into town lots, the development of the tract having made it one of the best residence districts of this thriving little city. Mr. Owens has always taken loyal interest in community affairs and has been inflexible in his allegiance to the democratic party, though he has manifested no ambition for political office. He is an appreciative and popular member of the United Confederate Veterans, through his association with which he vitalizes the more gracious memories and associations of his army life and his interest in his old comrades in arms. Through the influence of Major Littlefield and other representative veterans of the Civil war, Mr. Owens was induced to become a member of the board of trustees of the Texas Soldiers' Home, in the City of Austin, and he has served in this capacity since 1910. He is affiliated with the Independent Order of Odd Fellows and with his family holds membership in the Methodist Episcopal Church, South.

In Bastrop County, on the 1st of May, 1882, was solemnized the marriage of Mr. Owens to Miss Mary L. Carter, who is a daughter of Edward and Mary (Hutchings) Carter, both natives of Virginia. In conclusion is entered brief record concerning the children of Mr. and Mrs. Owens: Lucy, who was graduated in the Southwestern Texas University, at Georgetown, is the wife of Dr. Simon Wood, a representative physician and surgeon at Elgin; Janie, who likewise was graduated in the Southwestern Texas University, is the wife of Robert Carter, of Elgin; Clyde C., who died at Elgin in 1913, married Miss Lizzie Wills, who survives him, as does also their one son, Clyde C., Jr.; Arabella is the wife of Dr. Walter Brenley, one of the chief surgeons of the sanitarium at Temple, Bell County; Nellie and Ned are twins and both completed courses in Kid Key College, at Sherman, Texas, Ned being a member of the class of 1916 in the Texas State Normal School at San Marcos, and being associated with his father's business activities, to the control of which he is destined to succeed: he and his twin sister still make their home with their venerable parents, to whom they give the utmost filial solicitude and affection.

FRANK E. LEIDOLF. For more than half a century the agricultural development, the business interests and the work of social and civic betterment, in Colorado and Fayette counties, have had their chief source and most active influence from the sterling German-American citizens of those localities. The history of the town and surrounding country of Weimar for the past forty years could hardly be told without mention of the Leidolf family, which has in many ways been identified with farm, manufacturing, schools and church affairs.

Frank E. Leidolf was born in the Province of Mehern, Austria, June 6, 1868. His father was Mathias Leidolf, who was an Austrian farmer. In 1872 he embarked his family and some of their possessions on board the ship Koeln at Bremen, bound for Galveston, and accomplished the voyage without special incident. He came out to what was then the terminus of the Southern Pacific or the Galveston, Harrisburg & San Antonio Railway, at Weimar, and found but three houses in the settlement. It was a community of strangers, but he quickly adapted himself to circumstances and being of the same race and language as the other people in that community soon felt at home. The first year he spent as a tenant on a farm of William Oncken, and then invested his means in a farm of 125 acres. This farm was at Osage, where he lived until 1882, then removed to Old Moulton, bought another and larger farm, and was actively engaged as a cotton and corn producer there until 1897. His wife died in that year, and thereafter he lived at Weimar until his death in 1906 at the age of seventy-nine. He learned the new language of the New World, though never with perfect accent, became a naturalized citizen, with only casual participation in politics, was a democratic voter, and a member of the Catholic Church and one of the six founders of the German School at Weimar. He was himself well educated, and did much to advance community interest in good schools. Mathias Leidolf married Rosine Friederich, daughter of John Friederich. The children of this union were: Anna, who died in 1892 as the wife of Henry Michalke; Frank E.; and Amelia, wife of A. J. Ratleff of Weimar.

Frank E. Leidolf has been a resident of Texas since December, 1872, when he was about four years of age. His early life was spent on a farm, with an education in the schools at Weimar. His inclinations were for business, and at the age of twenty-two he left the farm and became a ginner and miller with Henry Michalke as a partner. They bought the combined gin and mill of Louis Pietsch and were associated until 1892, when they sold out and dissolved partnership. Mr. Leidolf then bought the Louis Fahrenthold, Sr., gin and mill plant, and has been connected with this industry ever since, though his milling plant and operations have been greatly extended. As an adjunct to his gin plant in 1896 he installed one dynamo and started to give electric light service to the Village of Weimar. Subsequent years saw a large development and increased demand for electric power in connection with lighting and other purposes, and by 1905 he separated the electric plant from the gin, enlarging it to twice its former capacity, and in 1914 built a second gin, which is now operated with power supplied from the light plant. The daily capacity of his gin is ninety bales, and he also has a mill sufficient to supply the needs of his corn meal patrons.

Mr. Leidolf's home is situated on twenty-two acres adjoining and within the corporation of Weimar. As a townsman of Weimar he has been fire chief for a number of years, has served on the German school board, and is a precinct chairman of the democratic party. He has landed interests which he operates through tenants, and has been a delegate to different farmers conventions. He is also a stockholder of the T. A. Hill State Bank of Weimar. Mr. Leidolf is a man of physical vigor and powerful frame, and combines with this strength a keen intelligence and business judgment.

He was married in Colorado County November 10, 1892, to Miss Josephine Hoelscher, daughter of Bernard and Elizabeth Hoelscher. Her father was born in Alsace, came to Texas before the war, and served as a Confederate soldier. Mrs. Leidolf is one of ten children, namely: Anna, wife of Emanuel Rabe; Henry; Joseph; Lena, who married Jacob Kromer; Willie; Mary, wife of Albert Kuhn; Mrs. Leidolf; Robert; Otto; and August. The happy little household of Mr. and Mrs. Leidolf is comprised of four children: Oswald, Edgar, Emil and Henrietta.

James F. Card. Of old American families that have been identified with the material development of Texas since it was a Spanish or Mexican province, none deserve more particular mention than that represented by James F. Card, who represents pioneer Texas stock on both sides of the house. Mr. Card is a well known farmer and stock man on the Cuero and Westhoff Road.

Though most of his active career has been spent in the vicinity of Cuero, Mr. Card was born at Flatonia, in Fayette County, Texas, January 27, 1872. The Cards were of Scotch and Irish ancestry, and early in the last century lived in Tennessee. Grandfather James Card, who was born in 1804 and died in 1870, joined almost the original American emigration to Texas. Coming from Tennessee, he reached Texas soil about 1832, four years before the winning of independence, and was identified with the little settlement at LaGrange. His old home was on Buckner's Creek on the west side of Colorado River, and he lived and died in that one community. In those excursions and expeditions which began in the early '30s as part of a general conflict between the Texas Americans and the Mexicans, and which continued with little interruption for fully ten years, James Card had his part as a member of the famous Dawson Company, the slaughter of whose members has resulted in one of the most familiar events of Texas history, the "Dawson Massacre." Fortunately a lame horse caused James Card to escape from that slaughter. He was a farmer and stock man, and never held any slaves. Grandfather James Card was the only one of his particular family to come to Texas. He married Jane Anderson. Her brother, William Anderson, was also a pioneer in Fayette County, Texas, and reared a family there. To the marriage of James and Jane Card were born: Sarah, who married Henry Redfield and spent her life about LaGrange; Joseph, who lived around Flatonia and left a family there; Samuel, who died in Fayette County; William, who also died in Fayette County with a family; Ann, who married John Moore and spent her life in Coryell County; James Neal; and Mary, who became the wife of J. Mahan of Leesville, Texas.

James Neal Card was born at LaGrange, Texas, November 27, 1841, and is one of the oldest native sons of that locality. He grew up and acquired a very limited education and during the war between the states served in Colonel Breckenridge's regiment of Texas troops. Most of his service was at Saluria Island and along the East Texas coast. After the war he took up the active life of a farmer and stock man and in 1880 moved his family to Dewitt County, locating on the Breeding Survey, where he still has his home. He has not been identified with local offices, is a republican in politics in spite of the fact that he was a Confederate soldier, and was reared in the Baptist faith. James Neal Card married Mary Merken. Her father, Ferdinand Merken, came to Texas from Germany prior to the war. Mrs. Card was born in Fayette County March 10, 1851, being one of a large family of children. To her marriage to James N. Card were born the following children: James F.; William, who was a farmer and died unmarried; Milton, who is a farmer, also in Dewitt County; Joseph, a stock man in the same locality who married Annie Howell; Samuel, a farmer around Cuero; Mary, wife of Henry Hillman of Bloomington, Texas.

Since he was eight years of age James F. Card has been identified with Dewitt County as his residence. He acquired his early training in the country schools and also attended the Nash School or Guadaloupe Academy at Cuero. Having remained at home and assisted his father in the management of the farm until past his majority, he then took up farming and stockraising on his own account, his first home being in the Breeding survey. In 1903 he moved to his present place, which had been settled before by a member of the pioneer Lane family. The previous owner, however, was James Robinson, also one of the old settlers of Dewitt County. Mr. Card's estate is situated in the Wentworth League, and he has been unusually successful in the breeding and raising of cattle, sheep, goats and hogs, and at different times has figured on the market as a shipper and dealer in live stock.

Many citizens of Dewitt County know him best for his work as a public official. He first began voting in 1892, and his first presidential ballot was given to Grover Cleveland, while in a year made famous in Texas politics by the battle between Hogg and Clark he supported James S. Hogg for governor. For twenty years or more he has exercised considerable influence in local democratic politics. In 1910 Mr. Card was elected county commissioner as the successor of A. W. Eatman. He represented Precinct No. 1 for one term, and his associates on the board were Judge Kleberg and commissioners George P. Willis, M. F. Mueller and R. C. Brown.

May 17, 1893, Mr. Card married Miss Claudia Wallace. Her father, Elias M. Wallace, was one of the early settlers of Dewitt County, having come to Texas from Mississippi prior to the Civil war, and served in the Confederate army from this state. Mr. Wallace married Saloma Stubbs. Mrs. Card is the third in a family of seven children, the others being named as follows: Ida, now Mrs. J. D. Hardy; Mrs. Abbie Hodge; Winnie, wife of S. D. Thomason of Wilson County, Texas; Elias, a farmer in Dewitt County; Bula, who died young; Martha, who married Bruce Roan of San Antonio; and William, a farmer of Dewitt County. The little family of Mr. and Mrs. Card contains the following children: Salome, Claudia, Victor, Buna and Bruce. In fraternal matters Mr. Card is only identified with the Woodmen of the World.

William Herder. Another of the native sons of Texas who has here achieved distinctive success in connection with the great fundamental industry of agriculture and who is the owner of a large, well improved and valuable landed estate near the Village of Shiner, Lavaca County, is William Herder, and he is entitled to recognition in this history not only by reason of his own achievement and advanced status as a citizen and man of affairs but also as a scion of a now numerous family that was founded in Texas more than eighty years ago and that has been one of prominence and influence in connection with the social and material development and progress of the southern part of this great commonwealth.

The honored father of William Herder figures as the founder of the family in the Lone Star State, and this sterling pioneer, George Herder, was a youth of sixteen years when he came from his German Fatherland and established his residence in Texas, then on the very frontier of civilization, other members of the family having later come to America and established their home in Texas, including his sister, Mrs. William Winkelmann, who passed the closing years of her life in Colorado County.

George Herder was born in the Grand Duchy of Oldenburg, Germany, in the year 1818, and there received good educational advantages. In 1834, at the age of sixteen years, he severed the home ties and set forth to seek his fortunes in America, though he could have little foreseen that it would be his portion to gain broad experience in connection with life on the frontier of civilization and to aid in gaining independence for what is now the largest state in the greatest of all American republics. In the year that marked his arrival in the United States he came to Texas, and his loyalty to the land of his adoption soon came into effective play, for he joined the forces of Gen. Sam Houston and did effective service as one of the valiant soldiers who won independence for the Lone Star State, which was freed from the domination of Mexico. He took part in the historic battle of San Jacinto and his record of gallant service as a soldier in the war for independence makes it but consistent that his name and memory shall be held in lasting honor and given recognition on the pages of Texas history.

George Herder, the youthful soldier and adopted son of Texas, was one of the pioneer German settlers in the vicinity of Frelsburg, Colorado County, where he reclaimed land and became actively engaged in agricultural pursuits. Just prior to the inception of the Civil war he removed to the High Hill community, in Fayette County, and there he continued his successful operations as a farmer for many years, besides building up also a substantial business as a general merchant, his ability and enterprise bringing to him splendid prosperity and giving him prestige as one of the most influential, even as he was one of the most honored, citizens of Fayette County. In the early '80s Mr. Herder removed to Lavaca County, where, in "half-moon Timber," he purchased a tract of open grazing land, over which occasional bands of cattle had roamed. He fenced his land and brought a portion of the same under cultivation, besides continuing his operations in the raising and handling of cattle. He remained on this place about three years, and the closing days of his long and useful life were passed at Schulenburg, Fayette County, where he died in 1887. He was a democrat in politics, was identified with no religious or fraternal organizations, was not given to garrulousness or self-exploitation, but was a strong, upright, reserved man who was a person of thought and action rather than of useless loquacity.

As a young man George Herder wedded Miss Minnie Wolters, a daughter of another prominent pioneer, Jacob Wolters, concerning whom special mention is made elsewhere in this work, in the comprehensive article dedicated to the Wolters family and its various representatives in Texas. Mrs. Herder passed her entire life in Texas and died at High Hill, Fayette County, in 1877. Of the children the eldest is Meta, who is the widow of Julius Seydler and who still maintains her home at High Hill; Annie is the wife of Charles Eschenburg, of Schulenburg;

Fritz, who died in Dewitt County, married Miss Ida Arnim, who, with several of their children, survived him; Augusta became the wife of Moritz Richter and both died at Shiner, leaving children; Minnie is the wife of Adolph Richter, of Weimar, Colorado County; Charles died in 1874, when a young man; August was a resident of the City of Houston at the time of his death in January, 1916, Eliza is the wife of Fritz Hillje and they reside in San Antonio; Henry, who died at High Hill, married Josephine Russek and left children; William, the immediate subject of this sketch, was the next in order of birth; George, who resides at Weimar, is one of the substantial capitalists of Southern Texas; and the other child of the twelve died in infancy.

William Herder was born at High Hill, Fayette County, on the 5th of April, 1861, and in that locality he was reared to adult age, in the meanwhile gaining youthful experience of practical order in connection with the work of the home farm. His education was not neglected and he was favored in being able to prosecute his studies under the direction of such able instructors as Professors Seydler and Heyer. He continued to be associated with his father in the work and management of the home farm until he had attained to the age of twenty years, and for the following year he was employed for wages in the vicinity of his home. Shortly before attaining to his legal majority he took unto himself a wife, and the youthful pair established their first home at Engle, Fayette County, where he purchased a farm, in the locality formerly designated as "Black Jack Oso." After having there been engaged in agricultural pursuits four years Mr. Herder purchased and removed to the Half Moon Ranch, in Lavaca County, where he and his wife have since maintained their home and where their lives are compassed by smiling plenty and fair prosperous days. Mr. Herder owns 446 acres of the old ranch bearing the name designated above and situated in the Lockhart League. The estate is given over principally to the raising of cotton and corn, and since the property has come into his possession Mr. Herder has effected the reclamation to cultivation of an additional area of about 100 acres of the tract, besides which he has made many substantial improvements of permanent order, including the erection of two tenant houses. In addition to this fine landed estate he is the owner of a well improved farm of 296 acres in Gonzales County.

Mr. Herder cast his first presidential vote for Grover Cleveland and has since continued his allegiance to the democratic party, though he has had naught of ambition for public office or the activities of practical politics. He was reared in the faith of the Lutheran Church, of which his mother was a communicant, but is not formally identified with any religious or fraternal organization.

In December, 1880, was solemnized the marriage of Mr. Herder to Miss Theresa Nitschmann, who was born in Fayette County, Texas, on the 27th of February, 1858, and who is a daughter of the late Frank and Anna (Gallus) Nitschmann. Mr. Nitschmann was one of the earliest of the German settlers of the High Hill district of Fayette County, and later removed to the vicinity of Engle, that county, where he was not only a successful farmer but also followed the trade of blacksmith. He had much mechanical and inventive skill, and is accredited with having invented the first turning plow and "middle buster," which he patented and for which a certain implement manufacturing company offered him the sum of $10,000. He declined to let the patent pass from his control and the same was later practically stolen from him, so that he realized but meager financial profit from a valuable device which brought large monetary returns to others, who had taken advantage of his genius. He was a resident of Schulenburg at the time of his death and his widow passed the closing years of her life in the home of her daughter Theresa, wife of the subject of this review. Concerning the other children of the Nitschmann family the following brief data are available: Joseph was a resident of Lindenau, Dewitt County, at the time of his death; Edward died at Flatonia, Fayette County; Mrs. Anna Bucek resides at Engle, Fayette County; Emil maintains his home in Victoria County; and Hermann is a resident of Guadaloupe, Victoria County.

This concluding paragraph is given over to a brief record concerning the children of Mr. and Mrs. Herder: Adaline is the wife of Edward Busch, of Shiner, and their children are Lonnie and Emmett. Edmund, the present postmaster at Shiner, is individually mentioned on other pages. Ella is the wife of Edward Cordes, a farmer near Shiner, and they have one child, Marvin. George remains at the parental home. Mrs. Annie Ahrens resides at Shiner and has two children, Avery and Melvin. Hattie is the wife of William Hewig, of Gonzales County, and they have one child Ed. Walter, who married Miss Eva Turk, likewise resides in that county.

John W. Kyle. While now living retired at Nixon, John W. Kyle for a great many years prosecuted his extensive business as a stockman and farmer over a wide range of country in Victoria and surrounding counties and for almost half a century he has borne an important share in the life and progress of his section of the state.

Of old Virginia stock and ancestry, he was born in Botetourt County, Virginia, June 11, 1847, and was christened John William H. Kyle. He grew up on a plantation where most of the heavy labor was performed by slaves, and received his education in the "pay" schools of his native county. As a boy he showed a special proficiency and handiness with mechanical tools. He developed a considerable skill as a blacksmith, as a harness and saddle maker, and in other lines, and this proficiency served him well after he came to Texas and he also did much as a practical mechanic though without charge, for his neighbors.

He was of a true Virginia family, and loyal to the institutions of the South. His father was too ill to bear arms and the duties of soldier fell upon John W. Kyle, who was at that time only a boy in years. In 1863, at the age of sixteen, he enlisted in the Flying Artillery under Thomas Jackson in the battalion of Major Johnson and in Gen. John A. McCausland's Brigade. While in the ranks he took part in the battles of Cold Harbor, at Morefield, West Virginia, where the Confederates were surprised and routed, and at the battle of Winchester. He was taken out of the ranks about that time to serve as courier, scout and guide for Major Johnson. He was a light rider and had a fine horse and he rendered much valuable service in this capacity. He was a courier at the battle of Fisher's Hill and in the battle of Cedar Creek. After Cedar Creek he and his command were in winter quarters in Southwestern Virginia, and remained there until almost the time of General Lee's surrender. He was on detail with some of his comrades picketing and scouting near Sweetwater, Virginia, when the end of the war came. He left the army at a point not more than twenty miles from his old home.

After the war he helped manage the dismantled home plantation for a time, but in 1867 he came out to Texas in company with his uncle, William H. Kyle, who had been a resident of Texas before the war, and who was long a prominent cattle man in Victoria County. The career of this uncle as a citizen of Texas was of such importance as to justify a diversion from the principal subject of this sketch for a paragraph or so.

William H. Kyle, who was long known as Major Kyle, was in Texas

W. H. Kyle

J. W. Kyle

W. H. Kyle

J. W. Kyle

before the war and beginning as a cowboy, he soon acquired stock of his own. In Texas he joined the Confederate army first in Terry's Rangers and afterwards in Shannon's Scouts. With the Rangers he served in Tennessee and Kentucky and over a great area of southern country, and took part in some of the heaviest fighting. He remained a private soldier and showed himself valiant and faithful to duty at every call.

After the war Major Kyle took up trail driving into Kansas, both for other cattle men and also for himself. He next joined Shanghai Pierce in the cattle business along the coast and his operations also extended into West Texas. In 1875 this firm lost heavily because of the great storm that destroyed Indianola. William H. Kyle had his principal ranch on the Guadalupe River above Victoria at a place called Nursery. For a time he was an active speculator in cattle but later his interests were concentrated in the natural growth of his own herd. He was an ardent democrat, a Mason, and was reared a Presbyterian and was always faithful to his religious convictions. Major Kyle was born December 9, 1836, and died March 21, 1907, highly respected and honored. He was laid to rest at Victoria and he was never married.

During the first two years he spent in Texas John W. Kyle worked for his uncle as a cowboy and in that way he gained much experience which proved valuable to him in the management of his subsequent interests. In 1869 he returned to Virginia, where he married, and resumed farming in his native county until 1877. He then came back to Texas, accompanied by his wife and three children, and again became associated with his uncle. They all lived in the same house near Nursery. John W. Kyle dissolved partnership with his uncle after about twenty-five years, and subsequently, until his own retirement, managed his livestock and directed his farm enterprise.

Mr. Kyle is a man who has rendered a great deal of gratuitous and none the less valuable service in a community way. He served many times as trustee of the school at Nursery, an institution which he practically founded. He has always been a democratic voter. A Presbyterian, he contributed substantially to the building of the Presbyterian Church at Thomaston, where he had his membership for many years. Among the people of the older generation in that section of Texas Mr. Kyle is kindly remembered for his services as a community doctor. Although he never studied medicine in college, he took it up from natural inclination, and in that way followed the example of both his father and grandfather and this family trait is now exhibited in the trained and scientific fashion of the present century in the person of one of Mr. Kyle's sons, a successful physician in Texas. Mr. Kyle while living in Nursery in the early days furnished his skill without charge to his neighbors over a country ten miles around, and he furnished his own medicines and his own transportation, seldom neglecting a call for his services.

Mr. Kyle's great-grandfather was Joseph Kyle, who, it is thought, was one of three brothers who came over from Ireland and settled in Virginia, the other two brothers being William and Robert. One of them settled in Rockingham County. Joseph Kyle married a Miss Diuguid, who was a lady of Scotch descent and their children were: Diuguid, Robert, Christopher and Virginia, who married Barney Pittser.

Christopher Kyle, grandfather of John W. Kyle, was born March 7, 1793, and married Hettie McFerran, who was born November 4, 1799. Her mother was a Miss Van Meter, whose parents were natives of Holland. Her father was Thomas McFerran. Their children were: Joseph; Ann, who married William McClaugherty; and William H., whose sketch has already been given and who was the Major Kyle, so long prominently interested in the cattle industry in Texas.

Joseph Kyle, father of John W. Kyle, was born in Botetourt County, Virginia, May 30, 1821. He married Mary Jane Peck, who died March 9, 1893. Her parents were Jacob and Patsy (Walker) Peck. Joseph and Mary Kyle had the following children: Elizabeth Ann, who married Jacob Kern and lived in Botetourt County, Virginia; John William H.; Lucy McFerran, who married Carper Williamson and died in Karnes County, Texas, being the wife of a Methodist minister; Martha Alice died in childhood; and Mary Hannah, who married Louis Carpenter, of Nursery, Texas.

John W. Kyle after his return from Texas to Virginia was married December 22, 1869, to Miss Penelope Biggs, a daughter of Allen and Patsy (McCartney) Biggs. Her father was a Virginia planter. Mrs. Kyle and her brothers James and John were the only children who grew up. Mrs. Kyle was born in August, 1849, and her death occurred on June 30, 1897. Of her children, Dr. John Allen is a physician at Houston and by his marriage to Stella Carr has a son named William Allen; Thomas McFerran, who lived in Victoria County until his death, married Glennie May Rylander, who became the mother of one daughter named Charlotte; Henry C. died in Victoria County and had two children—Henry C. and Medie Penelope—by his marriage to Medie Rylander; Martha Jane is the wife of Jeff C. West of Leesville and has two daughters, Charlotte Rebecca and Martha Florence; John Irvin, now deceased, married Edith M. Coffin, and was survived by a daughter, Madaline Lee.

On March 29, 1899, Mr. Kyle married for his second wife Elizabeth Lusby, a daughter of Joseph and Mary (Stennett) Lusby. Her father came to Texas from Lincolnshire, England, and died in 1879 just after his arrival. His widow subsequently died at Taylor, Texas. Mrs. Kyle's brothers and sisters were: Mrs. J. E. Smith of Waco; Joseph of Elk City, Oklahoma; Maidens of Canyon City, Texas; and Mrs. C. R. DeLong of Cress, Texas.

Frank J. Parma. In the little business community of Ammansville in Fayette County, the place of leadership was accorded to the late Frank J. Parma, proprietor of the only store there, and who after an illness of six weeks died August 14, 1915.

Frank J. Parma was all but a native of Fayette County, having come to this locality when a boy of ten years, with an uncle from the Province of Moravia, Austria. He was born in the Town of Frenstad February 17, 1870, and had acquired some education before he left the old country, and in Fayette County attended the common schools and was also a student in the Sam Houston Normal School at Huntsville. The father was Frank Parma and his mother was Veronica Krc (pronounced Kerch). His parents spent all their lives in the old country, and their children were: Leo, Richard, deceased, and Frank J.

Frank J. Parma at the age of ten years sailed from Bremen, Germany, on board the Brunswick, and with other members of the party landed at Galveston after an uneventful voyage of twenty-two days. Until ready to take up life independently he made his home with his uncle Ignaz Parma at Bluff, and his creditable position in life was altogether the result of his individual push and enterprise. As a boy he was well disciplined in the work of the farm, in raising cotton and corn, but at the age of eighteen took up the profession of school teacher. He taught his first school near Engel in Fayette County, and his work along that line continued for about twelve years. His last school was taught in Ammansville. He served as a county examiner under County Superintendent Heimann and under Superintendent Sterling. He gave up his profession as teacher to engage in merchandising at Ammansville.

He opened business with a stock and capital representing about $1,500. His goods were placed in a small house which he rented and which is a part of the large building he occupied. His record as a general merchant was one of steady growth. He sold his first goods in 1900, and his stock at the time of his death was four times as large as that with which he began business fifteen years ago. He had a double store building and the Bank of Ammansville occupies quarters in the same structure. In 1914 the Ammansville State Bank was established, with Mr. Parma as one of its active promoters and he was largely concerned with its successful management in the position as cashier. The bank has a capital stock of $10,000 and its president is George Herder, Jr., while the assistant cashier is I. C. Parma.

In politics Mr. Parma manifested considerable interest in the democratic cause, attended state conventions in Galveston and Houston, and in 1912 took up the cause of Woodrow Wilson for President. In Fayette County on November 10, 1891, he married Miss Agnes Cernosek, a daughter of Joseph Cernosek. Her father was a farmer who came out from Moravia, Austria, and reared a family of six children. The children of Mr. and Mrs. Parma are: Lillie, Ivan C., Vojtech, Helen, Frank, Agnes, Vaclav, Bertie, Stanislav, and Vit.

Gus E. Ruhmann. While the thriving little City of Schulenburg has several local factories and industrial plants, one of the most distinctly individual and important is the G. E. Ruhmann factory of steel metal and wire products. It differs considerably from the typical gins and cotton oil plants of most of the smaller cities of Southern Texas, and represents the original enterprise of its owner, Gus E. Ruhmann.

Gus E. Ruhmann is a native of Fayette County, born in LaGrange August 23, 1873, and grew up in that vicinity, with an education from the public schools. Leaving school at the age of fourteen, he was thenceforth on his own responsibilities, and while living with an uncle in Shiner learned the tinner's trade, and also acquired a knowledge of the hardware business. He lived with his uncle until past twenty, and at the age of twenty-one bought his uncle's business as a partner of C. B. Wellhausen in the firm of Wellhausen & Company. After two years and three months Mr. Wellhausen became sole proprietor, and Mr. Ruhmann then engaged in business on his own account in the hardware and furniture line, tinning and plumbing, and that was his regular business seven years. He finally sold out to some citizens of Shiner, and then came to Schulenburg. His residence at Shiner was for sixteen years, and though he went there without a cent of capital and with no experience, he came away with a well established reputation for successful business operations and with some capital.

On locating at Schulenburg Mr. Ruhmann engaged in the hardware and plumbing business as a partner of G. E. Ruhmann & Brother, but in 1908 sold his interest in the establishment to his brother and took up the manufacture of furnaces, sheet metal and wire goods. His wire goods include all kinds of muzzles and baskets, while his metal work comprises different lines of guttering and fittings, pipes, shingles, galvanized troughs, ridge rolls, cresting and flue caps, smoke stacks and steel furnaces.

It will be a matter of interest to describe some of the successive steps by which Mr. Ruhmann became engaged in manufacturing About the time the Spindletop oil fields inaugurated the era of fuel oil at a price so cheap that such fuel came into general use in the operating of gins and oil mills, there was a general demand for steel oil tanks for the storing of oils. It was while at Shiner that Mr. Ruhmann perceived the possibilities in the manufacture of such tanks, and accordingly acquired the machinery and necessary facilities for manufacture. He equipped several mills and two or three gins with the tanks, and then all at once the demand seemed to fall off. In order that his machinery might not stand idle or prove a useless investment, he looked around for some other article that he might manufacture. He thus turned his attention to the making of a furnace. The first furnace he made was after the plan of another party, but he saw the idea was a good one and set about to improve it. He added the "Flue Wing" around the kettle, this serving to economize half the fuel required, also made it adjustable and other valuable improvements, and after perfecting his furnace and assuring himself of its usefulness as a marketable commodity, he applied for a patent, which he secured in three weeks. He then became a salesman on the road, and the first week more than $800 worth of furnaces were sold, and Mr. Ruhmann devised and increased his factory equipment for the regular manufacture of the goods. He has since added and patented other improvements to his furnace, and now has on file an application for a patent to a basket.

The present factory at Schulenburg was erected in 1914, and at full capacity the plant requires the services of twenty-five employes. He has been engaged in the manufacture of furnaces since 1908 and has shipped his products all over Texas and other Southern States. The enterprise is all his own, and is managed and controlled by the man who left LaGrange more than twenty-eight years ago to seek his fortune in the world. Mr. Ruhmann also has a Canadian patent, and his furnaces for the Dominion market are made on a royalty by the Record Foundry & Machine Company at Moncton, Ontario.

Mr. Ruhmann is also president of the Baumgarten & Matula Company, a lumber business in Schulenburg. He is a member of the Fayette County School Board, but has filled no offices in his home town, and is not in politics, though in every sense a patriotic American and a public spirited citizen. He is a grandson of Edward Ferd and Helen (Moos) Ruhmann and a son of Philip Ruhmann, who was born in Colorado County, Texas, during the '40s, was a man who had little education, was a carpenter by trade, and spent most of his life in LaGrange, where he died at the age of forty-four in 1889. He left his widow with a family of eight children, of whom Gus E. was the oldest son, and he being the oldest most of the responsibility of taking care of the family depended on him. He had the unusual record of having served on both sides during the Civil war. He was forced into the Confederate service at the beginning, but as soon as opportunity presented itself made his escape and joined the Federal forces, and for this service his widow draws a pension from the Government. Philip Ruhmann married Lena Melcher, whose father was an early German settler. Their children were: Louisa, wife of Gus Worth of LaGrange; Gus E.; Max of Schulenburg; Albert, of LaGrange; John, of Ballinger, Texas; Louis, of Victoria; Lena, who married George Moos of LaGrange; and August, of LaGrange, who is in the hardware business.

Mr. Gus E. Ruhmann was married in Schulenburg June 11, 1896, to Miss Elizabeth Baumgarten, who is a daughter of the late Christian Baumgarten, one of the most eminent business men and citizens of the Schulenburg district, whose career is sketched on other pages of this publication. Mr. and Mrs. Ruhmann have four children: Ernstina, a student in the College of Industrial Arts at Denton, Texas; Gus, Jr.; Annie; and Agnes.

THE WOLTERS FAMILY. The historic record of a family which has been identified with the civilizing influences of a vast border domain from the beginning can not fail to prove of enduring and vital interest, but when that record concerns a family which has given to that one-time frontier wilderness men of renown in business affairs, in the professions and in other honorable walks of life, a perusal of the story of incidents which affected the lives of its pioneer representatives and a reference to the causes which led to their abandonment of domestic ties and the advantages of civilization for exile among the very enemies of civilization, claim the rapt attention of all students of history in the making. To the Wolters family of Fayette County, Texas, belongs this distinction, and this history of the state exercises an important function when it enters even the brief review that is incorporated at this point.

To the Wolters family of Southern Texas belongs primarily the distinction of having lived under the flags of three republics. Its original representatives came to the Republic of Texas in the morning of its birth and when the cause of the new government seemed just and righteous, those of the Wolters name lent aid, without ostentation, toward the maintenance of the new republic under a banner which proclaimed inviolability to favored and ancient institutions of the South, and when that movement failed, the members of this sterling pioneer family submitted to the results of the military contest which ensued, thereby returning to the protection of the stars and stripes and contributing further, with sincerity and industry, to the rebuilding of the mother republic of the world.

To Jacob Wolters it was given to found in the United States a home that should give to American civilization a new germ which added an element of strength to our continuous process of assimilation and amalgamation. To this sturdy old Prussian the fates decreed a part in the subjugation of nature and the introduction of the arts of progress and peace where the denizens of forest and plain were wont to hold dominion. He came from his native Elberfield, in Rhenish Prussia, to America in 1834, in company with his wife, three sons and one daughter. This action was prompted by his desire to find freedom from the monarchial restraint under the influences of which he was born and reared and under which the lives of men of independent thought and action were made a burden. His coming to the United States was several years in advance of the rebellion or revolution in his Fatherland, a rebellion resulting from the absolutism and oppression of the reigning house and the failure of which gave to America Carl Schurz, Kunkel and a score of other enlightened German minds and patriotic souls. It is possible that the old Texas pioneer foresaw this catastrophe in his native land and decided to avoid its consequences to himself by quietly removing himself beyond the influence of his sovereign.

Finding on a sailing vessel of the type common to the period the means of transporting his family and small amount of personal effects to the land of promise, Jacob Wolters severed the ties that bound him to his native land and set forth to establish a home in America. Upon arrival in the year 1834, he established his residence in the City of Philadelphia. His trade, that of a baker, proved to be somewhat in advance of American demands in that early day, as the average housewife yet felt an independence which prompted her to supervise the work of her kitchen and do her own baking,—a situation that implied disaster for the old craftsman when thinking to establish himself in the work of his trade. Every month of delay brought a diminution in his limited financial resources, and under these conditions Jacob Wolters decided to put even further to the test his strength and versatility in the land of his adoption. Fortitude and courage thus led him to bring his family into the wilderness of Texas, where the white men were then contending against the forces of barbarism, and in the spring of 1835 Mr. Wolters and his family embarked on a coasting vessel that transferred them to the City of New Orleans, Louisiana. Here transference was made to another boat, which finally landed the family at Velasco, Texas, from which point a primitive steamboat transported them up the Brazos River to Brazoria. Mr. Wolters was bent upon joining the little German colony that had been established in Colorado County, and with wagon and ox team he and his family were transported to the site of the present Town of Frelsburg, Colorado County, where, in May, 1835, he settled on a tract of land in the Piper League. His temporary home was a camp under a spreading tree, and before he could prepare his pioneer cabin his devoted wife sickened and died, her mortal remains being laid to rest in July, 1835, in a necessarily unmarked grave, so far as enduring designation was concerned. Sorely desolated and grieved, surrounded by conditions that must have been strange and bewildering, with no possibility of applying himself to the vocation in which he had been trained, Jacob Wolters may well have faltered in courage and purpose. He was not, however, a man of such caliber, and he set himself to mastering rather than yielding to the conditions of circumstance and place. He was compelled to invent a means of livelihood that would appeal to the few settlers throughout the wide area of country surrounding his home. He hit upon the manufacturing of rawhide chairs, and the popularity of his products established him in a good business, as gauged by the standards of the locality and period. As a matter of course, he made his way by primitive conveyances over the wide stretches of country, and as a pioneer manufacturer and commercial salesman he journeyed about with his wagon and ox team, hauling his products through a country infested with hostile Indians and over roads that were such in name only. He encountered his full share of dangers and hardships as he went about selling his chairs, and on one occasion it has been related that he and one of his sons met a situation in which only good fortune and circumspection saved their lives. On this particular occasion they discovered a band of Indians encamped between them and their home,—a menacing situation and one fraught with dire results if their presence were discovered. To determine the right move was a veritable problem, but the father and son finally determined to make an effort to pass around the Indian camp at night. Equipped with a bacon rind with which to grease the spingles of the ox cart and prevent their squeaking, the son Robert had ample demands upon his attention, and the father piloted the lumbering ox team on the perilous journey at dead of night, good fortune having attended the venture, as they arrived safely at their home without having attracted the attention of the Indians.

The home of Jacob Wolters continued to be maintained on the Piper League until 1838, when he contracted a second marriage, Louise Maybrink becoming his wife. He then removed to the Mill Creek community, near Industry, Austin County, where he passed the residue of his life and where his death occurred in 1865, his second wife having passed away three years previously. The following data concerning the children of the first marriage are properly entered at this juncture: Robert, who achieved business success at Schulenburg, died at that place when venerable in years; Mrs. Wilhelmina Herder died in Fayette County, and left children; August was a resident of Fayette County at the time of his death; and Ferdinand likewise was a resident and influential citizen of Austin County at the time of his demise, his posterity having made an enduring impress in various Texas communities. The children of the second marriage were: Edward, who died at Brenham, Washington County; Theodore, who is a resident of Schulenburg, Fayette County; Hermann, who died when a youth; and Frank, whose posterity are found at Flatonia, Fayette County. In an article which follows the one here presented further reference is made to the life of Robert Wolters, the eldest of the children.

Ferdinand Wolters, the youngest of the children of his father's first marriage, was born at Elberfield, Prussia, in 1827, and thus was about seven years old at the time of the family immigration to America. He was reared to manhood under the conditions and influences of frontier life in Texas, and his death occurred at New Ulm, Austin County, in 1866. His education was acquired largely through self-discipline and he was a man of strong character and well balanced mentality, his vocation during the greater part of his active career having been that of saddler. During the Civil war he was made exempt from military service in order that he might ply his trade in the manufacturing of saddles for the use of the Confederate soldiers. He had no desire for the honors or emoluments of political office, and was not active in religious affairs. He took life earnestly and hopefully, was genial, kindly and considerate in his association with others and commanded the high regard of those who came within the sphere of his influence. He married Miss Elizabeth Goeth, a daughter of Ernest Goeth, who came from Prussia to Texas in an early day. Mrs. Wolters was a child at the time of the family immigration to Texas and here she passed the remainder of her gentle and noble life. After the death of her first husband she became the wife of Charles Ernst, and she died in 1879, at New Ulm. Concerning the children of Ferdinand and Elizabeth (Goeth) Wolters the following data are available: Ernst, a saddler and harnessmaker by vocation, married Miss Annie Norhausen, who survives him, as do also a number of their children, he having died at Schulenburg, in 1914. Robert A. is a representative citizen and business man at Schulenburg and to him the publishers are indebted for the interesting data which form the basis of this article. Julius A. who married Emilie Koenig, was a prominent merchant at Shiner, Lavaca County, at the time of his death and is survived by several children, he having been a prominent merchant at Shiner. A special tribute to him is given in this work. Ferdinand, Jr., who died at Schulenburg, was a successful business man and public-spirited citizen. He married Norma Miller and they became the parents of several children. Max E. is a resident of Shiner and is individually mentioned in an appending article. The children of Charles and Elizabeth (Goeth Wolters) Ernst were two in number,—Mrs. E. Moeckel, of Shiner; and Charles, who died at Hallettsville, Lavaca County, leaving a family.

EDMUND F. WOLTERS. He whose name initiates this paragraph is an influential and honored citizen of Shiner, Lavaca County, and is a scion of the fine old pioneer family whose history is outlined in the article immediately preceding the one here presented, he being a son of Robert Wolters, the eldest of the children of that sterling pioneer, Jacob Wolters.

The late Robert Wolters was a lad of fifteen years at the time when he accompanied his parents to Texas, and from that time forward his youthful education of specific order was necessarily limited, owing to the conditions and exigencies of time and place. An alert and receptive mind enabled him, however, effectually to overcome this handicap of earlier years and he became a man of broad information and mature judgment. He assisted his father in the reclaiming of the pioneer farm and initiated his independent career as a farmer in Austin County. A number of years later he removed thence to Blanco County, where he was engaged in stock-growing for two years. He then returned to Fayette County, the original home of the family, and for many years he was one of the prosperous and representative agriculturists and stock-raisers near High Hill, that county. When the Civil war was precipitated he subordinated all personal considerations to tender his aid in defense of the cause of the Confederacy, by joining Captain Upton's Company of the Texas militia, in which connection he was in service in the local field when called upon, the command having not been regularly enlisted in the Confederate ranks.

Upon the restoration of peace and his resumption of the activities of civil life Mr. Wolters engaged in the general merchandise business at High Hill, where he continued his residence until the railroad line was extended through Schulenburg, when, in 1872, he removed to the latter place, where he continued in the mercantile business with marked success. He retired from this line of enterprise when past sixty years of age and thenceforward he gave his attention to his private affairs and varied capitalistic and real-estate interests. He was one of the foremost in effecting the material upbuilding and civic and business development of Schulenburg, where he erected a number of brick and stone business buildings which remain as enduring monuments to his memory and civic liberality. While he aided in the promotion and establishment of the first banking institution at Schulenburg he did not long maintain his active association with its affairs, it being evident that he preferred to associate himself with such enterprises as he could personally direct and control. He was loyal and progressive as a citizen, was a staunch supporter of the democratic party in state and national affairs, but never desired or held public office. Mr. Wolters had due appreciation of the spiritual verities but his convictions were such that he did not subscribe to any ecclesiastical dogma or creed and did not ally himself with any church organization. His vigorous mind was a veritable storehouse of most interesting reminiscences concerning the pioneer days in Texas and his facility in narrating tales of his personal experience and observance as well as those of which he learned through extraneous sources made him a most interesting reconteur, so that the younger generation who knew him felt a deep sense of loss and deprivation when his earnest and noble life came to a close.

At Cat Spring, Austin County, on the 26th of December, 1849, Robert Wolters wedded Miss Adolphine Welhausen, the marriage ceremony having been performed by Ernst Kleburg, who was the incumbent of the magisterial office of justice of the peace and who was the father of Congressman Kleburg, now representing Texas in the National Legislature. Mrs. Wolters was a daughter of Charles Welhausen, who came with his family from Germany and established his home in Texas in 1847. Mrs. Wolters was summoned to eternal rest, at Schulenburg, on the 20th of May, 1906, and thus was broken the devoted marital companionship that had continued for fifty-seven years, the venerable couple having celebrated their golden wedding anniversary in 1899, the occasion having been made memorable by the assembling of a large concourse of their friends and by their reception of messages and telegrams of congratulation from many representative Texas citizens, besides which tangible tokens of esteem were presented by old friends and neighbors. Mr. Wolters survived his wife by about six years and continued his residence at Schulenburg until his death, which occurred February 23, 1912, he having attained to the patriarchal age of more than ninety years.

Concerning the children of this revered pioneer couple the following data are given: Augusta is the widow of Oscar Roos and she now resides in the City of San Antonio. Edmund F. is the immediate subject of this review. Louisa is the widow of Emanuel Roos and resides at Victoria, judicial center of the county of the same name. Ottellie became the wife of Hugo Horner and her death occurred at Schulenburg. Mary is the wife of Edmund B. Kessler, of Schulenburg, and in the same city resides Ella, who is the wife of Hon. I. E. Clark, M. D., who is representative of the Schulenburg district in the Texas Senate at the time of this writing, in 1915.

Edmund Ferdinand Wolters was born in Austin County, Texas, on the 29th of September, 1852, and his early educational advantages were those afforded in the pioneer schools, but, like many another man of affairs, he has had the ability to widen his mental ken by reading and observation and to round out his education through the lessons gained under the direction of that wisest of all headmasters, experience. At the age of eighteen years he became associated with the mercantile business conducted by his father, and he eventually succeeded to the ownership of the store at Schulenburg, where he continued operations until 1887, when he disposed of his interests at that place and removed to Shiner, a newly founded town through which the first train on the Aransas Pass Railroad had been run in the preceding month. Here he purchased the lumber and hardware business of Mr. Woodley, and after conducting the enterprise about two years he sold the business to William Green and turned his attention to the ginning of cotton, in which line of industrial enterprise he is still actively engaged at Shiner, in association with the Trautweins. He has acquired also interests in high-grade cotton gins at other points, at each of which he is associated with partners who are his valued coadjutors, each of these enterprises having been developed and brought to prosperous status. A number of years ago Mr. Wolters became identified with the banking business, and he is at the present time president of the Yoakum State Bank, at Yoakum, Dewitt County, and vice president of the First National Bank of Shiner. Aside from the interests already noted Mr. Wolters has become a prominent and successful dealer in real estate, and he is president of the Shiner Oilmill & Manufacturing Company, of which he was one of the promoters and organizers. At Shiner the firm of Trautwein & Wolters operate not only a thoroughly modern cotton gin but also a creamery and an ice manufactory.

In connection with the physical upbuilding of Shiner Mr. Wolters has played as effective a part as did his honored father at Schulenburg. He has erected two brick business buildings and has otherwise shown his civic enterprise and loyalty. He has served as a member of the board of aldermen of Shiner and was the incumbent of this office at the time when the waterworks plant of the town was installed. His political allegiance is given to the republican party in national affairs, and in the Masonic fraternity he is affiliated with the blue lodge at Shiner and also with the Order of the Eastern Star.

At Meyersville, Dewitt County, on the 18th of June, 1890, was solemnized the marriage of Mr. Wolters to Miss Sophie Trautwein, a daughter of William Trautwein, who was a representative farmer of that locality and who came to Texas soon after his immigration from his German Fatherland. Mr. and Mrs. Wolters have two children,—Lillie A., who is the wife of William Wendtland, Jr., of Shiner, and Miss Stella, who is a member of the class of 1914 in Baylor University, in the City of Waco.

Julius A. Wolters. He to whom this brief memoir is dedicated well upheld the high prestige of a family name that has long been one of prominence in the annals of Southern Texas, as the foregoing genealogical record clearly indicates. He became one of the pioneer merchants of the Town of Shiner, Lavaca County, wielded large and benignant influence in the development and upbuilding of the village along both civic and material lines and his impregnable integrity, his worthy achievement and his usefulness in the community gave him inviolable place in popular confidence and esteem. He was a son of Ferdinand and Elizabeth (Goeth) Wolters, concerning whom adequate mention is made in the preceding article touching the general family history, so that a repetition of the data is not demanded in this connection.

Mr. Wolters was born in Austin County, Texas, on the 28th of September, 1860, and after an illness of less than two weeks' duration he died at his home in Shiner, Lavaca County, on the 17th of December, 1913, after having been one of the representative citizens and prominent merchants of Shiner for approximately a quarter of a century. He was a child at the time of his father's death and was reared to adult age in the home of his mother and stepfather, Mr. and Mrs. Charles Ernst, his educational discipline having been obtained in the rural schools of his native county and his initial business experience having been gained under the direction of Mr. Ernst, who gave to him true fatherly solicitude. After having served as a clerk in the store of his stepfather he eventually engaged in the mercantile business in an independent way, at New Ulm, Austin County, where he continued operations until his removal to the newly founded Town of Shiner, Lavaca County. Here he associated himself with his brother Max E., to whom specific attention is directed in an article following this memoir, and the firm of Wolters Brothers became one of the most aggressive and successful in the town. Among the business firms the two brothers were recognized leaders, and none excelled them in the furtherance of the physical and social upbuilding of the town.

Julius A. Wolters was a man of strong mind, strong character and strong physical powers, his comparatively sudden death, in the very prime of his useful manhood, having been the result of a disorder of the heart. From a newspaper tribute published at the time of his demise are taken, with certain paraphrase and elimination the following appreciative statements:

"The business of the firm of Wolters Brothers, of which he was the senior member, was very large and required much of his time and attention. In his business relations Mr. Wolters was strictly just in all his dealings. He had many hard problems with which to deal, but he generally solved them to the satisfaction of all persons concerned. He was a man of many sides. He was liberal with you when you were right and firm with you when you were in the wrong. On account of his fair dealing and good business qualifications Mr. Wolters numbered his friends by the score. He came to Shiner when the town was in its incipiency, about twenty-five years ago, and engaged in business with his brother Max. The partnership was ever congenial and it continued until the time of his death. His funeral was one of the largest ever held at Shiner. A special train was made up at Yoakum and brought twenty-five citizens from that city to attend the last sad rites. Other friends were here from Moulton, Flatonia and Hallettsville."

In a fraternal way Mr. Wolters was identified with the Hermann Sohns, the Woodmen of the World, the Ancient Order of United Workmen and the Knights of Honor. Reared in the faith of the Lutheran Church, he continued in the same until the close of his life and manifested it in his daily walk and associations. He was essentially public-spirited in his civic attitude, exercised his franchise in support of the cause of the democratic party, but he never had aught of ambition for political office.

At New Ulm, Austin County, on the 1st of May, 1883, was solemnized the marriage of Julius A. Wolters to Miss Emilia Koenig, a daughter of John and Annie (Meyer) Koenig, both of whom died at LaGrange, Fayette County, when in the prime of life, both succumbing about the same time, during a scourge of yellow fever. They became the parents of six children: John is a resident of LaGrange; Mrs. Augusta Zwiener is a resident of Halsted, Fayette County; Mrs. Wolters, who survives her husband, was the next child; Mrs. Paulie Jersig maintains her home in the City of Galveston; and Mrs. Lizzie Frohnapple is a resident of LaGrange. Mrs. Wolters was a child at the time of her parents' tragic death and was reared in the home of Mrs. Ernest Wangamann, of New Ulm.

In conclusion of this memoir is given a brief record concerning the children of Mr. and Mrs. Wolters: Edwin, who is an interested principal in the firm of Wolters Brothers, wedded Miss Henrietta Hollman and they have one son, Julius Henry. Ottillie is the wife of Hermann G. Hollman; Elo, who likewise has become a member of the firm of Wolters Brothers, married Miss Julia Runk. Edgar also has become a member of the firm of which his father was one of the founders, and the maiden name of his wife was Lassie Schaeffer, their one child being Carlton Edgar. Herbert, the youngest of the children, remains with his widowed mother and is associated with the firm of which his father was a member.

Max E. Wolters. In point of continuous identification with the business interests of the thriving Town of Shiner, Lavaca County, Mr. Wolters now holds the distinction of being the oldest merchant of the village, with whose civic and business activities he has been closely identified since 1888, he and his older brother, the late Julius A. Wolters, to whom the preceding memoir is dedicated, having been pioneer merchants of the town, where they initiated business in the month following the completion of the railroad through this place. In the generic sketch of the Wolters family that appears in foregoing paragraphs adequate mention is made of the life and services of Ferdinand Wolters, father of him whose name initiates this article and who is the youngest of the children of Ferdinand and Elizabeth (Goeth) Wolters.

Max E. Wolters was born at New Ulm, Austin County, Texas, on the 13th of July, 1864, and to the common schools of the locality and period he is indebted for his early educational discipline. He obtained his initial business experience in the mercantile establishment of his stepfather, Charles Ernst, at New Ulm, and later, in the latter's store at Schulenburg, Fayette County. He severed the home ties when eighteen years of age and became a clerk in the mercantile establishment of G. Bohms & Company, at Schulenburg. His salary as a general salesman in the store was of nominal order but he profited much through the experience that he gained during his service of somewhat more than five years in a clerical capacity. His wages were advanced by degrees and he carefully saved his earnings, so that he was finally enabled to join his brother Julius A. in the founding of their independent general merchandise business at Shiner, their combined capital having not exceeded $4,000 and their original place of business having been in a one-story frame building 24x60 feet in dimensions. In this building they continued operations during the first year, and the firm of Wolters Brothers was the fifth to engage in business at Shiner. In 1889 they erected a new and better frame building, and in this their business was successfully continued until its prosperity and increased demands led them to erect the substantial brick building in which the enterprise is still continued under the original firm name and of which Max E. has been the senior member since the death of his brother Julius. In 1911 the firm added to their original brick building a two-story brick structure 50x110 feet in dimensions, for the accommodation of the grocery and hardware departments of their establishment, and the aggregate floor space now utilized by the firm is 17,500 square feet, besides which they have a wareroom, 50x110 feet in dimensions, for the storage of surplus stock.

When the Wolters brothers began business at Shiner the two personally attended to all details of the enterprise, and the substantial expansion of the business is indicated by the statement that at the present time the corps of employes numbers eighteen persons. The establishment is modern in appointments and in the equipment of each department, and the extensive trade rests upon the high reputation the firm has ever maintained for effective service and fair and honorable dealings.

Mr. Wolters is president of the Farmers State Bank of Shiner and he and the firm of Wolters Brothers own extensive tracts of land in Wilson and Scurry counties, besides an appreciable acreage in Reagan County. They have been thus concerned with the bringing into effective cultivation many tracts of wild land, upon which numerous reliable tenants are supported. The original members of the firm continuously invested their surplus capital by making judicious investment in farm lands, and in the management and extension of this important feature of the firm's business Max E. Wolters has successfully continued operations since the death of his brother, who was his honored coadjutor in all of their activities.

For fifteen years Mr. Wolters was insistently retained in service as a member of the board of aldermen of Shiner, and his civic loyalty was further shown by a service of several years as a member of the board of education. He is affiliated with and is a former president of the Shiner Lodge of the Hermann Sohns, which he has represented in the grand lodge of the state, as has he also the local camp in the grand camp of the Woodmen of the World in Texas, he being likewise a valued member of the Rathbone Lodge No. 109 of the Knights of Pythias. In the Village of Shiner Mr. Wolters has erected as his place of residence one of the finest houses in Lavaca County, the same being a pretentious mansion of colonial architecture, massive columns carrying the two-story gallery and balcony, and the entire place being essentially metropolitan in appearance and appointments, even as the home is known for its gracious and refined hospitality and as a center of much of the representative social activity of the community.

In Fayette County, on the 5th of June, 1887, Mr. Wolters wedded Miss Annie Baumgarten, who was there born and reared and who is a daughter of Christian Baumgarten, long a representative citizen of that county. Mr. and Mrs. Wolters have two sons: Victor, who is associated with the firm of Wolters Brothers, married Miss Alvina Ehlers and they have one son, Max; Gustave, who is one of the eligible young bachelors of Shiner, is likewise actively concerned with the business of the firm of Wolters Brothers.

James Edward Lord. One of the best ranch homes and farms in Gonzales County is that owned by James E. Lord near Cheapside. Mr. Lord is one of the progressive and successful men of his section of

George Lord

Texas, and besides what he has accomplished in a material way he is worthily distinguished as being the son of one of the great Texas patriots, and one of the last survivors of the Mier expedition, which has served as a theme for as much historical narration as any other incident in Texas annals.

Mr. Lord is the youngest son of the late George Lord, who had a remarkably interesting career and who died when nearly eighty years of age in February, 1895. George Lord was born in County Essex, England, April 21, 1816, a son of Felstead and Anna (Siggs) Lord. His father was a bricklayer and while repairing a brick oven lost his life when his son George was only an infant. The mother married again and died in London at the age of eighty-two. Three of the sons came to the United States, William and Robert settling in McLean County, Illinois.

Educated in England, George Lord in 1834 crossed the ocean to Canada, two years later came to the United States, for several months was a Mississippi steamboat man, and at New Orleans on December 27, 1836, he joined a company of seventy-five under the command of Captain Lyons who had volunteered for service in the war between Texas and Mexico. He landed at Galveston February 27, 1837, when only a single frame building stood on the entire island. He was then ordered to Camp Independence on Lavaca River and joined John Holiday's Company of Second Regimental Volunteers under Colonel Wiggington. In June, 1837, this company was consolidated with Captain Jordan's company and went to San Antonio. The next year George Lord was discharged and for his service to the Republic received a grant of land. During the same year he was at Cibolo at the ranch of Colonel Patton, when about fifty Comanche Indians slew a man named Tolbert. After Colonel Burleson's fight with Cordova on the Guadaloupe near Seguin, Mr. Lord joined Captain Dawson's company in San Antonio.

About September 1, 1839, he joined the forces under General Canaliz on the Nueces River, and during the first campaign was at the taking of Guerro, Mexico, and was a participant in the battles at Alcantra, Matamoras and Monterey. During the second campaign he was at the taking of Laredo and in the battle of Saltillo with Colonel Jordan. These various campaigns were chiefly in the interests of the Mexican faction who were fighting to maintain or re-establish the Mexican Constitution of 1824.

In 1842 he took part in the famous expedition to the Rio Grande which included the capture of Mier and that town gave the name to the entire expedition. After the surrender at Mier Mr. Lord and his comrades made several attempts to escape while being taken into the interior. The third attempt was made at Salado, and that exploit was described in Mr. Lord's own words as follows: "When all was ready Captain Cameron said in a distinct tone 'well boys we will go to it,' and suiting the action to the words he seized one of the two sentinels while S. H. Walker seized the other. It was the work of only an instant to disarm the guard and get possession of the outer court, where the arms and cartridge boxes were guarded by one hundred fifty men. They then charged the enemy outside the building, including the 'Red Caps' and routed them in less than two minutes, with only two killed, two mortally wounded and five or six slightly wounded, while the enemy lost eight or ten men. The Texans traveled sixty-three miles before stopping after their escape and wandered for three days across almost a desert, suffering greatly from hunger and privation and on the 8th day they were captured and returned to Salado, where on March 25th the infamous lottery of the bean drawing took place.

Acting on instructions from superior officers, the Mexican guards informed the prisoners that they were to be decimated. Governor Mexia refused to perform the black deed and it was assigned to Col. Domingo Huerta. The decimation took place by the drawing of black and white beans from a small earthen mug, the white beans signifying exemption and the black ones meaning death. One hundred fifty-nine white beans were placed in the bottom of the mug and seventeen black ones on top. The beans were not stirred and had so slight a shaking that it was perfectly clear that it was the intention of the Mexican authorities to capture Captain Cameron and the other officers who had to draw first. During his lifetime Mr. Lord frequently recalled the scene and especially the manly temper and courage of those who participated.

Captain Cameron stepped up with utmost coolness and thrust his hand into the mug, but drew out a white bean. Others took their turn and made the drawing a matter of jest and sport. One of them said: "Boys, this beats raffling all to pieces," and another one said "this is the tallest gambling scrape I was ever in." Those who drew the black beans showed no emotion, not even changing color, and it was those who drew the white beans who exhibited the most concern. Many of the latter begged piteously to be allowed to take the place of their doomed comrades, and the scene even brought tears to the eyes of some of the Mexican executioners. Soon after the drawing the fated men were placed in a separate courtyard and executed. The victims were bound with cords, eyes bandaged and were seated on logs with their backs to the executioners. They all begged the officers to shoot them in the front and at a short distance, but this request was denied, and the firing squad continued shooting for ten or twelve minutes until the bodies were lacerated and mangled horribly.

After this execution Mr. Lord and some of his comrades were imprisoned at Tacubaya from May 1 to September 16, 1843, and was employed there in making streets. He was then moved to Castle Perote and liberated in 1844. On returning to Texas he received a patent for 1,280 acres of land which he located in Dewitt County at Cheapside, and it was there in quiet industry and the vocation of husbandman that he spent his remaining years. When the Civil war broke out he joined the Home Guard, although exempt from service on account of age, and served two years.

In 1849 George Lord went to California and for three years was in the gold diggings. He returned to Texas with $7,000, which he had coined at the New Orleans mint. This gold furnished the basis for his future success in life.

In politics he was independent and in religion an Episcopalian. He served his district as school trustee and enjoyed many places of trust and honor. At El Paso, Texas, December 30, 1849, George Lord married Miss Kate Myers, an orphan girl who was born in New Orleans October 15, 1832. At the time of her marriage she was one of a party bound for California. Mr. and Mrs. George Lord had eleven children, as follows: Cynthia, widow of John Johnson of Eldorado, Texas; George, who spent his life on a farm adjoining that of his father and died just before his mother; Robert F.; Emma, wife of H. M. Smith of Westhoff; Pleasant, who died in Gonzales County, and left children by his marriage to Mary Miller; Minnie, who married E. K. Smith and died near Sample, Texas; Henry, who lives on the old home farm; Sidney of Runge, Texas; James Edward of Cheapside; and Katie, wife of L. A. Carter of Cuero.

The youngest son of this splendid Texas patriot, James Edward Lord, was born in Dewitt County February 21, 1872. He grew up in that community, gained an education in the country schools, supplemented by a business course at San Antonio and in the George Soule Business College of New Orleans. He employed his talent as an accountant only a few months, but has found the knowledge useful in his increased business affairs of later years. While with his father he learned all the details of the cattle business, and on leaving home he started out for himself in the Cheapside community. He has lived at his present place for the past twenty years. His farm was first improved by Thomas Carter, the father of his wife. Mr. Lord began his operations there in 1896 and his first land was a part of the Carter ranch, but later he acquired by purchase a portion of the Houston ranch and his land now lies in the M. Cogswell, the Lott and the Hill leagues. As a cattle man he has fed rather extensively, has taken his stock to markets and sold as an individual, and at various times he bought cattle extensively in his home community for shipment.

His principal service Mr. Lord has rendered as a trustee of his home school district for many years. The splendid schoolhouse in the Cheapside community was erected by private subscription, and Mr. Lord was one of the generous donors to that fund.

On May 14, 1896, he married Miss Sarah J. Carter. Her father was Thomas Carter and her mother was an Arnold. To their marriage have been born three children: Grace, who died when almost three years of age; George J.; and Edna.

Rev. Joseph Szymanski. On May 26, 1914, the Church of St. Michael at Weimar was dedicated with impressive ceremonies, with the presence of Bishop Shaw from San Antonio and a large concourse of clergy and laity. This splendid church home, representing the religious ideals and activities of the Catholic people of Weimar and vicinity, is also a monument to the devoted and unselfish labors of the parish priest, Father Joseph Szymanski, who has been identified with the State of Texas since 1896 and has been pastor of the parish at Weimar since May, 1906.

Joseph Szymanski was born August 7, 1873, at Tuszewo, Prussia, and was a son of farming people. His father, Albert Szymanski, who was born in the same locality, married Catherine Lamparsky, who died at Bluff, Texas, in 1901. Albert Szymanski is still living in his home near Flatonia. These parents came to Texas when their son, Father Joseph, was a pastor at St. John. Their other children are: Frank, of Detroit, Michigan; John, a farmer in Fayette County; Antone, of Detroit; and Adam, at Flatonia.

Father Szymanski did his college work in his native land, and for nine years attended the higher school. After coming to America he spent two years in study in Sts. Cyril and Methodius Polish Seminary at Detroit, Michigan, then went to St. Meinrads Seminary, Spencer County, Indiana, and in 1896 came to Texas and for a year and a half was a student in the Victoria Seminary at Victoria. After being ordained to the priesthood, he did his first active church work at St. John, where he was pastor of the congregation for three and a half years. From there he went to Ammandsville and Bluff, in Fayette County, and continued his pastoral duties in those charges five and a half years.

His forte has been especially noteworthy as a builder and improver of church property. At St. John he improved the church building and had it painted and the same attention was given to the churches at Ammandsville and Bluff, and also the school property there. When he arrived at Weimar in May, 1906, he found the parish worshiping in an old frame church erected about twenty-five years before, and without any needed accommodations. He then set himself upon a campaign for the building and equipping of the new edifice, one that might properly accommodate the church interests of the parish and properly represent the dignity of the church in that community. The result of his work continued through eight years was seen in the dedication of St. Michael's Church in May, 1914. He was the pastor of a faithful congregation, ready and willing to sacrifice time and means, and with this backing he was able to achieve the grand work represented in the dedication of the church.

A brief description of the church edifice as given in a copy of the Southern Messenger is as follows: The new church is built of gray Elgin brick, with stone trimmings, on a reinforced concrete foundation. The body of the church measures 100 feet in length by 60 feet in width, while the sanctuary extends 30 feet further and measures 26 feet in width. On either side of the sanctuary is a sacristy, 16x16 feet. Underneath the sanctuary and sacristies is a fine basement for meetings, but may be used later for the installation of a heating plant. The tower and spire rise to a height of 144 feet to the top of the cross. The roof is of the best Pennsylvania slate, while the ceiling is vaulted gothic, plastered and tinted. Eight large art glass windows on each side afford light and air, while five smaller ones light up the sanctuary. For artificial lights about 200 electric lamps are supplied. The church is furnished throughout in keeping with its exterior beauty, with three beautiful altars, a handsome pulpit and communion railing, two double confessionals, a baptismal font and oak pews. The cost of the building proper was about $37,000, while the price paid for the lots and the cost of the furnishings brings the total investment to about $44,000.

The parish also maintains a parochial school, and its teachers are the Sisters of the Incarnate Word, comprising three teachers with a school enrollment of 120 children. The school was opened before the church was established here, and has been maintained for many years. Attached to St. Michael's is Dubina Mission, patronized by the German and Bohemian parishioners at Dubina, about five miles from Weimar. Father Szymanski serves this church as part of his general pastoral duties. The school there has eighty pupils and is taught by Sisters of the Incarnate Word.

Father Szymanski's literary work aside from his sermons comprises articles for newspapers, chiefly devoted to news of the church and replies to articles pertaining to church matters. He has exercised a wise leadership and benevolent influence in his community as presiding officer of meetings of his people and in his daily intercourse with his neighbors. Soon after coming to America he made his first declaration of citizenship and was fully naturalized in 1907. He has made a study of our political system, formed his conclusions as to the best policies for the promotion of prosperity and contentment, and has participated as a voter in national affairs.

Charles Henry Holland. The career of this well known citizen of Schulenburg has two interesting distinctions. The first is his long service for more than a quarter of a century in the employ of the Southern Pacific Railway, and railroading has been almost his entire life work, having learned telegraphy in a railway office in Indiana, his native state. The second is his proficiency in the traditional work of Masonry, and he is one of the few Masons clothed with authority to teach the unwritten rites and symbolisms of this great and ancient order.

Charles Henry Holland was born in Dublin, Henry County, Indiana,

July 12, 1859, and he spent his youth there and received an education in the public schools. His first work after leaving school was with some horse men in that locality, and he spent a couple of years training horses and then conducted a butcher shop in Dublin. While in this business he was taken ill, and while convalescing and still weak from the disease, he was spending a few days in Richmond, Indiana. While there his attention was directed to the study of telegraphy. He talked with the manager of a school which had that art in its curriculum, and was induced by the prospects to begin the study. After several lessons he visited a couple of friends, employes on the Grand Rapids & Indiana Railway, who advised him to give up the telegraph school and begin the practical work of a railway station and telegraph office. He found an opening in the office of the Grand Rapids & Indiana at Fountain City, in Wayne County, and there was converted from his former vocation as butcher and horse trainer to a telegrapher, and soon afterwards was given his first independent work at Kendallville, Indiana. He was stationed at several points, including Fort Wayne, Richmond, Kalamazoo, along the route of the Grand Rapids & Indiana and was finally induced to come South by Mr. Van Vleck, general manager of the Southern Pacific Railway system.

Mr. Holland came to Texas in December, 1888, was an operator at Rosenberg, and before he had been with the company two months he was given a day shift, and in April, 1903, was made agent of the Schulenburg Station, succeeding Agent R. S. Tanner, another old employe of the system who had left the service to engage in business for himself.

Mr. Holland is a grandson of Rev. Henry and Mary Holland. The grandfather was a native of Ohio, one of the early settlers in Henry County, Indiana, and entered Government land and was a farmer there until his death. He was also a Methodist preacher, and did circuit work over his section of Indiana before the advent of railroads. His ancestry was a combination of Irish and French. Rev. Mr. Holland and wife had eleven sons and a daughter, all of whom grew up in Indiana, and all those reaching maturity had families. Of these children the following are named: Joshua, Asbury, William, Andrew, Joseph, Elijah, Henry, Isaac, Emma, Emory, Adam and Elizabeth, who married Joshua Waddell.

Henry Holland, father of the Schulenburg railway man, was born in Henry County, Indiana, in 1826, and died at Dublin in 1904. His career was spent as a sawmill man, a farmer and carpenter. Owing to an injury he had sustained when a boy he was rejected for military service during the Civil war, but three of his brothers were soldiers in the Union army. Though a democrat in politics, he took little part and never held an office. He was a member of the Methodist Church. Henry Holland married Mary Swiggett. She was an only child of Andrew Swiggett, who came from North Carolina to Indiana as a pioneer. In the Swiggett household was reared another child, Isaac McNamee, who at his death left a family of six children. Mrs. Henry Holland died in 1901 at the age of seventy-nine. Her children were: Joshua, who died at Straughns Station, Indiana, leaving a son; Roy Holland, now a New York lawyer; Mary, who married Dill Waddell, of Straughns Station; Lydia, who married Nate Gaukher of same place; Charles H.; William A., of Elwood, Indiana; and Ella, who married William Gaukher, of Straughns Station.

Mr. Charles H. Holland owes his success largely to the fact that he has supported himself unreservedly to the business in hand, and has participated in no other lines of commerce or in politics, except to vote the democratic ticket. He is well known in different fraternal orders and fraternal work is his one absorbing interest outside of business and home. He belongs to the Knights of Pythias, the Improved Order of Red Men, the Woodmen of the World, the Modern Order of Praetorians. In Masonry he is member of both Lodge and Chapter, a past master of his lodge, and in December, 1914, was made deputy district grand master of the Thirty-third Texas District. It is given to few men to master the 42,210 words of unwritten work with such proficiency as to be able to communicate this as instruction to novitiates, and Mr. Holland is one of these few and occupies a place of high standing and esteem in his order.

Mr. Holland was married at Portland, Indiana, December 24, 1886, to Miss Harriet Winters, daughter of John and Margaret Winters. Her father was a miller at Portland, and met an accidental death at his mill at the age of seventy years. The children in the Winters family were: Mollie, wife of Doctor O'Neal, of Elwood, Indiana; Mrs. Holland; Addie, wife of A. Hamlett, of Portland; Thomas, of Pittsburgh, Pennsylvania; John, a resident of Pennsylvania; and Jay, of Huntington, Indiana. Mr. and Mrs. Holland have five children: Irene; Frank, who is employed in the railway station at Schulenburg; Mabel, Pearl and Donley.

Maj. John Barclay Armstrong. In business life a cattleman, the late Maj. John Barclay Armstrong was probably best known as a former Texas State Ranger and as a criminal officer in various capacities during the stirring days of frontier life in Texas. As an officer he was a remarkable man, and the story of his deeds of bravery and daring in capturing and arresting criminals, if written in full, would fill a large-sized volume. It can never be told in its completeness, however, for, as is often the case with those who are the bravest and strongest, he was an exceedingly modest man in relating his own achievements, and his reticence in this respect, even toward members of his own family, was one of his noticeable characteristics. Many of his most notable exploits he never spoke of to anyone, deeming them of no consequence, but rather considering them merely as a part of the day's work. Combined in him were the heart and courage of a lion; the gentleness and tenderness of a woman.

Major Armstrong was born at McMinnville, Tennessee, January 1, 1850, and died at his home at Armstrong, Texas, May 1, 1913. He grew up as a boy during the Civil war, and even as a lad his prowess and skill as a fighter asserted themselves and are still remembered by the very old-timers of his home community in Tennessee. He was born of the best Scotch ancestry, his father being Dr. John B. Armstrong, of Tennessee, and one of the girls of the Armstrong family, a cousin of Major Armstrong, became the wife of John Morgan, the famous Confederate raider. When he was eighteen years of age Major Armstrong went to Missouri and Arkansas, in which states he spent two or three years. He came to Austin, Texas, in January, 1871, and from that time until his death the Lone Star State continued to be his home. He was married at Austin, to Miss Mollie Durst, a daughter of Maj. James H. and Josephine (Atwood) Durst, themselves a noted pioneer family of Texas. Mrs. Armstrong died in 1897, having been the mother of seven children: Josephine, who is the wife of Andrew Stewart, of New Orleans, Louisiana; Jamie, who is the wife of John M. Bennett, Jr., of San Antonio, Texas; John B., Jr., who was killed by a horse on the ranch, at the age of twenty-two years; Charles Mitchell, a graduate of Princeton, and now manager of the ranch; Julia Catherine, the wife of Zeb Mayhew, of New York; Elliott Ropes ("Tim"), who died at Austin in 1898; and Tom, a graduate of Princeton, class of 1913, and Harvard Law School, 1915.

When he was eighteen years of age, Major Armstrong, as before noted, had gone to Missouri and Arkansas, and in those states had been engaged in a variety of pursuits. Soon after locating at Austin, Texas, he joined the old Travis Rifles, a military organization of state troops, and for a long number of years was a member and officer of the National Guard of Texas. About 1872, having had considerable experience in military affairs, he was asked by the late Captain McNelly, the famous ranger officer, to join the latter's company of rangers, which he did, and was put to work as drill sergeant, drilling recruits for the ranger service. Later he became a lieutenant of rangers and for quite a long time acted in the capacity of captain, although never commissioned as such, but he was always known as "Major" Armstrong.

One of Major Armstrong's most notable exploits as a ranger was his capture of John Wesley Hardin, one of the most desperate gunmen and highwaymen that ever came to Texas. He madé this capture in Florida, to which state Hardin had fled, a fugitive. Major Armstrong also at one time captured that other noted desperado, King Fisher, who was, however, later released and was finally killed in San Antonio. Major Armstrong's career as an officer, both as a ranger and a deputy United States marshal, brought him, in fact, in conflict with nearly all the famous criminal characters of Texas, the list including Sam Bass, Ben Thompson, Alfred Aylee, and numerous others. After retiring from the ranger service he was appointed deputy United States marshal and served in that capacity until the time of his death. He rendered most faithful service to the Federal officials and these were greatly appreciated by them.

In 1882 Major Armstrong, having acquired large land interests near the coast in Southwest Texas and entered the cattle business, removed to the ranch and there his home remained during the rest of his life. This is one of the finest ranches in Texas, consisting of 50,000 acres, lying originally in Cameron and Hidalgo counties, but now in the new County of Willacy. The ranch is divided in half by the St. Louis, Brownsville & Mexico Railroad, and Armstrong Station, on this road, is situated in the center of it, and is seventy-seven miles north of Brownsville. The family home is located two miles from Armstrong. On the ranch there are sixteen artesian wells, and the property is stocked with a notable herd of high-grade Shorthorn cattle, registered.

Major Armstrong was a noted shot with the rifle and six-shooter, and remained as such, with undiminished steadiness of nerve, up to the time of his death. His aim was unerring, and he never missed fire. His quickness with the gun was in keeping with his accuracy. With reference to himself, he seemed to lead a charmed life, for although shot at, at close range, on innumerable occasions, by desperate characters bent on killing him, he was never even wounded. Although a very powerful man physically, being 5 feet 11 inches in height, and weighing 190 pounds, with very broad shoulders, all his life he was very athletic, light on his feet and very active in his móvements. If unarmed, or if he did not wish to use his gun, he would fell the most powerful opponent with one blow of his fist. His true chivalry and valor were often displayed in the protection of the weak, and it was no doubt, secretly, one of the pleasures of his life to knock down some bully for terrorizing helpless persons: and in traveling, on trains, or in public places, wherever trouble of this sort was brewing, he would hesitate not a moment but get into action at once. In his mere presence one felt instinctively a sense of safety and protection. Withal, his gentleness and kindness of heart were very noticeable characteristics, as before mentioned. He had been known to shed tears at seeing even a stranger in trouble or distress, and to his friends and his family, his kindness, sympathy and generosity were unbounded. There could not have lived a more beloved man. He had that great gift, unconsciously, and possessed by so few, of winning the love, immediately, of all, high and low, in all stations of life. In a hotel lobby or any public place where his presence became known, he would soon be surrounded. On visits to New York and other northern and eastern cities, he made many warm friends and was taken at once into the best circles. Notwithstanding his long years as an officer dealing with the worst elements of the frontier, his polish and gifts of the gentleman, which were his by nature, were never missing in his manner and his conduct. He became wealthy in the cattle business and was lavishly generous with his family, giving his children the best of college and university educations. When he passed from life his adopted state lost a citizen who played a conspicuous and helpful part in its development and whose achievements have an established place in its history.

CHARLES G. SMITH. This well known resident of Cuero, who has for many years managed extensive farm and ranch properties in Dewitt County, is identified with one of the early families of that section of Texas. The Smiths located in Dewitt County about 1856, the family home having been established by the late Rufus Smith, who came to Texas from Kentucky.

The ancestors of Charles G. Smith were prominent in the very early day of New England, and there were three brothers of the name, active Puritans, and on account of the restrictions placed upon the practice of their faith in the mother country, emigrated to America in the second ship following the Mayflower. Of these three original settlers one was killed by the Indians in the early Massachusetts colony, his name being Samuel, and the colonial records speak of his loss to the colony as a serious one. It is certain that subsequent members of the family bore their part in the struggle for American independence. In all the generations one characteristic of the family has been free thinking and independent action, and those attributes have persisted from the time the family left England in the early part of the seventeenth century down to the present time.

One branch of the family subsequently moved from Massachusetts and became identified with one of the early colonies in Connecticut. It was at Wethersfield, Connecticut, that Rufus Smith was born May 27, 1827. He was a son of Josiah and Hannah (Goodrich) Smith, who were married at Wethersfield; most of their children were born there, but they spent their later years in Chautauqua County, New York, and they are buried at Fredonia in that county. A brother of Josiah Smith was Walter Smith, who became prominent as a citizen, merchant and man of affairs at Dunkirk, New York. It was common for his note to circulate as money throughout that section. He was a stockholder of the first railroad built through that part of the state, and when asked how he was going to use the railroad he replied that he was going to raise cattle in Ohio, ship them by rail and slaughter them in New York, a suggestion which excited considerable ridicule at the time, but the idea is now one of universal practice. He was a forerunner of thought and the spirit of progress, and he it was who dammed the creek and brought the water to his mill some distance away and established a new industry at Dunkirk.

The children of Josiah Smith were: Daniel, who died in Chautauqua County, New York, at the age of ninety-four, having for many years served as chief clerk of his Uncle Walter; Misses Hannah and Elizabeth,

RUFUS SMITH

both of whom spent their years on the old homestead in New York; Sarah, who married Mr. Goodrich and died in Illinois; Albert, who occupied the Chautauqua County homestead and died there; Rufus; and Ann, who died unmarried on the old Chautauqua County home.

Rufus Smith was educated at Fredonia, New York, and learned the profession of civil engineering from an uncle in Connecticut. After considerable training and preparation he went to Kentucky and did engineering work on a railroad from Louisville to Maysville. While there he became acquainted with his wife. The Hamiltons, his wife's people, went to Texas soon afterwards, and this induced him to follow. Then in Dewitt County on February 7, 1856, Rufus Smith married Miss Caroline Hamilton, who was born February 7, 1837.

After coming to Texas Rufus Smith abandoned his profession as engineer and engaged in the cattle business in Dewitt County, and his chief interests during his remaining years was the stock business. He died at the age of seventy-eight. His farm in Dewitt County was the Captain York section, which had been purchased from its original owner by John Hamilton, and which had been given by the Republic of Texas to Captain York for gallant service in the battle of Bexar. Rufus Smith took little part in politics, only as a voter of the republican ticket. A Union man in sentiment, during the war he joined the Home Guards for frontier service in order to avoid fighting against the flag of his country. He was a zealous Methodist; his home was the headquarters for all circuit riders of the Methodist faith and he entertained them well. The Methodist Parsonage of Cuero was a donation from his estate.

His first wife, Miss Hamilton, who died June 25, 1863, was the daughter of John Hamilton, who was born December 12, 1790, and who married on October 12, 1813, Kittie, a daughter of John and Sarah Rule. John Hamilton was a son of Daniel and Mary (Scott) Hamilton of York, Pennsylvania. Daniel Hamilton was born April 10, 1755, a son of William Hamilton of Londonderry, Ireland. Daniel Hamilton's wife, Mary Scott, was a daughter of John Scott of Scotland.

There were two children by the marriage of Rufus Smith to Caroline Hamilton: May, who married Herbert L. Willis; and Charles G. For his second wife Rufus Smith married Mrs. Victoria Leonard, but there were no children by that union.

Charles G. Smith was born in Dewitt County, June 11, 1860, and grew up on the farm where he was born. Up to the age of eleven he attended the neighborhood schools and his father then sent him to the grandfather's home in New York State, and he graduated from a New York Normal School. With his education completed he returned to Texas and took up ranching with his father, and before the latter's death he had succeeded to the active management of the ranch and farm and has found in this business his chief prosperity and success. For several years he has kept his home in Cuero in order that his children may have the benefits of the schools.

To the schools, in fact, Mr. Smith has given his chief public service to his community. For some time he was a member of the county board of education, and is now a member of the Cuero Board of School Trustees. He is consul commander of the Woodmen of the World of Clear Camp and is also affiliated with the Knights of Pythias. Mrs. Smith, his wife, and the children are members of the Methodist Church.

On June 17, 1896, Mr. Smith married Miss Eliza Edgar, daughter of Henry and Jane (Brown) Edgar. Her father was one of seven brothers, sons of Joseph Edgar, and founders of the Edgar community of Dewitt County. Henry Edgar was twice married, and his first wife had two children, Jane and Bammie, and by the second marriage the children were Sarah, Kate, Kittie, Henry, Lemuel and Mrs. Smith. The daughter Jane married Lemuel Bachelor; Bammie married Joseph Brown; Sarah married W. T. Knox; Kate married Will Guthrie; Kittie married Will Kellett; Henry married Mary Benbow; and Lemuel married Elizabeth Faulconer.

Mr. and Mrs. Smith have a fine family of nine children, most of whom are attending the public schools of Cuero. Their names are: Carrie, May, Annabelle, Marie, Edgar, Margaret, Rufus, Alexander and Eleanor.

Monroe R. Allen. Few families in Colorado County have been more closely identified with farm development and production, with merchandising and other business institutions, and with church and politics than the Allens, among whom the one selected for special representation in this sketch is Monroe R. Allen, of Weimar. The Allens were among the antebellum families of Colorado County, and are one of the few American families still left in this section of the state.

Monroe R. Allen was born in the Shimek locality January 7, 1860, just two years after his parents settled there. Prior to becoming Texans the family were Georgians, and in a generation before that were from Scotland. In Scotland Grandfather John Laird Allen was born, and served a thorough apprenticeship in the mechanical trade of carpenter in his native land. He came to America about the close of the Revolutionary war, and spent the rest of his life at Macon, Georgia, where his body is now at rest. He was one of the real mechanics of his time and a valuable addition to any community. John L. Allen married Nellie McMurrey, of Georgia, who died in Texas and is buried at Shimek. Their children were: Charles Alexander; John Laird; Matthew R.; Nellie, who married Wiley Wadsworth; and Jane, who married a Mr. Ross and died in Alabama. All the sons came to Texas together and settled in the same neighborhood, and all of them reared families except Charles Alexander.

Matthew R. Allen, whose middle name was Robinson, was born at Macon, Georgia, February 15, 1828, and learned the same trade followed by his father. In 1858 he started for Texas, and from New Orleans went by ship to Indianola, Texas, and finished his journey to Colorado County with wagons and ox teams. His skill as a carpenter was of material assistance in building a home and adding improvements to a new farm, but outside of his own requirements followed his trade very little. He bought land on the Jack Survey, farmed and improved it with free labor and remained a resident there twenty-three years. While a man of little education, he was kindly disposed, a man of peaceable inclinations, and was an excellent type of citizen for a new country. He was active in the Methodist Church and a meeting house was erected for that denomination on a part of his land. He believed in and heartily embraced the great American principle of free education, and was positively aggressive in aiding in the promotion of schools and other means of educational and intellectual and moral training in his community. Almost continuously he served as a member of the local school board. During the war between the states he was exempt from military duty on account of physical incapacity, but gave some aid to the Confederate Government as a freighter. Before the war he was opposed to the secession of Texas, cast his vote against such a measure, but like thousands of other southerners yielded his sentiment to the voice of the majority and did a modest part in upholding the new government and the new flag. Matthew R. Arnold died September 26, 1881, and his wife passed away November 11, 1907. Her maiden name was Martha Thomas Woolsey, a daughter of John M. Woolsey, who died in Georgia. To this union were born the following children: John Milton, who spent his life in New Mexico from early manhood and died at Magdalena, leaving a family of four children: Joel Madison, who died at Shimek in 1875, leaving a wife and child; Eliza Eleanor, who married Albert Grobe, of Shimek; Charles Alexander, noted below; Monroe R.; Edmon, of California; Minnie, who married Josephus Barnett, of Tampa, Arizona; Nellie, who died in Arizona as the wife of Howard Livingston.

This sketch must devote a paragraph to the late Hon. Charles Alexander Allen, a brother and long associated with Monroe R. Allen. He was born near Macon, Georgia, January 8, 1857, and his life was passed as a farmer and merchant. By dint of his own efforts he secured an education, and was active both in church and politics. For about eight years he was with his brother Monroe in merchandising at Shimek, and the two were also partners as large and successful farmers. He was an officer in the Methodist Church at Shimek from early life until his death, and in politics was a democrat and much inclined toward active participation in party affairs. He enjoyed the excitement of political contest, although never an active candidate himself for any office except as representative to the Legislature. In his time he attended all the state conventions and had a wide acquaintance among Texas politicians. In 1894 he was first elected to the lower house of the Legislature, again was returned in 1900, and in 1904, and for the fourth term in 1908, and died while still a member of that body. He did valuable work on several committees and among others was chairman of the committee on stock and stock raising. His best service in the Legislature was in offering an obstinate resistance to useless and trivial bills. He had the best qualities of a political leader, though not as a public speaker, and was a hard worker and capable business man. He married Miss Georgie Amanda Castleberry, who died about two years after his death, without children.

Monroe R. Allen attained his early education in the country schools near Shimek and his career has been one of steady progress as a farmer. He has done much to bring land under cultivation, introduced practical and successful methods of farming, and has one of the best estates in Colorado County. He is also president of the Weimar Creamery, and is a stockholder in the T. A. Hill State Bank of Weimar.

Politically he has been an interested democrat in about the same sense as his brother Charles, and formerly attended the local conventions regularly. In the early days he was a member of the Sull Ross state convention, was a Hogg delegate to the famous car-barn convention at Houston, where the Clark element bolted and nominated their favorite for governor, introducing the greatest factional fight ever known in the democratic party of Texas. He was a participant in various other state conventions up to 1910, when he abandoned politics. He has never been a candidate for an elective office, but in 1915 President Wilson, through the influence of Congressman Burgess, named Mr. Allen as postmaster at Weimar and in that office he is showing great capabilities as an executor and administrator. Mr. Allen is affiliated with the Masonic order through the Lodge Chapter and Knight Templar Commandery and also with the Woodmen of the World.

November 7, 1896, Mr. Allen married Miss Mollie McMurrey, daughter of William and Anne (Harbour) McMurrey. Her father was from Greene County, Georgia, an early settler in Lavaca County, and is now living at Sweet Home. The McMurrey children are: Mrs. Allen, Leroy, Lucy, wife of D. A. McCord, Samuel, Walter, Arthur and Lydia, twins. Mr. and Mrs. Allen have two children: Annie Lee and William Charley.

In his personal characteristics Mr. Allen shows the presence of a large physique, weighing about 280 pounds, has affable manners, has brought himself to a position of affluence, and while a man of positive opinion and action in present day affairs, finds great recreation and entertainment in a retrospect of the past and olden times in his part of the state.

WILLIAM STEINMANN, SR. One of the oldest residents of Fayette County is William Steinmann, whose home for nearly ten years has been in Schulenburg. He belonged to one of the German families that located about Central Texas in the decade before the war, and his own career comprises service as a Confederate soldier, with many years of prosperous and steady activities as a farmer and rancher in Fayette County.

William Steinmann was born at Kreitzburg, Saxe-Weimar, Germany, August 13, 1836. His father, Andreas Steinmann, born in the same locality, where many generations of the family had lived, was a saddler by trade, and was the son of a forester or overseer of the hunting grounds belonging to the crown. Andreas Steinmann married Caroline Yeager, and both brought their children to the United States in 1846. They took ship at Bremen, on board the Diermond, and after being on the Atlantic Ocean six weeks landed in Galveston. The first two years were spent in the City of Houston. Andreas Steinmann, like his father, was a great hunter, and indulged his inclinations to that pursuit in the woods and on the prairies of Southern Texas. He also had a garden, and from these two sources supplied most of the living for his family. In 1848 came an epidemic of yellow fever in Houston, and while both parents passed through the plague, two of their children died. In 1858 the family removed to Fayette County, settling near the place of Doctor Tell, an old countryman of the Steinmanns, his farm being between LaGrange and Schulenburg. Andreas Steinmann bought some land there, but spent most of his time in hunting. He not only supplied the larder of his home with the deer and turkey which fell before his trusty rifle, but also marketed some of the game. Finally, when his sons bought land on the East Navidad and settled there, he moved to the same locality and both he and his wife are buried in the old Philadelphia Cemetery. Andreas Steinmann died in February, 1885, and his wife passed away in 1870. The two children who survived to reach Fayette County were Chris Steinmann, a farmer near Schulenburg, and William.

William Steinmann had no opportunities for schooling after coming to Texas, and what he knows of the common branches was acquired in the schools of his native land. As a boy he learned the value of honest industry, and not long after coming to Fayette County he and his brother bought the 200 acres of raw land on the East Navidad, at $1.50 an acre, and devoted all their energies to improvement, farming and stock raising. They subsequently bought other land, and when the partnership was dissolved William Steinmann purchased all the available land adjoining his own share of the estate, and eventually acquired almost 400 acres in a single body. Many years ago he attempted to introduce the Durham cattle into his community, but after the Texas fever had swept away the entire drove with the exception of two heifers, he was satisfied to improve and raise the native stock.

With the outbreak of the war between the states Mr. Steinmann enlisted as a Confederate soldier. His company was at first an independent one under Captain Breckenridge, but was afterwards added to Colonel Duff's Thirty-third Texas Cavalry Regiment. This regiment operated on the coast of Texas, and at one time met the Yankees at Powder Horn, captured fourteen Federal cattle drivers, and took them into camp. The regiment was subsequently ordered north to Bonham, Texas, remained there several months and also did some service in the Indian Territory. Captain Breckenridge's company was later ordered to Dallas to look after some bushwhackers who were operating in that vicinity, and captured some of these while at a dance and placed them in the guardhouse at Dallas. There were many interesting and exciting incidents of his service, but Mr. Steinmann never participated in any important battle, and when the war closed he was with his comrades in the vicinity of Brenham, and left the army without any wounds and with only such marks as come through the hardships of military life. His chief privation as a soldier was from trials of hunger. For several days the only diet supplied the command was pumpkins, and Mr. Steinmann relates that he ate pumpkin so long that he has never liked this article of food since.

On October 5, 1876, in Fayette County, Mr. Steinmann married Miss Olinda Boling, who was born in Fayette County during the '50s, daughter of Dietrich and Augusta (Scherenbach) Boling, who came to America from Lippe Detmold, Germany, and settled in Texas. Her father died in this state in 1899 and her mother in 1902. Besides Mrs. Steinmann the Boling children were: Wilhelmina, wife of William Plaxka, of Lee County, Texas; Elizabeth, who married Albert Jochan, of Freiburg, Texas; Augusta, who married Henry Foerster, of Fayette County; Sophia, wife of Charles Briggeman, of Fayette County; Emma, now Mrs. Fritz Schumacher, of El Campo, Texas; Theodore, of Swisalp, Texas; Lavina, who married Frank Keder, of the same town; Mary and Caroline, twins, the first the wife of Julius Nolkemper, and the second the wife of Hermann Jocher; Louie, of Swisalp; Olga, wife of Richard Otto, of Swisalp; and Henry, who died unmarried in 1907.

The children born to Mr. and Mrs. Steinmann are mentioned briefly as follows: William, of Schulenburg, who married Minna Knappa, and has three children, Edwin, Melba and Walter; Caroline, who married William Thiel, of Palo Pinto County, and their children are Hermann, Hobert and Hugo; Edmon, at home; Louie, of Cuero; Augusta, wife of Fred Gresser, of Houston; Adelle, who married Charles Thiel, of Lee County, and has two children, Ruby and Cora; Lavina, who is the wife of Ernst Russek, of Schulenburg; Robert, of Cuero; Olga, Mrs. Fenton Konnelson; Laura, of Cuero; and Alfred. Mr. Steinmann has reason to be proud of his family as well as his own experiences and accumulations in life. He has eleven children and eight grandchildren, and most of them are well established in their respective spheres in the world's work.

Politically Mr. Steinmann has cast his vote as a democrat, but has participated to no extent in politics. He is a church member and has always given his share to the support of church and benevolent causes. In November, 1906, he removed his family to Schulenburg, constructed a large and roomy home for the children, and gave them all the advantages of the public schools. He and Mrs. Steinmann have now lived together and shared the responsibilities and joys of life for nearly forty years.

Rev. Joseph Meiser. Pastor of the St. Rosa Catholic Church at Schulenburg, Father Meiser has been connected with churches in Texas since 1904. He possesses rare accomplishments for his profession, both as a matter of scholarly training and natural fitness, and is one of the ablest younger priests in the San Antonio diocese.

Born November 1, 1876, Father Meiser's birthplace was in Wustweilerhof by Illingen, Ottweiler, in the Province of the Rhine. He grew up on a farm, and on completing the course of the elementary schools continued his studies in the Gymnasia at Neuenkirchen and Saarbruecken, studied philosophy in the University of Louvain, Belgium, finished four semesters in theology at Luxemburg, and for a like period was a student of theology in Freiburg, Switzerland. He was ordained at Freiburg by Archbishop Potron, one of the old missionaries of the church, on September 24, 1904, and was designated for service in the diocese of San Antonio, Texas. He at once came to this country, and was first assigned to the Sacred Heart Church at Red Rock. There in addition to his pastoral duties of a regular nature he proved his efficiency in building up the parochial school and erecting new school buildings at Spring Prairie. His pastorate at Red Rock, in the Sacred Heart Church, lasted eight years. His next duties were in St. Mary's Church at LaCroste, where he remained a year and a half and erected a parochial school and parsonage. On July 17, 1914, Father Meiser was transferred to Schulenburg to succeed Rev. Father Mathias.

Father Meiser is a son of Peter and Catherine (Schirra) Meiser. Of their nine children six died in childhood, and the other two now living are Catherine, who is one of the visitors of the poor at Bruegge, Belgium; and Anna, still at the old home in Germany. Father Meiser's father participated in the Prussian war against Austria during 1866, and in the Franco-Prussian war of 1870, his service consisting of those duties now designated under the general term Red Cross work.

Born a German, Father Meiser acquired Italian and Spanish during his courses in the gymnasia, also some knowledge of the English, and his study and associations in Belgium made him proficient in the French. He is a linguist of exceptional attainment even for the Catholic priesthood. Father Meiser is spiritual director of the Sterbekasse of the German Catholics of Texas, and is a member of the German Catholic Staatsverbund of Texas.

ARTHUR E. BECKER, M. D. Three successive generations of the Becker family have given physicians to South Central Texas, the representatives of the present generation, Dr. A. E. Becker, having been in active practice at Kenney for about fifteen years. This is one of the pioneer German families, to which as a class Texas owes so much. The Beckers were among the finest representatives of those liberty loving Germans who were driven out of the fatherland after the suppression of the insurrection of 1848. It was as a representative of the cultured class that Dr. Frederick Becker, the grandfather of the present physician at Kenney, came to Texas during the '40s, bringing with him not only the thrift and industry characteristic of his people, but also an acquaintance and deep culture in the philosophy, literature and art of his native land.

Dr. Frederick Becker was a highly educated man, having finished his work in the classical languages at the University of Berlin and being also proficient in the French language and a master of English before he left Germany. In that country the family were Catholics and Doctor Frederick's education had been directed by his father with a view to the priesthood. He preferred the science of medicine to that of theology and left Europe not only for political reasons but also to escape the influences that were trying to shape his future career. After a temporary sojourn in Houston he made his settlement at Frelsburg in Colorado county, where he practiced medicine for some time. He established the famous vineyard at Frelsburg now owned by Mr. Laake, and built the pioneer brick house on the site. He originated the famous Texas apple, "the Becker Apple," now exploited by the Austin Nursery. These interests and activities indicate the chief bent of his enthusiasm during

his life in Texas, and he was probably as much engrossed in his flowers and in his bees as in his medical practice. He entered into the spirit of American citizenship, and during the Civil war era was chosen major of a militia regiment. In religious affairs he was a Liberal or Free Thinker, and subsequently became an admirer of the Darwinian theory. Like most Germans, he had a deep love for and appreciation of music, and the walls of his living room were adorned with the portraits of the German masters. Toward the close of his career he moved to Brenham, and died there in 1891 at the age of eighty-nine. Dr. Frederick Becker married Miss Fernandina Biergans, who died at Frelsburg. Their children were: Dr. Edward; Charles, who died young; Bertha, who died unmarried; and Hugo, who married Isabella Wangemann and died at Brenham, leaving five sons.

Dr. Edward Becker, the second physician of the name to practice in Texas, was born at Muenster, Germany, the original home of the family in the fatherland. His birth occurred October 17, 1838, and he was a boy when brought to America. His education in preparation for his profession was finished in Jefferson Medical College at Philadelphia. During the process of his education he served in the Confederate army, belonging to Waul's Legion of Infantry, and participated in a number of campaigns in Louisiana, Arkansas and Mississippi, and went through the service without wounds. In the early '70s Dr. Edward Becker established himself in practice at Frelsburg, but in 1882 removed to Brenham and lived there nearly all the rest of his life. He died in 1913. He served as the first medical director of the Sons of Hermann and held that post many years. He was not in active politics, though voting the democratic ticket, and never affiliated with any church, taking somewhat of the same views as those held by his father. Dr. Edward Becker married Henrietta Wangemann, a daughter of Adam and Fredericka (Kling) Wangemann, her father a native of Saxony and her mother a native of New Orleans and daughter of a physician. The children of Doctor Edward and wife were: Dr. A. E.; Bertha, wife of Charles Wilkins, cashier of the First National Bank of Bremen; Ada, wife of Charles Carlisle, Jr., of Brenham; and Edward of Brenham.

Dr. Arthur E. Becker, who has had constantly before him the stimulus and example of his father and grandfather, was born at Frelsburg, Texas, December 26, 1875. His literary education came from the Brenham High School and St. Edwards College at Austin, and he began the study of medicine in the State University Medical School at Galveston, but finished the course at Baltimore, Maryland, where he graduated M. D. in 1899. After a short practice at Brenham he moved to Kenney in August, 1900, and has since given his time wholly to his professional duties. Doctor Becker is camp physician for the Sons of Hermann and the Woodmen of the World. In addition to his native ability and thorough preparation, Doctor Becker has apparently the best of physical and personal qualifications for the duties of the medical practitioner, is a man of great vigor and strength, of keen mind, radiates cheerfulness wherever he goes, and has the dignity of a man of the world.

Doctor Becker was married in Washington, D. C., October 31, 1901, to Miss Ella Gordon, who has brought into the family relationship a fine strain of Scotch and Southern States ancestry. Her father, David Gordon, was a native of Ohio and of Scotch ancestry, a son of Rev. D. Gordon, a Presbyterian minister whose father came from Scotland. Rev. David Gordon was a cousin of John B. Gordon, the great Georgia soldier and orator. Mrs. Becker's father was a prominent cattle man at Parkersburg, West Virginia, and her mother was Miss Jennie Cox. In the Gordon family were the following daughters: Mrs. Grace Hill of

Modena, California; Mrs. Becker, who was born September 19, 1875; Mrs. Bertha Jackson of Petroleum, West Virginia, and Miss Elizabeth of Petroleum, West Virginia.

The children of Doctor and Mrs. Becker are Eleanor, Gladys and Bernice Virginia.

Ernst Russek. A family that as much as any other has contributed to the development of the country in and about Schulenburg and that section of Southern Texas is the Russek, which was introduced to that vicinity in 1869 by Franz Russek. Many of the old time settlers in this community, especially the sturdy Bohemians and Germans, have many kindly memories of Franz Russek, whose chief business in life was in looking after the interests of his fellow countrymen during the early stages while they were getting located in the New World. Franz Russek was the father of the late Ignaz Russek, whose life was likewise one of boundless activity and countless benefits. The sons of Ignaz Russek are among the leaders in business enterprise at Schulenburg, one of them being Ernst Russek, above named.

Franz Russek came to Texas from Austria, having been born in 1816 in the Town of Mahren, Moravia. He acquired a liberal education, being well versed in the German as well as the Bohemian language. As a business man he owned a cloth mill at Hustopec, of which town he was one time mayor. He also owned large landed estates, but sold all his various property interests before coming to the United States. Franz Russek had a philosophic mind, and for a number of years had seriously considered the economic and political conditions under which he and his fellow countrymen lived. It was as a result of this thought and observation that he determined to come to the New World which exemplified human liberty to the highest extent, where opportunities were almost unlimited, and where less attention was paid to the military. He left with his numerous family in 1869, sailing from Bremen to New Orleans, and came out to the then terminus of the Southern Pacific Railway at Alleyton, and from there to Fayette County made the journey by team and wagon. He bought the farm which now constitutes the home of his grandchildren. This land and its first occupants have a history. It was part of the grant of the Austin Colony, and its first owner was Warren Lyons, who built, many years before the Civil war, a log house. The Indians on one of their raids killed the senior Lyons and carried off his son Warren, a lad of ten years. This son remained with the tribe on the plains, was adopted and adapted Indian habits and only when twenty-three years of age, when visiting San Antonio with his fellow tribesmen was recognized and induced to return to his old home and visit his mother. He had been led to believe that his mother was dead. He approached his mother's home decked out in all his Indian regalia, and the sudden appearance of the son whom she had long since thought dead so affected his mother that she fell in a swoon. The son was then induced to remain, and finally joined the Texas Rangers, a service which provided him with a life of excitement as a substitute for his former career as an Indian.

It was the old log house on the Lyons place that provided the first habitation for Franz Russek and his family. Though his enterprise in Fayette County was as a farmer, his main business for many years was emigrant agent for the Southern Pacific Railway. When this line was built through Schulenburg, the builder and superintendent, Mr. Pierce, gave Mr. Russek a life pass over the system. Mr. Russek probably used this road more than any other citizen in his business as agent in behalf of the German and Bohemian emigrants who were seeking homes in

Southern Texas. When families found themselves too poor to make the passage from Austria he many times advanced money, and after his countrymen arrived he helped them locate homes and taught them the art of farming in the United States, and in many ways proved himself valuable as an adviser, practical assistant and friend until they were well versed in the ways of the new country. Probably more than any other individual he deserves credit as a direct cause for the settlement and development of the whole country tributary to and beyond Schulenburg and Weimar, and it has been estimated that thousands of families sought homes in Texas through his influence.

When the town of Schulenburg was located on the newly constructed railroad, Franz Russek started the first store and for a short time was associated with his son Ignaz. Merchandising was only temporary, however, as his time was demanded by his business in looking after emigration. It was his practice to meet the emigrants at Galveston, and frequently had the responsibilities connected with looking after an entire shipload of newcomers. He was never active in politics, though he became a naturalized citizen soon after landing in Texas, and usually voted the democratic ticket. He belonged to the Catholic Church, was a contributor to church buildings, and gave some valuable donations in the way of decorations for the Schulenburg church.

Franz Russek's first wife, who died in Europe, left him one child, Anna, who married Frank Blumrich, of Lavaca County. For his second wife he married Miss Havran, whose children were Joseph, who lost his life in Bee County, Texas, leaving a family; Ignaz, who assumed many of the business responsibilities established by his father; Josephine, whose first husband was Henry Herder and her second Joe Schindler, and she left a family at her death in Gonzales; Frank, who lives in Skidmore; Theresa, who has a family by her marriage to I. J. Gallia of Houston; and Julia, wife of August Gallia, of Refugio. For his third wife Franz Russek married a widow, Mary Pivode, who came from Austria.

Franz Russek had a long and useful career, which came to an end by death in 1895. He was a man of rather small stature and medium weight, was smooth shaven, and possessed the quiet efficiency so characteristic of many successful business men. He talked very little except when business and business matters required it and though seldom found as a worshiper in church was consistent in his church creed and made his home a place of entertainment for priests and all his wife's circle of friends and acquaintances. He was perhaps the best known man Fayette County contained. Echoes of his popularity are still manifest towards his grandsons when his old friends meet them away from Schulenburg.

Ignaz Russek, who possessed so many of the sterling characteristics of his father, was born January 25, 1856, and was educated in both the Bohemian and German languages, most of his schooling being acquired at Neutitschein, in Germany. He was a boy of thirteen when he came to Texas, and thereafter attended no regular school. In 1870 he left the farm and became a merchant's clerk at High Hill for Mr. Seydler, and subsequently worked as bookkeeper and cotton buyer in Columbus until the yellow fever epidemic of 1873 caused his return to Schulenburg. About that time the railroad had been completed, and he became associated with his father in merchandising. Not long afterward he bought the interest of his father and conducted the business under his individual name, and until 1882 sold goods on the corner where his sons are now doing business as Russek Brothers. When Ignaz Russek sold his store he entered the banking business, starting the private bank of Ignaz Russek, and this was his chief business interest until his sudden death on January 6, 1908. At the same time he looked after the emigration business, the chief interest of his father, and did much in that line after the death of the elder Franz Russek. In the course of his business career he accumulated many property interests in Schulenburg, and is said to have built more houses of business and residences than any other man of the town. In October, 1894, fire destroyed all the frame business houses owned by him and fronting the main business street, and after this loss he replaced the buildings with substantial brick structures. Having lived in Schulenburg from its founding about the railway station, he possessed an extraordinary faith in the future and continued welfare of the little city, and never withheld his co-operation or effective helpfulness from any movement that would clearly benefit the locality. At one time he also had extensive interests in Skidmore in connection with his brothers. His farming interests were measured by his homestead on which he reared his children. Ignaz Russek, though a democrat, took little interest in national politics, but in his home city was an alderman and city treasurer, and at different times a trustee of the schools.

Ignaz Russek married Rosa Pivoda, whose father came from Moravia, Austria. To their marriage were born the following children: Gus, cashier of the First National Bank of Schulenburg; Ernst; Antonia, wife of Fred Bittner, of Schulenburg; Henry, who is associated with his brother Ernst in the firm of Russek Bros.; Lydia, who married J. M. Garret of Schulenburg; Emmie, wife of Isy Schwartz, of Schulenburg.

The late Ignaz Russek was a business man of rare attainments. He possessed the faculty of "getting ahead" to a marked degree, and yet all his transactions were within the recognized and legitimate lines of trade. He popularized himself with all his friends and business acquaintances through his scrupulous methods and his sincerity and friendly manner.

Ernst Russek, one of his sons, was born January 13, 1881, and is now manager of the property interests of his mother and a member of the firm of Russek Brothers, merchants, at Schulenburg, and is also interested in ranching in Lavaca County. He was educated in the Catholic school in San Antonio, and later in the A. and M. College at Bryan. His independent business career began at the age of twenty-two, though in the meantime he had acquired valuable experience with his father in banking and insurance. Ernst Russek lives adjoining the town limits of Schulenburg. He married Lavina Steinmann, daughter of William Steinmann, an old Confederate soldier and a retired farmer and stockman at Schulenburg.

ANTON KAHLICH. As an expression of positive leadership and forceful individuality in a community, one of the best examples is the career of Anton Kahlich, a highly successful German farmer of Fayette County, a man who has raised his individual and family fortunes from nothing to affluence, and in many ways has participated in those movements and developments which make a community prosperous. He has lived in the locality of High Hill since boyhood in 1870.

Anton Kahlich was born at the Village of Boelten, Mehren, Austria, May 8, 1857. In that locality his father Antone Kahlich was a miller, and spent his life, dying in 1863. He married Rosa Lopreis, and after his death she married Frank Marits. Her children by the first marriage were: Johanna, of Austin, Texas, wife of Charles Wild; Louisa, who married Charles Holles, and died at High Hill, leaving a family; Anton; Caroline, who married Henry Dreyer, of Linn County, Texas;

Rudolph, a farmer in Dewitt County. By her marriage to Mr. Marits the only child was Wilhelmina, who married Hermann Dreyer, and died at Shiner, Texas. Mrs. Marits died in 1907 at the age of seventy-seven.

On the 26th of March, 1870, the Marits and Kahlich family, consisting of Mr. and Mrs. Marits and five Kahlich children, sailed from Bremen on the steamship Koeln, and on the 2d of May arrived in Galveston Harbor. Thence they journeyed by rail as far as Columbus, which was the terminus of the railroad, and by ox team to High Hill. This family was one among hundreds of Bohemian people who were induced to settle in the State of Texas by Franz Russek, of Schulenburg. Mr. Russek was an uncle to Anton Kahlich. The family, on reaching High Hill, rented a house and for the first year the active members of the household found work at wages. The following year they rented a farm, but finally purchased the land included in the present estate of Anton Kahlich. It was prairie land, untouched with the plow, and a large number of acres in this vicinity have been brought into cultivation and made productive and valuable through this worthy family.

Anton Kahlich was still a boy in years when he came to Texas, but his strength was soon directed to useful purpose, and at the age of fifteen he drove an ox team to Columbus for the lumber with which to build a box house, 12 by 12 feet, with a small gallery, a habitation in which the family of eight people lived for a number of years. Ten years later their prosperity was sufficient to bring about the construction of the substantial residence in which Mr. Kahlich now lives. Like many new settlers this family was confronted with practically new conditions on reaching Texas. Back in Austria they had wheat and rye as their principal crops, but in Texas their chief dependence was placed on cotton, and in time they had the larger part of their one hundred acres in this crop. Since Mr. Anton Kahlich has assumed the active and independent management of the old estate, its acreage was increased to 476 acres, and some of this he has since given to his children for homes, since they in turn helped to improve the land and became valuable factors in the work of the locality. Mr. Kahlich has made it his practice to raise more meat than is needed for the consumption of his family, and nearly everything else for the table is supplied from his own fields and gardens with the exception of the wheat that supplies the bread.

After reaching his majority Mr. Kahlich began voting with the democratic party, but has never been a politician, has never attended conventions, and his one official service has been as trustee of the schools. He was reared in the Catholic Church, and his own family have been brought up in the same faith. He was a substantial contributor towards the erection of the new St. Mary's Church at High Hill, one of the monuments which marked the progress and ideals of the community.

On November 7, 1882, in the vicinity of High Hill Mr. Kahlich marriad Miss Therse Wick, daughter of Franz and Anna (Klos) Wick. Her father was a farmer and one of the first settlers in the vicinity of High Hill. He also came from Mehren, Austria. The Wick children were: John, a merchant of High Hill; Anna, who married Ferdinand Klesel, of Schulenburg; Mrs. Kahlich; Mary, wife of Franz Brossman, a farmer near High Hill. Mr. and Mrs. Kahlich may well take pride in their fine family of children, most of whom are already established independently in the world. Alvina, the oldest, is the wife of F. Heinrich, and her children are Herbert, Hugo, Erwin, Victor and Laura; Addie married Rudolph Bednatz, and her children are named Edwin, Alvon, Robert, Willie and Alvin; Rudolph, a farmer near High Hill, married

Amelia Holles, and has two children, Leo and Olivia; Mina is the wife of Joseph Bednatz, of the same locality, and their children are Elizabeth and Alexander; Charles married Otilia Bednatz, and has one child, Edgar; Antone is a business man of Schulenburg; Maria is the wife of Frank Lux, near Schulenburg; and the younger children still at home are Frank, Alfred, Rosa and Otto.

Mr. Kahlich is easily one of the most influential leaders among his countrymen in Fayette County, and in the achievement of financial success has spent his years most profitably. He is robust and vigorous in body and mind, and his locality has felt the influence of his citizenship in many ways.

Christian Baumgarten. With the death of Christian Baumgarten there was closed what, on the basis of service and in the estimation of many people, was the most important chapter in the history of the little City of Schulenburg in Fayette County. It is both important and appropriate, after the passing of a useful citizen, to narrate the simple story of his life. It is important because of its lesson to aspiring and ambitious generations in learning the conditions under which such a character labored and lived. It is appropriate because his achievements serve to stimulate the young to greater effort and nobler lives and to reassure our faith in the old saying that industry and integrity have their sure reward.

If the influences and environment under which Christian Baumgarten grew up had not impelled the virtue of industry from an early age, the blood of his nativity would have exerted itself in that direction. He was bred a Teuton and was a child of the modern Saxon whose forefathers gave to the world one of the greatest nations of the Middle Ages. Christian Baumgarten was born at Tartun, Saxony, March 13, 1836. His father was also named Christian and his mother was Maria Burgemeister. He was the oldest of four children, his brothers Adolph and Gustav live at Sweet Home, Texas, and his sister, Mrs. Paulsen, is a resident of Columbus. His parents both died at Tartun, Saxony, and the younger children followed their brother Christian to the United States.

Christian Baumgarten acquired his education from the popular schools about Tartun before he reached the age of fourteen. For three years he was apprenticed at the carpenter's trade, and then became a journeyman workman. At the age of eighteen he went to the coast and secured employment in the shipyards of Bremen as a mechanic. In this city of commerce and navigation he was brought into contact with the stream of emigration to the New World, heard the siren song of opportunity wafted across the waters from American shores, and breathed the air of liberty as it came fresh and untainted with autocratic inhibitions and monarchical limitations. It was not strange that he was inspired with the desire to find for himself a home where the joy of living abounded in every heart and where the authority of kings and princes knew no sway. Always a close observer of conditions, he was also impressed while living at Bremen with the tendency of political and social conditions towards centralization and autocracy, and the leaving of the fatherland was also due to a desire to escape the increasing burdens upon the plain people.

In the autumn of 1854 he embarked for America on a sailing vessel bound for Galveston. The rough sea dispelled the monotony of a voyage of eleven weeks, and when he landed at Galveston he found a small port and a town still insignificant as a commercial center. His trade brought the young man work without delay, and he spent fifteen months on the island. By that time he had saved $450, and the spirit of exploration seized him. He started inland, bought a pony and saddle from an Indian at the forks of Trinity River, and made a wide tour over the narrow limits of civilization in Texas in search of a more promising location. He was at that time twenty years of age, had a meager command of the English language, was untutored in the ways of the wilderness, and partly as a result of this inexperience he saw the bottom of his purse before he found a better location, and of necessity was compelled to return to Galveston and to his trade.

Having recuperated his finances after a few months of manipulation of the frow, the chisel and the saw, young Baumgarten went out to LaGrange and became a carpenter and builder in that essentially German community. He remained there until his enlistment in the Army of the South, early in the war. He was ready to serve his state, although he disapproved of the separation of Texas from the Union. When the strife actually began he enlisted in Company B of the Third Texas Infantry, but after a short time that regiment was transferred to the engineers corps, and served under General Magruder, who promoted him to first sergeant of the Second Engineers Corps, and in that capacity he was in the Trans-Mississippi Department until the close of the war. He then resumed his business as carpenter and builder. The mechanic of that day knew all about the builder's trade. Everything used in the construction of a house was made by hand. Nothing was carried in stock anywhere, and the mechanic proposing to build a house went to the woods for his lumber, selected his trees, took his logs to the nearest sawmill, had them cut to his liking, dressed the lumber by hand, made the window sash, doors and blinds, rived the shingles with the frow, and turned the house over to its owner, not in a month after its beginning, but in a year or two afterwards, and the evidence of workmanship was everywhere apparent throughout. Many buildings thus constructed by Mr. Baumgarten still stand in Fayette County, and the silent voice of the mechanic's skill of the olden times speaks audibly its disapprobation of the botched work of the commercially built structures of the present time.

Christian Baumgarten possessed a genius in the handling of tools. He could make everything out of wood that was needed in the activities of men. One of the most difficult tasks was the making of the old wooden screw used in baling cotton before the Civil war. He became a gin builder, erecting for his German friend, Mr. Hillje, of High Hill, the first gin there, and in 1867 erected the first Hillje oil mill in connection with the gin, and equipped it with machinery of German make. According to a report from the United States Central Bureau, of 1900, this mill was the first oil mill to be operated successfully in the United States.

With his savings as a building contractor while living at LaGrange, Mr. Baumgarten purchased a tract of land seventeen miles south of the county seat. It was this investment which proved the foundation of his financial success in life. In 1873 the Galveston, Harrisburg & San Antonio Railway built its lines through the south end of Fayette County and across Mr. Baumgarten's land. He arranged with the railroad authorities to locate a station, and today the thrifty Town of Schulenburg occupies the tract. Mr. Baumgarten was alive to the importance of the impetus given the community by the railroad, and instead of withholding his individual enterprise and allowing others to create wealth for him, he from the first became foremost in the activities of the young village. He established a lumber yard, erected several buildings and put in a stock of furniture and hardware. Later he erected a planing mill and sash and door factory, where he manufactured the first "curly pine" furniture that found a market in the state. He made a variety of articles in his mill—moldings, beehives, cypress cisterns and a number of farming implements. In the late '70s he opened a brick yard which supplied the town and country about with the brick necessary for its needs. In 1882 he built the Schulenburg Oil Mill, a large part of the machinery of which was ordered from Germany. This mill has been in continuous operation during each annual season, though the machinery has been several times renewed to keep the plant apace with the progress of invention.

The success of his oil mills led Mr. Baumgarten to engage in oil mill construction, and during the year 1890 he erected and equipped oil mills at Luling, Taylor, Caldwell and Hempstead, and the following year built mills at Hallettsville, Rockdale and Kyle. In 1882 he had invented and patented the Baumgarten hydraulic cotton baling press and in 1884 patented the perforated press plates for cotton seed oil mills which have replaced the old-style press boxes with the bulky hair mats then in use. The various oil mills he built were included in the "Baumgarten system" of mills, and their success was a strong factor in stimulating capital to this channel of investment in Texas.

As a citizen Mr. Baumgarten might probably be termed as the father of Schulenburg. He was not only its pioneer, but its leading spirit and venerated citizen during his life. His many inventions and investments gave much substantial aid through the domain of labor, and it was this phase of his busy life which brought him his pleasure and satisfaction, and it lends much to the appropriateness of this brief sketch. His generosities were represented in many homes and revived hope in many a disheartened and depressed soul. He loved the "open book" life of humanity because he lived it himself, and shams, pretentions and undignified show made him impatient. While he was a veteran of the Confederate war, there was that about the reunion of the old comrades that lent an air of superiority because of military service, and he declined to identify himself actively with the organization. A similar spirit was illustrated in his attitude toward politics. He believed in the tenets of democracy and voted the democratic ticket, but there were practices among political leaders that he strongly disapproved of and could never be brought to active participation in so-called practical politics. He held no office, and yet his life was that of a public servant, and through his business activities and personal influence effected more that is of lasting importance than could ever have been performed by the instrumentality of public position. A service he did for his county and which added much to the comfort of the early Bohemian and German settlers was the erection of housing quarters for them in Schulenburg. During the time of most rapid emigration by this foreign element many of the newcomers arrived without having notified sons or relatives, and oftentimes days and even weeks ensued before they could proceed to the homes of friends or become independently established. Frequently these arrivals were in such numbers that no accommodations could be provided in an already overcrowded village, and to remedy this defect Mr. Baumgarten erected an "emigrant house" for their use, and in this and in many other ways maintained an interest in his old country neighbors until they were settled about the country in new homes.

On June 6, 1859, Mr. Baumgarten married Ernstine Pannewitz. She was born March 12, 1841, in Pennig, Germany, and at the time of her marriage was making her home with an uncle in LaGrange. A few weeks after the wedding she accompanied her husband to the tract of land he had located on, and situated seventeen miles from the county seat and which later on became the site on which Schulenburg now stands. This virile, vigorous and energetic couple lived together more than fifty years, and passed away with the consciousness of duty well performed. They were Lutherans in training and belief, and reared their large household in the fear of God. They enjoyed life in all its best relations, both of service and of comfort. When in the fullness of years, armed with a United States passport issued by the then secretary of state, Elihu Root, they visited Old Mexico and traversed the region of the Aztecs for health and recreation. The death of Mrs. Baumgarten occurred June 23, 1909, and on September 29, 1912, the pulsations ceased of the heart of the great force which had contributed something worth while to the founding and growth of a community in a great Commonwealth, and side by side their bodies now are at rest in High Hill Cemetery.

The children of Christian and Ernstine Baumgarten are: Ernstine Mary, born February 19, 1860, was drowned May 31, 1872; Ernst, born October 4, 1861, is a resident of Schulenburg; Augusta, born January 24, 1863, died in February following; Gus A., born February 4, 1866, occupies largely the place left vacant by his father; Emil H., born September 8, 1868, is a merchant of Schulenburg; Elesa Anna, born August 29, 1869, is the wife of Max Wolters of Shiner; Lillie Erna, born August 7, 1873, died October 15, 1889; John C., born August 2, 1875, is a business man of Schulenburg; Bertha Elizabeth, born October 23, 1877, is Mrs. G. E. Ruhmann of Schulenburg; Fred Charles, born in February, 1879, and Paul Willie, born in June, 1881, are both residents of Schulenburg; Alfred Henry, born March 17, 1883, died September 29, 1912; and Fritz, born January 29, 1886, completes this numerous family.

As already stated, Christian Baumgarten entered earnestly into the spirit which dominated his adopted country, and took out his first papers of citizenship as soon as he felt qualified to act. November 22, 1859, he made his first declaration and in November, 1865, county clerk, Z. M. P. French of LaGrange, issued him the papers which separated him from every king, prince, potentate or power of the old world and brought him under the protection of the Stars and Stripes. He was a pioneer, and his going from the municipality he did so much to benefit brought a general response of grief and affectionate memory from his fellow townsmen. The funeral services was conducted October 1, 1912, under the magnificent live oak which sheltered his home for more than half a century and under which four generations of his family had gathered on many occasions.

GUSTAV A. BAUMGARTEN. Among the many children of the late Christian Baumgarten, whose career has been followed in the preceding sketch, Gustav A. Baumgarten has been most prominent in carrying out many of the plans and the scope of business enterprise formulated by his father to their logical conclusion. In the great cotton oil industry his name is one of the most prominent in the entire South.

Gustav A. Baumgarten was born February 14, 1866, on his father's farm upon much of which the Town of Schulenburg now stands, but which was then an untamed prairie. He grew up amid the scenes of improvement following the close of the Civil war. He was just old enough to go to school when the Southern Pacific Railroad came to the Baumgarten farm and caused the founding of the little city on what had formerly been a raw prairie. As a boy he attended common schools, later was a student in night school, and finally with his own savings entered the Gem City Business College at Quincy, Illinois, graduating in 1890.

At the age of fifteen he took up practical and self-supporting work, and was identified with the oil mill business from the erection of the first plant at Schulenburg in 1882. He aided his father in the erection of oil mills at various points in South Texas, and is one of the men whose experience in that industry practically covers all phases of its development. This line of enterprise has remained the field of his life labor, and he has not only gone far and become eminent in the business himself, but has prepared other young men for useful and conspicuous places as superintendents or managers over this state.

As an authority in oil mill matters Mr. Baumgarten was early recognized by the Oil Mills Superintendents' Association of Texas, and for a number of years was repeatedly elected its secretary and treasurer, and in 1901 was chosen vice president. His career demonstrates the value of the directing of human energy in a single plane to achieve the best results. Masters in business, as in other lines of effort, are not made in a mould, they come out of the fiery furnace of experience, and the example of Gustav A. Baumgarten is worthy the study and emulation of rising generations who have an ambition to succeed.

He has been the active force in the Schulenburg Oil Mill since 1882. More recently he has entered modestly upon the making of bread-flour from cottonseed meal. His is the only mill of the kind in the world, and its product, the "Allison Flour" is destined to popularize itself in the homes of bread eaters until it spreads a revolution in the food industry of the world. The Allison flour has been perfected by Mr. Baumgarten to a point where it can be depended upon as a pure and unfermenting article of diet, free from deleterious matter and a reliable article of commerce for human food. After others had failed in the production of a flour that could be stored without fermentation, and as a result of expenditure of $20,000 in his efforts, Gustav A. Baumgarten perfected a plan which met the difficulty and is producing such a commodity as the world food supply demands. Apparently Mr. Baumgarten brought his long course of experimentation to a successful conclusion at a most appropriate time, when the resources of production are largely perilized by war, and when the mounting prices of wheat have brought about a vigorous demand for other available forms of bread stuffs. As a contribution of the oil mills of Texas to the starving Belgians, and indirectly as an advertisement of the Allison flour, Mr. Baumgarten has recently shipped a consignment of the flour containing 60,000 pounds purchased through a fund raised by individual $10 subscriptions from each member of the cotton-seed trade of Texas. A brief extract from a letter written by Mr. Allison upon this subject will make clear the plan of relief and show to what extent the Schulenburg Oil Mill has invested its means in preparing itself to meet the demands made upon it for this new kind of flour. After speaking of instructions given at a general meeting in Houston to raise a sufficient fund from the cotton-seed oil mills and members of the cotton-seed trade to be used in the purchase of cotton-seed flour to be contributed to Belgium in the name of the Cotton-seed Oil Trade of Texas, the writer says: "Proceeding at once to carry out these instructions, I immediately entered into correspondence through Senator Morris Sheppard and Congressman H. W. Summers, with the proper representatives of the Belgium government at Washington, secured the necessary instructions for shipment in such way as to secure free transportation, made arrangements with the Schulenburg Cotton Oil Company, who have just installed at a cost of about twenty thousand dollars the only complete manufactory of cotton seed oil in all the world, for its manufacture and sale at, to us, a reduced price."

Mr. Baumgarten was married June 22, 1892, to Miss Ida Wallace. Their children are: Wallace, who finished the course of the Gem City Business College in June, 1915, just twenty-five years after his father

J N Gallagher

graduated from the same institution; Roy, a student in the Marshall Training School at San Antonio; Audry, Norma Madaline and Norine. Mr. Baumgarten, like his father, has eschewed politics, has never held any office, is not a fraternity man, and his whole life, outside the interests of his home and family, has been one of singleness of aim and large achievement in one industry.

James Nestor Gallagher. In San Antonio's colony of men and women devoted to literature and the arts there is probably no more interesting feature than James Nestor Gallagher. Mr. Gallagher is not a literary man by profession, so much as a means of expression for the rare charm of culture and sentiment that moves in him and as a result of his experience in the world of practical affairs. For many years Mr. Gallagher was a railroad man, and in recent years has been identified with the department of public works at San Antonio. He served seventeen years as roadmaster on the San Antonio and Aransas Pass Railroad, and two years as general superintendent of the Artesian Belt Railroad, resigning both positions.

James Nestor Gallagher was born in Concord, New Hampshire, July 5, 1848. His parents, Owen and Mary Nestor Gallagher, were both born at Castle Bar, County Mayo, Ireland. When he was two years of age his parents removed to Seneca, LaSalle County, Illinois, where he was reared and went to school, and later took a course in a commercial college in Chicago. Though only fourteen years of age at the time, in 1862 Mr. Gallagher enlisted in the Union Army as a drummer boy, and was in service until the return of peace. Most of his duties were performed in Virginia, and he left the army with the rank of sergeant.

Mr. Gallagher first came to Texas in 1871, locating at Palestine. He was engaged in the construction work during the building of the International and Great Northern Railway, and subsequently entered the train service of that road. For many years he was in the railway business, and in the meantime had located at San Antonio in 1880. That city has now been his home for thirty-five years.

Mr. Gallagher was formerly a prominent factor in local politics, and is still one of the influential men in San Antonio affairs. He served two terms, four years, as an alderman from the Second Ward, and for two years was an alderman at large representing the entire city. During his service as alderman San Antonio's splendid city hall on military plaza was constructed, and he deserves considerable credit for the location and erection of that edifice. In later years he has held an office in the department of public works.

Mr. Gallagher is thoroughly a literary man, and literature and associations with literary people are his greatest delight. He is widely known as a writer of both prose and verse. Almost throughout his residence at San Antonio he has been a frequent contributor to the local press, and has been a friend and associate of all the old-time literary lights in the city. His reputation in literary circles was first established by his book, "Let 'er Go, Gallagher!" which was published by Rhodes & McClure of Chicago in 1888, and had a large sale over the country, its title furnishing a current phrase which thousands will well remember. Several of his poems are published in the work "The Poets of America." At the present time Mr. Gallagher contemplates publishing another volume, a collection of prose and verse. The strength and rugged simplicity of his verse are well illustrated by his poem entitled "Gold" which he wrote at San Antonio about a quarter of a century ago, which has been widely reproduced in many magazines and daily newspapers, and which recently interpolated in the photoplay, "A Gilded Fool," and the words thrown upon the screen of several of the local playhouses in San Antonio. This little poem is as follows:

"An impress of satanic mold
Art thou, creation-hunted gold,
Which defies this pinch of earth
And classifies its current worth.

You arm the strong, enchain the weak,
And blanch the ruddy, virgin cheek;
And most the evil we behold
Originate from thee, oh gold!

Many in this mortal fold
By thee, alas, are bought and sold;
And yet, despite thy hellish mold,
We idolize thee, winsome gold."

Mr. Gallagher married Miss Calphurnia Forman, who was born and reared in Cherokee County, East Texas. Their eight children are: Thomas D. Gallagher, Mrs. Maggie Jones, Mrs. Mattie Reuter, Miss Stella Gallagher, Miss Bessie Gallagher, and David, Julius and John Seneca Gallagher. Masonically Mr. Gallagher is affiliated with Alamo Lodge No. 424, Ancient Free and Accepted Masons, and with San Antonio Chapter, Royal Arch Masons, and San Antonio Commandery No. 7, Knights Templar.

REV. JOSEPH SCHWELLER. Now serving as pastor of St. Mary's Church at High Hill, Rev. Joseph Schweller has been identified with the religious work of the Catholic Church since 1901, when he commenced as a new pastor at Red Rock and Smithville. He had charge of the Sacred Heart Church, with interests divided between the two communities of Red Rock and Smithville. He was the successor in that post of Rev. C. X. Neisens, and during the 3½ years of his stay in addition to the ordinary duties of the pastorate, built a new church at Spring Prairie or Rosanky Station. His next place was at Seguin as pastor of St. James Church, and his labors in that parish continued for nine years. His ability as a financier had successful play, nd he was able to lift the church debt, and left the parish preparing for the erection of a new building. The school in connection was maintained in a prosperous condition, and his pastorate was marked by a harmonious development of both religion and education. He was assigned to High Hill Church in August, 1913, succeeding Reverend Father Gerlach who left the parish in a flourishing state.

Father Schweller came to Texas from Maria Stein, Mercer County, Ohio, where he spent most of his boyhood from the age of ten years. He was born near Heidelberg, Baden, Germany, November 22, 1869, a son of Julius Schweller. His father was a merchant in the old country, but in Ohio spent his years as a small farmer, dying in 1887 at the age of fifty-one. Julius Schweller married Angeline Schleicher, who died at the Ohio home in 1898 at the age of sixty-three. Her children were: Michael, who died in Burkettsville, Ohio; Jacob, who died at Maria Stein November 26, 1895; Rev. Joseph; and Miss Elizabeth. of Maria Stein.

Rev. Fr. Schweller while in Germany attended the parochial schools, spent two years in the St. Francis School at Cincinnati, was in the parochial school at Maria Stein, and pursued his seminary work in St. Charles

Seminary at Carthagena in Mercer County. Father Schweller received his minor orders in the Carthagena Seminary from Most Rev. Archbishop Henry Elder of Cincinnati, and was ordained a priest at San Antonio by Rt. Rev. John J. Forest, bishop of San Antonio, on January 10, 1901. He was almost immediately placed in charge of his first assignment at Red Rock.

Father Schweller comes of a family which has given ministers, some teachers, farmers and business men to the world. His personal fitness, like his professional equipment, for this high calling is such as to mark his official tenures somewhat as epochs in the life of such congregations as he has attended as pastor.

JOHN C. BUCEK. One of the chief factors in the business life of Engel in Fayette County is John C. Bucek, whose family has been identified with this community nearly sixty years, having been founded in Fayette County in 1856. They represent the excellent Bohemian stock which has been so notable in the progress and development of this section of Texas, and the reputation of the family for industry, integrity and good citizenship has been maintained in every generation.

The head of the family in 1856, when they arrived in Texas, was Philip Bucek, who was a native of Bohemia, Austria. He brought his family to High Hill in Fayette County, and lived as a farmer. He had been engaged in business in Austria, and possessed exceptional qualifications and enterprise and was a helpful worker in the early community. He finally removed to the locality of Velehrad on the Fayette and Lavaca County line, where he donated twenty-five acres of land for a school and cemetery. He continued his life there as a farmer until his death in 1878. His death was the result of an accident when he was struck by a falling tree. He was specially prominent among his fellow countrymen, and his opinions were respected and his advice often sought. He came in advance of the great bulk of his countrymen, and by his experience and judgment was able to do a great deal in getting his compatriots well established in Texas. In this work he was a colleague of Franz Russek, of Schulenburg. Philip and Johanna Bucek had the following children: Johanna, who married John Hajek, and died near Praha; John; Anna, who married Frank Matula, and died at Moravia in Lavaca County; Mary, who married Frank Pesek, of Velehrad; Charles, who is a farmer in Fayette County; Frank, of Runge, Texas; Agnes, now deceased, who married Frank Chalupka, of Sweet Home, Texas.

John Bucek, father of John C., was born in the old country in 1846 and was ten years of age when he came with the family to Texas. He grew to manhood at High Hill, and the circumstances in which his youth was passed made an education almost impossible. He was still young when the war broke out between the states, and he enlisted in the Confederate army and gave his best efforts towards the cause of the South in that war. He reached his majority after the close of hostilities, and then took up his solid career as a farmer near Schulenburg, and in the course of time acquired an estate which represented a commendable degree of material success. He died at the home of his son in Engel. His characteristics were industry, intelligent management of his own affairs and useful relationship with his community. He was always a democrat, though never a candidate for office, and his public service was principally represented as a school trustee. He came of a Catholic family but took little interest in church affairs. He grew up with a knowledge of the Bohemian tongue, and afterwards acquired both German and English. He was a member of the Sons of Hermann. John Bucek married Bertha Ermis, who was born at Mistek in Bohemia, and came to the United States when about five years of age. She is still living and now resides in Wharton County. Her children are: John C.; Frank, of Wharton County; Charles, of Wharton County; Philip, of Port Lavaca; Alphonse, of Victoria; Lillie and William, of Wharton.

John C. Bucek was born near Schulenburg, Texas, November 12, 1872, and spent the years of his minority on his father's farm. His education came from district schools, supplemented by a business course in the Capital Business College of Austin. His entrance into business life was as clerk in Engel for I. J. Gallia, with whom he remained two years. He then engaged in the saloon business, and after two years put in a stock of general merchandise, conducting both establishments until his stock and store were wiped out by a disastrous fire in 1902. This was a heavy blow to his rising prosperity, but he set to work and has more than recovered the ground lost. When he resumed business he secured his stock on credit and has since acquired a substantial place in the village, and has a business that is known to all the residents of that locality. His property represents much labor and effort. Back of his place of business is the chief beauty spot of the village. It is a small park, with a band stand and with accommodations for the amusement and comfort of the villagers, who make that their chief place of resort during the summer evenings. From the front gate leading up to the building is a row of tall cedars, overarching the walk, and this feature alone makes his place the most conspicuous one in the town.

Mr. Bucek was married October 10, 1894, in Engel to Miss Anna Nitschmann, whose father came to Texas from Germany, and until his death followed farming near Engel: Mr. and Mrs. Bucek have one daughter, Blanche, now a young lady of sixteen and attending school. In politics Mr. Bucek is associated with the democratic party and is a member of the Sons of Hermann, of the S. P. J. S. T. and the Order of Puritans.

Rev. Louis P. Netardus. One of the flourishing Catholic parishes in the country around Flatonia is that of Praha, with its Church of the Assumption of the Blessed Virgin Mary. Father Netardus is the intelligent and hard working priest of this parish and is a churchman who has been identified with his calling in Texas for more than twenty years. Rev. P. Netardus was ordained at Victoria in 1894 by Right Rev. Claudius Neraz and was immediately assigned to work in Victoria as assistant priest for two years and as a professor of philosophy and Latin. His next position was at Hallettsville, where he remained six years, and had charge of the missions at Koerth, Smothers Creek and Nada. He built new churches at Smothers Creek and Nada. From Hallettsville Father Netardus came to Praha as the successor of Rev. J. V. Vrana. He also has charge of the mission of Flatonia, where he erected the church building and at Praha the pastor's residence, a commodious two-story stone structure, was built under his direction. Besides his ministerial and pastoral work Father Netardus is a frequent newspaper contributor, particularly to Bohemian publications, and under his name are occasionally published articles treating of Christian apologetics in the Houston Post.

Louis P. Netardus was born in the Province of Moravia, in the City of Frankstadt, June 22, 1866, and his family have been identified with Southern Texas for the past thirty-five years. His father, Francis Netardus, a native of the same community and of a family that was for many generations identified with the City of Vsetin, Moravia, and consisting largely of tradesmen, was a cloth dyer. Francis Netardus married Agnes Drozd. In 1880 the father, mother and all the children except Louis P. came to the United States, settled near Hallettsville, and took up farming.

Theo. Y. Hull, B.S. M.D.

The former is still living in that locality at the age of eighty-four years, while his wife passed away in 1898. Their children were: Frank, who died near Hallettsville leaving a family; Cyrill, a farmer near Hallettsville; Louis P.; Charles, a farmer in Lavaca County; Mary, wife of John Kalivoda, of Sweet Home, Texas.

Father Netardus spent the first fifteen years of his life in his native country. He attended the city schools of his native town for eight years, and in 1881 embarked on a vessel at Bremen, the Frankfurt, and a number of days later was landed at Galveston. He soon joined his parents at Hallettsville and spent four years on a farm. It was then decided that he should devote his life to the ministry and he took up his preparation at St. Joseph's Seminary in Victoria. He spent nine years there as a student of the classics, philosophy and theology and also became versed in various languages, particularly the English. Father Netardus preaches in Bohemian, German and English, and has a speaking command of the Spanish and Polish. Immediately after his ordination as a priest he took up the work of his calling and has shown remarkable energy and earnestness in looking after his people and in upbuilding the various churches of which he has had charge. In 1909 Father Netardus took out citizenship papers and for a number of years has interested himself in general civic, political and social movements.

Dr. Theodore Young Hull of San Antonio, Texas, the subject of this sketch, was born on the 24th day of August, 1860, in the City of New York. Just at this time the clouds of Civil war were lowering, and thinking men were asking what of the morrow. His parents, Peter H. and Mary J. (Lance) Hull, were natives of New Jersey. The family comes of that hardy New England stock which, transplanted from England in the early colonial days, did its part in developing the struggling colonies, and fought its way through the Revolution and other wars. When he was a child, Doctor Hull's parents removed from New York to the West, settling in Northwest Missouri, then on the very frontier of civilization. In this section of the West, noted for its rapid development and agricultural wealth, he spent the earlier years of his life, imbibing the spirit of the West and loving its frankness.

His early education was begun in the schools of Illinois and Missouri. He completed his literary education in Amity College in Southern Iowa, where he graduated with the highest honors in 1884, receiving the degree of Bachelor of Science. Amity College was one of those staunch Presbyterian schools which pinned their faith on hard work, and required it of their students. The following years wert devoted to educational work. Early in 1887 he entered the Government service at Washington, District of Columbia. During the years of educational work, he read both law and medicine in an effort to obtain a liberal education. The Government service not satisfying his ambition, though noticeably increasing the breadth of his outlook on life, he decided upon the profession of medicine as a life work. He thereupon entered the medical department of the Columbian University, now the George Washington University, at Washington, District of Columbia, where he graduated in 1892, receiving the degree of Doctor of Medicine.

In January, 1888, Doctor Hull was married to Miss Maud F. Hall, of St. Joseph, Missouri. Their son, Warren H. Hull, graduated from the West Texas Military Academy in 1912, and this year, 1916, received the degree of Bachelor of Arts from the Southwestern University, Georgetown, Texas.

Immediately after graduation, Doctor Hull took up the practice of medicine in the city of his Alma Mater, Washington. He was successful beyond his earliest dreams. At the time of this success, his wife, who had so ably seconded his every effort to advance, became an invalid. In his effort to save her life, he entered the largest institution of its kind in this country for the study of pulmonary diseases. He came to San Antonio in 1906, and again took up his life work, this time limiting his efforts to the treatment of the diseases of the heart and lungs. Whatever degree of success he may have attained in this most difficult of all special work in medicine, he feels that it is due to her who has always offered encouragement when it was needed, and who has shared every sorrow and rejoiced in every good fortune. Into this work Doctor Hull has thrown his whole soul. He is now medical director of the Lutheran Sanatorium in this city.

In his early professional life he became physician to Washington College for Young Ladies, located in Washington, District of Columbia. He held this position for five years, and incidentally conducted the classes in psychology, geology and botany in the institution.

Although coming of Presbyterian stock, he entered the Methodist Episcopal Church, serving as superintendent of Sunday school for eight years, and was licensed as an exhorter in that church. Fraternally he became a member of the Odd Fellows and the Masonic order. On the organization of the Texas State Society of Social Hygiene he became secretary. For five years he has been editor of the Medical Annals of Southwest Texas. For several years he has been a member of the San Antonio Scientific Society. For two years he has been a member of the San Antonio Board of Health. He is now a member of the San Antonio Press Club.

Many men in the medical profession are today devoting themselves in a large measure to the prevention of disease as well as its cure. In this way their efficiency as benefactors has extended much beyond the scope of the old fashioned practice when the physician's relation to his patient was confined to the attempt to relieve his present suffering. Doctor Hull has acted upon the belief that the physician was the semi-official guardian of the public health, and that his duty as physician did not end at the prescription counter. His literary efforts have been directed largely along the lines of preventive medicine and sociology. He has in frequent public addresses and in many newspaper and magazine articles advocated measures for the conservation of the public health and the betterment of the human race.

In his professional work he has contributed many articles on the subject of the treatment and prevention of tuberculosis. These articles have been published in the medical journals of this state and elsewhere. Some of those on the prevention of tuberculosis have been published in the lay press. Several articles have been prepared and published on the subject of Tuberculosis in Childhood.

As secretary of the Texas Society of Social Hygiene, he has contributed many articles which have appeared in the Club Women's Argosy, The Texas Motherhood Magazine, The Texas Medical Journal and other publications. Some of these articles were written in the effort of the Society of Social Hygiene to secure legislation to protect marriage, by preventing the marriage of those suffering from certain contagious diseases, alcoholism and drug addiction.

For the Texas Motherhood Magazine a series of articles was written on eugenics, heredity, the conservation of the child, and mothers' pensions. In all these he has sought to teach the principle that healthy offspring can come only from healthy parents, and that the welfare of the state and the future of the race depend upon the healthy normal children born. As a member of the Scientific Society he has contributed addresses on Inheritance, Tuberculosis, Cancer, Social Disorganization, etc. As a member of the San Antonio Board of Health he has made a study of the prevalence and fatality of infectious diseases in the city, and secured the passage of ordinances governing the control of tuberculosis so far as it relates to hotels, boarding houses, etc. As editor of the Medical Annals of Southwest Texas, he has contributed to the medical literature of the Southwest.

Through every article runs the ever present desire to help better the conditions of human life.

FRANK L. ERMIS. A retired business man of Engel, Frank L. Ermis is one of the early Bohemian settlers of Fayette County, having lived in the State of Texas almost half a century. He has risen from the discouraging conditions which confronted most men of foreign birth and training who arrived in Texas at that time, to a position such as only comparatively few reach in a business and civic way.

He was born at Frankstad in the Province of Moravia, Bohemia, April 11, 1848, and was eighteen years of age when he came to America. His father, Frank Ermis, a farmer and quarryman by occupation, embarked his family upon board the sailing ship Irish at Bremen in 1866, and after a voyage of twelve weeks, during which a storm drove the vessel four hundred miles out of its course, landed in Galveston. At that time, only a year after the close of the Civil war, the railroad mileage of Texas was very limited, and the family rode over the rails as far as the then terminus of the Southern Pacific, to Alleyton, on the Colorado River and thence a wagon and nine oxen conveyed them to High Hill, where they had friends living. Thence they continued on to Osso in Fayette County, their first point of settlement. Frank Ermis in the second year of his residence in Texas bought land at Praha, and spent the rest of his active career there as a farmer. He died in February, 1873, when a little past fifty-three years of age. He married Mary Hermis, who died in 1911 at Praha when eighty-four years of age. They were both active members of the Praha church, which they helped to build and in which they reared their children in religious instruction. These children were: Johanna, widow of Frank Jureka, of Praha; Mary, who married in Bohemia Cyrill Matula and remained in that country; Frank L.; Joseph, an extensive farmer at Shiner, Texas; Bertha, who married John Bucek and lives in El Campo; Annie, who married Nick Brod, of Shiner; and Agnes, now deceased, who married Charles Gallia.

Frank L. Ermis received his early education in the Village of Kozlovic in Moravia, and after coming to Texas acquired considerable instruction from local teachers. The beginning of his career was one of hard manual labor. For some time he was employed in a stone quarry and as a mason at wages of "four bits" per day with board. During two winters he clerked in a store at old Flatonia for $12 to $15 a month and board. From these occupations he returned to the farm, married, spent the first year in operating the old homestead for his mother, and then bought a place at Vellehrad on the Lavaca County line, which was his home for ten years. The land when it came into his ownership was absolutely unimproved, but he left it as a valuable farm, and was the owner of 300 acres when he sold out. His steady industry and good management gave him the foundation for his subsequent prosperity.

In 1880, having sold his farm, Mr. Ermis removed to Hallettsville and became a merchant. For five years he sold goods as a general merchant, and also was an extensive buyer of cotton. He had some business reverses and finally sold his interests in Hallettsville, and with three partners bought 9,000 acres of school land in Lavaca, Dewitt and Gonzales counties.

He at once removed to this land and undertook its improvement. He put up several tenant houses, built a gin, established a postoffice under the name Hermis, of which he was the first postmaster, and was succeeded by his son. After a few years he sold all his land, and concentrated his attention for seven years upon the management of the store and cotton gin. Eventually he sold this property, returned to Velehrad, bought another farm and of the 425 acres he still owns 208 acres. In 1912 Mr. Ermis removed to Engel and bought the various business interests of I. J. Gallia, consisting of houses, stock, land and other properties in the village. Here he again became identified with merchandising, but is only a silent partner in the firm of Engel Hardware & Furniture Company, handling a large stock of furniture, hardware, implements, wagons and buggies. Mr. Ermis owns a small farm of eighteen acres adjoining the village limits and his home is one of the best in that community. He has given extensive repairs to all his own business houses and has built several structures for the accommodation of his own and other enterprises.

Since reaching his majority Mr. Ermis has acted and voted as an American citizen and has manifested an intelligent interest in affairs around him. From association with neighbors and friends he naturally inclined to the democratic party and has served many times as school trustee while living at Hallettsville, Vellehrad and Shiner. His only other official service was as postmaster at Hermis as already mentioned.

On September 2, 1870, Mr. Ermis married Miss Clara Michni, daughter of Vancil Michni, who died at Refugio County, Texas, at the wonderful age of ninety-eight years. Vancil Michni was born in the same village where Mr. Ermis first saw the light of day. He married Mary Holub. The six Michni children were: Mary, who died as the wife of James Gahanak; Johanna, now deceased, who married Antone Gahanak; Mrs. Ermis, who was born June 5, 1852; Joseph, of Kennedy, Texas; Rudolph, of Wichita Falls, Texas; and James, of Refugio County.

The children of Mr. and Mrs. Ermis are mentioned briefly as follows: James, who died in Seymour, Texas, married Louisa Pacha; Frank, a farmer at Moulton; Joseph, who is a large farmer near Shiner, married Frances Malena; Charles, who married Annie Kosack and lives at Vellehrad; Louis, a farmer at Moulton, married Louisa Palica; Willie, a farmer at Vellehrad, married Miss Lelia Gahanak; Clara, wife of Lebo Jarosek, of Engel; Emma, who married Hendre Orsak, an Engel merchant; Lucy, wife of John Farek, of Engel; and Julia, a twin sister of Lucy, who is the wife of Joseph Farek. The son, Frank, mentioned among the above children, married Lillie Pecha.

AUGUSTUS F. VERDERY, M. D. A remarkably interesting personal and family history is that of this honored and representative physician of Fayette County, Texas, where he has been engaged in the active practice of his profession since 1868 and where he holds prestige as one of the most venerable physicians and surgeons still active in practice in the Lone Star State. Though he has passed the eightieth milestone on the journey of life, he has the mental and physical vigor of a man many years his junior and has no desire to withdraw from the unselfish and humane vocation which has engrossed his attention for many years. He is one of the revered and influential citizens of the Village of Winchester, a community in which he settled upon coming to Texas, within a few years after the close of the Civil war, in which he had given valiant and effective service as a surgeon in a Georgia regiment of the Confederate forces. The doctor is a native son of Georgia, where the Verdery family was founded in 1796, and the lineage traces back to staunch French origin, though the first representatives of the name in America came to Georgia from the Island of Hayti, in the West Indies. The name has been one of special prominence and distinction in Georgia and other sections of the South, and the doctor himself became its first representative in Texas.

Near the now metropolitan City of Augusta, Georgia, which was then in Warren County, but which is now the judicial center of Richmond County, Dr. Augustus Freeman Verdery was born on the 1st of November, 1832. He was reared in a home of affluence and refinement and was afforded the advantages of the excellent schools maintained at Augusta. His father was an extensive landholder and manufacturer of lumber; he built and placed in operation near Augusta the first steam saw mill in Georgia, and he cut much timber from several thousand acres of pine land which he owned in that section, the major part of the lumber product having been shipped by him in train-loads to Augusta, for local consumption and for further distribution.

Judge Augustus N. Verdery, father of the doctor, was born at Augusta, Georgia, on the 1st of November, 1804, and was a son of Nicholas Verdery, who had been a large slaveholder on the Island of Hayti and whose slaves voluntarily accompanied him when he removed to the present State of Georgia. With his family and fully a hundred of his loyal slaves he landed in Savannah, Georgia, in 1796, and soon afterward he settled near Augusta, where he became an extensive planter, much of his old plantation being now within the corporate limits of the City of Augusta. Nicholas Verdery, who was a brigadier-general in Napoleon's army, was a scion of a patrician French family and was born at Bordeaux, France, whence he went to Hayti when comparatively a young man. He was liberally educated and was a talented violinist, in which connection it should be noted that one of his prized possessions was a fine Cremona violin, this old and valuable instrument having been taken from the home of his son, Judge Augustus N., by some Federal soldier at the time of the Civil war, when such depredations were most frequent in devastated Georgia, and the instrument was never recovered by the family. Nicholas Verdery was long one of the prominent and influential citizens of Eastern Georgia, where he left a vast estate, his death having occurred in 1839, when he was nearly ninety years of age. Concerning his children the following brief data are available: Benjamin was a resident of Columbia, Georgia, at the time of his death and left several children; Augustus N. was the father of Doctor Verdery of this review; Dr. Mandos Verdery, next of the sons, was sent by his father to Europe, where he received a liberal literary and professional education, and he became one of the eminent surgeons of Georgia, his death having occurred at Augusta, that state, when he was sixty-six years of age, and several of his children having survived him; Eugene, whose wife was a native of South Carolina and bore the family name of Paul, became a prosperous business man, and died near Augusta, Georgia, some of his descendants being numbered among the wealthy and influential men of that state at the present time; Clio, the only daughter of Nicholas Verdery, became the wife of Pleasant Stovall, a prominent merchant of Augusta, where she died without issue.

Judge Augustus N. Verdery acquired his youthful education in the schools of Georgia and his father provided him also with excellent business training of a preliminary order. He became a substantial planter, and when the Federal Government removed the Cherokee Indians from Georgia to the Indian Territory, Judge Verdery purchased the old home and land of Chief Ridge, one of the most prominent of the Cherokees, and this property, in Northwest Georgia, the judge developed into a fine agricultural and live-stock farm. When he was a young man the country about Augusta was sparsely settled, and among the neighbors of the family were the Hon. George W. Crawford, who served as secretary of state in the cabinet of President Buchanan, later held the post of United States minister to Italy, and who still later became one of the most prominent figures in the secession movement in Georgia, where he served as president of the Secession Convention which brought that commonwealth staunchly into line in the support of the cause of the Confederate States during the climacteric period of the Civil war. Judge Holt, a justice of the Supreme Court of Georgia, was another honored neighbor and friend of the Verdery family, and still another neighbor was Thomas W. Barrett, who was engaged in the wholesale drug business in Augusta. It was thus in a community pervaded by fine intellectual and social atmosphere that the sons and daughters of Judge Verdery were born and reared. The judge married Miss Susan Hampton Burton, a daughter of Rev. William B. Burton, who accompanied Burnet's colony into Texas but who soon returned to Georgia, where he remained until his death, a prominent and able clergyman of the Baptist Church. He died at Cuthbert, Georgia. He wedded Elizabeth Hughes, of Virginia, and they became the parents of five children, the two sons being Joseph and Isaac W.; Mrs. Verdery being the eldest of the three daughters; Mrs. America McLendon died in Baker County, Georgia; and Mrs. Virginia Watson was a resident of Florida at the time of her death. Isaac W. Burton, younger of the two sons, came to Texas in 1832 and settled in the present County of Fort Bend. He was a pioneer who took part in the conflicts through which the Indians were kept in comparative subjection and otherwise aided greatly in the march of civilization and progress, both during the regime of the Republic of Texas and after the admission of the state to the Union. No representatives of his family are now to be found in Texas, and his older brother, Joseph, was a resident of Alabama at time of death.

At this juncture is entered brief record concerning the children of Judge Augustus N. and Susan H. (Burton) Verdery: Rev. William M., who devoted his life to the ministry of the Baptist Church, died near Augusta, Georgia, and left a large family of children. He served the Confederacy during the Civil war in the office of chaplain of the Fifty-ninth Georgia Regiment, which was a part of Gen. G. T. Anderson's Brigade, Hood's Division of General Longstreet's Army Corps. Emily became the wife of Dr. George M. Battey, of Augusta, and was a resident of the City of Atlanta at the time of her death. Thomas J. was lieutenant-colonel of the Twenty-first Georgia Infantry, with which he served in the command of Gen. "Stonewall" Jackson, he having been killed in the first Battle of Fredericksburg. He had become a successful lawyer before the inception of the war and sacrificed his life in the cause of the Confederacy. Mary F. became the wife of Col. Warren Aiken, who was a prominent member of the bar of Cartersville, Georgia, who later served as speaker of the House of Representatives of the Confederate States Congress, and whose son later served in the United States Congress. Susan is the wife of Col. John S. Prather and they still reside in the City of Atlanta, Georgia. Oriana married and passed the closing years of her life in Atlanta. George T. was a lawyer by profession and died in New York City as the result of a wound received at the Battle of Gettysburg, when he was serving as adjutant of the Fourteenth Alabama Regiment in the Confederate army; he was a bachelor at the time of his death. Pleasant S., the youngest of the children, read medicine under the preceptorship of his brother, Dr. Augustus F., subject of this review, was later graduated in the medical department of the University of Georgia, and thereafter was engaged in the practice of his profession at Douglasville, that state, until his death, his wife and children surviving him.

Dr. Augustus F. Verdery supplemented the early education which he received at Augusta, Georgia, as previously noted, by higher academic study under the direction of Prof. Benjamin Moultrie, of Rome, that state, in which city he also studies medicine under the direction of Prof. H. V. M. Miller, of the medical department of the University of Georgia. In this department of the university he was graduated on the 4th of March, 1854, and he initiated the practical work of his profession at Talladega, Alabama, but a year later he returned to Georgia and engaged in practice at Louisville. From that place he finally removed to the Shoals of Ogeechee, in Warren County, where he became a planter and also continued the practice of his profession until he responded to the call of higher duty at the inception of the war between the states of the North and the South. In the spring of 1861 he entered the Confederate army as assistant surgeon and a year later he was promoted surgeon of the Fifty-ninth Georgia Regiment of Infantry, and was ordered from Richmond, Virginia, to Charleston, South Carolina. He was on duty to give first aid to the wounded at Fort Sumter, the victims being transferred at night to the hospital in Charleston. He was next ordered or detailed to Savannah, Georgia, where he served as night surgeon of Hospital No. 2 with Surgeon William R. Waring, who was on duty during the days. The doctor next went to Quitman, Georgia, to establish a hospital and after conducting the work of this institution ten months he went to Thomasville, that state, where he continued in charge of a hospital maintained in the county courthouse until the surrender of General Lee.

After the close of the war Doctor Verdery returned to his plantation and, with the aid of his former slaves, raised a crop of cotton and with the proceeds from the sale of this product and the final sale of his plantation, of which he disposed when land in Georgia commanded a low price and industrial conditions were in chaotic state, he fortified himself measurably in a financial way for his new venture in the State of Texas. The results of the war were the industrial and commercial prostration of the South and the placing of former slaves on a plane of equality for which they were not in the least fitted, and under these depressing conditions Doctor Verdery decided to leave his native state and identify himself with the West. He came by rail to Brenham, Texas, and was led to come into the community of Winchester by reason of the fact that here the mother and stepfather of his wife, Doctor and Mrs. Jenkins, had established their home. His financial resources were meager, and here he forthwith engaged in the practice of his profession, in which he has continued during the long intervening years of a signally earnest, upright and benignant life.

With a single exception Doctor Verdery has emphasized his allegiance to the democratic party in every national election and this single exception was when he voted for Horace Greeley, the Greenback candidate for the presidency in 1872, this action having been taken principally because of his appreciation of the great editor's generous service, as bondsman, in effecting the liberation of Jefferson Davis, the former president of the Confederacy, from imprisonment by the Federal authorities. Doctor Verdery holds membership in the Methodist Episcopal Church, South, while his wife was a devoted adherent of the Baptist Church, and he has been not only affiliated with but has served as examining physician for the Knights of Honor, the Woodmen of the World, the Sons of Hermann, the Praetorians and other fraternal organizations, besides having been medical examiner locally for the New York Life Insurance Company.

At the Shoals of Ogeechee, Georgia, on the 17th of August, 1859, was solemnized the marriage of Doctor Verdery to Miss Mary Beall, daughter of Robert Beall, who was a representative agriculturist and a member of an old Georgia family. Mr. Beall met his death in a personal encounter, in the '50s, and his wife, whose maiden name was Martha Jones, survived by many years, finally becoming the wife of Doctor Jenkins, with whom she came to Texas, where she passed the remainder of her life. Of the three children of Mr. and Mrs. Beall the wife of Doctor Verdery was the eldest, the other two being Mrs. Thomas Coleman, of Dinwiddie Court House, Virginia, and Mrs. Julia J. Baker, of Colorado City, Colorado. The supreme loss and bereavement in the life of Doctor Verdery was entailed by the death of his devoted and gracious wife, who was summoned to eternal rest on the 24th of December, 1911, after their companionship had continued for more than half a century. In conclusion is given brief record concerning their children: Virginia is the wife of Charles S. Gates, of Winchester, Texas; Carrie V., who is the widow of John P. Jones, likewise resides at Winchester; Oriana is the wife of Theodore Secretan, of San Antonio; Robert N. is a representative business man at Shawnee, Oklahoma; Burton is the wife of Thomas Cowden, of Oklahoma City, that state; Felix Freeman, who resides in Houston, Texas; and David P. is married and resides at Achille, Oklahoma.

John F. Mohler. Born and reared in the Winchester district of Fayette County, John F. Mohler has here continued his residence during the long intervening years and here has found ample opportunity for the achieving of success and substantial prosperity through well ordered personal endeavor. He is a representative of one of the sterling German pioneer families of this now favored section of the Lone Star State, and the name which he bears has been long and worthily identified with civic and industrial activities in Fayette County.

Mr. Mohler was born near the present Village of Winchester, where he maintains his residence, and the date of his nativity was August 6, 1865. He is a son of Frank Joseph Möhler (this being the original German orthography of the name) and Catherine (Nink) Möhler, the former of whom died at Winchester, Texas, in 1911, a few months after having celebrated his eighty-second birthday anniversary, and the latter of whom still resides in this village, as one of its venerable and revered pioneer women. Frank Joseph Möhler, who ultimately simplified the spelling of his name to the present form of Mohler, was born in one of the Rhine River districts of Germany and was there reared and educated. In 1856, as a young man, he emigrated to the United States and in the same year he settled in Bastrop County, Texas, where he found employment at his trade, that of carpenter. There his marriage was solemnized and there he and his wife continued their residence until after the close of the Civil war, when they removed to Fayette County and established their home in the Winchester community. Here Mr. Mohler became a successful contractor and builder and during the later years of his life he was here engaged in the furniture business and in work as a cabinetmaker, lines of enterprise with which he continued to be identified until his death. He was a man of sterling character and ever commanded the respect and good will of his fellow men. A rupture made him ineligible for and exempt from service as a soldier during the Civil war; his political allegiance was given to the democratic party and he was a devout communicant of the Catholic Church, as is also his widow. He was a close student of the Bible and was one of the best informed laymen in regard to biblical history to be found in this section of the state.

In Bastrop County was solemnized the marriage of Frank J. Mohler to Miss Catherine Nink, who was born in Germany but who was reared and educated in Texas. She is a daughter of Madison and Ellen (Rauch) Nink. Her father came from Carlsbad, Germany, to the United States in 1845 and settled in Texas, this being the year in which the state was admitted to the Union. He landed at Indianola, which was then known as Powder Horn, and in the early days he became a prominent freighter between his home town of New Braunfels, Comal County, and the frontier towns of Austin and Houston. While he was engaged in this hazardous business he encountered at one time a band of 500 Comanche Indians and he feared that his life was to end. However, he treated the Indians to coffee and gave other evidences of friendliness, with the result that they finally left him unmolested. He kept watch all night, with his gun ready for service, but upon his arrival at New Braunfels on the next day he found the Indians peacefully encamped in the vicinity of the village. After his retirement from the freighting business Mr. Nink removed to Bastrop County, where he and his wife passed the residue of their lives. Of their children, Mrs. Catherine Mohler, mother of the subject of this review, is the eldest; and she was born at Carlsbad, Germany, in 1839; Mrs. Mary Brieger, the next in order of birth, died at Bastrop, Texas; Jacob continued his residence in Bastrop County until his death, as did also Madison; Margaret became the wife of Peter Braum and died in Bastrop County; and Bettie, whose death occurred in the same county, was the wife of John Michel.

Mrs. Catherine Mohler was about six years of age at the time of the family immigration to America and settlement in Texas, where she received her education in the pioneer schools, a few months having been the duration of her attendance in a school at Frelsburg, to which point she rode on horseback each day from her home, several miles distant. She recalls in graphic reminiscence the conditions and incidents of the pioneer days, especially in the struggle of the settlers to save their homes when prairie fires were started by the Indians. On the occasion of a visit to Ship's Lake she witnessed the gathering of fully 500 Indians who had assembled to witness an eclipse of the moon, an event of which they had been informed by the well known frontiersman, Grassmeyer. Mrs. Mohler knew the Goche family, members of which were massacred by the Indians, and she heard at first hand the story of the butchery and of the capture of the two Goche boys, Samuel and Riley, both of whom, with other captives, were rescued finally by Mr. Spalding, who later married a widow of one of the Goche family, she having been widowed at the time she was thus captured by the Indians.

Concerning the children of Frank J. and Catherine (Nink) Mohler the following brief record is given: Mary is the wife of Albert Shober, of Smithville, this state; Jacob is a prosperous merchant in the same town: Ellen is the wife of Edward Rasbery, an oil operator in that section of the state, their home being at Thorndale; John F., of this review, was the next in order of birth; Bettie is the wife of Robert Redfield, of Cameron, Texas; Mott resides at Winchester, as does also Miss Lela, who remains with her widowed mother.

John F. Mohler was reared to adult age on the old homestead farm near Winchester and such were the conditions and exigencies of time and place that his educational advantages in his youth were greatly limited. He assisted in the work of the home farm until he was about twenty-one years of age, when he made his first independent venture by engaging in business in the conducting of a meat market at Winchester, under the firm name of Mohler & Murphy. After his retirement from this line of enterprise he devoted his attention to farming for a period of about five years, and he then became clerk in the mercantile establishment of Roensch Brothers, at Winchester. About a year later he engaged in the retail liquor business in this village, and after conducting a successful enterprise in this line for somewhat more than a decade he turned his attention to farming and stock-raising, with which basic industries he has since continued his identification and in connection with which he has achieved distinctive success. In the live-stock business Mr. Mohler is associated with Hugh F. Little, concerning whom individual mention is made on other pages of this publication, and their several tracts of excellent grazing land, in the district surrounding the Village of Winchester, have an aggregate area of nearly 2,000 acres. The firm controls a large business in dealing in cattle and other live stock and at times large direct shipments are made by its members, both of whom are progressive and energetic men of affairs. They utilize on all their cattle the ear-crop method of identification, which has been found more effective and humane than the old branding system.

Mr. Mohler was one of the influential men identified with the organization of the Winchester State Bank, of the directorate of which he has been a member from the time of its incorporation and of which he was soon elected vice president, a position of which he continued the incumbent. He is broad-minded and public-spirited as a citizen and as such opposed the "State-wide" movement in Texas. By Governor Colquitt he was appointed a delegate to the Conservation Congress held in the City of Indianapolis, Indiana, but circumstances prevented him from attending the sessions of this body. He has been a loyal supporter of the cause of the democratic party and was a liberal contributor to the Bryan Campaign Fund in the election of 1908.

Mr. Mohler has been twice wedded. On the 20th of February, 1894, he married Miss Lizzie Phillips, daughter of John Phillips and a granddaughter of Thompson Phillips, who was a pioneer of Texas, where he settled in 1834. Mrs. Mohler's death occurred on the 18th of February, 1899, no children having been born of this union. On the 16th of December, 1899, was solemnized the marriage of Mr. Mohler to Miss Frances Hutcherson, only child of James F. and Martha (Brooks) Hutcherson, her father being a prosperous farmer and a representative of a family that was founded in Texas in the early pioneer days. Mr. and Mrs. Mohler have three children: Little Joe, Frank Leon, and Leslie Eugene.

MILES T. COGLEY. One of the strongest and most influential financial institutions of Texas, and particularly of the southwestern part of the state, the Milmo National Bank, of Laredo, is distinguished from the great majority of monetary enterprises in that it places the general interests of the community above self interest. At the head of this bank is found Miles T. Cogley, a capable financier, who in the capacity of president extends support to all enterprises and industries that are of general benefit to Laredo and the vicinity, regardless of whether the individuals behind such are patrons of his bank or not. It can be truly said of Mr. Cogley and the bank that the progress and welfare of the community are of much more importance to them than the dividends of the bank stock. Unlike many others, this bank has never been known to engage in an undignified competition for business, for the best class of business comes to its coffers without seeking. The bank has always been particularly strong in its cash resources, so that in times of financial stress or panic, neither the officials of the bank or its depositors have any cause for worry.

The charter of the Milmo National Bank was issued as a national institution July 12, 1882, and it has been in business at Laredo continuously ever since. Mr. Eugene Kelly, of New York, who was instrumental in its establishment, was the first president of the bank, and was later succeeded by Daniel Milmo, who was in turn succeeded by Miles T. Cogley,

[illegible] business in this village, and after conducting [illegible] for somewhat more than a decade [illegible] to farming and stock-raising, with which [illegible] continued his identification and in connection [illegible] has achieved distinctive success. In the live-stock business [illegible] associated with Hugh F. Little, concerning whom [illegible] made on other pages of this publication and [illegible] grazing land, in the district surrounding [illegible] Winchester, have an aggregate area of nearly 2,000 acres. [illegible] controls a large business in dealing in cattle and other live stock and [illegible] large direct shipments are made by its members, both [illegible] progressive and energetic men of affairs. They utilize on [illegible] ear-crop method of identification, which has been [illegible] and humane than the old branding-system.

[illegible] of the influential men identified with the organization [illegible] State Bank, of the directorate of which he [illegible] from the time of its incorporation and of which he [illegible] president, a position of which he continued the [illegible] broad-minded and public-spirited as a citizen and as [illegible] "State-wide" movement in Texas. By Governor Colquitt he [illegible] a delegate to the Conservation Congress held in [illegible] Indiana, but circumstances prevented him from [illegible] of this body. He has been a loyal supporter [illegible] Democratic party and was a liberal contributor to [illegible] in the election of 1908.

[illegible] wedded. On the 20th of February, 1894, [illegible] Phillips, daughter of John Phillips and a grand[illegible] who was a pioneer of Texas, where he [illegible] death occurred on the 18th of February, [illegible] born of this union. On the 16th of December [illegible] marriage of Mr. Mohler to Miss Frances [illegible] of James F. and Martha (Brooks) Hutcherson, [illegible] farmer and a representative of a family [illegible] in the early pioneer days. Mr. and Mrs. [illegible] Little Joe, Frank Leon, and Leslie Eugene.

[illegible] one of the strongest and most influential financial [illegible] particularly of the southwestern part of the [illegible] Bank, of Laredo, is distinguished from the great [illegible] in that it places the general interests [illegible] interest. At the head of this bank is found [illegible] who in the capacity of president [illegible] enterprises and industries that are of general [illegible] vicinity, regardless of whether the individuals [illegible] of his bank or not. It can be truly said of [illegible] that the progress and welfare of the community [illegible] to them than the dividends of the bank [illegible] this bank has never been known to engage [illegible] competition for business, for the best class of business [illegible] without seeking. The bank has always been particularly [illegible] resources, so that in times of financial stress or panic, [illegible] of the bank or its depositors have any cause for worry. [illegible] the Milmo National Bank was issued as a national [illegible] 1882, and it has been in business at Laredo continu[illegible] Eugene Kelly, of New York, who was instrumental [illegible] was the first president of the bank, and was later [illegible] Milmo, who was in turn succeeded by Miles T. Cogley.

The American Historical Society

Eng by E. G. Williams & Bro. N.Y.

in 1911, who up to that time had held the position of cashier from 1886. This bank, the oldest and first national bank to be established, has steadily improved its status ever since organization, and its general condition is now better and its deposits and resources larger than at any previous time in its history. As shown in the following statement, issued at the close of business, May 1, 1916, its individual deposits are considerably over $1,000,000: Resources—Loans and discounts, $990,815.11; U. S. bonds, $120,000.00; bonds, securities and claims, $531.14; stock Federal Reserve Bank, $6,000.00; banking house, $23,500.00; furniture and fixtures, $3,279.50; redemption fund, $6,000.00; cash and sight exchange, $773,423.04; total, $1,923,548.79. Liabilities—Capital, $150,000.00; surplus, $100,000.00; undivided profits, $36,136.67; circulation, $118,750.00; dividends unpaid, $1,880.00; individual deposits, $1,472,312.17; bank deposits, $44,469.95; total, $1,923,548.79. The present officers are: Miles T. Cogley, president; A. M. Bruni, vice president; G. P. Farias, cashier; and Albert Martin, assistant cashier; while the directors are Miles T. Cogley, Albert Urbahn, A. M. Bruni, T. A. Austin and L. J. Christen.

Mr. Cogley enjoys the friendship and financial co-operation of some of the strongest bankers and financiers in the country. He has always been the credit man of the bank—the one who passes upon the making of loans—and has seldom made a bad one, notwithstanding the fact that he almost invariably makes a loan to a man "on his face"—according to the moral risk, rather than upon his actual resources and security. The Milmo National Bank enjoys extensive and influential outside connections and has always held particularly confidential relations with the leading business men and enterprises of Laredo and the vicinity. This has been particularly so in connection with the new business and agricultural growth of Webb County, and newcomers, whether going into farming, stockraising or general business, have found this institution a most excellent medium through which to get and stay in touch with the life and business activities of this locality.

Miles T. Cogley was born in 1863, in the City of Cleveland, Ohio, and his entire career has been devoted to financial affairs. As a young man he entered the service of the Cleveland, Cincinnati, Chicago & Saint Louis (Big Four) Railroad, now a part of the New York Central System, as cashier, and in 1883 came to Texas and became cashier and paymaster of the "Tex-Mex" Railroad and the National Railway of Mexico, extending from Corpus Christi south through Laredo into the Republic of Mexico. In 1886 he went into the Milmo National Bank, was later advanced to the cashiership, and in 1911 was elected to the presidency, a position which he still holds. In December, 1914, Mr. Cogley was elected president of the Texas-Mexican Railway, of which he had been paymaster thirty years before, and under his wise and efficient direction the road has prospered greatly. He has always taken a keen and active interest in the affairs of Laredo, and has served as a member of the school board, of which he has also been president. His service to his community also includes eight years as commissioner of Webb County. In fraternal circles Mr. Cogley is well known as a member of the local lodges of the Benevolent and Protective Order of Elks and the Knights of Columbus.

Mr. Cogley was married in 1884, at Cleveland, Ohio, to Miss Rose Hungerford, daughter of Col. W. W. Hungerford, a widely known railroad official, now living in retirement in Mississippi. Mr. and Mrs. Cogley have one daughter, Mabel, the wife of Stephen M. Barlow, of Laredo. Mr. and Mrs. Cogley suffered great misfortune in the loss of their son, Dan Cogley, aged ten years, who was killed by the accidental discharge of a gun, in July, 1910. In his memory Mr. Cogley has dedicated the

Santa Rosa Ranch, in Webb County, ten miles below Laredo, on the Rio Grande. It is one of the show places of Texas, the tract consisting of 5,314 acres, of which 400 acres are in cultivation by irrigation. A specialty is made of Bermuda onions and alfalfa, and the ranch is used as a demonstration farm for products suitable for this part of the country. Here Mr. Cogley has had erected a first-class barn, a number of buildings for the employees, substantial structures for the shelter of machinery, stock and appurtenances, and a beautiful residence which is modern in every particular. Mr. Cogley has expended over $10,000 on this residence alone, and it now contains bath rooms, gas for cooking, electric lights and sanitary plumbing and sewerage, and is beautifully furnished.

Robert C. Botts. As the result of thrift and industry Robert C. Botts has become the owner of some 800 acres of land along the Guadalupe River and the same is devoted to the growing of cotton and corn, Mr. Botts having won splendid success as an experimental farmer. He was one of the organizers of the Farmers National Bank at Gonzales and is now vice president of that reliable financial institution. During his administration as county commissioner the roads in this precinct were graded and graveled and while he was a member of the school board a new high school was built in Gonzales. Accomplishment marks his every endeavor and he ranks as one of the prominent and successful business men of this section of the state.

The grandfather of Robert C. Botts was a native of Virginia and he was a slaveholder and planter in that commonwealth during the early part of his active career. Later he removed to Kentucky and in Bath County, that state, in 1808, occurred the birth of his son Benjamin. The latter was reared to maturity on the paternal farm and acquired such schooling as was afforded in that early day. In 1852, with his family, he made the journey to Texas, going down the Ohio River from Maysville, thence down the Mississippi to New Orleans and from the latter place to Port Lavaca. The trip by land to Gonzales was made by team and in this vicinity Mr. Botts purchased a small farm, on which he settled with his family and small family of slaves. Later he located on Smith Creek, a mile from his original place and there he passed away in 1892. While in Kentucky he raised grain, tobacco and stock but on coming to the Lone Star State he gave his attention to the growing of cotton and corn. He was a successful farmer and in politics was a democrat. He was interested in public education and was identified with the district schools as trustee on various occasions. He was a member of the Christian Church in Kentucky but was not identified with any special church after coming to Texas. He married twice, his second wife being the mother of the subject of this review. Her maiden name was Frances McIlvain and she was a daughter of Joseph McIlvain, of Kentucky. Mrs. Botts was a Methodist in her religious views and she took an active part in the upbuilding of the church of that denomination in her home community. The following children were born to Mr. and Mrs. Botts: Mattie J. became the wife of J. T. Conn and she resides in Ballinger, Texas; Robert C. is the subject of this sketch; and John H., now deceased, was a farmer and stockman near Gonzales during his lifetime, he married Elizabeth Davis and is survived by his widow and a family.

Robert C. Botts was born in Kentucky, February 27, 1848, and he was but three years of age when his parents came to Texas. He was educated in the country schools and for a short time was a student in the Gonzales High School. He was too young to participate in the Civil war, being but seventeen years of age when peace was declared. The first line of business to which he gave his attention was that of a merchant and he sold goods in Gonzales, at Rightsboro and South Riverside. Subsequently he became interested in farming and stock-raising and in this connection he began with but a small capital. He invested his profits in lands and now owns several fine farms along the Guadalupe River. At the present time he has 800 acres devoted to cotton and corn and he has met with marked success as an experimental farmer. By fertilization and intense cultivation he has succeeded in growing a bale of cotton to the acre in country where the surrounding land gives a yield of but half to three-quarters of a bale per acre. In addition to his farming interests Mr. Botts deals in real estate and he helped organize the Farmers National Bank of Gonzales, of which he is now vice president.

Mr. Botts has always taken a voter's interest in politics and he gives a staunch allegiance to the democratic party. For two years he gave most efficient service as county commissioner and during that period a bond issue of $150,000 was spent in precinct No. 1 in improving the roads. He has also served on the local school board for several years and was largely influential in securing a new high school for Gonzales. In a fraternal way he is a Mason and his religious faith coincides with the doctrines of the Methodist Church; he is one of the stewards of the Gonzales Church of that denomination and he was an active factor in securing the means for the erection of the present church.

Mr. Botts has been twice married. In 1879 he wedded Miss Cornelia Lovett, a daughter of Evan Lovett. She died in 1887, leaving two children: Lovett and Frances. Lovett Botts was educated in the Gonzales schools and he is now a prominent farmer and stockman in this section. He married Inez Thornton and has two sons, Robert and Gerald. Frances married R. S. Chambers, of Gonzales. In June, 1897, was solemnized the marriage of Mr. Botts to Miss Lilla Wood, a daughter of Harris K. Wood, a sketch of whose career appears elsewhere in this work. Mr. and Mrs. Botts have one daughter, Lillian Fay, who was graduated in the Gonzales High School, in 1915, and who is now a student in the Ward Belmont College, at Nashville, Tennessee. The Botts family have a beautiful home in Gonzales and take their recreation in the fine car recently purchased by Mr. Botts. He has ever been a strong prohibitionist, and can always be found on the moral side of all public questions.

HARRIS K. WOOD. The founder of the Wood family in America was an Irishman who settled in Virginia prior to the War of the Revolution. He had four sons, namely: Penial, Burrell, Jones and William, all but one of whom settled and reared families in Randolph County, North Carolina. Penial Wood, grandfather of Harris K. Wood, was born in the Old Dominion Commonwealth and as a young man settled in North Carolina, where he became a prominent planter and slave owner. He set his slaves free, however, prior to the outbreak of the Civil war, thereby setting a good example to others in his community. He married a Miss Kimbrell, a daughter of Buckner Kimbrell, commander of a company in the Revolution whose duty it was to pursue and capture Tories, who were hanged upon a certain tree when they refused to disclose the hiding places of their comrades. To Mr. and Mrs. Wood were born the following children: William, father of Harris K. Wood; Burrell, who died in Tennessee, leaving issue; Penial, Jr., who died in North Carolina, as did also Wiley and Priscilla, the latter of whom married a Mr. Wilburn; Sarah married John Kirk and they settled in the West many years ago; Patsy married Neeley Laughlin and died in North Carolina; and Irena married John Ridge and passed her life in North Carolina. By a second marriage Penial had three daughters: Jincy, who married Willis Carter; Samantha and Josephine.

William Wood was born in Randolph County, North Carolina, in 1799, and he died in 1844. He was a farmer by occupation, was a whig in politics and in religious faith was a Methodist. He married Henrietta Harris, a daughter of Wiley Harris, who passed the major part of his life in North Carolina as a farmer. Mr. Wood left his wife a widow in 1844 and she subsequently married Morgan Denman. To Mr. and Mrs. Wood were born the following children: Harris K. is he to whom this sketch is dedicated; Laura A. married Robert Nixon and died in Texas; Elmyra married Marion Foster and left a family in Guadalupe County, Texas; Alexander died, unmarried, at Crockett, Texas; and William is a farmer in Frio County, Texas. There was one child born to Mr. and Mrs. Denman: Leroy, who maintains his home in San Antonio. The mother of the above children died in 1862.

Harris K. Wood, who has resided for the past thirty years on a large farm adjoining the City of Gonzales, was born near Ashboro, Randolph County, North Carolina, April 4, 1827. His boyhood was spent on a farm on Caraway River and in that vicinity he received his preliminary educational training. His father died when he was but seventeen years of age and thereafter he helped support his mother and the younger children. He was twenty-five years of age when he came to Texas, his mother and the family of Robert Nixon coming across the country in covered wagons. The trip consumed three months and eight days and the party crossed the Mississippi River at Memphis, when that now famous commercial metropolis was but a country village. The party passed through Little Rock, old Lanesport and Houston and finally settled on the San Marcos River, just across the river from the present City of Ottine. In the following year they located in Guadalupe County, near Luling, on Smith's Creek. In the latter place the Wood family bought land, which was developed into a fine farm. Two years later Mr. Wood went to Bexar County, near San Antonio, where he was a farmer and stockman for the ensuing five years. During the Civil war he enlisted in Captain Kelly's company of independent troops and served along the gulf, attempting to keep back the Federal gunboats. He never left the state, however, was not in a battle, and was disbanded before the close of the war at Victoria. He then engaged in hauling cotton for the Confederate government, taking the same to Laredo, on the Rio Grande. After the war he came to Gonzales County and located on a farm near Belmont. There he was engaged in agricultural pursuits and in stock raising and eventually he located on his present fine estate of 379 acres just outside the city limits of Gonzales. He has substantially improved his holdings with good tenant houses and fine quarters for his stock and he has met with unusual success as a cotton and grain farmer. He is an industrious worker and, although well advanced in years, still he superintends the management of his large estate.

In politics Mr. Wood is a democrat and he has given efficient service as a school trustee in Guadalupe County. He is a Methodist in his religious faith and in a fraternal way is a Blue Lodge Mason.

January 3, 1855, in Gonzales County, was celebrated the marriage of Mr. Wood to Miss Nancy Jane Parchman, a daughter of James Parchman, who came to Texas from Mississippi, in which latter state Mrs. Wood was born in 1837. This union has been prolific of the following children: James is a farmer at Gonzales and is unmarried; Lucius is a stockman and farmer in Runnels County, this state, he married Lillie Nunn; Vida died unmarried; Ora resides at the parental home; Willie married Boone Jackson, of Gonzales; Dula is at home; Ruth died as the wife of Thad Cardwell; and Lillie married Robert C. Botts, a sketch of whose career appears on other pages of this work.

HERMANN ZILSS. A resident of Fayette County for more than thirty years, Mr. Zilss has been a citizen of the Village of Winchester, active and influential in both business and civic affairs and through his well ordered efforts has achieved large and worthy success. He has been concerned with mercantile enterprise, and has large farming interests and business connections at the present time, his success having been the direct result of his own ability and earnest endeavors. Prior to establishing his residence in Fayette County Mr. Zilss had passed a year in the City of Galveston, where, through his service as a laborer and in the driving of a street car, he was enabled to save about $250. With this money and a certain surplus which he had brought with him from his native land, he established himself in the general merchandise business at Winchester. Fair and honorable dealings and effective service to patrons conduced to the development of a large and prosperous business, and after a successful career of fifteen years as a merchant at Winchester he sold his stock and business to his younger brother, Emil, since which time he has given his attention principally to the supervision and management of his extensive landed estate and other capitalistic interests. He has done successful work in the buying and selling of real estate, principally farm property, and also controls a prosperous enterprise in the extending of loans upon approved real-estate securities.

Hermann Zilss was born in the Town of Buetow, in the Prussian Province of Pommern, or Pomerania, Germany, on the 8th of September, 1847, and his early educational advantages were of excellent order, as he completed a thorough course in the gymnasium, which is similar to the high school of the United States. He became an expert bookkeeper and accountant and his final service in this connection was given in the City of Berlin.

From the City of Hamburg Mr. Zilss sailed for Baltimore, Maryland, in 1881, on the steamship Braunschweig, and after his arrival on American soil he forthwith made his way to Giddings, Texas. Soon afterward he went to Smithville, where one of his first experiences in connection with his spirited welcome to his adopted country was that of being a member of a little party of men who were surrounded by robbers, were held up at the point of pistols and compelled to deliver their valuables, Mr. Zilss's pockets having been made to disgorge an appreciable amount of cash. Soon after this unseemly adventure he went to Galveston, where he began work as a common laborer, this being the only honest employment then offered. It was a proud moment in his career when he discovered at the end of a year that through such honorable toil and endeavor he had saved $250. He has had many "ups and downs" during the long intervening years but has persevered, has shown indomitable spirit in the surmounting of obstacles, has met emergencies and adversities with courage and has reached a certain amount of independence and prosperity, the while he has so ordered his course as to gain and retain the confidence and good will of those with whom he has come in contact in the various relations of an earnest and useful life. He has shown marked consideration for those who have been less fortunate than he in connection with business affairs. While he lends money to those who borrow for various purposes, there has been naught of the grasping, Shylock attitude on his part, and he has never charged more than 6 per cent interest on his financial favors to others, though there have been occasions when he could readily have exacted a much higher rate. In politics Mr. Zilss has been a supporter of the cause of the democratic party and thus has been in accord with the general sentiment of his friends and neighbors, the while he has given earnest and loyal support to measures and enterprises that have conserved civic and material progress and prosperity in his home community.

Christian Zilss, father of him whose name initiates this article, was a man of substantial means in Buctow, Pomerania, in which locality he owned and operated an excellent farm, his means and paternal fidelity being such that he gave to each of his children excellent educational advantages. He wedded Henrietta Grubert, and both continued their residence in Buctow until the close of their lives. Of their children Hermann, of this review, is the eldest; Julius is the executive head of a surveying bureau in the City of Berlin, Germany; Willhelm holds a similar administrative position with an important railroad bureau in the Fatherland; Emil, who came to the United States in 1884, is one of the leading merchants and representative citizens of Winchester, Texas, where he succeeded his brother Hermann in the mercantile trade; and Miss Emma still remains at the old home in Buctow.

In the period of his residence in Texas it has been the privilege and pleasure of Hermann Zilss to visit his old home in Germany on six different occasions.

Christobal Benavides. A life that was of extraordinary vigor, vitality, and wide and useful influence, was that lived by the late Christobal Benavides, one of the most striking characters in the modern history of the City of Laredo. He exemplified some of that loyalty, patriotism and business enterprise which have served to impress the name permanently upon the history of Southern Texas.

The prominence of the Benavides family is so well known that it is only necessary to note the relations of Christobal Benavides in the family lineage. His paternal grandfather was Jose Maria Benavides, who was a native of Mexico and was one of the pioneer settlers of Laredo. He married Dona Petra Sanchez, who was the granddaughter of Captain Tomas Sanchez, the founder of Laredo in the middle of the eighteenth century. Jose Benavides, Jr., father of Christobal, spent his entire life in and around Laredo, and was one of the large land owners and extensive ranchers of his time. He married Tomasa Cameros, and of their children one was the celebrated Col. Santos Benavides, whose name is especially familiar as a result of his exploits in guarding the southern frontier of Texas during the Civil war.

The third child of his parents, Christobal Benavides was born April 3, 1839, at Laredo, and received his education in his native city and at Corpus Christi. From early boyhood he was identified with the live stock industry, and with his headquarters in Webb County he handled cattle and sheep on an extensive scale. He developed a large ranch, consisting of many thousands of acres, and occupied a striking place in business life before the Civil war. Among other interests of that period he had contracts for carrying the mails through this section of the state.

In 1861 he entered military service as a sergeant in a company of state troops commanded by his brother, Santos Benavides. He was with the state troops for about a year and was advanced to the rank of lieutenant. The regiment was then reorganized and mustered into the regular Confederate service, with Santos Benavides as colonel and Christobal as captain of a company. This regiment became known in history as Benavides' Regiment. The command saw its principal service along the Rio Grande from Laredo to Brownsville, and played a valiant part in the fighting and campaigns commanded by Col. Rip Ford, the celebrated Indian fighter and soldier. This regiment was also in the last battle of the war, Las Palmas, fought after the surrender of Appomattox on the Rio Grande, a few miles above Brownsville, and not far

CHRISTOBAL BENAVIDES

from the scene of the first engagement which marked the beginning of the war with Mexico. By his record as a brave and efficient soldier and officer Captain Benavides shared the honors which are associated with his brother, Colonel Santos. One of the objective points of many Federal expeditions during the course of the war was the Rio Grande Valley, which was a frontier of great value to the Confederacy, since in the latter years of the war it was almost the only source of supplies. The Benavides' Regiment performed a splendid service in keeping this route of communication open.

When the war was over Christobal Benavides became associated with his brother Santos under the name S. Benavides & Brother in the mercantile business at Laredo. About 1875 Colonel Benavides retired, and the business was conducted under the name C. Benavides as sole proprietor. Colonel Santos lived retired from that time until his death in 1891. The house of Benavides, both wholesale and retail, was for many years one of the largest and most prosperous firms along the international boundary between Mexico and the United States. It supplied the merchandise handled by retail dealers for a radius of several hundred miles on both sides of the Rio Grande, and the name became a synonym for commercial integrity and success. At the same time Mr. Benavides developed his live stock interests on a large scale, and it is to be especially noted that he was among the first to introduce graded Durham cattle into the Rio Grande country.

His active career came to a close after nearly half a century of constructive business by his death at Laredo September 2, 1904. It was said that no man was ever more deeply mourned in that community than he, not only by his family, upon whom he lavished generously the love and affection of his heart, but by the entire community. He was charitable from impulse and principle, and the poor had in him their most steadfast friend. The concourse that followed his body to its last resting place was not only the largest funeral ever witnessed in Laredo but was a singular tribute of grief and affection rendered by an entire community to an individual. His life was honorable and upright, he was gifted with a great and noble nature, and he furnished his protection and sympathy to all who needed it. He deserved the large fortune which accumulated by reason of his judgment and enterprise, and all the more because he dispensed it with such liberality among his own family and in behalf of deserving charity.

On January 29, 1867, at Laredo, Mr. Benavides married Miss Lamar Bee, who is still living, and represents one of the notable families of South Texas. Mrs. Benavides is a daughter of Gen. Hamilton P. Bee of Texas, whose name is carried in one of the principal counties of that section of the state and whose record as a distinguished soldier is found in all the histories of the war between the states. Mrs. Benavides' maternal grandfather was Don Andres Martinez, a member of the distinguished Martinez family of Spanish ancestry in Mexico. He was Alcalde of Nuevo Laredo, Mexico, during the closing years of the decade of the '40s. Mrs. Benavides was liberally educated, and spent several years as a student in the East, principally at the Academy of Mount de Sales, five miles west of Baltimore. She has given her best devotion and the influence of a cultured mind and heart to her family, and the ten children she reared reflect honor and credit upon Mrs. Benavides and her honored husband. The family are of the Catholic faith, and the children were all educated in Austin, the sons in St. Edwards College and the daughters at St. Mary's College. They are as follows: Carlota, wife of M. Valdez; Marie, wife of Amador Sanchez; Santos M.; Lamar, wife of Dr. H. J. Hamilton; Aurela, wife of Francisco Garza Benavides; Christobal;

Eulolio; Luis; Melitona, who married Reyner K. Hymar, of Fort Worth; and Elvira, who married first Jack Duncan, of Columbus, Texas, and after his death married Ernest T. Laubscher, of New Brounfels, Texas.

Dr. A. M. Kotzebue. This well known physician of Flatonia, who has practiced medicine in Lavaca and Fayette counties for more than twenty years, is a native of South Texas, and represents a fine old line of German ancestors, several branches of which have lived in Texas since prior to the Civil war.

The history of the Kotzebue family dates back to 1420. The village that gave the name to the family was Kossebau or Kossebue, and was later named Kotzebue. This village is located in Prussia, at Arendsee in the Altmark or Old Market. Denning Kotzebue, the first of whom we have any knowledge, was born in 1420 in Stendal, and later lived at Salzwebel and also at Magdeburg in Germany. A direct lineage begins with Jacob Kotzebue, who was born in 1527 in Stendall and who was Rathskammerer at Magdeburg. His oldest son John, who was born in the Altstadt (old town) Magdeburg in 1591, was a minister or preacher. He had two sons. The older of these sons was the beginning of the Hanover line of descendants, while the younger son originated the Braunschweig or Russian line. The Kotzebue family in Texas are descended from the Hanover line.

A brief account of the Hanover line of the family is as follows: Johann Kotzebue, born at Quedlinburg in 1616, died in 1677. In 1658 he was ordained a Protestant minister at Hanover. Next comes Georg Carl Kotzebue, of Hanover, who died in 1730. The head of the next generation was Georg Christian Kotzebue who was born in 1706 and died in 1779. He was the father of four sons and five daughters. Of these Christoph Carl was born in 1740 and died in 1810; Albrecht David was born 1754 and died in 1839; and Georg Christian was born in 1752 and died in 1808.

The children of Georg C. Kotzebue last named were as follows: Julie, who was born in 1785 and died in 1861; John Carl Andreas, born in 1787 and died in 1788; Carl Ernst Leopold, born in 1789 and died in 1790; Peter Heinrich Albrecht, born in 1792 and died in 1862; Christian August Meinhard, born in 1795 and died in 1880; and Stats Franz Friedrich, born in 1801.

Stats Franz Friedrich Kotzebue, grandfather of Doctor Kotzebue, was born April 14, 1801, at Hoija in Hanover. He married Christiane Jorgensen, who was born in Denmark. Franz Friedrich Kotzebue owned land at Bocksee in Holstein, Denmark, but on account of the Danish military pressure upon settlers he sold it in 1853, and came to America with his wife and four sons, locating at New Ulm, in Austin County. Franz Friedrich Kotzebue died in 1864. Of his sons, Christian born in 1836, and Johannes, born in 1839, both died in 1857. The other two were Christian Meinhard, born in 1840, and Julius Kotzebue, born in 1842. Both these sons had to go to war in the Confederate army, and after the restoration of peace they both married, and Julius Kotzebue settled down on the farm in Colorado County, while Christian M. later moved to Lavaca County. Julius Kotzebue, who was born in 1842 in Denmark was married in 1866 in Colorado County to Bertha Donlevy. He is still living on his farm in Colorado County and has one daughter and four sons, namely: Lina, Julius, Heinrich, Wilhelm and Hilly, all living and married.

Christian Meinhard Kotzebue, father of Doctor Kotzebue, was born in Denmark in 1840. In 1870 he moved to Lavaca County, locating on a farm near Moulton, sold that place in 1890 and moved into the Town of Moulton, where for the past twenty-five years he has been in the hotel business. He was married in 1866 to Louise Bauer. Her father, George Bauer, was a baker by trade and was employed in that occupation in St. Petersburg, Russia, and after coming to Texas established a home on a farm near New Ulm. Mr. Bauer's wife was Anastasia Amalie Wiese, who was born in Germany. The Bauer children were: August; Amalie, wife of Rev. Rudolph Jaeggli of Moulton; and Mrs. C. M. Kotzebue.

Christian M. Kotzebue and wife are the parents of thirteen living children, mentioned as follows: August Emil Meinhard (Dr. A. M. Kotzebue), born in 1869; Louise, born in 1870, married F. J. Helweg of Moulton; Elise, born in 1873, married W. Graves of Moulton; Alexander F., born in 1875, in the drug business at Moulton, married Erna Fehrenkamp and has two sons and a daughter; Emilie, born in 1876, married F. F. Nesrsta of Flatonia; Selma, born in 1878, married Herman Chemnitz of Flatonia; Bertha, born in 1880, married John Brunkenhoefer of Moulton, and has two sons; Wilhelm, born in 1882, married Adela Helmkamp; Emma, born in 1883, unmarried; Julius, born in 1885, married Helen Goetz, and has one daughter; Amalie, born in 1886, married Vincent Rehmet and has one son; Linda, born in 1889, married William Franke, and has three children, two girls and one boy; and August, born in 1892, married Allan Baugh. Of the sons the oldest is Doctor Kotzebue, two others are engaged in the drug business at Moulton, and three have their homes at Flatonia, including Doctor Kotzebue, one of his brothers being in the employ of the Cowdin Grocery Company, while the youngest is a druggist.

Dr. A. M. Kotzebue was born near Columbus in Colorado County, January 13, 1869, and was reared on the old farm at Moulton. He acquired his early education in the Moulton Institute, took a correspondence course in pharmacy and then engaged in the drug business at Moulton as a partner of Dr. W. H. Lancaster and continued in that line for eleven years. He took his first course in medicine in the Kentucky University of Medicine at Louisville in 1889, and finished in the Illinois Medical College of Chicago in June, 1892. After this preparation he engaged in practice at Moulton, remained there until 1907, and has since had his office and home in Flatonia, and enjoys a large practice in the town and surrounding country. He is a member of the Lavaca County and the Fayette County Medical societies, and served as secretary of the former and has been representative of that society to three meetings of the Texas Medical Association. Ever since coming to Flatonia Doctor Kotzebue has served as city health officer, and for several years has been a member of the school board. For a time he was postmaster at Moulton. In politics he is a democrat with strong prohibition tendencies, is a member of the Lutheran Church, and has fraternal affiliations with the Woodmen of the World, the Sons of Hermann, the Knights of the Maccabees and the Order of Yeomen.

At Moulton, Texas, June 7, 1892, Doctor Kotzebue married Miss Leona Veliera Lightner. Mrs. Kotzebue was born on a farm at Clayton, near Montgomery, Alabama, a daughter of Thomas Smith and Nancy (Bishop) Lightner. Thomas S. Lightner was a son of William Michael Lightner, whose parents came to America from Holland. Mrs. Kotzebue's mother, Nancy Bishop, was a member of a well known Alabama family, and her mother was a Miss Pitts. Nancy (Bishop) Lightner had four brothers and four sisters. All the brothers lived and died in Alabama except William Bishop, who moved to Arkansas. The sisters became the wives of William Blair, Ryan Bennett, Concel Bush and Monroe Lasseter. Thomas S. Lightner's mother was a Miss Sophia

Mustgrove. Mr. Lightner had three brothers and one sister: Sarah, Samuel F., John and William. The sister married a Mr. Warren and after his death married Mr. Helms. The mother of William Michael Lightner, above mentioned, was a Miss Smith. Her first husband was named Harvy, an Englishman. They had been married only a short time before the Revolutionary war. Mr. Harvy was wrongfully accused of active sympathy with the English in that war, and without any trial was hanged before the eyes of his wife. She fainted at the spectacle and when she recovered consciousness found the dead body of her husband across her. At that time they lived in North Carolina. Mrs. Harvy afterwards married a man of German origin, named Leitner, the name which was subsequently changed to its present spelling of Lightner. Mrs. Doctor Kotzebue has three brothers and three sisters: Fannie, wife of L. T. Edwards of San Antonio, and the mother of three sons and one daughter; Alabama, widow of J. S. Burns of Brownwood, Texas, and has two daughters and one son; Mollie, now Mrs. G. W. Harrison of Cottonwood, Alabama, and has four daughters and three sons; William M. Lightner, of Arkadelphia, Arkansas, and has five daughters and three sons; C. E. Lightner, still living in St. Louis and Gus O. Lightner, who lives in Monterey, Mexico, and has two sons.

Mrs. Kotzebue was reared in Alabama, finished her high school course in the Clayton Female College of Clayton, and is a graduate of the Tuscaloosa Female College of Tuscaloosa, Alabama. Before her marriage she was a teacher in the public schools at Moulton, Texas. Doctor and Mrs. Kotzebue are the parents of two sons. Meinhard Henry Kotzebue, born May 9, 1893, was graduated from the mechanical engineering department of the Agricultural and Mechanical College of Texas in 1914, and is now manager of an automobile school at Houston. Leon Lightner Kotzebue, born September 29, 1896, is a graduate of the Flatonia High School and is now a student in the Agricultural and Mechanical College.

Alexander Ramsey. Now approaching the psalmist's span of three score years and ten, this honored and influential citizen of Fayette County has been a resident of Texas from the time of his nativity and is a representative of one of the sterling pioneer families of this section of the Lone Star State. Mr. Ramsey served continuously as postmaster of the Village of Winchester from 1895 until his retirement on the 1st of October, 1915. He is also president of the State Bank of Winchester, one of the staunch financial institutions of Fayette County.

Alexander Ramsey was born at Eagle Lake, Colorado County, Texas, on the 28th of August, 1846, and when he was a lad of five years his parents removed to Cryer's Prairie, near the present Village of Ellinger, Fayette County, where they remained until 1853, when they established their permanent home in the Winchester community, where the father passed the remainder of his life. Mr. Ramsey is a son of Martin D. and Margaret (Dabney) Ramsey, the former a native of Tennessee and the latter of Kentucky. Martin D. Ramsey was born at Bolivar, Hardeman County, Tennessee, in the year 1812, and was reared to manhood in his native state, where he received limited educational advantages, the schools of the locality and period being of meager order. In 1831 he came to Texas with the well known Burleson family which was destined to become one of distinction and influence in connection with Texas history, his first wife having been a member of this family. He first settled with the Burleson Colony in Bastrop County, and he became prominently identified with the movement that resulted in the freeing of Texas from the Dominion of Mexico. His active career was devoted to agricultural pursuits and stock-growing on a modest scale, and his old homestead place in Fayette County was on the John F. Berry league of land, near Winchester, where he continued to reside until his death, in 1866, at the age of fifty-four years. He was a son of William Ramsey, who removed from his native State of North Carolina and became a pioneer farmer of Tennessee, where he continued to reside until his death, Martin D. Ramsey having been the only member of the family who came to Texas. As a young man Mr. Ramsey wedded Miss Abigail Burleson, who died near Eagle Lake, Colorado County, Texas, leaving no children. He later wedded Miss Margaret Dabney, a daughter of John A. Dabney, who came from Kentucky to Texas about 1833, his home having been in such proximity that the members of the family could hear the firing incidental to the historic Battle of San Jacinto. Mrs. Ramsey was then a girl of thirteen years, her birth having occurred in 1822, and she now resides at Winchester, at the remarkable age of ninety-three years,—one of the revered and most venerable pioneer women of the Lone Star State. She well recalls the hearing of the tumult of the famous battle which resulted in gaining independence to Texas. Martin D. Ramsey is survived by four children,—Sarah A., who is the wife of William Faires, of Burnet County; John H., who resides at West Point, Fayette County; Alexander, who is the immediate subject of this review; and Minnie, who is the wife of William F. Brieger, of Winchester, individually mentioned on other pages of this work.

Alexander Ramsey acquired his early education principally in the schools of the Winchester community and at the age of seventeen years he enlisted as a youthful soldier in the Confederate service, at LaGrange, where he became a member of an independent company commanded by Capt. William G. Webb, and went to Columbia, Brazoria County, to do guard duty at the powder magazine. Six months later the company was reorganized and Charles Smith was elected captain. Under Captain Webb the company was stationed at Anderson, Grimes County, as guard over the pistol factory there maintained by the Confederate government. After its reorganization the command proceeded to the mouth of the Brazos River and shortly prior to the close of the war it was attached to Colonel Waller's regiment, with which it proceeded into the northern part of the state, for the purpose of effecting the capture of a regiment of Confederate soldiers who were attempting to desert. The command arrived at Gainesville and captured some of the men, but before it was possible to report with these disloyal soldiers the war came to a close, Mr. Ramsey's company having been disbanded at Hempstead, Waller County. The members of the company furnished their own horses, which they of course retained after the war, as did they also their arms. Mr. Ramsey vitalized his interest in his old comrades through his affiliation with the United Confederate Veterans.

After the close of the war Mr. Ramsey resumed his activities as a farmer and stock-grower, and with these basic lines of enterprise he continued to be successfully identified, in Bastrop County, until 1890, when he established his residence at Winchester, through which place the railroad had just been completed. Here he erected a building and opened the same as a hotel, under the name of the Ramsey House. He conducted the hotel somewhat more than a decade, and in the meanwhile was one of the dominating figures in connection with the development and progress of the community. About the year 1892 he was elected justice of the peace for Precinct No. 4, and of this magisterial office he continued the incumbent about ten years, previously having served eight years in the same office in Bastrop County. In January, 1895, Mr. Ramsey was appointed postmaster at Winchester, as the successor of

H. Zilss, and he continued the incumbent of this office without interruption until October 1, 1915. He is a stalwart advocate of the principles of the democratic party, though his first presidential vote was cast in support of Horace Greeley, the nominee of the ephemeral greenback party, in 1872. For more than twenty years Mr. Ramsey has been affiliated with the Knights of Honor and he is also past noble grand of Winchester Lodge, No. 125, Independent Order of Odd Fellows. He was one of the organizers of the Winchester State Bank, in 1910, and has served as its president since its incorporation.

In October, 1866, was solemnized the marriage of Mr. Ramsey to Miss Susan Redfield, daughter of Henry P. and Sarah (Card) Redfield, who passed the closing years of their lives in Bastrop County, Mr. Redfield having come from New England to Texas in the pioneer days. Of the children of Mr. and Mrs. Ramsey three attained to years of maturity: Wallace, a bachelor, died at Winchester when thirty-five years of age; Kittie is the wife of Samuel F. Drake, a representative merchant of Winchester; and Edward H., who married Miss Mamie Roensch, is the mayor of the City of Giddings, Lee County, where he is engaged in the buying and shipping of cotton.

FREDERICH T. FEHRENKAMP. It is gratifying to give recognition in this history to Mr. Fehrenkamp, who is to be designated as one of the pioneer business men and representative citizens of the Village of Moulton, Lavaca County, a place at which he established his residence when the town had but two stores and was otherwise in embryonic state, the railroad line having at the time been but recently completed through the place. For more than a quarter of a century he has been actively identified with the lumber business at Moulton and he is now the owner of the pioneer lumber yard of the town, the same being well equipped and controlling a substantial business in the handling of lumber and other building supplies. Mr. Fehrenkamp has been one of the aggressive and loyal forces in the development and upbuilding of his home village and is a substantial and honored citizen who further merits consideration by reason of his being a native son of the Lone Star State and a representative of one of its sterling pioneer families.

On the pioneer homestead of his parents, northeast of Liveoak Hill, Colorado County, Texas, Frederich T. Fehrenkamp was born on the 7th of July, 1857, and he was reared in that community, where his father was a representative farmer, his educational advantages having been those afforded in the common schools of the locality and period. His first independent venture was made by his entering the employ of the Ehlinger family, in the capacity of teamster on freighting wagons engaged in operating from the old Town of Ellinger to Columbus. After severing this association he served a practical apprenticeship to the carpenter's trade, and after becoming a skilled artisan he continued to work at his trade until after he had passed his majority and had taken unto himself a wife. He then removed to Lavaca County and engaged in farming in the immediate vicinity of the old Town of Bowersville, not far distant from the present thriving Village of Moulton, which at that time was "not on the map." He purchased his farm, made good improvements on the place and there continued his residence eight years, within which he brought the farm under effective cultivation. In 1888 he left the farm, of which he later disposed, and established his residence in the ambitious new Village of Moulton, where he became a clerk in the employ of J. W. Matteer, who was the first to establish a lumber business at this place, the village basing its claims for advancement on its newly acquired railroad facilities. After having been associated with Mr. Matteer for 7½ years Mr. Fehrenkamp purchased the yard and business, and he has continued the enterprise successfully since that time in an individual way. When he located at Moulton the town had only two mercantile establishments,—the Boehm Store and that of the firm of Jackson & Company. As a business man and progressive citizen he has been closely concerned with the upbuilding and development of Moulton, where he erected his attractive residence and made other improvements for the benefit of the town, besides being the owner of his well equipped lumber yard, with its substantial shed for storage purposes and with a building used for office purposes and as a store for the handling of paints, oils, glass and other building accessories.

The general civic interests of Moulton have received the earnest support and encouragement of Mr. Fehrenkamp, and he has given specially valuable service in the office of trustee of the school district, the first school having been established at Moulton after he had here taken up his residence and he having soon afterward been chosen one of the trustees, a position in which he has continued to serve for fully twenty years. He has shown no desire to enter the activities of practical politics but has been content to do his part as a loyal and public-spirited citizen and to support the mean and measures meeting the approval of his judgment. He was reared in the faith of the Lutheran Church but his wife and children are communicants of the Catholic Church. He is affiliated with the Blue Lodge and Chapter of the Masonic Fraternity and both he and his son Victor O. are members of the Hermann Sohns.

Mr. Fehrenkamp is a son of Gerhard and Christina (Frehrichs) Fehrenkamp, the former of whom died in Fayette County in 1879, at the age of fifty-six years, his devoted wife having passed away in 1869, and their remains resting side by side in the cemetery at Frelsburg, Colorado County. Gerhard Fehrenkamp was born in Germany and was a son of Bernard Fehrenkamp, his younger brother, Dr. Bernard J. Fehrenkamp, having become a representative physician and surgeon at Frelsburg. Christina (Frehrichs) Fehrenkamp was the oldest of the children of Frederich Frehrichs, who came from Oldenburg, Germany, and became a pioneer farmer in the Liveoak Hill District of Colorado County, Texas, where he devoted his attention also to fruit-growing and where he passed the residue of his life. In his native land he had followed the trade of watchmaker and had also been a musician in a semi-business way. Of his children Mrs. Fehrenkamp was the eldest, as previously noted; Frederich, Jr., resided in the vicinity of Frelsburg, Colorado County, until his death, and was survived by several children; William died in the Rock Hous community in Austin County and left children; Henrietta married Otto Baring and died near Oakland, Colorado County. In the appending paragraph are given brief data concerning the children of Gerhard and Christina (Frehrichs) Fehrenkamp:

Bertha became the wife of Alois Koniakowsky and died at Ellinger, Fayette County, in 1912, leaving seven children—Minnie, Bertha, Erna, Emma, Lizzie, Alois, Joseph and James. Bernard Fehrenkamp resides at Shiner, Lavaca County, and Gerhard at Ellinger, Fayette County; and Frederich T., of this review, is the youngest of the children. For his second wife Gerhard Fehrenkamp, Sr., married Mrs. Eliza (DeLaux) Giesbers, and the one child of this union is Otto Fehrenkamp, who resides at Temple, Bell County.

At Liveoak Hill, Texas, on the 20th of June, 1878, was celebrated the marriage of Frederich T. Fehrenkamp to Miss Hildegard Giesbers, daughter of Henry Giesbers, whose widow became the second wife of Gerhard Fehrenkamp, Sr., as noted above. Mr. Giesbers was one of the sterling German pioneers of Texas, where he established his residence in 1848, upon his immigration from Dusseldorf, Prussia. For a number of years he was a merchant at LaGrange, Fayette County, and he passed the closing period of his life at Rutersville, that county. Of his four children Mrs. Fehrenkamp is the only daughter; John is a farmer near Moulton; Charles resides at Temple; and Henry died a bachelor.

In conclusion are entered brief data concerning the children of Mr. and Mrs. Fehrenkamp: Ida became the wife of Vladimir Boehm and died at Moulton, in March, 1913, two daughters surviving her, namely: Helen and Marguerite. Lillie is the wife of H. George Bargmann, of Snyder, Scurry County, and they have two children—George and a daughter born in the spring of 1915. Erna is the wife of A. F. Kotzebue, of Moulton, and they have three children—Roy, Alice and Henry Earl. Louis, who resides at Moulton, married Miss Augusta Ullmann and they have one son, Harvey. Victor Otto, a popular young business man, is associated with his father in the latter's various business activities. Elois C., who is assistant cashier of the bank at Moulton, married Miss Della Boehm. Henry, who likewise is associated with his father's business activities, married Miss Emma Ullmann. Frederick has recently completed his studies in the public schools of Moulton.

Arthur Claude Hamilton. Vice president and general counsel of the Texas-Mexican Railway and general counsel for the National Railway of Mexico, Mr. Hamilton easily ranks among the best lawyers of Texas. For twenty years his home has been in Laredo, and besides his work as a railway attorney he has a large business in corporation, land and criminal practice.

Though a native of Canada Mr. Hamilton has spent most of his life in Texas. He was born at Barrie, Ontario, November 12, 1871, a son of Dr. Alexander and Katherine (Spohn) Hamilton. His mother was a sister to the celebrated surgeon, Dr. A. E. Spohn, who recently died in Corpus Christi. The grandfather of Mr. Hamilton was one of the pioneers at York in founding the modern City of Toronto, and had cousinship relation with the Countess of Dufferin and Lord Claude Hamilton of Ireland. Doctor Hamilton was a physician of high attainments both in Canada and the United States, having moved to Corpus Christi in 1875 on account of his wife's health. He was for several years surgeon of the marine hospital at Corpus Christi.

Arthur C. Hamilton acquired his education in Texas. After graduating from Coronal Institute at San Marcos in 1887, he entered the University of Texas at Austin, graduating Bachelor of Science in 1892 and from the law department with the degree of LL. B. in 1894. During his senior year in the regular college course he was a fellow in chemistry and taught that subject to several classes.

After a brief experience in practice at Austin, Mr. Hamilton came to Laredo in the fall of 1894, and that city has since been his home and professional headquarters. For about a year he was law partner of the late Charles C. Pierce. In 1896 he was elected district attorney for the Forty-ninth Judicial District, and by subsequent elections at the end of each two years served nearly eight years. Then for about two years he was assistant United States district attorney for the southern district of Texas.

Mr. Hamilton in 1910 became vice president and general counsel for the Texas-Mexican Railway and general counsel for the National Railway of Mexico, and besides these important offices is also local attorney for the International & Great Northern and the Southwestern Telegraph & Telephone Company. He enjoys a large practice in corporation law,

land litigation and criminal cases. In a great majority of the cases tried in the courts at Laredo many of the witnesses are Mexicans, speaking only their own language. On account of his proficiency in Spanish and a peculiar tact and diplomacy in dealing with the Mexican people, Mr. Hamilton is particularly well equipped for legal practice on the Texas border. His thorough ability and diligence have brought him a well deserved success in the law. Mr. Hamilton was married at Beaumont to Miss Henrietta A. Greer. Her father, Judge Hal W. Greer, was for years a leading Beaumont lawyer, but is now a law partner of Mr. Hamilton at Laredo.

Fritz Reinsch. By training and experience Mr. Reinsch has become a man of marked versatility in business and not only is he a worthy representative of the sterling German element of citizenship that has played an important part in the development and upbuilding of Southern Texas but he has also become known as one of the prominent, successful and influential business men and progressive citizens of Winchester, Fayette County, where he owns and conducts a well equipped blacksmithing and general machine shop and is also engaged in the general merchandise business. He has been a resident of Texas for somewhat more than thirty years and through his own ability and earnest efforts has achieved independence and definite prosperity.

Mr. Reinsch was born in the ancient and splendidly fortified City of Magdeburg, Province of Saxony, Germany, on the 31st of July, 1860, and his early advantages were of meager order, his father, Reinsch, having been a shoemaker by trade and vocation and in modest financial circumstances. Reinsch wedded Carolina Mathes, and he died when the subject of this review was a child, leaving his widow with four children, of whom Fritz was the youngest. The devoted mother made the best possible provision for her fatherless children and continued her residence in Saxony until the time of her death, both she and her husband having been consistent communicants of the Lutheran Church. Fritz, the youngest of the children, is the only representative of the immediate family in the United States, and all of the others are now deceased; Minna, the eldest, became the wife of Julius Bach; Julius served in the German army and after his retirement he died while still a young man and a bachelor; Mrs. Bertha Trener died in Saxony and left two sons.

After receiving such educational training as the family station and resources made possible, Fritz Reinsch entered upon an apprenticeship to the trade of lockmaker and machinist, in his native city, and he became a skilled artisan in both lines. After serving three years in the German army, as a member of the Twenty-sixth Regiment, Tenth Company of the Fourth Army Corps, he found employment in a railroad roundhouse near Magdeburg, and through his earnings in this connection he saved the funds which made possible his immigration to the United States, where he felt assured of better opportunities for the winning of independence through his individual efforts.

In 1884 Mr. Reinsch sailed from Hamburg to Liverpool, and at the latter port he embarked on the City of Rome, through the medium of which vessel he received transportation to the City of New York. From the national metropolis he continued his journey, by railroad, to Galveston, Texas, and for several years thereafter he was employed in a cotton gin at Paige, Bastrop County. He then devoted a year to independent operations as a farmer near the little Village of Hill's Prairie, that county, and he then found employment in a cotton gin near Eagle Lake, Colorado County. In 1899 Mr. Reinsch made permanent location in the

Village of Winchester, where he established a blacksmith shop. For several years thereafter he gave his attention to general blacksmith work, but in 1905 he engaged also in the general merchandise business, the expansion of which justified his erection of his excellent brick store building a few years later. His blacksmith shop now includes an excellent equipment for general machine and repair work, and not only does he give close attention to all departments of his business enterprise at Winchester but he is also the owner of a good farm, in the improving of which property he was effectively assisted by his wife and children, especially in the initial period when all took part in the removal of the setting of Johnson grass, with which the place had been liberally supplied. It will be seen from this statement that practical industry is essentially a family trait and that Mr. Reinsch has found able coadjutors in the members of his own household. In politics Mr. Reinsch gives support to the cause of the democratic party but has had no ambition for political office, though he has served as a member of election boards and is loyal and progressive as a citizen. He and his family hold to the faith of the Lutheran Church.

On the 18th of July, 1889, in Fayette County, was solemnized the marriage of Mr. Reinsch to Miss Anna Lowke, a daughter of Andreas and Henrietta (Deurlich) Lowke, who immigrated from Saxony, Germany and established their home in Texas in 1883. Mr. Lowke became a prosperous farmer in Fayette County, and his widow now maintains her residence in the Village of Winchester. Of their children it may be recorded that John is a resident of Vernon, Wilbarger County; Mary is the wife of John Grescher, of Winchester; Anna, who was born September 8, 1870, is the wife of Mr. Reinsch of this review; Lydia is the wife of Charles Grescher, of Houston; and Ernst is a blacksmith and machinist at Vernon, this state.

Mr. and Mrs. Reinsch have eight children, namely: Rachel, Esther, Hermann, Carl, Louise, Max, Martin and Leon. Rachel is the wife of Lucas Hart, of Winchester, and they have one child, Evelyn. Esther is a clerical assistant in her father's well equipped mercantile establishment. Hermann is employed in the blacksmith and machine shops of his uncles, the Lowke Brothers, at Vernon. Carl is his father's assistant in the blacksmith and machine shop. Louise is still attending school and assists at times in the store of her father.

John G. Guenther, M. D. Success is the ultimate criterion of ability in the medical profession, and guaged by this standard Doctor Guenther is fully entitled to designation as one of the representative physicians and surgeons of Lavaca County, where he is engaged in active general practice in the thriving Town of Moulton. Aside from his well earned professional prestige he is further entitled to consideration in this publication by reason of being a native son of the Lone Star State and a representative of one of the sterling and honored families that was here founded more than forty years ago. He is known as a physician of high attainments and is the dean of his profession in the Moulton community—a man of sturdy loyalty in all of the relations of life and one who commands unequivocal popular confidence and esteem.

Doctor Guenther was born at Schulenburg, Fayette County, Texas, on the 12th of May, 1872, and is a son of Franz and Magdalena (Seidenberger) Guenther, who still maintain their home at Schulenburg, where the father is engaged in the bottling of carbonated waters and is a citizen of prominence and influence.

Franz Guenther was born in the Town of Deutsch Jasnik, in the Province of Moravia, Austria, in which locality his ancestors settled more than a century ago, their emigration from their native Germany having been prompted by their desire to escape after the ravages of an epidemic or plague that was there raging at the time, the original home of the family having been in the Rhine country of Germany. In Austria representatives of the name in the various generations were found prominently identified with the agricultural and milling industries, and Joseph Guenther, grandfather of the doctor was long and prominently associated with what was perhaps the largest flour-milling enterprise in Austria, both he and his wife, who bore the maiden name of Magdalena Seidenberger, the same as that of the noble young woman who later became the wife of his youngest son, continued their residence in Moravia until the time of their death. Of their children, Franz, father of Doctor Guenther of this review, is the youngest; Joseph was for many years a resident of the City of St. Louis, Missouri, and late in life he came with his family to Texas, where he continued to reside until his death; John came to this state in 1867 and for many years was a prominent citizen of Weimar, Colorado County, where his death occurred and where he left a family of several children; Henry died in Austria and has no posterity; Rosina became the wife of Franz Stanzel and they were numbered among the pioneer settlers of Schulenburg, Texas, where she died in 1914, at the venerable age of eighty-six years; Elizabeth, the wife of Franz Brossmann, died at Schulenburg, in 1913, at the age of seventy-six years.

Franz Guenther was reared and educated in his native land and in his youth followed the miller's trade, though he subsequently served a thorough apprenticeship to the carpenter's trade and became a skilled artisan. He became a successful bridge contractor in Austria and had the supervision of the construction of many important railway bridges in that empire. There was solemnized his marriage to Miss Magdalena Seidenberger, and upon their immigration to America they were accompanied by their two children—Prof. F. P., who is one of the prominent and honored figures in educational circles in Texas and who now holds the professorship of German and history in the Northwestern Texas State Normal School, at Canyon; and Louisa, who is the wife of Henry Jeterka, of Schulenburg, this state. Upon coming to Texas, in 1871, Franz Guenther established his residence at Schulenburg, where he and his wife have since continued to maintain their home, and where all of their children were born except the two already mentioned. Concerning the American-born children the following brief record is entered: Dr. John G. is the immediate subject of this review; Ludmilla is the wife of Henry Friederich, of Schulenburg; Miss Theresa is a trained nurse and holds a position in the hospital at Moulton; Anna is the wife of Joseph Winkler, of Lockhart, Caldwell County; Doctor Frank is engaged in the practice of medicine at Moulton; Tillie is a popular teacher in the Moulton High School; and Charles, who was the second in order of birth, was a representative member of the bar of Travis County at the time of his death, which occurred at Moulton, in 1914. Charles Guenther was a man of distinctive intellectuality and fine professional ability, was a talented musician, and his wanderlust led him to travel extensively in all parts of the world prior to his engaging in the practice of law at Moulton. He was a bachelor.

Dr. John G. Guenther acquired his early education in the public schools of Schulenburg and his higher academic education was gained in the University of Texas. For one year he was engaged in teaching at Yorktown and a second year found him similarly employed at Moulton. In the medical department of the University of Texas, a department established in the City of Galveston, he was graduated as a member of the class of 1897, his reception of his degree of Doctor of Medicine having occurred on May 16th of that year. He forthwith established his residence and professional headquarters at Moulton and he has not only achieved unqualified success in the general practice of medicine and surgery but has also shown his humanitarian spirit and civic enterprise by establishing the Moulton Hospital, which was founded by him in 1913 and of which he has since continued the executive head. This institution, with excellent modern equipment and facilities, has proved of inestimable benefit and value to the local community and its advantages have been utilized by patients from a wide area of surrounding country. The doctor is actively identified with the American Medical Association, the Texas State Medical Society, and the Lavaca County Medical Society, which last mentioned organization he has effectively represented in the State Medical Society, besides which he has served as county censor of Lavaca County. He is one of the oldest members of the Moulton camp of the Woodmen of the World and also of the Hermann Sohns, which latter fraternal organization he has represented in the grand lodge of the state.

At Cuero, Dewitt County, on the 26th of December, 1900, was solemnized the marriage of Doctor Guenther to Miss Justina Kossbiel, a daughter of Charles and Helena (Moll) Kossbiel, who came to America from Cologne, Germany, and who became the parents of two sons and nine daughters. Doctor and Mrs. Guenther have three children—John C., Leo, and Marion.

Hugh F. Little. A prominent and popular exponent of the agricultural and live-stock industries in Fayette County, Mr. Little maintains his residence in the Winchester community of Fayette County and is well upholding the prestige of a family name that has been identified with Texas history since the early period when the now opulent commonwealth was still under the Dominion of Mexico. William Little, grandfather of him whose name initiates this paragraph, came from Tennessee and settled in Texas as a member of the American Colony founded by Stephen F. Austin, in the early '30s, and he obtained as his headright a league of land in what is now Fort Bend County. He endured the full tension of hardships and perils incidental to life on the frontier and did his part in furthering the cause of Texas independence. His marriage was solemnized in Texas, and here he and his wife passed the remainder of their lives. Among their children were John, Walter, William, Mrs. James Jones, of Fort Bend County, and George, of Columbus, this state, the two last mentioned being now the only survivors of the children of these sterling pioneers. It will thus be seen that the family of which the subject of this sketch is a scion of the third generation in Texas was one of the first to become identified with the settlement and development of the Lone Star Commonwealth.

Hugh F. Little was born at LaGrange, the judicial center of Fayette County, Texas, on the 30th of September, 1861, and is a son of Walter and Sarah (Wilson) Little. Walter Little was born on his father's extensive landed estate, twenty miles above Richmond, in Fort Bend County, Texas, in October, 1830, and he passed the last ten years of his life at Eagle Lake, Colorado County, where his death occurred on the 4th of March, 1913. He passed his early manhood as a cattle man in Colorado and Fort Bend counties, and prior to the Civil war he removed to LaGrange. During the progress of the war he was identified with the Government freighting operations between Texas points and Mexico, and this was the medium through which he served the Confederate government. After the war he removed to the district east of LaGrange, but several years later he returned to the county seat. He served for a number of years as a member of the Board of County Commissioners of Fayette County, and his services were frequently in requisition in the work of surveying, for which he had become well qualified. He did much speculating in lands in Fayette County, and represented the Vail-Evans heirs as agent for their extensive landed estate in Fayette and other counties of Texas. Walter Little was a man of well disciplined mind, broad information and special mathematical ability, and his life was guided and governed by the highest principles of integrity. Such was his natural reserve that he had no desire to enter the area of practical politics or to assume leadership in public affairs, the only public office of which he consented to become the incumbent having been that of county commissioner. He was reared in the faith of the Catholic Church but in the later years of his life he formed a definite religious affiliation with the Methodist Episcopal Church, South. In the Masonic fraternity he was raised to the degree of Master Mason, and he was a loyal and worthy citizen who ever commanded unqualified popular confidence and esteem. He had in the early days broad and varied experience in frontier life and was known as a fine pistol shot. In his younger life he drove cattle through to army posts in Northwestern Texas and incidentally had occasion to pass numerous Indian camps and to encounter at times the danger of attack by marauding bands of the Indians. Throughout his life he was aligned as a stalwart supporter of the principles of the democratic party.

As a young man Walter Little wedded Miss Sarah Wilson, daughter of Doctor Wilson, who came from Virginia to Texas and settled in Colorado County, where he passed the remainder of his life. Of the other children of Doctor Wilson it may be noted that Norval is a resident of Alleyton, Colorado County; Virginia became the wife of Vincent Allen and her death occurred in Colorado County; and Robert met his death in battle, while serving as a soldier of the Confederacy in the Civil war. Of the children of Walter and Sarah (Wilson) Little, Hugh F., of this sketch, is the eldest, and Mary is the wife of Edward McRea, of Eagle Lake, Colorado County. The first wife of Walter Little died in 1869, and he later married Maggie Laird, their children being Nellie, who is the wife of Walter Strickland, of Eagle Lake; Walter, who is associated with the Frank Stephens Company at that place; and Sam who is serving in 1915 as postmaster at Eagle Lake.

The public schools of LaGrange afforded to Hugh F. Little his early educational advantages, and when but a boy he initiated his business career by assuming charge of a bunch of cattle, of which he became the owner. By the time he had attained to his legal majority he had gained a substantial start in the cattle business. He first grazed his cattle on the old-time open range in Fayette County, and within a short time after becoming of age he engaged in the meat market business at LaGrange. Two years thereafter he disposed of his market and business and in the autumn which marked the construction of the railroad through the Winchester district of his native county he established his residence in the ambitious Village of Winchester, where he erected a business building and where for two years he was associated with William Loud in the retail liquor trade. He then purchased his partner's interest, and his association with this line of enterprise continued for an aggregate period of eighteen years. In the meanwhile he had continued to a certain extent his identification with the cattle business, and after his retirement from the liquor trade he engaged in the live stock commission business in the City of Fort Worth, as a member of the Flato Commission Company. After an experience of eighteen months he retired from this business and returned to LaGrange, where he again began handling cattle, in association with Mr. Juergens. In 1911 he returned to Winchester, and he has since found ample demands upon his time and attention in connection with his successful operations as a farmer and in the raising and handling of live stock. In politics he is arrayed as a loyal supporter of the cause of the democratic party, he is affiliated with the Independent Order of Odd Fellows, and he and his family hold to the faith of the Methodist Episcopal Church, South.

On the 4th of February, 1885, in Fayette County, was solemnized the marriage of Mr. Little to Miss Elizabeth Walker, a daughter of John Z. and Shields (Saunders) Walker, both of whom were residents of LaGrange at the time of their death. Mr. Walker came from Maryland to Texas, but Robert D. Saunders, maternal grandfather of Mrs. Little, was numbered among the pioneer settlers of the Lone Star State. John Z. Walker came from Mardela Springs, Maryland, his father, John Walker, having been a prosperous farmer of that state. Mr. Walker not only became a successful farmer in Texas but also worked at his trade, that of carpenter. He was a valiant soldier of the Confederacy in the Civil war, as a member of a Texas regiment. He and his wife became the parents of seven children: Ella married J. P. Wroe, of Houston; Elizabeth is the wife of Mr. Little, of this review; John Walter resides at Winchester; Mrs. Kate Joyner likewise maintains her home at Winchester; W. Alexander resides in the City of Houston; Margaret wedded William Caldwell, of La Grange; and Robert resides in the City of St. Louis, Missouri. Mr. and Mrs. Little have no children.

HON. JOHN COLEMAN JONES. For many years John Coleman Jones has been a distinctive figure in Texas life. A fitting honor was bestowed upon him in January, 1915, when Governor Ferguson appointed him to the position of commissioner of pensions of the State of Texas. No one could be better qualified than Colonel Jones for the responsibilities of such an office. He has been administering its duties since January 21, 1915. While his home for a great many years has been in Burleson County, he now has his temporary residence at Austin, his offices being in the State Capitol. Being a thoroughgoing business man, it is needless to say that Colonel Jones has rendered an inestimable service to his state as commissioner of pensions. Through his office are distributed large sums of money in the form of pensions to the deserving veterans of the Confederate army.

While Colonel Jones was not a soldier himself, being only eleven years old when the war broke out, he lived in the midst of the war's alarms, had four brothers in the army, and is one of the few persons now living who have something in the way of personal reminiscence to contribute to that memorable chapter in the nation's history which is concerned with the killing of Abraham Lincoln by John Wilkes Booth. Not long ago Colonel Jones wrote one of the most interesting articles that has ever appeared descriptive of the capture and killing of Booth, and from this article, which appeared in the Dallas News in December, 1915, some quotation should be made, not only to give permanent record to his story but also because it describes some of his own early environments.

"It was in April, 1865, that the news of Lee's surrender came to our home. Three brothers were with him, the fourth a prisoner in Elmira, New York. We were anxious about them, having had no tidings since the retreat from Petersburg. I was a mere boy, but this narrative so fastened itself on my mind that time can never efface. My old father would go on the porch every morning after the Lee surrender and look

J. C. Jones

up the lane to the gate opening to the public road with anxious longings for his boys. The morning of April 11 about 9 o'clock, someone came through the gate. It was too far to recognize but after he approached nearer my father with tear-stained eyes caught a glimpse of his boy coming from Appomattox. I shall never forget that anxious look from my dear old father when the embrace took place on the green sward at old Locust Grove in Caroline county, Virginia. The next day my other two brothers came home from Appomattox. The devastation of war had laid waste my father's fortune. Horses, mules, cattle, sheep, hogs and even chickens had been swept from our home; all the slaves had been forced to leave and march away to Washington City. Seated around the dining table on the morning of the 12th my father said: 'I have lost all my property, but I am thankful to God that my boys have been spared and this joy and pleasure to me makes the loss of material property pale into insignificance.' He arranged to turn over the thousand acre farm to the boys and devise means to repair the lost fortune."

Then Colonel Jones recalls the fact connected with the assassination of Lincoln, and how Booth, after his escape from Washington finally arrived at the home of Henry Garrett, which was only a few miles from the Jones homestead. The entire country was in a turmoil since Federal troops were scurrying hither and thither searching for the fugitives, but when Booth and his companion arrived Mr. Garrett, who was old and feeble, reluctantly consented that they should spend the night in his tobacco barn, thinking that they were Confederate soldiers on their way home. A little later Garrett's two sons reached home and were informed by their father about the two men asleep in the barn. The sons, fearing that the guests might steal away in the night with the two fine horses kept in the barn, went out and securely locked the door where Booth and his companion had gone for the night. From this point the narrative of Colonel Jones should be continued in his own words:

"In the meantime the posse headed by Sergeant Corbit, continued their journey to Bowling Green. They arrived there about 8 P. M. They made inquiries about Mr. Jett, learning he had put up at the hotel, and learning too at Port Royal that he had piloted those men across the river. Sergeant Corbit repaired immediately to the room of Mr. Jett at the hotel, aroused him with two pistols drawn, and told him he had but a few moments to live unless he told where those men were whom he had piloted across the Rappahannock River at Port Royal. Mr. Jett stated that he did not know but thought they had turned up the road toward Henry Garrett's home. He was ordered to get his horse and go with them to Mr. Garrett's. Arriving there about 9:30 p. m. Sergeant Corbit entered the Garrett home, dragged old Mr. Garrett from his bed, and told him he had only five minutes to tell where he had secreted those men who had come there for their lodging. Old Mr. Garrett was dazed and could not speak. In the meantime the sons, who were sleeping upstairs, heard the melee and came down in their father's room all excited and wanted to know the meaning. Corbit stated that they had but a few minutes to tell where they had those two men secreted. The sons said they were in the tobacco barn, and come and they would show him.

"On arriving at the barn, sentinels were stationed around it, and an order from Corbit was given for Booth and Harrold to surrender. Booth replied in the negative and stated he would fight the posse at forty paces. Corbit replied: 'We will take no chances, and unless you surrender we will fire the barn.' Booth said let her burn. At this juncture Harrold surrendered leaving with Booth his carbine and two pistols, Booth still refusing to surrender. A match was put to some straw and fodder through a crack in the barn, which was soon ablaze, and Booth was easily seen lying on a pile of straw. Corbit seeing that he would burn rather than surrender, ripped a plank from the barn and shot Booth and ran in and dragged him out from the burning building and took him in a dying condition to the porch of Mr. Garrett's home, where he expired in a short time. Just before he expired Miss Lucinda Holloway, a sister-in-law of Mr. Garrett, came on the porch on hearing the death groans of Booth and asked Sergeant Corbit to let her sit on the floor and hold the head of the dying man so that he might die easy. Corbit consented and just as he expired she took from her apron pocket a pair of scissors and cut from his head a lock of his hair, thinking that his mother or father if living or some relative would love to have it as a memento."

In telling this story Colonel Jones says that what he did not witness was told him by Willie Garrett, a schoolmate, and Miss Lucinda Holloway, his old and loved teacher. He of course witnessed the burning barn, and was at the Garrett home the morning following.

John Coleman Jones was born in 1850, and as already stated his birth occurred in Caroline County, Virginia. His parents were William I. and Sarah (Wharton) Jones, both members of old families in Virginia, where their ancestors settled in the earliest colonial days. On the paternal side they are of Welsh origin and were among the original settlers about old Jamestown. In ante-bellum days the members of the Jones family were on intimate terms with the Lees and other noted families of the time, and Fredericksburg, the scene of one of the greatest battles of the war, was not far distant. It was in such environment that Colonel Jones grew to manhood and the associations of his early childhood could not but enforce and train a vigorous character.

It was in 1873 that he came to Texas and located in Burleson County. For a time he worked on a farm in the same neighborhood where he has lived for more than forty years and where he now owns a fine place of 300 acres, located seven miles northeast of Caldwell, the county seat of Burleson County, on San Antonio Prairie. Colonel Jones for a great many years has been a successful general farmer and stock raiser, and by his own work has set an example for progressive agriculture in that section of the state. In fact he is quite widely known as "Farmer Jones," and in agriculture has found not only the opportunities to build up his personal fortune but also to serve the best interests of his home state.

At the same time he has always taken an active interest and has participated in public and political affairs in his county and state and it was his widely recognized prominence as well as his own fitness for the duties of his office that caused Governor Ferguson to select him for his present position as commissioner of pensions.

Colonel Jones has four children: Mrs. Bessie Wheaton Collins, Mrs. Civilla Jones Werner. Gabriel Jackson Jones and Miss Helen Jones. Miss Helen, who is a member of the class of 1916 in the University of Texas, has been very prominent in university and social life and was the sponsor for the Texas Division, United Confederate Veterans, at the last general reunion at Richmond.

Frank J. Knesek. The career of this native son of Texas has been marked by earnest and worthy endeavor, and through his own ability and efforts he has made his way forward and achieved definite success, as is manifest in his status as one of the representative business men of the thriving Town of Moulton, Lavaca County, where he has a large and well eqiupped hardware establishment and tinshop, in the conducting of which he is now associated with his only son, under the firm name of F. J. Knesek & Son.

Frank John Knesek, who established his residence at Moulton in 1902, was born on his father's farm, on Ross Prairie, Fayette County, Texas, on the 24th of February, 1862, and he was but four years of age at the time of his father's death, his mother passing to the life eternal when he was a lad of twelve years. His childhood and early youth were passed on the home farm and his rudimentary education was obtained in the rural schools of the locality and period. After the death of his mother he was taken into the home of Doctor Webb, of Flatonia, Fayette County, where he was reared to adult age, attended school for some time and finally served an apprenticeship to the trade of tinsmith, in the establishment and under the direction of George Yeager. He completed his apprenticeship at the age of eighteen years, and for some time thereafter he was not engaged in the work of his trade but was employed as clerk in mercantile establishments, his services in this capacity having been in turn in the employ of William Fortran, J. A. Nickol, and the firm of Harrison & Lane, all of Flatonia. He continued his clerical work for a time at Sweet Home and later at Schulenburg and Hackberry, so that several years elapsed before he again turned his attention to the trade for which he had admirably fitted himself.

His resumption of his trade was in association with Augustus Krook, at Schulenburg, in April, 1886, but after two years he sold his interest in the hardware and tinning establishment and removed to Fayetteville, where he engaged in the same line of enterprise in an individual way. He there remained nearly three years in the control of a prosperous business and was then induced to assume a position as clerk in the general merchandise establishment of the firm of Nehaus Brothers, of Schulenburg. He remained with this firm about eighteen months and then resumed his individual efforts in the hardware business and also conducted in connection a general tin shop. After an interval of about eight years he disposed of his business at Schulenburg and removed to Moulton, in 1902. Here he has developed a substantial and prosperous business as a tinsmith and a hardware merchant, and besides making various improvements upon his store and warehouse, of which he is the owner, he has erected his attractive residence. On the 15th of February, 1915, he admitted his son, Edwin J., to partnership, and the business has since been conducted under the firm name of F. J. Knesek & Son.

As a citizen Mr. Knesek is essentially loyal and public-spirited, and while he has had no desire to enter the arena of practical politics he accords staunch support to the cause of the democratic party, as does also his son. Both he and his wife were reared in the faith of the Catholic Church. He is affiliated with the Bohemian S. P. J. S. T. fraternity, for which he is eligible by birthright.

At Schulenburg, on the 29th of March, 1886, was solemnized the marriage of Mr. Knesek to Miss Johanna Chovanetz, a daughter of John and Apolonia Chovanetz, both natives of Silesia, Austria. John Chovanetz came to Texas in 1866 and established his home in Fayette County, where he became a prosperous farmer and valued citizen. He and his wife became the parents of two sons and three daughters, Mrs. Knesek being the youngest of the daughters and the date of her birth having been March 5, 1860; Bertha is the wife of Antone Knesek; Antonia is the wife of Charles Pustejovsky, of Moulton; Frank is a farmer near Hallettsville, Lavaca County; and Louis is a resident of the City of Houston. Mr. and Mrs. Knesek had five children. Two sons, Frank

William and Alfred August, died in infancy, and the three living children are: Edwin J., who is associated with his father in business, as previously noted, was born January 8, 1887, and in addition to receiving the advantages of the public schools he completed an effective course in the Massey Business College in the City of Houston; Edna is the wife of John Bucek, cashier of the First State Bank of Moulton; and Adela remains at the parental home.

Frank J. Knesek is a son of Albert Knesek, who came to Texas in 1856, a widower with four children. He settled on a pioneer farm near Fayetteville, Fayette County, but later bought a farm near High Hill in the same county, where he passed the residue of his life, his death having occurred in 1866, when the subject of this review was a child of four years. Albert Knesek was born at Frankstadt, Province of Moravia, Austria, where he continued to reside until after the death of his first wife, the four children who accompanied him on his immigration to America having been as here noted: Victoria, who is the wife of Rudolph Brauer, residing near Cuero, Dewitt County; Ferdinand, who died a bachelor, as did also Joseph; and Antone, who is a farmer near Engle, Fayette County. In Fayette County was celebrated the second marriage of Albert Knesek, who there wedded Mrs. Veronica Vanek, who was born in Moravia and who had two children by her first marriage—John, of whom all trace has been lost by other members of the family and who is supposed to be deceased; and Miss Veronica, who resides at Engle, Fayette County. Of the second marriage was born two children, Frank J., of this sketch, being the elder, and Ludwig being a prosperous farmer near Hallettsville, Fayette County.

WILLIAM F. BRIEGER. Senior member of the firm of Brieger & Kasper, which conducts a successful general merchandise business in the Village of Winchester, Mr. Brieger is known as one of the reprentative business men and progressive and public-spirited citizens of Fayette County and is a scion of one of the sterling pioneer families of this section of the Lone Star State. Gottlieb Brieger, grandfather of him whose name initiates this paragraph, was one of the early German colonists in the vicinity of Flatonia, Fayette County, where he developed a productive farm and where he continued his residence for many years, though he passed the closing period of his life at Bastrop, where his remains were laid to rest in the local cemetery. He died about the year 1899, at the venerable age of eighty-two years. He was three times married and reared children by each union. Of the children of the first wife the eldest was Charles, father of the subject of this review; Gottlieb Jr., was a resident of Fayetteville, Fayette County, at the time of his death, and the one daughter married and reared children. Three children were born of the second marriage—Robert, Ernst and Traugot, two of these sons passing their lives near Flatonia, Fayette County, and the other removing to the western part of the state. Two daughters were born of the third marriage.

William F. Brieger was born at Bastrop, the judicial center of the Texas county of the same name, and the date of his nativity was August 9, 1867. He is a son of Charles and Mary (Nink) Brieger, both of whom passed the closing years of their lives at Bastrop, where the former died in 1911 and the latter in 1901. Of their children William F. is the eldest; Albert J. is a resident of Denison, this state; Henry M. resides in the City of Houston; Reinholdt J. died at Taylor, Texas, leaving one child; Richard J., who resides at Bastrop, married Miss Annie Hasler and they have four children; Gustave B. resides at Taylor and he and his wife, Augusta, have four children; and the other three sons likewise maintain their home at Taylor—George D., who married Edna Hall and has two children; Louis, who is a bachelor; and Eugene, who is married but has no children.

Charles Brieger was born in October, 1834, acquired a limited education in the pioneer schools of Texas, learned in his youth the trade of tailor, and at the age of twenty years he settled at Bastrop, where he continued in the work of his trade during the remainder of his active career, save for the period of his valiant service as a Confederate soldier in the Civil war. He enlisted in the company commanded by Captain Petty, and with his gallant Texas regiment took part in many of the engagements marking the progress of the great fratricidal conflict. He served four years, a portion of the time in the command of General Beauregard, was a private in the ranks and was fortunate in having escaped capture or severe wounds. At the time of the war he walked from his home in Bastrop to Little Rock, Arkansas, and in later years he frequently reverted to this as the longest pedestrian tour of his life. He was a staunch democrat, was a communicant of the Lutheran Church, and was affiliated with the United Confederate Veterans. By his first marriage, to Caroline Jung, he had one son, Charles, who married Maria Matthews, their home being at Rockdale, Milam County.

William F. Brieger attended the public schools at Bastrop until he had attained to the age of fourteen years, and this discipline was later supplemented by study in night schools. Under the able direction of his father he served a thorough apprenticeship to the tailor's trade, and after following his trade ten years he finally became identified with the clothing business in his native city. In 1891 he established his residence at Winchester, where he engaged in the general merchandise business, as a member of the firm of Drake & Brieger, which was later succeeded by the present firm of Brieger & Kasper. The firm has a well equipped and appointed store and controls a substantial and representative trade, based upon fair dealing and effective service. In addition to his successful operations as one of the representative merchants of Fayette County Mr. Brieger has achieved prominence as a breeder of pedigreed cattle, with which line of enterprise he has been identified since 1911 and in which he takes specially vital interest. He has the "Flying Fox" strain of cattle, and his herd is descended from "Lady Merton's Rioter," some of whose descendants have become famous and brought phenomenal prices for breeding purposes. Some of the fine cows owned by Mr. Brieger have made records for high productiveness as milkers, with a product of four gallons a day. The herd is established on a well improved farm owned by Mr. Brieger in the vicinity of his home village.

Mr. Brieger is a man of distinctive civic liberality and progressiveness and he has been influential in political and other public affairs in Fayette County. He has assisted materially in the upbuilding of Winchester, where he has erected several houses, his own home being one of the attractive residence properties of the village. A stalwart in the local camp of the democratic party, he is chairman of its precinct committee at Winchester and has been a frequent delegate to its county conventions in Fayette County. He has served as a member of the board of trustees of the public schools of Winchester.

At Winchester, on the 8th of May, 1879, was solemnized the marriage of Mr. Brieger to Miss Minnie Ramsey, daughter of Martin D. Ramsey, an honored pioneer concerning whom specific mention is made on other pages, in the sketch of the life of his son, Alexander, postmaster of Winchester at the time of this writing, in 1915. Mr. and Mrs. Brieger have one daughter, Myrtle, who was educated in the San Antonio Female

College and who remains at the parental home—a popular factor in the representative social activities of the community.

Edwin Goddard Cowdin. It has been in the building up and extending of the Cowdin Grocery Company of Flatonia and its affiliated interests that Mr. Cowdin has expended the best efforts of his years and through which his success as a business man would be best measured. It is all a worthy achievement, and it is not surprising that it represents many years of consecutive endeavor.

Edwin Goddard Cowdin, who has lived at Flatonia since 1878, came to the state from the vicinity of Liberty, Mississippi, where he was born October 25, 1857. That part of his life when he gained his schooling fell in reconstruction days, and for the most part he attended private schools. His first regular enlistment in the army of self-support came at the age of eleven, when he entered the printing shop of the Southern Herald at Liberty, and spent about four years in learning and working at the printer's craft. There followed other employment as bookkeeper with a local store and work in various parts of the state.

It was in company with his mother and family that he came to Flatonia in 1878. His very first work here was as compositor on the Flatonia Argus, after which he did common labor and then began buying hides and wool. As a day laborer he was employed on almost all the brick buildings still standing as the old landmarks of the village. For a few years he was a farm renter near Flatonia, and while he pursued success earnestly he was far from being satisfied.

Finally the New Orleans wholesale grocery house of Zuberbier & Behan sent him on the road as their traveling representative in South Texas. He covered the territory well and built up a good trade during the thirteen years he sold goods for this house. In the same capacity and over the same country he next represented Wallis, Landes & Company of Galveston. When they first established a branch house in Flatonia in 1900 Mr. Cowdin was made manager, and some years later he bought the business and organized the Cowdin Grocery Company, of which he has since been president and manager. This is a wholesale grocery and coffee roasting concern, one of the chief business houses of Flatonia, and with a large connection with the retail trade in that section of the state. In 1914 a branch was established at Giddings, and five men are now employed on the road. Thus as a result of steadily pursued ambition, Mr. Cowdin has pulled himself from the position of day laborer to the head of a business employing a number of men and large assets of capital.

A few years ago he erected the present home of the company, a one-story brick store 50 by 125 feet. In an effort to stimulate local growing of cabbages he established a kraut factory in Flatonia, and this plant has the reputation of making the best kraut in the country, and the output is distributed through the Cowdin Grocery Company. The raw material consumed in this plant is the chief product of the experimental farm which Mr. Cowdin owns near Flatonia. He undertook its operation largely for the purpose of demonstrating to local farmers what amount of produce an acre of ground would yield under intensive cultivation. In one case he sold $54 worth of potatoes from one acre and $68 of cotton from the same ground in the same season. Both crops were growing at the same time. The potatoes were planted first, and in the water furrow he later planted the cotton. Another acre produced 20,000 pounds of cabbage, which was sold for $100, and when these were removed from the ground he planted cotton and secured a pick of half a bale the same year.

Robt. L. Knight

As to politics Mr. Cowdin does not even vote. He was reared in a home of Union sentiments so far as his father was concerned, although the family furnished five sons for the Confederacy. His father was born in County Tipperary, Ireland, and was married at Liberty, Mississippi, to Miss Virginia Poindexter. He died there but his wife died in Flatonia. Their children were: Thomas, who became a physician and died at Tangipahoa, Louisiana, leaving a family; Frank, who died at Liberty, Mississippi; Eugene, a Government specialist in agriculture at Bozier Parish, Louisiana, and the head of a family; Herbert, who married and died at Liberty, Mississippi; Louisa, who died unmarried; Carter, who died at Liberty; and Edwin G.

Mr. Cowdin was married at Moulton, Texas, in August, 1889, to Miss Bettie Thomasson, whose father was Buck Thomasson, a farmer and native of Fayette County, Texas. The three children of Mr. and Mrs. Cowdin are: Miss Lucile, who was educated in the Flatonia High School and graduated from the Denton School of Industrial Arts, now a teacher in the Flatonia schools; Miss Virginia, whose education came from the same sources as her sister's and is also a teacher in the local schools; and Edwin, now five years of age. Mr. Cowdin is a lodge and chapter Mason, a past master of Flatonia lodge, is affiliated with the Knights of Pythias and is a member of the Sons of Hermann.

Robert E. Lee Knight. A prominent Dallas lawyer and public spirited citizen, and a man of large influence in public and political affairs all over North Texas, Robert E. Lee Knight was recently made the recipient of an honor which confers upon him state-wide distinction. In December, 1915, he was elected president of the great Dallas Fair, an institution which as Mr. Knight properly pointed out after his election as president, is only localized and has been fostered and built up in Dallas, but is actually representative not only of the entire Lone Star State but of the Southwest.

It is peculiarly appropriate that this distinction should have come to a native son of Dallas and a representative of one of the oldest and most prominent pioneer families in this section of the state. Mr. Knight is a son of Obediah W. and Serena Caroline (Hughes) Knight. Obediah W. Knight, who died in 1868, was a member of that group of famous pioneers who were the founders of civilization in Dallas County and whose ideals and influence made it what it is, a center of the highest culture and refinement as well as the commercial metropolis of the state. The Knights were a family of wealth and substance, and O. W. Knight owned a large number of slaves in Dallas County before the war, although such were his humanitarian principles that he could never countenance the slave traffic which did so much to corrupt and degrade the institution in the South. He was born in Culpeper County, Virginia, in 1808, and afterwards moved to Bedford County, Tennessee, where he married. In 1846, the year after Texas had taken its place in the Union, he came West and arrived in Dallas County in November, settling in Precinct No. 1, four miles from where the little Town of Dallas was located at the forks of the Trinity. He bought a thousand acres of land, placed the tract under cultivation with his slaves, and the old Knight homestead was the center for some of the most prosperous agricultural enterprise in the county and the home of a large and cultured family. O. W. Knight was the leader of the faction which held out that the county seat should be located at Cedar Springs, close to the Knight homestead, though another faction was successful in establishing the nucleus of the present city four miles south, at what was then regarded as the head of navigation on the Trinity River. O. W. Knight was one of the men most interested in the navigation of the Trinity in the early days, and contributed $500, a large sum for the time, toward the cleaning up of the channel of the river. His progressiveness might be illustrated by many incidents. He introduced the first reaping machine into Dallas County, the first threshing machine, and was first in everything that meant development and progress. He stood firm for church and school, was long active in Methodism, and should especially be remembered for having contributed five acres of land and $300 in gold for the establishment of the Cedar Springs Academy, the first educational institution in Dallas County from which many later prominent men were graduated. The lumber for this schoolhouse was hauled from Louisiana by wagon and team.

Serena Caroline (Hughes) Knight, the mother of R. E. L. Knight, was the second wife of Obediah W. Knight. She died at her home in Dallas April 6, 1914, at the age of ninety-one, a venerable pioneer woman and one of the most notable characters of the county. At the time of her death she was probably the oldest living resident of Dallas County. She was born in Stokes County, North Carolina, September 30, 1822, and when four years of age moved with her parents to Columbia, Maury County, Tennessee, where she was reared and educated and where she married Mr. Knight. Seven of her sisters became residents of Dallas County prior to 1860. Of her three brothers, one of them is Rev. W. H. Hughes, often called "Uncle Buck," who still lives in Dallas, where he located in 1852 and is a noted pioneer Methodist minister. Mrs. Knight embraced Christian religion when quite young and continued an active member of the Methodist Church for more than eighty years. She was a splendid mother and not only reared twelve of her own children, but five stepchildren, and gave a home to five orphan girls and also had an active part in the rearing and training of ten grandchildren. For sixty-eight years her home was in or near the City of Dallas.

Born in Dallas in 1866, Robert E. Lee Knight grew up on the old family homestead north of the city, and was liberally educated and had every opportunity to develop his unusual talents. He was graduated Master of Arts from the Southwestern University of Georgetown in 1886, and in 1888 graduated LL. B. from the University of Texas, this being followed by post-graduate work under the late John B. Minor at the University of Virginia.

Admitted to the Texas bar in January, 1889, he has now been an active member of the Dallas bar for more than a quarter of a century. In 1890 he formed a co-partnership with the late J. L. Harris and still later with Judge N. W. Finley. W. R. Harris later became a partner, making the firm Finley, Knight & Harris, and at the present time the firm is Thompson, Knight, Baker & Harris. Mr. Knight is first and last a lawyer, a man thoroughly grounded in his profession, and has spent many years in the interests of his large clientage. He has been known in a quiet way in local and state democratic circles, but has never sought any office. As an honor and an opportunity to perform a great and lasting service he could not have desired a more substantial distinction than came to him with his election as president of the Dallas State Fair.

Mr. Knight married Miss Ann Armstrong. She was born in Brazos County, Texas, daughter of Cavitt and Ann Armstrong, and represents one of the oldest and most prominent pioneer families in this state, the Armstrongs having located in Texas while it was still a republic. Mr. and Mrs. Knight are the parents of six children: Thomas A., a graduate of Harvard University and of the University of Texas and a member of his father's law firm; Miss Mary Watts Knight, R. E. L.,

Jr., Henry Coke, Marion A. and Richard A. Three of the younger sons were students in the University of Texas during the scholastic year of 1915-16 and many favorable accounts of their work and positions as students have been received. The son, R. E. L., Jr., is a student in Harvard.

John Joseph Maurer. A well known citizen of San Antonio, John Joseph Maurer is to be especially remembered for his valuable work in building up and establishing several of the flourishing Baptist churches of that city. It is noteworthy that he was the first male person baptized in a Baptist church in San Antonio, and for a number of years he was active as a missionary and regular minister of that faith.

He was born in Fayette County near Cistern, March 18, 1873. His Elise (Jacquemart) Maurer. His father, who was born in the Rhine Province of Germany, coming to America when a youth, is now deceased, having for several years lived in San Antonio. The mother, who makes her home with her son in San Antonio, is now past ninety years of age. She was born in Northern France, daughter of a Protestant minister who was sent as a missionary to Montreal, Canada, where Mrs. Maurer lived as a girl.

John Joseph Maurer was about seventeen years old when his parents moved to San Antonio in 1875. After his education he took up the trade of sign painter, and since he gave up regular church work some years ago he has continued employment along that line and has done much of the artistic work found about the city.

He was converted at one of the early Baptist meetings held at San Antonio, and soon afterwards decided to enter the ministry. His conversion and baptism took place in the old First Baptist Church of San Antonio. After finishing the full English Bible course in the Southern Baptist Theological Seminary at Louisville, Kentucky, where he was graduated in 1886, he was ordained at Lawrenceburg, Kentucky, where he entered upon the regular ministry. However, he had begun preaching as early as 1880, and in the early years was the principal missionary of his denomination in San Antonio. It was due to his constructive labors as a preacher that three missions were established which subsequently grew into three flourishing churches, and are now known as the Prospect Hill Church, the Central Church and the Calvary Church. He was pastor of the Sunset, now the Calvary Church, for several years after its organization, and has also been pastor of a number of churches of his denomination at various places in Southwest and West Texas. Some of the towns where he is best remembered as a minister were Cotulla, Hondo City, Marfa and Marathon. While in recent years he has not taken any regular charge as a pastor, he is occasionally called upon to preach, and is one of the best beloved ministers of his denomination in Southwest Texas.

Rev. Mr. Maurer married Miss Ruth Hedger of Lawrenceburg, Kentucky. Their three sons are named Gus L., John J., and Charles W.

Albert Milton Gosch. One of the sterling old German families around Flatonia is represented by Albert M. Gosch, now the efficient incumbent of the office of postmaster at Flatonia. In view of his public position and his influence in local affairs, his personal career has considerable interest.

He was born at Port Huron, Michigan, in 1858, a son of J. J. and education came from the schools at Cistern and Elm Grove, followed by a course in the Walden Business College at Austin. During several years spent on the farm he married, and he soon afterward became mail carrier from Cistern to Flatonia. After four years he resigned, and entered the employ of J. J. Machann, the druggist at Cistern. At the end of two years he bought the business and conducted it until 1911, when he sold out and embarked in the same business at Flatonia, purchasing the J. J. Kotzebue stock. He was popular and successful as a merchant, and the same record has followed him into his position as postmaster.

Of a democratic family, he has been identified with politics in that part since reaching his majority. Since that date in his career he has attended nearly all the county, congressional and state conventions. He helped give Congressman Burgess his first nomination, supported Colquitt in his first aspirations for governor in 1906 and was influential in carrying Fayette County into the column of his supporters. He was a member of the state convention which finally nominated Mr. Colquitt, and also in the one which renamed him. There was hardly any competition when he sought the postmastership, and his name was sent to the Senate by President Wilson with the first twenty-three new postmasters. He succeeded Fred W. Laux.

Postmaster Gosch's father was the late Jacob Gosch, who spent nearly all his active life as a Texas farmer. He was born in Wuertemberg, Germany, April 27, 1834, and while growing up his education was directed with the idea of his becoming a member of the Lutheran ministry. His father, however, was an adherent of the Revolution of 1848, and in consequence the family had to leave Germany. Grandfather Jacob Gosch brought his household out to Texas, and landed at Galveston in the spring of 1851, after eight weeks spent on board a sailing vessel. From Galveston they proceeded to Columbus, spent a year on a farm at Cummings Creek, and then moved to the old Luck farm at Black Jack Springs, on the Lockhart and LaGrange road. Later Grandfather Jacob bought land near Cistern, improved a farm, and died in that locality in 1884 at the age of seventy-seven. His children were: Jacob, father of Albert M.; Christopher H., who spent most of his life in Chihuahua, Mexico, where he and his brother, Jacob, discovered the Torreon mine; Fritz, who also drifted into old Mexico and lived there from 1861, living at Parral; Lena, who married G. W. Michaels of Cistern; and Barbara, who died at Cistern as the wife of Z. H. Henry and was the mother of the county superintendent of schools of Dallas County.

Jacob Gosch, Jr., had spent about ten years in Texas prior to the outbreak of the Civil war. He enlisted at LaGrange in Captain Alexander's company, and was in the service of the South throughout the remainder of the war, entirely within the State of Texas. His command was almost destroyed at Brownsville toward the close of the war, and he then went into Mexico and remained with his brother Christopher until peace was restored. On returning to Texas he resumed his life as a farmer at Cistern, and thenceforward his career was one of quiet uneventfulness. Though a democrat, he took little part in politics, was a member of the Lutheran Church, and his only social connection was as honorary member of the Sons of Hermann. He died February 9, 1915, and his wife, whose maiden name was Mary Beck, a native of Germany, died in 1905. Their children were: Christian H., a farmer near Cistern; Fritz, of the same locality; Henry, also at Cistern; Charles J., who died in youth; William, a farmer in this locality; Albert M.; Monroe, of the old home community; Nancy, who married Joshua Singleton and died near Cistern; Caroline, who died unmarried; Micha, wife of Ernst Harsch of Flatonia; and Lena, wife of C. W. Churchwell of Uvalde.

Mr. A. M. Gosch was married at Cistern December 27, 1896, to Miss Lula Marburger, daughter of James and Mary (Doss) Marburger, a fine old German family of the Cistern locality. There were five sons and five daughters in the Marburger household. The children of Mr. and Mrs. Gosch are: Wilma, Lola, Vastine, James and Leonard.

CONRAD WENTWORTH. It is many years since the era of romance, so far as it concerned the conquest of the wilderness and the fierce battling with the wild tribes for possession, closed in the Far West. About thirty years ago the last great Indian battle occurred. Up to that time service in the United States army in the frontier posts meant adventure, danger, and the exercise not only of the qualities of discipline and fighting efficiency which are instilled into young soldiers as primary qualifications, but also those equally valuable qualities which prevailed among the old time woodsmen and frontiersmen of an earlier age in this country's life.

Surviving from that epoch of national history over which now the glow of romance and legend hangs, is the veteran Conrad Wentworth, who is today probably one of the oldest men still in the active service of the United States army. For a great many years his home has been in San Antonio, and he has been one of the most familiar figures among the military men of that city.

It is said that he possesses probably as many discharges from the United States army as any other man in the country, and in almost every instance across the discharge is written in red ink the words "Re-enlisted today," while his record of service is again and again stated as "excellent." He entered the service of the United States army at the outset of his career, and at the beginning of the Civil war. He spent many years as a scout and Indian hunter in the West, and although now seventy-five years of age and long since entitled to retirement on a pension, like a good soldier he prefers to die with his armor on rather than rust out in the quiet of retirement.

Conrad Wentworth was born in Florida in 1840 and during his infancy his parents removed to Missouri. He grew up in that state and in April, 1861, enlisted in the United States army. Since then he has been in active service with the exception of ten years from 1870 to 1883 when he was employed as a scout, Indian trailer and hunter. Much of his time during the last thirty years has been spent in and about the military post at San Antonio. For sixteen months during the war with Spain in 1898 he was with the army headquarters at Atlanta.

His experiences as a soldier, scout and hunter would fill a volume, and in fact his exploits and personality have been frequently pictured on the printed page. On account of his size, and his daring courage, he was given the sobriquet many years ago of "Little Buckshot," and many years ago the author Ned Buntline made him the hero of a story which ran in a New York fiction weekly under the title "Little Buckshot, the White Whirlwind of the Plains." Little Buckshot was a personal friend and closely associated with many of the western scouts whose names are famous in American annals. Among them was William Hickok, better known as Wild Bill, the noted Kit Carson, and he was a veteran in the service when Buffalo Bill gained his first lessons in the Wild West.

About forty years ago an Englishman, Rose Lambert Price, who had the title of baronet, and was also a major in the British army and a member of a number of learned societies, spent two years in the United States and South America and embodied his experiences in a work known as "The Two Americas." This book was published in 1877 and considerable space is given to the exploits and characteristics of "Little Buckshot" who accompanied Major Price on some of his expeditions in the Far West. One extract gives a pen picture of Mr. Wentworth that can be properly introduced into this brief article:

"We carried tents, had led horses and were guided by the scout and hunter from the post—Conrad Wentworth, better known as 'Little Buckshot.' Buckshot was quite a type of his class and an uncommonly good type into the bargain. Rather under the average height but perfectly formed and wiry as steel, about five-and-thirty, he was just the very cut of man suited to hunt elk, Indian or buffalo, and he knew the tricks of one quite as well as he did the habits of the other. At one time he hunted Indians and at another game, and was pretty successful at both."

One of the most exciting adventures Mr. Wentworth ever had was in the fall of 1869. He was then at Fort Fetterman in Wyoming. A corporal of the post had been killed and the murderer had joined a band of hostile Indians across the Platte River. Mr. Wentworth describes the ensuing incident as follows:

"Captain Egan of K Troop, Second Cavalry, was ordered from Fort Laramie to Fort Fetterman, and after we arrived he told me to take two men and a pack horse and go after the half breed murderer, John Reshaw. Several days later we made camp. That night was very cold and when I got back from a scout around I found that my companions had built a big fire. I told them this fire could be seen for miles and tried to induce them to put it out and move away, but they claimed they knew as much about Indians as I did and would not hear of it. Later on in the night I heard the horses snorting and told the man on watch to go see what was wrong. He came back and reported it was nothing but a coyote, and then crawled under the blanket. Hardly had he gotten settled when hell broke loose, and I never could remember everything that happened. There were shouts, yells, war whoops and shots. One of my men never even groaned and the other after an exclamation fell back, while I blazed away at the closest of the Indians and had the satisfaction of hearing one death yell. Why I wasn't hit I don't know, as we found later that the other men were literally riddled. Somehow I got to where the horses were picketed and there an Indian, thinking I was one of his fellows, addressed me in Sioux. I guess I started to shoot him, but I didn't, just lammed him over the head with my pistol, and he didn't even speak to me. If I had shot him the others would have heard it, and they did hear the horses galloping away and took after them. That gave me a chance and I put as much distance between myself and that place as I could for an hour or so. I was barefooted and the ground was rough and in places covered with cactus and other kinds of thorns, but I had to get back to the post. I wrapped my underwear about my feet but even then, when I got to the post about daybreak, my feet were in such condition that I couldn't walk for three months."

This exciting episode is described in detail by Major Price in his book, and there are many other incidents which are related and in which Little Buckshot figures prominently. With all this wealth of experience behind him it is not strange that Conrad Wentworth is one of the most interesting citizens of San Antonio, and he deserves all the literary monument that can be written with himself as a central figure of the pages.

Smith White Summers. It was a Texan distinguished in the field of invention and the larger affairs of business who died at Dallas, Texas, February 1, 1914. Smith White Summers had for many years been identified with the little community of Sulphur Springs in Hop-

as "Th[illegible]" [illegible] book was published in 1877 [illegible] [illegible] is given to the exploits and characteristics of [illegible] [illegible] accompanied Major Price on some of his exp[illegible] [illegible] W[illegible]. One extract gives a pen picture of Mr. Went[illegible] [illegible] introduced into this brief article:

"[illegible] had led horses and were guided by the sc[illegible] [illegible] post—Conrad Wentworth, better known as [illegible] [illegible] Buckshot was quite a type of his class and an uncomm[illegible] [illegible] to the bargain. Rather under the average height [illegible] [illegible] and wiry as steel, about five-and-thirty, he was just [illegible] suited to hunt elk, Indian or buffalo, and he knew [illegible] quite as well as he did the habits of the other. At one ti[illegible] [illegible] Indians and at another game, and was pretty successful at bo[illegible]

One of the most exciting adventures Mr. Wentworth ever had [illegible] in the fall of 186[illegible] He was then at Fort Fetterman in Wyoming. [illegible] corporal of the post had been killed and the murderer had joined a [illegible] of hostile Indians across the Platte River. Mr. Wentworth d[illegible] the ensuing incident as follows:

"Captain Egan of K Troop, Second Cavalry, was ordered f[illegible] Laramie to Fort Fetterman, and after we arrived he told me to [illegible] men and a pack horse, and go after the half breed murderer, John [illegible] Several days later we made camp. That night was very cold [illegible] I got [illegible] around I found that my companions [illegible] big fire [illegible] fire could be seen for miles and tried [illegible] them [illegible] away, but they claimed they kn[illegible] [illegible] would not hear of it. Later on in [illegible] [illegible] told the man on watch to go see [illegible] w[illegible] reported it was nothing but a coyo[illegible] [illegible] Hardly had he gotten settled [illegible] remember everything th[illegible] [illegible] whoops and shots. One of [illegible] [illegible] after an exclamation fell [illegible] [illegible] the Indians and had the [illegible] [illegible] Why I wasn't hit I don't know, [illegible] [illegible] literally riddled. Somehow I [illegible] [illegible] there an Indian, thinking I [illegible] [illegible] in Sioux. I guess I started to sh[illegible] [illegible] over the head with my pistol. [illegible] [illegible] I had shot him the others would [illegible] [illegible] horses galloping away and took after [illegible] gave [illegible] and I put as much distance between [illegible] place as I could for an hour or so. I was barefooted [illegible] was rough and in places covered with cactus and other [illegible] but I had to get back to the post. I wrapped my und[illegible] feet but even then, when I got to the post about daybreak, [illegible] in such condition that I couldn't walk for three months."

This exciting episode is described in detail by Major Pr[illegible] and there are many other incidents which are related and [illegible] Buckshot figures prominently. With all this wealth [illegible] [illegible] it is not strange that Conrad Wentworth is one of [illegible] [illegible] citizens of San Antonio, and he deserves all the lit[illegible] that can be written with himself as a central figure of th[illegible]

Smith White Summers. It was a Texan disting[illegible] [illegible] invention and the larger affairs of business who [illegible] [illegible]exas, February 1, 1914. Smith White Summers had [illegible] [illegible] identified with the little community of Sulphur Sp[illegible]

kins County, but after his first great success as an inventor he moved to St. Louis, Missouri, and was one of the leaders in mercantile affairs of that city for a number of years. In his later years he gave much study to the perfection of a process for making a superior varnish or lacquer, and the process which he finally brought out is the basis for the Lacquer-All Company, now one of the principal industries of Dallas.

Born in 1849 near Bladon Springs, Choctaw County, Alabama, he was the son of Jesse M. and Marie M. (Dunbar) Summers, both of whom came from North Carolina. It is a matter of interest that the late Mr. Summers' grand-uncle, named William Summers, was one of the martyrs of the Alamo massacre in 1836, and his name appears as such in the official records of the Texas Republic. In an early environment which had nothing to set it off from that which surrounded the majority of Southern boys who were his contemporaries, he was distinguished chiefly for an unusual keenness of mind and active curiosity. Early in his young manhood he came to Texas in the fall of 1871, locating first in Shelby County, where the following year he married Miss Eatha W. Gough. In 1879 he removed to Sulphur Springs, in Hopkins County, where he entered the drug business, and gradually expanded his enterprise to include groceries and dry goods. He built up a very successful business and accumulated a handsome fortune.

It was in the quiet routine of a mercantile experience at Sulphur Springs that Mr. Summers applied his genius to original invention. The most important product of his mind in those years was his automatic coupler and air brake. That was a time when the air brake was still far from perfect, and the automatic coupler was only being gradually introduced. In 1891 he left Sulphur Springs and removed to St. Louis, where he perfected the automatic air brake and car coupler. The Summers patents rendered these appliances well nigh perfect, and he sold them to the Westinghouse Company for a sum approximating a comfortable fortune, and the inventions are now of world wide use under the Westinghouse name and manufacture. In the meantime Mr. Summers became a partner in the Century Dry Goods Company, and established stores in Sapulpa, and elsewhere in Indian Territory. Returning to St. Louis he engaged in the grocery business, and became an important factor in mercantile affairs of large magnitude in that city. He was the leading spirit in the Rosenthal-Sloan Millinery Company, wholesale, and was treasurer of the company. He was also identified with Murray-Carlton, also a wholesale concern, with a wholesale dry goods house and other enterprises. In a few years Mr. Summers, who before had been chiefly known as a quiet and unpretentious merchant in one of the rural counties of Texas, was recognized in St. Louis as an astute and far-seeing man of commercial genius, with more than usual prescience, and was able in every way to hold his own in a great city noted for its brainy, successful business men.

While his home was in St. Louis Mr. Summers continued his investigations as an inventor. He centered his study and efforts upon making a varnish or lacquer that would be superior to all previous materials of the kind. He did much to unearth the secrets of paint making as known to the ancients, and which had become a lost art. He conducted his investigations regardless of time and money, and finally succeeded in producing what is known and manufactured as Lacquer-All, a secret formula and process. Lacquer-All as a varnish is the only material of the kind that has met practically every test to which a varnish might be subjected. It will not craze, check or crack, is waterproof, weather-proof, rust proof, and its qualities in combination make it superior to anything else now in use. Some of the principal qualities of Lacquer-All are quick drying, and when dry leaving a hard durable surface; elasticity and toughness and ability to withstand a high degree of heat, whether from the sun or from fire; resistence to acid, water, weather, and great ranges of temperature; possibility of being applied permanently to many classes of materials, including metals and glass; and the transparency and lüster which make it so valuable for fine cabinet work and furniture. While the base of all the product is the clear Lacquer-All, it is put up in many different forms for as many different uses. There is the clear Lacquer-All, the lacquer-all varnishes, aluminum paint, lacquer-all structural paint and individual make-up for different phases of architectural, woodworking and general manufacturing industries.

In the meantime Mr. Summers had removed his business headquarters from St. Louis to Dallas, became a prominent factor in general merchandise affairs of this city, but eventually perfected arrangements for the establishment of the Lacquer-All Manufacturing Company, which he located at Dallas and in which business he engaged to the time of his death.

The late Mr. Summers was a devout Christian, a member and deacon in the Baptist church, and at the time of his death a fine tribute to his work and character was paid by Rev. Dr. S. A. Hayden of Dallas in the Baptist Progress, and concerning his religious activities Doctor Hayden's words are herewith quoted in this article:

"Having removed to Sulphur Springs in 1879, he at once entered actively into church work, was ordained deacon, and was for several years superintendent of the Baptist Sunday School. In St. Louis he was a member of the Second Baptist church, and later assisted in organizing the Euclid Avenue Baptist church, of which Dr. S. E. Ewing was pastor. Of him the pastor wrote: 'When I think of Euclid Avenue I invariably associate Brother Summers with it.' He has ever been an energetic, wise and generous church worker. He never allowed his prosperity to abate his activity in any church where he has lived. He was by Dr. S. J. Anderson, with whom he was closely associated for over ten years, as Jonathan with David, when they were pastor and deacon, respectively, at Sulphur Springs. This friendship lasted so long as either lived. When Dr. Anderson was founding Burleson College, Brother Summers frequently sent him checks of $250.00 and $500.00 to help, counting it all joy that he could render such assistance. Full of enterprise and resourcefulness, he ever lent the sunshine of his nature to every church purpose. No one ever desponded after he spoke. He always backed his optimism by liberality according to his strength.

"Brother Summers was an affectionate husband, a devoted father, a faithful church member and a loyal citizen. His presence and service in the First Baptist Church of Oak Cliff, in which he died an enthusiastic member, will ever be missed. Few men made as many friends and as few enemies in the span of his life. He died in what ought to have been the zenith of his power, having barely crossed the crest of the mountain slopes toward life's sunset."

By his marriage to Miss Gough, who was born in Choctaw County, Alabama, and is still living, there were six children. The three now deceased are Ina B., Ernest G. and Miss Vera. Those living are: Mrs. Clara H. Bryan of Timpson, Texas; Harry W. and Raymond W., of Dallas.

The remains of the late Mr. Summers were laid to rest at Sulphur Springs with Masonic honors. He was one of the organizers of the lodge there, and always took a very prominent part in Masonic affairs.

He was one of the first seven Masons to take the Shriner's degrees in Texas. He attained the thirty-second degree of Scottish Rite, was a Knight Templar, and was one of the organizers of the Knights Templar Commandery at Greenville, Texas. He was a member of Hella Temple of the Nobles of the Mystic Shrine, and the Shriners jointly with the Sulphur Springs Lodge had charge of the funeral.

Harry W. Summers and Raymond W. Summers, the only two sons of the late Mr. Summers, are both members of the Lacquer-All Company, are interested in both the technical and business features of the industry, and are assiduously and conscientiously carrying out their father's desires and plans.

In the summer of 1915 the Lacquer-All Company was organized in Dallas, and the factory established for the manufacture of the varied products above mentioned on Wall Street near South Lamar. This factory is completely equipped with the necessary machinery, which is now in constant operation, while the goods are finding a steadily increasing sale on the general market. Wherever used the Lacquer-All products have made friends, and even now the business would go forward successfully and with increasing volume on the basis of the reputation made by the output. This gives promise of being one of the greatest industries, not only of the South, but the United States as well, since Lacquer-All had practically revolutionized the varnish business. The company that is manufacturing the Lacquer-All products is a Texas corporation, and is composed of some of the best known and most substantial business men and capitalists of Dallas.

Martin Van Buren Meyer. As a Southern Pacific Railway man, Mr. Meyer's rank is that of the seventh oldest agent on the division between Houston and Del Rio. For a number of years he has been a resident of Flatonia and agent of the Southern Pacific in that city. His connection with the Southern Pacific Road in Texas dates back to 1888, and he not only possesses the efficiency which comes from long discipline in railroad work but also the affability and desire to serve the patrons which give special value to his office.

Martin Van Buren Meyer was born on the Ohio River at Belleview, Kentucky, September, 1867. He comes of a German-French family, his father being a Frenchman, Martin Meyer, born at Passy in the Department of the Seine, and growing up in France and serving as a soldier in the Crimean war in 1853. He was born in 1833, and after his discharge from the French army following the Crimean war he came to the United States, locating in Kentucky. He was married at Newport to Miss Mary Miller, a daughter of Fred Miller, a German Bavarian. Martin Meyer was a skilled mechanic having a long and thorough experience in machine shops and foundries, and had inherited that trade from his father. He was employed in the steel mills in Newport and Covington, later at Aurora, Indiana, and after leaving mill work entered the employ of the Pennsylvania Railway as a blacksmith at Cincinnati, and continued with that company until his retirement. He died in Cincinnati in 1902 while his widow passed away in Norwood, Ohio, in January, 1915. Their children were: Kate, who married W. L. Mersfelder and died in Cincinnati; John, of Cleveland, Ohio; Minnie, who married E. T. Hoppy, of Norwood, Ohio; Martin Van Buren; William L., a telegraph operator of Webster, South Dakota. During the Civil war Martin Meyer, though he had already passed through one experience as a soldier, entered the Union army, in Company K of the First Kentucky Volunteers. His captain was Captain Jones and he went through the war with his regiment and had only a slight wound, which gave him a crooked toe.

Martin Van Buren Meyer received his early education in the public schools of Cincinnati, Ohio, and left school when about fifteen years of age, having mastered the common branches. He soon afterwards took up the study and practice of telegraphy with the Western Union Telegraph Company at Cincinnati, and his first regular position was as an operator with the Pennsylvania Company at Pendleton, Ohio. He worked along the route of that company at different points for a year or so, and then came West. He was with the Missouri Pacific in Kansas, beginning at Kirwin went to St. Louis and became operator at Kirkwood, and finally came south into old Indian Territory as operator at Durant, Oklahoma. He was at several points along that road, Atoka, Eufaula and McAlester, and from Oklahoma came into Texas and joined the service of the Southern Pacific. His first position was as operator at Smith Junction, after which he was in the same service at Rosenberg, and has his first position as agent at Stafford, following which he was at Marion, Waelder, and in 1902 came to Flatonia as agent succeeding R. B. Tanner.

Mr. Meyer has identified himself actively with local affairs at Flatonia, and for a number of years has been a member of the school board. He is a past chancelor of the Flatonia Lodge of Knights of Pythias, and has spent a number of years as deputy grand chancellor of that order. Mr. Meyer was married in Houston, Texas, on March 5, 1890, to Miss Laura Birdsong, who was born in Hockley, Texas. Her father, Dr. G. G. Birdsong, was a native of Mississippi, came to Texas in early life, locating in Waller County, saw active service in the Confederate army, while his last days were spent at Hockley. Doctor Birdsong married Mrs. Wheeler, of Tennessee, who brought him several children by a former marriage, namely: John, of Houston, and Frank, of Wharton, Texas. Mrs. Meyer has one brother, William Birdsong, of Hamilton County, Texas. To the marriage of Mr. and Mrs. Meyer have been born the following children: James, a student in the Agricultural and Mechanical College at Bryan; May, a junior in the University of Texas and a teacher in the public schools; Stella, a junior in the West Texas Normal at San Marcos; Louise, who is taking post-graduate work in the Flatonia public schools and is an assistant teacher; Mildred, Harry, Merwin and Grace, who are still school children.

Hon. Edward H. Lange. It is unusual for the honors of legislative position to fall upon a young man at the outset of his professional career, though in the case of Edward H. Lange, who was chosen at a special election in October, 1915, to represent the eighty-fifth district comprising Bexar County, the choice was exceedingly well bestowed, and it brings into the Thirty-fourth Legislature, which meets in 1915-16, a young lawyer of brilliant qualities and of great promise of usefulness both in his profession and in public affairs. Mr. Lange succeeds as representative from the eighty-fifth district the late B. Schwegmann. His influence, as shadowed forth by his professional interests and his political campaign, is likely to be specially directed toward legislation favoring the establishment and growth of Texas industries. As Texas heretofore has not ranked as a great industrial state, though that feature is now developing rapidly, it is evident that a great field of usefulness is presented for wise and well studied legislation affecting industrial interests.

Born in San Antonio May 14, 1892, the honor of election to the Legislature came to Mr. Lange in his twenty-fourth year, and without doubt he is the youngest member of the thirty-fourth session. He is a son of Bernard J. and Emily (Schiebel) Lange. His father was born in Bastrop County, Texas, in 1861, of German parentage, and has lived in San Antonio since 1886. In 1900 he established the Lange Soap Works, of which he is president, and this is one of the leading manufacturing industries of San Antonio.

Edward H. Lange acquired part of his early education in old St. Mary's College at San Antonio and he also spent nearly three years in the University of Texas at Austin. While in the university he gave most of his time to the regular literary course, but also gained the fundamentals of his legal education there. From Austin he entered the law department of Georgetown University at Washington, District of Columbia, where he was graduated LL. B. in June, 1915. He had also specialized in patent law and was awarded the degree Master of Patent Law. Nowhere are the environment and influences more advantageous for the prospective lawyer than the national capital, and Mr. Lange also acquired some practical experience there as an associate with the law firm of Maddox & Gatley. Returning to San Antonio Mr. Lange took up active practice in the summer of 1915, and has since handled cases in all the courts. As a solicitor in patent and copyright causes he occupies a new field in Southwest Texas, but with the rapid growth of industrial enterprises there is great opportunity for the trained and competent patent lawyer.

EDWARD LINDEMANN. Few of the early German families of Austin County antedate that bearing the name of Lindemann, of which a worthy representative at Industry is found in the person of Edward Lindemann, head of the firm of E. Lindemann & Son, vice president of the Guaranty State Bank of Industry, and a citizen who has contributed in full measure to the needs of his community and its growth and development. This family was established in Austin County in 1854, its founder being August Lindemann, now an aged resident of the community of Rock House, where he settled upon coming to Texas.

August Lindemann was born in a district known in German as Hertzogtum, Wittenberg, Germany, and belonged to a family which followed the custom of bauerngut, in which the eldest son succeeds to the family estate. August Lindemann's mother belonged to the Straach family, and was the mother of six sons and two daughters, those of them coming to America being: August, the father of Edward Lindemann; Andrew, whose death occurred at Bartlett, Texas; Johanna, who married Gottfried Boencke, and died at Hallettsville, Texas, with three children; Christina, who became the wife of Andrew Hirtze, and died near Burton, Texas; and Fredericka, who married August Wilke, and died at Welcome, Texas.

August Lindemann was born February 13, 1833, and in his youth worked faithfully on his father's farm and secured such educational advantages as were granted to one of his station. He came to the United States like many others of his countrymen, for the reason that opportunities were far better and more numerous than in his native land, and sailed from Bremen on a sailing vessel, duly landing at Galveston, Texas, after a more or less eventful voyage of nine weeks. The little party of which he was a member came out to Rock House in an ox team from Houston, and Mr. Lindemann here purchased a tract of virgin soil, which he began to cultivate during the following year. Until he was ready to settle on his own property he worked for wages, with native thrift and industry, and when all was ready for the establishment of his home he was married in that locality. Mr. Lindemann made that spot of ground his home as long as he was engaged in active pursuits, passed his active career as a cotton and corn grower, and increased his land holdings, as his finances permitted, until he owned, perhaps, a half-section.

Prior to the coming on of the Civil war, August Lindemann had taken out his citizenship papers, and when the trouble between the North and the South came to a head he did not seem to favor the cause of secession, as he did not volunteer in the Confederate service. However, he was later conscripted and served on the coast of Texas, in Wall's Legion, first in the military and later as a teamster engaged in the freighting of supplies out to the Rio Grande country. After the war he returned to the farm and took up the duties of his pastoral pursuits. In his political activities, August Lindemann voted the republican ticket, but he never sought nor cared for public office of any kind. From the time of his arrival in Texas he was a member of the Methodist Church, and during the active period of his life served in the capacity of steward.

Mr. Lindemann married Miss Fredericka Straach, who was born in August, 1833, in the same community as her husband, a daughter of Gottlieb Straach. To this union there were born the following children: Alwina, who is the wife of Henry Baeke, who is engaged in farming near Rock House, Texas; August, a well-known resident and successful farmer of Gonzales County; Edward, whose name heads this review; Charley, who is engaged in farming in the community of Rock House; William, who is engaged in merchandising in the vicinity of Cost, Texas; Minna, who is the wife of August Baeke, of Gonzales County; Otto, who occupies the old family estate at Rock House, where he is engaged in farming; and Willibald, who is his brother William's partner in business at Cost.

Edward Lindemann was born at Rock House, Texas, May 18, 1859, and there passed his boyhood and youth, his education being secured in the district schools. He remained under the parental roof and assisted his father in agricultural pursuits until reaching the age of twenty-four years, at which time, because of bodily ailments, he decided to enter mercantile lines. Accordingly, he came to Industry and established himself in business almost on the exact location of his present store, his business here being a modest one, as his stock of goods did not exceed $3,000 in value. Mr. Lindemann succeeded in business F. Holtze, who was the founder of the store at this location, and in connection with the place of business there are forty-seven acres of land, in addition to which a farm near Industry belongs to the Lindemann family at this time. Mr. Lindemann's expectations during the first year were well met, the business attracting a large and growing trade from all over the countryside, and after 2½ years he purchased the interest of his partner, Franz Getschmann. About that time he took in his brother, William, and the firm then became E. & W. Lindemann and continued as such until 1908, when his brother retired and Mr. Lindemann admitted his son, Edward H., to partnership, when the style became as at present, E. Lindemann & Son.

Mr. Lindemann aided in the organization of the Guaranty State Bank of Industry, the first bank Industry has had and which has continued to be the only organization here, a very successful enterprise of which he is a stockholder and the first vice president, as well as a member of the board of directors. He stands high among business men of Austin County, where his associates have the utmost confidence in his foresight, judgment and absolute integrity. Mr. Lindemann's religious connection is with the Methodist Church, and at the present time he is one of the stewards of the Industry congregation. In politics he has

O. P. Bowser

seen fit to give his support to the republican party, but has never devoted any time to the promotion of party affairs. He is not interested in lodge work. As a builder of Industry, he has done all the substantial improvements connected with his business, and has erected his own residence as well as the building in which his enterprise is located.

Mr. Lindemann was married in Austin County, Texas, January 9, 1883, to Miss Julia Fisches, a daughter of Fritz and Julia (Specht) Fisches, the former from Württemberg and the latter from Baden, Germany. They came to America and to Texas prior to the outbreak of the Civil war, passed their lives in the peaceful pursuits of the soil, and reared a family of eighteen children, only seven of whom came to mature years, they being: Fritz, born October 28, 1859; Mrs. Lindemann, born September 16, 1861; Augusta, born in 1863, who became the wife of Charley Lindemann; Hermina, born in 1865, who became the wife of William Moeller; William, born in 1874, and now a resident of Industry; Ida, born in 1876, who became the wife of Emil Moeller; and Betty, who was born in 1880, and is the wife of W. O. Moers.

To Mr. and Mrs. Lindemann there have been born two sons: Edward H., who is his father's partner in the business at Industry, married Minna Graeter, and has three children, Marvin, Olivia and Reuben; and Monroe, also in the business, married Ella Ott and has two sons, Milton and Elbert.

Col. Oliver P. Bowser. A city becomes really great only in one way—through its men of light and leading, whose lives enter into the warp of the municipal fabric and whose loyalty and influence extend like shining threads across the pattern of civic greatness.

When Col. Oliver P. Bowser died suddenly at his home in Dallas December 14, 1915, one prominent citizen, a friend of his, spoke of him as one of the last old timers who had found Dallas a mud hole and left it a city. In fact, he worked shoulder to shoulder not only with those who upreared a city at the original forks of the Trinity, particularly after the first railroad came to this point, but also with that generation of Dallas men of a later day who enjoyed some of the fruition of the early pioneers and who enlarged the foundations and framework of the city structure.

He is one of the men whose lives can be best interpreted through the city which was his home for so many years. A suggestive outline of his own career is all that can be attempted at this place. He was born March 21, 1842, near Dayton, Ohio, and was seventy-three years of age when he died. His parents were David and Mary A. Bowser and his ancestors were Virginia people originally, while his mother's family, the Bookwalters, were of Pennsylvania. In 1849, when Colonel Bowser was seven years of age, his parents removed to Central Illinois, and remained there for seven years. He was accordingly fourteen when he accompanied them to Texas and located in Dallas County in 1856, five years before the outbreak of the war and when Dallas was isolated from all the outside world by a radius of sparsely settled or wilderness country extending in every direction for several hundred miles.

Reared on a farm, he had the strength and rugged constitution of a country bred man. In 1861, at the age of nineteen, he enlisted as a private in Company E of the Eighteenth Texas Cavalry under Capt. W. M. Allison and in General Granbury's brigade. He was captured at the surrender of Arkansas Post, and was held in prison for some months at Camp Douglas, Chicago, but was exchanged at Petersburg, Virginia, in 1863. He was wounded on the first day of the fighting at Chickamauga, but recovered within six months and rejoined his company at Atlanta, being promoted to lieutenant. After the fall of Atlanta he was with Hood in the Tennessee campaign, and participated in the battles of Franklin and Nashville. At the close of the war he returned to Dallas County without a dollar in his pocket and helped his father re-establish the farm. For about three years he farmed independently near Reinhardt, five miles northeast of Dallas. Somewhat later, early in the '70s, he took a large contract for the furnishing of ties for the construction of the Texas and Pacific Railway into Dallas and west from that city.

It was soon after Dallas realized one of its early dreams and became a railway terminal that Colonel Bowser became associated with the late Capt. W. H. Lemmon in the old firm of Bowser & Lemmon, whose activities should always be recorded as an important part of the commercial history of early Dallas. This was one of the original pioneer firms in the implement business at Dallas, a business which as developed in later years has made Dallas the second largest market for implements in the United States, and there is more money invested in that than in any other business or industry in the city. This firm started out with a modest capital in 1873, and continued it successfully until about the middle of the decade of the '80s.

In the meantime the firm had acquired such valuable resources in lands and lots in Dallas that they retired from the implement business in order to devote all their attention to the development of real estate. It was the firm of Bowser & Lemmon that promoted and developed that beautiful section of the city known as Oak Lawn, where Lemmon Avenue and Bowser Avenue were named in their honor. They spent thousands of dollars in improvements, building sidewalks, pavements, laying sewers, and in other ways, and made of Oak Lawn an ideal residence section which has subsequently been built up with some of the most beautiful and costly residences of the city.

It would be impossible to estimate the total of the many thousands of dollars which Colonel Bowser gave at different times and in different ways in behalf of a greater Dallas. He assisted in getting railroads, interurban, factories and good roads. He was one of the big men of his day and age, practical, progressive, constructive, and the usefulness of such a character and life can hardly be underestimated. As a business man and citizen he associated with the best and greatest of his home city, was a close friend of many of the men of wealth and prominence, though it was a characteristic of his that he never hesitated to take up the cause of the underdog.

While essentially a business man, he also had a public career in addition to his service as a soldier during the war. For three years he was a deputy under Sheriff J. M. Brown, served a term in the lower house of the Legislature and in 1892 was elected state senator and served one four-year term and two two-year terms. Following that he was again elected a representative. While in the Legislature he became the author of the Dallas County Road Law, the County Auditor Law, and the Texas Home Insurance measure; assisted in passing the Fee Bill, most of the local option laws on the statute books of the state, the law providing for teaching in the public schools the effects of alcohol and narcotics on the human system; but above all else he gave his time and influence while in the Legislature to state finances and to the promotion of Texas educational interests.

One of his associates in the Senate was Gen. M. M. Crane, who after the death of Colonel Bowser spoke the following tribute: "Mr. Bowser was a good roads advocate and knew how to educate the public to the need of better public highways. He encouraged the building of factories and had an intelligent view of the proper way to encourage factory building. He was always ready to work for the promotion of general good and he held the respect and confidence of all his associates."

He is especially to be remembered for his work in behalf of good roads, and he was a pioneer advocate of that development. He believed in home industry, and he gave money and time to promote factory establishments particularly in Dallas. He helped organize and for three years served as president of the State Good Roads Association, and helped organize the first State Manufacturers Association, serving as its president for the first two years. For three years he was president of the Dallas Commercial Club and held active membership in that body fifteen years. Though he did so much for Dallas, he could never be drawn into municipal politics, declining many honors of that kind, and twice being nominated for mayor over his strenuous protest. He was a member of the Christian Church, and his membership was with the East Dallas Christian Church.

In July, 1866, Colonel Bowser married Virginia L. Murray, who survives him. There is also one son, David Watt Bowser, who was born and reared in Dallas County, and since his admission to the bar in 1896, has become a prominent Dallas lawyer.

Above all his material accomplishments there stood pre-eminent his splendid personal character. One of his old friends and long time associates said of him: "He was one of the finest men that I have ever known and one of the finest citizens that Dallas ever had. He has always been one of the foremost in the upbuilding of Dallas' material, spiritual and financial prosperity." Another tribute was this: "He was one of the first men to agitate organization for a movement of manufacturing in the state. He always voted on the right side of every worthy movement that I can remember while he was in the senate." Still another tribute that may be briefly quoted was this: "He was incorruptibly honest in every walk of life and his daily life was an inspiration to all who came in contact with him; he was big and broad in his views, kind and charitable in his judgment; he reached heights only the pure in heart would attempt to scale. He was ever to the forefront in every move that made for the advancement of Texas and of Dallas. He kept perfect step with every forward movement and to the very day almost the hour preceding his death his great brain was busy with those things that would be a help and a resource to our city. Almost his last conversation was of plans and suggestions in connection with the new interurban station now in its initial stage of construction. In his death education has lost one of its stanchest advocates; the people one of their strongest supporters; the state one of its ablest partisans; Dallas one of her most loyal citizens and tireless workers."

Bernard J. Fehrenkamp, M. D. Of the large and valued contingent of sturdy German colonists who settled in Southeastern Texas in the pioneer days a worthy and honored family was that of which this representative physician of Colorado County is a member, and he has been engaged in the active practice of his profession in the community that was the place of his birth for the long period of forty years—a period marked by large and worthy achievement on his part. He is now the dean of his profession at Frelsburg, which was made the central point of an appreciable German colony fully seventy years ago and which claims today many representatives of these sterling pioneer families, to the third and fourth generations.

Doctor Fehrenkamp was born at Frelsburg on the 6th of March, 1855, and is a son of Bernard A. Fehrenkamp, who was born in the

Village of Varrel, Grand Duchy of Oldenburg, Germany, in 1800, and who came with his family to America and established a home in the Frelsburg district of Colorado County, Texas, about the year 1848. In his native land the father received limited educational advantages in his youth, and there he learned the trade of cobbler, which he continued to follow until his immigration to America. His first wife died at Frelsburg, Texas, and was survived by two sons and four daughters: Meta became the wife of Theodore Becker, and passed the remainder of her life in Frelsburg; Mrs. Anna Klump is a resident of New Ulm, Austin County, Mr. August Klump being dead; Mrs. Sophie Heinsohn is a resident of Fayetteville, Fayette County; Helena is the wife of Dietrich Pophanken, of Frelsburg; Gerhard was a resident of Liveoak Hill, Texas, at the time of his death; and Bernard died when young. After the death of his first wife, Bernard A. Fehrenkamp married Mrs. Rosa Schiller, whose only child by her first marriage was Vincent Schiller, he having died when a young man, unmarried. He served throughout the Civil war, and died with typhoid fever which he contracted during his enlistment. Of the children of the second marriage Doctor Fehrenkamp, of this review, is the firstborn; Mary became the wife of Gustav Hoppe and was a resident of New Ulm, Austin County, at the time of her death; and Eliza is the wife of George Winkelmann, of Burlington, Milam County.

Like most of his Texas compatriots who settled in Texas in the early days, Bernard A. Fehrenkamp turned his attention to the great fundamental industry of agriculture after his arrival in the Lone Star State. He and his family came across the Gulf of Mexico and landed at Galveston, and thence made their way with ox teams to Frelsburg, which was then one of the leading communities of this section of the state—a veritable mecca for German immigrants. Mr. Fehrenkamp purchased from Herman Frels a tract of land and he developed this into a good farm, this homestead having continued to be his abiding place until the close of his long and useful life. He died in 1874, and his widow, who was much his junior, survived him by thirty years, she having been eighty-seven years old at the time of her death, in 1904. Both were devout communicants of the Lutheran Church, and Mr. Fehrenkamp supported the democratic party after he had become a naturalized citizen. Living in a German community, he acquired but slight familiarity with the English language and used that of his native land until the close of his life. He aided in building the Lutheran Church at Frelsburg, and was a man whose integrity and upright life gave him secure place and popular esteem. His sympathies were with the cause of the Confederacy during the period of the Civil war, in which none of his relatives served as a soldier except his stepson, Vincent Schiller.

In the schools of Frelsburg, Dr. Bernard J. Fehrenkamp acquired his early education, and as may well be understood, he has virtually equal facility in the use of the German and English languages. He was about eighteen years old at the time of his father's death and thereafter continued to assist in the care of his widowed mother and the younger children by supervision of the home farm until he had attained to his legal majority. For a time thereafter he was employed as clerk in a drug store at Columbus, the judicial center of his home county, and later he was in the employ of a firm conducting a wholesale drug business in the City of Galveston, where he continued to be thus engaged somewhat more than two years. This incidental experience caused him to become deeply interested in the subject of medicine and he finally determined to prepare himself for the exacting profession in which he has labored for so many years, and with so much success and unselfish zeal. While still employed in the wholesale drug house he initiated the study of medicine, and his earnestness, ambition and sterling character gained to him the kindly encouragement and assistance of his employer, who presented him with free tuition for one year in the celebrated old Jefferson Medical College in the City of Philadelphia. He entered that great institution in 1874, and was graduated in March, 1876, with the degree of Doctor of Medicine, his fortification for his chosen vocation having been further increased by his incidental service as interne in the German Hospital, Philadelphia, during a period of six months.

In 1876 Doctor Fehrenkamp engaged in the general practice of his profession at Industry, Austin County, Texas, where he remained until 1878, since which time he has been continuously following the work of his humane calling in his native town of Frelsburg, where he has long controlled a large and representative practice and where he has served as physician to and is held in affectionate regard by prominent families throughout the wide radius of country through which his practice has extended. When he began practice at Frelsburg the community had such other honored representatives of the medical profession as Dr. Frederick Becker and his son Edward, Doctor Herald and Doctor Neal, the last mentioned and veteran physician being the only one of the number except himself now left to continue active professional work. Doctor Fehrenkamp was one of the organizers of the Colorado County Medical Society and has been one of its most active and honored members for many years, besides which he holds membership in the Texas State Medical Society. For nearly thirty years the doctor served as president of the Hermann Seminary, an institution now transformed into one of the public schools of Frelsburg. He has never faltered in his allegiance to the democratic party, has been broad-minded and public-spirited as a citizen, but has deemed his profession worthy of his undivided fealty and thus has never consented to become a candidate for public office. The doctor is a man of broad intellectual ken, has been a close student along both professional and scientific lines, besides reading widely and with discrimination in the domain of general literature. He is a member of the National Geographical Society, and both he and his wife are communicants of the Lutheran Church.

At Frelsburg, on the 13th of February, 1877, was solemnized the marriage of Doctor Fehrenkamp to Miss Helena Hillje, who likewise was born and reared in this section of Texas, and who is a daughter of the late John Hillje. She is a sister of the well-known Hillje brothers, who are prominently identified with the cotton-seed oil industry in Texas, with mills at San Antonio, Hallettsville and Weimar. Relative to the children of Doctor and Mrs. Fehrenkamp the following brief data are available: Fenton, who served four years in the United States Navy and was on active duty on a torpedo boat destroyer during the Spanish-American war, now resides at Elmdorf, Texas; Nora is the wife of Louis Heinsohn, of Fayetteville, Fayette County, and they have one daughter, Lillie; Ellerslie married Miss Drew Pempell, a native of Missouri, and now resides in Kenedy, Karnes County; Stella is the wife of Henry F. Bretschneider, of Anadarko, Oklahoma, her husband being in Indian service for the Government, and their two children being Fenton and Drew; Fred Fehrenkamp resides at Kenedy, and Louis still remains at the parental home.

The residence premises of Doctor Fehrenkamp are perhaps the oldest of Frelsburg, the property having first been improved soon after the town was founded, and the original owners having been those honored pioneers, Messrs. Zimmler and Geogs, who conducted a mercantile business in a log house that stood on the site of the present brick building which is owned by Doctor Fehrenkamp and in which he maintains his well appointed office. The substantial brick house on the place was erected by Mr. Malsch, from whom the doctor purchased the property.

FREDERICK B. MILLER. In that prosperous rural community of Austin known as Postoak Point, the chief business man and merchant for many years has been Frederick B. Miller. It is a rural community with important commercial features, and was established by Frederick E. Miller, father of the present merchant. The elder Miller as a title of distinction was often referred to in the early days as "Postoak Point" Miller.

Frederick E. Miller was born at Kreutznach on the Rhine, in 1813, and in Germany the name was spelled Mueller. He was well educated, and his father desired that he should enter the priesthood, but that calling he considered suitable neither to his talent nor to his inclination. It was largely to avoid the persuasions of his father that he left his native land and started alone for America in 1831. Landing in New York he was employed for two years in a book bindery, and left that city to come to Texas. Texas was still a Mexican province when he arrived in 1833. He was one of the earliest German arrivals in Austin County, and on reaching the vicinity of Postoak Point, being without business or other professional training, he worked one year as a farm hand for Mike Muckelroy. For this year's work he was given 100 acres of land, and in some ingenuous way managed to secure a yoke of cattle. With this team he engaged in hauling freight from Houston to Austin, and later participated in the emigrant business as a freighter from Indianola to the interior. While thus engaged he met his future wife, who belonged to one of the emigrant parties of the Prince Solm Colony. He continued freighting and farming until the war, and as a result of judicious investment was the owner of a large amount of land in Austin County. His first improvement in that section was in the shape of a log house of small proportions. His second home was a much more pretentious and comfortable dwelling, and was built for him by Dietrich Schweke, and has been in use for sixty-five years, and is located on the land owned by Frederick B. Miller. On coming to America Frederick E. Miller at once identified himself both in spirit and in practice with his adopted country, he mastered the English language without difficulty, and was a keen observer and a student of American customs and politics. He was a republican at the organization of that party, and as the owner of slaves in Texas was a stanch friend of the Union, and a man of considerable influence in behalf of the Federal Government during and just after the war. He died September 8, 1867, at Hempstead, where he is buried. At the time of his death he held the office of justice of the peace, and was engaged in administering oaths and preparing citizenship papers when the yellow fever struck him down. He was a level headed man, wise as to the purposes and activities of life, and possessed a fine sociable and moral nature, enjoying the confidence of his fellows, who sought his advice in all kinds of problems and difficulties. When the occasion demanded he could make an address in public, and was one of the few members of the Masonic Order in Texas at that time.

Frederick E. Miller married Miss Philippine Holzmann, who was born in Langenschwalbach, Germany, in the '20s, and died when about seventy-three years of age. Her father came to Texas with the Prince Solm Colony of German emigrants, and spent the closing years of his life in the vicinity of Shelby and Round Top. Mrs. Miller had a brother, William Holzmann, who died in Austin County, leaving a family. To Frederick Miller and wife were born the following children: Charlotte, who married George A. Doss and is buried at New Ulm; Mary, whose first husband was Charles Eversberg, and her second Fred H. Kothmann, and now resides at Loyal Valley; Wilhelmina, who married Hermann Knolle, and now lives with her son, Dr. W. H. Knolle, at New Orleans; Josephine, the wife of Ernst H. B. Witte, of Shelby, Texas; Annie, who married August Jones, of Mason County, Texas, and died at Postoak Point; Frederick B., who is the seventh child and first son of the family; Emma, who married William Mogford, and lives in Mason County; Dr. Kenney N., of Houston, who married Laura Koch; Adolph G., who lives at Clairville, Bee County, Texas, and has a number of children by his marriage to Fredericka Luedecke; and Norma, widow of F. C. Wolters, of Schulenburg.

Frederick B. Miller has spent practically all his life in the vicinity of the old homestead at Postoak Point. The schools at home supplied his early training, and he also attended the old Soule University, of Chapel Hill. When about seventeen he took up the serious responsibilities of life, and had charge of his mother's property and made himself useful in saving her farm and other land to the family. His life was spent as a farmer up to the age of twenty-seven, when he engaged in merchandising with Mr. Adam Wangemann, under the firm name of Wangemann, Becker & Miller. Their store was located on Mr. Wangemann's land and was known as the "Lone Star." After some five years in business the firm sold out with the intention of becoming the first merchants of the Town of New Ulm, to which the Missouri, Kansas & Texas Railway was then building. However, the railway was delayed at Pisek so long that Mr. Miller changed his plans, and determined to resume business on his own farm at Postoak Point. He opened a store there in 1887, and it has since grown to be one of the chief commercial points in this rural district of Austin County. While a merchant, Mr. Miller is also still identified with farming, and his home is on the Dunlavy headright, which lies next to the headright of his father. He owns extensive tracts of land both in Austin and in other counties. In politics he takes no part, and fraternally is identified with the Woodmen of the World and the Sons of Hermann.

On February 3, 1881, Mr. Miller married Miss Hedwig Wangemann, a daughter of his former business partner, Adam Wangemann. Adam Wangemann was born in Saxony, and married Fredericka Kling, a native of New Orleans, and they were the parents of five children, four daughters and one son. Mr. and Mrs. Miller have the following children: Frieda, Texanna, Eugene A., Elsie, Robert F., and Dessie. The oldest, Frieda, was educated in Brenham High School and Blinn College, and by her marriage to Theodore Pophanken, of Postoak Point, has two children, Bernyna and Leroy. The daughter Texanna was educated with her sister, and also attended the School of Industrial Arts at Denton, and married George H. Zeiss, of Brenham. Eugene A. is a graduate of the Agricultural and Mechanical College at Bryan, went from that institution to Cornell University in New York, and from there to Poughkeepsie, where he finished bookkeeping and banking courses, and was offered a chair in the school, but declined. While at Bryan he was second lieutenant in his military company. He is now pursuing his favorite line, as a horticulturist, in the employ of the Louisville & Nashville Railway Company with headquarters at Etowah, Tennessee. The daughter Elsie, who was educated in Blinn College and in the Denton School of Art, married Dr. K. C. Knolle, of Wesley, Texas, and has two children, Evelyn and Kinch, Jr. The son Robert graduated from the Agricultural and Mechanical College, in animal husbandry, took a post-graduate course in the Iowa Agricultural College at Ames, Iowa, spent four years as an instructor at Bozeman, Montana, then had the Chair of Animal Husbandry at the University of California, and is now located at Davis, California. He served as first lieutenant of his military company at Bryan, and married Roxie Knolle. Arthur C., who is next to the youngest in the family, spent a year in Allen Academy at Bryan, followed by five years in the Agricultural and Mechanical College, where he was graduated after a special training in agriculture. He is now a student of medicine in the University Medical School at Galveston. He left the Agricultural College as major of his military company. The youngest, Miss Dessie, finished her education at Blinn College in Brenham, where she graduated.

Mr. Miller deserves much credit for what he has accomplished in life, both in a business way and for the fine family which he has reared. He is a large man physically, but active both in body and mind, has a keen business judgment, is very sociable, and is a positive force and leader in his locality.

Hon. George Alexander McCall. For more than sixty years members of the McCall family have held useful and prominent positions in the professional and civic life of Northern Texas. The family is most particularly identified with Weatherford, where the late Judge George Alexander McCall was a distinguished lawyer. A representative of the family now living in Dallas is Edward F. McCall, who has gained considerable prominence in the field of civil engineering and is now assistant city engineer.

The late Judge George Alexander McCall, who died at his home in Weatherford, Parker County, Texas, May 29, 1915, was born in Kentucky in 1849, and was about four years of age when the family came to Texas. The McCalls first lived at Waco and were among the pioneer settlers of what later has become the metropolis of Central Texas. Judge McCall was the son of James L. L. McCall, who was also a native of Kentucky and of Scotch ancestry. In coming to Texas the McCalls made the journey by the familiar pioneer conveyance, a wagon drawn by an ox team. James L. L. McCall was also a lawyer by profession, and in the days preceding, during and after the war was a prominent figure in Texas. He held the positions of judge and district attorney for the Confederate States government at Waco during the war, and otherwise took a leading part in collecting funds to sustain the Confederacy during the four hard years it was struggling for its principles. After the war he became a law partner of Hon. Richard Coke, who was governor from 1874 to 1876. Also at one time he was a law partner of the late Judge Sleeper of Waco. In 1871 James L. L. McCall moved to Palo Pinto County, and from there to Weatherford, the county seat of Parker County in 1873. Parker County forty years ago was on the frontier, and the echos of the last Indian raid had hardly died away. From 1873 forward the McCalls, father and son, lent distinction to the Weatherford bar, which has long contained some of the most brilliant attorneys of the state. James L. L. McCall was retired from the active work of his profession for several years prior to his death, which occurred at Weatherford in 1903.

In the City of Waco the late Judge George A. McCall was reared and as the son of a prominent father was given the best educational advantages. He graduated from the University of Virginia at Charlottesville in both the academic and law departments. In law he also had the advantages of study and experience in the office of his father. About the time his father removed to Palo Pinto County he also went

George A Kimball

to that locality, and in 1873 he identified himself with the Weatherford bar. At the time of his death he was the senior member of the Weatherford bar, where for more than forty years he had been a man of distinction and a leading practitioner. For several years he was a law partner of the late S. W. T. Lanham, who is well remembered as governor of Texas for a term of three years. Judge George A. McCall was elected and served one term as judge of his judicial district. He was twice married, and his first wife was Miss Emily Lanham, a sister of Governor Lanham. The Lanham family is referred to on other pages of this work. Mrs. Emily Lanham McCall died in 1889. Mr. McCall married, the second time, Miss Nannie Alexander of Sportenburg County, South Carolina, who survives, also the following children: Dorothy McCall, of New York City; James L., a lawyer of Weatherford, Texas; Dr. Joe M., of Dallas; E. F., of Dallas; and George Alexander, a teacher of Weatherford, Texas.

Ernst H. B. Witte. The residence of Ernst H. B. Witte in the vicinity of Shelby has covered a period of approximately sixty-five years, and during the greater part of this time he has been identified with the rising commercial and agricultural interests of Austin and Fayette counties. He is a son of the late pioneer, William Bernard Witte, who spent fifty-five years in this section of Texas, where he resided from the year 1845 until his death. William Bernard Witte was a native of Hanover, Germany, born near the City of Hanover, March 27, 1827, a son of Dr. Ernst Witte, who came to the United States in 1858, located in Texas, and established himself on a farm which is now owned by Mrs. Schmied.

Dr. Ernst Witte had been a lawyer in his native land, where he had acquired the degree of doctor of laws, hence his title. On coming to this country he did not resume the practice of his vocation, but instead turned his attention to agricultural pursuits, lived quietly and unobtrusively, and at the time of his death in 1869, at the age of seventy-seven years, was the owner of 1,400 acres of good land in the vicinity of Shelby. He married Miss Lizette Linemann, and they became the parents of the following children: Victor, a veterinary surgeon who spent his life in Washington County, Texas, and left a family at the time of his death; Charles Otto, who died at Charleston, South Carolina, one of the leading business men and financiers of that city, and left a family; Eugene, who met an accidental death, as will be further related; William Bernard; Ernst, who came to America, graduated in dentistry at Philadelphia, Pennsylvania, returned to Hanover, Germany, and continued to be engaged in practice until his death; George, who passed his life at Charleston, South Carolina, in association with his brother, Charles Otto, and died there leaving a family; Herman, who died in Hanover, Germany; Armin, who lives at Charleston, South Carolina; Frances, who married Paul Due, of Christiana, Norway; and Johanna, who married Emil Trenckmann, and died at Shelby, Texas.

William Bernard Witte was given a splendid education in the schools of his native land and became an excellent Greek and Latin scholar. He was eighteen years of age when he came to the United States in 1845, being accompanied by his brother Eugene, who was accidentally killed by the discharge of his own rifle, while he, his brother and a friend were in camp at San Felipe, Texas. Soon after this event, William B. Witte completed his journey and enlisted for service in the Mexican war, in a Tennessee regiment that was passing through Texas bound for the Mexican battle front. However, by the time he reached LaGrange, he was taken sick and never reached Mexico nor saw service during the war.

During the first few years, or until he returned to Germany for his bride, Mr. Witte and a party of rather well-to-do young men of his community kept "bachelor's hall" and enjoyed themselves in various ways, particularly in hunting and fishing. When he returned from Germany, however, in 1849, with his wife, Mr. Witte located on Mill Creek, near Shelby, where he bought land of William Duff, and there commenced his mercantile career. After a time he moved to Shelby and continued merchandising at this place until interrupted by the Civil war, and in 1862 left this locality and went to Mexico, fearing the consequences of his strong sympathy with the Confederate cause. In 1864 Mr. Witte made a trip to Europe, where he collected a legacy due him, and then once more returned to Mexico and was located at Matamoros and later at Monterey, at both of which places he was engaged in merchandising. In 1866 Mr. Witte returned to Texas and resumed merchandising at Shelby as a partner of James Marburger, a connection which was mutually dissolved in 1870. Following this, Mr. Witte continued in business alone until 1877, when he retired from his activities and from that time until his death in 1900, had but little to give his attention to save his work as a notary public.

Mr. Witte was long active in local politics. He was a democrat, and his interest in the cause of the South was enthusiastic. He was able to make a speech when called upon, and being a learned man and able scholar learned the English tongue easily and was a master of its complexities. Mr. Witte belonged to no church as a professed believer and seemed to give spiritual matters little or no concern. In his early years he was fond of the sport of hunting, which the opportunity afforded here so well, and he was the organizer and manager of a local theatrical or literary troupe, which entertained the people of this locality on occasions and in which he was perhaps the most active participant in the proceedings.

William B. Witte married Ida Woehler, a daughter of Capt. Henry Woehler, a military man who took part in the battle of Waterloo, and died as a result of his wounds received therein. His widow came to Texas with her daughter in 1849, and died at Shelby, Texas. Mrs. Witte, who was also splendidly educated, died at the age of fifty-six years, the mother of the following children: Ernst H. B., of this review; Dr. Otto, a resident of Shelby; Antonio, who is the widow of Emil Surmann and lives near Shelby; Dr. B. E., who lives at San Antonio, Texas; Laura, who is the wife of Dr. George Gevers, of Hildasheim, Hanover, Germany.

Ernst H. B. Witte was born November 14, 1850, near Shelby, Austin County, Texas, and has lived here all of his life. He acquired a somewhat limited education in the common schools here, and when the war came on he was anxious to enlist, although only a boy. A friend, Capt. M. von Huevel, raised a company in this locality for the Confederate service, and the boy Ernst begged hard to be allowed to join it, but he was refused. He continued as a family aid after his father went to Mexico, until 1865, when he joined his father, as did the whole family, and spent more than a year in that country. The youth learned the merchandising business in the store with his father, and in 1870, fully prepared, established himself in business as a merchant on the farm, four miles south of Shelby, at Rock House, where he also conducted a gin, continuing there until 1890. In that year Mr. Witte moved to Shelby and engaged in the raising of and dealing in horses. At the present time he is the owner of a farm of 200 acres, located in the West Southerland League, the old home of his brother-in-law, Doctor Gevers, and also continues to be interested in merchandising as a partner in the firm of

Pophanken & Witte, at Shelby. Mr. Witte is a democrat, has attended the county conventions of his party, and has rendered efficient public service as a member of the board of school trustees of his district. Fraternally he is connected with the Sons of Hermann, the Woodmen of the World, the Woodmen's Circle, and the Puritans.

On November 29, 1869, Mr. Witte was married to Miss Josephine Miller, a daughter of Fred E. Miller, from the Rhine country of Germany. Mrs. Miller bore the maiden name of Philippina Holzmann, and she and her husband had thirteen children. Mr. and Mrs. Witte's children have been as follows: Ida, who is the wife of Dr. B. E. Knolle, of Industry, Texas; Antonio, who is the wife of Otto Pophanken, of Shelby, Texas; Dr. W. S., a practicing physician of Waco; Norma, who married Henry Hodde, of Ansley, Louisiana; Dr. Kinnie L., a practicing physician of Leland, Mississippi; and Miss Birdie, who is unmarried and resides with her parents.

William W. Brown. Of the contracting builders who have contributed much to the past of San Antonio and who, because of their superior equipment and progressive ideas may be counted on to share in the development of the city in the future, mention is due William W. Brown, who has been a resident of this city since 1910. The trade of building, of housing the people, and enterprises which make up a community, not only is one of the oldest known to man, but its ranks include a far greater number than those of any other kind of skilled labor. Mr. Brown is a capable and progressive representative of his calling, and although a recent acquisition to the business world of the city has already made his name known in commercial circles.

William W. Brown was born at Prescott, Nevada County, Arkansas, in 1873, and is a son of W. S. and Sarah Luthera (Long) Brown, the former a native of Tennessee and the latter of Mississippi. At the age of nine years he accompanied his parents to Texas, the family settling at Hubbard City, in Hill County, where his father turned his attention to agricultural pursuits and where William W. was reared on a farm. His early education was secured in the public schools of Arkansas and Texas, following which he became a student at Trinity University, and there spent six years, that institution being then situated at old Tehuacana, but now at Waxahachie. He was graduated from that excellent school of learning with the class of 1898 and the degree of Bachelor of Arts, and at that time entered upon his active career in the capacity of educator, subsequently teaching school in various parts of Texas, although principally in Limestone County. Finally deciding that educational work was not congenial, he laid aside the cap and gown to enlist as a worker in the busy marts of commerce and trade. At Hubbard City he became the proprietor of a lumber business, which he continued most successfully until 1910, when he moved his offices to San Antonio. His connection with the lumber business brought him into contact with large building interests, and he eventually entered the latter vocation as a general contractor. He is master of a business singularly adapted to his inclinations and abilities, and the fact that his work is congenial adds not a little to his possibilities of continued advancement. As an employer of labor he is considerate and appreciative, and has the happy faculty of securing from his men the best work of which they are capable. He enjoys a splendid reputation for fidelity to the duties of citizenship and for probity in his dealings with the public.

Mr. Brown was married at Hubbard City, Hill County, Texas, to Miss Josie Wright, who was born in this state, and to this union there has been born one son: Wylie D. Mr. and Mrs. Brown are members of the Cumberland Presbyterian Church.

William A. Buenger. Of the residents of Austin County who have passed their lives largely upon the farms on which they now reside, William A. Buenger, of Industry, is deserving of more than passing mention. During the period of his long residence in this locality he has been a witness to and a participant in the development and advancement of this fine agricultural country, and has lent his encouragement to enterprises which have added to its prestige. His record in both private and public life is one worthy of emulation.

Mr. Buenger was born in the old house which is still used as a part of the homestead accommodations, May 25, 1852. His father was Andrew Buenger, who came to the United States and to Texas in 1846, with the Bock family, some of whose descendants are now residing in the vicinity of Weimar, Texas. Mr. Buenger was born in Prussia, April 15, 1824, and there received a good education and learned the trades of wagonmaker and millwright. When he located in Texas he secured work as a mechanic, building grist and sawmills and cotton gins, erected the first sawmill erected in this part of the country, an ox-tread mill for the pioneer, Charles Fordtran, and also constructed numerous gins and mills for the old-time plantation owners of that day, the excellence of his work bringing him all the business he could handle. He finally settled down to farming, when his sons came to an age to be of service to him, and long before the outbreak of the Civil war purchased the farm in the Petes League on which his son, William A., now resides. The house he erected here was of split and hewed logs, weatherboarded and ceiled, and his children were born in this home, where the greatest happiness of Mr. Buenger's life was achieved. He passed his active career as a modest farmer, having no office or public responsibilities, except in his church relations in the Lutheran and later the Methodist church. During the great Civil war, Mr. Buenger was a prison guard for the Confederacy for a time, when he was not assigned to duty as a wagonmaker and repairer for that government. He voted the democratic ticket in political affairs. Mr. Buenger was noted for his great industry and energy, as well as for his thrift and economy, demonstrated to his sons the value of these homely virtues, sent his children to the community schools, and saw to it that they were properly trained along useful lines, so that in after life they might take their place in the activities of life as useful and well-trained citizens.

Andrew Buenger married Miss Annie Rosky, born April 12, 1833, a daughter of a German emigrant and farmer of Texas, and she died February 3, 1899, Mr. Buenger following her to the grave on October 31, 1904. They were the parents of the following children: William A., of this notice; Hermann, a resident of Halsted, Texas; Charles, who died at Yoakum, Texas, leaving a family; Miss Emily, who resides at Industry; Adolph, a farmer near this place, a sketch of whose career will be found elsewhere in this work; Emil, of Grayson County, Texas; Ida, who married Rudolph Franke, of Industry; and Lena, who is the wife of Eddie Rinn, of Yoakum.

William A. Buenger was reared in the house of his birth, was educated in the community schools, and grew up on the homestead, being trained for the vocation of farmer, which he entered first when beginning his personal career. Later on, however, he engaged in merchandising in company with Emil M. Knolle, at Industry, and remained six years as clerk and bookkeeper and in other capacities. Leaving this store, he went to Brenham and clerked for a time in the store of Voss

Brothers, general merchants, and when he left their employ he became the operator of a gin, his residence at Brenham extending over a period of three years. Returning to Industry, Mr. Buenger became a freighter, a vocation which he followed for a few years, hauling the merchandise for the storekeepers at New Ulm to this point. Finally Mr. Buenger returned to his first vocation, that of farming, and he has since been so engaged, being the owner of the old home place in the Pettes League, in addition to a tract of timber land in Hill's League. He has been identified with the common money crop of the country, cotton, as a grower, and has also produced the necessary crops and truck for the use of his household. He is a seller of pork, instead of a buyer, and his feedstuff is also plentiful.

In 1913 Mr. Buenger rebuilt the family home, replacing the old house with a new one of four rooms which, joined to his main building, makes ten rooms in his home. His main building is one of two stories and stands upon a hill, thus giving its occupants an excellent view of the surrounding country. The place is made doubly attractive by a well-kept yard, with flowers, trees and shrubs, in charge of one of the sons of the family. Mr. Buenger served his school district as a trustee for a period of ten years, and is now a member of the board of county trustees, a capacity in which he has acted for many years, there being four other members at this time. He was one of the charter members of the Knights of Honor, and is a member of the Sons of Hermann, being a member of the board of managers of this order, in which he is very popular.

Mr. Buenger was married at Fayetteville, Texas, July 24, 1886, to Miss Agnes Mangliers, a daughter of Henry and Theresa (Fengler) Mangliers. Mr. Mangliers was born at Frankfort-on-the-Oder, Germany, and came to the United States after the close of the Civil war. He was a shoemaker in his native land, having had a factory there, and followed his vocation at Fayetteville until his removal to New Braunfels, Texas, late in life, where he died. His children were as follows: Mrs. Annie Scholandt; Mrs. Buenger, born January 15, 1863; Otto, who met his death in the great Galveston flood; Frank H., a jeweler of Columbus, Texas; Lizzie, who married Frank Burchard, of Gonzales; and Magrette, of Los Angeles, California. The children born to Mr. and Mrs. Buenger are as follows: Harry, who died in 1913, aged twenty-four years, a saddler of Brenham; Eldie; Norbert, who is the florist and landscape gardener of the family; Arno, who died as a lad of thirteen years; Anita, and Nessie.

Kirk Towns. It was one of several distinctions which mark out the Southern Methodist University at Dallas as one of the foremost institutions of higher education in the South when the noted musician of international reputation, Kirk Towns, was secured as dean of the department of fine arts and also to head the vocal department. Dean Towns has such standing in the musical world that he would lend distinction to any institution with which he was affiliated. And it can be said also that his affiliations with such an institution as the Southern Methodist University is of itself not without significance to those who understand what a splendid program this ambitious new school has undertaken and what resources are behind it.

The Southern Methodist University of Dallas is the great new university of the Methodist Episcopal Church South. Its first year began in September, 1915, and with an enrollment of over 500 students, said to be a larger number than any other university ever had in its first year.

It seems peculiarly fortunate that Dean Towns should begin his career in Texas with this splendid institution.

Like many men who have attained some of the highest points of fame in the fine arts, Dean Towns had an early life of struggle. He was born at Des Moines, Iowa, and left there with his parents when four years of age, and when fourteen went to Omaha, Nebraska. For four years he was employed in a large book and stationery house of that city. At the age of eighteen he went to New York City, and there he began his musical studies and the training of a fine natural voice and exceptional native talent. Since then his entire life has been devoted to the great art of music.

While he was a student in New York it is recalled that he was selected as a member of the famous quartet in Denman Thompson's celebrated play, "The Old Homestead," and was the youngest member of that quartet, in which Chauncey Olcott was the tenor. Kirk Towns is an artist and teacher of international reputation. For fourteen years, with the exception of the years 1902-04, during which he was one of the principal teachers in the Chicago Musical College, he resided abroad, in France, Germany and Italy, and attracted attention to his work as a teacher and singer. His own studies were carried on under the direction of George Sweet of New York; Bouhy and Leroux of Paris; Prof. Alfred Blume, George Fergusson, Edourd Behm; Hugo Kaun and Prof. Otto Lessmann of Berlin; and Francesco Mottino of Milan. His voice is baritone, and while in Berlin he appeared frequently in musical circles of the higher quality, and gained many favorable comments on his work from criticis whose opinions carry weight wherever spoken. During his long sojourn in Berlin he had pupils from all parts of America, from England, and also a number of German pupils.

For four years before coming to Texas Mr. Towns lived in Chicago and for three years was under contract with the Chicago Musical College as one of the directors of the vocal department. In that work he was associated with Herman and Maurice DeVries, Mrs. O. L. Fox and Adolph Muelmann. Concerning his work with the Chicago Musical College the vice president said: "We have never had a teacher in the institution whom we considered more painstaking or thorough than yourself, and the splendid results which you achieved in your work proved your efficiency most conclusively." Mr. Towns gave up his connection with the Chicago Musical College in order to open a studio of his own in the Fine Arts Building. While in Chicago he was also soloist in Doctor Gunsaulus' church of that city. He has been associated in recital and concerts with some of the greatest artists of the present time, including Emile Sauret, Rudolph Ganz, Harold Bauer, Clara Butt, Jane Osborne-Hannah, Arthur Hartmann, Theodore Spiering, Hugo Kortschak, Bruno Steindel, and others. His work in concert and recital has brought forth favorable comments from all the critics and it would take many pages to include even the more noteworthy and significant press notices. A layman's view of his art is well expressed by Dr. George B. Foster, the head of the theological department of the University of Chicago, in the following words: "While I have no scientific right to an opinion of the musician's technique, I am a lifelong lover of music, and as such it gives me singular pleasure to speak of the joy and elevation of soul I experience while listening to the singing of my good friend, Kirk Towns. With the best musical education that the Old World and the New can give, and with a wide and abundant practice in singing and teaching, to say nothing of his rich and manly personality, the power and charm of his work are of the highest order."

Dean Towns came to Texas largely through the advice and recommendation of his good friend, Harold von Mickwitz, of Chicago, the distinguished musician who gained fame in Texas as the head of the Kidd-Key Conservatory at Sherman. Dean Towns feels that he owes much to this eminent Chicago musician, and the latter in a personal letter expressed the following flattering but sincere opinion of the younger man: "Your voice is a superb organ, and your interpretation as artistic, full of dramatic force and charm, as I ever expect to hear from any prominent artist. You compel your hearers to listen. As for your teaching, I could not wish anyone a more competent instructor. I take very great pleasure in expressing to you my opinion of your work, both as a pedagogue and as an interpretive artist."

Kirk Towns first came to Texas a number of years ago with David B. Clarkson of Chicago, formerly of Mart, Texas. Mr. Clarkson is a wealthy business man who was giving large sums of money to the Texas Agricultural and Mechanical College, and Mr. Clarkson and Kirk Towns drove in an automobile all the way from Chicago to Dallas. While Dean Towns was teaching in Berlin, three daughters of Sam Davidson of Fort Worth and William Way, another Texan, residing at Austin, studied with him. Thus his name came to mean something in Texas many years before he knew that state or so much as thought of making it his place of residence. While in Chicago also Mr. Towns had a number of young ladies from very prominent Texas families among his pupils, and for this reason it was by no means as a stranger that Dean Towns came to Dallas in September, 1915, to take up his work as dean of the musical department. Thus his introduction to Texas was so favorable and auspicious in every way that he at once gained a following of more pupils than he could teach. In addition to his work at the university as dean of the fine arts department he has private pupils and a private studio in the city.

Henry August Wunderlich, who is now living a partially retired life on Fayetteville R. F. D. No. 3, has passed his entire career within the community of Shelby, having come hither as a child of three years with his father, John Wunderlich. The family came from Westphalia, Arnsberg, Germany, where Henry August Wunderlich was born December 1, 1844. John Wunderlich, his father, was born at the same place, and the forefathers had lived there for generations, and as far as is known all followed the pursuits of agriculture. John Wunderlich married Mary Wiet, of whose family little is now known. With his family, Mr. Wunderlich sailed from Bremen and landed from a sailing vessel at Galveston, the little party going at once to Austin County, where a few German emigrants and friends of the family had preceded them, among them being the Marburgers, the Wagners and the Roeders, the two latter families having since become in a manner extinct in the locality. There were also the Vogelsangs, Ploegers, Genskes, Bernshausens and Wittes, as well as the Hebels and Voelkels, who belonged to families that preceded the Wunderlichs and have posterity to preserve the names here.

The career of John Wunderlich was one which was characteristic in many ways of the early German settlers. Like many others he had not been satisfied with the progress he was making in his native land and accordingly determined to try his fortunes in the United States, and also, like numerous of his countrymen, he did not allow the lack of funds to keep him from coming here to face the hardships of an unknown land. He was possessed of but $24 in money when he arrived, but soon secured employment at the Roeder mill and gin, at a wage of $5 per month, with two bushels of meal thrown in, and continued to work there for a period of two years, in the meantime renting a house close to Shelby. Following this, he made the first payment on a small farm nearby, and there passed the remaining years of his life at agricultural work, succeeding because of his industry and close application. Considering the scant education he had received, he was a good business man, and when he died at the age of sixty-three years left a good estate.

Mr. Wunderlich had come to the United States to locate a home, but he had also come to be a citizen, and took that step not long after his arrival. He was too old for military service during the war between the North and the South, and was opposed to secession, yet when the issue came to a head he saw two of his sons give active service to the Confederate cause. He voted the republican ticket, but was not known in politics, and his religious faith was that of the Lutheran Church, of which he was a lifelong member. Mr. Wunderlich passed away in 1872, while Mrs. Wunderlich survived him until 1899, and was eighty-eight years of age at the time of her death. Their children were as follows: Frederick, who reared a family in this section and spent his life as a farmer; Henry Augustus, of this notice; William, who died as a boy during the war; and Elizabeth. The last named was the only child of Mrs. Wunderlich by her first husband, Mr. Witt; Frederick was a child by his father's first wife, and Henry and William were born to John and Mary Wunderlich.

Henry August Wunderlich secured the foundation for his education in the rural schools, and was purely a farm lad as a boy. He was seventeen years of age when he enlisted, in 1862, in the Confederate service, as a wagon man, and in the fall of the same year took up service as a conscript in the cavalry division, Colonel Lykens' regiment, with which he continued along the coast during the four months that he was out. In the spring of 1863 he returned to the freighting service, hauling cotton from this section of the state to Brownsville and Eagle Pass and returning with flour and bacon for the Confederate army. He left the service during that year and again identified himself with the farm at home.

After several years under the parental roof, Mr. Wunderlich was married, February 17, 1866, to Miss Frederica Treybig, a daughter of Nicholas Treybig, who came to Texas from Saxe-Weimar, Germany, and was a farmer by vocation. He died here, as did also his wife Mary, they having been the parents of five children, namely: Frederick; Benjamin; Carolina, who married George Wasserman; Eliza, who died young; and Frederica, who married Mr. Wunderlich. After their marriage, Mr. and Mrs. Wunderlich went to housekeeping at Shelby, and there maintained their first home. Mr. Wunderlich purchased his first tract of land in 1870 in the Southerland League, a tract of 150 acres, which was only fenced. There he made all the substantial improvements, including the erection of a good residence, commodious barns and other buildings, and made that property his home until 1911. In that year he felt that he had contributed his share of hard work to the development and improvement of the community, and therefore was indisposed to continue in active participation in agriculture. Accordingly he retired and moved to his present home on the Jones League, where he has sixty-four acres and has improved it to suit his family needs. To his original purchase in Southerland League, Mr. Wunderlich had added sixty-eight acres, which he devoted to farm and pasture. As a farmer and stock raiser he was known to favor the most progressive methods, and at all times was ready to give innovations a trial, thus helping to elevate agricultural standards in his section.

Mrs. Wunderlich died in 1897, leaving the following children: Henry, of Brenham, Texas, who married Emily Warnasch, and has four children,

Harry, Winfield, Zuleme and Robert; Ernst, who married Louisa Schulze, and left three children, Willie, Ella and Anita; Emma, who married Adolph Schroeder, of Dewitt County, Texas, and has eight children, Otto, Erna, Arnold, Addie, Leona, Hulda, Edwin and Emma Anita; Emily, who married Emil Petrich, of Lavaca County, Texas, and has six children, Emma, Agnes, Hilda, Meta, Willie and Mildred; Emil, a farmer of this locality, who married Anna Holocher, and has five children, Edward, Lena, Olga, Laura and Hugo; Mina, who married Ernst Warnasch, of Washington County, Texas, and has five children, Clinton, Margaret, Alice, Louisa and Carrie; Hetwig, who is the wife of Henry Warnasch, of Washington County, and has three children, Clinton, Elizabeth and Gilbert; Lena, who married Paul Hetgel, of Shelby, and has one son, Lynn H.; Edwin, of Shelby, who married Hulda Hermsdoerfer, and has three children, Delwin, Hilbert and Roy; William, who married Emily Dochel, a farmer of Fayette County, and has four children, Perry, Willie, Lillie and Ruby; and Miss Eda, who resides at home with her father. Mr. Wunderlich was married the second time to Mrs. Johanna Vetter, but there have been no children to this union.

Mr. Wunderlich has lived a private life. He served his community as a trustee of the public schools for many years while his children were growing up, and uses his own judgment in the matter of voting. He opposed Mr. Bryan in his three campaigns for the Presidency, voting for both Roosevelt and Taft, and in 1912 supported Mr. Wilson. In the famous political battle for the governorship in 1892, he voted for Clark, and opposed the aspirations of Senator Joseph W. Bailey. He is a firm believer in the value of a public school education, and sent his eldest son to commercial college. Mr. Wunderlich is a member of the Sons of Hermann, of which he was president for a time, and of the Woodmen of the World, of which he was consul commander. He is a stockholder of the First Guaranty State Bank of Industry.

Frederick H. Niebuhr. One of the pioneer residents of the Industry community, Frederick H. Niebuhr has lived in Texas since 1847, having sailed from the old country in November of the previous year. His father, Frederick H. Niebuhr, Sr., was the head of this family, and was a native of the Kingdom of Hanover, having been born in the Village of Broma, between Braunschweig and Prussia, where he subsequently became a small farmer and also followed the trade of tailor. He was born January 12, 1812, and was accompanied to America by his father, who died near Houston during the first year that the family was here. A brother of the father, Henry Niebuhr, came to Texas also and passed away near Houston, leaving an only son who subsequently died in Bastrop County leaving a family. A sister of the father remained in Germany and nothing has been heard from her branch for years.

Frederick H. Niebuhr, Sr., married Henrietta Holze and when they came to Texas they had a family of five children. They sailed from Bremen on the sailship Babohlen, bound for Galveston, and after fair sailing for seven weeks entered the Galveston harbor. The father was a man of ambition and industry and had not been satisfied with the future as he saw it spreading out before him in his native land, and accordingly determined to try his fortune in the new country, where he felt there were better opportunities awaiting him and his growing family. The family spent three years in the vicinity of Houston, then settling in Fort Bend County, at Stafford's Point, where they resided for ten years. They were originally a part of a colony intended for settlement on the Llano River, but because of Indian troubles and the danger attendant thereto did not go to their intended destination but instead founded their home near settlements and safety. In 1859 the Niebuhr family came on to Austin County and the father purchased land close to Industry, in the Ernst League, a tract of 500 acres of raw soil. They built the first house on the land and it still stands, a landmark of the pioneer period. The father continued to occupy this home while he was an active factor in life's labors, and spent his last years at Brenham, where he passed away. His wife survived him about eight years, and they were laid to rest side by side in the cemetery at Industry. Mrs. Niebuhr was born in 1817. They were the parents of the following children: Frederick H., of this review; William, who passed away in Fort Bend County when still a boy; Charley, who was unmarried when he passed away during the period of the Civil war; Ferdinand, a resident of Brenham, Texas; Caroline, who died as Mrs. Henry Hempel; Miss Louisa, of Brenham; and Henriette, who was killed by lightning when a schoolgirl.

The father of these children took out his naturalization papers and voted at elections and followed his neighbors into the democratic party. He was against the secession of Texas from the Union and took no part in the Civil war. Mr. Niebuhr was no politician or office seeker, but did his full duty as a citizen, and won and retained the full confidence of his neighbors and associates. He was a consistent member of the Methodist Church.

Frederick H. Niebuhr was reared in the country and as a youth learned farming in all its various branches. He went to school a little in Fort Bend County and he, too, thought that Texas would not secede, although he did not say so with his vote at the election as, to use his own words, "he thought it useless." He entered the Confederate army as a member of Captain Vogt's company, of Wall's Legion, in 1863, and saw service from Fort Pemberton, on the Mississippi, to the end of the struggle. His chief fight was at Fort Pemberton, above Vicksburg, and he was at Yazoo City when Vicksburg fell, being there taken prisoner with the other members of his company. He was sent to the military prison at Indianapolis, Indiana, and remained incarcerated there for twenty months, during which time he served as a member of the kitchen force. On March 4, 1865, he left Indianapolis for Richmond, Virginia, and remained there only two days when he was paroled and given transportation wherever there were railroads left in the South. He was compelled to walk, however, from Jackson, Mississippi, to Beaumont, Texas, and then went by rail to Houston, finally reaching home in April, after the surrender of General Lee.

Mr. Niebuhr's personal injuries received during the period of his service included a scarred face from a bullet fired through the wall of the kitchen in which his work was done. He escaped all the bullets meant for Confederates at the front, but it was his misfortune to be struck by a bullet meant for another when a prisoner.

Soon after his return home, Mr. Niebuhr was married, and at that time established his household and began farming on the tract which he now owns in the Ernst League. He commenced with a part of the paternal homestead and by corn and cotton growing has demonstrated his ability and achieved marked success. He owns here 200 of the 500 acres he accumulated during his active career, and is regarded as one of the strong men financially of his community. He has kept out of office, votes independently, is a gold standard man with republican leanings, and has served his community merely as a trustee of schools.

On November 12, 1866, Mr. Niebuhr was united in marriage with Miss Antoinette Hander, of Schleswig-Holstein, Germany, who died in 1901, having been the mother of the following children: Miss Henrietta, a resident of Industry; Hermann, a farmer of this locality who married Mary Martin and has three children, Gertie, Marie and Ruth; Amelia, who is the wife of William Lindemann, of Cost, Texas, and has four children, Nettie, Alfred, Milton and Ruby; Ida, who became the wife of Dr. Lee Knolle and died leaving two children, Nita and Luella; Matilda, who married W. F. Lindemann, of Cost, and has two children, Alice and Mae; Louis, who still resides on the homestead, where he is engaged in superintending the farming activities; and Angelica, a former student of Brinn College, the San Marcos Normal School and the University of Texas, who holds diplomas from the Brenham school and the San Marcos State Normal School, and was a teacher in the schools of Falls County, and at this time is a student in the University of Texas, taking a special course. Louis Niebuhr married Miss Alma Leifeste, the oldest of the nine children of Charley and Amelia (Lehmberg) Leifeste, of Mason County, Texas, where Mr. Leifeste was born. Mr. and Mrs. Louis Niebuhr are the parents of two children: Lorina and Estella.

JOHN R. SIMMONS. A member of the retired colony of Industry, John R. Simmons is still remembered as one of the most popular and efficient teachers of his day and locality, and as a farmer who through industry and energy developed a substantial property, so that his declining years are being passed in the midst of comforts that in part reward an individual for a useful and active life. Mr. Simmons was born December 19, 1841, in Richland County, Ohio, and is a son of Amasa F. Simmons. His grandfather, Thomas Simmons, was born in Loudoun County, Virginia, where he married for his first wife a Miss Flaharty, and they moved to Ohio, where they passed the remaining years of their lives as farmers. They were the parents of two children: Samuel, who moved to Iowa; and Amasa T. Thomas Simmons married for his second wife a Miss Piper, and they became the parents of the following children: Nathan; John, who served as a soldier during the Mexican war and later as a soldier in the Union army during the Civil war; Nicholas; Jacob, who also served in the Mexican war; Otho and Abraham. Amasa F. Simmons' family comprised the following children: John R., of this notice; Thomas, a resident of Independence, Ohio; Miss Isabel, also a resident of Independence; Andrew, who died in Richland County, Ohio; Martha J., unmarried, of Independence, Ohio; Dr. N. R., of Toledo, Ohio; A. Bidison, a resident of Kingfisher, Oklahoma; and Harmon M., of Fredericktown, Ohio.

John R. Simmons came to mature years as a farm youth, and secured his final educational training in Bellville (Ohio) High School. Following this he taught four school terms in his native county before enlisting in the volunteer service of the United States for the Civil war. At Mansfield, Ohio, Mr. Simmons enlisted and was mustered into Company B, 120th Regiment, Ohio Volunteer Infantry, October 14, 1862. His first captain was Rufus M. Brayton, and Joseph P. Rummel his second lieutenant, while Mr. Simmons was orderly sergeant of the company from its arrival at New Orleans on to the regimental consolidation. The second captain of the company, Joseph P. Rummel, is still a resident of Ohio, his home being at Mansfield.

The regiment rendezvoused at Mansfield, and was moved first to Covington, Kentucky, and then on to Memphis, Tennessee. In December, 1862, it went up the Yazoo River and attacked Fort Pemberton and after a week's effort to capture that stronghold the assault was given up and General Sherman moved his troops up White River to Arkansas Post, which Confederate point was captured with its troops. The command then returned to Young's Point, above Vicksburg, and when General Grant moved below that place the Young's Point troops crossed to the

Mississippi side and fought the battle of Grand Gulf. Mr. Simmons took part in that struggle, but not in the battle of Champion Hills, because he was assigned with others of his regiment to the performance of another duty. However, he took part in the first day's fight at Vicksburg and in the fight of the 22d of May there. Mr. Simmons' command was then moved back to Big Black River, to prevent General Johnston from relieving Vicksburg and raising the siege, and remained there until after the surrender and fall of Vicksburg. Being ordered to other work, the command was sent to Port Hudson and from there, after a short stay, to Baton Rouge. The One Hundred and Twentieth Ohio was among those ordered up Red River to relieve General Banks' army, which was being hard pressed. When the boat encountered the Confederate troops up the river and was shelled, Mr. Simmons missed being captured with about half his regiment, and those that remained accompanied Banks' army down the Mississippi to the Atchafalaya River. From there the regiment went to New Orleans and in November, 1864, was temporarily consolidated with the One Hundred and Fourteenth Regiment, Ohio Volunteer Infantry, and was afterward known by that number.

In the construction of the Fort Plaque mine, in Louisiana, Mr. Simmons served in the capacity of shift foreman. He next went with his regiment to Pensacola, Florida, and marched from there around to the rear of Mobile, taking part in the fight at Fort Blakely and helping to capture that stronghold. Following the fall of Mobile, his command went up the Alabama River to Selma, returned soon to Mobile and went into camp and remained there until ordered to Texas, reaching Galveston June 19, 1865. The Texas division was in command of General Granger, and the One Hundred and Fourteenth was at Galveston three days when ordered to Houston and then to Milliken, the terminal at that time of the Houston & Texas Central Railroad. Captain Eberhart was then in command of the company in which Mr. Simmons served, Company E, which after a short stay went back to Houston. At Orange, where the company went next, the oath of allegiance was administered to those who had not yet taken it and a week later the company went to Sabine Pass, then to Beaumont, by the Neches River, and on back to Houston. Then, when the work of re-establishing peaceful conditions had been practically completed, Mr. Simmons was mustered out of the service, October 14, 1865, that being the expiration of his term of enlistment.

Begining life once more as a civilian, Mr. Simmons was employed in the provost marshal's office at Houston until the spring of 1866 when he resigned, and found a partner and engaged in the photographic business. He possessed a theoretical knowledge of the business and his partner the practical side of it, and they opened a gallery in Houston. After a few months they came to Hempstead and later still to Bellville, and a month later Mr. Simmons went to San Felipe and made positive pictures for a month. He then bought out his partner at Bellville, and soon afterward started for Industry, but was taken ill en route and stopped at Nelsonville. After three months he came on to Industry, reaching here in December, 1866. He opened a gallery at this place and continued to be its proprietor for ten years.

Mr. Simmons became identified with the school of Industry in 1868 and taught here until 1894 when he abandoned the profession to give all his time to farming, a vocation which had claimed his attention for some time before. As a teacher he helped to educate many of the men now prominent in business and professional affairs in Austin County. He voted in Texas first at Nelsonville and was one of the election clerks at that place. He has always confessed to being a democrat, although he

J. K. Winston

voted for William McKinley in opposition to the "free and unlimited coinage of silver."

On January 5, 1868, Mr. Simmons was married at Industry, Texas, to Miss Philippina Harting, a daughter of Henry Harting. Mrs. Simmons was born at Preusse-Minten, Germany, in 1845. Her mother was formerly Charlotte Enke, a widow, who had one son by her first marriage, August, who died at Columbus, Texas. Mr. Harting was a shoemaker at Industry for a number of years, and had three children: Sophia, who is now Mrs. Boeker, of Gay Hill, Texas; Henry, who died as a Confederate soldier; and Mrs. Simmons. To Mr. and Mrs. Simmons there have been born the following children: Eleanora, who is the wife of M. F. Glenn, of San Marcos, Texas; Leanora, who is the widow of H. G. Scharnberg, of Port Arthur, Texas; Miss Anna, of Industry; George C. and Clotilda, twins, the latter of whom died as an infant, while the former is a reporter at Houston; Arminda, who became the wife of W. H. Fehrenkamp, of Lockhart, Texas; and Homer G., of Brenham, Texas, who married Clara Haaskarl, a daughter of the Reverend Haaskarl, pastor of the First Lutheran Church of Galveston. Mr. and Mrs. Simmons and their children are all well and favorably known.

Joseph K. Winston. He whose name introduces this review may consistently be termed one of the pioneer citizens of Fort Worth, where he has maintained his home for nearly forty years and where he has been a prominent and influential factor in civic and material development and progress. He has been prominently identified with industrial and business enterprises in the city and its tributary territory, and when he established his home in Fort Worth it was a typical western town and its life and vitality rested chiefly upon its being a trade center for the great open ranges devoted to the cattle industry under the conditions of the old regime in the Lone Star State. Mr. Winston has been a leader in furthering the development and upbuilding of the fine City of Fort Worth, is here the owner of valuable realty, besides having other real-estate interests, and is a man of lofty integrity and commands high place in popular confidence and esteem.

Joseph K. Winston was born in Logan County, Kentucky, in the year 1854, and is a son of Joseph K. and H. O. (Trabue) Winston, both likewise natives of the old Bluegrass State, the former having been born in Green County and the latter in Adair County, and both having been representatives of families that were early founded in Kentucky. The parents of Mr. Winston joined him in Texas shortly after he had established his residence in Fort Worth, and here they passed the remainder of their lives, their remains being laid to rest in a local cemetery.

Joseph K. Winston was reared to adult age in his native county and there acquired his early education. In 1877, as a young man of twenty-three years, he came to Texas and established his home at Fort Worth, where he has resided during the long intervening years and where he has assisted in the transforming of a frontier town into a metropolitan city. During the earlier years of his residence in Texas Mr. Winston gave his attention largely to the handling of cattle and land, and later he engaged in the grain and fuel business in Fort Worth.

Taking lively interest in all that has touched the general welfare of his home city and state and according unequivocal allegiance to the democratic party, Mr. Winston was early called upon to serve in public offices of distinctive trust. For four years he held the office of state and county tax collector in Tarrant County, and in later years he gave effective service as a member of the Board of Education of Fort Worth.

He is a member of the College Avenue Baptist Church and has been most generous and liberal in its support and in the furtherance of the church work in general. He wielded much influence in gaining Fort Worth the Southwestern Baptist Theological Seminary and was prominently identified with the erection and equipment of its present buildings, besides having made liberal donations of land for its site and to aid in its support. He is secretary of the board of trustees of this institution, and further reference to his service in this connection will be found in the article descriptive of the seminary and its work, on other pages of this volume.

Within a few years after becoming a resident of Texas Mr. Winston wedded Miss Lily Frazer, daughter of the late Judge Charles A. Frazer, of Marshall, Harrison County, who was one of the distinguished lawyers and eminent and honored citizens of Texas for many years prior to his demise. The supreme loss and bereavement in the life of Mr. Winston came when his gracious and devoted wife passed to eternal rest, her death having occurred in 1910. She is survived by five children—Paul F., Thomas L., Joseph K., Jr., Helen F., and Alexander F.

William Mieth. A pioneer farmer in the New Ulm community, William Mieth has lived a more than ordinarily eventful life. He was a soldier of the Civil war, and then took up farming in the community where he grew up. His distinguishing charactertistics have probably been a forceful activity, thrift and sound judgment. He was able to leave off hard work at the age of sixty, having accumulated ample provisions for his family needs, and not only has a reputation for success in a business way, but as a man of high character.

William Mieth was born at Anhalt, Dessau, Germany, March 31, 1840. He came to America in 1852 with his parents, and located in the Duff settlement of Austin County. His father was Gottlieb Mieth, who was born in 1810, served his time in the German army, and during the war between the American states was a strong Union man. On leaving Germany the family embarked on a sailing vessel at Bremen, bound for Galveston, and they spent ten weeks and four days in crossing the ocean. The voyage was without special incident, and the ship had 110 immigrants aboard, all Germans and bound for Texas. The majority of these people settled in Austin County, and among the families still here whose ancestors were aboard that ship are the Eckarts, of Cat Spring, Wilkens, of Welcome, and the Lindemann family of the Rock House community. After arriving in Texas Gottlieb Mieth, who was a shoemaker by trade, followed that business for the first four or five years in the Duff settlement just north of New Ulm. When he abandoned his trade he took up farming, acquiring a small tract in the same locality, where he spent the rest of his life. He died in 1890 at the age of eighty years. He was a voter at elections, but otherwise took little interest in politics, and was only a passive member of the Lutheran Church. Gottlieb Mieth married Wilhelmina Schulze, who died at the age of sixty-five and is buried beside her husband at New Ulm. Their children were: William; Sophie, who married Ludwig Rinn of Postoak Point; Charles, who lives in the same community; Mary, who married Charles Weige, of the New Ulm settlement; Clara, who was the first of the children to be born in the United States, and who is the wife of Joseph Foerster on the old Mieth homestead near New Ulm; and August, a farmer east of New Ulm.

William Mieth was about twelve years old when the family came to this country, and all his regular schooling was acquired in the fatherland. Though he had no educational advantages in Texas, by his own efforts he acquired the English language, and reads and writes it just as well as the German. He found exercise for his developing muscles on the home farm, and lived there until after reaching his majority.

Mr. Mieth has the unusual distinction of having fought on both sides during the great American Civil war. He was conscripted by the Confederate government in June, 1862, and assigned to Company K of Wall's Legion. He went to Mississippi with the regiment, and a few months after his enlistment, in December, 1862, was captured with others of his company, at Oxford, Mississippi. Taken to Cairo, Illinois, he was one of eighteen men, all of them from Austin County, who were given the alternative of being exchanged or joining the Federal army, and all of whom enlisted in the Twelfth Illinois Cavalry. This regiment was sent to Virginia, where Mr. Mieth saw active service in the battles of Chancellorsville, Gettysburg, Brandy Station, and Rappahannock Station, besides numerous small skirmishes and much scouting duty. Before the war was over his command was sent back to the Mississippi River Valley and was twenty miles north of Memphis, Tennessee, when the hostilities ceased. He escaped wounds, and after the surrender of Lee's army his company came to Texas with Custer's Cavalry and was engaged in scouting duty over the state from September to November, 1865. At the latter date he was mustered out at Columbia, Brazoria County.

After this long service as a soldier Mr. Mieth returned to the home of his childhood and resumed his occupation as a farmer. Soon afterwards he married Elizabeth Rinn, daughter of Andrew Rinn, whose widow brought the family to America from Germany and settled on the farm where Mr. Mieth now has his home, in the Daghtry league. Mrs. Rinn before her marriage was Margaret Neseldreher. She died in 1880 at the age of seventy years, and left the following children: Ludwig, who died in Austin County leaving a large family; Philip, who died about forty years ago and is survived by a numerous posterity; Jacob, who died in 1913, leaving many children and grandchildren in Milam County; John, of New Ulm; Mrs. Mieth, who was born January 21, 1844; and Daniel, a farmer in the Postoak Point locality.

To the marriage of Mr. and Mrs. Mieth were born the following children: Miss Charlotte, of the New Ulm community; William D., a farmer in the same locality; Adolph, also a farmer; Albert, who conducts a farm adjoining that of his father; Lena, wife of William Kuehn, a farmer in the vicinity of Industry; Mrs. Louisa Muench, who lives near New Ulm; Anna, wife of Emil Krause, near Industry; and Alma, who married William Krause, and lives with her father. Mr. and Mrs. Mieth now have twenty-eight grandchildren. It is a goodly family, and one that has rendered a splendid service in many ways in this prosperous section of Texas.

Mr. Mieth has seldom respected party affiliations in his political action. He is a wide reader of political subjects and other current topics, and has usually cast his vote in presidential elections for the republican candidate. His chief public service has been as reporter for the agricultural department of the Government for the past thirty years. During that period he has made his reports every month on crop conditions.

JOHN C. HELBLE. The possession of marked business talents, enterprise and aggressiveness, has placed John C. Helble in a position where he is contributing materially to the good government of the prosperous little City of Fayetteville. A product of the farm, in young manhood he turned his attention to business affairs, and through perseverance, energy and strict integrity built up a paying venture. In the meantime he acquired experience in business affairs and the management of men, so that his fellow-citizens have chosen him on numerous occasions to act in positions of public importance, and during the last thirteen years he has served very acceptably as both alderman and treasurer of Fayetteville.

Mr. Helble is a native son of Fayette County, Texas, born in the Biegel settlement, January 5, 1867. His father, also named John C. Helble, came to Texas in 1844, when a man of thirty years, and with a wife, and settled near Biegel. He was there only four years when he left for California with a party of gold-seekers, leaving his family alone in Texas for four years while he was engaged in prospecting and mining, in which, however, he met with but little success. Finally he gave up his idea of accumulating a rapid fortune, and in 1852 returned to Texas, where, until his retirement from active life, he followed the peaceful pursuits of the farm. During the period of the Civil war Mr. Helble sympathized with the cause of the South, and rendered some small aid to the Confederacy. In his political views he was a democrat, but he never desired public office. He was a well informed man, keeping himself thus by constant reading, although in his youth he had received only scanty educational training. He had no interest in fraternal matters and belonged to no orders, nor was he a member of any religious denomination.

Mr. Helble, Sr., married his first two wives in Germany, but had no children by either. His third wife was Johanna Gieshen who was born at Oldenburg, Germany, while he was from Wittenberg. Mrs. Helble still survives at the age of seventy-eight years, and has been the mother of the following children: John C., of this notice; Bertha, who married J. J. Tschiedel, a farmer of Fayette County; Joseph, who is a resident of Spokane, Washington; Otto, a resident of Halstead, Texas; and Julia, who married R. M. Oetken, of Fayette County.

John C. Helble of this review was reared at Biegel and secured his education in the country schools. He worked on the farm until reaching the age of twenty-two years, when he engaged in the retail liquor business at Warrenton, and remained there not quite two years. Subsequently, he went to Walhalla and continued in business until the fall of 1899, which year marked his advent at Fayetteville, with which place he has been identified as a business man and public official ever since. He is a man of high business attainments, progressive spirit and broad-minded views on various subjects. All movements which promise to be of business or civic betterment enlist his heart support and co-operation. In politics, his first office was that of alderman of Fayetteville, a capacity in which he has served for thirteen years, and during the same period he has acted as treasurer of the city. In 1903, under Sheriff August Loessin, he acted as deputy sheriff. He has always been known in office as a man who could accomplish things, and his community has benefited materially by his capable executive management. Mr. Helble has never been a convention man. He belongs to the Blue Lodge of Masons, is a Knight of Honor, and holds membership in the S. P. J. S. T., a Bohemian fraternal order, and to the Sons of Hermann. In business and public life, as well as in fraternal circles, Mr. Helble has a wide circle of friends, attracted to him by his whole-hearted geniality.

While a resident of Walhalla, Texas, January 6, 1888, Mr. Helble was united in marriage with Miss Emma Imken, daughter of Gerhardt Imken, who came to the United States from Oldenburg, Germany. Mr. Imken married Johanna Oetken, and Mrs. Helble is the youngest daughter of the family of seven children. Mr. and Mrs. Helble are the parents of four children, namely: Monnie, John, Herbert and Gilbert.

THE SARRAZIN FAMILY, which belongs to the pioneer element of Fayette County, is still worthily represented at Fayetteville by Edward and Leopold Sarrazin, sons of the original settler, Joseph Sarrazin, who came into Texas, it is believed, as early as 1834 and was a compeer of the pioneer Henry Scherrer, of Biegel, both being factors in the pioneer affairs of this county.

Joseph Sarrazin was a native of Westphalia, Germany, born near the Town of Paderborn, in 1809, and was there educated. He came to America alone, but soon met his countryman, Scherrer, with whom it is said that he lived at Biegel for several years. He was an aid to the women and children in the "Run-away Scrape," such an historic event in Texas history, and if he was not a participant in the Battle of San Jacinto he was very close by when that struggle occurred. Joseph Sarrazin was granted a third of a league of land in Gonzales County, as a reward for pioneering here, the grant being dated in 1845, under the authority of Pinkney Henderson. However, Mr. Sarrazin settled permanently in Fayette instead of Gonzales County, his home being located three miles west of Fayetteville.

Mr. Sarrazin had come to America somewhat as an early settler, being possessed of no settled trade or profession, and he was mixed up in much of the exciting experiences of the days of the Revolution and for some years following that struggle. He had a slave property, being one of the early Germans in Texas to own such a possession.

Mr. Sarrazin was a native of Germany and he was the only one of his family to reach America as far as there are any records to relate. He arrived in Texas in 1834. That he learned the English language is evidenced by the fact that the records show that he served on a jury here and from reports obtained from people who associated with him and knew him personally. During the early '50s, Mr. Sarrazin erected a cotton gin on his farm, and the property continued to be a live factor in the affairs of the family throughout the period of the war between the North and the South. This was a horse-power gin, operated by the members of Mr. Sarrazin's family, and remained as one of the institutions of the community until early in the '70s. That Mr. Sarrazin's business ability was far beyond the mediocre is shown by the fact that his estate at the time of his death was valued at $13,000. While he made money through his operations in the cattle business and in numerous other legitimate ways, he made it a point and part of his creed throughout his life to give freely and open-handedly of his means to those whom he thought needed it, and his numerous charities, the extent of which will never be fully known, did much to lessen his fortune. The sick, the unfortunate and always the lowly found in him a true and generous friend, whose heart could always be touched, and whose hand and purse could always be opened. If the full history of the life of this man, at once an early settler and pioneer, steady man of business and the head of an honored and respected family, public-spirited citizen and earnest philanthropist, could be written in its entirety, it would make very interesting and instructive reading, but the records have been lost, and he lives only in the memories of a few old-time friends, and in the hearts of the members of his immediate family.

Joseph Sarrazin was a member of the Catholic Church. His wife, who bore the maiden name of Miss Augusta Ploeger, was also a native of Westphalia, Germany, and a daughter of a judicial official of that country. She was a finely educated lady who came to Texas early in the '40s and was married in 1844, and who died in 1882. She was the mother of the following children: Arnold, Joseph, Edward, who is a member of the firm of E. Sarrazin & Brother, of Fayetteville; Gertrude and

Leopold, of Fayetteville, a member of the firm of E. Sarrazin & Brother.

Edward Sarrazin was born in August, 1850, and is about the oldest merchant in active business in Texas, and the oldest of Fayette County. He started in 1874 and has carried on his enterprise without finncial misfortune. For a long period he has been prominent in public affairs of Fayetteville, of which thriving little city he has been mayor for many years. As a citizen he is widely known and highly respected. Politically he is a supporter of democratic principles.

Leopold Sarrazin, youngest son of Joseph Sarrazin, and junior member of the firm of E. Sarrazin & Brother, was born on the farm near Fayetteville, March 30, 1854, and his education was secured in the country schools. Following this, his business experience added much to his practical knowledge. Mr. Sarrazin entered business in 1888, having passed his life prior to this time on the farm, but in the year mentioned associated himself with his brother, Edward, and the firm of E. Sarrazin & Brother has been doing a constantly increasing business ever since.

Mr. Sarrazin is a democrat in his political views, and has long taken an active part in local politics. He has served Fayetteville as its mayor, and served as a member of the executive democratic committee of Fayette County. Mr. Sarrazin is unmarried.

Elisha T. Tyra. To be the mayor of one of the largest and most rapidly growing cities of the Southwest is in itself no small distinction. But too often the holder of such an office is content to reap the honor without an adequate amount of service. The mayor of a modern American city stands in much closer relation and has more responsibility to the citizens than the President of the United States has to individual Americans. It requires courage, ability and competent efficiency to be a real mayor.

The people of Fort Worth generally express their opinion that in the person of Elisha T. Tyra they have a mayor who has given a vigor and vitality to the office such as it has not known for many years. Mayor Tyra is conducting a strictly business administration of his office, eliminating politics altogether, and he gives his entire time and disinterested labor to the business to which the votes of his fellow citizens called him. It is not strange therefore that Fort Worth has experienced a marked change from the old time ways of political machine government. Mr. Tyra acts entirely upon his own judgment on all matters, though he has never been accused of snap judgment and is always sure that he is right before he goes ahead. The main point is that he does not play politics, and is not subservient to the political leaders. Mayor Tyra would be the last to confess that he knows it all about a city government. He is an everyday student of municipal problems. He works, gets things done, observes closely, and every day he starts out afresh with some new ideas gained by experience.

This is a high and important honor for a man who thirty years ago was an uneducated farmer's son in Mississippi. Elisha T. Tyra was born at Booneville, Prentiss County, Mississippi, in 1864, a son of E. H. and Elizabeth (Stennett) Tyra. His father died in 1879, when Elisha was fourteen years of age. The mother is still living at the age of eighty-five at the old home in Mississippi, enjoying the best of health and spirits and possessing remarkable physical and mental vigor for one of her age.

It was on a farm back in Mississippi that Mayor Tyra was reared. In the years succeeding the war most farmers in Mississippi had a very hard struggle to make both ends meet, and Mayor Tyra suffered the additional handicap caused by the death of his father when he was

E. T. Tyra

still young. There were no opportunities, and his time was required at home so that he could not create advantages for himself in the way of schooling. Thus he arrived at his majority with hardly any education worthy of mention and had attended school only a few days all told. But by that time he had acquired a small store of money, earned by hard manual labor. He had a use for that money, and he invested it in the best possible way, in acquiring an education. He entered a good private school at Jacinto in Alcorn County, Mississippi, and remained a student five years, completing a very thorough course. He started in far behind where most boys of his age were, but made rapid advancement. After completing his course he was elected first assistant teacher of the school, and had already had some experience as a teacher in small country schools. After one year he resigned his position in the school of which he was a graduate, and became principal of the Cleveland High School in Prentiss County, Mississippi. He remained at the head of this institution two years, and was then elected county superintendent of Prentiss County. In that position he continued four years, and thus made a very creditable record as an educator, all the more so because he had educated himself by hard work and much self sacrifice.

It was in December, 1894, that Mr. Tyra came to Texas, locating at Ennis in Ellis County, where for five years he was in the mercantile business. He came to Fort Worth in 1904, and was soon recognized as a forceful and energetic citizen of the growing City of North Texas. His business until he accepted the post of mayor was as traveling salesman, and Mr. Tyra still has the good will and friendship of the large trade which he regularly visited for more than fourteen years. He continued on the road until October, 1914, when he turned his experience and ability as a salesman to good advantage in campaigning for the office of mayor. He was nominated on November 3d, and at the general election was the choice of the people, beginning his duties as mayor on April 15, 1915.

Mayor Tyra already had had experience in conducting municipal affairs at Fort Worth, since for five years he had been a member of the board of education and for four years was president of that body. It was during his term as president of the board of education that all the fine modern school buildings in Fort Worth were erected. The schoolhouses are without question equal to any found in the entire Southwest.

Mayor Tyra is a popular member of several fraternal orders, being a Knight Templar Mason and Shriner, and wherever known he is esteemed as a man of the highest standard of efficiency and honor. He married Miss Luella Lollar. Their three children are Gladys, Ruby and Curtiss.

John D. Saunders. In the Winchester community of Fayette County Mr. Saunders has maintained his residence from the time of his nativity, and not only is he a representative of one of the sterling pioneer families of this county but he also holds precedence as one of the substantial and progressive agriculturists and stock-growers of this section of the Lone Star State, his home being near the Village of Winchester and his unqualified popularity setting at naught in his case any application of the scriptural aphorism that "a prophet is not without honor save in his own country."

Mr. Saunders was born on the homestead that is now his place of abode and the date of his nativity was September 26, 1857. He is a son of Robert D. and Missouri (Carter) Saunders, both of whom were born and reared in the historic State of Virginia, where their marriage was solemnized. From the Old Dominion State Robert D. Saunders and his wife immigrated to Texas in the early '50s, the voyage across the Gulf of Mexico having been terminated when they landed at Galveston, which city was then a mere frontier village. From Galveston they made their way by the old-time overland freighting system to the interior of the state, and after remaining for a time on the Colorado River, in Bastrop County, they came on to Fayette County and numbered themselves among the early settlers on the land or survey on which their sons are now living, this tract being a part of the Whiteside League. Here Robert D. Saunders engaged in farming and in the raising of horses and cattle on modest scale, and with the passing years his earnest efforts were rewarded with definite success and prosperity. He was an unassuming, steadfast citizen who was honored for his uprightness and civic loyalty, and he continued his residence in Fayette County until his death, about the year 1905, when he was of venerable age, his devoted wife having preceded him to eternal rest by many years. Mr. Saunders was not actively concerned with military operations during the Civil war, but his sympathies and support were naturally given to the Confederate cause. Of the children the eldest was Shields, who became the wife of John Z. Walker; Payne married Richard McKinney and was a resident of Bertram, Burnett County, at the time of her death; Robert met his death while serving as a loyal soldier of the Confederacy in the Civil war; Jennie, who became the wife of Thomas Young, died near Winchester, Fayette County; Lou is the wife of James Hill, of Cleburne, this state; Carter died a bachelor; John D., of this sketch, was the next in order of birth; Rodney, a traveling commercial salesman, resides at San Marcos, Hays County; William died at Smithville, Texas, where a number of his children still reside; and Edward resides on the old homestead of his parents, near Winchester.

John D. Saunders was reared to adult age on the farm which is still his place of abode, and he availed himself of the somewhat limited educational advantages afforded in the schools of the locality and period. Upon attaining to his legal majority he engaged in farming and cattle raising in an independent way, and for many years his operations were conducted on rented land on the line between Fayette and Bastrop counties, where he farmed in turn the Stribling, the Roensch and the Zilss places. Finally he returned to the portion of land which he had inherited from his father's estate, and this property, adjoining the old homestead of his father, he has improved and brought under most effective cultivation. He owns about 140 acres, representing practically all of the old home place of his parents, and he has eighty acres under cultivation. On the farm he erected his substantial and commodious residence, a good barn and other buildings that are utilized for the accommodation of his live stock and farm products, and from his early manhood he has been actively identified with the raising of and dealing in cattle, his brand being the figure 7.

Mr. Saunders has passed his days as an energetic and productive worker, with naught of desire for public office or active association with political affairs, but he takes loyal interest in all that touches the welfare and progress of the community and is arrayed as a staunch supporter of the cause of the democratic party.

Just antecedent to Christmas day of the year 1881 was solemnized, in Bastrop County, the marriage of Mr. Saunders to Miss Mattie Taylor, a daughter of James Taylor, who was a prosperous farmer of that county and who came to Texas from the State of Georgia. In Georgia Mr. Taylor had served as sheriff of his county and after his removal to Texas he continued to be actively concerned with political affairs of a local order. He and his wife, Amanda, became the parents of seven children: Mary became the wife of Richard Smith; Fannie wedded Newton Wilson; Ella became the wife of Charles Clark; Mattie, the wife of the subject of this review, was called to eternal rest in 1913; Thomas, the eldest of the children, was a soldier of the Confederacy during the Civil war and still resides in Bastrop County; James died a bachelor; and Frank, the youngest son, is a resident of Weimar, Colorado County. Mrs. Saunders is survived by one daughter, Eva, who is the wife of Charles Bohannan, a prosperous farmer near Winchester, their children being Ruth, Saunders and Walter Edward.

THOMAS E. COCKRILL. The family of which the subject of this review is a prominent and popular representative is a numerous one in Fayette County, with whose history the name has been identified for more than half a century, and he whose name introduces this paragraph is a scion of the third generation of the family in Texas. Through devisement by the will of his uncle, the late Bush Cockrill, who died in 1914, at the age of seventy-five years, Thomas E. Cockrill inherited a substantial competency, and he is now the owner of a well improved farm near the Village of Cistern, Fayette County, and is successfully engaged in business as a trader and dealer in live stock, his modern and attractive residence property in the Village of Cistern being one of the best in this part of the county.

In the village that is now his place of abode Thomas Edward Cockrill was born on the 11th of March, 1869, and here he acquired his early education in the public schools. He began his independent career as a day laborer and continued his activities along this line until about 1905. Then he began trading in cattle and branching out into broader fields of endeavor, in which his success vouches for his ability in the handling of business affairs of important order.

Edward H. Cockrill, father of Thomas E., was born near the City of St. Louis, Missouri, and, the youngest child, he was a lad of six years at the time of the family removal to Texas, his death having occurred at Jeddo, Bastrop County, this state, on the 26th of June, 1913. His father, Starks S. Cockrill, came with his family to this state about the year 1852 and first settled at Milton, Fayette County, the place later becoming known as Cockrill's Hill and finally the name of Cistern being applied to the village, which has since borne this title. Starks S. Cockrill was a farmer and also conducted a modest mercantile business for a number of years, his death having occurred when he was virtually in the prime of life. His wife died just before moving to Texas. Concerning their children the following data are available: Milton, familiarly known as "Chig," devoted the major portion of his active career to mercantile pursuits, at Flatonia and Cistern, and during the Civil war he served as a soldier of the Confederacy. He married Sallie Chunn and was survived by several children. Arthur A., commonly known by the nickname of "Pod," made the trip from Missouri to California on horseback when a young man, and after remaining a few years in that state he made the return trip to Texas by the same means of locomotion, his vocation in Fayette County having been that of a teamster and stock-raiser. He married Riddie Bishop and upon his death was survived by one daughter. Newton was a successful stockman in Fayette County, was influential and useful as a citizen and was called upon to serve as county commissioner, besides which he was a loyal soldier of the Confederacy in the Civil war. He was survived by a large family of children. Bluford, who likewise accumulated a nickname by which he was familiarly known, that of "Bush," was one of the extensive and successful representatives of the cattle industry in this section of Texas and in the early days drove many cattle overland to Kansas. He married Mattie Chunn and they were survived by no children. The only daughter married a Mr. Williams of whom she had one child. After the death of Mr. Williams, she married James Crozier and died in Gonzales County, leaving a large family of children. Edward H., father of the subject of this sketch, was the youngest of the children, as previously stated. By his first marriage Starks S. Cockrill became the father of three children, William, Starks S. and Susie, and they passed their active lives as representatives of the live-stock industry in Fayette County, all having married and all having passed the closing years of their lives in the vicinity of Cistern, Starks S., Jr., having served as a Confederate soldier. The daughter, Susie, married Ezra Brown.

Edward H. Cockrill received in his youth very limited educational advantages but he became a man of broad information and mature judgment, his active life was devoted principally to agricultural pursuits and he was highly respected in both Fayette and Bastrop counties, in each of which he was well known. He married Miss Sarah Wier, who still resides at Jeddo, Bastrop County, and who celebrated her sixty-seventh birthday anniversary in 1915. She is a daughter of the late John Wier, who came to Texas from Mississippi and who established his residence in the southern part of Fayette County. In the following paragraph is given brief record concerning the children of Edward H. and Sarah (Wier) Cockrill:

Etta first wedded Wiley Obar, who was survived by two children, and she later became the wife of Thomas Terrell, to whom she bore four children, who survive her, her death having occurred in Fayette County. William, who is a resident of Hays County, where he is a prosperous farmer, married Della Robbins and they have no children. Thomas Edward, of this article, was the next in order of birth. James Oliver, who is a locomotive engineer, with residence in Denver, Colorado, married Della Lang. Margaret married Joseph Hallmark and died at Jeddo, Bastrop County, leaving three children. Lulu is the wife of Shook Galloway, of Lochart, Caldwell County, and they have two children. Bluford, a farmer and operator of a cotton gin at Jeddo, married Rhoda Fike and they have three children. Lizzie is the wife of George Bartlett, of Jeddo, and they have two children. Ulysses Owen, the maiden name of whose wife was Nora Crenshaw, resides in Hays County; Arthur A., who is a progressive farmer of Fayette County, married Jennie Davis and they have two children.

Thomas E. Cockrill was reared in the faith of the democratic party and in his mature years he has not departed or swerved therefrom, though the only public office of which he has been the incumbent was that of deputy sheriff of his precinct, under the regime of Sheriff Loessin. He takes loyal interest in the civic and material welfare of his native county and as a citizen is liberal and progressive.

On the 28th of January, 1906, was solemnized the marriage of Mr. Cockrill to Miss Cora Davis, a daughter of Tip and Sarah (Hodges) Davis, who became the parents of several children. Mr. and Mrs. Cockrill have no children, but in their pleasant home is being reared Roy Alexander, a son of one of Mrs. Cockrill's sisters, this boy having been given into their care but not having been formally adopted.

Rudolph D. Franke. One of the pioneer families of Austin County is that of Franke, represented by Rudolph D. Franke, who for a number of years has been known as a farmer and business man at Industry, and whose career is especially commendable for the efforts and enterprise which have enabled him to climb from a humble position to one of comparative affluence.

The Franke family was established in Austin County in 1856 by Ernst Franke, grandfather of Rudolph D. Ernst Franke was born at Oldenburg, Saxony, in 1806. He was a shoemaker by trade, and after his marriage to Catherine Hoffman left Saxony and moved to St. Petersburg, Russia, where he followed his trade and where all his children were born. From that country he brought his family to America, taking ship at Bremen on the brig Anna, and landing at Galveston, Texas, November 22, 1850. A few years later he made settlement about Industry and spent there the rest of his life. After his sons were grown, he abandoned his trade and took up farming, which he followed on a small scale. During the war he furnished several sons to the Confederacy, and only one of them, Charles Franke, is still living. Charles Franke was married at Industry October 5, 1860, Miss Agnes Bittner, and they have eleven children living. The children of the grandparents were: Rudolph; Charles; John, who was in Captain Vogt's Company of Wall's Legion in the war; Louis, who also served in Wall's Legion; and August. The son John spent his life as a farmer in the vicinity of Welcome, Louis was also a farmer and died near McGregor, while August died at Industry.

Rudolph Franke, father of Rudolph D., was born at St. Petersburg, Russia, in January, 1840. He came to his majority with a liberal education, and for two years after the war was a teacher at Industry. He entered the Confederate army in Company D, under Captain Vickland, in Wall's Legion, and was in service until the surrender of Vicksburg, where he was paroled and returned home. He and his brother Charles were together in the war, and both returned to Texas. Rudolph Franke learned the shoemaker's trade, the vocation of his father, but later became a farmer, his homestead being almost against the Village of Industry. On that farm he passed away in 1906. He gave little attention to politics, though voting the democratic ticket, and was a member of no church nor social organization. His wife Louisa came to Texas from Germany when a young woman, and is now living near Glenflora, Texas. Their children were: Emma, wife of William Schramm of Glenflora; Rudolph D.; and Ed, a farmer at Industry.

Rudolph D. Franke was born on the old homestead farm at Industry September 7, 1866. His training for life was a practical combination of books with hard work. He attended the village schools, and at the age of nineteen started out for himself as a dealer in cattle. He soon afterwards took up butchering, and that industry he followed in this vicinity for twenty-six years. He started without capital, and at first had a small shop 12x14 feet. He did all the work both of killing and cutting the meat on the block and selling it. He paid close attention to his work, and with increasing means expanded the scope of his operations. Eventually he became a large dealer and shipped extensively to the markets of Houston and Fort Worth. He also dealt in horses, and bought land which he farmed to the extent of growing his own feed. During his career Mr. Franke improved two farms near Industry, and has made one of the most attractive residences in the village. He is a stockholder of the First Guaranty Bank of Industry. He owns land in the Ernst and Pettes leagues, having 472 acres at Industry and 160 acres in Fort Bend County. Mr. Franke is a member of the Sons of Hermann, and carried a policy issued by the Mutual Life Insurance Company.

He was married at Industry in December, 1894, to Miss Ida Buenger, a daughter of Andrew and Anna Buenger and a sister of William A. Buenger of Industry. To their marriage have been born the following children: Lee, who graduated from the Belleville High School and subsequently from the Sam Houston Normal School, and is now a junior in the University of Texas, being a young man of great promise and no little ability; Lena, who is a student in the Sam Houston Normal School at Huntsville; Nora, a student in the public schools at Industry; and Walter and Edwin, both young children at home.

When Mr. and Mrs. Franke started in life after their marriage their possessions comprised a few old ponies and some household goods given to Mrs. Franke by her people. Their first housekeeping was on his father's farm, where he built a small house, and then with the savings from his business invested in two acres of land, situated on the main road in Industry. He moved his first home to the village lot, and around that nucleus has developed the commodious home and substantial property which he now owns.

Tom F. McClure. When Tom F. McClure, widely known in Texas as the "six-shooter-less sheriff," entered upon his new duties as captain of the North Side Police Station in Fort Worth in August, 1915, he accepted as a part of his official equipment, the regulation six-shooter for the first time in his life. Mr. McClure brought to his service in his new position the benefit of a lifetime of experience in the hunting and handling of criminals, for he began his official career when not more than sixteen, as a deputy in the service of his uncle, J. H. Mershon, deputy United States marshal for the Western District of Arkansas. Mr. McClure is a native Texan, born on his father's farm, twelve miles southwest of Decatur, Wise County, in 1868. His parents were John and H. E. (Mershon) McClure, both now deceased.

John McClure was born in Missouri and he was one of the early pioneers to Texas, coming to this state in the early '50s. He first settled in Hays County in Southwest Texas, but later, and just prior to the war, he settled in Wise County. There he was one of the pioneer white settlers, and he lived through the dread period of the Indian raids and depredations that made the life of the white man an insecure and uncomfortable existence, to say the very least. This condition obtained before the war and continued through it into the later '70s, making the history of Texas in those years a particularly bloody one. John McClure enlisted in the Confederate army under Sull Ross, who later became governor of Texas, and he served throughout the war with valor and distinction under that gallant solder and officer. He was a stockman by way of occupation, following the natural trend of the state, and he had a nice ranch at the vicinity of Decatur. It is recalled, however, that he was the only man among the pioneers of that part of Wise County who was a skilled carpenter and woodworker, and in that capacity he was called upon time without number to make coffins for white settlers that were the victims of Indian depredations in their vicinity.

Mrs. McClure was a native daughter of Kentucky and she came with her parents to Texas, also pioneers to Wise County, when she was yet a child in years. She married John McClure there, and there she spent her life.

Tom McClure was sixteen years old when in 1885 he left his father's home and went to Fort Smith, Arkansas, to be with his maternal uncle, J. H. Mershon, then deputy United States marshal for the Western District of Arkansas, with jurisdiction over Indian Territory. At that time the United States District Court of Indian Territory was noted for the great number of criminal cases, outlaws and desperadoes, that were tried there. Young McClure was appointed by his uncle as his assistant or deputy, and then began his thrilling career as an officer of the law in the most lawless period of that district.

TOM F. McCLURE

In 1891 Mr. McClure returned to Wise County, settled down and engaged in the cattle business. Later he became deputy sheriff of Wise County. In 1899 he became sheriff of the county and he served in that office for four years. Subsequently he went to Jones County and interested himself again in the cattle business, and was there elected sheriff, serving a four year term in his official capacity in that county. While there he was by appointment of Governor Campbell a member of the Live Stock Sanitary Commission of Texas for two years, in which post, as in all others, he gave an excellent account of himself at all times. His duties as sheriff of Wise and Jones counties took him in pursuit of criminals as far east as the Atlantic coast of Tampa, Florida, and as far west as California and through to British Columbia and Northern Canada, and in those years he established a reputation for fearlessness and all around efficiency that will never be outlived.

In 1914 Mr. McClure was a candidate for the office of state comptroller on the prohibition-democratic ticket, but for personal reasons he withdrew from the race while the campaign was yet in its earliest stages. In the summer of 1915 he moved to Fort Worth and in August followed his appointment to his present position, captain of police in charge of the North Fort Worth Police Station.

At the time of his appointment a local paper commented on the man and his career in this manner:

"Tom McClure, famed over Texas as the 'six-shooter-less sheriff,' first of Wise, then of Jones county, has been appointed Captain of Police in charge of the North Side station. He will begin work Sunday.

"McClure will be the successor of Capt. G. Frank Coffey who was killed two months ago by Tom Cooper. Captain George Cooper, transferred to the North Side temporarily, will be returned to headquarters.

"But McClure will no longer be known as a six-shooter-less officer. He will break his record of a life-time Sunday when he buckles a belt and pistol around his waist.

"'I guess I'll have to wear one,' he said Saturday. 'I don't expect ever to have to use it, but it is probably best to wear one. My experience as an officer has always been in the small towns and open country, and I did not need a pistol. But as a policeman I expect I will have to deal with many classes—that is why I'm going to use a gun.'

"Retiring as sheriff of Jones county after a service of four years, McClure entered the race for state comptroller, but withdrew before the election a year ago. He then moved to Fort Worth and became a qualified voter. The most exciting days of his career as an officer happened during the five years he served as a deputy United States marshal at Fort Smith, Arkansas, over which district the famous judge, I. C. Parker, presided. Judge Parker bore the reputation of having sentenced more men to the gallows than any other judge, and McClure participated in the arrest of many of these men.

"Lawlessness ran rife over the Indian Territory then, and McClure spent most of the five years on the trail of bad Indians and outlaws. Many of the Indian Territory cases were tried at Fort Smith. He was one of the officers who helped to break up the Belle Starr gang and the Pickens gang. two famous bands of territory outlaws. He left the Federal service, however, and came to Texas just as the Dalton gang was budding out into outlawry. He was intimate with them, and worked with them in Arkansas when they were deputy U. S. Marshals in Fort Smith.

"Although he had many fights with bad Indians and outlaws. McClure fought with Winchesters and shot guns, and never carried a pistol. 'Those were exciting days,' he said Saturday. 'We would go out in wagon trains to gather up prisoners. We would catch a man, chain him up in the wagon and drive on through the country looking for others. We would be gone as long as three months at times before we would drive into Fort Worth with three and four wagon loads of prisoners. I remember one time we drove to within sight of Decatur before we caught a man charged with assault to murder. I was hoping we would not catch him until we got into Decatur, because I wanted to see some of the home folks, but we turned around and drove back to Fort Smith.'

"McClure served as deputy sheriff for six years in Wise county before he ran for sheriff and was elected. After four years as sheriff at Decatur he went to Stamford. He lived two years in Jones county before he was elected sheriff and held the office four years. A chase of 9,000 miles after an alleged kidnapped boy of Stamford featured the closing days of his service as a Jones county sheriff. He brought the boy back."

Mr. McClure married Nannie Simmons, a Mississippi girl and the sister of Judge Tom Simmons and Dr. C. B. Simmons. They have their home on the north side.

Roger Byrne is a man of unusual enterprise and initiative and has met with such marvelous good fortune in his various business projects that it would verily seem as though he possessed an open sesame to unlock the doors to success. Self-made and self educated in the most significant sense of the words, he has progressed steadily toward the goal of success until he is recognized today as one of the foremost business men and citizens of Smithville, where he has resided since 1894. Formerly he was engaged in the retail liquor business in this city but since 1913 has given up that enterprise in order to devote his attention to his farming and banking interests. At one time he served this city as mayor and at the present time, in 1916, he is a member of the State Legislature.

A native of Ireland, Roger Byrne was born at Kilcar, County Donegal, September 20, 1858, and he is a son of Patrick and Bridget (McGuire) Byrne, both of whom are now deceased, their entire lives having been spent in the Emerald Isle. The Byrnes were driven out of the Wicklow mountains in the sixteenth century and they then settled in the mountain county of Donegal. Representatives of the name always stood for the government and were strongly opposed to revolutionary movements, for which reasons they were driven out of their native haunts in the Wicklow mountains. Mr. Byrne, through his parents, is part Cunningham and part Curran, but all Irish to the core. There were five sons and one daughter born to Mr. and Mrs. Patrick Byrne, namely—John, James, Patrick, Timothy, Roger and Mary, all of whom came to the United States except Patrick. Mary is now Mrs. Michael Leonard, of Austin; John died in Austin, leaving a large family; and James and Timothy are both unmarried and reside in Austin.

Roger Byrne was reared to the age of fifteen years on his father's farm in Ireland and there received his early experience as an agriculturist on a small scale. He attended school in the home community and in December, 1873, immigrated to the United States, coming hither aboard the steamer San Jacinto. The journey lasted twenty-six days and on reaching Texas Mr. Byrne stopped for a time at Bryan, where he visited an acquaintance. He then proceeded to Corsicana, where his brother James had previously settled. After a conference with his brother he decided to engage in peddling. He procured a "pack" of Irish linens and visited the towns along the railroads in the vicinity of Corsicana. His stock of merchandise was worth about $50 and he met with exceptionally good luck from the first. He traveled over the state and devoted his attention to that business for nine years, during the last three of which he carried his stock of goods in a spring wagon, which he drove from town to town. He did his last work in this line at San Marcos, where, by accident, he purchased a saloon, the owner of which was in jail. He then disposed of his team and outfit and began a new business in the retail liquor line there. He resided in San Marcos from 1884 until 1894, in which latter year he came to Smithville and embarked in the liquor business here, continuing until June, 1913. He became a citizen of the United States in 1884 and in 1892 returned to Ireland on a visit. Shrewd and energetic as a business man, he was not content to confine his interests to a saloon and in 1903 helped organize the First National Bank of Smithville, of which he was a director for several years and of which he is now president. In 1905 he became interested in farming operations and in recent years his investments in that line have extended to Lavaca and Bastrop counties, where he grows cotton and corn, several tenants being engaged to do his work. He built the block in which his saloon was located for some twenty years and he has substantially improved other property which he owns in this city.

In getting ready for citizenship Mr. Byrne made it a point to post himself on American affairs and when he settled down permanently he began a career which led to activity in political matters. In 1885 he was elected a member of the city council in San Marcos and held that office continuously there until his advent in Smithville, taking an important part in the improvement of streets and in the formation of a fire department. He cast his first presidential vote in 1884 for Grover Cleveland and has always given his support to democratic candidates since then. He has figured prominently as a democrat in state convention work and he supported Governor James S. Hogg in all his campaigns; he believed strongly in the issues of Jo Bailey and has always favored and fought the battles of the so-called Gainesville statesman. In the presidential line-up of 1912 he supported Mr. Harmon in the preliminaries but he is now thoroughly in accord with the policies of President Wilson. Mr. Byrne was first elected to the State Legislature in 1904, as the successor of Capt. J. S. Jones. He entered the Twenty-ninth Legislature and his committee assignments have been without chairmanships at his own behest. His chief and most important committee was that of Common Carriers and Labor and he introduced nearly all the bills passed affecting labor. He has been the champion of the union labor people in all his legislative work and for that reason the bulk of labor legislation devolved on him. In the Thirty-first Legislature he secured the passage of sixteen bills affecting labor and devices for its safety. The child labor bill, the electric headlight and the switchlight measures were all passed largely as the result of his efforts. He has also manifested interest in the subject of education and fought for all the recent legislation pertaining to public education, the University and Normal School, with the exception of the measure pertaining to the selection of the county superintendent of schools by a county board instead of by vote of the people. At one time he filled a vacancy as mayor of Smithville and during that period and as city alderman he made a point of improving the streets and it was during his regime that the present fine high school building was erected. It will be seen from the foregoing that Mr. Byrne has accomplished much both in the business and political world of his home community. His success is due entirely to his own efforts and for that reason is the more gratifying to contemplate.

In San Marcos, Texas, July 16, 1890, Mr. Byrne was united in marriage to Miss Addie McGehee, a daughter of Charles L. and Sallie (Humphrey) McGehee, who formerly lived in Texas, but who are now residents of Granite, Oklahoma. Mr. McGehee's father was a member of the firm of McGehee & Nichols, builders of the state capitol of Texas. Mrs. Byrne was the only daughter in a family of six children. Mr. and Mrs. Byrne have the following children: Roger H. is a student in Notre Dame College, Indiana; and Marie, Walter, Louise and Lewis (twins), and Joseph Weldon are all at the parental home in Smithville. Mr. Byrne was reared in the faith of the Catholic Church and he is a generous contributor to the financial needs of that organization. The Byrne home is a modest cottage in this city and is the scene of many convivial gatherings.

BERNHARD ERNST KNOLLE, M. D. Among the prominent pioneer families of Texas, one which has contributed to the growth and development of various sections is that which bears the name of Knolle, members of which have attained positions of prominence in agriculture, in business and in the professions. A worthy representative of the name is found in the person of Dr. Bernhard Ernst Knolle, of Industry, one of the leading medical practitioners of Austin County, and a man widely known in his profession.

The Knolle family was introduced into Texas by Ernst Frederick Gottlieb Knolle, the grandfather of Doctor Knolle, who was born at Krebshaven, near Stadthaven, principality of Schamberg-Lippe, Germany, January 12, 1814. He acquired a good education and became a teacher in the fatherland, and was also identified with the Lutheran ministry. In 1844, at the age of thirty years, he emigrated to the United States and located at or near Industry, and four years later was followed by his two younger brothers, Fritz and William Knolle, and all resided about Industry until just after the close of the Civil war, when William went to Pennsylvania, his family and posterity still living in the vicinity of Pittsburgh. Fritz Knolle became a farmer on a large scale at Industry and was a slaveholder of the olden time. A stanch supporter of the South, he sent his son Fritz to the Confederate army during the Civil war, and the latter was captured at Yazoo River, Mississippi, and died in the northern military prison at Indianapolis, Indiana. He could have evaded detention in the northern prison, by declaring his allegiance to the Union, when he would have been allowed to return to his home in Texas, but he was a true son of the Southland and gave up his life, as it were, for the cause for which he fought. Fritz Knolle, Sr., died during the early '70s, leaving a widow.

Ernst Frederick Gottlieb Knolle was the ship preacher on the vessel which brought him to America, and subsequently after his arrival engaged actively in church work among the settlers around Industry. He was not an ordained minister, but rather an exhorter, and made himself useful in the church as well as in civil life. On settling at Industry, Ernst Knolle erected an adobe house, which soon, however, gave way to a larger and permanent residence in which he entertained largely all the travelers passing through or stopping here for settlement, and aside from this feature of his life he was also one of the first merchants of Industry. He sold goods practically all of his life, both at Industry and on his farm near by, and spent his final years here as a merchant. As a farmer, he carried on extensive operations, and prior to the Civil war owned a large number of slaves and was a prosperous cotton planter. He built the first mill here, which he operated with mule power, as he did also the gin which was worked in connection. Later he added steam power to these enterprises, which were conducted by him for perhaps twenty years, it being then sold to Theo Daum, who in turn sold it to Frank Schramm, and it is now owned by the latter's son.

Another matter of importance with which this sturdy old pioneer was connected was the manufacture of leather. Some evidence of the location of his old tanyard still remains and the product from his yard was even better than is produced today. He sold his leather to the cities, and some of it is said to have been exported, the excellence of its quality bringing it a ready sale wherever displayed. It would seem that there was no limit to the activities and usefulness of Mr. Knolle. He erected a flour mill at Industry and induced his neighbors to grow wheat, but because of the climate wheat did not thrive here and the industry languished and was finally totally abandoned. At various times he was instrumental in bringing on craftsmen of the various trades and industries from the old country, and employed them wherever he could to advantage, Industry thus becoming the center of all things commercial and industrial in this part of the state. All his produce to and from market at Houston he hauled with his own ox-teams.

Upon the issues between the North and the South during the '60s, Mr. Knolle was a fiery secessionist, and supported the Confederate cause with his own money, raised money for the cause in various sections and provided goods and property wherever he could in aid of the cause. He cast all his fortunes with the Confederacy and was so confident of final success that he took Confederate bonds and accepted Confederate money for his goods. The fall of the Lost Cause was a severe blow to him, as his property was all swept away, as well as his many slaves, and he was comparatively a poor man when the war closed. However, he did not allow himself to become discouraged, but set to work to recuperate his fortunes, and made another modest competence in the old channels of trade before he died.

In politics Mr. Knolle was as much interested as he was in business affairs. He possessed great energy and determination, was wiry and sinewy and accomplished feats of endurance that few men would undertake. He was wont to ride his favorite saddler to Houston during a night, buy his goods in the markets the next day, and ride back to Industry again, sixty-five miles that night, and be ready for business the next morning. After the close of the Civil war he was ever a democrat in politics. He was a fighting man, by nature, and anything which smacked of the policies of the republican party was abhorrent to him. He was a Blue Lodge Mason, and his strong interest in the order was emphasized by his riding to the lodge meetings which were held at Belleville.

Mr. Knolle was married at Petzen, in the principality of his birth, December 24, 1837, to Miss Dorothea Frederike Charlotte Elenora Brandt, who was born October 5, 1811, and died March 21, 1868. He married the second time Mrs. Augusta Boesche, and they had one child, Arthur, who is now a resident of Brenham, Texas. By his first marriage Mr. Knolle was the father of the following children: Hermenia Sophia, born in Europe, who died unmarried; Herminia Amelia, who died as a child in Europe; Wilhelmina Sophia, who married Dr. Christof Kubitz, and died in Industry; Ernst Hermann, the father of Dr. B. E. Knolle; Ernst Emil (known as "E. M."), a resident of New Ulm, Texas; and Ernst Paul, who died at Flatonia, Texas, leaving a family. The father of these children passed away November, 1880, when the community of Shelby lost one who, probably, had done as much as any other man to develop its interests.

Ernst Hermann Knolle, father of Dr. Bernhard Ernst Knolle, was born February 9, 1844, in Germany, and there received an education in the country schools. He early became a farmer and superintended the work done by the slave labor, managing the interests of the farm, hauling the freight and taking charge of the outside matters of his father's numerous enterprises. When the Civil war broke out he enlisted in Captain Voigt's Company of Wall's Legion, and was captured in the defense of Vicksburg, at Yazoo River, Mississippi, and was imprisoned in the Federal prison at Indianapolis, Indiana. After twenty months there he was taken to Richmond, Virginia, and there released when General Lee surrendered. He walked back to Texas and after partial recuperation resumed farming, and belonged to the modest class when he died. He was famous for his personal industry and died prematurely because of his hard work and exposure, September 20, 1873. Mr. Knolle married Caroline Scherrer, a daughter of Bernhard Scherrer, another of the very earliest settlers of the Southwest, who came to the United States in 1829, from St. Gallen, Switzerland, and settled at Biegel, Fayette County, in 1833, spending the remaining years of his life there as a successful planter. Mrs. Knolle died the year after her husband, and their children were: Bernhard Ernst, of this review; Dr. Edmund Robert, a practicing physician of Brenham, Texas; and Dr. A. P., of Ellinger, Texas.

Bernhard Ernst Knolle was born November 24, 1866, and grew up in the home of his uncle, E. M. Knolle, who now lives at New Ulm. His childhood and youth were spent at Industry, and after he finished the public schools he took a course in the Agricultural and Mechanical College at Bryan. His professional training was secured at Tulane University, New Orleans, Louisiana, where he was graduated with the degree of doctor of medicine in 1886, and in further preparation for his chosen life work he took a post-graduate course of one year at the same school. Doctor Knolle began his practice among his old neighbors and friends, and has been actively engaged in his professional work at Industry ever since, having built up a very large and important practice. His connection with societies of medicine comprises membership in the Texas State Medical Society, the District Medical Association and the Austin County Medical Society.

In politics Doctor Knolle simply participates in elections as a democrat, and his only official positions have been those of county health officer and president of the school board, holding the latter at present. He is president of the First Guaranty State Bank of Industry, of which he was one of the promoters, and is a participant in all matters pertaining to the welfare of the community. Fraternally, Doctor Knolle is connected with the Sons of Hermann, the Knights of Honor and the Woodmen of the World, and has passed through all the chairs in the two latter lodges.

On May 14, 1889, Doctor Knolle was married to Miss Ida Texanna Witte, a daughter of Ernst H. B. Witte, of Shelby, a review of whose career will be found on another page of this work. To this union there have been born the following children: Roxie Minnette, born March 4, 1890, married Robert F. Miller, professor of animal husbandry in the agricultural department of the University of California, at Davis, California; Roger Edmund, born October 30, 1891, a medical student at Tulane University; Waldo Austin, born August 15, 1893, who is also a medical student at that institution; Sadie May, born May 27, 1897, who is a student at the Texas Presbyterian College, Milford, Texas; Josephine Iola, born September 21, 1899; Bernice Ida, born September 21, 1905; and Ben Ernst, born October 22, 1911.

John Lee Brooks. While now a successful lawyer of Dallas, the interests of John Lee Brooks have been widely and usefully diversified. He is an educator, a finished speaker, a trained debater, an original thinker, writer and lecturer, a native Texan and the finished product of

Sincerely, Jno. Lee Brooks

numerous enterprises. When the Civil war broke out he enlisted in Captain Voigt's Company of Wall's Legion, and was captured in the defense of Vicksburg, at Yazoo River, Mississippi, and was [illegible] in the Federal prison at Indianapolis, Indiana. After twenty [illegible] there he was taken to Richmond, Virginia, and there released when General Lee surrendered. He walked back to Texas and after [illegible] resumed farming, and belonged to the modest class when he died. He was famous for his personal industry and died prematurely because of his hard work and exposure, September 20, 1873. Mr. [illegible] married Caroline Scherrer, a daughter of Bernhard Scherrer, [illegible] of the very earliest settlers of the Southwest, who came to the United States in 1829, from St. Gallen, Switzerland, and settled at [illegible], Fayette County, in 1833, spending the remaining years of his life there as a successful planter. Mrs. Knolle died the year after her husband. [illegible] their children were: Bernhard Ernst, of this review; Dr. Edmund [illegible]ert, a practicing physician of Brenham, Texas; and Dr. A. P., of [illegible], Texas.

Bernhard Ernst Knolle was born November 24, 1866, and grew up in the home of his uncle E. M. Knolle, who now lives at New Ulm. His childhood and youth were spent at Industry, and after he finished the public school he took a course in the Agricultural and Mechanical College at Bryan. His professional training was secured at Tulane University, New Orleans, Louisiana, where he was graduated with the degree of doctor of medicine in 1886, and in further preparation for his [illegible] a post-graduate course of one year at the same [illegible] Doctor Knolle [illegible] his practice among his old neighbors and [illegible] and has been actively engaged in his professional work at [illegible] built up a very large and important practice [illegible] of medicine comprises membership in the [illegible] Society, the District Medical Association and the [illegible] Society.

[illegible] Doctor Knolle simply participates in [illegible] only official positions have been those of [illegible] of the school board, holding the latter [illegible] of the First Guaranty State Bank of Industry [illegible] promoters, and is a participant in all matters [illegible] community. Fraternally, Doctor Knolle [illegible] Hermann, the Knights of Honor and the [illegible] passed through all the chairs in the [illegible] 1889, Doctor Knolle was married to [illegible] of Ernst H. B. Witte, of [illegible] on another page of this work [illegible] following children: Roxie [illegible] F. Miller, professor of [illegible] of the University of [illegible], born October 30, [illegible] Waldo Austin, born [illegible]

Sincerely, Jno. Lee Brooks.

the best universities of America. He has come into close contact with the leading men and movements, philanthropies and affairs of the world.

Broad humanitarianism, intense patriotism, love of truth and justice, cultured courtesy, and prodigious capacity for hard work, are keynotes to the many-sided character and busy life of John Lee Brooks. Successively, he has mastered three distinct professions; namely, theology, pedagogy, and law. His deeply philanthropic bent early led him into profound theological and philosophical studies, later broadening out into science, history, economics and law.

However, while a deep student of comparative religions and ethical systems ancient and modern, the strongly scientific bent of his versatile mind early brought him into hopeless disharmony with accepted orthodox standards; so that he was never ordained, nor qualified for entering the ministry, for which his mother had designed him, but turned inevitably to the field of professional education, economics, business and law.

Having qualified fully as a professional educator by a four years course for the degree of doctor of philosophy, under Dr. Nicholas Murray Butler, and at Teachers College, Columbia University, New York City, and successfully pursued that calling for some years in Washington, District of Columbia, he finally finished his law course at Columbian University, and settled on law as his life-work.

By instinct and training, Mr. Brooks is a scholar. As a thinker, he is rigidly thorough, intellectually honest, conservatively progressive and fearless. As a writer, he is clear, logical and forceful, vivid and original; as a speaker and debater, he is clear, logical, persuasive and convincing. He is possessed of a well-trained, powerful voice, fluent, accurate diction, and a fiery, stirring eloquence, characteristic of his Scotch-Irish ancestry, which together with a fund of humor, irony and satire, makes him at home on the stump or in the court-house. His long residence in leading commercial and university centers, his extensive travels and observation as an educator, has laid broad and deep the foundations for the highest success in law, and justly merits his popular reputation as "one of the best educated lawyers at the Texas Bar."

On the other hand, his boyhood spent on the farm; six years on a Texas ranch, three years as farm and ranch superintendent; more than ten years active business career—as postmaster at Georgetown, Texas, under Cleveland's second administration; two years oil lands and brokerage business in New York City, as the eastern representative of the Hogg-Swayne Syndicate of Beaumont, of which his brother, Judge R. E. Brooks, of Houston, was a member; four years in the hay and grain, land and real estate business at Muskogee, Oklahoma, Wills Point, and Dallas, Texas; in addition to his many other business interests, has made Mr. Brooks a practical man of affairs, absolutely essential to the highest success in law and business.

Mr. Brooks' ten years residence in the East has put him in close sympathetic touch with modern economic and business needs and conditions, and peculiarly fits him as a lawyer to render an invaluable service to his native State, in the formative period of her modern business development. While a keen student of state, national and international politics, Mr. Brooks has no political aspirations whatever. His one aim is to become a really great lawyer, and as a private citizen help make Texas the first state of the Union, and America the greatest nation on earth!

John Lee Brooks, son of a native Texas mother, of Scotch-Irish and English extraction from the best Alabama and Virginia stock, was born at Elgin, Bastrop County, Texas, July 2, 1870. Originally named John Leander Brooks, after a Virginia gentleman kinsman of his mother, he changed his name at majority in honor of Gen. Robert E. Lee, his life-long exemplar and ideal of Southern manhood.

Mr. Brooks is the seventh child in a family of nine, five brothers and four sisters, and the fourth of five sons born to the Brooks family, four of whom, lacking thirty days in his case, were born exactly three years apart, namely: Walter, killed by a vicious horse he was handling at eight years of age; Itasca, named by her patriotic mother after Lake Itasca, source of the Father of Waters, and who died from exposure in a storm at fifteen years of age; Texas Cassandra ("Texie"), eldest living sister, named for her native state, a fine business woman, mother of a large interesting family, and wife of Col. John E. Jones, banker, of Fullerton, California; Nannie Roline, a talented musician who gave promise of a brilliant operatic career, cut short by a tragic accident and spinal injury, from which she died after a lingering and pathetic illness at twenty-three; Richard Edward, eldest living brother, for eight years judge of the 26th Judicial District at Austin, Texas, who after a brilliant though brief judicial career, retired to join ex-Governor Hogg in the organization of the Hogg-Swayne Syndicate, on the discovery of oil at Beaumont, Texas, and for several years past has been prominently connected with the Texas Company, and allied oil interests, and the leading financial institutions of Houston, Texas; James Robert, ranchman and planter of Mertzon, Irion County, Texas, a leading Mason and Methodist; John Lee, lawyer, Dallas, Texas, subject of this sketch; Mary, an accomplished vocalist, wife of J. E. Jordan, planter, of Mertzon, Texas; Charles Wesley, Jr., oil man and ranchman of the latter address.

Mr. Brooks' father, Charles Wesley Brooks, of English descent and named for the eminent English Methodist divine, was descended from the numerous branch of that family name in Alabama and Georgia, and traced his family tree back to the days of King John and Magna Charta. He was the son of a prominent Alabama planter, and was born at Florence, Lawrence County, Alabama, December 25, 1830.

Charles Wesley Brooks' name was a synonym of honor and integrity, and a passport to his children wherever he was known. He did much of his large and extensive business on his word of honor, which was as good as his bond. He was a man of fine physique and commanding appearance. He stood over six feet in his sock feet, and in his prime was a man of fearless courage and great physical prowess. He was a man of strong native ability, of sound business judgment, a scientific planter, stock-raiser and an expert horticulturist. He was a good veterinary surgeon, and, but for the misfortune of having his education cut short by family reverses, he would undoubtedly have achieved great wealth and distinction, as a man of the highest integrity, force of intellect and character. He was a life-long Mason, a Methodist, and a staunch Jeffersonian democrat, a teetotaler, but a militant believer and champion of local option and state rights. He took little stock in national prohibition, nor in woman's suffrage. He deplored "a short-haired woman" or a "crowing-hen!" and often prayed: "From such, good Lord, deliver us!"

In his early youth Mr. Brooks became an overseer and planter by profession. He came to Texas in 1854, in his twenty-fifth year, bringing fifty slaves to Texas for Judge John C. Townes, Sr., father of Judge John C. Townes of Austin, Texas, and opened up a six-hundred acre plantation for the elder Townes on the Yeghua Creek, below Manor, in Bastrop County, Texas.

Soon after completing this work, and over Judge Townes' protest, he left the latter's employ, and in 1854 married Elizabeth ("Bettie") Burleson, youngest sister of Gen. Edward Burleson, prominent in Texas history as a pioneer Indian fighter, at the battle of San Jacinto, vice president of the Republic of Texas under Sam Houston, and great-uncle of Albert Sidney Burleson, postmaster general, and one of the mainstays in President Wilson's cabinet.

Removing to Young's Prairie, now Elgin, in Bastrop County, Texas, Mr. Brooks opened up a big plantation and stock-farm of his own, on a large body of lands partly inherited by his wife from her pioneer father, James Burleson, and soon became one of the leading planters and ranchmen of that section of the State.

Charles W. Brooks gave four of the best years of his young manhood to the "Lost Cause," under Hood, Jackson and Lee. While a firm believer in Jeffersonian democracy and state rights, he deplored secession, leaning strongly to Sam Houston's view that it was unnecessary, and doomed to failure. Four times was he honorably discharged from the war for wounds and serious illness; four times did he voluntarily return to the fray, as soon as he was able to sit his horse. For seven years after the close of the war, he was an invalid, but finally recovered his health by his own efforts as a weaver of fine cloth, sitting at an old-fashioned hand-loom, under a giant cottonwood tree, in the open air of his own front yard.

The war had left him financially ruined, yet his noble wife, with indomitable courage and resourcefulness, took full charge of the big plantation, renewed farming operations, and with one old-time slave-darkey, a mule, and a bull-tongue plow, successfully piloted the Brooks family through the dark and tragic years of the Civil War, and Reconstruction in Texas until the father had recovered his health, and in large measure rebuilt his family fortunes.

For fifteen years after the close of the Civil War the little Town of Elgin, in Bastrop County, was noted as "one of the worst towns on the Texas border." The town was in the hands of the saloon gang; the county was dominated by the liquor interests; law and order were prostrate; cattle and horse thieves and desperadoes of the worst type infested the surrounding country. Elgin and the wild "Yeghua Country" of Bastrop County was the rendezvous of the noted Sam Bass, Bill Longley, and John Wesley Hardin gangs, the latter the son of a pioneer Methodist preacher, so tradition says!

The "Yeghua Notch-Cutters" and the "Vigilance Committee" was the answer of the law-abiding citizens to such lawless and desperate conditions in Texas, as was the "Ku-Klux Klan" in the old South. The "Notch-Cutters," so tradition tells, got their peculiar name from their unique method of recording their verdict in "notches" cut deep in the body of the tree which constituted the "gallows" for their victims. One "notch" meant he had been guilty of murder; two "notches" branded him as a horse-thief; three "notches" was a blanket verdict, covering cow-theft, minor offenses, or meant that he was hung on general principles as an undesirable citizen. Such verdicts, though crude, were not reversible by legal technicalities, were usually based in substantial justice, were never questioned, and usually ended the case.

The Masonic Order and the Methodist Church, organized and led by such men as Charles W. Brooks, and Josiah Whipple, a fearless itinerant Methodist preacher of that day, constituted the first nucleus around which rallied the elements of law and order, and which, after a score of years of fierce conflict, brought order out of chaos, and made Elgin, Texas, what it is today, one of the cleanest, most cultured and law-abiding communities in the State.

Charles W. Brooks was one of the first men in the Elgin of that day to lift his voice against the saloon, and the organized liquor traffic in politics; and for the sanctity of the home and the church, for the protection of property and the rigid enforcement of the law against murder and mob-rule; for the improvement of the schools, and the restoration of law and order. For fifteen long years in this time he led a bitter and relentless warfare against these organized forces of lawlessness and evil, part of which time he sat in an invalid's chair by his loom, under the big cottonwood tree in his own front yard, weaving, preaching Masonry, and pleading with his neighbors to rise up and destroy organized vice and crime, and fearlessly and impartially to enforce the law in Bastrop County!

For many years he was foreman of the grand jury, and in the face of bitterest threats, vilest calumny and denunciation from the powerful saloon and political factions of the day, who did not hesitate to mob or assassinate their enemies, good or bad, he finally won the fight for local option, law and order in Bastrop County, and destroyed the liquor power in politics in that whole section.

More than once during this time did he face without flinching the deadly threats and armed intimidation of desperate law-breakers. On one such occasion he stood with his back to a brick wall, bared his breast, scarred with the wounds of the "Lost Cause," scathingly denounced the enemies of law and order, refused to keep silence or go home until the final victory for local option had been won, and defied his enemies to "shoot the heart out of an ex-Confederate soldier, a Mason, a Methodist, and a free-born Texas and American citizen!"

This remarkable exhibition of unarmed moral heroism so aroused public sentiment, and smote the consciences of his cowardly enemies, that they hastily retreated as from a superior armed force; the country-side was swept by a tidal wave of victory for local option, law and order, which never afterwards receded. They knew him as a fearless soldier in the Confederate ranks, and recognized the folly of resisting further the even higher quality of moral courage, manifested in defense of the home, the church, law and order, property and life, the like of which they had never before beheld until that day!

After the triumph of his cause at Elgin, to save his family from the terrors that beset him, and give them the best educational advantages, he removed in the fall of 1878 to Georgetown, Texas, and entered his children in Southwestern University. This important move, made about the time the buffalo disappeared from the rolling plains of Texas, marked an epoch in the history of the Brooks family, destined to influence most profoundly the history both of that family and of the State.

When the Brooks family landed in Georgetown, Texas, that famed educational center was cursed with seven saloons, frequent murders and the customary attendant evils. Charles W. Brooks again entered the ranks of the forces of law and order, and did yeoman service in banishing the saloon and the liquor traffic from the sacred precincts of that classic seat of learning.

The records of such victories of peace richly deserve a place in the annals of Texas, as matchless exhibitions of moral courage and heroism, no less deserving of grateful commemoration than those of war; no less honored and glorious than the battles of the Alamo, and of San Jacinto!

Charles Wesley Brooks died while postmaster at Georgetown, Texas, August 28, 1898, mourned and honored by a host of friends and acquaintances throughout the State, as one of the best citizens Texas ever had. He was a thirty-second degree Mason, and a devout member of the Methodist Church, South. He was buried with highest Masonic honors in the old Odd Fellows Cemetery at Georgetown, where a noble granite shaft marks his final resting place. His life was lived for Texas, the old South, and the American Union; his name is unstained by dishonor; peace to his hallowed dust!

In any publication devoted to the lives of the founders of Texas, no space could be used amiss devoted to the character and influence of the heroic wives and mothers of the Lone Star State. Few deserve this highest tribute of respect more than does Elizabeth Burleson Brooks, wife of Charles W. Brooks, and mother of John Lee Brooks.

Mrs. Brooks is a member of the noted Burleson family of Texas, and is one of the truly great pioneer women of the State. Elizabeth Burleson, popularly known as "Bettie" Burleson, was the youngest of a large family of children, and was born near old Fort Bastrop, Texas, April 11, 1835. From her father, James Burleson, and her mother, Nancy Christian, on both sides of the house she is descended from the first families of Virginia; from the Buchanans, the same line from which came President Buchanan, and the Christians, after whom is named Christian County, Virginia. She is of the purest strain of Scotch-Irish stock in America, whose forefathers fought in the American Revolution, and have been prominent in the history of this country.

As soldiers, statesmen, educators and citizens, the Burleson clan has been conspicuous in the annals of Texas, as appears from other pages of this history, in the war for independence from Mexico, in border Indian warfare, in the Mexican War of 1848, and in the Civil War.

The maternal grandfather of Elizabeth Burleson, John Christian, came to Texas among Stephen F. Austin's first colonists, located thousands of acres of rich lands on the Colorado River below Austin, and was killed while surveying land near Manor, in Bastrop County, just prior to the war for Texas' independence. Her father, also a noted Indian fighter, died as the result of wounds received in battle with marauding Indian bands early in the '30s.

Elizabeth Burleson was the frequent companion of Gen. Edward Burleson, and imbibed freely of the patriotic zeal and heroic spirit of her illustrious brother. For thirty years as the captain of the famous "Minute Men" General Burleson defended the "Cross-Timbers Country" along the Texas border, during which time he fought thirty-six hard battles with hostile bands of marauding savages. Thousands of bullets used in the old "Kentucky rifles" of General Burleson and his men, that laid low the proudest warriors and chieftains of the dreaded Comanche, Tonkawa, and Apache tribes, were moulded by the hands of "Bettie" Burleson, along with the "jerked beef," and "parched corn" with which she often packed their "war wallets."

Gen. Ed Burleson, Aaron Burleson, his brother, and others of the Burleson clan were in the thick of the fight at San Jacinto, the former brothers, the latter close kinsmen of Elizabeth Burleson. It was the "grape and canister," made from cut up horse-shoes and stay-chains from the "Twin Sisters," two small brass cannon presented to the young republic by sympathizers of Cincinnati, Ohio, under the skillful and daring direction of General Burleson, that opened the first breach in the Mexican breastworks at San Jacinto, through which the Texans poured with resistless fury, and contributed so largely to the most wonderful victory ever won by a like number of citizen soldiers in human history.

Aaron Burleson, brother of Gen. Ed and of Elizabeth Burleson Brooks, was a distinguished scout and Indian fighter, along with Deaf Smith, the famous scout who cut Vince's Bridge at San Jacinto, cutting off the retreat of Mexicans and Texans alike, and forcing the finish death-grapple between Houston and Santa Anna. Aaron Burleson was one of the party of Texans who captured Santa Anna and dragged him before Sam Houston, after the battle of San Jacinto.

Both Edward and Aaron Burleson appear in the lifesize painting, "The Surrender of Santa Anna," which hangs on the walls of the Texas State Capitol today. General Burleson is seen standing in the background by the Texas flag; Aaron Burleson, in the buck-skin garb of the Texas scout, is seen standing near and looking with sinister mien towards the Mexican dictator, lariat in hand. He strongly favored hanging the "Napoleon of the West" to the limb of the tree under which Sam Houston reclined with his wounded foot, but wiser counsel prevailed.

Dr. Rufus C. Burleson, deceased, a cousin of Elizabeth Burleson Brooks is widely known and his memory deeply revered as one of the great pioneer Baptist preachers of Texas. His fame as a writer and educator is inseparably bound up with the founding and history of Baylor University at Waco, Texas.

Elizabeth Burleson Brooks is the great aunt of Albert Sidney Burleson, present postmaster general in President Wilson's cabinet, and one of the most trusted pillars of the present administration.

Elizabeth Burleson was born, reared and educated amidst the perils and hardships of the pioneer days of Texas. During the "Mexican Runaway Scrape," when Houston was retreating before Santa Anna to San Jacinto, in company with hundreds of the fleeing settlers of Texas, she was carried by her heroic mother, a babe in arms and on foot, for 300 miles, from Fort Bastrop to the Sabine River, through flood and famine, wild beasts and hostile Indian bands to final safety.

Twice in her girlhood did she escape capture and worse than death by marauding Indian bands, by defending herself, single-handed. On one occasion, armed only with a stick of stove-wood, and nerved by sheer desperation, she felled and whipped in fair fight a stalwart Indian warrior, escaping amid a shower of arrows, to the keen disappointment, but evident amusement of the savage band. Mrs. Brooks is proud of her native Texas and Virginia blood, and is a worthy representative of the noble and heroic women of that historic clan in Texas and in the Old Dominion.

As a young woman "Bettie" Burleson, as she was known, was a popular belle, of fine physique and appearance, vivacious, high-spirited, ambitious and daring. She was well educated for her day, largely through her own efforts. She was an accomplished horsewoman, a good rifle shot, a beautiful dancer, fearless as any man of her clan, and famed for her public spirit and philanthropies.

She often visited the friendly Indian camps, and frequently sat with her brother, General Burleson, in counsel with the chiefs of friendly tribes, assisted him in entertaining them and was his frequent companion in her early womanhood. She learned much of their language, songs, traditions, customs, frequently took part in their games, witnessed their war dances, attended their funerals and studied their mystical religious rites. Even yet she is a veritable mine of Indian lore, tradition and an original source of Texas history, which she delights to relate to her grandchildren around the evening fireside. She is possessed of an inexhaustible fund of incidents and stories of the tragic struggles and heroic battles of the early pioneers with the cruel and crafty red men of border days in Texas, and was herself a conspicuous actor in many of those stirring and thrilling tragedies.

Elizabeth Burleson was married to Charles W. Brooks in her twentieth year, 1855, at Bastrop, Texas, at the home of her older sister, Mrs. Martha Reynolds, wife of Sherman Reynolds, a public-spirited and prosperous merchant from New York State, through whose assistance she had mainly received her educational advantages. Of this union nine children were born, as appears elsewhere in this sketch.

As the wife of Charles W. Brooks, Mrs. Brooks carried her full share of the burdens and hardships incident to the opening up of the family plantation at Young's Prairie, now Elgin, in Bastrop County, just prior to the Civil War. She passed through four years of that fratricidal strife, with its untold privations and perils, and the awful period of Reconstruction in Texas, handicapped by her large family, and part of the time by the care of an invalid husband. By her matchless heroism, resourcefulness and executive ability, she held the family affairs and fortunes well together, often with her own hands slaughtering and selling beef to the countryside.

Mrs. Brooks retained most of her lands by selling much of it at as low as 25 cents an acre to raise money for carpet bag tax collectors. She supported and educated her large family for useful and honorable careers, frequently teaching them at night by pine-torchlight from books she had studied in girlhood. She kept her home well supplied with the best books and magazines of the day, borrowed from her New York brother-in-law's more prosperous home. In later years Mrs. Brooks provided music and musical instruments for her home, dispensed generous hospitality and charity to her less fortunate neighbors, kept open house for the ministers of all denominations, and especially for the Methodists, of which she was a "shouting member." She entertained leading public men of her day as a set policy of education for her children; her "latchstring always hung out for God's poor;" she created a home life of Christian culture and refined hospitality, the memory of which yet lingers like a benediction and an inspiration to her children and her hosts of friends throughout the State.

One of the most delightful memories of that early home life lingers around the family orchestra of six instruments, purchased by her for $1,200 on the family's removal to Georgetown in 1878. It was played entirely by members of the Brooks family and often afforded pleasing entertainment for neighborhood gatherings for the singing of sacred hymns on Sunday afternoons. On week-nights the same performers furnished music for friends in the innocent home dance, in which as a young woman Mrs. Brooks excelled, and often led, until advancing years had made heavy her once nimble feet, but could never dim her twinkling eyes, nor quell her joyous spirit.

In the darkest hour of family or neighborhood adversity her courage was invincible, her optimism unbounded, both based in her abundant health, alike inspiring and uplifting to all with whom she came in contact. One of her favorite proverbs, of which she was full and very fond, was: "A cheerful spirit will get along quick, while a grumbling soul in the mud will stick." In the full tide of her womanhood she was possessed of a remarkably clear, active mind and most marvelous memory, an iron will, infinite resourcefulness and a fighting spirit that might be annihilated, but conquered, NEVER! She was a great singer and possessed a beautifully clear, sweet voice; she often boasted that when she was married she knew the words and music from memory of a thousand different songs, learned from an old pioneer song-book, known as "The Thousand Songster."

Elizabeth Burleson Brooks, universally known as "Bettie Burleson" and "Bettie Brooks," is yet living, feeble in body, but fairly clear of memory at the advanced age of eighty-one years, with her eldest daughter, Mrs. "Texie" Jones, at Fullerton, California. Mrs. Brooks will soon "return to Texas," so she says, "to sleep forever in the bosom of her beloved Texas," whose sod for her is consecrated by the patriot life-blood of her father, her brothers, uncles and numerous kinsmen of the hardy Burleson clan in Texas, so freely poured out for the freedom of Texas from Mexican tyranny and the depredations of hostile Indians in pioneer days of the Lone Star State.

She has promised her son, John Lee Brooks, to give to him the heirlooms and assist him in compiling the reminiscences of her long and eventful life for permanent preservation among the historic annals of this great commonwealth.

John Lee Brooks is a Burleson to the bone. He is more like his mother in temperament and tastes than any other member of the Brooks family. He has the tall, wiry, athletic build and soldierly bearing, the square jaw, head and facial expression, the brown twinkling eyes, the restless energy and keen intellectual activity of his mother's clan to a marked degree.

Up to his eighth year Mr. Brooks' education was begun in a private school, taught by a Professor Stephens, a highly competent teacher, at Elgin, Texas. Mr. Brooks distinctly remembers two striking incidents in connection with these early school days; first, his standing at the head of the class for several weeks at one time, during which time the class was reviewed through the first half of "Webster's Hand School Dictionary," spelling and giving definitions, without once being turned down; second, his seeing as many as three horse-thieves at one time hanging by the roadside on his way to school, captured from the many gangs of desperadoes that infested that section, and given "hemp-justice" by the "Vigilance Committee."

On removal of the Brooks family to Georgetown in 1878, Mr. Brooks was placed in an excellent private school, Polytechnic Institute, taught by the Rev. Abram Weaver, a retired Baptist minister and teacher of some ability. From twelve to fourteen years of age Mr. Brooks was in the preparatory department of Southwestern University, leaving in 1884 on account of his health.

Up until his fourteenth year Mr. Brooks was considered a frail lad, weighing but eighty pounds, his growth having been somewhat stunted by malarial fevers and an accident to one of his limbs in baseball, which threatened to make him a permanent cripple. He went on crutches at one time for eighteen months. At fourteen, on his own initiative, he left school and home and spent the next four years on his father's ranch in Lampasas County, on the Colorado River, near old Fort San Saba, punching cattle and building up his present fine physique.

Mr. Brooks has often said that this was the most valuable four years of his life. During this time, by correspondence courses and persistent reading of standard works of history, science, literature and biography, rising regularly at 4 o'clock A. M., to read and study, Mr. Brooks not only regained his health, attaining a standard weight of 175 pounds, but laid broad and deep the foundations for his future intellectual career.

At twelve years of age, by special rule suspending the age limit of the constitution of sixteen years, Mr. Brooks was admitted to membership in the San Jacinto Literary and Debating Society at Southwestern University. Under the skillful tutelage of his older brother, Judge R. E. Brooks, who has always taken a deep interest in and has been his unwavering backer in his educational efforts, and himself an able debater, Mr. Brooks began active training in public speaking and debate, and a general course of reading of standard works, which has profoundly influenced his educational and intellectual development.

During this four years of ranch life Mr. Brooks achieved considerable local reputation as a stump speaker and debater. In his seventeenth year he met and defeated in joint debate Lossie Herrington, a shrewd lawyer from San Saba, Texas, in the first campaign for State-wide prohibition in Texas. In a free-for-all fight raised by some ruffians from the anti-crowd, a nearly successful attempt was made to assassinate the victorious young pro champion, and fortunately resulted in his leaving for college a few weeks later.

At that time, contrary to his father's advice, Mr. Brooks was an ardent supporter of the State-wide movement, and favored woman's suffrage. He has come around to his father's view today, namely, that local option or, at most, State-wide prohibition, is the true Jeffersonian theory of control for the liquor traffic in America and Texas; and that the suffrage should be left to state control, and should be greatly restricted, rather than extended, but should be conferred upon a basis of character, intelligence and property, and the full discharge of all the duties of American citizenship by voters, regardless of sex, color or creed. In politics Mr. Brooks has always been a staunch Jeffersonian and Cleveland-Wilson democrat.

In the fall of 1888, in his eighteenth year, Mr. Brooks entered Southwestern University, Georgetown, Texas, and took the seven years' course from Prep. to the A. M. degree in five years, reviewing all past work, and graduating in 1893 with first honors of his class, in company with Dr. R. W. Baird of Dallas, Dr. H. A. Boaz of Fort Worth and many other men who have since become distinguished in Texas. At different times in his college career Mr. Brooks was schoolmate with such men as R. E. L. Knight, William H. Atwell, Robert F. Allen, Congressman R. L. Henry, Sam Streetman, Frank Andrews, Robert L. Saner, Will C. Hogg and scores of other graduates of Southwestern University and the State University, and Vanderbilt University, whose names are synonymous with distinguished success in Texas today.

In college Mr. Brooks took active leadership in all departments of college life. He was a hard student, active in athletics, attained unusual success in essays, oratory and debate, winning several gold medals and valuable prizes in each, was editor of the University Monthly for one year, enlarging, illustrating and greatly enhancing its literary value, and placed the publication upon a new and permanently successful financial basis for the first time in its history. As a citizen of Georgetown he also took an active interest while yet a student in city affairs, college and local politics, and rendered valuable service with the local volunteer fire department. During his five years at Southwestern University, Mr. Brooks boasted that he knew by name every student in the university, practically all the citizenship of the town and most of the men of the county.

He entered Vanderbilt University on a scholarship from Southwestern University in the fall of 1893, and remained one year, taking courses in theology and modern languages, French and German. After six years of hard work in college, his health being poor, Mr. Brooks returned to Texas, spent another year on his father's ranch, completely recovered, and after a year or more in business succeeded his father as postmaster at Georgetown, in 1896, and for three years served acceptably as a public official of his home town.

Mr. Brooks attributes the best he has done or ever expects to do in life to the influence of his mother and his splendid wife. Early in his term as postmaster, on November 3, 1896, at Georgetown, Texas, he married Miss Eunice McLean, eldest daughter of Dr. John H. McLean, for many years president of Southwestern University, a noted educator, and for fifty-five years a prominent minister of the Methodist Episcopal Church South, in Texas.

Mr. and Mrs. Brooks had been raised up from childhood together at

Georgetown, and have a host of friends throughout the State. Mrs. Brooks is a graduate of Southwestern University, but cut short her educational career, voluntarily retiring from school at eighteen years of age and taking charge of her father's large household for two years to relieve her mother during a prolonged illness, thus illustrating one of the most noble and admirable traits of her beautiful Christian character that has made her married life a benediction to her husband and children alike.

Mrs. Brooks is a woman of strong intellect, deep sweet sympathy and steadfast in her many friendships; she is a devoted daughter, wife and mother, entirely practical and domestic in her tastes, a frugal housewife and fine disciplinarian, having taught for one year in a Mexican mission school at San Luis Potosi, Mexico, prior to her marriage. She was a fine student in college, is quietly ambitious and determined, and has a fair command of the Spanish language. She has no social aspirations, having practically been an invalid for many years, but is utterly devoted to her life-work of being a daughter, wife and mother, her ideal of southern womanhood. However, she is a strong believer in woman's suffrage and takes a keen intelligent interest in public affairs. She is also strong for national prohibition, holding that America cannot afford longer to stay behind benighted Russia. Her two fine boys hold their mother's views; her husband's more radical views are not given out for "home consumption." Mrs. Brooks is a devout Methodist, and, with her children, active in her church work.

Four children have blessed the happy union of Mr. and Mrs. Brooks, namely: John Lee Brooks, Jr., a fine specimen of young Texas manhood, six feet tall, nineteen years of age, a football player and all-around athlete, now finishing his third year at Terrill's School for Boys at Dallas. He has taken three gold medals for scholarship in Latin and English, two in the latter subject, and the highest rank in his third form class this year, at this splendid school where Yale standards of scholarship prevail. He is a special protege of his uncle, Judge R. E. Brooks of Houston, is being prepared for the Texas State University and a career in law. Mary Olivia Brooks, "Little Brownie," as she named herself, the first daughter born to the family, a most beautiful and promising child, died of pneumonia after a brief and tragic illness, at 2½ years of age, while Mr. Brooks was a student at Columbia University, New York City, in 1902, and was buried at Georgetown, Texas. John H. McLean Brooks, named for his distinguished grandfather, aged fifteen, is a good match for his older brother in physical prowess and scholarship. He is taking high rank in the Oak Cliff High School at Dallas, and gives promise of a splendid manhood. Eunice Elizabeth Brooks, named for her mother and her grandmother Brooks, aged eleven, is the physical image of her mother, and the intellectual and temperamental duplicate of her father. She is a fine student and gives promise of decided musical and literary talent; she is especially fond of her violin and the standard works of literature.

Next to his father and oldest brother, Judge R. E. Brooks, Mr. Brooks said that three men of all others had most profoundly influenced his life and intellectual development, namely: his father-in-law and first college instructor, Dr. John H. McLean, who grounded him in religious faith and first taught him how to think for himself; Dr. Robert Stewart Hyer, now president of Southern Methodist University, Dallas, his science teacher at Southwestern University, who first taught him intellectual honesty, love of and loyalty to truth for its own sake, and first introduced him to the master minds of modern science and philosophy; Dr. Nicholas Murray Butler, president of Columbia University, New York City, who completed the work so well begun by Doctor Hyer, opened to him the treasure house of universal knowledge in the greatest universities of two continents and made of him a national and world citizen.

Doctor McLean was brought to Texas from his native State of Mississippi at one year of age, the family settling at Marshall, in Harrison County. He is of pure Scotch and American descent; his father, Alan Ferguson McLean, was a prominent man of South Carolina. In the maternal line his great-grandfather, Capt. William Pinckney Rose, fought under General Jackson at the battle of New Orleans, and a great-great-grandfather, John Rose, fought under Gen. George Washington for American independence. Doctor McLean is a brother of Judge William P. McLean, one of the leading legal lights of the Texas Bar at Fort Worth, Texas, and prominently connected with the early history of the Texas Railroad Commission.

John H. McLean graduated from the old McKenzie College, which from 1841 to 1871 was one of the most important educational institutions west of the Mississippi, was a notable school of the Red River country of Texas and contributed some of the most brilliant minds to the early history of the Lone Star State. For three years after graduation Doctor McLean taught in McKenzie College, but in 1860 entered the ministry of the Methodist Episcopal Church as a member of the East Texas Conference.

In 1866, on the division of that conference, he became identified with the North Texas Conference, and was a member of that conference up until his recent retirement. In 1880 he was elected to the chair of mental and moral philosophy at Southwestern University, Georgetown, Texas, and for several years was president of that seat of learning, and has left his lasting impress upon hundreds of the leading men of Texas who graduated under his administration.

For nine times, or thirty-six years, did he represent his conference in the general conference, the highest legislative body of his church; in the last general conference attended by him he was the oldest delegate there, and had served by two general conferences longer than any other delegate elected to that office. In 1891 he was a delegate to the ecumenical conference of world-wide Methodism at Washington, District of Columbia, and was a delegate to the conference of world-wide missions held in New York City in 1900. For nineteen years he was on the Board of Publication of the Texas Christian Advocate, the leading organ of his church in Texas, and for seventeen years was president of that board, and guided the editorial policy of that publication, which is the chief voice of the powerful Methodist denomination in Texas, and has done so much to shape the moral and religious ideals of the people of Texas since the Civil War.

On March 22, 1866, Doctor McLean married Miss Olivia McDugald at Rusk, Texas. Mrs. McLean is descended from a prominent old Mississippi family and is related to ex-Governor James Stephen Hogg and to John H. Reagan, both prominent in the history of Texas and of the old South. Mrs. McLean is a cultured woman of great practical wisdom, sound common-sense, devout spirit and strong Christian character. Doctor and Mrs. McLean recently completed an unbroken record of fifty-five years in the itinerant Methodist ministry in the pioneer days of Texas. During all this time Doctor McLean missed but two appointments, owing to sickness in his family. At one time in his career he received but $30 for one year's salary as a pastor; the salary of a regular pastor in the Methodist ministry was but $150 a year. It was frequently necessary to carry a rifle on his rounds, for protection against "the world, the Indians and the devil!"

Doctor and Mrs. McLean recently celebrated their golden wedding in the Chamber of Commerce Building at Dallas, at which time scores of old-time pioneer Texas friends, and the hosts of friends and former students of later days, gladly did honor to this aged and truly great couple whose noble and heroic lives have been builded into the foundations of this great commonwealth, like the great stone of the ancient temple which the Master Builder took and made of it the "Head of the Corner." Doctor and Mrs. McLean are now living in quiet retirement in their elegant new home, recently presented to them by their children and former pupils and friends in University Park, near Southern Methodist University, Dallas.

Next to Doctor McLean, Doctor Hyer was most influential in awakening and directing the inquiring mind of John Lee Brooks, and in starting him on a line of reading and investigation, along with three other young men at Southwestern University, that finally determined the intellectual bent and destiny of Mr. Brooks along entirely different lines than those originally outlined by his early guide. Of that original four, W. K. Clement, a rare spirit, is dead; Samuel James Rucker is in the regular orthodox Methodist ministry in Texas; Hiram Abiff Boaz is president of an orthodox Methodist school for girls at Fort Worth; John Lee Brooks, originally designed by his mother for the ministry and subject of this sketch, is a lawyer and not a member of any church. This remarkable statement of facts, while not reflecting upon any of that goodly company, nor upon their scholarly and devout instructor, is full of meaning and deserving of fuller elucidation in this sketch, as typical not only of the intellectual and religious evolution through which many individuals are passing today, but of the renaissance of theology, science and philosophy which American popular thought is undergoing today in all parts of the country.

After finishing his term as postmaster at Georgetown, still being deeply interested in working out to a harmonious conclusion a fierce conflict in his own thought life between science and religion, the Darwinian theory of evolution and the scholastic philosophy underlying orthodox faiths since the days of Martin Luther and of John Wesley, Mr. Brooks went East in the fall of 1899, entered Drew Theological Seminary of the Methodist Episcopal Church at Madison, New Jersey, and spent two years delving into the mysteries of this historic problem, graduating from Drew with the B. D. degree in 1901. Mr. Brooks' graduating thesis was mainly an attack on the orthodox theory of the atonement, which was "viewed with alarm" by some, but was finally permitted to pass by the faculty. During his stay at Drew, Mr. Brooks also took lectures and read extensively in comparative religions and kindred lines at Union Theological Seminary, New York City, the highest institution of its kind in America.

In 1900 on a scholarship Mr. Brooks also entered Columbia University, New York City, taking the full four years' course for the degree of Doctor of Philosophy in education, philosophy and psychology, with side lectures in history, economics and law, with extensive courses of private reading along lines in which he was personally interested. Mr. Brooks has always said that, next to his four years on the ranch, this four years at Columbia University, with its opportunities for quiet but rapid intellectual development and ripening, was the next most important four years in his intellectual history.

During his stay at Columbia Mr. Brooks taught Latin, Greek, history, mathematics and kindred subjects, preparing young men for the leading college entrance examinations of America, in which work he attained marked success.

He also spent two seasons on the lecture platform, using such subjects as "Texas and the Empire of the Great Southwest" and "The Dollar and the Man." The former lecture treated mainly of the romantic and heroic past of his native State, of the historic importance of the life and work of Sam Houston in its bearing on the history of the map of the United States and of the American Union, of our relations to Mexico, the Latin-American republics, the Orient, the nations of Europe and the Monroe Doctrine. The latter lecture was along the lines of the conflict between capital and labor, or trusts, and the necessary economic and industrial evolution of modern business and finance; of our national maritime and commercial expansion and trade, and their effects on the fundamental principles of American constitutional government and of human liberty, individual and racial. In addition to these two lectures, the one historical, the other economic and commercial, Mr. Brooks also frequently lectured and wrote on educational subjects while a student at Columbia University.

Mr. Brooks was also an active business man while a student at Columbia; for nearly two years he was successfully engaged in the oil land and brokerage business at 141 Broadway, New York City, as the eastern representative of the Hogg-Swayne Syndicate of Beaumont, Texas, of which his brother, Judge R. E. Brooks, was a member. At one time, during this student period, Mr. Brooks ran successfully and contemporaneously four distinct lines of business, namely, teaching a night school in New Jersey, running a brokerage office in New York City, taking the full course of lectures for the Ph. D. degree in Columbia University, and delivering a course of popular lectures in off evenings in and around New York. During two years of this time he worked an average of sixteen hours daily, maintained his health, cleared several thousand dollars in money, and achieved more than average success in all four lines of activity.

Having finished his course and passed his examinations successfully for his doctor's degree at Columbia in 1904, Mr. Brooks removed to Washington, District of Columbia, for the purpose of completing and publishing his dissertation for the doctorate on "The Evolution of the American Denominational College," a study of the law of successful growth by which the leading American universities, like Harvard, Yale, Princeton and Columbia, have evolved from the denominational into the modern non-sectarian type of control and organization by throwing off the shackles of orthodoxy and sectarianism and adopting a non-sectarian type of the self-perpetuating board of trustees.

Solely on account of safeguarding sacred church, family and friendship ties that might be jeopardized by the premature publication of this thesis, already worked out to a demonstration convincing to any rational mind, Mr. Brooks, at the cost of the formal conferring of his hard-earned degree of Doctor of Philosophy, for which the publication of his dissertation was the last condition, considerately deferred the publication of this important investigation until some later date in life. His work has been pronounced by the highest university authorities as a most vital and important contribution to the literature of modern scientific education, and its completion and publication as greatly needed by American educational institutions today. The subject was assigned to Mr. Brooks by Dr. Nicholas Murray Butler, then president of Columbia University, and for two years Mr. Brooks' personal instructor in philosophy and education.

Having finally completed his own personal investigations and come to a definite conclusion, representing his own matured evolution of thought in science and religion, theology and philosophy, and covering ten of the best years of his life, Mr. Brooks finally offered his services as a minister to the Baltimore Conference of the Southern Methodist Church, at Washington, District of Columbia, in 1904. After two years' trial on probation, during which time he attained unusual success, though not an ordained minister, he came up for final examination and ordination by the conference.

The examining committee, so he was informed, consisted of five ministers, two of common school education, two graduates of high school and one a college man. On examination he was found practically book-perfect, so far as the contents of the standard orthodox works of the prescribed course of study were concerned. On oral examination, however, his views were found to be hopelessly out of harmony with the accepted standards of the church, held for nearly three centuries back, in theology, science and philosophy.

For the first time in life, with infinite regret, Mr. Brooks realized that he was a hopeless misfit so far as the church was concerned, but with characteristic intellectual honesty and moral heroism did the only thing any self-respecting, honest man could do under the circumstances—he promptly resigned his "first credentials," together with his membership in the Southern Methodist Church, the church of his mother and father, of his wife and her parents, and of his family and people, and has never united with any other church since.

At the earnest solicitation of Dr. William E. Chancellor, a brilliant author and educator, then superintendent of the city schools of Washington, District of Columbia, Mr. Brooks immediately took the teachers' examinations for a position in the schools of the Capital City, and from the first took high rank as a teacher of history, English and mathematics in the business and classical high schools of that city.

In 1905, foreseeing his inevitable break with the church, Mr. Brooks entered Columbian University Law School and completed the course in 1907, being prevented from graduation by only a few weeks on account of the dangerous illness of his wife, which necessitated his bringing her South for her health, which he did in the fall of 1907, taking her to his brother's ranch and 3,000-acre plantation, "Broadmoor Ranch," at Wills Point, Texas, of which place he was superintendent from 1907 to 1909.

In 1909 Mr. Brooks opened up a hay and grain business in Dallas, and at Muskogee, Oklahoma, where he lived until 1911, doing an extensive and successful business. He also dealt extensively in land, business and residence property during this time, owning a half business block and building in Muskogee and putting on a successful subdivision in Oak Cliff, at Dallas.

In 1911 Mr. Brooks sold out his business in Oklahoma, moved to Dallas and bought a home in Oak Cliff, where he has resided since. He engaged in the real estate and building business in Dallas from 1911 until the early summer of 1914, when, owing to financial depression incident to the European war, he closed out his real estate holdings, and, after a brief vacation traveling through West Texas, he entered the law office of Gen. M. M. Crane at Dallas and fitted himself for the local bar examinations, which he passed successfully with high standing in February, 1915. Since that time he has been successfully engaged in the practice of his profession at the Dallas Bar, where he is held in high esteem, being associated with Cecil L. Simpson, with offices in the Commonwealth Bank Building, Dallas.

Since becoming a citizen of Dallas, at different times, Mr. Brooks has been actively identified with the Dallas Real Estate Exchange, the Chamber of Commerce, the Automobile Club and various civic and educational movements. As chairman of the educational committee of the well-known North Loop League, the most active civic league in Dallas,

Mr. Brooks took active leadership in the recent local campaign for educational reform and new buildings that has resulted in securing two new high school buildings for Dallas and a splendid new high school building for Oak Cliff.

While somewhat restricted since his entry into the legal profession, the patriotic public spirit and love of reform so charactercistic of the Burleson clan in Texas has not slumbered in the heart and brain of John Lee Brooks. He has been active in the promotion of higher ideals and closer fellowship among the members of the legal profession. Until its recent consolidation with the Bar Association of Dallas, Mr. Brooks was an active vice president of the Dallas Lawyers' Club, and was one of the quiet but most active promoters of that most notable and commendable movement for judicial and legal reform in Texas projected in recent years.

Mr. Brooks is a member of the Masonic order and of the Order of Elks, though not active in either just now on account of the pressure of his legal practice. Though now giving his best time to his profession, Mr. Brooks is not exclusively a professional man. He quickly manifested a deep and intelligent interest in affairs of state history, biography, educational reforms, music, science, philosophy, literature, art and religion, and takes a deep interest in all matters of civic, social and labor reform, politics and business, and affairs, national and international. He is a deep student of men and of all important movements, from Dallas to the world-war, is a voracious reader of newspapers, magazines, books, in his own and numerous other lines, is an interesting speaker and writer on various themes, is a careful, successful lawyer, a good business man, philanthropic and public spirited, a type of the well-rounded, well-balanced citizen of the world whose need is apparent in every progressive community.

While not a member of any particular church, Mr. Brooks is thoroughly religious in spirit, mainly following the teachings of the Nazarene. He is a regular attendant on divine service, holding with Emerson that it is well for every man to cultivate weekly the plant called "reverence" in the garden of his heart, alternating among the orthodox churches, and frequently attending the Unitarian and occasionally the Christian Science, Jewish and Roman Catholic churches.

From his broad and deep researches in comparative religions, various systems of ethics, science and philosophy, Mr. Brooks has developed a system of philosophy, personal ethics and religion fundamentally in harmony with the best thought and practice of the good men of all ages and based upon the fundamental and immutable principles of truth, justice and mercy that affords him an abiding foundation of religious faith, a code of moral and ethical principles which constitutes a safe guide of life and practice, and meets and satisfies his every spiritual need.

While Mr. Brooks for years has been a deep thinker and close student of men and of affairs, and has written much, yet, on account of the mixed state of popular thought of this age, especially on scientific, philosophical and theological lines, he has deemed it wise to wait, and as yet has published little. When he has achieved recognized success and comfortable competence in his chosen profession, Mr. Brooks expects to devote much of his time to investigation, writing and publishing the results of his work on legal, economic, ethical, educational and kindred lines, that he hopes will be constructive and helpful in the development of his native State and of the country he loves so well.

One of the most intensely interesting, pathetic and all but tragic phases of Mr. Brooks' intellectual career grows out of the keen disappointment of his aged mother in his failure to realize her ideal for him, formed before he was born, that she should be privileged to give at least one son to the Christian ministry. Mr. Brooks is devoted to his wife and mother. With great reluctance he has consented to the incorporation here of an extract from a beautiful Christmas letter, written to his mother last Christmas, published without correction or being put in correct technical form as poetry, just as it was written, which reveals poetic gifts out of the ordinary, as well as something of the tragic struggles through which he has had to pass, and the awful price he has had to pay for his present intellectual and religious freedom.

The extract from the letter of Mr. Brooks to his aged mother is as follows:

"DALLAS, TEXAS, December 22, 1915.

"Dearest Mother:

"* * * At one time in life, during my university career in New York City, I was like an ancient mariner, storm-tossed, without chart or compass, disabled, drifting upon a wide, wide sea of scientific and philosophic thought and had lost my grip on God, the God of my fathers.

"During that tragic time, my little family circle, though humble, had no vacant chair. The brightest jewel in that circle was our little 'Brownie,' a mere baby of two and one-half years of age; but undoubtedly she was the most beautiful, sweetest, fairest spirit my life had ever known. As I remember her, for it was in the bleak December that she left us, she was as beautiful and pure as a spotless lily of the valley, her favorite flower. It was then that a fearful snow-storm came, scattering death and untold suffering throughout the land. In a few short days of unspeakable agony, with the horrible pneumonia, our rare and radiant flower was faded and gone.

MY CONFESSIONAL, IN MEMORIAM *

"Three days and nights mine eyes were dry,
  My grief too deep for tears;
Three nights did I lone vigil keep,
  Beset by countless hopes and fears;
Beside the bier of my infant child,
  In bleak December, white and chill;
Without, the night was dark and wild,
  Within, was blackness deeper still.

"Not once leaving, only gazing,
  On her form so wondrous fair;
As though chiseled by a sculptor,
  From the Parian marble rare;
Only thinking, fearing, wond'ring,
  Whether Hope or black Despair;
Ever more would bid me clasp her,
  And, if so, when? and where?

"As I sat there still, confronting
  Sorest loss my life had known,
And a Force I could not fathom,
  Faith was dead, and Hope had flown;
Love had turned to bitter Hate,
  Reason reeled upon her throne;
Black Despair beside me sat,
  And I was helpless and alone.

"I turned to Science for some ray
  Of hope to lift the Stygian pall;
I searched Philosophy's deepest depths
  To ask of her, if this was all?
I tried to pray the infant prayer
  I once had learned at mother's knee;
But only Darkness and Despair
  Echoed back in fiendish glee.

"Get thee hence, thou Thing of Evil!
  Cried my soul in anguish wild;
Whether spirit, man or devil,
  Thou hast not my vanished child;
Where is God? I must find Him,
  If there be one up on high;
For where He is, there my child is,
  I must find Him or I die!

"I must tell Him all my trouble,
  He must bid me hope once more;
He must tell me I shall see her,
  On that fair and radiant shore;
Then my heart grew strangely quiet,
  Reason sat upon her throne,
Faith and Hope and Love return'd,
  And black Despair at last was gone.

"Then I heard her sweet voice calling,
  As I oft' had heard before,
When at ev'ning home returning,
  She would meet me at the door;
'This way, Daddy, come this way,
  Here is God above the night!'
Then I 'roused, and it was morning,
  And the day was wondrous bright.

"Then I walked upon the mountains,
  And my soul was bathed in light;
I had risen above the shadows,
  Of a long and rayless night;
I had found God all around me,
  Above, below, without, within,
But a veil had come between us,
  And a mist of doubt and sin.

"I had lost my chart and compass,
  Faith, and Truth, and Hope, and Love;
I had drifted on the waters,
  Far away from things above;
Until His infinite Wisdom,
  Saw that I must have a star;
Upon which to fix my vision,
  And make port across the bar.

"It was then He took my darling,
  In His everlasting arms;
From this world of sin and sorrow,

From its cares and wild alarms;
And the brightness of her mem'ry,
Like a fix'd and guiding star,
Still is shining o'er the waters,
Like a light-house from afar.

* * * * * * *

"Mother, dearest, if His foot-steps,
Now be hastening to you;
And you soon must hear the summons,
That shall take you from us too;
As you rise above the shadows,
To the mountain tops of light;
Bear this message to my darling,
Far above the realms of night.

"Tell her, 'Daddy' still is sailing,
With his eye upon her star;
And some day he too shall anchor,
In her port across the bar;
And whene'er the storm-clouds gather,
And obscure that distant shore,
I will listen for her calling,
And but strive the more and more.

"I'll still keep my good ship pointed,
Through the darkness and the gloom;
To her port beyond the breakers,
Toward God, and her, and home;
For I still can hear her calling,
'This way, Daddy, this way, come;
Here is God, and I am with Him,
And where we are is your home.'

"Your affectionate son,
"JOHN LEE BROOKS."

AUGUST HEINSOHN, of Fayetteville, belongs to the pioneer element of the citizenship of Colorado County, and is a native of that county himself, having been born September 27, 1858. His father, Gerhardt Heinsohn, the founder of this branch of the family in America, came to this country in 1848, a young man, having just completed his service in the German army. He followed four brothers to come to the new world. Gerhardt Heinsohn was born at Oldenburg, Germany, February 13, 1822, and in his native land learned the trade of wheelwright and received a common school education. He sailed from Hamburg on an old sailing vessel, which brought him to the City of Galveston, Texas, where he found his brothers who were doing carpenter work for a time before seeking the rural precincts in Colorado County.

The Heinsohn brothers were as follows: William, who spent his life as a farmer in the vicinity of Frelsburg, Colorado County, and left a family there at the time of his death; Frederick, who spent his life at Galveston as a mechanic and left a family there when he died; Gerhardt, father of August; John, who lived at New Ulm, where he was engaged in farming, reared a family, and died; Henry, who died during the first year that he was in Texas, as did also his wife, they leaving a son, George, who also passed away and left no issue; and Antone, the youngest of the brothers, who lived near Frelsburg, Texas, as a farmer, and left a large family at the time of his demise. All the brothers were industrious, hard-working men, of honest purpose and determination, honest men who combined in their characters the best traits of their race.

Gerhardt Heinsohn had some military experience during the war between the states, hauling flour for the Confederate Government as a teamster and occasionally making a trip to Mexico from whence he hawked supplies. Almost immediately following the close of hostilities, he engaged in farming, his property being located near Frelsburg, where he made his influence felt in both a business and a social way. His handiwork is yet observable in the improvements of his farm, and the property is still held in the family name and possession. Mr. Heinsohn took no particularly active part in politics as a politician, although he was a naturalized citizen of the United States and voted at elections in support of the principles and candidates of the democratic party. A devout and consistent member of the Lutheran Church, he was one of the founders of the congregation at Frelsburg and took an active part in its work. Also, he manifested a strong interest in public education, and was one of the makers and sustainers of the old Frelsburg College, and continued as its permanent friend throughout his life.

Gerhardt Heinsohn was united in marriage in 1854 with Miss Sophia Fehrenkamp, a daughter of Antone Fehrenkamp, who came from Oldenburg, Germany, also. Mr. Fehrenkamp was a farmer in Texas, and at his death left a family which included: Mrs. Meta Becker; Mrs. Anna Klump; Mrs. Sophia Heinsohn; Mrs. Helena Pophanken, and Gerhardt, who died leaving three sons and a daughter. Mrs. Heinsohn still survives, at the age of seventy-eight years, having been born in 1837. The children of Mr. and Mrs. Heinsohn have been as follows: Mamie, who married William Schwecke, of New Ulm, Texas; August, of this review; Emma, who is the widow of Albert Wagner, of Bartlett, Texas; Mary, who married Charles Zapp, of Houston, Texas; Gerhardt, who engaged in farming in Fayette County; Emily, who is the wife of Monroe Johnson, of Fayetteville; Louis, a public weigher of Fayetteville; Matilda, who became Mrs. Adolph Krueger, of Fayetteville; Ida, who became the wife of Rev. August Beteit, a Lutheran minister at Hempstead, Texas; and Ella, who is the wife of the Rev. Hans Krause, a minister of Fayetteville. The children were brought up to value honesty and integrity above all things, to know the value and reason for hard work, and to render their community their best service, and all have since filled well the positions in life to which they have been called.

August Heinsohm passed his boyhood up to the age of fifteen years near Frelsburg, and then came with his parents to Fayette County. His education was secured in the public schools of his native locality, following which he began assisting his father in the work of the home farm, where he remained until he was twenty-seven years old. At that time Mr. Heinsohm engaged in the lumber business at Ellinger, this being a rather small undertaking, to which he devoted his attention for a little less than two years, moving to Fayetteville at the time of the building of the Missouri, Kansas & Texas Railroad. There he put in a lumber yard, which has been the only enterprise at that place in all the years that have followed, of its kind. In addition to this Mr. Heinsohn has extended his interests until they include the stock business, the raising of hogs and cattle. He has also become a farmer, has done much farm improvement, building cattle and hog sheds, and has erected two silos, of which he is also the agent for this county. Mr. Heinsohn owns more than one thousand acres of land, 100 acres of it being farmed, while the balance is his pasture, where he has but recently engaged in the breeding of Hereford cattle, while his hogs are of the Poland-China strain. He attends the Fort Worth stock shows and frequently returns to his home with something new to add to the blood of his fine herds.

Mr. Heinsohn has let politics alone. He votes the democratic ticket, and although he has not been an office holder, was made trustee of the school board before he had children, remained so while he was rearing his family, and continued to act in that capacity until his children had all passed through their educational experiences. He belongs to the Woodmen of the World and the Sons of Hermann, and is a Lutheran in his religious belief, as is Mrs. Heinsohn, their children having also been reared in that faith. Mr. Heinsohn erected his home, one of the substantial and modern ones of Fayetteville, and has added to the growth of the town by doing other building of a small residence character.

Mr. Heinsohn was married January 4, 1887, to Miss Adele J. Scharnberg, a daughter of Fred Scharnberg, who married Anna Albrecht at Shelby, Texas. The parents were born in Germany, Mr. Scharnberg at Mecklenburg and the mother at Pommerania. Mr. Scharnberg was a carpenter by trade, but in his later years took up agriculture, and died on his farm in Fayette County, Texas, in 1898, aged seventy-eight years. He was a Confederate soldier during the Civil war, and was a Lutheran in his religious belief. To Mr. and Mrs. Scharnberg there were born the following children: Anna, who became the wife of Ferdinand Menking, of Fayette County; Mrs. Heinsohn, born November 22, 1866; Ida, who died as Mrs. Gus Giese; Mary, who married Albert Heinz, and died at Gonzales, Texas; Hugo, who died at Port Arthur, Texas; Helmuth, a resident of Bartlett, Texas; Otto, who resides in Fayette County; Charles, a resident of Houston; John, also residing at Houston; and Fred, of Bastrop, Texas. To Mr. and Mrs. Heinsohn there were born several children, of whom the only survivor is Lee, who married Miss Agnes Sump, and is engaged with his father in the lumber business. He is a member of the Woodmen of the World.

RUDOLPH SCHMIDT. Through persistent determination and unceasing labor Rudolph Schmidt has won his way to a position among the substantial agriculturists of Fayette County, and his entire career has been devoted to the pursuits of the soil, he being at this time the owner of 170 acres of the Shepherd League, located on Fayetteville R. F. D. No. 3. He is a native of Fayette County, born near Shelby, on the Fayette and Austin County line, September 9, 1861, a son of Fred and Elise (Wunderlich) Schmidt.

Fred Schmidt was born at Witchenstein, Prussia, was there reared and aducated, and in young manhood took up the family vocation of farming. Although industrious and ambitious, he made but unsatisfactory progress in his native land and in 1852 emigrated to the United States, a married man in very moderate circumstances. Sailing from Bremen, he landed at Galveston, from whence he went by wagon and on foot to Shelby, Austin County, where he joined relatives who had preceded him, and for a time was a renter of land, but soon became able to purchase a property of his own near Shelby, on which he continued to carry on operations until 1869, when he located on the farm now owned by Rudolph Schmidt, which at that time was a new tract of land in the W. W. Shepherd League. There he began the improvement of a farm, and at the time of his death, in 1879, at the age of sixty-five years, was the owner of 158 acres. He led a strictly agricultural life, being content to devote himself to his own affairs, learned to speak English but poorly, became a citizen after several years of residence here, and voted the democratic ticket in elections. He was a consistent member of the Lutheran Church. Mr. Schmidt was married in his native land to Miss Elise Wunderlich, who survived her husband several years, and they became the parents of the following children: Catherine, who died unmarried; Lena, who married Fred Spies, and died in Fayette County; Louisa, who became the wife of Ernst Schulze, of the Fayetteville locality; Gustine, deceased, who was the wife of Fritz Menking, of Lavaca County, Texas; Caroline, who married Louis Ilse, of LaGrange; Henry, who died in this locality with a family; William, who died unmarried; August, who is engaged in farming near the home of his brother Rudolph; Rudolph; Fred, who is also a farmer in this locality; and Alvina, who died as Mrs. Fritz Scheu.

Rudolph Schmidt was eight years of age when his parents moved to his present locality and his education was secured in the Haw Creek country school, after leaving which he began to devote himself to farming. He remained under the parental roof until his marriage, December 21, 1886, to Miss Gesine Kerlers, who was born at Oldenburg, Germany, a daughter of Fred Kerlers. She died May 22, 1911, having been the mother of the following children: Alma, who is the wife of Rudolph Cordes, a farmer near Warrenton, and has a son, Jesse; Erwin, a farmer near his father, who married Emma Gerdes and has an infant daughter; Otto; Herbert; Elda, who is the wife of Lupold Steenken, of Wilson County, Texas; Emma; Louis; Wallie; Milton and Lydia. On June 21, 1913, Mr. Schmidt was again married, being united with Mrs. Rosa Schilling, who was born near LaGrange, Texas, and died December 7, 1914.

Mr. Schmidt is the owner of 170 acres of the Shepherd League, some fifty acres being cleared up and brought under the plow out of the heavy timber. He produces corn and cotton, which are the popular crops of this section, and also carries the stock that his pasture will support. In religious belief he is a Lutheran and his fraternal connection is with the Woodmen of the World.

George L. Cheek, retired bandmaster, United States Army, has led a most interesting and active life, much of it in Texas, and though retired from the army service nine years ago has continued to take a great interest in military men and affairs. From early youth he displayed marked talents of a musical character, as well as a predilection for army life, and his career as a musician and soldier took him into active service during the Indian, Spanish-American and Philippine wars.

He was born in the City of Boston, Massachusetts, in 1863, a son of G. W. and Alta A. (Bailey) Cheek. His father was born in Massachusetts, and though he always retained his home at Boston he became a pioneer in Indiana, moving to that state long before the Civil war and even when the Indians were still there. During the Civil war he enlisted in the volunteer service of the Union army in Indiana, and while a soldier in one of the Indiana regiments he engaged in the battle of Chickamauga and was severely, almost fatally, wounded, an injury which disabled him totally and which was ultimately the cause of his death. His wife was a member of an old and well-known family of the State of New York.

George L. Cheek grew up in the City of Boston, received a rudimentary education in the public schools, and when but eight years of age began the serious study of music on the violin, and for fourteen years was constant to that instrument, attaining such proficiency as to entitle him to a place in the professional class. In later years he had the misfortune to have two fingers broken, which necessitated his giving up the violin, but in the meantime he had become proficient in other band

and orchestral instruments, particularly the clarinet, and that instrument was his specialty as a professional musician.

When only sixteen years of age, in 1879, Mr. Cheek came to the West, and became a trumpeter in the Third Cavalry at Fort Fred Steele, Wyoming. After a few months the commanding officer transferred him to the regimental band and for thirty years thereafter he remained in the regular United States Army as a musician and bandmaster. In 1882 he went with his regiment from Fort Fred Steele to Fort Apache, Arizona, from which base the United States troops conducted their campaign along the Gila River and other parts of Southern Arizona against Geronimo and his Apaches. From Fort Apache he went to Whipple Barracks, Arizona, and then left the army for a time to return home, but soon afterwards was again in Arizona, joining the army as a musician at Fort Wingate, Arizona, in 1884. From there he was transferred to Fort Leavenworth, Kansas, as a member of the Eighteenth Infantry Band. Later he was assigned to the Third Cavalry at Fort Davis, Texas, from which point he was transferred to Fort Clark, Texas, with the Third Cavalry, and from there to Fort McIntosh at Laredo, and again to Fort Reno, Indian Territory. His next move was half way across the United States to Fort Ethan Allen, Vermont, where he was stationed in 1898, when the war broke out with Spain. He went out at once with the Third Cavalry, which was a part of General Shafter's army, and from Tampa, Florida, was sent to Cuba, where he remained during the entire campaign and until hostilities ceased. Honorably discharged, he soon re-enlisted as a musician in the Forty-sixth Infantry, at Boston, his old home. From Boston he was sent across the continent to San Francisco, from there to the Philippines, and spent three years in the islands, the greater part of the time at Silang. Near that post, while he and other members of the band were out picking bananas they were ambushed by natives and three of them, two trombone players and a piccolo player, were killed, the rest escaping. On returning to the United States Mr. Cheek re-enlisted in the Twelfth Cavalry at Fort Sam Houston, Texas. From there he was sent to Fort Clark, Texas, and then with the Twelfth Cavalry departed to the Philippine Islands again and saw another two years of service in the Far East, returning by way of Japan, Midway Island and Honolulu to San Francisco, and thence to Fort Ogelthorpe, Georgia. In the meantime, several years previously, he had become a bandmaster in the army, and it was as such that he was retired with pay June 29, 1907, at Fort Ogelthorpe.

Ever since early youth Mr. Cheek has been an adept at rifle and revolver shooting, and without any particular training or preparation became an expert shot. This talent developed particularly during the last years of his service in the army, and becoming competent in practice at Fort Oglethorpe, he won a medal, a marksman's pin, as a rifle sharpshooter, and in addition was mentioned in general orders for his efficiency as a mounted pistol shot. Besides these he has received a number of medals and decorations from the army for his service as a bandmaster.

After retiring from the army in 1907 Mr. Cheek removed to San Antonio. Since then he has tutored and organized a number of bands in Texas and particularly in San Antonio and the southwest part of the state. In 1911, at Eagle Pass, Texas, he organized and led the band that, heading Francesco Madero and staff, who were on their way to Piedras Nigras, Mexico, from El Paso, crossed the International Bridge and passed through the lines into Mexico City. This was at the time when the Madero revolution, which led to his subsequent election as president of the Mexican Republic, was at its height. Mr. Cheek has

Mrs Ella Caruthers Porter

Saml Carruthers

for many years been brought in contact in the most pleasant social as well as official ways with prominent officers of the United States Army, to whom he is greatly attached. He has also made two trips to Europe, in addition to the extensive travels already noted.

His home after retiring from the army was at San Antonio until quite recently when he moved to Gonzales and became bandmaster of the Gonzales Band. He has been married twice, his first wife having been Tillie E. (Hauser) Cheek. Their only son, Dr. G. L. Cheek, was graduated from a San Francisco medical college, and is now a successful physician at Santa Barbara, California. Mr. Cheek's present wife was before her marriage Miss Hilda A. Bergren. They have an adopted daughter, Pocahontas Cheek, who was born in 1911. They have in their home also a boy of Mexican parentage, Manuel T. Nieto, who was born in 1897, and was given to Mr. Cheek to bring up at Eagle Pass, Texas, when the lad was eight years of age. He has been reared and educated by Mr. Cheek and has developed into a young man of splendid talents and promise. His father was Poncho Nieto, whose life was one of romance and adventure. He had been captured by the Indians when only four years of age, and was rescued on the Texas side of the Mexican border by General McKenzie of the United States Army near Fort McKavett, Texas.

MRS. ELLA CARUTHERS PORTER. In the organization of the Texas Congress of Mothers Mrs. Porter of Dallas was the leader of a movement whose results have already been as important as any single constructive enterprise ever undertaken in the material development of Texas, and the future influence and scope of whose work must transcend in vital value many of those enterprises which in other fields have brought enduring fame to the men who conceived and carried them out. It is evident that in the future the work of the world must be carried on by organization rather than by individual units, and it is probable that the tributes of history will go chiefly to those individuals who were pioneers in great movements which in the next generation will have most influence on human destiny. From this point of view Mrs. Porter is one of the pioneers in the great twentieth century social program, especially in the State of Texas, where she has spent most of her life and where she represents one of the fine old pioneer families. She is well known both in and out of the state as a practical sociologist, and has been distinguished by her activities in welfare work, temperance and many other movements for bettering the condition of mankind.

Mrs. Porter is a daughter of Captain Sam and Lulu (Cox) Caruthers. The Caruthers family originated in Annandale, Scotland, a place distinguished from an early period of Scotch history. Members of this family emigrated to America about the middle of the eighteenth century, locating in Pennsylvania, with descendants afterwards going to North Carolina, Virginia and Tennessee. A number of them were Continental soldiers in the Revolutionary war. The Caruthers were a noble line of Scots. Most of them both in the earlier and later generations have been distinguished by very praiseworthy characteristics. In earlier times the members of the clan were very closely knit together, and family pride has always been a strong feature. They are noted for hospitality and generosity, for their devotion to religion, of the old Scotch Presbyterian type. Other characteristics are highly retentive memories and very alert mentalities.

Captain Sam Caruthers was born in Arkansas, a son of John Caruthers, a native of Pennsylvania and a distant relative of Judge Ardan Caruthers who founded the Lebanon Law School in Tennessee. William Caruthers, an uncle of Capt. Sam Caruthers, came to Texas in 1836, and was one of the followers of Gen. Sam Houston in the winning of Texas independence. He had an arm shot off in the battle of San Jacinto. Not long afterwards he participated in the famous Mier expedition to Mexico, was captured by the Mexicans along the Rio Grande, and participated in that famous bean lottery the incidents of which are familiar to every Texas schoolboy or girl. It will be remembered that these prisoners who were fortunate enough to draw white beans were allowed to go free, while those who drew the black beans were promptly executed. History recalls that William Caruthers was fortunate in this lottery, and later with some of his companions found his way back to Texas, though after the greatest of hardship and suffering.

John Caruthers, grandfather of Mrs. Porter, came with his family to Texas in the early '40s. They first located near what is now the Town of Mexia in Limestone County, but later moved to Bosque County, and perhaps no name was more closely identified with the early and later history of that section than Caruthers. The family owned a large body of land along the Brazos River located in Hill and Bosque counties, and that particular section has for many years been known as Caruthers Valley. Capt. Sam Caruthers, father of Mrs. Porter, enlisted from that locality at the outbreak of the war between the states, was assigned to the command of a company, and made a gallant record as captain. He was a man of uncompromising honor and integrity, and his dignity of bearing commanded the love and respect of all who knew him.

Mrs. Porter's mother, Lulu (Cox) Caruthers, was a native of Virginia and a woman of remarkably literary ability and intellectual attainments.

Mrs. Porter was born and spent her early girlhood in Kimball, Bosque County. She was married at the tender age of sixteen, and a few years later was left alone a mother with two small children. While her little girls were still very young, in order to fit herself more perfectly for educating them and rearing them to ideal womanhood—a task which in her extreme youth and inexperience she realized she was not then prepared to undertake—she went to Nashville, Tennessee, accompanied by her daughters. There she entered Nashville College for Young Ladies, specializing in literature and history. Three years later she went to the University of Chicago, where she pursued special sociological studies under Doctor Vincent, now president of the University of Minnesota. While in Chicago her daughters, who had in the meantime been growing up to young womanhood, enjoyed the superlative advantages of Chicago University High School.

There is something inspiring in the efforts of this young mother to realize the utmost attainments in her natural profession as a mother and also to enable her to extend by her influence and leadership the modern ideas of woman's mission and work. She spent several years in study and research, taking an especial interest in child welfare, and her efforts in this direction were brought to the attention of Mrs. Helen M. Stoddard, president of the Woman's Christian Temperance Union of Texas. That official urged her to establish a mother's department of the Women's Christian Temperance Union in Texas. In carrying out this suggestion Mrs. Porter organized the first Mother's Club in Texas at Hillsboro. She was herself still a young mother and undertook the founding of that club long before the organization of the National Congress of Mothers.

The club at Hillsboro was followed by the organization of similar clubs in other parts of the state. When the National Congress of Mothers was organized at Washington, Mrs. Porter was sent as a delegate to represent Texas and was by that organization appointed state organizer for

Texas. She ably filled that position for fifteen years and she more than any other individual has been responsible for that campaign of education which has made motherhood a word of dignity and real meaning in her state.

The climax of her work as state organizer in Texas came when, after realizing the advantages of having a regular state organization, she called a meeting in Dallas for the purpose of establishing a State Congress of Mothers. This meeting took place in the old First Methodist Church in Dallas on October 19, 1909. Every organization in the state having any department bearing upon the welfare of the child, and every mayor in the state, were invited to send delegates and many of them responded. In the enthusiastic meeting which followed a strong organization was formed. Mrs. Porter was elected president; Miss Eleanor Brackenridge of San Antonio, first vice president; and Mrs. John S. Turner of Dallas, recording secretary. The motto adopted was "A Little Child Shall Lead Them." Headquarters for the organization were established at once in the Methodist Publishing House in Dallas, and Mrs. Porter gave almost her entire time to congress work. During the first year hundreds of letters were written and thousands of pages of literature were sent out. An official organ, The Texas Motherhood Magazine, edited and published by Mrs. N. B. Ford of Dallas was also launched.

The second annual meeting of the Texas Congress of Mothers was held at the State Capitol in Austin in October, 1910. Some of the most prominent speakers of the state were represented on the program; among others was president of the State University, Dr. S. E. Mezes, Prof. E. M. Bralley, superintendent of public instruction. Other speakers of distinction from outside the state appeared on the program, including Dr. J. H. Kellogg of Battle Creek, Michigan. A brilliant reception was tendered the congressman by the wife of the governor, Thomas M. Campbell, at the executive mansion.

At this time the leading educators of the state realizing the wonderful possibilities of organized motherhood, gave their enthusiastic endorsement of the Congress of Mothers and promise of co-operation in every way possible. The conference for education extended to the Congress material financial aid to enable it to carry out its undertakings for child welfare.

On the last day of this meeting Mrs. Porter called together and presided over the first Child Welfare Conference ever held in Texas. The following organizations were represented: State Teachers' Association, Conference for Education, State University, College of Industrial Arts, Federation of Women's Clubs, Young Women's Christian Association, Young Men's Christian Association, Daughters of the Confederacy, Farmers Congress, Texas Sunday School Association, Social Hygiene Association, and the State Reformatory. The intent of the conference was to co-ordinate the work for child welfare in the state, and to prevent duplication of effort. It was agreed that its specific work would be to unite the efforts of all these organizations toward the passing of legislative measures that would better conditions for children in Texas.

During Mrs. Porter's administration of the Congress of Mothers the first Child Welfare exhibit ever held in the state was successfully maintained at the Texas State Fair in Dallas. The object of this exhibit was to show the great need for a more intelligent parenthood and a closer co-operation between the home and school. Demonstrations showing the danger to the child of the common house fly, the mosquito and of impure milk were also in operation. A telling exhibit showing the danger of the common drinking cup was a part of the demonstration. This, followed up with an active educational campaign, resulted in the establishment of sanitary drinking fountains in almost all the public schools of the state. Individual drinking cups were installed on all the railroads and in many places of public business.

Through Mrs. Porter's efforts a bill providing for a child welfare commission was formulated and introduced into the Legislature, but failed of passage on account of a small appropriation asked for its maintenance. An educational campaign was also begun looking toward the introduction of a bill providing for state aid for needy mothers—mothers who, alone and unprovided for, are struggling to bring up good citizens for the state.

During the first three years of the life of the organization 165 local clubs became members of the state body and the membership increased to almost 8,000. The state had been divided into five districts, each with its president and corps of officers. Many parent-teacher county conferences had been held by county chairmen of congress extension; "Mothers' Congress Day" had been made a feature of the annual state fair in Dallas, and by request of the president of the congress the governor had issued a proclamation designating the second Sunday in May as mothers' day, when all Texas should do honor to motherhood.

A constantly increasing membership, a greater demand for literature to aid in organizing local clubs, attested the growing appreciation of the work of the Congress of Mothers. There were no complexities in the work of the organization or in its appeal. Child welfare formed the burden of every program and the constant endeavor was to understand childhood and to come to know better how to provide for its best development physically, mentally and spiritually.

At the close of the third year of the congress Mrs. Porter declined to serve the organization longer as its president, though persistently urged by friends all over the state to do so. She was then elected honorary president and a life member of the executive board, an honor fittingly bestowed on one who is devoting her life to movements for the uplift of mankind.

In the field of temperance and the abolition of the liquor traffic Mrs. Porter has taken an equally active interest. She was sent as a delegate from Texas to the great World's Temperance Convention held at Edinburgh, Scotland, in 1900. At this meeting she stood in the reception line with Lady Henry Somerset and the lord provost of Edinburgh as well as other notables, and received great inspiration from that historic gathering. She has attended many annual meetings of the National Congress of Mothers as a representative from Texas. She was appointed by the governor to represent Texas at the first International Child Welfare Convention held in Washington, District of Columbia, under the auspices of the National Congress of Mothers, in 1908. This great world-wide conference verified the statement of the founder of the National Congress of Mothers that "the love of childhood is the common tie that should unite us in holiest purpose."

It need hardly be stated that Mrs. Porter is an ardent equal suffragist. She advocates that cause because she believes that the interests of the home and the welfare of the child demand it.

Mrs. Porter's beautiful home is known as "Lakeview," in Highland Park, Dallas. She personally superintended the building of this home, and it not only presents artistic architectural lines, but in many ways constitutes a model of comfort, convenience and the ideal atmosphere of a home environment. Her two beautiful daughters, Misses Stella and Lillian Porter, radiate the culture and refinement developed by educational advantages and opportunities for travel. Miss Lillian is thoroughly accomplished as a reader; Miss Stella is a musician and possesses unusual business ability.

William D. C. Jones. The Jones family, of Tennessee, has contributed many brilliant men to the State of Texas. This family was founded in Bastrop County by William Dandridge Claiborne Jones, grandfather of him whose name initiates this article. He was born in the vicinity of Fayetteville, Tennessee, in 1799, and died in 1892, living to the patriarchal age of ninety-three years; his remains are interred in the cemetery at Belmont, Gonzales County. He came to Texas with the Burleson family, by ox team, in 1835, and he married one of the Burleson girls in Alabama. He left four brothers and a sister behind him in Tennessee and never saw them again until his visit home some fifty-eight years later, at which time all were still living. One of his brothers, George W. Jones, of Fayetteville, who for twenty-eight years represented Tennessee in the United States Congress, was one of the prominent citizens of that state. After his arrival in Texas Mr. Jones located some three miles west of Smithville. He was a large slaveowner and stockman, and while he himself lived out his life as a private citizen, many of his posterity have won fame in political and military circles, five of his sons having been Confederate soldiers. He was a devout Baptist and a stalwart democrat, although he was opposed to the separation of Texas from the Union. He married Rachel Burleson, first cousin of Gen. Ed. Burleson, one of the heroes of San Jacinto. Among their children was George Washington, known throughout Texas as "Wash" Jones. He was born in Alabama in 1833, grew up in Bastrop County, Texas, as a ranchman and Indian fighter, and was commissioned colonel of a regiment in the Confederate Army, serving throughout the entire period of the Civil war. He was a lawyer by profession and he held the offices of district attorney and lieutenant governor under the administration of Governor Throckmorton. Subsequently he served for eight years in Congress and on one occasion came near being elected governor of the state. He was a law partner of Governor Jo Sayers, as Jones & Sayers, and he well demonstrated his ability as a counsellor and pleader at the bar. He was an able business man and founded a factory for the manufacture of cotton cloth in Bastrop, for which Texas transferred to him 55,000 acres of land. He showed exceptional ability as a financier. He was in thorough sympathy with the unfortunate, and educated some forty orphans, many of whom were not even related to him. He was married but never had a child of his own.

James S. Jones, another son of William and Rachel (Burleson) Jones, died as a farmer soon after reaching manhood. Charles Hill was father of the subject of this sketch and he is mentioned at length in a following paragraph. William Henry, another son of the old pioneer, was a farmer and stockman of note in the vicinity of Belmont, Gonzales County; he was a Confederate soldier and prior to his demise served his section in the State Legislature. Benjamin F., also a farmer and stockman, lived and died on the old Jones homestead in Bastorp County; he was likewise a member of the State Legislature. In addition to the foregoing sons, Mr. and Mrs. Jones had three daughters: Mariah married Joseph Rogers, of Travis County; Rachel married Jonathan Rogers; and Patsy married John S. Wilson, a farmer and tax collector in Bastrop County.

Charles Hill Jones, father of the immediate subject of this review, was born in Bastrop County, Texas, and there was reared to maturity and educated. During the Civil war he organized a company of cavalry for the Confederate service, was made captain of the same, and was promoted to the office of major of his regiment before the war ended. He served during the entire period of that sanguinary conflict and participated in the battles of Mansfield and Pleasant Hill. He was a merchant at Woodville, Tyler County, Texas, after the close of the war and was also interested in farming enterprises in that section, where he continued to reside until his demise in 1880. He served a term in the lower house of the State Legislature, was a democrat in politics and was a Master Mason. He married Sarah Ann Gilder, a daughter of U. M. Gilder, a native of Forsyth, Georgia, and a pioneer settler in Tyler County, Texas, where he passed to eternal rest; he is survived by several children. Following are brief data concerning the children born to Mr. and Mrs. Charles H. Jones: Charles H., Jr., died as a youth, in 1879; George M. died at Bastrop in 1887; Emma R. is the wife of Dr. J. H. Stovall, of Los Angeles, California; and William D. C. is the subject of this review. Mrs. Jones died in 1867 and for his second wife Captain Jones married Annie F. Ratcliffe, who survives her honored husband and is now living in Giddings, Texas. The following children were born of the second marriage: Oliver P., of Bastrop, this state; Charles H., Jr., a cotton broker in Bastrop; Ethel is the wife of Dr. G. C. Harris, of Courtney, Texas; and Laura married Dr. John Johnson, of Giddings, Texas.

William Dandridge Claiborne Jones, of this notice, youngest in order of birth of the four children born to Capt. and Mrs. Charles H. Jones, was born in Woodville, Texas, August 15, 1866. He lost his mother when he was but a year old and he was reared by his stepmother until his father died, in 1880, at which time he went to Bastrop and lived in the home of his uncle, Colonel "Wash" Jones, mentioned above. After a thorough preliminary education in the public schools of Texas he entered the University of Texas, at Austin, and was a student in that institution during the years 1884-85-86. Tiring of study and confinement he then spent a year on a cattle ranch owned by his uncle, in Coryell County. In 1888 he returned to Bastrop and engaged in the general merchandise business and in farming. He came to Smithville in 1892 and here he has been almost continuously engaged in buying cotton to the present time, in 1915. He is an extensive farmer in Bastrop County, his land lying chiefly in the Loomis and Sterling surveys. His farms are splendidly improved and seven families are employed as tenants to cultivate his fields. He is interested in banking in Smithville, being vice president of the First State Bank, which he helped organize. He is now investing money in the development of an oil field in the vicinity of Smithville. He has never mixed in politics and has never sought public office of any description. He stands high in Masonry, being a member of Blue Lodge, of Smithville Chapter, Smithville Commandery, and Ben Hur Shrine, in Austin. He is a business man of unusual merit and his interests cover many different lines of enterprise. He is jolly and good-natured and is extremely popular with his fellow men.

In Bastrop, Texas, October 20, 1889, occurred the marriage of Mr. Jones to Miss Jessie B. Young, a daughter of M. H. Young, a prominent farmer and stock raiser in Bastrop County. Mrs. Jones is the eldest in a family of eight children. She and her husband have one son, George M., who was graduated in the Carlisle Institute, at Arlington, Texas, in 1908, and who received a Bachelor of Science degree in the Texas Agricultural and Mechanical College in 1912. He is now a senior in the medical department of Tulane University at New Orleans. The Jones home is in a beautiful colonial residence in the eastern section of Smithville.

FRANK J. KROULIK. Man's greatest prize on earth is physical health and vigor; nothing deteriorates mental activity so quickly as prolonged sickness, hence the broad field for human helpfulness afforded in the medical profession. The successful doctor requires something more than mere technical training—he must be a man of broad human sympathy and genial kindliness, capable of inspiring hope and faith in the heart of his patient. Such a man is he whose name initiates this article. Doctor Kroulik has devoted the past twelve years to his work as a general physician and during ten years of that time has resided in Smithville.

A native son of the Lone Star state, Doctor Kroulik was born near Industry, in Austin County, Texas, January 13, 1877. He is the fourth in order of birth of the eight children born to John and Fannie (Pačhr) Kroulik, the latter of whom is dead and the former resides in Industry, Texas. After a preliminary education in the country schools of his native place, Doctor Kroulik completed the prescribed course in the Belleville High School. He then pursued a commercial course in the Metropolitan Business College, of Dallas, and for a time thereafter clerked in a store in New Ulm. Later he worked as a clerk in Brenham, whence he returned to Dallas to complete his business course. For a short time thereafter he clerked in San Felipe and in 1899 he was matriculated as a student in the University of Louisville. One year later he entered Tulane University at New Orleans, in the medical department of which excellent institution he was graduated April 29, 1903, with the degree of Doctor of Medicine. He entered upon the active practice of his profession in LaGrange, where he remained for three months. In the fall of 1903 he came to Smithville and here was engaged in practice for three years, when he went to Cistern, remaining there for the ensuing two years. In 1908 he returned to Smithville and this city has since represented his home and professional headquarters. During the intervening years to the present time he has built up a large and lucrative practice and he now holds prestige as one of the most prominent and efficient doctors in this section of the state. In connection with his life work he is a valued and appreciative member of the Bastrop County Medical Society, of the Texas State Medical Society and of the American Medical Association. In politics he is a democrat, and fraternally he is affiliated with the Sons of Hermann and with the S. P. J. S. T.

June 8, 1910, was solemnized the marriage of Doctor Kroulik to Miss Mathilda Rosanky, a daughter of Ed and Mary (Zimmer-Hanzl) Rosanky, residents of Rosanky. There are six children in the Rosanky family, namely: Mrs. Annie Morgan, of Smithville; Mrs. Emelie Heckle and Mrs. Minnie Naumann, also of Smithville; Mrs. Kroulik; William, of Bastrop County; and Miss Emma, of Smithville. Doctor and Mrs. Kroulik have one son, Frank Jack.

ADOLPH ENGELS. A career of persevering and untiring industry, covering a period of many years, has advanced Adolph Engels from the capacity of a worker for others to a position of independence, in which he is accounted one of the substantial men of the New Breslau community of Colorado County. The circumstances of his life teach the old lesson that persistence, steady application and honest, straightforward effort, intelligently directed and given the proper opportunity, will eventually lead to success, and to the attainment of that regard and esteem by which mankind measures accomplishment.

Mr. Engels was born in Dewitt County, Texas, March 19, 1862, and is a son of Bernard Engels, who came to the United States from Germany, and married his second wife at Galveston. He brought two children with him from the old country: August, of Lavaca County; and

Bertha, who married Henry Hinkel, of the Oakland community. Mr. Engels' second wife was Ernestine Quast, who outlived her husband, married Gottlieb Buske, and died in February, 1914. Bernard and Ernestine Engels were the parents of seven children, as follows: Emma, a resident of Bosque County, Texas, the wife of John Oswald; Adolph, of this review; Hulda, who married Charles Hoegemeyer, of this locality; Frank, who was twice married but left no children at his death; Eda, who married August Dahse, of Colorado County; and Paulina and Alvina, twins, the former the wife of Charles Gerstenberg and the latter the wife of Herman Sachs. Mr. and Mrs. Buske became the parents of three children: Clara, who became the wife of Henry Laas, of Columbus, Texas; Olga, who married Antone Guenther, of Weimar; and Alfred, who died in 1914, leaving one child. Bernard Engels died in 1871.

Adolph Engels was five years of age when he was brought to Colorado County by his parents, and here he has continued to reside and to be identified with the growing agricultural and other interests of the community. The old Engels home was on Sandy Creek, about two miles south of Weimar, and in the country school of Content and the public school of Weimar, Adolph Engels received his education. He remained at home until reaching the age of twenty-eight years and then rented land for two years on the home place of his stepfather, Gottlieb Buske. Moving to Weimar at that time he engaged in a kind of work in which he had had much experience, the running of the Buske gin, a country gin located on the old Engels (subsequently the Buske) homestead. Mr. Engels continued to be thus engaged, but in 1898 moved from Weimar to his present home. He bought here 110 acres of plow land and forty acres of post oak land, upon which the improvements amounted to practically nothing. The farm boasted of a log house of three rooms, with a log corn crib, and the former was made his home for three years before he began the erection of his present residence. This extensive and somewhat conspicuous country home has been many years in completion, for he has added something to its size practically every year he has been here. It is of eight rooms, and the barns and other improvements give ample accommodation for many horses and other stock. He has been grubbing every year and adding to his tillable land until there is now nearly fifty-five acres under the plow. He has devoted it to corn and cotton, he and his son having carried on the farm alone, and his milk cows constitute his cattle. When he came to this place Mr. Engels found it nearly entirely covered with stumps, and he was compelled to hire hands to remove them, so that to gain a self-supporting farm has been an uphill task. He has persevered, however, and today has a nice property. Mr. Engels is not in politics, never served in any public capacity, and as a voter has acted rather independently.

Mr. Engels married Miss Selma Gerstenberg, a daughter of August Gerstenberg, who came from Germany and was a farmer of this community. His wife was Minna Reichert, and in addition to Mrs. Engels they had four children: Charley and August, twins; Eda and Adolph. To Mr. and Mrs. Engels there have been born the following children: Clara, who married Otto Hovemann; Frank, who is a student in Byrne's Business College, Tyler, Texas; Lenora; Lillie; Hulda; Selma; Viola and Erna.

EMIL G. BUSKE. One of the vigorous and representative business men of the Town of Shiner, an important trading and industrial center in Lavaca County, Mr. Buske is here the proprietor and operator of a well equipped cotton gin of the most approved and modern type, and he also has other important capitalistic interests in this section of the state.

Mr. Buske is a native of Lavaca County, his birth having occurred on the homestead farm of his father, near Content, on the 19th of August, 1875. His father, William Buske, has been a resident of Texas since he was about thirteen years of age, he having accompanied his parents on their emigration from Germany and the family home having been established in the fine old German colony known as Kinkler, Lavaca County, where the father and mother passed the residue of their lives and where their home farm was well improved ere their death, their remains being laid to rest in the little cemetery at Kinkler, where they settled about the close of the Civil war. Of their children the eldest was Charles, who died at Weimar, Colorado County; Henry was a resident of the City of Houston at the time of his death and is survived by a number of his children; Gottlieb is a resident of Weimar; Emilie became the wife of August Wustenbard and is now deceased; Minnie is the wife of Ferdinand Treptow and they reside near old Kinkler; and Mrs. Annie Schuetts is deceased.

William Buske, father of him whose name initiates this article, was reared to manhood in Lavaca County and here he has continued his active and successful association with agricultural pursuits throughout his mature life. As a young man he wedded Miss Christina Oswald, and she was yet a comparatively young woman at the time of her death. Concerning the children the following brief record in consistently entered at this juncture: Henry is a farmer in the vicinity of old Kinkler, and after the death of his first wife, whose maiden name was Paulina Frehner, he married Mrs. Mary Schroeder, his present companion and helpmeet; Emil G., of this sketch, was the next in order of birth; Minnie is the wife of Louis Klaer, and Anna is the wife of Emil Treptow, both families being residents of Lavaca County. After the death of his first wife, William Buske married Mrs. Anna Schroeder, and their children are: Benjamin, Alfred, Martha, Louisa and Ella, the last mentioned remaining at the parental home. Martha is the wife of Richard Mertz, of Lavaca County, and Louisa is the wife of Henry Renger, of Shiner.

Emil G. Buske is indebted to the schools at old Kinkler for his early educational discipline, and he continued to be associated in the work and management of his father's farm until he had attained to his legal majority, after which he was for three years engaged in farming in an independent way. His next venture was made when he entered the cotton gin business at Witting, in partnership with Edward Fertsch and under the firm name of Fertsch & Buske. After three years Mr. Buske purchased his partner's interest, and about two years later he sold the plant and business at Witting and removed to Shiner, where he purchased the gin of William Hillmann. When he assumed control of this plant its equipment consisted of four stands, of the Murray patent, and he has since remodeled and enlarged the ginning establishment, which now has nine stands, of the Munger and Murray gins, the output capacity of the plant being eighty bales of cotton a day.

In addition to his control of the above mentioned and signally prosperous business enterprise, Mr. Buske is the owner of two well improved farms in the William Hill League, of Gonzales, the respective areas of the two farms being 177 and 196 acres. He has effected the reclamation of a considerable part of each of these farms, which are being brought under effective cultivation. In Lavaca County he owns an excellent farm near the old village of Kinkler, and this place is improved with good buildings, a windmill and other modern appurtenances. On one of his farms in Gonzales County Mr. Buske has erected tenant houses. He is a stockholder in the Shiner Brewing Association and also in the Johnson Oil Company, controlling valuable properties in the Electra field. His political allegiance is given to the democratic party, his support is extended to measures and enterprises tending to advance the general welfare of the community, and he is a public-spirited citizen of Shiner, where he has maintained his residence since 1906. In a fraternal way he is affiliated with the Hermann Sohns.

On the 24th of June, 1904, Mr. Buske wedded Miss Hedwig Fertsch, a daughter of Charles and Paulina (Beneker) Fertsch, who came from Germany to Texas and settled near old Kinkler, where the father became a prosperous farmer. The children of the Fertsch family are: Edward, Charles, Oscar, Albert, Linn, Paul, Miss Antonia, Mrs Anna Bonerden and Mrs. Buske. Of the children of Mr. and Mrs. Buske, the firstborn, Melvin, died in infancy, and the three surviving are Roxie, Veree and James.

COL. WILLIAM WHIPPLE JOHNSON. The boundless natural resources of any section of country may continue entirely unknown for centuries for Nature has a cunning skill in hiding her mysteries. Her secrets are uncovered only when human enterprise, in the person of men of courage, will, foresight and scientific knowledge, enters the field and with organizing power makes possible the uncovering of the hidden treasures. To the late William Whipple Johnson the State of Texas owes a debt of gratitude, for through his untiring efforts as discoverer and developer, the stupendous coal wealth of the state was made available. He was the pioneer operator in Palo Pinto and Erath counties, which comprise the largest and richest producing coal mining territory in the whole state. Colonel Johnson has been justly called, because of the extent and importance of his work, the father of the coal industry in Texas. He was almost equally prominent in developing oil and gas properties, and additionally, in furthering the livestock industry. So numerous and so important were the many activities of his life, that on every hand throughout the Panhandle are memorials that recall his years of usefulness to his state and fellow citizens.

William Whipple Johnson was born at Ionia, Michigan. He died at his home in Mineral Wells, Palo Pinto County, Texas, October 19, 1914. His parents were Ethan S. and Jane (Whipple) Johnson. On the paternal side his ancestry was of substantial Rhode Island stock. On the maternal he was descended from distinguished lines. His great-great-grandfather, William Whipple, was one of the signers of the Declaration of Independence and all down the line men of that name attained eminence in American life. The late Bishop Whipple, the venerable prelate of the Episcopal Church of Minnesota, was a member of this family as was also Edward Percy Whipple, the author and critic.

In the schools of Ionia and Ypsilanti, Michigan, the youth was afforded excellent educational opportunities, after which he became associated with his father and brother in a mercantile business at Ionia. Mr. Johnson came to Texas in 1880. He located at first at Fort Worth and two years later began prospecting for coal at Thurber, in Erath County, extending his operations through the extreme southern part of Palo Pinto County. His efforts, directed by good judgment and scientific knowledge, were successful and he put down the first shaft and operated the first mine at Thurber. He had ventured much and his success was beyond expectation and created widespread interest. Some time afterward, in association with a Mr. Ray, now a resident of Midland, Texas, opened the first mine at Strawn, in Palo Pinto County, and subsequently

[illegible] Johnson.

of his farms in Gonzales County Mr. Buske has erected tenant [illegible]. He is a stockholder in the Shiner Brewing Association and also [illegible] Johnson Oil Company, controlling valuable properties in the [illegible] field. His political allegiance is given to the democratic party [illegible] port is extended to measures and enterprises tending to advance the general welfare of the community, and he is a public spirited [illegible] of Shiner, where he has maintained his residence since 1906. In a [illegible] way he is affiliated with the Hermann Sohns.

On the 24th of June, 1904, Mr. Buske wedded Miss Hedwig Fertsch, a daughter of Charles and Paulina (Beneker) Fertsch, who came from Germany to Texas and settled near old Kinkler, where the father became a prosperous farmer. The children of the Fertsch family are: Edward, [illegible], Albert, [illegible] Paul, Miss Antonia, Mrs. Anna Bonerden and Mrs. Buske. Of the children of Mr. and Mrs. Buske the firstborn, [illegible] died in infancy, and the three surviving are Rosa, Veree and [illegible].

Col. William Whipple Johnson. The boundless natural resources of any section of country may continue entirely unknown for centuries [illegible] skill in hiding her mysteries. Her secrets [illegible] only when human enterprise, in the person of men of [illegible] and scientific knowledge, enters the field and with [illegible] possible the uncovering of the hidden treasures. To [illegible] Whipple Johnson the State of Texas owes a debt [illegible] his untiring efforts as discoverer and developer, [illegible] of the state was made available. He was the [illegible] Pinto and Erath counties, which comprise the [illegible] coal mining territory in the whole state. [illegible] justly called, because of the extent and im[illegible] father of the coal industry in Texas. He was [illegible] developing oil and gas properties, and addi[illegible] livestock industry. So numerous and so im[illegible] of his life, that on every hand through [illegible] memorials that recall his years of usefulness to [illegible]

William Whipple Johnson was born at Ionia, Michigan. He died [illegible], Palo Pinto County, Texas, October 19, 1914. [illegible] and [illegible] (Whipple) Johnson. On the pat[illegible] was of substantial Rhode Island stock. On [illegible] from distinguished lines. His great [illegible] Whipple, was one of the signers of the [illegible] all down the line men of that name [illegible] America life. The late Bishop Whipple, the [illegible] Episcopal Church of Minnesota, was a [illegible] was also Edward Percy Whipple, the author [illegible] of Ionia and Ypsilanti, Michigan [illegible] educational opportunities, after [illegible] and [illegible] in a mercantile [illegible] in 1880. He located at [illegible] prospecting for coal at [illegible] through the [illegible] Pa[illegible] directed by good [illegible] kn[illegible] down the [illegible] th[illegible] ventured [illegible] widespread [illegible] Mr. Kay now [illegible] Palo Pinto County [illegible]

William Whipple Johnson.

he located a mine at Rock Creek which he sold to the Texas Pacific Coal Mining Company, and which made possible the bringing of the Weatherford, Mineral Wells and Northwestern Railroad, a branch of the T. P., to Mineral Wells. Colonel Johnson was the pioneer operator at all three points and for several years he continued extensively engaged in coal mining operations in this county. To all who are familiar with the history of coal development and the present status of the industry relative to state wealth, the name of Colonel Johnson stands for executive ability of the highest order and business acumen far beyond ordinary.

Not content with being the pioneer in the coal industry, Colonel Johnson became wide awake to other natural sources of wealth in the state, particularly in the oil and gas deposits at Wichita Falls, in Wichita County. His investigations led to his investing and he organized and became president of the Forest Oil Company of Wichita Falls, an organization that became one of the most extensive producers of oil in that section. Other enterprises that offered wide opportunity likewise were not neglected. He invested in land and went into the cattle business on a large scale. He improved a ranch comprising many thousand acres, situated in the southern part of Palo Pinto County, five miles north of the Town of Gordon. He gave the name of Elmhurst to this beautiful estate and made the place his home and here his ashes rest in a mausoleum.

At Fort Worth, Texas, in 1880, Colonel Johnson was united in marriage with Mrs. Anna F. (Fatzinger) Campbell. Mrs. Johnson was born at Waterloo, Seneca County, New York, and is a daughter of Samuel and Fannie (Cook) Fatzinger. On the paternal side the family was prominent in the military life of the country, serving in the early colonial wars and in the Revolutionary struggle and her father, in 1845, served in the Mexican war. She can also claim descent on the maternal side from Revolutionary patriots. She was brought to Illinois by her parents when three years old and they resided at Morris in Grundy County until she was ten years old, when they moved to Ypsilanti, Michigan, and later to Chicago. In all these cities Mrs. Johnson had both educational and social advantages. Two children, a son and a daughter, were born to Colonel and Mrs. Johnson, neither of whom survived early youth, the son, William Harvey Whipple, dying at the age of six years, and the daughter, Marion, at the age of three years. Both rest with their father in the mausoleum at Elmhurst. Although she makes her home at Mineral Wells, Mrs. Johnson still keeps the home at Elmhurst intact and among her plans for the near future is the building on this estate of a beautiful and artistic memorial church.

Colonel Johnson was an exceptional man in many ways. The coal industries, of which as has been noted, he was the father, in themselves comprise a lasting monument to his enterprise and public spirit. Another side to his character was his generosity and his recognition of the responsibilities that his wealth entailed. It is recalled that in the '80s, during an unusually prolonged drouth when many people were thereby brought almost to starvation in Palo Pinto County, he opened up the cedar post industry, giving profitable employment to a large number of men and at the same time utilizing another of the natural products of the country. Thus, in his charities he was, if possible, practical, helping others to help themselves. He was very benevolent but so unostentatious in his giving that few beneficiaries ever knew the source of their help. Personally he was a polished, educated gentleman, dignified but approachable, and fortunate were those who were admitted to close friendship.

JAMES W. NIXON, M. D., long a physician and surgeon of prominence in Gonzales, is now living retired in that city. In his professional service he was prompted by a laudable ambition for advancement as well as by deep sympathy and humanitarian principles that urged him to put forth his best efforts in the alleviation of pain and suffering. He gained recognition from the profession as one of its able representatives and the trust reposed in him by the public was indicated by the liberal patronage awarded him. In addition to his medical work he has long been a prominent agriculturist in this section of the state, having 700 acres of land under cultivation at the present time, in 1915.

A native son of Texas, Dr. James W. Nixon was born on the parental homestead in Guadalupe county, the date of his birth being April 20, 1855. The founder of the Nixon family in America was born in Scotland, was a Quaker in religious faith and was a member of the colony of William Penn. His descendants located in North Carolina and his son, John Nixon, was a member of the committee that drew up the Declaration of Independence. Dr. Phineas Nixon, son of John Nixon, contrary to the religious views of the family, was a soldier in the war of the revolution. He spent his life in North Carolina and married Millicent Henley, who was part Indian. To them were born the following children: Jesse, Mrs. Mary Casand, Thomas, Mrs. Nancy H. Winslow, Barnabus, John, Mrs. Simon Jones, Gabriel, William Penn, Stephen and Zachary. Of the foregoing Zachary Nixon was the lineal ancestor of Dr. James W. Nixon. He lived in North Carolina until old age came on, when he started by boat to Texas and was lost en route. He married Mary Thomas, a sister of John W. Thomas, the founder of Thomasville, North Carolina. This union was prolific of the following children: Robert T., father of the subject of this review; Margaret married Rev. David Bruton and to them was born John F. Bruton, a lawyer and banker in Wilson, North Carolina; Stephen moved to Texas, where he was a teacher, rancher and stockman for many years; he married Caroline Hysaw and left issue; and John T. was a merchant and farmer and died in Gonzales; he married Lucinda Askey and left a daughter. Three children were born to Zachary Nixon by a second wife, namely: J. King, a Confederate soldier and now a resident of Hondo, Texas, where he is a farmer, miller and stock raiser; Jesse died in childhood; and Zella is the wife of a Mr. Green, of Gonzales.

Robert Thomas Nixon, father of Doctor Nixon of this review, was born in Randolph County, North Carolina, in 1827. He was educated in the country schools of his native place and farming became his life work. In 1852, with a young wife and four orphan brothers, he came from North Carolina to Texas by wagon. For a time after arriving in this state he was a renter in Gonzales County, and then he settled permanently in Guadalupe County, near Luling, where he died in 1897. He served as captain of a company in the war of the Rebellion, being a Confederate, and most of his service was within the state. He was a democrat in politics and his religious faith was in accordance with the tenets of the Methodist Church. He married Laura Ann Wood, a daughter of William Wood, of North Carolina; she died in Texas at the age of forty-two years. The following children were born to Captain and Mrs. Nixon: John T., of Hondo, Texas; Stephen, a resident of New Mexico; Margaret, wife of W. B. Stevens, of Texas; Ella, wife of Doctor Champion, of Luling, Texas; Violet, wife of H. G. Wilson, of Hondo, Texas; Sam H., owner of the Nixon homestead in Guadalupe County, this state; and Dr. James W., of this notice. For his second wife Captain Nixon married Fannie Andrews and to them were born: Beulah, wife of Ed Wood, of Luling, Texas; Corenna, wife of Walter Hyman, of

Luling; Alta, wife of J. E. Fisher, of Luling; Dr. Pat Ireland, of San Antonio, Texas; and Zeb Vance, of Kingsville, Texas. The posterity of Captain Nixon, including children, grandchildren and great-grandchildren number seventy-five.

It is interesting at this point to note that a member of one of the branches of the Nixon family, either John or Thomas Nixon, was the first man in North Carolina to free his slaves. He hired a sailboat to take them back to their native land, Africa, entirely against the wishes of the blacks themselves. After a lapse of two years he learned that the majority of them had died. He removed to Ohio, where he passed the rest of his life.

Dr. James W. Nixon lived in Guadalupe County, Texas, the place of his birth, until 1890. He was educated in the Seguin High School and for a time taught a country school. He attended the University of Virginia in 1878-79 and in the latter year was matriculated as a student in Tulane University, in the medical department of which excellent institution he was graduated in 1890, with the degree of Doctor of Medicine. He initiated the active practice of his profession in Guadalupe and Gonzales counties, and for ten years he maintained his office on his farm in the latter county. In 1890 he located in Gonzales and here built up a splendid practice. Prior to his retirement, in 1915, he ranked as one of the most efficient and successful physicians in this section of the state. He took a post-graduate course in the medical department of the University of Texas, at Galveston, and was a valued and appreciative member of the Texas State Medical Society for a number of years. During the past thirty years Doctor Nixon has been a farmer as well as a physician. He owns 700 acres of land in Gonzales and Medina counties and the same is devoted to the growing of cotton and corn. He was one of the founders of the Gonzales Cotton Oil Company and is a stockholder in the Farmers National Bank of Gonzales.

In 1892, in Gonzales County, Texas, was solemnized the marriage of Doctor Nixon to Miss Mary King, a daughter of William and Mary (Grubbs) King, the former of whom died in Georgia and the latter of whom subsequently came to Texas. Mrs. Nixon is a descendant of William R. King, once vice president of the United States. Following are the names of the King children: Mrs. Nixon, Mrs. Willie Jones, Mrs. Ella Harris and Mrs. Belle Combs. Doctor and Mrs. Nixon have three children: Robert Leroy is a ranchman in Medina County. He was a student in the Agricultural and Mechanical College of Texas for some time and pursued a special course in business in the University of Texas. James is a medical student in the University of Texas, and Luella is at the parental home.

Doctor Nixon's political interests have been confined to his efforts as a voter and in that connection he is a staunch democrat. He and his wife are devout members of the Methodist Episcopal Church and their home on East Avenue is one of the most beautiful ones in this city. Doctor Nixon is a fine, congenial gentleman and he commands the unalloyed confidence and esteem of all with whom he has come in contact.

Rev. Frank Machan. The Catholic parish of the Church of Saints Cyril and Methodius at Shiner, Lavaca County, has its spiritual and temporal affairs admirably ordered under the regime of Father Machan, who has been the incumbent of this pastoral charge since the spring of 1913. His consecrated zeal and devotion are on a parity with his high intellectual attainments and marked executive ability, and as a true shepherd of his flock he has the affectionate regard of all of his parishioners, as well as the confidence and esteem of the entire community.

Father Machan was born at Val Mezirici, Province of Moravia, Austria, on the 15th of April, 1865, and is a son of Anton and Christine (Repa) Machan, both of whom passed their entire lives in that section of the Empire of Austro-Hungary, where the respective families were established many generations ago. Anton Machan was a skilled mechanic and both he and his wife were devout communicants of the Catholic Church, in the faith of which they carefully reared their children. Of the children, Father Machan, of this review, is the oldest of those surviving; Anton still resides in Moravia; and Josephine and her husband maintain their home at Radomsk, Russian Poland, a section that is the stage of horrific military conflict at the time of this writing.

In the excellent government schools of his native place Father Frank Machan acquired his early educational discipline, and after completing the curriculum of the gymnasium, corresponding to the high school of the United States, he pursued higher academic studies in the seminary or Catholic theological school in the City of Brünn, the capital of Moravia, where he completed his philosophical, classical and ecclesiastical courses and was prepared for the reception of holy orders. In 1889, in the ancient cathedral in the City of Brünn, as a member of a class of more than thirty young men, he was ordained to the priesthood by Cardinal Bauer. Soon after his ordination Father Machan was assigned to the professorship of pedagogy and methods of teaching and also church history, in the karlin or boys' high school maintained under church auspices in the City of Prague, Bohemia. His service in this institution continued somewhat more than six years, and he then came to the United States.

As soon as he had received holy orders Father Machan applied for a position as chaplain in the Austrian army, and he was assigned to the Forty-eighth Regiment. Each year thereafter until he came to America he reported to his command, appeared before his superiors and gave active service as chaplain during the prescribed period. The incidental oath which he took in this connection was of such character as to bind him conscientiously and loyally to his native land, with the result that he has never felt justified in applying for citizenship in the United States.

In 1895, in the City of Bremen, Father Machan embarked on the steamship Trave and by the same found transportation to New York City, from which point he came forthwith to Texas and was assigned, by Bishop Gallagher, to parish work at Granger, Williamson County, where he remained four years. There he not only exercised his sacerdotal functions and taught in the parish school, but he also had supervision of the work of the missionery parish at Corn Hill. At the expiration of four years he was assigned to the parish of St. Joseph's Church, at Bryan, Brazos County, where he remained two years, within which he effected the erection of a new church edifice and also established a parish school. After leaving this charge Father Machan served as supply priest to a Polish parish at Bremond, Robertson County, until a Polish pastor could be provided, and he was then appointed pastor of St. Mary's Church at Sealy, Austin County, besides which he prepared plans for the small church and school buildings in the Bohemian settlement of Frydek, at San Felipe, that county. He retained his pastoral incumbency at Sealy one year and then became pastor of the parish of the Church of St. John the Baptist, at Ammansville, Fayette County, where he remained two years, within which time the new church edifice was erected. Impaired health compelled his retirement, and after a year of rest and recuperation he was assigned to his present charge, that of pastor of the one Catholic parish at Shiner, as the successor of Father

Hudecek. In this large and prosperous parish, like in all other charges in which he has served, Father Machan has labored with indefatigable zeal and devotion and has greatly vitalized the spiritual and temporal activities of the parish. As a preacher he has excellent ability, and his addresses invariably bear the stamp of consecrated sincerity as well as of practical and vigorous humanitarianism, his aim at all times being to aid and uplift his fellow men in all of the stations and walks of life.

JOSEPH J. FIETSAM. A man who has won success by hard directed effort, Joseph J. Fietsam is one of the large land owners and business men of the Ammansville locality in Fayette County, and is known all over the county for his efficient service as county commissioner, an office from which he retired in 1914. He is a man of large physical proportions and splendid constitution, from whom one would expect vigorous accomplishment, and while he began life with only the capital of willing hands he has secured a reasonable degree of material prosperity and at the same time has not neglected his obligations toward the community and his fellow men.

Joseph J. Fietsam was born in Fayette County, at Bluff, on February 6, 1856. His father was Joseph G. Fietsam. The latter was one of those German pioneers who came into Texas in the great movement of German colonization during the decade of the '40s. He was born at Herzogthum in Nassau, in what is now the German Empire, on February 12, 1825, and was reared on a farm, being the son of a surveyor. He acquired a more liberal education than could usually be obtained from the popular schools of his time. He learned the trade of wheelwright, and when about twenty years of age, in 1845, took passage on a sailing vessel at Bremen, and some weeks later landed at the old Texas port of Indianola. He was still unmarried, and joined the old German community of New Braunfels, and soon took service with the Texas Rangers. He became a wagoner, and worked along the frontier and in the Indian country for some time. On leaving the ranger service he moved to LaGrange, and took up work at his trade as wheelwright at 50 cents a day. He soon found reason to give up this business, and engaged in farming. He was married in 1852, and then located on a farm at Rock Prairie in Fayette County. From there he moved to the Bluff community, and in that locality bought his first land. His home was there until 1887, when he went to Weimar, and died in that village in 1906. Joseph Fietsam had no part in the war between the states since he was physically incapacitated for active service. Not long after coming to Texas he took out citizenship papers and in politics was a republican. At one time he served as county commissioner of Fayette County, and for many years was a trustee of the public schools at Bluff. After removing to Weimar he was appointed postmaster by President Harrison, and had begun a second term when the democratic party came into power and replaced him with a new appointee. He was an active member of the Catholic Church. Joseph G. Fietsam married Catherine Laux, daughter of Peter Laux, who came also from the Province of Nassau, Germany. She died in 1898. Her children were: Henry, who died at Weimar, leaving three children by his wife whose maiden name was Thekla Goeph; Joseph J.; Mary, who married Oscar Hilden of Weimar; Bertha who married William Tell of Weimar; and Miss Emma, still living at Weimar.

Joseph J. Fietsam has spent practically all his life in Fayette County. He grew up on a farm and while learning the duties of the household and the fields attended the public schools at Bluff. After his marriage at the age of twenty-two he removed to the Ammansville community. He bought his first farm, comprising seventy-one acres of raw land in the Jesse Barton Survey. Confronted with the heavy task of improving new land and making a home for himself and family, he set about his business with characteristic vigor and was soon on a fair way to prosperity. For many years he has been engaged in growing cotton and corn, and has also kept stock so far as his range would permit. His material prosperity has been indicated by the addition of new lands from time to time, until at this writing he is the owner of more than 500 acres, with 125 acres under the plow, and with three complete sets of farm improvements.

In the meantime for many years Mr. Fietsam has been a worker in local affairs. Politically he has been a democrat, since 1906, and has supported all the party nominees since that time. In 1892 he was elected justice of the peace, and served four years, making a favorable record in the routine duties of that office. In 1898 he was elected county commissioner for the fourth beat of Fayette County, succeeding Commissioner Neal McKinnon. His services as county commissioner, which has been the chief event of his public career, was for sixteen continuous years. Besides the usual duties connected with the administration of that office his administration was marked by the refunding of the courthouse bonds, which were sold to the school fund; proper provision for precinct government; and extensive road improvements and the building of a number of iron bridges in his precinct. With many high testimonials commending his service in this office he retired in December, 1914, being succeeded by Robert Williams. Mr. Fietsam was also one of the organizers recently of the Ammansville State Bank, and is first vice president and one of the directors.

In December, 1877, he married Miss Ida Albrecht, daughter of Fritz and Christina (Suren) Albrecht. Her parents came to America from Mecklenburg. Mr. and Mrs. Fietsam have the following children: Sophie, who married Charles Munke, and their children are Emma, Hilda, Edna and Katie; Walter, a farmer of Fayette County, married Rosa Munke, and has two children, Thelma and Jo. Katie married Willie Munke and has a son Clarence; Laura is the wife of Adolph Schindler of Weimar, and their two children are Ida and Oscar; Lillie married Hermann Munke, of Fayette County, and has a daughter Josephine; the younger children are Judith, Bruno and Arnold.

Otto Koehler. With the death of Otto Koehler on November 12, 1914, there passed from the active citizenship of San Antonio one of the most valuable factors in that city's commercial development and civic life. For more than thirty years he had been closely identified with San Antonio, and his loss was not only a personal one but also left a gap to be filled in the business world. Mr. Koehler was the leading spirit and the executive genius of the San Antonio Brewing Association from its organization until the time of his death. Of a genial and generous disposition, he made friends wherever he was, and his undoubted ability and a capacity for hard work made him a valuable man in all his associations. He possessed the ability to handle large practical interests and men, had a thorough sympathy and understanding of human nature, and while in the course of his career he amassed a fortune, his liberality was as conspicuous a trait of his character as his business ability.

Otto Koehler was born in the Town of Aldfeld, Hanover, Germany, April 28, 1855, and while his own life came to a close shortly before his sixtieth birthday, both his grandparents and his parents lived to celebrate their golden wedding anniversary. He was one of the ten children of August and Johanna Koehler and of all these children Otto became the wealthiest and most influential. His twin brother Karl,

his senior by a few hours, died several years ago. Another brother, Herman C. Koehler, is auditor of the San Antonio Brewing Association; Louis is in business in St. Louis; and Albert is a farmer in Germany. The three surviving sisters are: Mrs. Johanna Graef of St. Louis; Mrs. Hermine Froehlich of Hamburg; and Mrs. Anna Koopman of Holstein.

Otto Koehler acquired his schooling in the Seminary School of Aldfeld, and early in life showed the boundless energy and steadfastness of purpose which were among his conspicuous qualities of character. His father was a grain and coal merchant, but the son had little inclination for that line of work, and after securing a substantial education, including both business and military training, he crossed the Atlantic in 1872, and his first experience was as a clerk in St. Louis. He applied himself vigorously to the mastery of the English language, and in a few years was equipped for more extended ventures in the American fields of business. At that time his brothers were engaged in merchandising in St. Louis, but the experience which furnished him the foundation for his future career was employment with the firm of Griesedieck Brothers, brewers at St. Louis. During those early years Mr. Koehler also spent some time in Arkansas representing business interests for capitalists. At St. Louis he devoted himself with steadfastness of purpose toward acquiring a knowledge and mastery of all branches of the brewing industry, and after a few years sought a newer field in the Southwest.

It was in 1884 that Mr. Koehler came to San Antonio and first became identified with the Lone Star Brewing Company, which had only recently been organized. A short time later there was a disagreement in the management of that company, and Mr. Koehler withdrew and became associated with John J. Stevens, Otto Wahrmund and Oscar Bergstrom in the organization of the San Antonio Brewing Association. From the beginning Mr. Koehler was the practical spirit in this enterprise. The company bought a small brewery, known as the Beloradsky Brewery, situated on the present location of the San Antonio Company's plant. This was the first commercial brewery in San Antonio. Under the management of Mr. Koehler the enterprise had a rapid growth, has been enlarged and rebuilt many times, and for a number of years has been the largest brewery in the South, with a standard reputation for its products all over the Southwest. It was known for a number of years and is still known among local citizens as the City Brewery. Early in the history of the enterprise Mr. Koehler became president, with Col. Otto Wahrmund as vice president. Mr. Koehler was frequently given the credit of being the father of the brewing industry in San Antonio, and his enterprise resulted in making that city the brewing center of the state.

As a business man and capitalist Mr. Koehler showed his enterprise and public spirit in many ways, often through financial aid of enterprises that were not profitable to him personally but were of value in advertising the city. He organized the Hot Sulphur Wells Company, building a fine hotel, of which he was the principal owner, and thus gave to San Antonio the famous health resort of Hot Sulphur Wells, lying south of the city. That was one of the factors that attracted tourists to San Antonio. A number of years before his death Mr. Koehler became interested in mining operations in Mexico, and was remarkably successful. He organized the Jimulco Mining Company and the Panuco Mining Company, being president of both concerns, and was also president of the National Rubber Company, owning and operating a rubber factory at Torreon, was president of the Continental Mining Company, the Monarch Mining Company, of the Panuco Mountain Railroad, of the Texas Transportation Company, and of the American

Lignite and Briquette Company, with headquarters at Rockdale, Texas. He was one of the organizers, one of the largest stockholders, a director and vice president of the Central Trust Company of San Antonio, and with Adolph Wagner was an organizer of the Star Product Company and also a stockholder. Altogether Mr. Koehler was president or director in about fifteen different corporations. At the time of his death his estate was estimated in value at about $3,000,000, and included a large amount of valuable business property in some of the central sections of San Antonio. He also had property in Atlanta, Georgia, and was interested in brick manufacturing in Louisville, Kentucky.

About fifteen years before his death Mr. Koehler acquired a block of land in San Pedro Place, Laurel Heights, long before modern development had made that the most exclusive residence section of San Antonio. On that land Mr. Koehler erected an attractive and beautiful residence, one that has long been a landmark in San Antonio, attractive both for the architectural lines and for the unusual setting in which the house is placed. For a number of years at least it was regarded as the most costly private residence in the city. Mr. Koehler took the greatest pride and pleasure in his home and the grounds, and adorned it with the choicest specimens of the landscape gardener's art. He also carried out his interest in landscape gardening by planting many trees around the brewery, and it is said that he never left San Antonio for an extended absence without special caution and instruction to the gardener for care of his flowers and trees.

Mr. Koehler was married at St. Louis to Miss Emma Bentzen, who belonged to an old and respected family of that state. While Mr. and Mrs. Koehler had no children of their own, they had in their home two of his nephews, Charles and Otto, sons of his twin brother.

Both business associates and fellow citizens felt the greatest sense of loss at the news of Mr. Koehler's death. An expression of the general feeling of the community was voiced by one of his long standing business associates, who said: "He never saw an opportunity to do good that he did not act to his fullest ability. Every man in his employ was devoted to him, and this spirit of friendship for the chief dominated every man in the employ of the brewery. Mr. Koehler was not only very methodical, but was a very hard worker and the constant tax on his energy was beginning to tell on him." Mr. Koehler had many associations with the city which he was always proud to call his home. He was one of the supporters of the Chamber of Commerce, both financially and personally, and always gave substantial support to any enterprise sponsored by that organization. His charities were known to be large, though the specific directions they took will never be known, since it was a part of his modesty to do good by stealth. While devoted to family and home, he was also a member of many clubs, was one of the most influential in the organization of the Travis Club, and belonged to the San Antonio Club, the Rockhill Golf Club, golf being his favorite diversion, the Casino, the Beethoven Maennerchor, the Turn Verein, the Elks and the San Antonio Automobile Club. He was also affiliated with Alamo Lodge of the Masonic Order.

HERMANN SCHROEDER. A capable representative of the agriculturists of the vicinity of Industry, Hermann Schroeder is a native of the County of Austin and at the present time commissioner of Precinct No. 4. He was born at the old Town of Industry, June 30, 1858, his father being Fritz Schroeder, a German, who came to America in 1848, or about that time, and located at once at Industry, to which place his refugee brother, Christian Schroeder, had come previously.

Fritz Schroeder was born at Lippe-Detmoldt, Germany, in 1827, and passed away in 1872. A tailor as a tradesman in his native land, on coming to Texas he adopted the vocation of farmer and gin man, and continued to be engaged in operations along these lines until the time of his death. Mr. Schroeder married Mrs. Carolina Sieper, a daughter of Frederick Ernst, whose wife was the first German woman to come to Texas. Mrs. Schroeder had issue by her first marriage: August, who died unmarried; Mrs. Amelia Baring, who is now deceased; Johanna, who married Albert Baring and lives at Eagle Lake, Texas; Louisa, who became the wife of Henry Brill, and is now deceased; Mary, who became the wife of Max Schmidt and both are now deceased; and Lena, who is the wife of Charles C. Gollmer, of Industry. To Mr. and Mrs. Schroeder there were born the following children: Hermann, of this review; Mrs. Elam Lockwood, who is deceased, as is her husband; Otto, who lives on the old Schroeder place in the locality of Industry; and Edward, who has a family and resides at the old home. Mrs. Schroeder passed away at the historic farm at the age of eighty-two years. The Schroeder family from the old country comprised, beside Christian and Fritz, William and Ferdinand, the latter of whom still resides at Kennedy, Texas, while the former died at New Ulm. Both reared families.

Hermann Schroeder grew up in the old Town of Industry and in the atmosphere of the Industry pioneers. He was a schoolboy of the days following the close of the Civil war, and left his studies with a fair education, at that time taking up farming as a member of the family group and remaining under the parental roof until he reached the age of twenty-five years. He was married at that time and began farming, but subsequently became star route mail carrier from Industry to Brenham, and from Industry to Columbus, both of which routes he contracted for. He abandoned the business with the expiration of the long contract and the introduction of other plans, and resumed farming. In 1900 Mr. Schroeder located on his present property, located in the Pettes League, where he has 100 acres of good land formerly owned by Emil Knolle, and has devoted himself to corn and cotton growing, in the meantime participating in the neighborhood affairs as a progressive citizen always does.

Mr. Schroeder became identified with politics as a voter and, in a measure, as an earnest supporter of democratic success when still a young man. Unlike his father, he has permitted himself to be drawn into official life, his first office being that of constable of his precinct, in which he served two years. He is a trustee of the schools here, an office in which he has frequently served for a number of years, and in 1914 was elected to the position of county commissioner of Precinct No. 4, as the successor of Oscar Fissler. He is serving on the board with Judge Krueger and Commissioners H. Waak, Henry Peters and Julius Schofner. Mr. Schroeder's public career has been one upon which there is no stain or blemish, and his fellow-citizens have every reason to continue to hold him in the highest confidence and regard. As a farmer, he is progressive and energetic, liberal-minded in experimenting with new ideas and inventions, and always ready to lend his support to anything that promises the elevation of agricultural standards. His fraternal connection is with the Sons of Hermann.

Mr. Schroeder was married at Industry, December 12, 1882, to Miss Annie Voelkel, a daughter of William Voelkel, who came from Wichenstein, Germany, was a farmer by vocation, married Margaret Fimdt, and died at Yoakum, Texas. The Voelkel children were as follows: Henry, who died leaving a daughter; William, who passed away without issue; Louis, who is also deceased and left two children; Mrs. Schroeder, born April 30, 1861; Louisa, who married Emil Rinn and lives near Industry;

Ernst, of Yoakum, Texas; Sophie, the wife of Gustav Rinn, of Yoakum; Amelia, who married William Poth; Emma, who married Doctor Beckman, of Yoakum, died March 21, 1916; and Edmund, a resident of Austin, Texas.

To Mr. and Mrs. Schroeder there have been born children as follows: Louisa, who married Ernst Dippel, of Industry, and has two children, Eldis and Leroy; Doctor Ervin, of Boston, Massachusetts, a veteran surgeon and graduate of the Agricultural and Mechanical College of Texas and of a Louisville school of veterinary surgery, and married in Massachusetts; Ella, a teacher in the Belleville schools, and a graduate of the School of Arts, at Denton, Texas; Alfred, who is engaged in the carpenter's trade at Industry; Lillie, who acquired an advanced education at San Marcus, Texas, and is now a teacher in the schools of Sealy, Texas; Bennie, a student at Boston, Massachusetts; Herbert and Herder, twins; and Otto.

James Marburger. In the year following that of the admission of the former Republic of Texas as one of the sovereign commonwealths of the United States, James Marburger, of Cistern, Fayette County, became a resident of this state, as a lad of about five years. He accompanied his parents on their immigration from Germany and the family home was established in Austin County, Texas. Here Mr. Marburger maintained his home during the long intervening period of seventy years, and it was his privilege and satisfaction to have witnessed and assisted in the civic and material development and upbuilding of the Lone Star State and through his well ordered endeavors to achieve independence and substantial financial success. He was one of the pioneer citizens of Fayette County, where he accumulated a large landed estate, and he was prominent and influential in civic affairs and in industrial and business activities, the while his course was ordered according to the principles of integrity, fairness and steadfastness, so that he fully merited the confidence and good will that were uniformly accorded to him.

Mr. Marburger was born in Witzenstein, Prussia, on the 22d of March, 1841, and was a son of Henry and Mary (Wolf) Marburger, both natives of Preis-Witzenstein, where the former was born August 20, 1805, and the latter on the 19th of February, 1803. Henry Marburger acquired a common-school education in his native land, was reared in the faith of the Lutheran Church, and he developed much musical ability, especially as a vocalist. In his Fatherland he had direction of a church choir, and he continued his activities in this line after becoming a pioneer in Texas, having been a leader in the religious activities in the Shelby community of Austin County.

In 1846 Henry Marburger and his family embarked on a sailing vessel in the port of Bremen, Germany, and set forth to establish their new home in America. Their voyage was continued through the Gulf of Mexico to Texas and they landed at Galveston, five days having been required for them to make the trip between that place and Houston, from which latter point they were transferred to their destination to the Shelby community, in Austin County, by the old-time freighter and pioneer German citizen named Rinn. In the vicinity of the present Town of Shelby Henry Marburger purchased and improved a tract of land, and prior to the war between the North and the South he owned a few slaves. When the war was precipitated he vigorously upheld the cause of the Union, but his three sons all served as soldiers in the Confederate ranks. He was a staunch democrat, an honest, upright and unassuming citizen, he became only measurably familiar with the English language, and on his farm he continued to live a quiet and uneventful life until he was venerable in years, when he became a welcome member of the home circle of his son James, of this review, at Cistern, where he died on the 11th of January, 1893, his loved and devoted wife having passed away June 14, 1886. Of their children it may be recorded that William died near Cistern, at the age of sixty-five years, he having been a soldier in Waul's Legion in the Confederate service in the Civil war; his wife, Anna, having survived him by a number of years; Henry, who likewise served in Waul's Legion, died at his home near Cistern, Fayette County, at the age of seventy-six years, the maiden name of his wife having been Bertha Wunderlich; James, of this sketch, was the next in order of birth and is the only surviving member of the immediate family; and the one daughter, Mrs. Louisa Bernhausen, died near Welcome, Austin County, when seventy-six years of age.

In Austin County James Marburger was reared to manhood under the conditions of the pioneer days on the Texas frontier, and such educational advantages as came to him were those offered in the somewhat primitive schools maintained in the Shelby community. As a youth he entered the employ of William B. Witte, the leading merchant of Shelby, and was assigned to the work of hauling merchandise and other commodities from Houston to Shelby. After experience in this capacity he was given a clerkship in Mr. Witte's store at Shelby, and his compensation for the first year included his board and lodging and the stupendous emolument of $5. The second year, however, he prevailed upon his employer to accord to him a cash compensation of $12.50, and he continued his faithful clerical labors in this connection until he went forth in the Civil war as a youthful and loyal soldier of the Confederacy.

In November, 1861, Mr. Marburger enlisted in Company G, commanded by Captain Hauvel, in Colonel Riley's Regiment of General Sibley's Brigade. With this valiant command he proceeded into New Mexico, where he took part in the battles of Fort Craig, Valverde and Santa Fe, besides a long-resisted engagement at Beralda after the return of the brigade to Texas. After remaining a few weeks in camp at Milliken Mr. Marburger's regiment went with his regiment to the vicinity of Harrisburg, where some of its members, concerning one of whom Mr. Marburger was prone to keep wisely silent, did effective foraging and captured a number of semi-belligerent hogs, and the command thence proceeded to Galveston. From the rank of private Mr. Marburger was promoted sergeant, later was made orderly sergeant, and finally was commissioned first lieutenant. After the battle of Galveston he was assigned to guard duty, with sixty men, on the wharf of that city, where they endured much hardship in the loss of their tents and being compelled to sleep unprotected from the rain, besides meeting other unseemly exposure to the elements. From Galveston the command returned to Houston, and prior to the close of the war Mr. Marburger received his honorable discharge, on account of physical disability. Prior to his discharge he had been assigned to hospital service at Hempstead, but he was soon ordered to Houston, with his men and equipment, and in that city he was finally retired from further service.

After having recuperated his physical powers Mr. Marburger joined his old friend, the pioneer freighter, Mr. Rinn, and engaged in the buying of cotton, which they hauled to the Rio Grande, where they sold the product at the rate of 40 cents a pound. He paid for the freighting of his cotton across the plains to Rio Grande at the rate of 11 cents a pound, in gold, and even under these conditions he realized large profits. Before the close of the war Mr. Marburger became associated with his former employer, Mr. Witte, in the general merchandise business at

Shelby, and though much the junior in years he was made senior member of the firm of Marburger & Witte, his capitalistic investment being the heavier of the two and representing his profits from his transactions in cotton, notwithstanding he had been compelled to pay one-fifth of his gross receipts to the Confederate government, as a war tax with incidental privilege of conducting his business enterprise. After six years of successful merchandising at Shelby, Mr. Marburger dissolved his partnership with Mr. Witte and engaged in the same line of enterprise at Haw Creek, a village in Fayette County. He established the first mercantile store in the place and the building which he there erected for the purpose is still used for business purposes. He developed a specially large and prosperous enterprise, was the first country merchant in this locality to buy his goods by the car-load lot, and he continued in business at Haw Creek nearly five years, besides which he conducted a similar or branch enterprise about three years at Rock House, in the meanwhile having opened also a general store in Cistern, where he occupied the old adobe building that had been erected by the Goshia firm some years previously. At Cistern Mr. Marburger continued his successful business as one of the leading merchants of Fayette County for the long period of twenty-two years, his retirement having occurred in 1900.

While engaged in the mercantile business Mr. Marburger was investing his profits judiciously in real estate. He bought lands in the Whiteside League, near Cistern, and brought much of the same into effective and profitable cultivation. He is still owner of an extensive landed estate in Fayette County and has set apart a large amount of his holdings for his children. At Cistern he erected the fine and essentially modern house which was afterward his place of residence and which became a center of genial hospitality. For many years Mr. Marburger was engaged in the raising of cattle on an extensive scale, and until within a recent period he had many head of high-grade cattle on his range. His brand was the anchor, and it is used on the Anchor Brand Ranch, of which one of his sons has the active supervision.

In politics Mr. Marburger never deviated from a line of strict allegiance to the democratic party, but in local affairs he was inclined to subordinate mere partisanship to give his support to men and measures meeting the approval of his judgment. He was for many years arrayed as a foe of the liquor traffic and was in full accord with the prohibition movement. Mr. Marburger was reared in the faith of the Lutheran Church, maintained an abiding appreciation of the spiritual verities of the Christian religion and was always liberal and helpful in church support, holding it not in derogation of the cause that he himself has had his confidence abused and sustained losses through the medium of hypocritical clergymen and other church members from whom he had expected honest and sincere treatment. At Round Top he became affiliated with the Masonic fraternity more than forty-five years ago, but he was not in active affiliation with the order at the close of his life. He signified his birthright eligibility by holding membershp in the Sons of Hermann. In addition to Henry Marburger, grandfather of the subject of this sketch, three of his brothers, William, Ludwig and Jacob, likewise became early settlers of Texas, and their only sister passed the closing years of her life at Shelby, this state, the name of her first husband having been Voelkel and that of her second, Hetzel, she having had children by both marriages.

In Austin County, on the 10th of January, 1865, was celebrated the marriage of James Marburger to Miss Mary Doss, a daughter of Charles and Augusta (Schneider) Doss. Mr. Doss came from Potsdam, Germany, and was a skilled mechanic as well as a talented vocalist. In his native land he was a music leader in the service of his Prussian king, and after he came to Texas he served as leader of the Gesangverein in Austin County. He was one of the German revolutionists of 1848 and on this account, with many of his fellow patriots, was compelled to flee his Fatherland and establish a home in the United States. Of his children Richard died at Victoria, Texas; George is a resident of Rockdale, this state; Mrs. Marburger, the elder daughter, was born in the City of Berlin, Germany, August 14, 1846, and was a young child at the time of the family immigration to America; and Johanna, who became the wife of Andreas Schucaney, was a resident of Shelby, this state, at the time of her death. In the concluding paragraph is entered brief record concerning the children of Mr. and Mrs. Marburger:

Antonia died at the age of three and one-half years; Hedwig, born March 14, 1867, is the wife of William Mennicke, of La Grange, judicial center of Fayette County; Paula, born March 11, 1869, is the wife of E. A. Arnim, of Flatonia, this county; Walter, born August 8, 1870, is a resident of the City of Galveston, the maiden name of his wife having been Antonia Paul; Johanna, born June 6, 1872, is the wife of W. C. Miller, of Smithville; Lula, born August 26, 1874, is the wife of A. M. Gosch, of Flatonia; Felix J., who was born March 12, 1878, married Miss Georgia Blanchard and they reside in the City of Galveston; Max, who was born November 8, 1879, and who married Miss Clara Mensing, is a successful ranchman near Cistern; Beno D., who was born December 10, 1882, and the maiden name of whose wife was Eva Rich, resides at Kingsville, Texas, and is a civil engineer by profession, he being identified with railroad work in a professional capacity; Valeska, born November 25, 1884, is the wife of Dr. O. Davis, of Anderson, this state; Arnold, born November 15, 1889, is a scientific farmer on a portion of his father's landed estate, near Cistern, and the maiden name of his wife was Dovie Knight.

James Marburger, the subject of this sketch, died at Flatonia, Texas, October 3, 1915, and was buried under the auspices of the Sons of Hermann at the family buying ground at Cistern, Texas, October 4, 1915, at the age of seventy-four years and six months, his entire family being present.

WESLEY KINGSTON SULLIVAN. One of the oldest residents of Flatonia, having located there soon after the railroad was built, is Wesley K. Sullivan, cotton buyer and broker. Among the cotton planters and growers in Fayette County his is one of the most familiar names and his record as a dealer has been so consistently maintained on the par of truth and fairness that every one of his many customers places implicit faith in his word and his representation. In many ways outside of his business he has identified himself with the community interest and has been an aggressive improver and developer of this section.

Wesley Kingston Sullivan was born in Pontotoc County, Mississippi, March 1, 1862. His grandfather, John Sullivan, was of Irish stock, and was born in March, 1772, just ninety years before the birth of his grandson Wesley K., and died in July, 1871, in his hundredth year. He was of a revolutionary family and had seven brothers who served on the American side in that struggle for independence. John Sullivan's wife lived to be almost ninety years of age, and both are buried at the Bethlehem Church near Moscow, Tennessee. Among their ten children were: John; Caleb; Jesse; Elkanah J.; Mrs. Elizabeth McPhail, who died in Houston County, Texas; Mrs. George Green of Tippah County, Mississippi; and one daughter who died at Mount Pleasant, Texas.

Elkanah Jasper Sullivan, father of Wesley K., was born in Yallabusha County, Mississippi, and grew up on a plantation worked by slaves. He acquired a liberal education, and was an able business man. When his son Wesley was three years of age he took the family to Moscow, Tennessee, and became a large land owner and practical farmer in that locality. In 1880 he moved to Texas, and a few months later died at Flatonia. During the war he was in the Confederate service, served as a justice of the peace in Tennessee, was an active democrat, and a man of special prominence and influence in the Methodist Church. He filled several of the church offices and frequently was an exhorter. He was affiliated with the Lodge of Masons, and was the first man buried by the Flatonia Lodge of that order. He possessed unusual financial ability, and invested largely in lands and left a considerable estate. Elkanah J. Sullivan married Bettie Howell, whose father was a farmer in Middle Tennessee. She died in 1864; her children being briefly mentioned as follows: Mary, who married Joseph Rose and died in Yazoo, Mississippi; Nannie, who married David McDonald and lives in Texas; Virginia, who became the wife of William Jackson of Tippah County, Mississippi; Frances, wife of Wilson Slaughter, M. D., of Mississippi; Florence, wife of G. W. Perry of Pine Bluff, Arkansas; Samuel S., a farmer near Flatonia; America, who married John Teague and died in Fayette County, Tennessee; and Wesley K.

Wesley K. Sullivan spent his youth up to the age of eighteen at Moscow, Tennessee, attended the schools in Macon and also the Macon College. He has been a resident of Flatonia since 1880, and on coming to Texas engaged in the cattle business for a short time. C. S. Wigg of Houston then made him cotton buyer at Flatonia, and later on he was associated with Blakely & Brown as buyer, subsequently bought for Inmann & Company, and finally represented Ralli Brothers, cotton factors of Liverpool, with offices in Houston. Mr. Sullivan finally established an independent business as a cotton broker, for one year was a partner of A. B. Slack, and has since conducted business on his own account. He is a "fob" broker, buying and selling cotton according to that commercial principle at Flatonia.

Mr. Sullivan has been a notable influence in this section of Texas for his part in the development of agriculture and in the improvement of good roads. He invested largely in farm lands around Flatonia, and had improved almost a section of land before selling. He still owns an experimental farm, which he employs for the production of cotton and corn under intensive methods and with appropriate use of fertilizer to demonstrate what can be accomplished. In his home community he has built the street adjacent to his home, and confesses to being a "good roads crank." He constructed the first split log road drag and for years at his own expense kept the roads around his farm in fine condition. His own home in Flatonia is one of the show places in the residence district. It is located upon the high point in the heart of the residence section. He is also the owner and has built houses which he rents in the town. The Sullivan home is one that shows an artistic taste in planning and construction both inside and out. It is surrounded by a beautiful landscape of lawn, shrubs and trees, and in this happy setting the lines of the home have a harmonious part. His residence is built in the most modern style and with exceptional comforts and conveniences. Attractive features are the sun parlor, the summer dining room, sleeping porch, and a large sitting room furnished in that simplicity which is the acme of good taste. His ideas of comfort and luxury find their best exemplification in the bath room, furnishings and equipment of which were put in at an expense of $1,000.

In local affairs Mr. Sullivan has concerned himself chiefly with those movements which would bring direct and practical benefit to the community. He is a democrat in politics and has occasionally attended conventions as a delegate and in the primaries of 1912 supported the candidacy of Mr. Wilson, and is one of the thousands of men who have found reason to approve the high-minded course of that scholar statesman. Fraternally he is active in Masonry, is a past master of his lodge, past high priest of his chapter, and it is largely through his influence that the Knights of Pythias Lodge was established at Flatonia, in which he is a past chancellor and for ten years was a member of the grand lodge of the order. His church is the Methodist and he is a steward in the Flatonia congregation.

In September, 1894, Mr. Sullivan married Miss Ella Wheeler, daughter of William H. Wheeler of Flatonia. William Harrison Wheeler has been a resident of Flatonia almost continuously since 1877, was a liveryman for more than thirty years, and is now living retired. He was born in Alabama, a son of Richard and Katie (Church) Wheeler. His father, who died when about fifty years of age, in Jackson County, Alabama, was a farmer and a son of Amos Wheeler, a Georgian, and of the same family as Gen. Joseph Wheeler. Mrs. Richard Wheeler died in 1848, leaving a number of children. William H. Wheeler came to Texas in the fall of 1858, by boat from Memphis to New Orleans and to Galveston, and then went over the only Texas railroad as far as Hempstead. He soon afterward took up a career as freighter with ox teams between Austin and Port Lavaca. He carried goods to and from Bastrop, Gonzales, Lockhart and Austin. It was the custom to load their wagons with cotton from the interior towns to the gulf port, and the two wagons drawn by six yoke of steers brought back various goods and merchandise.

When the war came on Mr. Wheeler left his wagon below Hallettsville and joined Company D under Captain Walker, which went to San Antonio to enter the State Ranger service. The company was later assigned to the Second Texas Cavalry, Col. John R. Baylor, and later Colonel Byron. The regiment took part in the New Mexico campaign, and at the end of the year returned to San Antonio. The regiment then became a part of the Confederate army which recaptured Galveston, then went into Louisiana, and participated in the battles of Mansfield, Yellow Bayou, and finally returned to Texas and was operating in the country between Corpus Christi and Brownsville in the last months of the war. His comrade tried to persuade him to leave Texas and join the Maximilian invasion in Mexico, but Mr. Wheeler rejected the proposal and returned to Hallettsville to take up the occupations of peace. He worked as a clerk at Hallettsville, subsequently became a partner in the firm of Walker & Wheeler, spending a part of the time traveling for the firm, and about ten years later became traveling representative for a Galveston wholesale house. He then located in Flatonia, established the Wheeler House and conducted that as a hotel for several years, though the building is now used as his residence, having been remodeled and improved. For many years he conducted both a hotel and livery. He finally purchased the old Leceister Hotel, ran it for eight years, then managed the Cleburne Hotel at Cleburne for a year, since which time he has lived quietly retired in Flatonia. Mr. Wheeler is a democrat but has been strongly adverse to any notoriety, and has not even attended Confederate reunions except the meetings of his old Green brigade.

Mr. Wheeler was married in Lavaca County in 1873 to Emma Arnim, daughter of Albert Arnim, who was for many years a merchant of Hallettsville. Mr. Wheeler's children were: Ella, wife of W. K. Sullivan; Richard A., a cotton buyer of Flatonia; Katie, wife of N. Lyon of Flatonia; Willie of Flatonia; Dr. Leslie, a dentist at Flatonia; and Margie, wife of R. D. Clancy of Flatonia.

CHARLES E. NESRSTA. For upwards of half a century the Nesrsta family has been one of prominence and valuable service in Fayette County. Charles E. Nesrsta, of the second generation, is well known as a Flatonia lawyer, and his father before him was one of the ablest and best known educators in this section of the state.

Antone Nesrsta, founder of the family in Fayette County, was born in the Town of Zlin, in the Province of Moravia, Austria, on September 8, 1851. In 1869 he came to the United States with his mother and brother, landing in New York after seven weeks spent on board a sailing vessel in crossing the ocean. From New York they came South, locating in the southern end of Fayette County. The father of Antone, who died in Europe, had been a government forester, and had also served his regular enlistment as a soldier. After coming to Texas the members of the family took up farming, rented land for several years, and finally got themselves established in a degree of comfort and with rising prosperity. Antone's inclinations, however, were all towards the profession of educator, and he soon took up teaching. He had received a liberal education in his native land and may possibly have received some instruction in the English language before coming to this country. Anyhow, he had a fluent command of that tongue and made his mark as a teacher in public schools. That was his profession, carried on at Praha, continuously for a period of thirty-seven years, with only one year of interruption, during which twelve months his family induced him to rest. He then returned to his work at the same place and died while still practically in the harness. The Praha school was graded under his supervision, and it was noted as one of the best schools in Fayette County. Professor Nesrsta turned out many young teachers during those years and his popularity and efficiency made his school much above the average and pupils from outside the district often came to attend his classes. He possessed not only the gift of imparting information, but also that of inspiring others to work and cultivate their minds and ambitions at the same time. Though not gifted as a speaker, he could express himself forcibly as a writer. His penmanship was extraordinary, and samples of his handwriting were almost as regular and perfect as a copy book. For a number of years he was a notary public, and in that way his penmanship was introduced into many public documents. The people in that section frequently exhibit with pride old deeds and other legal instruments bearing the impress of his penmanship.

Antone Nesrsta became a citizen soon after coming to America and was always allied with the democratic party. He satisfied himself with merely voting, was frequently an election judge, but had no higher political aspirations. He was a leader in the Catholic Church and an active factor in establishing and maintaining the church at Praha, having aided in the erection of its new building. Like many of his fellow countrymen he had a talent for music, played with considerable skill on the flute and violin and occasionally formed one of the church orchestra for special occasions. The mother of Antone Nesrsta was Rosa Krupala who died at the age of eighty-three years in 1905. Her other son was Charles Nesrsta, a farmer near Praha.

Antone Nesrsta was married in 1874 to Miss Anna Kubicek, a daughter of Frank Kubicek, who came to this country from Bohemia. Mrs. Nesrsta was born on board the sailing vessel which brought the Kubicek family to this country. She died in November, 1897. The children were: Charles E.; Frank A., a banker of Flatonia, who married Martha Zuhm; Cecilia, wife of A. F. Kubala, of LaGrange; Annie, wife of I. J. Parma, of LaGrange; Felix F., a merchant in Flatonia, who married Amelia Kotzebue; Emma, wife of Charles E. Hackebeil, of

LaGrange; Anita, wife of Thomas Prajer, of Eads, Colorado; Roy, of LaGrange; and Adella, wife of Gus Herzik, of Engel, Texas.

Charles E. Nesrsta was born at Praha in Fayette County, November 6, 1875. He was educated in the school conducted by his father, and has inherited the scholarly traits of his elder. He began life as a teacher at the age of seventeen and for six years taught in the vicinity of Flatonia. He then took a course in the Alamo Business College at San Antonio, where he was graduated August 6, 1897, following which a Flatonia firm employed him as bookkeeper. With the closing out of the business he took up the study of law in the firm of Lane & Lane at LaGrange and continued until admitted to the bar in June, 1899.

Mr. Nesrsta was examined for admittance to the bar before Judge H. Teichmueller, the committee being Judge C. E. Lane, J. F. Wolters and Judge L. B. Moore. The examination covered the usual grounds for admission and the committee recommended that a license be issued. Judge Teichmueller was not satisfied and wanted a more thorough examination made. He felt that the young man had not read law long enough to be qualified to join the bar and requested the privilege of putting a few questions of his own on a certain date. At this private examination Judge Teichmueller touched on many matters of which Mr. Nesrsta knew little or nothing, and finally, feeling his weakness on many points, he declared to the judge frankly that he was unable to reply adequately to the questions at issue. Feeling that the applicant possessed merit and a considerable judgment, the judge asked for another hearing, and at the end of a series of questionings finally asked: "What would you do if you were a district judge and a young man came before you as plaintiff in a suit for damages against a young lady who had broken her contract of engagement with him and refused marrying him?" Mr. Nesrsta answered that a young lady was responsible for her contract after attaining the age of eighteen, but notwithstanding this fact, he considered marriage so important that if she discovered before the ceremony that her fiance was unfit for her life companion and that they could not live in peace and harmony together, he would concede her the right to break off the engagement and refuse the young man a judgment. The judge said: "Young man, that is just what I did in a case at Victoria, and you watch the case to see what becomes of it in the higher court. You are entitled to your sheepskin."

Following his admission to the bar Mr. Nesrsta took charge of the branch office of the firm of Lane & Lane at Flatonia and continued practicing with that firm until the Lane Brothers dissolved partnership. Since then he has carried on an individual practice, in which he confines himself to civil business and to the execution of conveyances and office work. He is city attorney of Flatonia and in 1910 in that capacity prepared the bond issue for the public schools. For eight years he was justice of the peace of his precinct. He is a democrat, confining his work largely to local affairs and has been an occasional attendant at state conventions.

On February 7, 1899, Mr. Nesrsta married Miss Annie Ziegelbauer, daughter of Mat and Annie Ziegelbauer. Both her parents were natives of Texas and of Bohemian parentage. While Mr. Nesrsta has made an enviable record as a citizen and as a lawyer, it is with commendable pride that he regards the fine family of children in the household over which he presides. These eight young people are named Annie, Olga, Marie, Charles, George, Edith, Alice and Benjamin. It is a musical household. The talent is inherited from both sides, but particularly from the Nesrsta family, and it has already been mentioned that the late Antone Nesrsta had considerable skill as a performer on the flute and violin. The

Nesrsta family orchestra is one of no mean distinction and ability. Mr. Nesrsta and five of his children comprise this talented group of performers. He and one of his daughters play the violin, another daughter is the piano accompanist, still another takes the cornet part, while one of the boys handles the trombone and the youngest, a boy of seven, plays four instruments, usually designated as tympani, including the bass and snare drum, the bells and triangle. This little organization not only finds pleasure for its members and affords entertainment to others, but through its work is acquiring a degree of culture such as no other one agency could supply.

CHARLES C. GOLLMER. This well known business man of industry represents another of the early settler families of Austin County. The family name was introduced into this section of Texas about seventy years ago by Christian and Christoph Gollmer. Christoph Gollmer, who followed his brother to Texas after an interval of several years, was a cripple and never married. A sister of these men, Christina, came with her husband Christoph Straele to the same locality and spent her life on a farm about Schoenau, and died without children. The prominent characteristics of the Gollmer family during their residence in South Texas have been useful industry, largely as mechanics, neighborliness, serious and practical citizenship, and honorable relations with all men.

Christian Gollmer, the founder of the family in Texas, was born September 7, 1815, in the Town of Oberleningen, Wuertemberg, Germany. By the death of his father he was left an orphan as a lad and was put to learning the wagon maker's trade. He escaped the military service usually required of German citizens, and was married in his native land to Fredericka Fischer. She was born in Wuertemberg January 24, 1818, and died October 14, 1894. Her husband passed away July 7, 1889, and they lie in the Industry Cemetery.

Christian Gollmer sailed from a French port for America, with a party of colonists bound for Texas under the general auspices and leadership of Prince Solms, who was then undertaking to establish a German colony at New Braunfels. The boat was driven by a storm on a reef in the English channel, and the passengers were compelled to take another ship. The second boat, from an English harbor, was also lost on the coast of England. Again the Gollmers were rescued with their belongings, and the third boat on which they embarked finally landed them at Galveston, instead of Indianola, the port to which it was destined. The journey across to the arrival at Galveston took them eleven months. On arriving at Galveston Christian Gollmer decided to leave the colony, and settled in Texas independently of that movement. From Galveston he and his family proceeded by boat up the bayou to Houston, and thence in wagons drawn by ox teams to Austin County. On leaving Houston they had no definite destination in mind, but the teams brought them out and unloaded them at Industry, and Mr. Gollmers decided to stay. The journey from the coast to Industry required four weeks and was made with ox teams.

Arriving at Industry, Christian Gollmer entered upon his work as a wheelwright and wagon maker. He set up a shop just below the cemetery at Old Industry. When the new town took on form and showed signs of permanency, he erected a shop where William Boelscher now lives, and there finished his active career as a mechanic. He was at his bench until almost the last day of his life, and the only important interruption to his work at Industry came during the war. He was conscripted for service and made saddletrees for the Government in Houston from

1863 to the end of the war. As soon as possible Christian Gollmer took out citizenship papers, and became an earnest and serious American citizen. While he voted the democratic ticket, he never filled an office. He knew the English language well, and in religion was of Lutheran training, though he drifted away from that church when the local society was turned over to the Methodists.

The children of Christian Gollmer and wife were: Susan, who was born in England while the family were en route to America, married Christian Wolfer and died in Galveston October 24, 1913, leaving five children who reached mature life; Catherine, who married Henry Grusendorf, died in April, 1905, at Galveston without children; Charles C.; Henry, who perished in the Galveston flood in 1900, with his wife and five children, and the only child left of that family now lives at Welcome, Texas; Christian, who died in December, 1887, and one of his children now lives near Industry.

The little Village of Industry is the birthplace of Charles C. Gollmer, who first saw the light of day there April 8, 1851. The years when boys usually attend school were those that were vexed by the Civil war period, and few successful men of the present generation have done so well on so little schooling as Mr. Gollmer. From the age of fourteen he took his place in his father's shop, and is a practical graduate of that training school. After his marriage he began his independent career at Haw Creek, in Fayette County, where he conducted a shop for almost fourteen years. With the death of his father he returned to Industry, and resumed his trade as the successor of the elder Gollmer. He has been at Industry uninterruptedly for more than a quarter of a century, and his reputation in his line of business extends over a wide stretch of country about Industry. He builds vehicles as well as repairs them, and for fourteen years conducted the undertaking business of the village.

In politics Mr. Gollmer is a republican voter, the "gold standard" having been the influencing motive for his change from the democratic affiliation. A service of one term as school trustee, presiding at local elections for sixteen years, and an occasional attendance at county conventions, comprise his political activities. Mr. Gollmer is also a social member of the Schoenau Gesang Verein, a singing society, which has been an organization of no little benefit to the musical training of the young German people in its membership.

On March 9, 1875, Mr. Gollmer married Miss Caroline Siepert. She was born in Austin County, Texas, December 25, 1853, and represents some of the oldest stock in Texas. Her father, John Siepert, was born at Duesseldorf, Germany, and died in 1856. He married Wilhelmina Ernst, daughter of Frederick Ernst, who came to Texas as early as 1831, five years before the independence of the province, and was one of the first Germans to locate at the little community of Industry. One of the best known tracts of land in that section is the Ernst League, which was granted to this early German pioneer. Frederick Ernst married Louisa Weber, and their posterity are now numerously distributed about Industry and over South Texas. John Siepert and wife had five daughters and one son, namely: August, who died unmarried during the war while in business as a miller at Industry; Emily, who married Louis Baring, both now deceased; Johanna, who married Albert Baring, and lives at Eagle Lake, Texas, the mother of four daughters and three sons; Louisa, who married Henry Brill and died leaving a son August Brill of Austin; Mary, who married Max Schmidt, and spent her life near Industry, leaving three daughters; and Mrs. Gollmer, the youngest child. For her second husband Mrs. John Siepert married Fritz Schroeder, and information concerning this connection of the family will be found under the name Hermann Schroeder elsewhere in this publication.

Mr. and Mrs. Gollmer are the parents of three daughters. Miss Hedwig, the oldest, is a seamstress and dressmaker at Industry. Miss Hulda, who completed her education in the Sam Houston Normal School, has for the past five years been a teacher and is now assistant in the Industry schools. Miss Edna is employed in the Lindemann store at Industry.

DANIEL RINN. A resident of Texas since June, 1856, Daniel Rinn is numbered among the successful farmers, and has a most attractive homestead between Postoak and Industry in Austin County. His residence, at the top of one of the high points on the Industry and Frelsburg Road is almost hidden by the grove of trees that were planted and nurtured by the owner. The neatly kept yard, the fresh and attractive appearance of the surroundings, make this one of the fine homes to be long remembered by the traveler in this section of Texas.

Daniel Rinn was born in Hesse, Germany, January 7, 1848, and was a boy of eight years when brought to Texas. His father was Andrew Rinn, who died in the fatherland. His widow Elizabeth subsequently brought her children to Texas and located in Austin County, where she lived to the age of seventy years, passing away in 1880. Her children were: Philip, who died about forty years ago; Jacob, who died in 1915; John, of New Ulm; Mrs. William Mieth, of Austin County; and Daniel.

Daniel Rinn had some schooling at New Ulm after arriving in this state, but took up the serious and practical responsibilities of life with very little education so far as schools were concerned. He was not old enough for military service during the war, but four of his brothers, Ludwig, Philip, Jacob and John, were Confederate soldiers. Of these brothers only John is now living, a retired farmer at New Ulm.

When Mr. Rinn married and started life for himself, it was on his present farm. He started in a limited way, with a team, a few implements, and a meager stock of household goods. His house was a frame 14x24 feet, and in that humble abode some of his children were born. His next home was the commodious residence which he now occupies, which is a well built and substantial structure erected in 1885. All the other buildings and conveniences that complete his cluster of improvements were put here by his own hands. Mr. Rinn began with a tract of fifty-one acres in the Pettes league, but his success has been represented by additions to it from time to time until his ownership now extends over 127½ acres. He has been raising corn and cotton, the staple crops of the South, and his success is largely due to the fact that he has devoted himself with both diligence and intelligence to the management of his personal affairs. Mr. Rinn is a democratic voter, but has never held office and is a member of no order.

In September, 1870, Mr. Rinn married Miss Matilda Gross, daughter of Fritz Gross, who brought his family to America from Werdorf, Prussia. Mrs. Rinn was born in Texas in 1851, and died in September, 1891. She became the mother of twelve children, and those who grew up were as follows: William, a farmer near Postoak Point, married Louisa Heinsohn, and their children are Elsa, Isabella, Roxie and Edward; Bertha is the wife of Charles Peske, a farmer between New Ulm and Industry, and her children are Monroe, Otto, Adella and Matilda; Daniel, a farmer at Postoak Point, married Lena Heinsohn, a daughter of his brother's wife, and they have one child, Beona; Edmund, the youngest of the twelve children, lives at Schulenburg, unmarried. On July 11, 1893, Mr. Rinn married for his second wife Wilhelmina Schmidt, daughter of Frederick and Sophia (Havercamp) Schmidt. Her parents spent their lives in Hanover, Germany, where Mrs. Rinn was born in 1867, and she was the only one of the three daughters and one son to come to America.

Mr. and Mrs. Rinn are the parents of the following children: Rosa, Adaline, Lillie, Erna, Alma, Alvin, Walter, Robert and Eddie.

VINCENT M. WEST. One of the most interesting pioneers of the Southwest Texas frontier is now living retired at San Antonio. Vincent M. West was for thirty years or more closely identified with the ranch and range in the country southwest of San Antonio, but while a very successful stock man and well known among all the old timers in that industry, his career has a special value and interest because of his effective influence in behalf of the cause of Christian education, not only in the outlying districts in which he was a pioneer settler but also in later years in behalf of that wide movement for higher education and the extension of church influence over the entire state.

Born in Wayne County, Mississippi, July 1, 1849, he was the son of Hon. John and Eleanor (Odom) West. His father was a wealthy planter and slave owner in Wayne County and for many years represented the county in the State Legislature. Eleanor Odom belonged to a family several members of which were Methodist ministers and laymen and early settlers in East Texas. John West died in Mississippi and his widow afterwards moved to Texas and died at the home of her son Vincent in Uvalde. Four of Mr. West's older brothers were Confederate soldiers and two of them gave up their lives as sacrifice to the Southern cause.

This was not the only sacrifice which the family made to the Confederacy, since the fortune was ruined by the ravages of the war and by the blight which fell upon southern industry and prosperity in the dark days of the Reconstruction period. It is interesting to recall that Vincent M. West as a boy was a member of the Ku Klux.

He had had some educational advantages before the outbreak of the war and he finally managed to acquire a good academic education sufficient to enable him to become a teacher. Before leaving Mississippi he was principal of the Waynesboro Academy, a private school of distinction from which were graduated several young men who attained to prominence.

In frail health and fearing that he was threatened with tuberculosis, Vincent M. West came to Texas in 1879 and located on the then unsettled frontier in Zavalla County. Referring to his life in Southwest Texas Mr. West recently wrote a very interesting letter which was published in a church journal. This letter affords some striking comments that illustrate the religious and social conditions on the Southwestern frontier thirty-five years or more ago. A portion of that letter is real history and is accordingly given a place in this sketch:

"I settled in an unorganized county, twenty-eight miles from a postoffice and a hundred miles from a railroad. I pitched my tent on Nueces River in Zavalla County, in the midst of a gang of desperadoes, the notorious King Fisher, the Burtons, Steadams and others. These men and their families never attended church, their children sadly needed religious instruction. Desiring to be helpful to my neighbors, also to hold myself in line religiously, I procured suitable literature and started a Methodist Sunday school. King Fisher and the other squatters seemed glad to have a Sunday school in their community and treated the tenderfoot superintendent with much consideration. Anxious to manifest his appreciation of the school, Fisher sent me word to bring the school some Sunday to a beautiful grove on the river, he would kill a calf, we could catch fish, and thus have a Sunday school picnic. This invitation perplexed me. He was a dangerous character when opposed, reputed to have slain many men. I knew it was improper to desecrate the Sabbath with a picnic and I was afraid he would regard it as an offense to decline. Seeking an interview, I told him we appreciated his kind invitation, but that it was inappropriate to have a Sunday school picnic on the Sabbath; that if he would name any other day we would gladly attend. This was his reply: 'God! I didn't know; I thought Sunday was the right day. Any day will suit me. I couldn't tell when Sunday comes if it wasn't for that school.'

"With such environments I felt the necessity of church fellowship, and ascertaining when the circuit rider would preach at Uvalde, I appeared at the service and deposited my Church letter. William Monk was the preacher,. I took him to our camp. He preached for the settlers and reported the Sunday school to the Quarterly Conference. The next appointment was Quarterly Conference occasion, no one present save the presiding elder, preacher in charge and this new superintendent. I was elected to the District Conference to be held at Center Point, about a hundred miles from my camp. . . . I put Uvalde in nomination for the next conference, arguing that it was a frontier town, the people never had seen a conference, needed to hear some good preaching, etc. . . . That fall I was elected principal of the public school in Uvalde. It did not require much scholarship to be a principal in those days. Religious standards were very low in the town. Not being acquainted with Texas statutes, I did not know that it was unlawful to read the Bible and pray in the public schools, neither did my trustees, or if they did know they did not object, for I opened school with Scripture reading and prayer the whole two years I taught."

Thus Mr. West was a means of introducing the Christian religion into a wide region where it had never been anything but lightly esteemed if considered at all. He has often wondered himself what direction his career would have taken had he not held to and practiced the principles to which he had been trained as a boy. He served not only as a delegate to the annual conference at Center Point in 1879 but also in 1912, and from almost the beginning of his Texas residence he has attended regularly all the quarterly, district and annual conferences of the church.

After giving up his school at Uvalde Mr. West went into the cattle business and for eighteen years made his home at Uvalde in Uvalde County. For several years he was a member of the well known cattle firm of Piper & West, conducting a large cattle business in Uvalde and adjoining county. His family moved to San Antonio in 1898, though he spent most of the several succeeding years with his cattle interests and with headquarters at Uvalde. For several years now he has been retired from active business and keeps his home in San Antonio.

One of the greatest pleasures and comforts of his life has been his active church membership and he is recognized as one of the prominent laymen of the Methodist Episcopal Church South. Many times he has been a delegate to the General Conference of the church. He has supported actively all progressive and modern educational movements of the church, and has given church and other worthy movements the benefit of his intelligence, ability and means. It is noteworthy that Mr. West has long advocated the union of the southern and northern branches of the church in order to eliminate the necessary duplication of church officials, missionary work and also bring about the benefits of good feeling and harmony that would result from such a union. Mr. West enjoys a large acquaintance and friendship with bishops, editors, educators and other prominent leaders in both the southern and northern branches of the church. Mention should also be made of his enthusiastic support of the movement for building the great Southern Methodist University at Dallas, an institution which began its first year in the fall of 1915. He

is properly considered one of the founders of that institution and one of those who supplied enthusiasm as well as practical means to its beginning. He has always strongly advocated higher education and it is noteworthy that all his children received a college training.

When Mr. West first located in Southwest Texas he was married and had two children by his marriage to Miss Ida Parsons. She was born in Alabama, though her people were New Englanders, her father an architect and builder, having come south before the war. Mr. and Mrs. West are the parents of six children. Thomas [illegible] West is a graduate of the Southwestern University at Georgetown and is now a lawyer at San Antonio. E. J. West is graduated from the University of Tennessee and is now enjoying a large practice as a lawyer in New York [illegible]. Mrs. [illegible] Hopkins is a graduate of Oberlin College at Oberlin, Ohio. [illegible] West is a young cattleman at [illegible], Texas. Miss Anna West graduated from the San Antonio Female College and the Oberlin Conservatory of Music and is now a teacher of [illegible]. Miss Ida [illegible] West graduated from the San Antonio Female College and Ohio Wesleyan University at Delaware, and has also taken post-graduate work in [illegible] University at New York.

FRED House is generally spoken of in this section of the state as being a "regular [illegible]" and he lives well up to the description. He has been a resident of Yorktown since 1849, and is one of the most conspicuous [illegible] DeWitt County. When he came to this [illegible] was a settlement of four families, and he has been [illegible] its growth and its fortunes [illegible] then down to the present day.

Mr. House was [illegible] when he came to Texas from Germany. He came with his parents [illegible] from Bremen [illegible] and located first in Galveston, after spending several months in making the passage. After arrival at Galveston [illegible] as it was called, and [illegible] the death of his mother [illegible] his father's marriage to a woman who did not make [illegible] the [illegible] boy. He made his way to San [illegible] "[illegible] Campbell" as he said, on Campbell's [illegible] in San Antonio for a while, and was [illegible] to his annoyance. Soon thereafter [illegible] Frenchman, Colonel Bouqua of San Antonio, [illegible] him nothing but a grievance. He [illegible] and making himself generally useful [illegible] his way in the four years of his service [illegible] old when his time was out, and he came straight [illegible] has already been mentioned four families [illegible] the community then. They were the [illegible] and Peter Metz. John King lived near [illegible] belong in it, and Fred House hired out to King [illegible] chore-boy. During that time he chopped wood [illegible] and did whatever needed to be done to [illegible] King was the stage man and he in 1852 sold out [illegible] started on its run from San Antonio to Port [illegible] the first one pass. It carried mail and passengers [illegible] stage came through loaded, drawn by four [illegible]. When the stand was first established [illegible] occasional trips, one stage each way [illegible] trips were made and the line was [illegible]. Mr. House, out of his excellent memory [illegible] bits about the life in the country [illegible]

F. House

is properly considered one of the founders of that institution and one of those who supplied enthusiasm as well as practical means to its beginning. He has always strongly advocated higher education, and it is noteworthy that all his children received a college training.

When Mr. West first located in Southwest Texas he was married and had two children by his marriage to Miss Ida Parsons. She was born in Alabama, though her people were New Englanders, her father, an architect and builder, having come south before the war. Mr. and Mrs. West are the parents of six children: Thomas M. West is a graduate of the Southwestern University at Georgetown and is now a lawyer at San Antonio. E. J. West is graduated from the University of Tennessee, and is now enjoying a large practice as a lawyer in New York City. Mrs. Sue Hopkins is a graduate of Oberlin College at Oberlin, Ohio. Fred Waller West is a young cattleman at Brackett, Texas. Miss Anna West graduated from the San Antonio Female College and the Oberlin Conservatory of Music and is now a teacher of voice in Oklahoma. Miss Ida Bess West graduated from the San Antonio Female College and Ohio Wesleyan University at Delaware, and has also taken post-graduate work in Columbia University at New York.

Fred House is generally spoken of in this section of the state as being a "regular character," and he lives well up to the description. He has been a resident of Yorktown since 1849, and is one of the most conspicuous pioneers in Dewitt County. When he came to this city it was a settlement of four families, and he has been conversant with its growth and its fortunes from then down to the present day.

Mr. House was nine years old when he came to Texas from Germany. He came with his parents who sailed from Bremen in 1849 and landed first in Galveston, after spending several months in making the crossing. After arrival at Galveston they reshipped to Indianola, or Powderhorn, as it was called, and while there Fred ran away from home, because of the death of his mother which was followed by his father's marriage to a woman who did not make herself especially agreeable to the motherless boy. He made his way to San Antonio, riding behind "old man Campbell" as he said, on Campbell's mule. He stayed with Mr. Campbell in San Antonio for a while, and was finally restored to his father, much to his annoyance. Soon thereafter he was bound out to a Frenchman, Colonel Bouqua of San Antonio, for four years. This experience netted him nothing but a grievance. He worked incessantly, driving a cart and making himself generally useful, and many a sound beating came his way in the four years of his service. He was thirteen years old when his time was out, and he came straight to Yorktown. As has already been mentioned, four families comprised the population of the community then. They were the Streibers, the Hoppes, the Hardts and Peter Metz. John King lived near the settlement, but he did not belong in it, and Fred House hired out to King for a term of two years as chore-boy. During that time he chopped wood, drove team, washed dishes and did whatever needed to be done to keep King's place going. King was the stage man and he in 1852 sold out to Daniel Friar. The stage started on its run from San Antonio to Port Lavaca, and Mr. House saw the first one pass. It carried mail and passengers, and that particular stage came through loaded, drawn by four horses and driven by Tom Fuqua. When the stand was first established in Yorktown there were only occasional trips, one stage each way, and later, as business grew, daily trips were made and the line was maintained until after the Civil war. Mr. House, out of his excellent memory, is able to tell many interesting bits about the life in the country in the later '40s and early '50s. The country in those days were overrun with mustang horses, deer and other wild creatures native to the state, and their trail passed near Yorktown, and was very conspicuously marked, and indeed, is very distinctly apparent even at this late day. The horses were wiry and tough, and when they passed through the country they traveled in pairs. In 1858, following the scourge of grasshoppers, they practically disappeared, and in 1857-8 the black tongue almost completely wiped out the deer that had been so plentiful for so long.

School facilities, of course, were practically nil. The first school in the Yorktown section was located between the two Yorktowns, where Peter Metz lived, and it was erected in 1853. The house was originally designed for a residence, and had but two sides, both ends being open. The first school was presided over by Mr. Davis, an Iowa man, and the children came, in charge of their parents, for twenty-five and thirty miles around to attend the sessions, the parents meanwhile camping round about so as to be near the children. Times have changed, as the excellent school equipment in Yorktown today will amply testify.

The first church was erected in 1857-8. It was in a building designed for a Masonic hall, the upper story being used for the lodge room, and the lower served as a church and Sunday School room. The people gathered there weekly for worship, and Coletto Creek served them as a baptismal font. It is related that on one of the occasions when converts were to be immersed at the Pirtle Tank, when they reached there found to their surprise that a half-wit of the community had forestalled them by taking the opportunity to go in swimming, or as he said, baptizing himself. A Methodist itinerant preacher was sent there from time to time, and he finally died in the community. In those days preachers did not depend on voluntary contributions for their support, but maintained themselves at some occupation, such as sheep-raising. Just whether that method was conducive to a higher quality of spiritual guardianship or otherwise is not clear, but the fact remains that the system is practically obsolete in America today. Camp meetings were popular with the brethren, and the first one of the kind ever held in Dewitt County was at Shiloh. The people flocked in from over the entire county, and Fred House butchered for the gathering, according to his statement. That is, they fed them bread and beef from the commissary, and much spiritual agony was suffered—and enjoyed—during that time.

Mr. House was still but a boy when he hired out for two years to John King, the contract providing that he was to get for his services ten acres of land, five cows and calves and a horse. At the end of that time he got the live stock, but failed to get title to the land. He traded the land to Judge Kilgore, long his friend, for a coat and hat, and the cattle he traded to a soldier for a six shooter. With his horse, saddle and pistol, he was quite ready to cross the San Antonio River and "split the wild west" as he expressed it. There were less than half a dozen families on the river then, and he went to work for Wesley Yow on his cattle range, and stayed there for about a year. His next employer was Elijah Ray, and his occupation was the same, his activities being in the vicinity of where the Town of Kenedy is now. He stayed with Ray several months and in 1854 went to old Mexico with a Mr. Newman, taking cattle down and bringing horses back.

Mr. House was now twenty-two years old, and he thought he would do well to marry. When he had been married twenty-four hours to Sarah Powell, he awakened to the fact that while it was all very well and proper to have a wife, the possession of one rightfully called for certain other possessions as well. For instance, he had a wife, but no place to keep her. He was never slow to act, once an idea had struck home with him, and the morning after his wedding he saddled his pony and announced that he was going out to split rails for a house for them to live in. It was January, and the weather was wintry, but he applied himself with all diligence to the business in hand and soon had a shelter in readiness. His next move in preparing to go housekeeping was more simple. He traded some calves for a bed and some beef for some chairs and a small table. Then he "swapped" a horse to Judge Kilgore for enough other household furniture to make the little place habitable. And soon they were settled in comparative comfort. Indeed, for one of his station in that day, it was almost luxury. His first house was in upper Yorktown, near where Henry Menn's place is, and near to his butchershop, which was situated under the live oaks there. He hung up his meat in the open and sold it out by the "quarter" at 2½ and 3 cents, and many a man complained about the price even at that and resented the fact that the critters had bones. After he had been in the butcher business for three years and making some money, he abandoned the business and engaged in other business. During that time Mr. House killed many a fine steer that would have been a dead loss but for the hide and tallow, for beef went begging, but tallow was worth 10 cents and cured hides worth 15 to 18 cents a pound.

Out on Salt Creek Mr. House gathered up a little bunch of cattle and applied himself to ranching. He squatted on the land to gain possession, and used all the country round about him for pasture. He ran stock there and his herds grew until he had more stock than he could handle. At that time he furnished cattle for the Kansas drive and was agent, under power of attorney, for 700 brands, over territory extending from the mountains to the Rio Grande. He worked for outside men under power of attorney for ten years without once seeing his principals, getting his authority by mail. He kept all records himself, and when settlement day came he would simply say: "I branded so many thousand calves and sold so many beeves." That was sufficient testimony for his employers. His own brand was "House-F," which he still uses, and it is perhaps among the oldest brands in use in the state today. He located his land on Salt Creek and patented much of it, and before he divided with his children he had accumulated several thousand acres. He stayed on the ranch with his family until 1910, when he came to Yorktown and took up his residence here.

Mr. House began his military career by driving beeves for the Confederate government in 1861 to New Iberia, Louisiana, when he made the trip with 1,220 head. In 1862, some time in January, he enlisted for service as a member of Company K, Twenty-fourth Cavalry, with Captain Cupples, and Colonel Wilkes in command. The regiment dismounted before it reached Arkansas and went to Arkansas Post. In the fight there Mr. House was captured and taken to Camp Butler, Springfield, Illinois. The capture was made on January 11th, and he was exchanged the following April at City Point, West Virginia. The regiment was retained for a time at Richmond and then sent to join General Bragg's army in Tennessee. There Mr. House was in the battles of Chickamaugua, Missionary Ridge, Lookout Mountain, and at the latter engagement he pulled the first battery up the mountain for the army. He was later in the Atlanta campaign, where he was fighting every day down to the battles of Ringgold and Dalton. His youngest brother was killed in action at Resaca. At Dalton Mr. House got into difficulties with his lieutenant, expressed himself in plain American, left the command then and there and walked 500 miles back to Texas, rather than face the alternative of a court martial. He rode a mule from

Shreveport, Louisiana, and got into Yorktown in the latter part of 1864. This ended his military career, but the reconstruction and its logical effect brought on a kind of war among the settlers that lasted almost ten years.

Mr. House has been twice married. He married first in January, 1855, when Sarah Powell became his bride. She was a daughter of Samuel and Agnes Powell, Kentucky people, from the vicinity of Richmond. She bore him several children and died in January, 1895. Their children were John, of Runge, Texas; Jane, who married Henry Byran, and later married Will Potter, and is now deceased; Annie, who died as Mrs. John Grun; Laura, who married Ed Buschick and lives in Dewitt County; Martha, who married Albert Potter and lives on the House Ranch at Davey; Chris, who is a farmer there; Elizabeth, who married Henry Burt, of Davey; Mrs. Mary Dromgoole of Davey; Henry, of Hondo, Texas; Ola, who first married Doctor Hall and is now the wife of Charles Gardner of Davey.

On December 23, 1899, Mr. House married a second time, Mrs. Ada Coleman, a daughter of A. J. Tully, becoming his wife. Her father came to Texas from Mississippi after the close of the war. Of this second marriage there is one son—William Frederick. By her first marriage Mrs. House has three children: Bert Coleman of Davey; Oscar of Pecos County, and Ruby, the wife of W. J. Lyons of Runge, Texas.

Mr. House is a democrat, and he has participated less in actual politics than in any other phase of civil life. He is a member of the Modern Woodmen, and being "liberal" in his theological convictions, claims friendly relations with all churches. Now in his eighty-third year, Mr. House enjoys a strength and vigor that a man of sixty-five might well be proud of. He has no hospital record, has never lost a tooth since his milk teeth disappeared, and in every way is in a splendid state of preservation.

James Hector Morgan. The superintendent of schools of Eagle Lake, James Hector Morgan, has held his present position for five years, but has been identified with educational work for a period of fifteen years. Since coming to Eagle Lake, Mr. Morgan has set a new standard for educational development and progress, and under his able direction the school system here has progressed so rapidly that it is serving as a model for many older communities of the state.

Prof. James Hector Morgan was born near Seguin, Guadaloupe County, Texas, December 19, 1879, and is a son of Haines L. Morgan, who was born at Seguin, spent many years there as a merchant and subsequently went to Kingsville, Texas, where he also carried on mercantile pursuits. He was a son of Dr. John B. Morgan, who came from Marion County, Virginia, and settled in Texas about the year 1836, making his home at Seguin. Doctor Morgan married a Miss Hector, and they had but one child. Haines L. Morgan was the father of the following children: Dr. John B., of Robstown, Texas; James Hector, of this notice; Robert T., a banker of Eagle Pass, Texas; Solomon Guy, a business man of Corpus Christi; and Haines L., Jr., chief clerk of the commissary department of the Frisco Railway at Kingsville.

The boyhood of James H. Morgan was passed at Seguin, where he was graduated from the high school at the age of sixteen years, and for a time thereafter he was engaged as a clerk in his father's store. Entering the state university in 1897, he spent two years in the academic department, and on leaving that institution went with a cotton classifier, intending to become a cotton broker. He became proficient in that work and was put in charge of the cotton office at Seguin, but after eighteen months thus spent, and at a time when he was not especially busy with this work, he was asked to take the class of Texas history in the summer normal held there. Accepting this offer, Mr. Morgan entered upon the work in which he was to make his real success. He was particularly qualified for the phase of normal work in which he engaged, for he had made a special study of Texas history, and his work in this department was therefore not only efficient but congenial as well. Soon after, Mr. Morgan began to teach a country school near his home town, the school being known as the Dale. When he finished his work there, he took the Pettis school, in the capacity of principal, and was then chosen principal at Mendoza, Caldwell County. Later he became principal of the grammar school at Seguin, where he remained two years, and was then elected superintendent of schools at Sabinal for one year and at Falfurrias for four years, coming to Eagle Lake from the latter place.

Professor Morgan served on the state summer normal examination board in 1903, and taught two normal schools at Seguin and one year in the summer normal at Rockport. He has served as secretary and president of the agricultural section of the Texas State Teachers Association, and as vice president of the South Texas Teachers Association, and is now treasurer of the latter body. His connection with the work of the State Teachers Association placed him on the legislative committee of the association, the purpose of which was to achieve the foundation of the proposed senatorial agricultural high school, and the sentiment so created will eventually bring into existence this needed institution. Mr. Morgan has been on the sectional and general programs of the association, and on one occasion presented particularly the conditions prevailing in the border counties with reference to public education, and suggested a remedy whereby funds intended for school work there could reach its proper channel and be expended as intended, without being diverted elsewhere. Many Mexican teachers along the border were found unable to speak English, whereby they were drawing salaries unlawfully, some of them doing absolutely no work. Graft was something rather common in some of the Mexican counties, and vouchers for salaries were padded, others were discounted for "campaign purposes" and one fellow admitted that he had had two pupils in his school, having paid them 50 cents a month to attend, but that now they had left the locality and he was unable to induce others to come to his school!

At Falfurrias, Professor Morgan first achieved the organization of an independent district, and by throwing together schools formed the first consolidated district and introduced the practice of hauling pupils to school from all parts of the district. He inspired a school spirit which resulted in the erection of a $25,000 building, equipped with auditorium and paraphernalia for school work, and the success of his labors there led to his invitation by the board of Eagle Lake to visit this locality and look over the situation here. Professor Morgan came over, found a new building just completed, barren of furnishings and equipment and with no school spirit at all. The utmost chaos prevailed in the town and there was all but war on between patrons, superintendent and teachers. With the agreement of the board to turn over the entire management of the school to him, he decided to accept the superintendency and started in on his work with three industrial departments added to the course, i. e., agriculture, domestic science and manual training. The building basement, which had formerly sheltered the "town cow," was converted into classrooms, and a force of eleven teachers is now preparing the graduates for high work in the state institutions. The city district organization has been abolished and an independent district created, and bonds have been voted almost unanimously for such aid as the schools need for doing the most efficient and effective work. He added the eleventh grade to the high school and under the new course, three classes, including twenty pupils, have graduated from the high school. Six of these are teaching, two are students in Rice Institute, one in the State University, three in the normal schools and several in the Agricultural and Mechanical College. A recent article in the Galveston News, speaking of Eagle Lake's schools, said in part: "Eagle Lake is making a fine record in the upbuilding of her public schools. She has a splendid brick building. The rooms are large, airy, well furnished and comfortable. There are 360 pupils enrolled in this excellent school. While the departments of domestic science and art and agriculture and manual training are well equipped and doing fine work, every effort is being made to maintain a uniform excellence throughout all departments of school work. The advancement during the past few years has been marked. The school is affiliated with the State University. Five of its former students attended the Rice Institute last year and two of this year's graduates have just entered that institution. The school spirit is said to be excellent, the people believing that nothing in the way of education is too good for the Eagle Lake boys and girls. The district has a property valuation of more than $2,000,000, on which was voted and levied a 50c maintenance tax with but seven opposing votes. The city levies 15c to carry an outstanding issue of bonds that has been reduced to $10,000. A unique feature is the $500 lyceum course that is given free to the children. Sufficient seats are available in the spacious auditorium for the children and the citizens who purchase the season's tickets, making it possible for every child to come in contact with the most elevating and instructive forms of entertainment. The athletic spirit is strong. The school is a member of the University Interscholastic League and expects to have a strong football team in the field this fall. Baseball has always been quite strong. The girls have been organized into basketball and tennis clubs. A gymnasium with shower baths has been provided and an instructor in German and Swedish physical education has been secured. The boy scouts are now erecting the aerial of their wireless plant on the school building. The high school attendance has increased 30 per cent during the past year, nearly all the older pupils remaining in school. The district is fortunate in having a fine board of trustees."

Professor Morgan is interested in politics merely at the time of elections, although he never fails to do his full part in securing good legislation for his schools. Fraternally, he is connected with the local lodges of the Masons, in which he has the master's degree, the Independent Order of Odd Fellows and the Knights of Pythias. With his family, he is connected with the Methodist Church.

On June 19, 1905, at Seguin, Texas, Professor Morgan was married to Miss Blanche Woods, a daughter of James W. and Emma (Dunn) Woods. Mr. Wood's father was Don A. T. Woods, and Mrs. Woods' father was William Dunn, an old settler and for years sheriff of the county and prominent in Texas as an Odd Fellow. Mrs. Morgan finished her school work in the Seguin High School and became a teacher, and although she was out of the schoolroom for two or three years succeeding her marriage, now supervises the intermediate department of the Eagle Lake schools.

William W. Johnston. At this juncture in a volume devoted to the careers of representative citizens of Texas, it is a pleasure to insert a brief history of William Warren Johnston, who has ever been on the alert to forward all measures and enterprises projected for the general welfare and who has served his community in various official positions of trust and responsibility. He was city marshal of Gonzales for two years, was sheriff of Gonzales County for twelve years and is now devoting the major portion of his time and attention to ranching and stock-raising, his fine estate being located on the Guadalupe River, some miles distant from Gonzales.

William Warren Johnston was born near Wharton, in Wharton County, Texas, March 9, 1869, and he is a son of James C. and Kate (Warren) Johnston, both of whom were born and reared in North Carolina, the former having been born in 1832. The father was a man of splendid education and he was a Confederate soldier in the Civil war. He was of Scotch descent and was a son of the Rev. Samuel I. Johnston, an Episcopal minister, who was likewise a slave owner and a planter in North Carolina, in the vicinity of Edenton. Mrs. Johnston was a daughter of Dr. William Warren, a descendant of an old and prominent Virginian family. She and her husband passed the closing years of their lives on a farm near Hochheim, Gonzales County, and there both are buried. He died in 1889 and she passed away in 1900. Following are brief data concerning their children: Katie is the wife of Walter FitzGerald, of Haskell County, Texas; Fannie married Lee FitzGerald and they are both deceased; Jane is the wife of S. S. Cobb, of Gonzales; Annie is the wife of John FitzGerald, of Yoakum County, Texas; Samuel I. is a ranchman in Lubbock County, Texas; and William W. is the immediate subject of this sketch.

In the Hochheim community and in Gonzales William Warren Johnston grew to maturity and was educated. At the age of fourteen years he became identified with the range as an employe of Robert FitzGerald, with whom he traveled the trail to Dodge City, Kansas, their route being the western trail which crosses Red River at Doan's store and proceeds thence northward. They grazed the stock for five months en route. Mr. Johnston returned home in the fall and when he left again it was for Haskell County, where he remained as a range man, with Walter FitzGerald and William Ward, for the ensuing three years. In 1887 he returned to Gonzales and in the following spring he went to Alpine and helped drive a herd of cattle for L. M. Kokernot, of Gonzales, to Hunnewell, Kansas. Returning to Gonzales he spent the following two years as a rancher and stockman on his own account. He then engaged in the restaurant business in Gonzales and while devoting his time to that line of enterprise was elected city marshal; he had to maintain law and order in the face of gambling and drinking Mexicans and some bad whites. In 1902 he was elected sheriff of the county, succeeding Sheriff Fly in that capacity. He was re-elected in 1904, 1906, 1908, 1910 and 1912, running three straight races against his predecessor: in the last three elections he was without an opponent. He was unusually efficient as a sheriff, his work as a cattle ranger having made him well acquainted with the country. He traced fugitives from the law in all directions, bringing one back from San Bernardino, California, one from Lawton, Oklahoma, and a few from old Mexico and elsewhere. While he rounded up a number of murderers and other blackguards, of whom some were sentenced to the penitentiary for life, he was not called upon to use the "rope." His last term of office expired in December, 1914, and he has since refused to run for office of any kind. He is a member of the Sheriffs Association of the state. During the last couple years he has settled down as a stockman and rancher, his place being located on the Guadalupe River. He has entered into the spirit of development which pervades Gonzales and here has erected a number of residences and improved property which he owns. In politics he is a stalwart democrat and in a fraternal way he is affiliated with the Independent Order of

Odd Fellows, the Modern Woodmen of America and the Woodmen of the World. He and his wife are connected, as members, with the Church of God.

In 1889 was celebrated the marriage of Mr. Johnston to Miss Nannie Lipps, a daughter of William E. Lipps, a German farmer in Gonzales County. Following are the brothers and sisters of Mrs. Johnston; Charles; John; Aryannie, wife of John W. Crawford, of Gonzales; Abbie, wife of A. J. Martin, of Brownwood, Texas; Libbie, wife of B. Brewer, of Gonzales; Fred; Mrs. Johnston; Mrs. Nettie Patterson, of Bay City, Texas; and Otis. Mr. and Mrs. Johnston have four children, as follows: Katie married Arthur Ward, of Gonzales, and they have a son William Arthur; Ernest L., engaged in the restaurant business in Gonzales, married Cholisse Barlieman; and Robert Scott and William Warren, Jr., are both at the parental home. Mr. Johnston is possessed of a congenial disposition and is very popular amongst his fellow citizens, who honor him for his native ability and straightforward methods.

Adolph Buenger. The second generation of the Buenger family to maintain the farming and stockraising prestige of Austin County, and to contribute also to the large wealth and promise of the locality of Industry, is ably represented by Adolph Buenger, the owner of ninety acres of good land located in the Pettes and Dotries leagues. Mr. Buenger was born August 14, 1864, on the old Buenger homestead place, now the property of his brother, William A. Buenger, a sketch of whose career will be found elsewhere in this work.

Andrew Buenger, the father of Adolph Buenger, was born April 15, 1824, in Prussia, received a good education and learned the trades of millwright and wagonmaker, and in 1846 came to the United States with the Bock family, some of whose descendants are still residing in the vicinity of Weimar, Texas. When he located in this state, Andrew Buenger secured work as a mechanic, building saw and gristmills and cotton gins, and erected the first sawmill built in this part of the country, an ox-tread mill for the noted pioneer, the late Charles Fordtran. He also constructed numerous cotton gins and mills for the old-time plantation owners of this locality, his fine workmanship and fidelity to agreements attracting business to him from distant points. Mr. Buenger finally settled down to operations as an agriculturist, when his sons came to an age to be of service to him, and long before the outbreak of the conflict between the South and the North he had purchased the farm in the Pettes League which is now occupied by his son, William A. The house he built here was of split and hewn logs and was weatherboarded and ceiled. Here his children were born, and here the greatest happiness of Mr. Buenger's career was attained. He passed his active life from that time forward as a modest farmer and raiser of cattle, and had no office or public responsibilities save those in his religious relations with the Lutheran and later the Methodist Church. During the period of the Civil war, Mr. Buenger was a prison guard for the Confederacy for a time, when he was not assigned to duty as a wagonmaker and repairer for that government. In political affairs he always voted the democratic ticket. Mr. Buenger was widely noted for his great industry and energy, as well as for his habits of thrift and economy, the value of which he communicated to his sons. His children were given good educational advantages in the public schools of the community, and were brought up to lives of honesty and integrity, so that when entering upon their individual careers they were ready to capably fill the positions in life to which they were called by choice or circumstance.

Andrew Buenger was united in marriage with Miss Annie Rosky, who was born April 12, 1833, a daughter of a German emigrant and early farmer of Texas, and she died February 3, 1899, Mr. Buenger passing away October 31, 1904. They were the parents of the following children: William C., before mentioned; Herman, who is a resident of Halsted, Texas; Charles, who died at Yoakum, leaving a family; Miss Emily, a resident of Industry; Adolph, of this review; Emil, a resident of Grayson County, Texas; Ida, who is the wife of Rudolph Franke, of Industry; and Lena, who is the wife of Eddie Rinn, a resident of Yoakum.

The boyhood and youth of Adolph Buenger were passed at the place of his birth, in which vicinity he was given his education in the public schools. He was reared as a farmer, and remained with his parents until the time of his marriage, November 10, 1889, at which time he moved to his first permanent home, located near Skull Creek, at Shelby. He was there engaged in farming on the property of his father-in-law, Charles Schulze, for four years, following which he came to his present home in the Pettes and Dotries leagues, this being the old Max Meisner farm, where Mr. Buenger has ninety acres. This property was once the scene of activity as a cotton gin point, the plant (the shell of which is still standing) being erected by C. C. Koch. It went next into the hands of Robert Vogt, who was succeeded as owner by Mr. Buenger, who conducted it with a fair measure of success for a period of twenty years, then disposing of the machinery, when the plant became silent. It is one of the evidences of the old-time industry and is now a silent witness of the things of the past.

As a farmer, Mr. Buenger is a corn and cotton grower, and aside from this is interested with his son, Jesse, in the well-drilling business. This latter enterprise has been in operation since 1911, and seventy-three wells located about over this locality of their manufacture are supplying the agriculturists with water. Their experience in drilling developed, in one instance, strong signs of oil, and after the water had been used for some time from this well oil showed so strongly as to compel its abandonment. In political matters Mr. Buenger is a democrat, but not a politician. His fraternal connection is with the Woodmen of the World.

Mr. Buenger married Miss Johanna Schulze, the only daughter and youngest child of Charles and Louisa (Weige) Schulze, and to this union there have been born two children: Jesse and Wanita. Charles Schulze was born in Anhalt-Dessau, Prussia, April 14, 1841, and secured the education common to his station in life. His father was a cabinetmaker, David Schulze, who died in Germany, and his mother bore the maiden name of Johanna Kötteritzsh, and they had two children: Charles; and Louisa, who died as Mrs. Carl Lange. Mrs. Schulze was married a second time to August Kettner, who brought the family to the United States in 1872, was a cabinetmaker by trade, and died in Texas in 1909, leaving two children: Augusta, who is now Mrs. Max Gross, of Yorktown, Texas; and Johanna, who is Mrs. Max Meitzen, of Hallettsville, Texas. In his native country Charles Schulze learned the cabinetmaking trade, and this he followed as well as farming after coming to Texas in 1866. He sailed from Bremen on the Iris, a sailing vessel, and made port at Galveston, from whence he made his way by rail to Alleyton, and then by ox-team to New Ulm and two years later to Industry. He married Miss Louisa Weige, who was born May 1, 1841, at Herford, Province of Westphalia, Germany, daughter of Antone Weige. They became the parents of three children: Charles, Otto and Johanna. After coming to America Mr. Schulze continued to spend his life as a mechanic and farmer, and through his good citizenship and sterling characteristics won and held the esteem of those among whom he made his home.

Alberto M. Cassini Garcia. The gracious art of musical thought and interpretation has a distinguished and talented exponent in the person of the popular violin virtuoso and teacher whose name initiates this paragraph and who maintains his residence and professional headquarters in his native City of San Antonio, where he was born May 8, 1876, a scion of one of the patrician old Spanish families of Texas, his maternal lineage tracing through many generations of distinguished Italian ancestry, so that by very birthright he has the temperament that makes for great musical appreciation and genius.

A son of J. E. and Isabel (Cassini) Garcia, both now deceased, Mr. Garcia is a representative of families whose names have been long and prominently identified with the history of the fair City of San Antonio. His paternal grandfather, a Spaniard of distinctive ability and culture, settled in San Antonio in 1820, Texas having been at that time still a part of Mexico. J. E. Garcia was a man of fine intellectual and musical attainments, his musical studies having been in part pursued in the City of Boston, and though he became a talented violinist he never adopted music as a profession. He was born in San Antonio, his literary education included a course of study in Williams College, in Massachusetts, and he continued to maintain his home in his native city until the time of his death.

In the agnatic line the subject of this review is a kinsman of the well known Raymond Martin family, of Laredo, Texas, one of the wealthiest in the state, Raymond Martin having been a Frenchman and his wife having been a member of the Garcia family. The mother of Mr. Garcia was a member of a distinguished Italian family, one of her uncles having been a cardinal of the Catholic Church and other members of the family having been prominent and influential in divers fields of activity. Her father was the only one of the family to come to America and he settled in San Antonio, where his daughter Isabel, Mrs. Garcia, passed her entire life, a woman of education and gracious personality and one who was a popular leader in the best social life of her native city.

Alberto M. Cassini Garcia acquired his early education in San Antonio, where he attended the high school and later became a student in St. Mary's College, in which he was graduated. He completed also a course in a local commercial college. When but fifteen years of age, and before he had completed his educational discipline, Mr. Garcia assumed a position in the famous music house of Thomas Goggan & Brothers, of San Antonio, the oldest concern of its kind in Texas, and he continued in the service of this firm until he was thirty-five years of age, his position during the major portion of this period having been that of cashier and accountant. During virtually all these years Mr. Garcia devoted close attention to the study of the violin, his ambition being to become a successful interpretive artist of the king of solo instruments and to make music his life profession. His study and preparation were marked by the most thorough care and close application, and he held as satisfactory to himself nothing less than the highest mark of proficiency at each successive stage of advancement. Upon severing his association with the music house mentioned he went to New York City, where he became a pupil of the world renowned violin virtuoso, Ovide Musin, whose studio in the national metropolis is at 51 West Seventy-sixth Street, and who, until the recent cataclysm of war that has ravaged his native land, made to Belgium annual visitations for the purpose of there giving instructions to advanced violin students. With his honored preceptor Mr. Garcia was thus enabled to pass one season in the Belgian Royal Conservatory, in the now devastated city of Liege. He was asso-

A. M. C. GARCIA

ciated with Musin as a pupil and assistant instructor from 1911 to 1913, and within this period he was also associated with and studied the methods of other great violin masters, in Belgium and in the City of Paris, the Musin studio in New York being recognized as the greatest school of violin playing in the United States. None but those who manifest sufficient talent to give assurance of their becoming true artists are accepted as students, and this great master will insist on nothing short of perfection in the study and work of his pupils, whom he turns out of his institution as finished artists. Students are perfected in the ancient and modern classics of music and in complete repertoires of the world's greatest composers, the school being exclusively one for virtuosi. It is greatly to the distinction of Mr. Garcia that he not only qualified as a pupil of Musin but also that he was accepted and retained as a member of the faculty of the Musin studio and school.

In the spring of 1915 Mr. Garcia returned to San Antonio, where he has entered upon his professional career as a teacher of the violin and as an interpreter of the instrument on the concert and recital stage. His studio and home address is 118 Yndo Street, and he retains a professional address at South Texas Music Company on Avenue C, San Antonio. Texas is favored in having this native son as one of her distinguished representatives of the finest type of musical art, and it is pleasing to be able to make the following quotation from an appreciation commendation written and signed by the great violin maestro, Ovide Musin:

"Mr. Alberto M. C. Garcia has pursued his musical studies with me for the past two years, which time he has devoted most assiduously to furthering himself in his chosen profession, in which he is ambitious to attain the highest goal. As regards Mr. Garcia's violin playing, I take pleasure in saying that the progress he has made has been remarkable. He has a nice position, beautiful tone, precision of technic and elegance of style. As a performer he will give satisfaction to the most critical audience, and to the student desirous of learning the best methods Mr. Garcia will prove to be an instructor of sterling value and an acquisition to any community."

John Kubena. As a lad of sixteen years Mr. Kubena accompanied his parents on their immigration to America from the Province of Moravia, Austria, and the family home was established in Texas, where he was reared to manhood and where he has so availed himself of opportunities and so utilized his powers as to achieve large and worthy success and become a prominent and influential citizen of Lavaca County, his fine homestead place being situated a short distance east of the Town of Moulton. He is one of the extensive landholders and representative agriculturists and stock-growers of this section of the state, and his civic loyalty, as well as his personal popularity, is indicated by the fact that he has served continuously and efficiently as a member of the board of county commissioners of Lavaca County since 1906.

Mr. Kubena was born at Stromberg, near the City of Neutittschein, in the Province of Moravia, Austria, and the date of his nativity was December 28, 1857. He is a son of John and Susan (Janek) Kubena, the parents of both of whom passed their entire lives in Moravia, where the respective families have been established for many generations.

In his native land John Kubena was engaged in the manufacturing of and dealing in lime, besides having other business interests. In 1873, at Bremen, Germany, he embarked with his family on the steamship "Koeln," which afforded the transportation to the United States. They landed in the City of New Orleans, and thence came across the Gulf of

Mexico to Galveston, Texas, from which point the journey was continued overland, with four yoke of oxen, to Frelsburg, Colorado County, where the family remained until the autumn of the following year when they came to Lavaca County and established a home in the vicinity of the old Town of Moulton and Young's Store, both of which settlements have since been obliterated. In 1878 John Kubena here purchased a tract of wild land, from Henry Fordtran, and the original family domicile on this pioneer prairie homestead was a primitive box house of the type common to the locality and period. Mr. Kubena reclaimed his land to cultivation and became a successful agriculturist, his attention being given principally to the raising of corn and cotton. On his old homestead he continued to reside until his death, on the 24th of June, 1893, at which time he was seventy-one years of age. This sterling citizen acquired measurable familiarity with the English language and was able to utilize the same with discrimination in connection with his business affairs. After becoming a naturalized citizen he espoused the cause of the democratic party, with which he continued to be aligned during the remainder of his long and useful life. In a sense he was a political refugee from his native land, where his boldly expressed opinions had brought to him no little trouble, and he was thus doubly appreciative of the individual freedom and independence which became his after establishing his residence in the United States. Both he and his wife were communicants of the Catholic Church, in the faith of which they earnestly reared their children. Mrs. Kubena survived her husband by nearly fifteen years and was summoned to the life eternal in December, 1907, at a venerable age. Brief record concerning their children is here given: Annie is the wife of Emil Gieptner, of Lavaca County; John, of this review, was the next in order of birth; Mrs. Susie Leidolf resides at Hallettsville, judicial center of Lavaca County; Mary is the wife of Joseph Klekar, of Novohrad, this county; Matthew resides at Flatonia, Fayette County; Jeffrey died at Flatonia and is survived by three children; and Albert is a resident of the State of New Mexico.

John Kubena acquired his early education in the schools of his native land and, as before stated, was sixteen years of age at the time of the family immigration to America. After the home was established in Lavaca County he supplemented his education by attending a night school near the old Village of Moulton, where he devoted himself principally to the study of the English language. He assisted his father in the reclamation and other work of the home farm and as a young man instituted his independent career as a farmer on rented land. Not until seven years after his marriage did he feel that his financial circumstances justified him in making his first purchase of land, and it is greatly to his credit that he has so brought to bear his energies and business ability as to make his way forward to his present status of substantial prosperity, his success being in all senses the result of his own efforts, and his career having been marked by that sturdy integrity and uprightness that always beget popular confidence and good will. His first land purchase was a tract of 160 acres, 1½ miles east of the present Village of Moulton, and he made various improvements on this place, which he still owns and on which some of his children now reside. Mr. Kubena's next purchase was of a tract of 200 acres near Flatonia, Fayette County, in the Cottle League, and this land is farmed by reliable tenants, the property still remaining in his possession. About the same time Mr. Kubena purchased land adjoining his home place, the area of which was thus increased to 340 acres. He next purchased the old homestead of Samuel Moore, acquiring this property from the widow of Mr. Moore. It comprised 218 acres, of which he has since disposed of ninety acres. His homestead farm comprises 130 acres, and the same has the very best of modern improvements, making it one of the model rural estates of this part of Texas. On a rise of land just east of Moulton Mr. Kubena erected his substantial residence, which is conspicuous for its size and which is recognized as one of the finest farm dwellings in Lavaca County. On the homestead is also a good tenant house, and on his large landed estate Mr. Kubena has a total of seven tenant families. He is one of the progressive and specially successful agriculturists and stock-growers of this part of the state and has not hedged himself in with mere personal advancement but has shown himself loyal and public-spirited as a citizen. In addition to the lands previously mentioned he owns a tract of 145 acres five miles west of Moulton, in Gonzales County, and six lots in the City of Yoakum, Dewitt County.

At Hallettsville, in 1889, Mr. Kubena took out his final naturalization papers and became a full-fledged citizen of the United States. His first presidential vote was cast for Grover Cleveland, after he had received his first papers of citizenship, in 1884, and he has ever since given unqualified allegiance to the democratic party, whose every presidential candidate he has voted for since that time. In 1906, as representative of precincts Nos. 2 and 6, he was elected a member of the board of county commissioners, as successor of Emil Gieptner, and each successive election, at intervals of two years, has shown his re-election to this office, his continuous retention of which affords the best voucher for his efficient service and the verdict passed upon the same by the qualified voters of Lavaca County. His associates on the board of commissioners in 1915 are Louis Waggoner, August Eilers, and Calvin Deborah. In a fraternal way he is affiliated with the Hermann Sohns, and the religious faith of himself and his family is that of the Catholic Church.

At Praha, Fayette County, on the 20th of November, 1882, was solemnized the marriage of Mr. Kubena to Miss Mary Caka, a daughter of Joseph and Mary (Riha) Caka, who came from Bohemia, Germany, and settled near Flatonia, Fayette County, Texas, in 1881, Mr. Caka become one of the prosperous farmers of that county. Of the children Mrs. Kubena is the eldest; Martin is engaged in farming in Austin County; Katherine is the wife of Antone Jemelka, of Shiner, Lavaca County; Albert is a farmer near Shiner; Lizzie is the wife of Frank Janecek, of that place; and Sophie is the wife of James Lahodny, likewise a resident of Shiner.

Mr. and Mrs. Kubena have eight children, concerning whom the following data are consistently entered in conclusion of this sketch: Hedwig is the wife of Ignatz Jalufka, of Moulton, and they have two children, Emil and Annie. Frank, who is a prosperous farmer in Lavaca County, married Miss Agnes Kubenka, and their one child is Millie. Mary is the wife of Adolph Hoffner, of Charlottenburg, and their children are Mary and Edwin. John is a representative farmer near Moulton, the maiden name of his wife having been Katie Tylich and their one child being a son, Erwin. Susie is the wife of Henry Bucek, of Hackberry, Lavaca County; Annie is the wife of Frank Jurek, of Flatonia; and Joseph and Jeffrey remain at the parental home.

HON. JOHN R. KUBENA. A resident of Fayette County since 1882, Hon. John R. Kubena has been engaged in general merchandising at Fayetteville since 1899, and here has built up a reputation as a business man, public servant and dependable citizen that makes him one of the leading men of his community. His business establishment has been developed from modest beginnings to one of large proportions, and would do credit to a much larger community than Fayetteville; his signal services in various public capacities have been of a nature to contribute materially to the general advancement of the county, while as a public-spirited citizen he has promoted and supported various movements for the welfare of the county and its people.

John R. Kubena came to Texas in 1882 as a lad of thirteen years, having accompanied his parents from Moravia, Bohemia, where he was born June 10, 1868, at the little Town of Lichnov, where his ancestors had lived for several generations and where they had passed their lives in agricultural pursuits. Mr. Kubena is a son of John Kubena, who died at Fayetteville, in 1898, at the age of sixty years. The father's career in America was passed as a farmer, he settling among his Bohemian countrymen here and becoming a real friend of the institutions of the United States. He became naturalized, and in politics identified himself with the democratic party. He was a lifelong member of the Catholic Church, in which faith the members of his family were reared. Mr. Kubena married Miss Veri Kahanek, who still survives and makes her home on the farm on which the family settled upon first coming to Fayette County. The following children were born to Mr. and Mrs. Kubena: Jane, who became the wife of E. J. Knesek, of Fayetteville; John R., of this notice; Miss Rosalia and Miss Rosa, both of Fayetteville; Agnes, who is the wife of Joseph Zapalac, of Fayetteville; Joseph, a resident of Crosby, Texas; Rudolph, who is in the employ of his brother John R.; and Anton, who is residing with his mother and operating the old homestead farm.

John Kubena came to America as the only one to emigrate of the children of his father, John Kubena, who died at the age of thirty-six years. John Kubena's only brother died in Moravia, and his sisters both married and live there. His first wife was Veri Miculka, who bore him a daughter, Veri, who is now the widow of Adolph Polansky, and resides at Caldwell, Texas. The Kubena family sailed from Bremen, Germany, for the United States on the ship Elbe, which on a later trip met disaster in a collision at sea, but on this voyage reached New York without undue incident, making port March 16, 1882. The family then came directly to Texas, where the father purchased property in the near vicinity of Fayetteville, and in this locality the children entered the public schools and secured their first lessons in English.

John R. Kubena gained his education from the public school during two winter terms, and farmed with his parents until reaching the age of twenty-two years, at which time he left home and went to LaGrange to enter upon his mercantile experience. He entered the employ of C. J. VonRosenburg, as a clerk, and remained until the spring of 1896, when he was married and moved back to Fayetteville. Here Mr. Kubena worked for his brother-in-law, Mr. Knesek, for one year, and in 1897 went to Moulton and became a clerk for Ed Boehn, a merchant, with whom he remained until January 31, 1899. On March 1st following, Mr. Kubena formed a partnership at Fayetteville with Mr. Knesek, as Kubena & Knesek, and this association continued until the concern was mutually dissolved, January 1, 1905, Mr. Knesek retiring and Mr. Kubena continuing in business. His stock comprises general merchandise, implements and vehicles and occupies a frontage of three stores. Mr. Kubena owns the property and was the erector of two of the buildings which accommodate his stock. In addition to his extensive mercantile interests, he has been identified with other enterprises, having been one of the promoters of the New Ulm State Bank, of which he served in the capacity of vice president for several years.

In political matters, Mr. Kubena began taking an interest as soon as he attained his majority. He cast his first vote for President for Grover

Mr and Mrs. Joseph G. Braun

Cleveland, and early became a convention man. He attended every state convention for several years, and in the famous Hogg and Clark campaign of 1892 he was a supporter of George Clark for governor. He was an alternate at large to the National Democratic Convention held at Denver, Colorado, in 1908, and attended that body as an alternate-at-large for M. M. Brooks.

Mr. Kubena's first office was as mayor of Fayetteville, a capacity to which he was elected and served one term. Following this, he was sent to the Twenty-eighth Legislature, as flotorial representative for the counties of Fayette, Bastrop and Gonzales. He served through the Lanham administration and two years under Governor Campbell, but, having been on the losing side of the house in the speakership contest was overlooked in the chairmanship assignments Mr. Kubena was in favor of Governor Campbell's "full rendition" scheme, and helped to elect Senators Bailey and Culbertson during his terms. He retired in 1908, and was soon appointed by Governor Colquitt to an official position at the State Insane Asylum at Austin, but resigned that office in 1915 to become a member of the board of managers of the Agricultural and Mechanical College, by the appointment of Governor Ferguson.

Mr. Kubena is a Pythian Knight, a past chancellor and present chancellor of the Fayetteville Lodge, is a Woodman of the World, and has served as camp clerk, and is a member of the Sons of Hermann and the Bohemian lodges S. P. J. S. T. and C. S. P. S. In the S. P. J. S. T., he was an active figure in the organization at LaGrange, and has been secretary of the supreme lodge of the state since its organization.

On January 21, 1896, Mr. Kubena was married to Miss Julia Sladek, a daughter of John Sladek. Mr. Sladek came to America from Moravia prior to the Civil war, married Miss Mary Polak, and passed away in 1908 as a merchant at Fayetteville. The children born to Mr. and Mrs. Kubena are nine in number, as follows: Jerome, John, Ladimir, Joseph, Rudolph, Lambert, Julia, Anita and an infant son, Woodrow Wilson. Mrs. Kubena has two brothers, Raymond and Rudolph, and one sister, Mrs. Bertha Foitik.

Joseph G. Braun. Among the men whose work naturally tends toward the development of the mineral resources of Texas, as well as of Mexico, Joseph G. Braun, of San Antonio, analytical and consulting chemist and mineralogist, occupies an important place. A man of broad and comprehensive learning, native talent and acquired experience, during the fifteen years that he has been located in this city he has reached an eminent place in his profession, and by frequent contributions to the literature of his calling has made himself widely known throughout the Southwest.

Joseph Maria Alfons Georg Braun was born at Kosten, in Bohemian Austria, August 12, 1876, and is a son of Gustav and Meta (Schlessinger) Braun, the former deceased, and the latter still living. The parents were both of pure German stock, Mrs. Braun being a native of Saxony, while Mr. Braun's ancestral home was in Vienna. The uncle of Mr. Braun, Dr. Joseph von Wild, was surgeon to the Duke of Lobkowitz, in Kosten, Austria, and the family resided in that city for many years. Their ancestors were members of the nobility, and several of them achieved prominence in the professions and in military life. Gustav Braun was educated as a chemist and mineralogist in the famous School of Mines of the University of Freiberg, at Freiberg, Saxony, and adopted these as his callings. He came with his family to the United States in 1887, locating first at Seguin, later removing to Boerne, and finally settling at San Antonio. While living at Boerne, Mr. Braun published and was the editor of The Texas Pioneer, a weekly newspaper printed in the German language.

Joseph G. Braun, following in the footsteps of his father, became a chemist and mineralogist. He studied under his father, also in St. Mary's College, at San Antonio, and in the Catholic Seminary at Victoria, Texas, and for five years applied himself to the study of Latin and Greek. Mr. Braun established himself in his profession at San Antonio, in 1900, under the name of the San Antonio Assay Office, which is located at No. 1618 South Presa Street. He is an analytical and consulting chemist, making laboratory tests and solutions of metallurgical difficulties, assays of ores and analysis of petroleum, minerals, waters, soils, etc. His specialty is mineralogy, and he has taken an important part in the assays of ores in Mexican mining properties, and in various minerals in Texas. His work is of the highest efficiency and in Texas he has made tests of some valuable minerals, particularly in the extreme western section, that will, no doubt, some day lead to the establishment of important industries. His tests of fire clays, etc., are worthy of note in connection with industries using such materials in the vicinity of San Antonio, and his work naturally plays an important part in the development of the mineral region of the Southwest. As a writer on subjects closely associated with his profession, Mr. Braun's services are in demand by the leading magazines and periodicals, and one of his recent contributions to the literature of mineralogy was a masterly-written article which appeared in the San Antonio Express, December 6, 1914, and which attracted widespread attention. In its composition the wonderful range and extent of his professional knowledge is clearly set forth.

Mr. Braun was married at San Antonio, to Miss Kate Dunlap Quillian, a native of Georgia, and to this union there have been born two children: Josephine and Alfred.

Frank A. Laake. When a lad of fourteen years this well known citizen of Frelsburg, Colorado County, accompanied his parents on their immigration to America from the Province of Silesia, Prussia, and the family home was established in Texas soon after their arrival in the United States, in 1856. In the period prior to the Civil war the father of Mr. Laake had become one of the progressive agriculturists of the Lone Star State, and the family name has been prominently and worthily linked with the civic and industrial history of Texas during the long period of nearly sixty years. Frank Albert Laake has not only been a successful farmer and stock-grower in Texas but has here shown his initiative ability and progressiveness by the developing and carrying forward of a substantial and prosperous enterprise in the growing of grapes and in manufacturing therefrom the finest type of wines, this line of industry having enlisted his attention for nearly forty years and his gratifying success having demonstrated the great possibilities in this line of business in Texas. He is senior member of the firm of F. A. Laake & Son, proprietors of the Oak Hill Vineyards, eligibly situated in Colorado County, near the line of Austin County, and on rural mail route No. 2 from New Ulm, in the latter county. The Oak Hill wines, the result of Mr. Laake's many years of experience in the scientific growing of grapes and the making of wines, have gained reputation and sales that far transcend local limitations, and the founder of this flourishing enterprise is known as one of its foremost exponents in the Southwest.

Frank Albert Laake was born in the Village of Gerlachsdorf, Province of Silesia, Prussia, in the district of which the ancient Town of Nimptsch is the seat of government, and the date of his nativity was

August 10, 1842. In Silesia the family had been actively concerned with agricultural pursuits for many generations, and the grandparents of the subject of this sketch were Carl and Caroline Laake, who passed their entire lives in their native province. They reared a large family of children, of whom Ernst, father of him whose name introduces this article, was the only one of the children to come to America, though some of the children of his brothers and sisters eventually came to the United States and settled among the German colonists of Southern Texas.

Ernst Laake was born at Baerdorf, Silesia, on the 1st of July, 1815, and died at Frelsburg, Texas, on the 13th of January, 1884. In his native land he acquired his early education and also learned the tailor's trade, to which he there gave his attention besides maintaining supervision of his small farm. He married Clara Hilgner, daughter of John Hilgner, a substantial Silesian farmer, and she was the only one of the children who came to the United States. Mrs. Laake was born May 11, 1817, and she was summoned to the life eternal June 6, 1884, about six months after the death of her husband, their remains resting in the Frelsburg cemetery.

On the 5th of September, 1856, Ernst Laake and his family embarked on a vessel at Bremen, Germany, and set forth for America. On the 5th of the following November, after voyaging across the Atlantic and the Gulf of Mexico, they landed in Galveston, Texas, from which place they made their way by one of the old-time steamboats up the Buffalo bayou to Houston, where a wagon and ox team were driven to the boat landing and became the means of transporting the family and their belongings to their destination in Austin County. Eight days were required to make this overland journey of eighty miles to the Village of Industry, and for the ensuing two years the family resided in the new Schoenau community in that county. They then removed to the Frelsburg community, and here the parents passed the residue of their lives, many of their posterity still remaining in this district of the state. After devoting himself to farming on rented land for a time Ernst Laake purchased a tract of raw land, to the reclamation and modest improvement of which he directed his energies. This homestead, in the Muckelroy League, he developed into a fine farm, and on the same he and his wife continued to reside until their death,—folk of industry and sterling integrity and pioneer citizens who commanded the high regard of all who knew them. Ernst Laake became a supporter of the democratic party as soon as he acquired citizenship in the land of his adoption, and when the Civil war was precipitated his sympathies were with the cause of the Union, but he was of too advanced age to be eligible for military service. Both he and his wife were zealous communicants of the Catholic Church, in the faith of which they carefully reared their children, of whom Frank Albert, of this review, is the eldest; Anna became the wife of Jacob Poth and died near Cuero, Dewitt County, leaving a large family of children; Bertha married Justin Stein, of Frelsburg, where she still maintains her home; and Paul, the only one of the children born in Texas, is a prosperous farmer near Cameron, Milam County.

Frank A. Laake is indebted to the schools of his native land for his early educational discipline and after the family immigration to America, as a strong and vigorous lad, he gave his father effective service in connection with the work of the home farm. Later, in association with the breaking of prairie with ox teams, he gained ample experience, and finally he engaged in the freighting business, in connection with which he frequently drove six or seven yoke of oxen to a single wagon, the only way of traffic in those days. The youth of the present day would consider almost marvelous the patience and dexterity demanded in driving such teams through thick timber and over a section without roads and with a plethora of obstacles of varied kinds, but Mr. Laake usually manipulated his slow-moving teams without difficulty and traversed the country with as much facility in a comparative way as could be done with a team of horses over the roads of the present time. As a freighter Mr. Laake hauled produce and other material to and from Houston, and when the Civil war started his objective point was transferred to Matamoras, Mexico, where a market was found for the cotton raised in Southwestern Texas. As a freighter Mr. Laake thus continued his operations along the frontier trail until the third year of the war, when a provost marshal of the Confederacy made him a subject of conscription, at Columbus, the judicial center of Colorado County. He was given sufficient furlough to permit him to take his team and wagon home, and this incident closed his career as a freighter. Rather than to take up arms against a cause which he believed to be just, he broke his furlough and made his way into Mexico, thus evading service in the Confederate ranks.

At this critical juncture Mr. Laake found employment as waiter in a restaurant at Bagdad, Mexico, and there he was receiving good pay when friends in the City of New Orleans induced him to report there and join the Federal troops that were then in control of the city. Upon his arrival he duly enlisted in Company D, First New Orleans Infantry, and his company, commanded by Captain Boothby, was detailed for service on Lake Pontchartrain, Mr. Laake himself being detailed as mounted orderly for Colonel Allen, who was in charge of all the water transportation. Thus Mr. Laake served as messenger in the carrying of orders to company commanders about that section of the country, and his regiment was one of the last to be mustered out of the United States service at the close of the war. He received his honorable discharge on the 1st of June, 1866, in the City of New Orleans, and before the close of the same month he had returned to his home in Texas. He is one of Uncle Sam's pensioners.

In the following autumn Mr. Laake took unto himself a wife, and after remaining two years on the farm of his father he purchased a new farm for himself, near his present homestead. In a primitive dwelling he established his home and then instituted the clearing off of the timber and otherwise improving his land, even as he had assisted his father in similar work about a decade previously. In 1878 Mr. Laake purchased the Dr. Frederick Becker farm in Pieper's League, and he then removed with his family to the substantial brick house that had there been erected in 1858 and which is said to have been the first brick house built in Colorado County. This well preserved and attractive old homestead has many points of historic interest, especially in its fittings of the ancient type common to the pioneer era when dwellings of superior order were to be equipped. The house has heavy black-walnut doors and casings, and the locks on the doors are of the old-time hand-made type. Honest and substantial is every detail of construction, signalizing the enterprise and good judgment, as well as the prosperity of the pioneer builder and owner. There remain in service some of the window-panes that were imported from Germany and there are divers other evidences of the substantial way in which the building and equipping of a house was done by a pioneer of the more prosperous order. The house is 1½ stories in height, is situated in a fine grove of forest trees, and the entire environment is most attractive, making the ancient domicile one of ideal order and one suggesting thrift, prosperity and happiness.

Mr. Laake has never severed his allegiance to the fundamental industry of agriculture, but when he removed to his present fine homestead he found that here had been made an initial and successful undertaking of grape-culture. Here he made his first barrels of wine from the old Mustang grapes that had been planted by Doctor Becker. In 1883 he instituted the development of his present large and splendid vineyard. After clearing out the timber he first planted potatoes on the land designed for his vineyard, and his next operation was the propagating of grape cuttings as the basis of his future vineyard. In the development of this interesting and profitable line of industrial enterprise on his fine farm Mr. Laake has shown the utmost discrimination and judgment. He has made a careful study of grape cultivation and wine manufacturing, has brought to bear the most approved and scientific methods, and his vineyard and its ultimate manufactured products constitute a valuable adjunct to his general agricultural operations. The Laake vineyard comprises about fifteen acres and Mr. Laake may consistently be designated as the only grape-grower and wine manufacturer in Southern Texas who has had the vigor and enterprise to make of this line of business a distinctive success, his example being one well worthy of emulation. Of the many varieties of grapes with which he has experimented for the purpose of obtaining types best suited to the soil and climate and to the production of wine of maximum excellence, he has selected as his leaders the Herbemont, the Black Spanish and the Elvicand varieties, the latter one of Professor Munson's excellent hybrids,—a cross between the Elvira and the Mustang types.

As a wine-maker Mr. Laake obtained his first premium in 1889, at the Colorado County Fair, and in 1910 he made an exhibit of his wine at the International Fair in the City of San Antonio, where likewise he obtained a premium and diploma of merit.

In 1913 he secured a diploma on his exhibit at the State Fair at Dallas, and in the same city he obtained in 1914 a first premium for the best selection of Texas wines, besides which he took the blue ribbon for the best plate of Texas persimmons, and two premiums on pears raised in the state,—one for the largest pears and one for the best plate of this variety of fruit.

For many years Mr. Laake has served as a correspondent of the United States Department of Agriculture, and he receives each week from Washington the official agricultural and horticultural reports and bulletins, as does he also those issued by the same departments of the Texas government. He has carried his research, study and experimentation to broad limits, and is a prominent and influential member of the Texas State Horticultural Society and the Texas State Agricultural Society, and before the horticultural congress held at Agricultural and Mechanical College Station, Brazos County, in 1912, he read an article or paper on agriculture in Texas and another series of papers having been prepared by him at the suggestion of Prof. George Husmann, of Washington, District of Columbia, to whom he dedicated the same. The articles were widely published in newspapers and other publications throughout the state and have proved to be a specially practical, authoritative and valuable treatise on the subject of grape-culture and wine-making in Texas.

Mr. Laake has been essentially loyal and progressive as a citizen but has held aloof from practical politics, though giving staunch allegiance and support to the democratic party. He has held no public office save that of school trustee and that of election officer. He was a delegate to the state democratic convention, in San Antonio, that nominated Governor Colquitt for his first term, and these services have fully satisfied his ambitions in the matter of political activity.

On the 30th of October, 1866, was solemnized the marriage of Mr. Laake to Miss Louisa Werlla, a daughter of John and Anna (Wacek)

Werlla, who came to America from Maeren, Austria, although Mr. Werlla was a native of Hungary. John Werlla was a man of superior education and was a skilled mechanical engineer. He came to the United States in the early '50s and he thereafter erected many cotton gins through Southeastern Texas. He became also a successful agriculturist and operated a sawmill and a cotton gin. His wife died at their early home, on Little Bernard Creek, Austin County, and he passed the closing period of his life at Millheim, this county. Of their children Mrs. Laake is the eldest; Anna is the wife of Jacob Swearingen; and Carl is a resident of Eagle Lake, Colorado County. After the death of his first wife John Werlla wedded Mrs. Willrodt, a widow, and the two children of this union are John, a resident of Colorado County, and Mrs. Mary Anderson, of Wallis, Austin County.

At this point is entered brief record concerning the children of Mr. and Mrs. F. A. Laake: Louisa, who became a member of the Catholic Sisterhood of the Divine Providence, died on the 22d of March, 1904. Clara is the widow of William B. Niehues, of Hydro, Oklahoma. Mary is the widow of Henry B. Niehues and resides at Westphalia, Falls County, Texas, where her husband died. Frank W., who was born September 20, 1873, and who is a prosperous farmer near Hobson, Karnes County, married Miss Lizzie Gully. Cecelia, who was born September 25, 1875, married Wendelin Stock, and resides at Hamlin, this state. Carl J., who was born September 23, 1877, and who married Johanna Reinhardt, was a railway fireman when he met an accidental death, September 22, 1906, near Bobstown. Alois Albert, who was born July 6, 1880, wedded Miss Emma Franke and resided at Hallettsville, but is now at Oak Hill Vineyards as a partner; Angela F. remains at the parental home and was born September 28, 1882. Edward J., who was born November 18, 1884, completed the short course in the Agricultural College at College Station and was associated with his father in the ownership and operation of the Oak Hill Vineyards, under the firm name of F. A. Laake & Son. He died September 1, 1915. Ernest William, who was born September 22, 1887, was graduated in the Texas Agricultural & Mechanical College on the 10th of June, 1913, with the degree of Bachelor of Science, and he is now in the service of the United States Department of Agriculture, as an entomologist, with headquarters in the City of Dallas, Texas. As a student he was a member of the college athletic team, was a lieutenant and musician in the College Cadets' Band, and he won many collegiate honors and distinctions in the line of medals in athletics and also in his undergraduate work as a student. Mr. and Mrs. F. A. Laake and all of their children are communicants of the Catholic Church and he and all of his sons except the youngest are affiliated with the fraternal organization known as Hermann Sohns, he himself being an honorary member.

Adolph Krenek was born at Fayetteville October 17, 1880, a son of Ignaz Krenek, who for many years was one of the leading ginners in the Fayetteville community. Ignaz Krenek was born at Bordovice, Bohemia, in 1853, and came to America at the age of eighteen. He had gained practically no education in the old country, and such schooling as he had in Texas was of a most primitive character. In fact, he learned to read and write after his marriage. For a few years following the establishment of a home of his own, he was a farmer, and then demonstrated his first stroke of business genius by establishing a cotton gin. His capital was exceedingly limited, and he secured machinery for a gin of one stand, which he put up on his farm, and the power for its operation was supplied by his mule. In connection with the gin he also set up, as his own millwright, a molasses mill. He made the rolls out of liveoak blocks. For several weeks in each season he operated his molasses mill, and after that did the ginning for the cotton growers of that locality. With increasing business and capital he finally installed a modern steam gin, put in a new molasses plant and grist mill, and thus established on his farm three miles south of Fayetteville an institution which gave his place the name of Krenek, an independent village. As a result of increasing financial success he finally bought the gin at Live Oak Hill, rebuilt it, and after operating it for a number of years sold to his son-in-law Joseph Jasek. The plant on his home place he finally sold to his son Ignaz Krenek, and on retiring from active affairs erected a comfortable residence on his adjoining farm. In 1900 Mr. Krenek attended the exposition in Paris, France, and visited the localities in his native land where he had grown up. He was attacked by a severe illness during this trip abroad, and died in 1902 after returning to Texas. In every sense of the term he was the architect of his own destiny, and his success in business was very unusual. Though a democrat, he was never in public office, and his social relations were largely with the Knights of Honor, the Bohemian Orders of C. S. P. S. and the S. P. J. S. T.; while in religious affairs he was a Freethinker. Ignaz Krenek married Anna Bubela, daughter of John Bubela, who came to America about the same time as Mr. Krenek and from about the same locality in Bohemia. Mrs. Krenek is now living in LaGrange. The children of their marriage were: Joseph, who was killed in a railroad wreck near Chihuahua, Mexico, in 1902, and was still unmarried; Ignaz, a farmer at Crosby, Texas; Agnes, whose first husband was Joseph Jasek, and who is now the wife of Joseph Franta, and lives at Crosby; Amalia is the wife of John Kubala of Granger Texas; Annie, married J. H. Schamburg of Bartlett, Texas; Rudolph E., a veterinary surgeon in Kansas City, Missouri; and Emil, a graduate of the Kansas City Veterinary College; Alvina who married W. H. Hruska of LaGrange.

Adolph Krenek spent his early life in the Fayetteville community, attended school at Ellinger, and for one year was a student in the Agricultural and Mechanical College at Bryan. He inherited many of the practical qualities of his father, and was well trained for his future career under the direction of that self-made business man. When still a boy he acquired a minute knowledge of the ginning business, and helped to remodel the home plant and the Live Oak Hill plant. Thus he brought experience with him when he moved in 1901 to Engle and bought the William Hillmann gin. After conducting this plant four years it was destroyed by fire, but he at once replaced it with one of the best plants of the kind in Fayette County, a five stand gin of the Murray system. The ginning plant is located in a galvanized house, and adjacent is a corn mill. The mill and surroundings are a model of neatness. In November, 1915, Mr. Krenek sold his business at Engle and moved to Crosby, Harris County, where he again went in the gin business. He made this change in order to afford his children better educational advantages.

There was hardly any more important institution at Engle than the Krenek Cotton gin, and its proprietor was one of the leading citizens of that community and a vigorous and progressive business man who usually succeeds in everything he takes hold of. His family were identified with Fayette County for many years, and their activities sufficed to accumulate a number of honorable associations around the name.

In fraternal matters Mr. Krenek is affiliated with the Bohemian Order S. P. J. S. T., with the Woodmen of the World, the Sons of Hermann, and carries insurance policies issued by the New York Life Company, the Merchants Life Association of Burlington, Iowa, and the Amicable Life of Waco.

Every visitor to Engle carried away impressions of the Krenek home, one of the most attractive in all Fayette County, and few if any of the towns can compete with it for beauty. This residence is a two-story frame building, set in the midst of an attractive lawn, covered with luxuriant grasses, with substantial walks, the evergreens and other shrubs carefully shaped by the tools of the landscape gardener. Mr. Krenek was married at Engle, Texas, July 8, 1902, to Miss Albina Herzik. She was born in Fayette County, and one of a large family. Her mother was a Russek. Mr. and Mrs. Krenek are the parents of three children: Adella, Walter and Wilbur.

HANNIBAL PIANTA. The picturesque little City of Varallo, on the Sesia River, Province of Novaro, in the Piedmont region of Italy, figures as the ancestral seat of the Pianta family, and this Alpine town, 7,000 feet above the sea level and near the remarkable hill known as Sacro Monte, figures as the place of nativity of Hannibal Pianta, who is now numbered among the successful business men and highly esteemed citizens of San Antonio, Texas, where he is a manufacturer of decorative composition, plaster ornaments and cement architectural products. In his important and prosperous business enterprises he gives evidence of the artistic ability and appreciation that has ever denoted the race from which he is sprung, though virtually his entire life thus far has been passed in the United States, so that he is thoroughly in touch with American sentiment and progressiveness.

Mr. Pianta was born in the year 1874, and is a son of John Pianta, who likewise was born at Varallo, where he was reared and educated and where his marriage was solemnized. In 1869 John Pianta came to the United States, where his wife joined him within a short interval thereafter, the family home being established in the City of Chicago. He was by trade and vocation an ornamental plasterer and staff worker, and some of the earliest art work along these lines to be manufactured in America was done by him. His home in Chicago was destroyed in the historic fire that swept that city in 1871, but he erected a new residence and for many years he was manager of the staff work for the well known Chicago firm of Smith, Crimp & Eastman, as representative of which he had the supervision of more than a million dollars' worth of the beautiful staff work that had so much to do with making the buildings of the World's Columbian Exposition, in 1893, a marvel of picturesque and esthetic values, these structures having been virtually the first of the finer type of staff buildings to be produced in America and making the famous "White City" an artistic ideal whose charms have not been surpassed in any of the later expositions in the history of the world. Mr. Pianta also completed a large and important contract of similar order in connection with the construction of the buildings of the great Louisiana Purchase Exposition of 1904, in the City of St. Louis. It is specially worthy of mention in this article that he had the supervision of the plastering and similar decorative work in the magnificent state capitol of Texas, in 1885-86, this being recognized as one of the finest state buildings in the Union. Mr. Pianta attained to high reputation in his chosen field of enterprise, became a successful contractor in an independent way and did a large amount of fine work in many different states and many of the leading cities of the land of his adoption. From Texas he went to Georgia, where he carried out an effective contract in connection with the erection and decorating of the admirable capitol of that state, in the City of Atlanta. In later years he returned to Texas and established his home in San Antonio, where he became associated with his son Hannibal, of this review, in the equipping of a plant for the manufacturing of ornamental building work of staff and cement. With this enterprise he continued to be actively identified until his death, which occurred in 1911. Since that time the business has been successfully continued by the son, who is fully upholding the artistic and civic prestige of the name which he bears. In 1874 the wife of John Pianta returned to her old home in Italy, where their son, Hannibal, was born in that year and where the mother remained until her death, a few years later, her intention having been to rejoin her husband in the United States.

Hannibal Pianta acquired favorable academic education in the schools of Italy and those of the City of Chicago, and in his native land he received also excellent training along the line of the profession of which he is now a prominent and successful representative, his further experience of preliminary order having been obtained under the direction of his father, principally in the City of Chicago, where he was reared to maturity. In an independent way he has handled fine work at his trade or profession in thirty-eight different states of the Union, but for a number of years he has maintained his residence in the City of San Antonio, where he has been the sole proprietor of his large and successful business since the death of his honored father. His manufactory represents one of the important industrial plants of San Antonio and its products have wide reputation for artistic values and for being of the highest class of work utilized in modern architectural achievement. The buildings and yards of the plant are eligibly situated on a triangular tract of land with a frontage of 145 feet and Fredericksburg Road, 215 feet on Sandoval Street, and 100 feet on the line of the International & Great Northern Railroad, so that the best of facilities are afforded for both local and railroad transportation.

Mr. Pianta is a contractor for and manufacturer of modern decorative composition, plaster ornaments and cement-stone work for public and private buildings, bridges and other structures where the element of decorative art supplements that of practical utility. Much of the work done by Mr. Pianta follows the designs of sculptors and other artists, and in material evidence of this fact stands the beautiful public fountain on the new Commerce Street bridge in San Antonio. This fountain was completed in the autumn of 1915 and the cast was made by Mr. Pianta from the design of a pupil of the well known sculptor, Pompeo Coppini. Another work of great artistic beauty that was manufactured in the Pianta establishment in San Antonio is the great municipal fountain at Corpus Christi, Texas, this having been designed by Coppini himself. Mr. Pianta constructed also the ornamental and decorative work for the new courthouse at Corpus Christi, one of the finest buildings of its kind in the state and did all the decorating work on the new $125,000 Majestic Theatre in Austin, Texas, including all the interior finish, this theatre now being considered the most beautifully finished one in Texas. Mr. Pianta employes only skilled and efficient workmen, and his establishment has attained to the highest reputation for the beauty and utility of its products, the while he is constantly called upon to assume important contracts in connection with architectural activities in the leading cities of the Lone Star State.

At Charleston, Illinois, was solemnized the marriage of Mr. Pianta to Miss Rose Nees, who was born and reared in that city and who has the distinction of claiming fine Indian lineage, her paternal great-grandfather having been a full-blood Cherokee Indian. Mr. and Mrs. Pianta have four children,—John D., Emanuel, Eugene and Catherine.

Franz F. A. Kotzebue. It has been given to this well known and representative citizen to gain status as one of the influential business men of his native county and to play prominent part in the civic and material advancement of his home town of Moulton, where he is engaged in the drug business, is a director of the village waterworks system, and is president of the board of education. He is a son of one of the honored pioneer families of this county and further details concerning his parents are given on other pages of this publication, in the sketch of the career of his brother, Dr. A. M. Kotzebue, who is now a resident of Flatonia, Fayette County.

On the old homestead farm of his father, within 1½ miles of distance of Moulton, Franz Frederick, Alexander Kotzebue, who in business connections signs his name A. F. Kotzebue, was born on the 5th of May, 1875, and the conditions and influences of the farm continued to compass him until he had attained to the age of sixteen years, his educational discipline in the meanwhile having included that of the high school at Moulton, and later it having been his privilege to attend for one year the Lutheran College at Brenham, Washington County.

After leaving the home farm Mr. Kotzebue was variously employed, and at the age of twenty-one years he initiated his active business career by purchasing an interest in the drug store then conducted at Moulton by his brother, D. A. M. Kotzebue, who is now one of the representative physicians in the thriving little City of Flatonia. After two years Dr. A. M. Kotzebue sold his interest to F. P. Guenther and the firm was then Kotzebue & Guenther. Two years later he purchased the interest of his partner, Professor Guenther, and since 1900 he has been the sole proprietor of the substantial and representative business, which is conducted in one of the best business blocks in the village. This building, a substantial brick structure of two stories, was erected by him and has a frontage on each of two streets, the building being virtually in the form of an L, and the intermediate or corner building being that of the Moulton State Bank. The upper story of the Kotzebue Block is excellently fitted up as an opera house and gives to the community a most attractive place of entertainment. Mr. Kotzebue has further added to the material upbuilding of Moulton by the erection of his fine residence, a modern house of two stories and fourteen rooms, with expensive grounds that have been beautified with trees and effective landscape gardening.

As may naturally be inferred, Mr. Kotzebue is found aligned as a staunch supporter of the cause of the democratic party, and he is recognized as one of the most vital and public-spirited citizens of Moulton, where he has been influential in the furtherance of those measures and enterprises that make for the general well-being of the community. Since 1909 he has been a valued and progressive member of the board of trustees of the public schools of Moulton, and he has served as president of the board since 1912. He is a member of the directorate of the Moulton Water Works Company, in the promotion and chartering of which he was primarily influential, the installing of the effective water system having been instituted in 1913. Of the local camp of the Woodmen of the World he has been an active member from the time of its organization, and he has served as its clerk since 1908. Since 1898 Mr. Kotzebue has been the manager of the local telephone exchange, and in a fraternal way he is further affiliated with the Moulton Lodge of Ancient Free and Accepted Masons and its adjunct organization, the chapter of the Order of the Eastern Star, and with the Hermann Sohns, his wife likewise holding membership in the Order of the Eastern Star and both being members of the Woodman Circle. They are leaders in the representative social activities of the community and their beautiful home is a center of gracious hospitality. Their religious faith is that of the Lutheran Church.

On the 22d of October, 1902, was solemnized the marriage of Mr. Kotzebue to Miss Erna Fehrenkamp, daughter of Frederick T. Fehrenkamp, a prominent and influential citizen of Moulton, and the names and respective dates of birth of the three children of this union are here noted: Roy Louis, October 16, 1903; Ida Alice, October 13, 1905; and Henry Earl, February 13, 1908.

JAMES C. MCGREGOR, M. D. For fully sixty years members of this family, many of whom have gone into the profession of medicine, have been identified with Central Texas. Dr. James C. McGregor is a physician of nearly thirty years' experience, and for the past ten years has been located at Caldwell.

It was in 1856 that his father, C. Gilbert McGregor, also a physician and a graduate of a regular medical college, located in Washington County near Greenvine. C. Gilbert McGregor was born in Robinson County, North Carolina, a son of Malcolm McGregor, who settled in that section of North Carolina after coming from Argyleshire, Scotland. Dr. C. G. McGregor followed his brother, Dr. G. C. McGregor, to Texas, and not only practiced medicine but also followed farming in Austin County until his death in 1861. He married Miss Ann Wilkinson. Their children were William Harvey, who died unmarried at Chapel Hill, Texas; Dr. James C.; Dr. John D. of Lobo, Texas, who married Hattie Smiley, a native of Selma, Alabama; C. Gilbert, Jr., of Houston, who married a sister of his brother John's wife, Callie, also a native of Selma, Alabama. After the death of the senior Doctor McGregor his widow married Thomas E. Woods, and she died at Salado, Texas, in 1903. Her children by the second marriage were: Thomas E., who died at Salado, unmarried; Alice, who married Macklin Robertson of Georgetown, Texas; and Mamie, wife of Fuller Griffith of Quanah, Texas.

Dr. James C. McGregor was born in Robinson County, North Carolina, November 30, 1855, and was still an infant when his parents moved to Texas. He was reared in the Wesley community of Washington County, had a public school education, and also did three years of work in the Baylor University. He was twenty-eight years of age before he entered upon the study of medicine. In the meantime he had followed farming and ginning in Washington County. In the medical department of Tulane University at New Orleans he spent one year, and then finished his course in the Louisville Medical College at Louisville, Kentucky, where he was graduated in 1887. In the meantime he had two years of experience in a drug store at Kenney. After graduating he practiced for a few months at Yarbor in Grimes County, and then established his home and office at Nelsonville in Austin County, a community to which he furnishes capable services as a physician and surgeon for sixteen years. In 1903 he located at Kenney, but two years later, in 1905, moved to Caldwell, where his ability as a physician is rated second to none in that locality.

He is a democrat, has usually cast his vote at every campaign and in the interests of good government, but his only official service has been as trustee of schools at Nelsonville.

In Austin County, Texas, November 30, 1893, Doctor McGregor married Miss Fannie Daughtrey. She is a daughter of Ed and Nettie (Dixon) Daughtrey. Her father was born near Nacogdoches, Texas, about 1821. The Daughtrey family were among the first Americans to locate in Texas and the father of Ed Daughtrey died at San Antonio, the father of James, Ed, Felix, Elisha, Joseph, Mrs. Doctor Ross, Mrs. Judge Cheshire, Mrs. Judge Munger, and Miss Ann. Mr. and Mrs. Ed Daughtrey were the parents of thirteen children.

Doctor McGregor and wife have a son and a daughter. Gilbert E., the son, is a rancher at Lobo, Texas. Miss Antoinette is a student in the Denton Normal. In the Caldwell High School, in 1915, she took the Morgan Medal as the best student in her classes. Doctor McGregor is a Chapter Mason and is also affiliated with the Woodmen of the World and the Sons of Hermann. His family are members of the Presbyterian Church. When he leaves his practice for recreation he finds it chiefly in hunting.

John M. Smith, who for the past seven years has been superintendent of the schools of Caldwell, comes of a family of educators, his father and grandfather before him having been prominent in the schoolroom, and special honor should be paid to his father, the late William T. Smith, as one of the oldest and best known of Texas educators. The first children taught by the grandfather came from the country communities of the South before the Civil war, before any general system of public free education had been established. John M. Smith is an exemplar of the modern ideals of school work, and since taking charge of the schools at Caldwell has done much to broaden and give efficiency to the course of instruction.

His grandfather was James Smith, who was born in Alabama, and devoted most of his years to the schools of that state. He married a Miss Lovelace. When he gave up teaching he was succeeded in the schoolroom by his son, the late William T. Smith.

William T. Smith was born at Camp Hill, Alabama, in 1844 and died while still in the harness as an educator at Denton, Texas, in 1913. He was reared at Dadeville, Alabama, and attended the Alabama Agricultural and Mechanical College. For several years before reaching his majority he faced the stern realities of civil warfare. As a Confederate soldier he served under General Jackson in General Longstreet's corps, and was in much of the hard fighting done by the army of Northern Virginia. Once severely wounded, he recuperated and returned to the service as soon as possible, and still later lost his right arm in battle. Even after this he continued with the Southern armies until the close of the war and was with General Lee at Appomattox at the time of the final surrender.

Immediately after the war he began his teaching career, and for twenty-four years was county superintendent of Talapoosa County, Alabama. His first teaching in Texas was done at Waelder, then at Port Lavaca, Dawson, Meridian, Rogers, Godley and at Denton he concluded his long career as a school man. He was chairman of the board of examiners at Port Lavaca and served on several state examining boards, while three of his sons were similarly honored. In politics a democrat, he was an ardent supporter of Governor Hogg as long as that figure remained dominant in Texas affairs, and also supported the election of State Superintendent Cousins. He was an active Methodist and attended district conferences and was steward of his home church.

William T. Smith married Miss Fannie Virginia Ingraham, who was one of the several children of Rev. Jonathan Ingraham. Her ancestors were Virginia people and Rev. Mr. Ingraham was a minister of the Methodist faith.

Professor and Mrs. Smith had the following children: Mrs. Emma Phillips of San Antonio; Mrs. Leila Ward of Bishop, Texas; James W., who is secretary of the Denton Normal School; Miss Lora H., instructor in English at the University of Texas; Miss Ruby C., a student in the University of Texas; John M.; Mrs. S. W. Horne, a teacher in the Austin

High School; and Lewis I., superintendent of schools at Jefferson, Texas. All these children became teachers and six of them are still in the work.

John M. Smith was born at Walnut Hill, Alabama, May 5, 1882, and was brought to Texas when a child of eight years. He never recited a lesson to anyone outside of his own family until he entered the University of Texas, where he pursued his studies at different times, giving altogether about two and a half years to the Bachelor of Science course. In 1905 he received a diploma from the San Marcos Normal School. His first work as a teacher was done at the age of eighteen in a rural school near Port Lavaca, where he remained two years, then went to Kerens and worked up in the grades to the principalship, and was identified with the school work of that community four years. He next became high school principal at Rogers for two years, and following this was elected superintendent of the Caldwell schools. Mr. Smith came to Caldwell in 1909 as the successor of his brother, James W. Smith, and has already completed seven years of successful work. In the meantime three teachers have been added to the school faculty, and the course of instruction has been broadened to meet the requirements for affiliation with the State University and the State Department of Education.

For four summers Mr. Smith has been employed in the Denton Normal and is under contract for a similar engagement during the summer of 1916. He has taken an active part in the meetings of the State Teachers' Association, has served as a state examiner under Superintendent Cousins and was in his office for a time as certificate clerk. He also attended the meeting of the National Educational Association at Richmond. In 1909 he conducted the Washington County Normal, but has since confined his efforts during the summer to teaching in the State Normal School. Fraternally he is a Mason, is a past chancellor of the Knights of Pythias, and past consul of the Modern Woodmen of America.

In June, 1911, at Temple, Texas, Mr. Smith married Miss Willie V. Burleson. Her father was Henry Burleson and her grandfather Ed Burleson, who was a nephew of the pioneer Burleson of Bastrop County. Henry Burleson had two children, Edgar and Mrs. Smith, the latter a native of Texas, who received her education at Temple and in 1905 graduated from the Sam Houston Normal School. Before her marriage she taught at Rogers and Temple. Mr. and Mrs. Smith have one son, John M., Jr.

Fritz Kraege. Representing a family which has been identified with Texas since 1859, Fritz Kraege, of Yorktown, has been connected with the business and civic affairs of his community during a long period of years, and belongs to that class of energetic and enterprising men who have built up their own fortunes and made their own reputations. He was born in the Town of Friedeberg, Province of Brandenburg, near Berlin, Germany, September 16, 1855, and is a son of August and Wilhelmina (Heinrich) Kraege.

August Kraege was born in that same town in Germany, the son of a baker who passed his entire life there, but did not take up his father's vocation, learning instead the trade of tanner. He was one of three children, the others being a brother Ferdinand and a sister, Mrs. Alvina Noster. He was married in his native place and in 1856, after the birth of one child, set sail from Bremen for Galveston, Texas, where he duly arrived, subsequently making his way to Indianola and thence to Yorktown. He was possessed of but a small amount of capital when he joined his native countrymen here, but soon managed to establish a tanyard on the creek, gathering his own tanbark from the trees nearby, grinding it up and tanning his hides in the vats of the olden times, when it took eight months to complete a hide. He followed this business until 1867 and was not interrupted but once for his service during that time. On one occasion he was taken away by the Confederate authorities for military duty, but was absent only a short time, when he bought himself off and resumed his work. In 1867 he had accumulated some $10,000 in gold, an amount which would have allowed him to live in ease in his native land during the remainder of his life, and his longing for Germany at that time caused him to take his family back to the fatherland, sailing from Galveston to Liverpool on the old sailing vessel then still in use, crossing through England to Hull, and going then on a small sailboat to Hamburg. Arriving in his native Town of Friedeberg, he established a tanyard and remained three years, but the importunities of his children, who were American reared, caused him to come once more to Texas. Here, at Victoria, Mr. Kraege once more engaged in the tannery business and conducted his yard for one year, at that time coming back to his old location at Yorktown. He abandoned the tannery for a time to engage in mercantile affairs with F. B. Gohmert, and the firm of F. B. Gohmert & Company continued to exist for five years. The business, however, was not at all profitable to Mr. Kraege, and he resolved to resume tanning, in which he had shown that he could make money. He put up a new yard at Yorktown and prepared to duplicate his former success, but after operations extending over a period of eight years he found that changing times and conditions mitigated against his business and he gave up tanning for good and all. At that time, in 1880, he began work in the store of his son, Fritz, who had embarked in business at Yorktown, and remained with the business until his death, in March, 1906, when he was eighty years of age. He took out his naturalization papers and became a good citizen, and although he never sought office was a consistent voter, and gave his support as his principles prompted to the republican party, being one of the few men who had the courage to do this in his locality during the early days. He was not a church man, and his only fraternal connection was with the blue lodge of the Masonic order. Mrs. Kraege, who still survives him, is eighty-two years of age. They were the parents of the following children: Fritz, of this review; Alvina, who is the widow of August Ladner, of Yorktown; Mrs. Anna Meyer, of Runge, Texas; Emma, who married F. M. Braunig, of Yorktown; August, who is associated with his brother Fritz in business; Otto, who died at Runge, Texas, in 1895, leaving children; Mrs. Helena Hinueber, of Yoakum, Texas; and Miss Hulda, of Yorktown.

Fritz Kraege was still a small child when the family first came to Texas, and here his education began at the age of six years under a German teacher of Yorktown, Professor Schumacher, who was a Maximilian soldier in Mexico and died at Yorktown. He also had three years of instruction in the gymnasium in Germany during his life there, and while his father was engaged in merchandising at Yorktown he entered upon his career as a clerk in his store. He worked for a year also in the tanyard, but after his marriage resumed clerking with C. Eckhardt & Sons, one of the pioneer concerns of Yorktown. In 1880, having the experience and some small capital, Mr. Kraege gave up clerking to establish himself in business as the owner of a small grocery, located on the lot where the State Bank of Yorktown now stands. His capital consisted of the money which he had saved from his wages, but he was able to borrow some more, and two years later took in his brother-in-law, August Ladner, as a partner, they doing business together for six years as Kraege & Ladner. As soon as he accumulated the means he began buying property and improving it, and in 1886 the old frame store house was built, and in 1890 he added another section to it, making a frontage of seventy feet. Mr. Kraege's business continued to grow steadily, under his able and energetic management, and in 1901 he found it desirable to seek more commodious and modern quarters. Accordingly he erected his new business house, a one-story brick structure, with a frontage of 45 feet, but 100 feet deep. Here he has a full and up-to-date line of the finest goods and caters to a high-class and representative trade. He also owns a home in the same block with his business house, but it is his old home. As a promoter and developer of other enterprises, Mr. Kraege is acting vice president of the First State Bank of Yorktown, of which he was an organizer, and in the development of which he has been a forceful factor. He has at all times been interested in the welfare of the city, and has served as an alderman for a quarter of a century and as long as a school trustee, which latter position his son, Otto, now holds.

Mr. Kraege was married at Yorktown, October 14, 1877, to Miss Malvina Heissig, a daughter of Charles H. Heissig, and to this union there have been born the following children: Ferdinand, of Yorktown, who married Bertha Peterson; Otto, a member of the firm of F. Kraege, who married Ida Thuem; Olga, who is the wife of William Stuermer of Yorktown, with a daughter, Marian; Ella, who married A. J. Fimbel and has two children, Elsie and Addie; Ida, who is the wife of G. M. Hinsey, of Yorktown, with a daughter, Melba; and Albert, of Yorktown, who married Thea Grunewald, of this city.

JOHN JANCIK. For nearly thirty years John Jancik has been a factor in local business affairs in Caldwell. While he did not attract much attention at first, since he was only a boy worker in a lumber yard, he has for a number of years kept one of the principal stores of the city and has been a factor in local banking, and the upbuilding of all the concerns of that community.

Though not a native of Texas, he was hardly a year old when his parents brought him out of Europe to this country. He was born at Moravia in Austria, April 20, 1870. His father, John Jancik, and family sailed from Bremen, Germany, on a sailing vessel, and they were eleven weeks four days on the ocean before reaching Galveston. They brought a very little capital, less than $200, and for a few years they lived at Nelsonville in Austin County, then moved to a place two miles east of Caldwell in Burleson County, and the parents devoted their remaining years to making a success as farmers, and their thrift and enterprise were well repaid, since they acquired not only a good property in the rural district east of Caldwell but also a home in the city. John Jancik, Sr., died in Caldwell in July, 1915, aged seventy-seven years, six months and twenty-eight days. His widow, Antonia Janick, is still living at Caldwell at the age of sixty-five. Their children were: John; Fannie, wife of Paul Lukas of Milam County; William, who died at Caldwell leaving a family; Charles, a business man at Caldwell; Teresa, wife of Frank Kristof, a farmer near Caldwell; Mary, now deceased, who married William Zalobny and left two children; and Frank, of Caldwell.

Mr. John Jancik was reared in Burleson County, gained a limited education in the country schools, and lived with his parents on the farm until he was sixteen. He then came into Caldwell and found employment in a lumber yard. He afterwards for two years worked for W. F. Gay & Company, a liquor firm, and after his marriage engaged in the retail liquor business for himself. This was his line for about sixteen years, and one year of that was spent as clerk for Womble, Jenkins & Jenkins. In 1907 Mr. Jancik gave up the saloon business and engaged in the grocery and hardware trade. He owns the building in which his large stock is carried, so divided as to make a double store, and he is regarded as one of the principal merchants of Caldwell.

A few years ago Mr. Jancik helped to promote the Caldwell National Bank, of which he was a director for about seven years. He also helped to organize and build the opera house in Caldwell, and he has also contributed two dwelling houses to the town, his own home being one of the best there, a large roomy house, surrounded by wide lawns, and making a picture of cleanliness and attractive comfort.

He has never worked in politics except for his friends and has held no public office except that of school trustee, a position he is still filling. He is a democrat, a member of the S. P. J. S. T. and the C. S. P., Bohemian orders which are popular among his countrymen, and is also affiliated with the Woodmen of the World and the Burleson County Home Circle.

At Caldwell April 15, 1890, Mr. Jancik married Miss Frances Skrivanek. The Skrivaneks came from the same part of Moravia as the Janciks. Her father, Frank Skrivanek, was a farmer, and married Mrs. Teresa (Masik) Wunderlich. The Skrivanek children were: Mrs. Jancik, Mrs. Antonio Dusek, Mrs. Stannie Rippel, Mrs. Winnie Dusek, Mrs. Lillie Shiller, Rosa, Frank and Annie. Six children have been born into the home of Mr. and Mrs. Jancik: Lottie, wife of E. S. Dusek, who is connected with the Caldwell National Bank; Ella May, who died when eighteen months old; John William; Alvin Frank; Olga and Robert Lee.

Casper Landolt. Much of the important history of the flourishing little town of Somerville may be told incidental to the activities of Casper Landolt, who in 1891 settled at what is now Somerville and had soon made himself known as the pioneer truck grower in that locality. He first purchased a hundred acres of timberland, cleared it and began raising something besides the staple crops of corn and cotton, specializing in sweet potatoes, cabbage and tomatoes. He was really the first man in that locality to grow anything in the way of crop of an extensive scale, and even the great staple of cotton was given more attention by him than by most of the farmers then living in the community.

Somerville at the time Mr. Landolt came, had but five small houses scattered around the depot, with all the rest of the site woodland. The townsite proper embraced about two blocks square on each side of the railroad, and it had been platted by the Gulf, Colorado & Santa Fe Railway some years before Mr. Landolt arrived.

The Santa Fe acquired its land from a tract of 8,000 acres in the Hardeman and other leagues formerly owned by Messrs. Pennington and Snyder. It was on a part of the Santa Fe holdings that the town of Somerville stands. The Lastly League faced the Hardeman League, the line being the stake in front of both, and Mr. Landolt purchased his small tract out of that league from Pennington and Snyder. Besides his original 100 acres he bought another 100 of James Wishard and still other lands from the railroad company. Of his original 100 acres all of it has come into the corporation and forms a part of the residence portion of the town, while other purchases of land have also been platted as additions.

Somerville is made up of the original townsite, platted by the Santa Fe Railway Company, and of the Alford addition, the additions of Tom Watson and J. W. Lauderdale, the Oak Hill addition laid out by Charles

Parks, the Thomas Ralph addition and the additions of Rufus Going, W. A. and J. R. Lyon, W. A. Lyon and George L. Edwards.

In addition to the above Mr. Landolt himself platted eleven additions to the town, embracing altogether 233 acres. His first addition was laid off by January 1, 1897; the second in the same year; the third in 1899; the fourth in 1900; the fifth in 1902; the sixth and seventh in 1903; the eighth a year or so later; the ninth in March, 1907, the tenth in May, 1911. What is known as the Brenham Addition, platted in 1907, also belongs to Mr. Landolt, and every lot in it was a corner lot. All the others carry the name of C. Landolt according to the number of the addition.

With the location of the railroad division at Somerville the town advanced rapidly and for the first ten years its growth was somewhat phenomenal. The first store was put up by Mr. Gabert, confectionery being his chief stock. In 1895 a real mercantile establishment was brought in by W. A. Lyon, and Casper Landolt put in the second one, carrying groceries, drugs and also having an ice cream and confectionery parlor. Charles Parks established the first dry goods store, and these pioneer stores were all located where the business portion of the town still is. The first brick building was erected by Landolt, Havecotte & McCoy, a row of brick structures built in 1903 and still forming the main portion of the business center.

Mr. Landolt from the beginning has been an active factor in the material development of Somerville, having erected some sixty buildings of various kinds, and has been the chief individual contributor to the upbuilding of the town in that way. He is still the largest property owner and taxpayer.

He was also one of the first school trustees before the Somerville School District was separately laid off, and after that district was formed and bonds issued to build a $10,000 school house he was elected district assessor and collector, and served so for many years, finally resigning the office in order to get rid of the responsibility. He was also the first president of the Bank of Somerville, which he assisted in organizing, but later he resigned that position also. When the town was incorporated he was elected the first mayor, and after serving a term declined to run again, and that ended his official participation in local affairs.

In the town of Neffels, Canton Glaris, Switzerland, Casper Landolt was born August 24, 1851. His father, Casper Antone Landolt was born September 22, 1822, and the mother, who was of German stock and whose maiden name was Elizabeth Feldman, was born in Neffels December 11, 1829. Grandfather Landolt was also a native of Switzerland and a farmer. The Landolt family arrived in America March 24, 1854. The father was a cooper and brewer by trade, and after landing at New Orleans he moved to Louisville, Kentucky, where he followed his trade, and for a time owned a small brewery in Elizabethtown, Kentucky, where he died in 1865. He left a family comprising Casper, William, Joseph and Lizzie, the last two now deceased. Joseph left a large family in Columbia, South Carolina, while Lizzie died in Cincinnati, Ohio. The widow Landolt married for her second husband Jacob Kurtz, and for her third husband Joseph Recks, and she died in Houston and is buried in Somerville.

Casper Landolt acquired his early education principally in night schools. By working during the day he learned the painter's trade in Newport, Kentucky, and in time became very proficient with his services much in demand as a house painter and decorator. Much of this skill was due to the supervision and direction of his employer, George

Teichmoeller. After leaving Mr. Teichmoeller's employ he engaged in contracting for himself, and in 1878 he moved from Newport, Kentucky, to the old community of Cottelsville in St. Charles County, Missouri, where for about a dozen years he followed the painter's trade.

On coming to Texas and locating at Somerville he had a desire to get away from his trade and engage in something more agreeable to his tastes at that age. He therefore experimented with the trucking industry and was soon well established in the business. He kept up trucking as his regular business for a number of years after he had begun improving and developing the city, but made his last crop about 1905. His principal business connection at present is as partner in R. M. McCoy & Company, operating a feed store.

Ever since reaching his majority Mr. Landolt has been a democrat, but his chief work has been as a voter. He is affiliated with the Lodge and Royal Arch Chapter of Masonry at Somerville, has passed all the chairs in Somerville Lodge of the Independent Order of Odd Fellows, is past consul in the Woodmen of the World, and also affiliated with the Knights of Pythias. His church was the Catholic.

At Newport, Kentucky, October 5, 1875, Mr. Landolt married Miss Annie M. Sauer, a daughter of Frank and Louise Sauer. Her father was born September 19, 1823, in Scheinheim by Schaffenberg, Kingdom of Bavaria. He came to America in 1846, while his wife, whose maiden name was Louise Busch, came over in 1849. Their children were: Henry and Louis, both deceased; Mary Schoo of Newport, Kentucky; Mrs. Frances Burding of Cincinnati, and Mrs. Landolt. Mrs. Landolt, after nearly forty years of married life, died July 26, 1914. Her children were: Casper Jacob, who died at the age of thirty-two unmarried; Elizabeth, wife of Henry Millard of Houston; Miss Annie of Somerville; Rosa, wife of Otto Seeger of Somerville; Caroline, wife of Charles Balke, Jr., of Somerville; Clara, who died in young womanhood; and Wilkie J., the youngest, still at home. Mr. Landolt also has twelve surviving grandchildren.

Robert A. Brantley. That type of public spirit which is always ready to sacrifice the individual for the community interests, and which is one of the best qualities in any citizenship, is well exemplified at Somerville by Robert A. Brantley. He is a young business man, vigorous and versatile, with much pride in his home town, and is usually consulted and advised with when Somerville's welfare is at stake.

His home has been at Somerville since 1897, a year which practically marked the beginning of the town as an organized community. It was as a railroad man that he first came to this locality, but left a clerkship in the station department to enter merchandising, and it is as a merchant that he is best known. He established a grocery stock and for a number of years has sold that class of merchandise to a constantly expanding trade. His citizenship has been exemplified in many ways. He was one of the first board of commissioners after the incorporation of the town, and helped to put the town's affairs on a business basis. He also used his influence in organizing the school district. He has also actively promoted an industry in the mining of Fuller's earth. Mr. Brantley has been active in organizing all the lodges represented at Somerville except that of the Odd Fellows, is past chancellor of the Knights of Pythias and represented his home lodge in the grand organization. He has also been a factor in county politics, has attended party conventions and during the Bailey fight was a strong supporter of the junior senator.

Robert A. Brantley was born in Brazos County, Texas, March 9,

1872. He grew up in his home town of Bryan, where he attended the public schools and also the Agricultural and Mechanical College for two years. He has never married. When a little past sixteen years of age he started out to win the battle of life by his own efforts. He was first in the express business, employed in various minor services by the local company, and then went to railroading with the Santa Fe at Milano, and before going to Somerville was in the clerical department in different places on the Texas system. His father, Robert A. Brantley, Sr., was born in Georgia in 1839 and belonged to a slaveholding family of that state. One of his brothers, Edward Brantley, settled in Texas between Houston and Galveston, and left some descendants at the time of his death. Robert A. Brantley had a very meager education so far as schools were concerned, and gained most of his education by his own efforts. He came to Texas alone in 1859 and located in Montgomery County, where some relatives lived. From there he enlisted in Hood's Brigade at the opening of the war and was sent into Virginia, and remained with his command in its important engagements until he was captured at Gettysburg. He remained in the Federal military prison at Fort Delaware until the close of the war. At one time he made an effort to escape from prison by trying to swim the Chesapeake Bay, but was apprehended before he got away. He fought in the ranks, and besides the ordinary hardships of a soldier's career he suffered wounds from Federal bullets. After being released from a Northern prison he returned to Texas, and soon afterwards settled in Brazos County, where for many years he was a merchant at Bryan. He finally became an organizer for the Ancient Order of United Workmen and represented its interests over the state, and associated with Mr. Hassell organized nearly all the lodges of that order in the state. Since giving up lodge work he lived quietly at Somerville and was associated in business with his son, Robert, until his death. He was a very close student of the Bible, and once wrote a treatise which he called the "Key to the Bible," a manuscript which is still preserved. He was an active member of the Methodist Church.

In Brazos County Robert A. Brantley, Sr., married Miss Anna Wilson. Her father, Thomas Wilson, a native of Alabama, came to Texas about the time the state was admitted to the Union. He served as a soldier in the Mexican war from 1846 to 1848 and then spent a number of years as a farmer near old Washington, and died while serving in the Confederate army stationed at Galveston. Thomas Wilson married Patience Edwards of Prattville, Alabama. She is still living as Mrs. Robert Alexander of Chappel Hill, widow of the pioneer Texan, Parson Alexander. Mrs. Robert A. Brantley, Sr., died January 4, 1916. Her children were: Helen, who died as the wife of B. F. Gafford at Rogers, Texas, leaving two children; Robert A., Jr.; Thomas Wilson, who died at the age of twenty-one; and Mary, wife of B. P. Wellborn, who is an engineer and has his home at Longview, Texas.

NATHANAEL WILSON has an enviable record as an educator in this section of the state. He has been identified with the public schools hereabouts since 1895, and few have done more to advance the local standards of education than has this man. Mr. Wilson is a native son of Georgia, born in Buchanan, Haralson County, on May 11, 1871, and he is the son of William J. and Mary Adeline (Ayres) Wilson and the grandson of John J. and Elizabeth (Phillips) Wilson, all native Georgians.

John J. Wilson reared a large family. Three of his sons served as Confederate soldiers, and he died in Haralson County, where he had passed his entire life. His son, William J. Wilson, father of the subject, was born in Polk County, Georgia, and spent much of his life in that county, and all of it in his native state. His wife, Adeline Ayres, was a daughter of Austin Ayres, of an old established Georgia family. Mrs. Wilson died the mother of six children. Nathanael was the eldest. Nancy, now deceased, was the wife of W. E. Gilbert of Georgia. Kenneth A. is a farmer of Haralson County. Ida married B. F. Williams; Arabella is the wife of a Mr. Jeffries, and Viola married a Mr. McCollum.

The early education of Nathanael Wilson was gained in the public schools of his native community, followed by attendance at Piedmont Institute in Rockmart, Georgia. He began teaching in his native county when he was twenty years old, at a time when Webster's old blue-backed speller was still in use, and even in that early day did he change from the old "a-b-c" method to the method now in use in the instruction of reading. Mr. Wilson did rural school work for eleven years, teaching four years in his native county and then coming to Texas.

Beginning his school work in Texas, Mr. Wilson taught in Hunt County, not far from Greenville, and after a year he moved out toward the frontier, and did the remainder of his country school work in Montague County. He was assistant at St. Jo one year while in Montague County, and then was elected superintendent of schools at Lot, Falls County. He spent a year there, and was in that time instrumental in bringing the change in the standing of the school from a common school district to an independent school district, brought about the sale of a bond issue for new buildings, and saw the house erected. He next went to Mt. Calm, Hill County, where he passed another busy year in the development of a course of study, placing the schools in a good, healthy condition before his year was ended. His next move took him to Sam and Will Moore Institute at Moulton, where he spent a year, and then took the superintendency of the Meridian schools, after which he went to Morgan, then to Bells, Grayson County, and then came to Yorktown, spending a year's time in each named place.

The condition of the schools in Yorktown were not particularly inviting in 1909 when Mr. Wilson assumed charge of the system. The white school was an old frame building of five rooms, and five white and one colored teacher did the work of the city. In the first year was started the movement for a new school building. Bonds were issued and in 1910 a new brick school house of nine rooms and an adequate auditorium was completed. The cost of the building and its fittings was $22,500, and it was completed in six months after the formal laying of the corner stone, an event that took place under the auspices of the Masonic fraternity, Rev. C. H. Dobbs of Gonzales making the principal address of the day.

In 1909 the colored school was a shack somewhat removed from the center of education, and in time this gave way to a new building. Not long, in fact, after the dedication of the new Central High School. The colored school now has two rooms and an enrollment above 200. It is in charge of a negro principal with numerous diplomas showing him a graduate of several schools, while his assistant is a product of the Negro Normal at Prairie View.

In 1909 the Yorktown high school had but a single teacher. Since then it has been developed into a school of the second class, and its management has in mind its further development into a high school of the first class. During the years of Mr. Wilson's incumbency the attendance has increased 150 per cent, and the attendance in the entire school has increased about 70 per cent. In 1909 there were

210 enrolled, while in 1915 it was 345. The course of study was brought to conform to the course prescribed by the state in this class of school, and the school is now affiliated with the A. & M. College and with the state normals of Texas. In 1910 the high school began graduating its pupils with formal exercises and the issuing of diplomas, and since then there have been graduated twenty-six pupils in all. A laboratory equipment worth $200 and a library of 600 volumes are a part of the facilities now available to the pupils. The spirit of the school is of the finest, and the needs of the district are being taken care of by the management as rapidly and promptly as financial conditions will warrant.

Mr. Wilson was married in Jack County, Texas, to Miss Lula Addie Raines, a daughter of Judge Cadwell W. Raines, of Austin. The judge was a native of Georgia who came to Texas before the Civil war and served as a Confederate soldier. He married Mary Bowden, taught school for a while, spent some time as a newspaper man, was county judge of both Wood and Van Zandt counties, and was appointed state librarian by Governor Hogg. His children are Lela, the wife of Rev. D. W. Gardner; Mrs. Wilson, born November 9, 1871; Caddie, the wife of R. L. Scarborough, and Dr. S. W. Raines, who is next older than Mrs. Scarborough.

Five children have been born to Mr and Mrs. Wilson. They are Bowden Walton, Raines Ayres, Gladys Carmen, Gordon Winston and Lulu Kae.

Mr. Wilson is a member of the Baptist Church and his fraternal connections are with the Woodmen of the World and the Masons. He is secretary of the blue lodge of Yorktown.

JESSE M. BURFORD, M. D. It has been within the compass of Doctor Burford's ability and ambition to achieve distinctive prestige as one of the representative physicians and surgeons of his native state and he is a scion of a family whose name has been worthily linked with the annals of Texas history for more than sixty years. He is engaged in the successful practice of his profession at Independence, Washington County, and as one of the leading physicians and public-spirited citizens of this county he is properly accorded specific recognition in this history of Texas and its people.

At the old family homestead situated eleven miles northwest of Columbus, Colorado County, Texas, amidst the rock hills along the Colorado River, Dr. Jesse M. Burford was born on the 15th of September, 1861. His father, Francis Marion Burford, who became widely and familiarly known as "Dick" Burford, was born in Bolivar County, Tennessee, on the 5th of May, 1826, and in his native state he acquired a limited common school education,—the best available under the conditions and exigencies of time and place. He began his independent career as a slaveholding farmer in his native state, and upon coming to Texas, in 1850, he brought with him his contingent of slaves, to the number of which he added by later purchases, his retention of slave property having continued until his vassals were freed by the Emancipation Proclamation issued by President Lincoln, in 1865. At the beginning of the Civil war he was the owner of a productive cotton and corn plantation in Colorado County, and was prominent and influential in connection with the political, civic and religious affairs of his county. He was one of the uncompromising democrats who advocated without reservation the secession of the Southern States, and while he five times tendered his services as a soldier of the Confederacy he was on each occasion assigned to the charge of the commissary maintained in his section for the maintenance of the Confederate troops in the field. Finally he made his sixth attempt to enlist, and on this occasion he realized his ambition. More than this, he was commissioned major, but when he had proceeded with his command as far as the Mississippi River the war came to a close and he was denied the opportunity for battling for the cause in the justice of which he firmly believed. He made great financial sacrifices in connection with the great conflict that left the South with prostrate industries and other unmerited burdens, and though he found himself in debt to the amount of $12,000 and without a dollar to apply in the liquidation of this formidable indebtedness, he had the vigor, self-reliance and courage that counted no obstacle as insuperable, with the result that he gallantly set himself to the task of recouping his fortunes. Through the medium of his farm he so applied his energies and business ability that within the remaining ten years of his life he accumulated $30,000, besides freeing himself from debt and providing his children with excellent educational advantages. Though he was possessed of admirable business acumen and constructive ability, the judgment of "Dick" Burford was frequently made subservient to his generosity and kindliness, with the result that he became sponsor for the financial obligations of others and through lending his name in such connection was compelled to pay about $40,000 from which he had received no return. He was one of the charter members of the lodge of Ancient Free & Accepted Masons at Osage, Colorado County, and his entire life was guided and governed by his unfaltering Christian faith. He was a most zealous member of the Methodist Episcopal Church, South, as was also his wife, and he assisted liberally in the erection of two or more churches, besides having served as steward of the church at Osage.

In Tennessee was solemnized the marriage of Major Burford to Miss Cordelia Ann Shaw, daughter of Thomas T. Shaw, an extensive planter and slaveholder of that state. Mrs. Burford was summoned to the life eternal in 1889 and her remains rest in the cemetery at Osage, beside those of her husband, whose death occurred in 1877. Of their children the eldest was William T., who was sheriff of Colorado County at the time of his death; Mrs. Cyrus O. Weller died in the city of Austin; Dr. John E. is a representative physician engaged in practice at Patterson, Waller County; Robert F. was a prosperous farmer near Osage, Colorado County, at the time of his death; Dr. Jesse M., of this review, was the next in order of birth; Mrs. Annie Townsend maintains her home in the city of San Antonio; Mrs. Sallie Bock resides at Weimar, Colorado County; and Mrs. Belle Odom is a resident of the city of Dallas.

Francis Marion Burford was a son of Dr. Jonathan and Euphemia (Chafin) Burford. His father was born in one of the northern counties of Ireland and upon coming to the United States he first located in Pennsylvania, whence he finally removed to Tennessee, where he passed the remainder of his life. He there became the owner of a substantial landed estate and a large number of slaves, and he not only served effectively and earnestly as a physician but also became a clergyman of the Methodist Church, so that he was able to minister alike to the physical and spiritual needs of his fellow men. His first wife, Euphemia, bore him eleven children and by his second marriage he became the father of four children. Among the children of the first union were: Dr. Jesse, Dr. Jonathan E., Mrs. Rebecca Grace, Mrs. Elizabeth Tuggle, Mrs. Puss Norment, Francis Marion ("Dick"), Mrs. Euphemia Shaw, Mrs. Sallie Simmons, and John David, the last mentioned having been a noted spy in the service of the Confederacy during the Civil war.

All but three of the children just named came to Texas, and three of the four children of the second marriage likewise became residents of the Lone Star State. For his second wife Dr. Jonathan Burford wedded Mrs. Harry Yates, and of their children the youngest, Harriet, died in infancy. The three who attained to maturity and became residents of Texas were Andrew Linn Burford, familiarly known as "Step" Burford, R. Phillip, and Mrs. Mary Matthews. From the data given in the foregoing paragraphs it will be discerned that the Burford family has given a number of representatives to the medical profession, and in this domain the prestige of the name is being effectually upheld by him to whom this sketch is dedicated.

Dr. Jesse M. Burford was reared to adult age on the old homestead farm which was the place of his birth, and after due preliminary discipline he entered the Texas Agricultural & Mechanical College, in which he was graduated as a member of the class of 1882. In consonance with his ambition and well formulated plans he soon began the study of medicine, and in 1887 he was graduated in the medical department of Tulane University, in the city of New Orleans. After receiving from this fine Southern institution his well earned degree of Doctor of Medicine he returned to his native state and engaged in the practice of his profession at Moravia, Lavaca County, where he remained five years. He then, in 1892, removed to Independence, Washington County, where he has since continued in active and successful general practice, where he succeeded to the business of the honored pioneer physician, Dr. H. W. Waters, who was killed by an accident, in January, 1894. Doctor Burford controls a practice that extends throughout a wide area of country and his efficient and unselfish service in the community has given him inviolable vantage-place in popular confidence and appreciative esteem. He keeps in line with the advances made in medical and surgical science and by his character and achievement has lent dignity and honor to the profession of his choice. He is identified with the Texas State Medical Society and the Washington County Medical Society, and he subordinates all other interests to the demands of his exacting profession, through which he has won merited material prosperity.

Dr. Burford accords unswerving allegiance to the democratic party and is liberal and progressive in his attitude as a citizen. Though he has not desired or held political office he has been influential in local politics and has been on numerous occasions a delegate to the democratic county conventions in his county. He is affiliated with the Benevolent and Protective Order of Elks.

In the year 1891 Doctor Burford wedded Miss Pattie McLeary, a daughter of Dr. W. T. McLeary, who was a sterling pioneer and prominent physician of Colorado County. Mrs. Burford died without leaving any children who attained to years of maturity, and on the 24th of June, 1903, was solemnized the marriage of the Doctor to Miss Kate Clay, who was born and reared in Washington County, a daughter of Atreus M. and Pauline (Thornhill) Clay, representatives of sterling pioneer families of this section of Texas, where both families were founded in 1840, the paternal grandfather of Mrs. Burford having been Tacitus Clay, who came to Texas from the state of Kentucky. Atreus M. Clay was a valiant soldier of the Confederacy in the Civil war and he maintained his home in Washington County during his entire life. He was a citizen of much influence in the community and served for a number of years as postmaster at Independence. Mr. Clay first wedded Miss Sue Robertson, who died without issue. By his marriage to Miss Pauline Thornhill were born the following named children:

Mrs. Lela Watson, of Newark, New York; Mrs. Alice Watson, of Temple, Texas; Thomas T., a resident of Independence, Texas; Mrs. Kate Burford, wife of the subject of this review; Nestor A., of Navasota, Grimes County; Mrs. E. O. Routt, of Chapel Hill, Washington County; and Tacitus W., of Independence, this county. Doctor and Mrs. Burford have one child, Catherine Clay Burford.

William Bauer. The president and manager of the Burton Cotton Oil Company, William Bauer has lived in Texas since 1867. He came to the United States in 1864. His early experiences were in the baking trade in the city of Philadelphia. When he came to Texas he was practically without funds. In the scale of progress he has been gradually ascending, impelled by exceptional vigor and industry and a thorough talent for business affairs. He is now one of the recognized leaders in Washington County's business and civic circles.

A native of Germany, he was born in the Kingdom of Wurtemberg in the city of Tuebingen, on February 18, 1844. His parents were William A. and Margaret (Hahn) Bauer and his mother died in Germany. Of eight children five are living, and four are married and have families. William A. Bauer was a miller by trade, and on bringing his children to the United States located in Pennsylvania, but died some years later in Louisville, Kentucky. The Bauer family sailed from Antwerp, Belgium, on a sailing vessel, and landed in New York after a voyage of seventy-eight days. There were no trans-Atlantic liners at that time, and many of the sailing vessels had almost intolerable conditions. This particular schooner was barnacled and keel-mossed, moved sluggishly under the best of winds, but on this trip was becalmed, and provisions ran short so that the passengers were confronted with famine.

Twenty years of age when he left his native land, William Bauer had secured the equivalent of a liberal education. He had been a member of a Latin class taught by the family pastor. He had also gained some knowledge of the baker's trade, and when he landed at Philadelphia a baker came around looking for a helper and he responded. He remained in that bakeshop practically the entire two years he was in the city. When the Civil war ended the return of the soldiers to their homes threw him out of employment, and he borrowed the money that brought him to Texas. His first stop was in Houston, where he found work as a carpenter, but in July of the same year, 1867, in company with his brother Charles, he left Houston because of the yellow fever epidemic, and came out to Fayette County and found work as a carpenter at Warrenton. In that county he remained until 1871, and then hired to Mr. Weyand, a large planter near Nassau. After working for him about two years he went east to Louisville, Kentucky, for several months and conducted a bakery. Selling out he returned to Texas and henceforward has been permanently identified with this state.

For another two years he remained an employee of Mr. Weyand, and he then came to Burton in Washington County and opened a lumber yard. This was in 1874, and he then, in company with his brother, established another lumber yard at Ledbetter. This was sold after two years, and on returning to Burton he engaged in merchandising. For upwards of forty years his business activities have covered a gradually enlarging field. He entered the ginning business and succeeded to the ownership of the first gin built at Burton. For about a dozen years he and his brother, Charles, conducted a general store and cotton gin, and he also bought the second gin in the town. In 1900 Mr. Bauer converted one of the gins into a cotton oil mill with a twenty-ton capacity.

He formed a stock company, of which he was made president and manager, and is also the principal stockholder. The Burton Cotton Oil Company is perhaps the most important industry in Burton, and Mr. Bauer's name is most closely associated with this institution.

For many years his operations have also extended to the buying and selling of farm lands. When he first took up that line of business the average of prices was $7 an acre for raw land and between $18 and $20 an acre for farming land. He has himself been instrumental in introducing many solid and substantial agricultural settlers in this section of Washington County and has witnessed a great rise in agricultural values. Mr. Bauer helped to organize and is one of the directors of the Burton State Bank. He has helped the growth of Burton as a town, having erected a store building and his own residence, which is one of the best in the village.

While living in Washington County Mr. Bauer took out citizenship papers. On choosing a political party he identified himself with the republicans. He made this selection on his own judgment, and in politics, religion and all other matters, he has held to the principle that he was entitled to his own opinions and has always conceded the same right to others. He never filled a public position, had no desire for politics in that sense, although at different times he was urged to make the race for county commissioner. He is a member of no church, and believes that a man may live up to the best standards of morality and good citizenship without active church affiliations. Fraternally he is a member of the Sons of Hermann and also belongs to the Order of Cardinals.

In Ledbetter in Fayette County in September, 1877, Mr. Bauer married Miss Annie Wendorf, a daughter of Frederick and Doris (Hartz) Wendorf. Both her parents were born in Kiel, Germany, and her father, who was a carpenter and farmer, came to Texas before the Civil war and died in Carmine. Mrs. Bauer's sister and two brothers are Mrs. Lena Blum, Henry and Adolph. The two other children are now deceased. To the marriage of Mr. and Mrs. Bauer were born three sons. William, of Pflugeville, Texas, married Nora Homeyer and their daughter is named Mary B. Alexander, who lives in Belton, Texas, is married and has three children named Will, Annie Louise and Bud. Felix, the youngest son, lives at Robbstown, Texas.

THOMAS WATSON. The enterprise of Thomas Watson has been responsible for giving the village of Burton in Washington County a department store out of all proportion to the size of the town. Mr. Watson is a very capable business man, a merchant of long training and experience, and his success may be ascribed to the fact that he has devoted himself to practically one calling since early youth.

The Watson family came into Texas in 1856. Its founders were three brothers, Branch A., Armsted and Jacob Watson. They came across the country overland from their native county of Prince Edward, Virginia. Branch A. Watson was born June 20, 1836, and was the son of a planter, James Watson. He belonged to a family of means, and in consequence received a liberal education, having finished his course and taken a diploma from the Hampden Sidney College of Virginia. In his early youth he taught school, and on coming to Texas he located at Old Washington, the former capital of the republic, and there resumed his work as a teacher. He brought with him several slaves from old Virginia, and he employed their services in clearing up land and opening a farm. Not many years afterward he entered the Confederate army as a private in Colonel Giddings' Regiment, and was connected with the Trans-Mississippi department during the war.

After the war Branch A. Watson moved to what was known as Union Hill in Washington County and established a store. The war had freed his slaves, and he felt that he could have no further profitable use out of his land. At Union Hill he continued to sell goods to the surrounding rural community until the Houston and Texas Central Railroad was built through the county and the new station of Burton established. The village of Union Hill then migrated bodily to Burton, and Mr. Watson moved his store to the new location. From 1875 he was out of business until 1884, but then continued merchandising in this locality until his death in 1906.

In early manhood Branch A. Watson cast in his lot with the democratic party and remained with it to the end. For ten years he served as justice of the peace, and was always interested in local affairs. He was a member of the Masonic Order and also of the Methodist Church. At the town of Old Washington in 1858 he married Miss Ann Gay, daughter of Thomas and Eleanor (Hope) Gay. Thomas Gay was one of the original settlers of Texas, having come as a member of one of the Austin colony. By profession he was a surveyor, but spent much of his life on a farm and ranch. Mrs. Branch A. Watson is still living. Her children were: Joseph W., who died in December, 1914; Thomas; Frank, who died leaving two children by his wife Viola Leonard; and Quintus Ultimus, who is well known all over the state as a lawyer and public leader, whose home is in Giddings, and who served as president pro tem of the Texas State Senate and was acting governor during the absence of Governor Colquitt from the state.

A member of this very substantial family, Thomas Watson, was born August 17, 1861, at Old Washington. He received all the education necessary for a business career, and at the age of sixteen left the Hermann Seminary, where he had been pursuing his studies, and went to work in H. Knittel's store at Burton. Since then for a period of almost forty years he has never at any time been out of merchandising. He and his father jointly purchased the store of H. Knittel, and the firm name then became Thomas Watson & Company. He has always managed the business under his direct supervision, and it is now a store of metropolitan proportions, employing four buildings, with 140 feet of frontage, and the stock is well arranged in various departments so that it is a veritable department store in the city sense of that term.

However, he has from time to time taken upon his shoulders other responsibilities. He is now manager of the Burton Cotton Oil Company and is vice president of the Burton State Bank. He was one of the three men who started and installed the Telephone Exchange at Burton, and for a dozen years he served as one of the local school trustees. His interest in politics is confined to voting for the principles and candidates which he believes are most deserving of his support. Since the age of twenty-one he has been affiliated with the Masonic Order, and for three years was master of his lodge. While he believes in the work of the church, he is not a member, but gives liberally toward the organization which appeals to him most strongly and to other denominations as well.

While living in Burton Mr. Watson married Miss Emma Knittel, a daughter of Hermann Knittel, whose career is sketched in following paragraphs. Their children are: Branch C., who was educated at Toby's Academy in Waco and is now bookkeeper in his father's business and married Clara Von Bluecher; John F., also a graduate of Toby's Academy who is associated with his father, married Louise Fischer, and their children are Allyne, Lucile and Fischer; Louise is the wife of H. H. Fischer of Burton, and their two children are named Nevilee and Elwood; Eleanor Gay Watson died when a young woman of sixteen.

Hermann Knittel, the father of Mrs. Thomas Watson of Burton, was in his time one of the splendidly vigorous characters and upright citizens of Washington County. He was born in Silesia near the Riesengebirge December 4, 1835, and died at Brenham, Texas, March 4, 1899. He had only a common school education, and was employed for a time as a clerk in his native village. In 1852 with his widowed mother, Christina Knittel, he came to America, landing in Galveston, and thence going by wagon and ox teams to Brenham. His mother's first husband was a Seidel, and people of that name were living around Brenham and Hermann Knittel worked among them for a time at wages. When about twenty years of age he married and started his independent career as a trader with ox teams from Houston to various points in Washington County. That was his regular business for a number of years, though later he became identified with farming and other lines of business.

At the outbreak of the war he gave up his trading enterprise to enter the Confederate army. He was a member of Capt. Robert Voight's Company, General Waul's Legion, Hood's Brigade. He saw a great deal of active campaigning and fighting, and participated in the engagement of Holly Springs, Grenada, siege of Vicksburg, Yazoo City, and at the last named place was taken prisoner and was confined for six months in the Federal prison on Johnson's Island in Lake Erie. After being released, he rejoined his command, was made a lieutenant and continued in the war until the close. He came home without wounds.

After the war he took up merchandising in Berlin, Washington County. He was too poor himself to buy a stock of goods, and was furnished a supply by his brother. He remained at Berlin until 1871, and then moved to Burton and continued a merchant here for many years. He was prosperous and much of his surplus revenue was invested in lands around Burton and he did much to improve them, and was a strong factor in the development of the village of Burton. He was especially fond of live stock, and had some very fine horses on his ranch.

In 1884 he was elected on the democratic ticket to the Texas State Senate, and was reelected to that party. He was one of the strong members of the legislature during that time, and among other committees he served on the finance committee and was chairman of the committee of retrenchment and reform and contingent expenses. He was a believer in fraternalism, attained high rank in the Masonic Order, was long identified with the Independent Order of Odd Fellows, and also belonged to Washington Camp of the United Confederate Veterans. About two years before his death he gave up his business affairs in Burton and moved to Brenham. He was a member of the Lutheran Church.

On August 28, 1857, Hermann Knittel married Miss Johanna Heinecke. Her family came from Brunswick, Germany. Mrs. Knittel is still living and celebrated her seventy-fifth birthday on December 18, 1915. The children in the family were: Ida, widow of William H. Hons of Burton, and she has one daughter; Estelle, the wife of Harry Korthauer; Emma, wife of Thomas Watson of Burton; Hermann, a merchant of Burton; Ernest; Alvina, who is the wife of Max Eversberg and lives at Fort Worth; Charles, of Fort Worth; George, of Burton.

August and Otto H. Riedel. One of the old business houses of Yorktown, which has always borne a high reputation in commercial circles, is that of M. Riedel & Sons, which was established in 1885. Its founder has now passed away, but its reputation for straightforward and honorable dealing still continues under the management of his sons, August and Otto H. Riedel, who are not only well known in business life but have served their community faithfully and well both as citizens and as public officials.

The name of Riedel has been identified with South Texas since 1848, having been introduced here by Moritz Ferdinand Riedel, the grandfather of the brothers. He was born August 29, 1809, in the town of Kahla, Saxony, Germany, where he learned the baker's trade and married Jane Heinrich, and following on the heels of the German Revolution they departed from the Fatherland on a sailing vessel which required many weeks to carry them to their destination across the ocean. The family remained at Indianola for a short time, then removed to Victoria, and soon came on to Dewitt County, making their settlement two miles from Yorktown. One of Mr. Riedel's first labors was to get ready to do mill work, in accordance with which he built a dam across Smith Creek and erected the first gristmill here. However, with the washing out of the dam, the mill was moved by the sons to Yorktown and converted into a steam mill, and for years continued to be operated by them. Moritz Ferdinand Riedel died August 29, 1862, and his widow April 15, 1874, and both were laid to rest in the Yorktown Cemetery. Their children were as follows: Moritz Ferdinand, the father of August and Otto H. Riedel; Carl, who has passed his entire life at old Riedelville, now Gillette, where he still makes his home; Caroline, who is the widow of Charles W. Nau, of Yorktown; Franz, who died in 1865, unmarried; Adolph, who was a soldier in the Union army during the Civil war and subsequently a farmer of Dewitt county, dying near Nordheim and leaving several children; Fritz, who built the first brewery at Yorktown, subsequently engaged in the retail liquor business, proved himself one of the substantial builders of the town, and left a numerous posterity at his death; Ernst, who was a Confederate soldier during the war between the states, and subsequently passed his life as a farmer near Yorktown, living a private life, as did most of his brothers; Joseph, who was engaged in ginning at Yorktown throughout his career and was married but had no children; and Gus, the youngest, who was also for many years a ginner but is now one of the leading farmers of Karnes County.

Moritz Ferdinand Riedel was born December 4, 1832, in Saxony, Germany, and in early years displayed decided musical talent, learning to play the violin and cornet. In after years he played these instruments at Yorktown, and was the organizer of the first band here. For several years after his marriage he was engaged in farming, but at that time the Civil war came on and he entered the Confederate service as a musician. He was captured at Arkansas Post and held in a military prison until being paroled, following which he remained in the North until the close of the war. On his return home Mr. Riedel engaged in mercantile lines with his brother-in-law, Charles W. Nau, who died in 1882, and he then continued with Mrs. Nau until 1887, Mr. Riedel's sons subsequently purchasing her interests from his estate. From that time to the present the business has been conducted as M. Riedel & Sons, and Moritz F. Riedel remained as an active factor in its management until his death, June 30, 1912. In politics, Mr. Riedel was not a party man, although it is believed that he inclined toward republicanism. He was postmaster at Yorktown from 1883 until 1910, when

Aug. Riedel

Moritz Riedel

he was succeeded by Mr. Stark, and during this period did much to improve the service. He also served as one of the best mayors Yorktown ever had, and as a justice of the peace displayed his judicial capacity and ability in the adjustment of tangled affairs. A consistent churchman, he was one of the founders of the First Lutheran Church at Yorktown.

Mr. Riedel married Mrs. Sophie (Afflerbach) Scheffe, who was born near Berlin, Germany, September 23, 1827, and who died in 1905. By her first marriage she was the mother of one daughter: Caroline, who is now Mrs. Henry Jacobs. To Mr. and Mrs. Riedel there were born the following children: Emma, who is the wife of Louis Riedesel, of Nordheim; Hermann, who is corresponding secretary of the Annheuser Busch Brewing Company of St. Louis, Missouri, married Augusta Mueller; August; Richard, who died at the age of twenty-one years; Bertha, of Yorktown; and Otto H.

August Riedel, senior member of the firm of M. Riedel & Sons, is a native of Yorktown, born January 17, 1861. He was educated in the public schools here as was his brother, and as a youth learned the trade of wheelwright and conducted a shop until he was twenty-nine years of age. At that time, with his brother, Otto H., he entered his father's business, which they have continued to conduct since the elder man's demise. The general merchandise house changed to a drug house in 1876, and the old home of the business gave way to the new brick establishment in 1911. This modern structure is a two-story buff brick edifice ninety feet in depth, with a frontage of ninety-two feet, the main floor being devoted to the business of the firm, while the second floor is given over to offices and lodge and club rooms. The Riedel brothers have always been energetic and enterprising, prominent in business life and supporters of their community's best interests. They were among the promoters of the Yorktown Cotton Oil Mill, and both have served as city assessor and collector of Yorktown, as well as trustee of the school board, August having devoted some twenty years to that position. August Riedel is a member of the Woodmen of the World and the Independent Order of Odd Fellows, while Otto H. belongs to the Sons of Hermann and the Knights of Pythias.

August Riedel was married at Yorktown, November 4, 1882, to Miss Ida Heissig, daughter of Charles Henry Heissig, who came to Texas from Landsberg, Prussia, and at Yorktown kept stage headquarters for a time, his later years being passed in the management of a saloon, mercantile establishment and boarding house. Two children have been born to Mr. and Mrs. Riedel: Alfred, connected with the American Exchange National Bank, of Dallas, married Tempest Kingston; and Hendia, of Yorktown.

Otto H. Riedel was born at Yorktown, August 11, 1871, and was married November 6, 1893, to Miss Hendia Heissig, the sister of his brother's wife. Two children have come to them: Lelia and Wilfred.

F. W. E. Fischer. A vigorous pushing business man of Burton, Mr. Fischer has been identified with that community fully forty years. He is a merchant. Beginning with a capital of less than $100, he has built up an enterprise that might well be envied by many men whose fortunes were better at the start. His fortunes have been those of the prosperous little village, which had been founded only a few years before he identified himself with that locality. The town has helped make him successful and he in turn has given his influence and activity towards building up the community.

Ed Fischer, as he is most familiarly known, was born August 3,

1849, near Magdeburg in Saxony. His father, Henry Fischer, was a government forester. The maiden name of the mother was Minnie Simmon. They were the parents of five children: Rudolph, who is still in Germany; Minnie, who was the first born, married Ferdinand Jahn, a teacher, and she died in her native land; Henry, who died in the old country; Herman, who died in Brenham, Texas, leaving three daughters and two sons; and Ed, the youngest.

It was in 1870 that Mr. Ed Fischer came to Texas. His brother, Herman, had come to the state in 1865, and when joined by Ed was engaged in merchandising in Brenham. Ed Fischer acquired an education in the Volk Schule in his native locality, and learned the rectifier trade in a distillery, and also gained considerable knowledge of merchandising. He was twenty-one years of age when he left Germany, sailing from Bremen on a vessel bound for Galveston and landed after a voyage of four weeks. He went on to Brenham, where he worked for his brother for six months, and then took up a career entirely different from the lines of his previous experience. He was employed by the International & Great Northern Railway between Hearne and Longview in the bakery department, while that road between those points was being constructed. When he left the employ of the railway he established his home for a time in Mineola, working as a baker, and later followed the same employment in Tyler. He spent a month in Dallas, and then returned to Brenham where he was a clerk for his brother until 1875, when he looked for a new location.

When Mr. Fischer came to Burton it was with the intention of establishing a business of his own. With about seventy-five dollars in real cash, he installed a stock of groceries, liquors and a bakery. His first store was on the hill a block from where he finally located. Success came to him from the start. He is a man of genial manners, makes friends wherever he goes, and even now, after forty continuous years of merchandising, attends to his business with the snap and vim of a man many years his junior. In 1878 he moved to his present location, where he constructed a double wood building, using the front part for his store, while his family lived in the rear. The next stage of progress was indicated by the erection of a brick store building in 1900, a double store 50x80 feet, and for the past fifteen years he has conducted here a general merchandise business, with stock of hardware and groceries and a saloon. Mr. Fischer also owns stock in the Burton Cotton Oil Company, and in the Burton State Bank of which he is vice president.

A few years after coming to Texas Mr. Fischer became a naturalized citizen and gave his first presidential vote to a republican candidate. In recent years, however, he has supported democratic candidates. His only public service has been on the school board. He is a member of the Lutheran Church.

In Burton in May, 1878, he married Miss Louisa Reichmann, a daughter of Henry Reichmann. Mr. and Mrs. Fischer have the following children: Minnie, wife of Robert Wirren, of LaGrange, Texas, and their children are named Robert, Eddie and Karl; Herman, who is associated with his father, married Louise Watson; Eddie R. is also helping his father; Louise is the wife of John Watson; Busch is at home; and Mamie is the youngest of the family. Mr. Fischer is actively identified with the Sons of Hermann and was the first president of that order in Burton. Some years ago he erected as his home a commodious residence in the village and also owns a small farm near town.

Charles W. Homeyer. As a progressive citizen Washington County has no more useful member of the community than Charles W. Homeyer, who is perhaps best known in a business way as president and cashier of the Burton State Bank, in the organization of which he took a prominent part. Most of his life has been spent in the Burton locality, and for thirty years or more he has helped to uphold material prosperity and to carry the banner of progress in all things.

He was born near Burton December 11, 1855, and is a son of substantial early German colonists in this part of Texas. His father, William D. Homeyer, who was born in 1816 and died in 1896, was a native of Vinzlar, a small town in the Kingdom of Hanover, and the son of a farmer Henry Homeyer. The Homeyers in Hanover were landowners, and the old farm there is still owned by descendants of its earlier possessors. William D. Homeyer acquired a fair education, and had made some progress in farming before he left Germany.

It was in 1846 that he came with his first wife to Texas. His wife died at Buckhorn in Austin County, Texas, and had two children, who are deceased. William D. Homeyer was a younger son in the family, and therefore had little prospects of any legacy from home. Hence he came to America in the hope of profiting from the generous abundance of public lands open to entry, and after arriving in Texas he secured a tract of land in McCulloch County, but never used it. For a few years he remained about Burton as a tenant farmer and then bought 250 acres within four miles of the village. That land was sold by the family some years ago. On that old homestead he reared his children, including Charles W. Homeyer, and was a man generally successful in all business affairs. Being afflicted with rheumatism, he was exempt from military service during the Civil war but reached a good old age. Soon after coming to America he took out citizenship papers, and was an earnest student of American politics and became identified with the republican party. He was opposed to secession and was always noted for an independence of opinion and the courage of his convictions, which were reached only after deliberate study. In the early days he served as superintendent of schools in Washington County. He was reared in the faith of the Lutheran Church. In Washington County William D. Homeyer married for his second wife Caroline Koenig, who also came from Hanover, Germany. She died at Burton in 1900. Their children were as follows: William H. of Walberg, Texas; Minnie, wife of Fritz Bredthauer of Weir, Texas; Charles W.; Frederick A. of Burton; Caroline, wife of Theodore Granzin of Weir; Dora, who married E. A. Matijowsky of Lyons, Texas; Albert G., who died in Washington County, leaving a family; and Frank J., who is also deceased.

Charles W. Homeyer was about six years of age when the war between the states broke out. Part of his education was acquired during that dark and troublous period when very little attention was paid to maintaining the facilities of public education. He grew up on the old homestead farm of his father, learned all its duties, and was an active helper there until he was twenty-two years of age. Since then his career has had a wide and varied scope. For about five years he served as deputy tax collector under Collector R. A. Harvin, and as deputy tax assessor under Joe Hoffmann. In December, 1881, he engaged in the lumber business in Burton, and it is as a lumber dealer he was chiefly known for a period of more than a quarter of a century. He disposed of his interests in that line in 1908.

In 1906 Mr. Homeyer organized the State Bank of Burton, of which he became president and cashier, and has had the active management ever since. The State Bank of Burton opened with a capital stock of $10,000. A few years later the capital was increased to $20,000. With the exception of the second vice president the officers have been the same since organization. The management has been more successful than the most sanguine expectations entertained at the beginning. The bank now has loans and discounts totaling over $67,000, with a surplus of $8,000 and $6,000, certainly an excellent showing when the several successive hard crop years in this section of the state are considered. Mr. Homeyer has also been a director of the Burton Cotton Oil Co. since its organization in 1902, and president of the Burton Telephone Company since its organization in 1912.

To politics he has not been much inclined. He is a republican voter and in 1896 was a delegate to the republican state convention at Austin. Fraternally he is affiliated with the Woodmen of the World.

On November 17, 1880, he married Miss Mary D. Korthauer. She is a daughter of Henry and Caroline (Broesche) Korthauer, both of whom were from Hanover, Germany. The Broesche family came to Texas in 1846 and the Korthauers in 1854. Mrs. Homeyer's two brothers are William H. and Henry Korthauer. They are deservedly proud of their own children. Nora, the oldest, is the wife of William Bauer, Jr., one of the substantial business men of Pflugerville, Texas. The son, Charles W., Jr., completed his course in the Texas Agricultural and Mechanical College in 1908, then went East to the Boston Technological Institute, where he was graduated in 1910, and has since been identified with some important engineering work in Texas, and is one of the very capable civil engineers; while in college he was very popular socially, and was senior captain in the A. & M. College, and was elected president of the final ball, an honor much coveted by the socially ambitious young seniors there. Mary Blanche, the youngest child, was valedictorian of her class at Kenilworth Hall in Austin, in June, 1915, and is now engaged in teaching music in Burton.

Gustav A. Broesche. Now living virtually retired, after many years of successful endeavor along normal lines of industrial enterprise, Mr. Broesche is essentially one of the representative and influential men of Washington County, within whose limits he has maintained his home from the time of his nativity and in which he is a scion of a pioneer family that was here founded in 1846. He is a citizen whose high civic ideals and distinct loyalty have been at all times in evidence and that his is the strongest of vantage-ground in popular confidence and esteem needs no further voucher than the statement that he served continuously for a score of years as a member of the board of county commissioners of his native county,—a position in which his progressive policies and liberal views enabled him to do much for the furtherance of the best interests of the county along both social and material lines. The founder of the family in Washington County was William Broesche, and his numerous posterity constitute a valued and honored element of citizenship in this section of the state at the present time, this sterling pioneer, who came from Germany to the United States and established his home in Texas, having been the father of him whose name initiates this review.

Gustav A. Broesche was born on the old family homestead, on the James McCain League of land in Washington County, and the date of his nativity was November 22, 1848. He was reared under the conditions and influences of the early pioneer days, and as definite schools in this frontier section were conspicuous for their absence, he gained his early education chiefly under the direction of a private teacher employed by his father and a few neighbors. While he continued at the parental home he put forth arduous efforts in aiding in the maintenance of the family, and much of his work in his youth was in connection with the herding of cattle on the great open range and on the ranch which was developed by his father. He continued to live beneath the parental rooftree until he had passed his legal majority, and he then established a modest home for himself, on the same league of land.

In 1871, at the age of twenty-two years, Mr. Broesche purchased a small tract of land on credit, and this, as combined with that which his wife received at the time of their marriage, gave him ample opportunity to initiate his steady progress toward the goal of independence and definite prosperity. Bringing to bear energy, industry and good judgment, he began the improving of his land and brought its cultivated area of large dimensions each successive year. All this implied a continuity of responsibility and close application, but the ends justified the means and as a citizen and a captain of industry he has lived to receive the gracious benefices of fortune and to prove well his value as one of the influential citizens of his native county. His home life has been one of ideal associations, and he and his gracious wife have walked side by side down the pathway of life for a period of forty-five years, sharing in their joys and sorrows, their hopes and ambitions and in the filial love of their children and their children's children, so that now in the gentle twilight of their long and useful lives they may well feel content with their stable prosperity and rejoice that their lines have been cast in pleasant places. The temporal advancement of Mr. Broesche has been won through his long and active association with agricultural and live stock industry, and in addition to his well improved homestead place he is the owner of a valuable ranch of 1,000 acres in Burleson County, a property which has been effectively developed and improved under his personal direction. It will thus be understood that he has been more than ordinarily prominent and influential in farm development in this section of the state, for he has brought under effective cultivation not only his old homestead place, which comprises 400 acres, but has also achieved a similar development of hundreds of acres on his ranch in Burleson County, where he has erected good dwellings and made other consistent provisions for his tenants and others who have been his valued assistants in his various operations on his extensive landed estate.

From 1875 onward Mr. Broesche stood prominent also as a grower of and dealer in cattle, and for a number of years he was associated with the Blackburn-Turner cattle enterprise, represented in a business that covered a wide scope of territory in Washington and Burleson counties, besides which he devoted considerable attention for some time to the shipping of cattle. By the introducing of pedigree strains of horses and cattle he effectively raised the grade of his stock, but, notwithstanding his activity in this direction, his experience with the native "longhorn" of the pioneer days as compared with the bluer bloods of the present, was such that he is convinced that the best all-round results were to be gained through the old type, to which he would return if such a thing were possible. Since his retirement from his protracted service as county commissioner, in 1910, Mr. Broesche has lived practically retired in his pleasant home near Burton and has assigned to his sturdy sons the active management of his extensive landed estate and its various operations.

In 1884 Mr. Broesche initiated his activities as an influential figure in local politics, and both by conviction and inherent predilection he has been constrained to accord unfaltering allegiance to the democratic party. In 1890 he was elected a member of the board of county commissioners, as successor of E. J. Neinast, and by successive re-election he continued the incumbent of this office for twenty consecutive years.

With all of consistency may it be said that few men in Texas have filled this office with such uniform satisfaction to the constituency for so long a period. That period, as a matter of course, was one of marked transitions, for the older policies gave way to those of more modern and progressive order, and in all this advancement Commissioner Broesche stood well to the forefront,—a wise and loyal leader in popular sentiment and action.

Within his regime as a member of the board great progress was made in Washington County and its governmental affairs were systematized and made steadfast. Within his term of service was eliminated the indebtedness incidental to the erection of the courthouse; he advocated and assisted in supervising the purchase of the county farm; he supported the policy of so employing the county convicts as to make this branch of the county affairs self-sustaining; he aided in making provision for the remodeling of the office of the county clerk, especially in the installing of a modern fire-proof vault, and was similarly influential in repairing the county jail and placing new vaults and cells therein; and shortly before his retirement from office he gave his support to the order under the provisions of which each precinct in the county was supplied with eight mules to be utilized in connection with the improvement of highways, this provision virtually marking the initiation of the building of good roads in the county.

Mr. Broesche is affiliated with the Sons of Hermann and the Woodmen of the World, and he and his family hold to the faith of the Lutheran Church, of which both he and his wife are zealous communicants. He gave liberal aid in the erection of both the first and the second edifices of St. Paul's Church, at Burton, and his liberality has been shown also in his material contributions toward the support of other religious denominations. His Christian faith is one of tolerance and of good works, and in all of the relations of life he has proved considerate, kindly and helpful. He has been specially zealous in his support of the cause of education, the great value of which he fully appreciates as a phase of civic life, and he has served as a member of the board of trustees of his school district. Mr. Broesche is a man whose strong individuality is shown form in his facial lineaments and general bearing, and he gives the evidence of much reserve power as well as distinctive mentality and mature judgment.

On the 16th of November, 1871, was solemnized the marriage of Mr. Broesche to Miss Mary Turner, who is a member of another of the old and honored families of this section of the state and whose brother, William, is now serving, 1915-16, as a member of the board of county commissioners of Washington County. In conclusion is given brief record concerning the children of Mr. and Mrs. Broesche: Emma is the wife of Albert Neinast, of Gay Hill, Washington County; Henry E. is a representative farmer and stockman of Burleson County, where his operations are on the extensive landed estate of his father; Frederica is the wife of A. F. Lepping, of Travis County, and they have one child, Loretta; William married Minnie Kiel and their children are Floy and Marie; Mary and Louise died in childhood; and the three younger daughters, Celeste, Caroline and Mattie, remain at the parental home.

Rev. John Jachtyl, pastor of the Roman Catholic Church of the Holy Cross of Yorktown has been a factor in the work of the church in Texas since 1908. Still young in years, he is old in experience in affairs relating to his chosen work, and in the various communities where he has performed the duties of pastor he has left a splendid record for human helpfulness among his parishioners.

Rev. John Jachtyl.

Rev. John Jachtyl came to the United States from Galicia, Austrian Poland and is a native of Boleslaw in Galicia, born on May 15, 1871. He is the son of Joseph and Theckla (Skotnicki) Jachtyl, natives of Galicia, and the parents of four children. Sylvester, their eldest son is still living in Boleslaw, Austria. Helen also makes her home there. Julia married Joseph Mettig and lives in Ware, Massachusetts. Rev. John Jachtyl of this review is their youngest child. The father was a miller in his native community, where he passed away in 1912. The embryo churchman was reared in his native community, had his early education in the parish schools of Boleslaw, followed by a course in the gymnasium in Tarnow, and then entered the diocesan seminary of the same city. He completed his theological studies there and was there ordained on June 30, 1895, by Bishop Ignatius Lobos, eleven other young men taking the ordination at the same time. Young Jachtyl in the following five years served as assistant priest in various places. His first pastoral work as priest was at Roznov, Galicia, where he remained five years, and where he built the church. When he left that city it was to come to the United States. He sailed from Bremen on the Saxonia, bound for Boston, and the journey was made without incident. His first American post was in Newark, New Jersey, to which diocese he had been assigned, and from that state he came to Texas in September, 1908. He was first assigned to the church at Falls City and spent a year in service there. In addition to his regular pastoral duties he undertook the building of a parochial school, which he carried to completion, and from there he went to St. Hedwig Church in Bexar County, where he continued for 2½ years. When he left, all obligations against the congregation which were pending when he took charge had been wiped out, and the parish had a clean slate, the property being in better condition than when Father Jachtyl took charge. His next post was at Cestohawa, Karnes County, where he was pastor of the Church of the Nativity, and he also had as a part of his assignment Panna Maria—the oldest Polish parish in the United States. At the latter place during his service he erected the priest's house, renewed the church and school buildings, all within eighteen months of his service. From that locality he was transferred to Yorktown, coming here in May, 1914, as the successor of Rev. Father S. Przyborowski. Less than a year later, on April 7, 1915, the church was destroyed by an incendiary, and the reverend father began at once restoring the property. The church was dedicated in May, 1916, and is considered one of the finest churches in this part of the state.

Father Jachtyl is a worker, and is so known in the church. He is a linguist of splendid ability, speaking Polish, German, Bohemian, Spanish and English, with a thorough working knowledge of Latin and Greek.

Ludwig Voelkel. The career of Ludwig Voelkel, whose home is located on Cummings Creek, adjacent to Warrenton, is an illustration of the possible control over early limitations and the wise utilization of ordinary opportunities. He received only limited advantages in his youth and left the parental roof at an early age, determined to make his own way in the world, and through industry and enterprise his ambitions have been realized and at this time he is the owner of a valuable property of 265 acres in the Logan League, six miles east of Warrenton. Mr. Voelkel was born January 25, 1846, at Wichenstein, Prussia, and is a son of John J. Voelkel.

The Voelkel family left Prussia in 1849, sailing from Bremen and landing at Galveston after a trip of thirteen weeks, and then went to

Houston by boat and on by ox-wagon to Shelby, Austin County, Texas, where the father died in the same year. The family was left in fair circumstances, the father having purchased a small tract of land on which was located a log house, this latter being soon replaced by Jacob Voelkel, the grandfather of Ludwig Voelkel, whose death occurred in 1850. Mrs. Voelkel subsequently married Ferdinand Hezel and continued to live in that locality, dying in Austin County, Texas, at the remarkable age of ninety-six years, and being buried at Shelby. By her first marriage she was the mother of three children: John J., who is a retired farmer living at Houston; William, who is engaged in farming at Rutersville; and Ludwig, of this review. By her second marriage Mrs. Voelkel was the mother of one son: Richard, who is a resident of Shelby.

Ludwig Voelkel has lived in Fayette and Austin counties practically throughout his life. He was three years of age when brought to the United States by his parents and he grew up amid pioneer surroundings, obtaining his very limited education in the country schools. At the age of nineteen years he left home and began to learn the trade of carpenter, which he subsequently followed in Austin and Fayette counties, also doing some work in Washington County. Always a skilled and conscientious workman, a number of the buildings erected by him still stand as monuments to his contributions toward the building up of the community, these including several schoolhouses, among them the Haw Creek and Nassau, the Haw Creek store and a number of the business houses of Shelby.

Mr. Voelkel turned his attention to agricultural pursuits and located on his present property on Cummings Creek in 1893, buying 305 acres of the Logan League, much of it on the Creek bottom, for $10 an acre. He cleared 100 acres of the tract, and of the 265 acres he now owns, 55 acres are under the plow. Mr. Voelkel has devoted his activities to the growing of cotton and corn, the popular crops of the community. Mr. Voelkel was not called upon to serve in the army during the Civil war. In national political matters he has steadfastly voted the democratic ticket, but in local matters is inclined to be independent and to give his support to the candidate whom he deems best fitted for the office at stake. He never has been active politically, but has led a quiet, unostentatious life, content to devote himself to his estate and to supervise its many and extensive interests. He has done much to elevate the local standard of agriculture and to strengthen the popular regard for thoroughness, thrift and integrity.

Mr. Voelkel was married in Austin County, Texas, in 1869, to Miss Catherine Schlabach, a daughter of Alexander Schlabach, who came from the part of Prussia which produced Mr. Voelkel. Mrs. Voelkel died in 1876 and left these children: Louis, of LaGrange, Texas; Hedwich, who is the wife of John Lenert, of Warrenton, Texas; Walter, who is a farmer on Cummings Creek, married Augusta Schultz; Zelma, who married Otto Menking, of Haw Creek; and Frieda, who is the wife of Fritz Bauerkemper, of Warrenton. Mr. Voelkel was married a second time to Mrs. Wilhelmina Kramer, a daughter of John Michess, of Prussia. There have been no children born to this union.

Ernest Fricke, of Round Top, is a typical Texan, born in Fayette County, September 19, 1875, prominent in business as a young man, and of more recent years a leading merchant and in the forefront of movements beneficial to the material and moral uplifting of the community. As far as his education is concerned he is also a product of the Lone Star State. Starting his business in a modest way, relying upon the local patronage for its support, by untiring energy and remarkable initiative he has built up a large and prosperous enterprise, which attracts its trade from all over the county.

Mr. Fricke is a member of a pioneer family of Texas, and a grandson of the founder thereof, George H. Fricke, who was born in Hanover, Germany, September 19, 1821. In 1846 George H. Fricke sailed from the city of Bremen, Germany, to Galveston, Texas, and subsequently removed to Washington County, where he soon enlisted for service during the Mexican war under the flag of the United States. He was soon taken ill and sent to a hospital at Houston, and after his honorable discharge and recovery returned to his native land where he was married to Miss Behren. Again coming to this country, he settled on his first property, and being a man of excellent education took up the vocations of teaching and farming. In 1864 he removed to Fayette County, where he continued his educational labors for many years and died in 1893. He had come to Texas during a time when many of its heroes of the Revolution were still living, and among whom he formed a wide acquaintance, one of these being Gen. Sam Houston, whose opinions as to the Civil war Mr. Fricke shared. He was a republican in his political views, was an able and fluent speaker, and frequently was called upon to preside at meetings of various kinds in his community. His religious faith was that of the Lutheran Church, in which he was confirmed. Mrs. Fricke died March 12, 1880, having been the mother of the following children: George, the father of Ernest of this review; Paul, who resides at Brenham, Texas; Dora, who married first Otto Grumbka and second Charles Schreiber and died at Rutersville, Texas; Mary, who died in Austin County, Texas, as Mrs. Theo. Buehrina; Susan, who became the wife of Julius Holckamp and died in Kendall County, Texas; Fred, who is president of the First State Bank of Round Top and a well-known business man; Regina, who died as Mrs. Charles Huth, at Austin; and Ida, who became the wife of Albert Real and lives near Herrville, Texas.

George Fricke, son of the pioneer and father of Ernest Fricke, was born July 3, 1849, in Washington County, Texas, and has spent his life about Round Top since 1864. He married Matilda Henkel, a daughter of Edward Henkel, who was justice of the peace for the Round Top locality for years and a native of Hessen-Castle, Germany, coming to the United States in 1848 and settling in Fayette County. He was an early merchant at Round Top, and after the war between the North and South devoted his life chiefly to public affairs. He erected some of the first structures at Round Top, was active in democratic politics, served his community ably as public official and private citizen, and died in 1894, one of the best known men of his locality. Mr. Henkel married Miss Louisa Schoenwerk for his first wife, and after her death was united with her sister, Matilda Schoenwerk. Of the Henkel children there were: Charley, who died unmarried; Mrs. Matilda Fricke; George, who resides at Dallas, Texas; and Albert, who died without issue. George Fricke has passed his life in agricultural pursuits, and his home is now near Round Top. He has had the following children: Ernest, of this review; Edward, a successful merchant at Woodsboro, Texas; Miss Louisa, who is engaged in teaching in Caldwell County, Texas; Albert, who is engaged in teaching in Refugio County; and Annita, the youngest, who is a schoolgirl.

Ernest Fricke received his educational training in the public schools of Round Top, under the preceptorship of the present county clerk of Fayette County, P. Klatt, who was then in charge of the schools here. He left his school books before he was eighteen years of age to begin to work on the home farm, in addition to which he became skilled in handling live stock, in which he was engaged for a period of about two years. Just before he became twenty-one years of age he secured his first business experience as a clerk in the mercantile line for Alex von Rosenberg, of Round Top, at the same time being employed in the post-office here. In 1897 he was appointed postmaster under the McKinley administration, and this office he has continued to retain to the present time, having passed the civil service examination for the office in 1914 and being reappointed as a result of that examination. Mr. Fricke went into business on his own account, August 1, 1898, with a grocery stock valued at $400. He was aided financially by an uncle for some years until he reached a point where he could go on alone, and for four years was a partner with Arthur Fricke, as Fricke & Fricke, but finally bought his partner's interest and since that time the establishment has been conducted under the business style of Ernest Fricke. In addition to being a general merchant, Mr. Fricke is engaged in buying cotton, poultry and country produce, in which he also deals. He has always warmly accorded to Round Top the same stanch support which its people have given him as an honorable and successful merchant and eminently useful citizen. Mr. Fricke has always practiced temperance. It has always been his endeavor to bring to Round Top the best trade, whether it patronizes his establishment or not, and for this reason may be placed in the booster class. He is vice president and a member of the official board of the First State Bank of Round Top, of which he was one of the organizers in 1912. A stalwart republican in his political views, Mr. Fricke was a member of the state republican convention held at San Antonio in 1900, and has served Round Top as its mayor four years. His administration was made notable by a businesslike handling of the town's affairs and the innovation of a number of needed civic reforms. Fraternally, he is also well known, being consul commander of the Woodmen of the World and treasurer of the Sons of Hermann, which latter lodge he has represented in the Grand Lodge of Texas.

On November 1, 1899, Mr. Fricke was married at Round Top to Miss Elizabeth Ginzel, a daughter of William Ginzel, an interesting figure of the locality and a business man of importance. Two children have been born to this union, namely: Mignon M. and Elmo Arthur.

Fred Fricke. Of the men of Fayette County who have contributed to the material growth and development of this part of Texas, few are more widely or favorably known than Fred Fricke, of Round Top. During his long and active career his experiences have included operations as a merchant, traveling salesman, stock dealer and banker, and at the present time he is president of the State Bank of Round Top and one of the most influential and progressive men of the village.

Mr. Fricke was born in Washington County, Texas, June 28, 1856, and is a son of the pioneer founder of this German family, George H. Fricke. The father was born in the city of Hanover, province of Hanover, Germany, September 19, 1821, a son of Louise (Rehren) Fricke. The grandfather was an official in the service of the government. Among the children of the grandparents' family were: several daughters who remained in Europe; August, who remained in Hanover and served his government; George H., the father of Fred; and Dr. Fred, who came to the United States and located first at St. Louis, Missouri, but later went to Pine Bluff, Arkansas, where he died in 1873 unmarried. A son of August Fricke, Fred Fricke, is a well-to-do druggist of Nebraska, and another son, Ernst, came to the United States, married in New

Orleans, was a civil engineer and machinist, and died in Cuba while on a mission in connection with his profession.

George H. Fricke sailed from Bremen, Germany, in 1846, and after his arrival at Galveston, removed to Washington County, Texas. He was not there long before he entered the service of the United States as a soldier for duty during the Mexican war, but after six months of military life became ill and was recuperated in a Houston hospital, then receiving his honorable discharge. Upon his recovery he returned to Europe and married Miss Rehren, with whom he soon returned to his first permanent place of settlement in Washington County, Texas.

George H. Fricke was a well-educated man, and when he first began civic life in Texas it was as a teacher and farmer. He followed his educational career during almost all of his life, finishing his work in Fayette County, whence he had moved in 1864. He was several times justice of the peace in Washington County, and was busy with the duties of that office and his educational labors when the Civil war broke out. Mr. Fricke had early taken out his citizenship papers, and as he was a friend of the Union he espoused the cause of the republican party. He had come to Texas during the formative state of the commonwealth and at a time when many of her heroes of independence were still living, among whom he formed a wide acquaintance. He knew personally the great leader, Gen. Sam Houston, and it is probable that his warmth of feeling for the Union was inspired by the attitude of the general. Mr. Fricke was a man able of expressing himself on public occasions, and during gatherings in his community of any nature he was invariably called upon to preside or to speak. He was confirmed in the Lutheran Church, but never was connected with a fraternal order. His death occurred in October, 1893, Mrs. Fricke having preceded him to the grave, March 12, 1880. Their children were as follows: George, who is engaged in farming in the vicinity of Round Top; Paul, who resides at Brenham, Texas; Dora, who married first Otto Grumbka and second Charles Schreiber and died at Rutersville, Texas; Mary, who died in Austin County, Texas, as Mrs. Theo. Buchrina; Susan, who became the wife of Julius Holckamp and died in Kendall County, Texas; Fred, of this review; Regina, who died as Mrs. Charles Huth, at Austin; Ida, who married Albert Real and lives near Kerrville, Texas; and Clara, who married Albert Giebel and resides on a farm near Industry.

Fred Fricke was a lad of eight years when he accompanied his parents to Fayette County, and his education was secured under the preceptorship of his father, with additional schooling at LaGrange. He had a teaching experience of one year in a country school before he entered business life, and in 1873 went to Brenham and became a merchant's clerk. Three years later he engaged in mercantile pursuits on his own account there, conducting a store until 1878, when he went on the road as a traveling salesman, a vocation in which he followed the "trail" until January 1, 1897. Mr. Fricke started on the road for W. D. Cleveland, of Houston, was later with Ullmenn, Lewis & Company, and subsequently spent thirteen years with Foche, Wilkins & Lang, covering Texas territory throughout this long period, and becoming widely and favorably known throughout the state. When he left the road Mr. Fricke turned his attention to the stock business and farming in Fayette County, and became rather extensively identified with these lines, which he followed until 1908. He introduced a good blood of cattle into the country, occasionally shipped his stock, and as a farm improver added homes to the farm for tenants and gave an impetus to an already wakeful spirit there. On December 19, 1912, Mr. Fricke became identified with financial matters when he became the founder of the State Bank of Round Top, an institution with a capital of $10,000, of which he has since been president and his son, George H. Fricke, cashier. In the direction of this enterprise Mr. Fricke has displayed the possession of marked business and financial ability, a natural courtesy and broad-mindedness, a knowledge of affairs and human nature gained in his long years of travel and experience, and good business and financial judgment, which, combined with his high reputation for stability and substantiality, have gained the confidence of the depositors of the bank, as well as a high standing for the institution in financial circles. Mr. Fricke has not entered actively into political life, but has cast his presidential vote always with the republican party.

On February 20, 1880, Mr. Fricke was married to Miss Louisa Weyand, a daughter of George Weyand, a merchant of this community, a large real estate dealer, and a sterling citizen. Mr. Weyand married Christina Becker, and their living children are: Mrs. E. Nagel, Mrs. Alex von Rosenberg, Mrs. Louisa Fricke and Mrs. Lena Kaiser.

The children born to Mr. and Mrs. Fricke are as follows: Paul, a business man of El Campo, Texas, who married Adelia Hahn; Arthur, a business man of Carmine, Texas, who married Irene Vogelsang and has a daughter, Eveline; Fred, Jr., a stockman of this locality, who married Eugenie Vogelsang and has a son, Clinton; George H., who is cashier of the State Bank of Round Top, and married Louisa von Rosenberg, has two children, Helmer and Vernon; Lydia, the wife of Walter von Rosenberg, of Malone, Texas, a merchant, who has two daughters, Loraine and Loretta; Edgar, a student in the Blinn College, Brenham; and Estella, who is attending the public schools.

Joachim von Roeder, of Yorktown, the oldest living representative of this pioneer German family, and perhaps the oldest native Texan now living in Dewitt County, was born in Nacogdoches County on November 9, 1836, and is the son of Rudolph von Roeder, one of the founders of this prominent family. The family history is an interesting one, but space forbids any but most cursory mention of the early annals of the house of von Roeder. Their connection with the State of Texas has been highly creditable to them and to the land of their adoption, and they are justly entitled to mention in a work of the nature and purpose of this publication.

The von Roeder family was of the German nobility. They were natives of Paderborn, Prussia, where Ludwig von Roeder, grandsire of the subject, Joachim, was an army officer, with the rank of lieutenant. He married Caroline Louise Sack, a woman of excellent family, but not of the nobility. Their difference in rank excluded her from presentation at court with her husband, a fact which stung his pride and eventually caused him to resign his commission in the army and withdraw from the court life. Von Roeder was deeply devoted to his wife, and that she was not received with him was an indignity to which he would not submit. Upon his withdrawal from the army he retired to his country estate near Paderborn, where he reared his large family. The estate was heavily taxed by the government, and the demands of his family after his resignation from the army made heavy inroads upon his wealth. A growing dissatisfaction with his government caused him to make up his mind to release himself and his family from its operation, and after some thought he determined to bring his family to America where liberty existed in fact as well as in theory and where independent action on his part would not result in censure. Accordingly von Roeder disposed of his property, provided himself with what he considered an adequate material equipment for life in a new land, and with his family set sail for American shores. They sailed from Bremen on November 1, 1833, on the sailing vessel Congress, and were nine weeks in making the crossing. Through a seeming accident or miscalculation, the vessel landed on Galveston Island. They knew not whether it was the mainland or an island, and while they rested and made ready to continue the men of the party busied themselves in bringing down the wild game then so plentiful on the island. From there the von Roeder family went to San Felipe and soon thereafter went to Cat Spring, at which place Ludwig von Roeder died soon after Texas was admitted to the American Union.

In the family of Ludwig and Caroline von Roeder were several children, of whom brief mention may here be made. Theodore, the eldest, remained in Germany. Otto became a large slave holder, built the von Roeder mill in Austin County and owned the Nassau farm in Fayette County. He later moved to Dewitt County and is buried in Corpus Christi. He was twice married. His first wife was Paulina von Donop and his second was Mrs. Theodora Sack. He had children of each marriage. Louis von Roeder was one of the San Jacinto veterans who passed all through the war for Texas independence and also was in the battle of the Alamo, when General Houston took it away from Santa Anna. He married Caroline Ernst, a daughter of Frederick Ernst, the founder of Industry. Rudolph, father of the subject, spent his life as a merchant. He located the first store in Austin County at Cat Spring, to which place he moved from Nacogdoches County, where he had also been engaged in the merchandise business. While living in Cat Spring he went to Houston on a buying trip, and contracted yellow fever while absent. He came home, sickened and died soon after. Joachim, an elder brother, died in Austin County unmarried. He was one of a small party of the family who came to Texas in advance of the main family, and settled at Industry. Albrecht, who also was with General Houston at the battle of the Alamo, and who aided the family to escape the Mexicans in what was long known as the "runaway scrape," spent his life in Texas as a farmer and stockman. He married Caroline Ernst, the widow of his brother Louis, and died in Dewitt County, leaving a family. William, the youngest son, was a farmer and stock man and he died in Dewitt County of yellow fever prior to the Civil war. The daughters of Ludwig von Roeder were Valeska, who was one of the small advance party headed by her brother, Joachim, and died in Industry, unmarried. Louise, who married first Louis and then Ernest Kleberg, and died at Cat Spring, leaving a family. Rosa, who married Robert Kleberg and became the mother of a future congressman, Rudolph Kleberg, and lived to a fine old age, dying in Yorktown, Texas. Lena, who married Ferdinand Engelking and spent her life in Cat Spring, where she is buried, and where she left a large family.

Rudolph von Roeder received an excellent education in his native land before the removal of the family to America. He was a business man all his life, successful and prosperous. He married Antoinette von Donop, who was a sister of his brother Otto's wife. He died October 10, 1839, and his wife passed on a year prior to that time. The von Donops were from the same Prussian community that produced the von Roeders and the two daughters who married the von Roeder brothers were the only members of the family who came to Texas.

Joachim von Roeder was the only child of his parents. He was born in Nacogdoches County on November 9, 1836. His parents died when he was a small boy and he grew up in the home of his aunt, Mrs. Robert Kleberg, and attended the schools of Austin and Dewitt counties. He came to Dewitt County in 1847, when he was nine years old and lived at the old county seat, Clinton, until he had passed his majority. He well remembers the "hard times period" of those days, common to all, as well as the "era of plenty," for the wild game of the country in those early days made the problem of living much simpler than it is today. When he began life on his own responsibility he settled between Clinton and Mayersville, and entered into the stock farming business. He lived in a cabin there until after the Civil war and then moved to Yorktown. He later established himself on a ranch on Salt Creek and was identified with the cattle business there for something like seventeen years. Today Mr. von Roeder owns more than 3,000 acres, but the bulk of it is in the old Hill league. His cattle brand in the days when he was prominent in that business was the well known six round-pointed star, the use of which is continued in the family to this day.

Mr. von Roeder enlisted for service in the Southern army in 1862. He was with Capt. Josiah Taylor, in Company G of the Thirty-second Cavalry, Colonel Woods in command. His first service was on the frontier, where they were stationed for a time at Fort Clark, and later moved east to Louisiana. His first engagement was at Blair's Landing on Red River, then the Mansfield campaign, ending with the battle of Yellow Bayou. Following the last named engagement the command returned to Texas and was disbanded at Houston. Mr. von Roeder was promoted to the rank of sergeant and came through his service without a wound.

Returning to the pursuits of peace, Mr. von Roeder resumed activities in the cattle industry, and while he continued in that business he shipped largely to New Orleans, Fort Worth and Galveston. In fact, he was one of the earliest shippers to New Orleans.

On November 4, 1858, Mr. von Roeder married Miss Louise Eckhardt, a daughter of Caesar Eckhardt, who came to America from Ansberg, Prussia, in 1848. Mr. Eckhardt landed at Indianola and made his way direct to Yorktown, where he knew he would find fellow-countrymen. Here he engaged in the merchandise business and was one of the foremost merchants of his time. Farming, too, claimed his attention, and he was successful in every enterprise he entered into. His wife was Louise Fischer, and their children were eight in number. Robert, the eldest, died in Dewitt County, leaving a large family. William is a prominent merchant of Yorktown. Louise, who married the subject, and who was born in Laspha, Prussia, on July 27, 1840. Emily married Gustav Schmelzer and both died in San Antonio, leaving a family. Jane married Edward Fechner and left a son at her death in Yorktown. Mary, the wife of Robert Gohmert, died near Yorktown, leaving a family. Herman, a stockraiser, died at his home in Yorktown. Matilda is the wife of Rudolph Kleberg, of Austin, former member of Congress.

To Mr. and Mrs. von Roeder were born nine children. Antoinette, the eldest, is the widow of Herman Dahlman of Cuero, and the mother of several children. Jane lives in Yorktown, unmarried. Mary married Kirk Lynch of Westhoff, Texas. Hermann, a farmer near Yorktown, married Ida Korth. Mrs. Matilda Thergood, of Runge, Texas. William, a ranchman of Dewitt County, married Louise Menn. Ludwig, of New York City, is a graduate of the medical department of the University of Texas at Austin, graduate of Bellevue in New York City, and he finished his medical training in the universities and hospitals of Vienna. He married Alice Seibert, daughter of Doctor Seibert of New York City. Lula married Charles Flato of Kingsville, and Rudolph, the youngest, is a farmer and stock man of Dewitt County. He married Augusta Hauerman. The grandchildren of Mr. von Roeder number nineteen and he has one great-grandchild.

Some years ago Mr. von Roeder retired from business, and has been living quietly on his record, which is highly creditable to him. He is a democrat, and all his life has he supported the democratic ticket and candidate. He never manifested any interest in politics beyond the demands of good citizenship, and never served in a convention. He had declined to affiliate himself with the leading fraternal orders, or any of them, and has never been a member of a church, though he was baptized a Lutheran and believes in a supreme being. He has been content to leave theology to those who appreciated it, to live a clean and wholesome life, to be a good neighbor, measuring his actions by the golden rule and to owe no man anything. All his life he has enjoyed the esteem of his fellow men, and the entire family stands high in their various communities.

Charles W. Ehlinger. The thriving little town of Ellinger in Fayette County was named for the notable Ehlinger family, and the difference in spelling is due to the fact that the railway company used the other form as the name for its station, and from that the spelling was transferred to the Government records in the name of the postoffice and has so continued. The leading merchant of the village is Charles W. Ehlinger, whose grandfather was one of the earliest German emigrants into Texas, and who helped to establish Texan independence as a soldier under Houston in 1836.

Charles W. Ehlinger was born at the old Town of Ehlinger, now Live Oak Hill, in Fayette County, October 8, 1866. His grandfather, Joseph Ehlinger, was a native of Alsace, France, now a part of the German Empire. He served under the great Napoleon in the European wars during the early part of the nineteenth century and acquired both a practical and theoretical knowledge of military tactics. He brought his family to America and arrived in Texas just before the war for independence, locating in the vicinity of Houston, which had not yet been laid as a town. In the War of 1836 he joined Houston's army on the Colorado River at about the site of the present City of Columbus, and owing to his previous military experience as a French soldier was appointed drill master for the Texas Cavalry. He proved a valuable man to the cause, and went with Houston's army in its retreat across Texas, and participated in the battle of San Jacinto, and was present when the Texans captured the Mexican president, Santa Ana. With the success of the Texans in their struggle for independence, Mr. Ehlinger, after performing his own important share in that conflict, settled in the vicinity of Houston and became a farmer and stock man. His name is identified with the City of Houston because of the fact that he platted Ehlinger's Addition, which is now in the heart of the city, but which, during his lifetime, was of little importance. His later years were spent quietly, and he died in 1853 and is buried at Houston. He was a member of the Catholic Church. His wife, Mary, is buried in the little cemetery on the Joseph Ehlinger League in Colorado County. This league was a tract of land which came to the old soldier as a reward for his services in the revolution. All of it has long since passed out of the ownership of the Ehlinger family. The children of Joseph Ehlinger and wife were: Charles; Henry, who died unmarried at Fayetteville; and Elizabeth, who married Jacob Hahn and is buried at Live Oak Hill.

Charles Ehlinger, father of Charles W., was born in Alsace, France, July 2, 1823, and was about ten or twelve years of age when he came with the rest of the family to Texas. He was a man of considerable education considering his opportunities, and in the early development of Texas made himself useful both in business and official life. He was a practical surveyor and did a great amount of work in that profession, surveying leagues and smaller subdivisions, and is credited with laying out the old Town of Ehlinger, now Live Oak Hill. He was the first merchant of that place and he conducted the postoffice there at a time when the stage coach carried all the passengers and mail through the country. As a merchant he carried a very extensive equipment, and all his goods were hauled by ox team from Houston. Other improvements which he introduced to the community were cotton gins, grist mill, and flour mill, and much of the wheat ground in his mill was raised on the Ehlinger League, which he put in cultivation. He owned a number of slaves, and many of these after getting their freedom as a result of the war continued to linger about the old plantation for some years.

During the war Charles Ehlinger, who was a loyal supporter of the Southern cause, organized a company for the Confederate army. Before leaving for the front he was advised to sell fifty bales of cotton he had on hand, but declined, saying that his negroes would kill every Yankee who offered to touch it. Nevertheless, before he had been away a month the Federal soldiers came through and took away the cotton. He was elected captain of his company, and during the greater part of the war was engaged in scouting duty. He was a man of strong prejudices, was a democrat, though not very active politically, and his loyalty to the cause which he espoused as a soldier is indicated by the fact that during the war he paid $1,800 in gold for a negro, which was perhaps the strongest proof of his faith in the ultimate success of the Confederacy. In the years immediately following the war he served as a justice of the peace. With the close of the war he continued merchandising, and was as successful then as he had been before. His death occurred in 1872, and he is buried at Live Oak Hill, where he gave thirty-five acres of land towards the church and school, and also erected the original church and school and gave them to the community.

Charles Ehlinger married Wilhelmina Miller, whose father came from Oldenburg, Germany. Mr. Ehlinger died in May, 1883. Her children were: Joseph Ehlinger, Jr.; Elizabeth, who married C. J. H. Meyer of Ellinger; Elo F., county and district clerk of Calhoun County, Texas; John P., who is in the office of the comptroller of state at Austin; Lena, who married D. F. Meyer of Ellinger; Minna, wife of C. C. Girndt of Ellinger; Charles W.; Dr. Otto, who is state physician to the Agricultural and Mechanical College at College Station. The oldest of these children, the late Joseph Ehlinger, Jr., died in January, 1913, for six years conducted a cotton gin near Ellinger, was elected a county commissioner, though not a candidate for the office, and after six years in that office became county clerk and gave sixteen years in continuous attention to that office. He subsequently engaged in the general merchandising business at La Grange two years, and on selling out was elected county judge, an office he filled with distinction four years. He then retired to his farm near Ledbetter, where he died, leaving a family.

Charles W. Ehlinger, the fortunes of whose family have thus been briefly traced, spent his boyhood at the old Town of Ehlinger up to the age of sixteen, getting his education chiefly at home and afterwards taking a course in the Capital Business College at Austin. His business career began at the age of nineteen, at which time he had the disabilities of his minority removed. He sold his first goods in the present Town of Ehlinger in 1895. His original stock was worth perhaps $2,000, and his store was in the same block in which he is still doing business. His present business house, the chief one of the town, was erected in 1910, to accommodate a business which has seen many years of gradual expansion and development. The building is 32 by 135 feet, and the stock includes everything in general merchandise and implements. The postoffice is also in the building, and Mr. Ehlinger has served as postmaster altogether eleven years. Another service has been as notary public, for which office he has held a commission twenty-two years.

While a merchant Mr. Ehlinger has also been actively identified with farming for many years, and has done much to develop the land in this section by the introduction of better methods and improved facilities. He is one of the directors of the First State Bank of Ellinger, and for twelve years has been a trustee of his school district. Several years ago he discovered the existence of an unliquidated obligation in the shape of a donation of $1,000 from Mr. Pierce, the noted railway man who built the Southern Pacific line west of San Antonio, and Mr. Ehlinger promptly took measures to make collection of this amount. His activity as the leading merchant and business man of the Ellinger locality has prompted him to avoid party politics, though he is a democratic voter, and though a man of unusual influence has never attended a political convention as a delegate.

On April 9, 1891, in his home locality, Mr. Ehlinger married Miss Nannie Birkmann, daughter of Henry and Nannie (Elerbush) Birkmann, both of substantial German stock. The Birkmann children were: John; Mary, who married Eugene Koehl; Amelia, who married Emil Koehl; Henry, of Weimar; William, of Shiner; Mrs. Ehlinger; and Louisa, who married Theodore Beyer of Ellinger. Mr. and Mrs. Ehlinger have the following children: Norma, who married Charles Meyer and has a son named Charles Henry; Leona, who married John Meyer and has a daughter named Jonnie May; Clara; Isabel; and Lottie Lee.

Mr. Ehlinger's family have been brought up as Lutherans, his wife being an active member of that church. While he comes of purely German family, and acquired that language while growing up, in the course of his business career Mr. Ehlinger has mastered the Bohemian tongue, and both reads and writes it, a feat that is not an easy one of accomplishment. He has thus been able to serve in many ways the community where he resides, made up of residents who speak German, Bohemian and English. He is frequently called upon to write contracts, translating from both the German and the Bohemian into the English. He has served as secretary and is a former president of the local lodge of Sons of Hermann.

GERHARD D. WESSELS. One of the men of whom the Town of Rutersville owes its present business prosperity, Gerhard D. Wessels has been the architect of his own fortunes, and from a boyhood and youth filled with hard work and numerous discouraging experiences has steadily advanced to a position of importance and influence to his community. He was born at Oldenburg on the Jade, Germany, January 11, 1867, and is a son of George and Sophie (Lange) Wessels.

Mr. Wessels' father died when Gerhard D. was still a youth, and shortly thereafter, in 1872, the widowed mother brought her little family to the United States, sailing from the City of Bremen on one of the vessels of the North German Lloyd line, the Frankfort, bound for Galveston, Texas, at which place the family duly arrived. From Galveston Mrs. Wessels took her children to Fayette County, where she had relatives, and during her first year in this country she was engaged in a small way in farming. She was married during the next year to William Hancord, a farmer and sheepman of Fayette County, and who later identified himself exclusively with farming operations near Rutersville, where Mr. Hancord resided until his death. Mrs. Hancord still survives and resides on the old homestead farm. The Wessels children were as follows: J. H. Wessels, a leading farmer and merchant of Halsted, Fayette County; George D., of Rutersville; Fred, who died at La Grange and left a family; and Gerhard D., of this notice. Mr. and Mrs. Hancord had one son, Willie, who died in childhood.

Gerhard D. Wessels was a lad of four years when he came to the United States with his mother and brothers, and grew up in the vicinity of Rutersville, where he received his education in the public schools. He was a farmer for a few years and an aid to the Hancord household after leaving school, later spent a short time in selling fruit trees, and then became a clerk in the store of Herman Amberg, whose employ he left to accept a similar position with August Heinze & Company, of La Grange. He was careful of his wages and finally accumulated a small capital with which he entered the retail liquor business at Rutersville, and also for several years was clerk for his stepfather, whom he succeeded in business, continuing in that line until July 11, 1914, when he sold out. At this time Mr. Wessels is engaged in buying and selling real estate, in loaning money and in conducting the saloon and dance hall property at Rutersville. He is well and favorably known in business circles of this locality, and his means have been accumulated solely by himself and through the exercise of stalwart business ability, good judgment and clear foresight. Mr. Wessels is one of the substantial improvers of Rutersville, having erected one of the best residences of the village.

In local politics Mr. Wessels has not been engaged actively, having aimed to vote for the best business interests of his community. However, he is primarily a democrat, having cast his first presidential vote for Grover Cleveland in 1888.

Mr. Wessels was married at Rutersville, May 28, 1891, to Miss Emma Voelkel, a daughter of William and Christina (Weyand) Voelkel. Mr. Voelkel, who was born December 13, 1841, came to America from Germany and was brought to Austin County, Texas, in 1848. During the Civil war he served for some time as a Confederate soldier, following which he took up farming in Fayette County. Mrs. Voelkel was a member of the well known Weyand family of Round Top, Fayette County, in which vicinity she was reared, and they were the parents of the following children: Robert, a resident of Rutersville; Mrs. Lena Koepke, of Ellinger, Texas; Mrs. Wessels; Gus, deceased, who married Frances Hardler, also deceased, and had three children; Amelia, who married Frank Hackebeil, of the Ruterville community; Otillie, who is the wife of H. O. Hackebeil, of this locality; R. W.; Herman; Alvin; Lydia, who is the wife of Charles Maas; and Willie A. Voelkel. To Mr. and Mrs. Wessels there have been born five children: Alma, Alfred, Welma, Gilbert and Milton, of whom Alfred is one of the salesmen for Herman Amberg, of Rutersville, one of the leading merchants of Fayette County.

Arthur Fricke, who is successfully engaged in the general merchandise business, as a cotton buyer and produce man at Carmine, is a worthy representative of the younger business element of Fayette County. To a very considerable extent it is this element in any locality, and particularly in those outside of the large cities, which infuses energy and progress into the activities of the place. The enthusiasm of this element, whose entrance upon the arena of business life dates back not much further than a decade, which contributes the spirit and zeal which

Mr & Mrs Robert J Jennings

THE CHILDREN OF MR. AND MRS. ROBT. J. JENNINGS

Standing left to right: Marion Elizabeth, age 11; Walter Pulliam, age 8; Charlotte May, age 5; William Ashton, age 1

keep commercial and industrial activities in a healthy condition. A pronounced type of this class of energetic workers is Mr. Fricke.

Arthur Fricke was born on his father's farm in Fayette County, near Round Top, April 1, 1884, and is a son of Fred Fricke, a sketch of whose career will be found on another page of this work. Arthur Fricke passed his boyhood and youth in the country, where his early education came from the country school, this being supplemented by a course in the commercial college at Brenham. Mr. Fricke's career was commenced in the field of education as a teacher in the district schools in Washington County and continued to be thus engaged for a period of three years, during which time he gained an excellent reputation as a capable and popular teacher. He then entered merchandise at Round Top in 1904 in partnership with Ernest Fricke, a cousin, the firm style being Fricke & Fricke. This existed until 1910, when the partnership was dissolved with the withdrawal of Arthur Fricke, who engaged next in the cotton business as a buyer for the exporting firm of the A. D. Milroy Company of Brenham and Galveston. After two years' of experience secured in this line he again turned to mercantile pursuits, and in 1913 came to Carmine and bought the stock and good will of F. Eichler. Since that time the business has been conducted under the style of Arthur Fricke, general merchandise, cotton buyer and produce man. Under his capable and energetic management the business has grown and developed into one of the paying enterprises of the village and one which attracts its trade from the best class of people. The straightforwardness of his dealings is fully recognized by his fellow townsmen, and although his advent in Carmine is of but comparatively recent date, the patronage which he has already enjoyed presages a very successful future.

Mr. Fricke was married in Fayette County, Texas, October 11, 1908, to Miss Irene Vogelsang, a daughter of Paul and Emma (Kraus) Vogelsang. Mr. Vogelsang is a representative of an old and honored German family of Austin County and was born near Shelby, his father having been the founder of the family in the Lone Star state. Mrs. Fricke is the third in order of birth in a family of five children, and she and Mr. Fricke are the parents of one daughter, Evelyn, four years old. Mr. Fricke is a member of the Woodmen of the World. He owns the property where he does business, as well as his own home, one of the choice residences of Carmine.

ROBERT JACKSON JENNINGS. The old time cattleman and trail driver of Texas is a vanishing race of men, who in their time represented the hardiest qualities and the acme of personal efficiency and courage. One of the survivors into the present era is Robert Jackson Jennings, in recent years established in the quiet routine of farmer and stockman and owning one of the splendid ranches close to the City of San Antonio. For more than half a century the name Jennings has been one of prominence in the livestock industry in Southwest Texas.

Robert Jackson Jennings was born in Lavaca County, Texas, March 23, 1856, a son of Joseph P. and Susan E. (Crunk) Jennings. His father, a native of Mississippi, came with his family to Texas in 1853 and located on the beautiful San Marcos River about twelve miles below its sources in Guadaloupe County. From there he moved to Lavaca County, but about the close of the war returned to the old place on the San Marcos. In that vicinity Joseph P. Jennings became a prominent cattleman with large interests, and was one of the pioneers in this great Texas industry. He developed an extensive and valuable ranch, lying in that section of Guadalupe County where it corners with Hays County, and extending over into that county. Joseph P. Jennings during the war between the states was member of a Texas regiment in the Confederate army. There are two other sons, William H. and Ira C. Jennings, the former a resident of San Antonio and the latter of Laredo. Both are prominent old time cattlemen, and William H. is particularly well known for his interests in that business, and during his active career owned many large herds of cattle and extensive lands.

Robert J. Jennings spent his life on the ranch in Caldwell County until 1883. He then became an independent cattle operator for several years in that section of Southwest Texas lying south of San Antonio. His first location was in Frio County, next in LaSalle County, and finally in Webb and Zapata counties along the Mexican border. In the latter county he owned a ranch of 13,000 acres, and in 1910 he traded it for a farm in Bexar County adjoining the City of San Antonio, to which place his family removed in 1911 to make it their permanent home.

Mr. Jennings had many interesting experiences as a trail driver during the late '70s and early '80s. His first trip over the trail was made in 1876, with his brother William H. and his uncle. They drove a herd of 3,600 cattle over the old Chisholm trail to Dodge City, Kansas, and Mr. Jennings was herd boss on this drive. His next trip over the trail was for John R. Blocker in 1881, and on his last trip in 1886 he was in charge of the Driscoll, Blocker and Davis cattle. This last trip was made in the year that witnessed almost the last of the driving over the open trail to the north, and the year is also memorable among all old stockmen as one of the hardest and most disastrous periods in the history of the Texas cattle industry on account of the terrible drought of that year. On this drive Mr. Jennings left Duval County with 1,100 head of Spanish cattle and on reaching Dimmit county his herd was increased by 1,500 head of fat cattle. From Dimmit County until he reached the Pease River in Vernon County not a drop of rain fell, and his herd suffered great losses from lack of water. He finally delivered his cattle at Trail City, Colorado.

Mr. Jennings' farm near San Antonio, to which he now gives his active supervision, is one of the most complete and most valuable stock farms in Southwest Texas. It comprises 195 acres of land, every acre under cultivation. It is situated about four miles from the city, a little south of west, on the Cupples Road and between that road and the Castroville Highway. His crops are cotton, corn and other grain, and he also has a fine pear orchard and a garden that produces all the vegetables that is consumed in his home. In 1914 his cotton crop aggregated nearly a hundred bales. His specialty is fine stock. He handles mixed cattle, any kind that is profitable, but shows a preference for Durhams. He also has some registered hogs of both the Berkshire and Essex varieties. This is a highly improved stock farm in every respect, and its value is greatly increased by its convenient location to the splendid metropolitan City of San Antonio.

The farm also furnishes a beautiful home to Mr. Jennings' happy family. He has been twice married. His first wife was Miss Dorcas Farmer, daughter of Rev. W. H. Farmer, a well known Baptist minister. The two children of this marriage are Mattie, wife of S. R. Harcourt of Chicago, and Robert F. Jennings, a stockman of Christine, Texas. After the death of his first wife Mr. Jennings married Miss Nannie Hazlerigg of Dimmit County, Texas, daughter of the late Judge Ashton W. Hazlerigg, a noted pioneer of Southwest Texas, a soldier in two wars, and distinguished both as a lawyer and judge. Judge Hazlerigg was born in Kentucky, and was the first cousin of Judge John T. Hazlerigg, chief justice of the Supreme Court of Kentucky. While still a youth he joined the United States army in the war with Mexico and continued until its close. This experience led to his location in the Southwest, where he became a pioneer in opening up the southwestern section of Texas. He laid out and organized Dimmit and several other counties, and established the Town of Carrizo Springs, county seat of Dimmit County. In North Central Texas he also organized Johnson County and built the first courthouse at Cleburne, the county seat. In the meantime he had made several trips back to his old home in Kentucky, and studied law in a college at Lexington, where he was admitted to the bar. During the war between the states he was in a Kentucky regiment of the Confederate army, rose to the rank of lieutenant colonel, and his record was that of a brave as well as efficient officer. Returning to Texas after the war, he located at Carrizo Springs, and in addition to handling a large law practice in the courts of Southwest Texas acquired extensive property and cattle interests. He became judge of the District Court of the district that then embraced a large number of counties lying south and southwest of San Antonio, and his career on the bench was distinguished by the same high qualities which characterized his every undertaking in life.

Mr. and Mrs. Jennings have four living children: Miss Marion Elizabeth; Walter Pulliam; Charlotte May; and William Ashton Jennings.

CHARLES BAUER. Although now living a somewhat retired life at Carmine, where he has resided since 1894, Charles Bauer still has large holdings in business and financial enterprises here and maintains an interest in the affairs of the thriving community to the development of which he has contributed so largely. A man of sterling ability in numerous directions, he has been an important factor in the work of development which has characterized Carmine during the past two decades, and his citizenship has always been of a character worthy of emulation.

Mr. Bauer was born June 5, 1845, at Oberensingen, Wurtemburg, Germany, a son of William and Margaret (Hahn) Bauer. His father was born in May, 1810, at the same place and was given a fair education. He came from a family of millers and was not called upon for military service in his native land, but was not satisfied with the progress he was making there, and determined to come to the United States. Accordingly, in 1864, he went with his family to Antwerp, Belgium, where he took passage on the sailing vessel Ellen, Captain Wilson, and after an uneventful voyage the journey was completed and the vessel reached port at New York City October 18th. The family at that time consisted of the father and six children, the mother, who was the daughter of a farmer, having died in Germany in 1855. The children were as follows: Wilhelmina, who died at Louisville, Kentucky, as Mrs. Charles Schaeffer; Caroline, a resident of Middletown, Delaware, and the wife of George Eckenhoffer; William, who is a resident of Burton, Texas; Charles, of this notice; and Misses Mary and Pauline, who reside with their sister at Louisville, Kentucky.

At the time of his advent in the United States, William Bauer located at Louisville, Kentucky, where he soon took out his citizenship papers. In his native land he had been a miller, but here engaged in the grocery business, and continued to be engaged therein until his death in 1896. Mr. Bauer took no part in politics, save as a republican voter and belonged to no fraternal order, but was a consistent member of the Lutheran Church.

The education of Charles Bauer was secured in the public schools of his native country, after leaving which he was apprenticed to the trade of carpenter, thoroughly mastering every detail of that vocation.

He was nineteen years of age when the family emigrated to the United States, and instead of going to Kentucky, as did the others, came almost at once to Texas and located at Round Top, where he engaged in work at his trade. He was industrious and thrifty, and after a few years had accumulated money enough to go to Burton, Texas, and engage in the lumber business, being associated with his brother under the firm style of W. Bauer & Brother. They bought out the first yard established at that place and conducted it successfully for a period of twelve years, after which Charles Bauer disposed of his interests and went to Pomona, California. He first engaged in farming in that community, later became the proprietor of a feedmill, and finally opened a laundry, but after seven unprofitable years he decided that his best opportunities lay in Texas, and he accordingly returned to the Lone Star state. Here, in 1894, Mr. Bauer entered the lumber business, buying out J. C. Hillsman & Son and conducting a yard until April, 1914, when he sold out and practically retired from active participation in business operations. He has been identified with a number of the industries which have given prestige to this thriving little city, being a stockholder in the Carmine Creamery and in the oil mill here, and a director and one of the organizers of the Carmine State Bank. He has erected some of the residences which make up Carmine's substantial improvements, including his own home. During several years, also, he has been a farmer by proxy, his property consisting of 174 acres and being located in the Obediah Hudson League, near Carmine.

In his political relation to the county and state Mr. Bauer is a stanch republican. He took out his first citizenship papers at La Grange, Texas, and his final papers at Brenham, and his first presidential vote was cast for James A. Garfield, in whose administration he served as postmaster at Burton for two years. Since that time he has been contented with voting at each recurring election. His fraternal connection is with the Sons of Hermann.

Mr. Bauer was married at Round Top, Texas, November 17, 1871, to Miss Mary Ernst, a daughter of Fred and Mary (Krum) Ernst. Mr. Ernst's mother, Louise Ernst, was the first German woman to set foot on Texas soil. Her husband was Frederick Ernst, and their advent here was in the early '30s, when they settled at Industry. There Mr. Ernst built a tavern and mill and he and his good wife entertained many German travelers there. They experienced trouble with the Indians, and on one occasion were driven from their home by the redmen. The old Fordtran place, near Industry, is a part of the league they obtained as pioneers, and there they are buried. Their sons to reach mature life were: John, Frederick and Herman. The daughters were Mrs. Caroline Von Hinueber and Mrs. Minna Sieber.

Fred and Mary (Krum) Ernst were German born, the former in Oldenburg and the latter in Baden. They were farming people, and Mr. Ernst came to Texas in the early '30s, living first at Industry and later at Round Top, and dying as a lieutenant in the Confederate army during the Civil war. Their children were: Mrs. Bauer; Mrs. Augusta Korff, now deceased; Mrs. Emily Korff, of Beaumont, Texas; and Herman, of Burton, Texas. Prior to her marriage to Mr. Ernst, Mrs. Ernst was the widow of Mr. Prey, who met his death in the ill-fated Mier expedition to Mexico, and left two children: Mrs. Johanna Gross, of San Antonio, Texas, and Mrs. Louisa Vogelsang, of Burton.

To Mr. and Mrs. Bauer there has been born a daughter, Miss Norma, who has been well trained, is a young woman of exceptional talents, and received her liberal education in Compton, California, and as a graduate pupil of Professor Jaekel, of Brenham, Texas, in music.

Herman Amberg. A representative of one of the oldest German families of Fayette County, Herman Amberg has resided in his present community of Rutersville throughout his life and in various ways has contributed to its material development and advancement, having been prominent in business and agricultural enterprises, as well as in public affairs, his incumbency of the position of postmaster being of twenty-seven years' standing. His father was Carl Amberg, who added his presence to the Rutersville community during the early '50s, being at that time an immigrant from his native land.

Carl Amberg was born in Hanover, Germany, in 1828, and there acquired a splendid literary and mercantile education, being brought up in the home of a merchant. As a young man he left his home and crossed the ocean in an old sailing vessel, and when the water supply of the ship became low and the calms held the vessel, the passengers and crew were in danger of death. However, after a long voyage of six weeks the ship made port at Galveston, and Mr. Amberg came on to Houston, Texas, with freighters who were going into the interior with ox-wagons. Mr. Amberg was at this time a young man of twenty-four years, and established himself in the mercantile business at Rutersville, then important as an educational center of Texas and even of the whole South, and a community at that time practically all American. A few Germans lived nearby, among whom were Joseph Beigel, Bernard Scherrer and Otto D. Lassaulx, who were older settlers than Mr. Amberg and all prominent men of the locality. Rutersville College attracted a large student body here before the Civil war, and a few old people still reside in Texas who remember the days of its prestige in the educational field. The town entered the list of contestants for the permanent capital of the state and was a popular candidate for the honor for a time.

Mr. Amberg continued his mercantile career here until his death, in May, 1884. As a man, Carl Amberg possessed the milk of human kindness. Some of his countrymen came to America with the money loaned them by him, and he saw to it that no one suffered for the lack of the necessities of life as the instances were presented to his notice. He seemed not to care for great accumulations or great wealth and never seemed to realize the value of real estate in the future as it lay out before him in its untamed state. He became a citizen early and cast his lot with the republican party, but was not loud in the expression of his views, and as a fair-minded and just man served his community as justice of the peace for several years. While he was not inclined to public speaking, it lay within his power to express himself clearly and intelligently upon questions, because of his superior educational and intellectual attainments. As a neighbor, Mr. Amberg was interested in those living about him and sympathized with those in sickness or distress. During the epidemic of yellow fever at LaGrange he was wont to visit the county seat and lend whatever assistance was possible as long as he was needed. He belonged to the Lutheran Church, and fraternally was a Mason of high rank.

Carl Amberg was married before he left Germany to Miss Emma Dietrich, a sister of Wilhelm Dietrich, who spent his life in Fayetteville and is mentioned elsewhere in this work. Mrs. Amberg died in 1901, and was laid to rest beside her husband at LaGrange. They were the parents of five children, namely: Mrs. Fannie Schueck, of Rosenberg, Texas; Olga, who is the wife of Otto Moellenberndt, of LaGrange; Herman, of this notice; Otto, who is engaged in mercantile lines at LaGrange; and Carl W., a business man of that place.

Herman Amberg was born at Rutersville, May 11, 1862, within 150 yards of his present dwelling, and was educated in the schools of Ruttersville, where he began business for himself at the age of twenty-two years. It might almost be said that he was born behind the counter, and the inside knowledge of merchandising was gained by practical experience. When his father died, the Amberg business was continued by Herman, and for more than sixty years this name has been conspicuously identified with the history, business and official, of Rutersville. Herman Amberg erected a new store house, two stories and of brick, in 1885, and it now constitutes the conspicuous business center of the village. Some twenty years ago Mr. Amberg identified himself with farming, and at this time he employs from eighteen to thirty families on his lands, a large part of his real estate being located on the Colorado River, between LaGrange and Ellinger. He has some 1,400 acres in cultivation and is easily the largest farmer in Fayette County. Mr. Amberg is also president of the LaGrange Cotton and Oil Manufacturing Company, is vice president of the Schumacher Bank of LaGrange and one of its organizers into a state institution, is a director of the LaGrange-Lockhart Compress Company, and is secretary and a director of the Farmers Lumber Company of LaGrange.

While his father was a republican, Mr. Amberg has been identified with the democratic party throughout his life. His father was postmaster of Rutersville for about twenty-two years and was succeeded by one of the family, and his son Otto came to the office next, and the latter was succeeded after four years by Herman, who has held this position continuously since 1888, when he was appointed during President Cleveland's administration. Although he has repeatedly been requested by republican administrations for campaign contributions, he has invariably replied that his political contributions were for the democratic party, having steadfastly maintained his courage in his convictions. He has been an active man in party affairs, attending state conventions and meetings, and was a member of the "Car Shed" convention of 1892 as a supporter of Governor Hogg. Subsequently he was a stanch adherent of the aspirations of Senator Bailey. A distinctive fact concerning the family is, that they have held the office of postmaster for over fifty years.

On April 15, 1886, Mr. Amberg was married to Miss Emma Luecke, a daughter of Fred Luecke, who has lived at Rutersville for more than sixty years, coming to Texas from Germany, where he was born during the '40s. He has been a successful farmer and is widely known in Fayette County. Mrs. Luecke is now deceased, and Mrs. Amberg is their only child. Three children have been born to Mr. and Mrs. Amberg, namely: Leonida, who is the wife of John C. Schumacher, of LaGrange, and has three children—Nolie, John Herman and Ruth; Edgar, of LaGrange, who completed his education in Southwestern University, Georgetown, and is now connected with the Texas Oil Company; and Miss Edith, who resides at Austin, Texas, married, in June, 1915, V. M. Ehlers, who is sanitary state engineer.

Jacob Koehl. Among the substantial and highly regarded agriculturists of Fayette County, who have contributed to the welfare and material advancement of their communities both as farmers and as the heads of families, Jacob Koehl is deserving of mention. He has been the author of his own success, and has spent his active career in Fayette and Colorado counties, and his present farm comprises a part of the Petty League.

Mr. Koehl was born at Saint Marie, Alsace, France, April 16, 1853, and the next spring his family came to America by the old-time method of ocean travel—the sailing vessel. Landing at New Orleans, they continued their journey by boat to Houston, Texas, and by ox-team to their destination in Colorado County, settling on Bee branch, about four miles east of Old Ellinger, near Connor's Creek. There the elder Koehl bought new land and opened up a farm, passing the remaining years of his life there and dying in 1908, at the age of eighty-five years. Jacob Koehl, the father of Jacob of this notice, was born in the same locality in which his son came to life, in Alsace, and came from a family of agriculturists. He himself demonstrated his ability in that field in the new world. During the Civil war and the events preceding it, his sympathies were with the South, and what brief service he rendered was done in behalf of the Confederacy, although two months of service in the field was all that he was able to render, he being honorably discharged at the end of that time because of physical disability. Mr. Koehl took no active part in politics, preferring to confine himself to the discharge of the duties of good citizenship. He was a consistent member of the Catholic Church throughout his life, and his children were reared in that belief. Jacob Koehl, Sr., married Mary Cubala, who survived him some three years and died in June, 1909. They were the parents of the following children: Walburga, who was the widow of John Bezung, and resided at Ellinger at the time of her death, February 14, 1916; Joseph, who died near Ellinger, leaving a family; and Jacob, of this notice.

Jacob Koehl, of this review, as above suggested, was reared at the point of the pioneer settlement of the family, and his education was acquired at Frelsburg, with a priest of the Catholic Church as his teacher. Under this preceptorship he was prepared for teaching himself, and for a period of three months was an assistant teacher at Liveoak Hill—Old Ehlinger. For five years succeeding this, Mr. Koehl drove a team for his cousin Ehlinger, freighting between Old Ehlinger and Columbus, this being previous to the advent of the railroads. When he stopped freighting, he clerked in a general store for his cousin at Liveoak Hill, and then engaged in the butcher business on his own account for two years, this being succeeded in turn by his operations in farming.

Mr. Koehl made his first home as a married man on Ross Prairie, but in the following year removed to his present location, in the Colorado River bottoms. His first home here was a frame house, 14x16, "with back room and gallery," and this continued to be his place of residence where several of his children were born. He lost his wife there, and then ceased his agricultural pursuits for twelve years. Following the period he was away from the farm, Mr. Koehl was a cotton weigher at Ellinger, and then engaged in merchandise here in company with Charles W. Ehlinger, whose partner he remained for four years. Mr. Koehl then sold out his stock and bought his present farm of 646 acres, and has been in possession of it since that time, and has continued to carry on active and successful operations. The Koehl farm, as previously noted, is a part of the Petty League, and was formerly the property of John H. Meyer. Here Mr. Koehl is cultivating some 450 acres to corn and cotton. The farm is practically all bottom land and the farm is among the most desirable and valuable on the Colorado River. His home is a two-story frame residence, of the ante-bellum pattern, erected by Colonel Jarmon, in 1853, and its appearance gives the spectator the idea of the days of slavery and the affluence of the Southern planters of that period.

In political matters Mr. Koehl is a democrat, but, like his father, he has given little time to political matters. However, while he was engaged in weighing cotton, he served in the capacity of deputy sheriff under Nat Reeves, John Rankin and Lit Zapp, and in his official capacity was called upon to make a few arrests of men charged with murder, and for minor crimes and misdemeanors. Mr. Koehl's fraternal affiliation is with the Sons of Hermann.

Mr. Koehl was first married in the fall of 1872, his wife being Miss Nancy Meyer, a daughter of John H. Meyer. She died at his first home in the Colorado River region, leaving him the following children: Caroline, who is the wife of Gus Tiemann and has three children—Erwin, Gussie and Dorsy; Willie, who married Sophie Jannek, and has two children—Nancy and Walter; and Charley, who married Pearl Anderson, has a son Charley, and is a resident of Wharton, Texas. Mr. Koehl was married in the fall of 1881 to Miss Antonia Neitzen, who died in 1888, leaving the following children: Max, a resident of Houston; Mary, who is the widow of J. V. Opert, and has two children; Lillie, who died in young womanhood; and Bessie, who is a clerk in a general store at Comfort, Texas. On February 24, 1891, Mr. Koehl was united in marriage with Miss Mary Krenek, a daughter of Joseph and Rosa (Bambu) Krenek, who came to Texas from Bohemia. Mr. Krenek was a farmer near Ellinger and died in 1891, while Mrs. Krenek survives. There were eight Krenek children in the family and Mrs. Koehl is the oldest. To Mr. and Mrs. Koehl there have been born seven children, namely: Jacob, who met an accidental death at the age of twenty years; Eugene Henry; Ora Rosa; Rudolph Edward; Eddie; Pearlie, and Lillie Bell. Mr. Koehl is the father of fifteen children, and has eight grandchildren. He is well known and highly respected in the vicinity of his home, where he has a wide circle of acquaintances and numbers his friends by the score.

Dr. Robert Lee Rhea. Among the men who are occupying important positions in the life of San Antonio is found Dr. Robert Lee Rhea, who has contributed materially to the city's welfare in his various capacities as chemist and scientist, veterinary surgeon and city veterinarian, a bacteriologist of more than local reputation, and city chemist in charge of inspecton of milk and dairies. Still a young man, with the best years of his life still before him, Doctor Rhea has already accomplished what it would require most men the better part of a lifetime to achieve, and while winning personal success and reputation, has made it his task to look after the best interests of his adopted city and its people.

Doctor Rhea was born near McKinney, Collin County, Texas, October 10, 1882, and is a son of Mr. and Mrs. J. C. Rhea, both of whom still reside at McKinney. His father, like so many North Texans, was born in Tennessee, and came to Texas in the late '50s, being a pioneer settler of Collin County. He was a Confederate soldier throughout the war between the North and the South, and was in Gen. Robert E. Lee's Army of Northern Virginia, distinguishing himself for bravery and soldierly qualities. He has for a long number of years been a successful farmer and stockman of Collin County, and for the past twenty-five years has lived in the county seat city, McKinney, retired from active duties, although he still retains his valuable land interests in that rich county.

Dr. Robert Lee Rhea is an accomplished gentleman of scientific education of the highest order. He was educated in the public schools of McKinney and in the Missouri Valley College, at Marshall, Missouri, from which he was graduated with the highest honors in 1902. He studied veterinary science in the Kansas City Veterinary College, Kansas City, Missouri, being graduated therefrom in the class of 1905, and following this spent four years as a member of the biological staff, experimental department, in the house of the Parke-Davis Chemical

R. L. Rhea

Company, Detroit, noted all over the world as leaders not only in commercial chemistry but as philanthropists in the field of scientific and biological investigation. This firm, without applause, in an entirely disinterested manner, and without the actual knowledge of the general public, has done an incalculable amount of good in the experiments it has carried on and is still prosecuting, in chemistry, biology and bacteriology, at the expense of hundreds of thousands of dollars, in protecting and preserving human and animal life against disease.

After four years of this excellent training, Mr. Rhea, resigned his position in Detroit and came to San Antonio, in 1909, which city has continued to be his home. Here he established the San Antonio Veterinary Hospital, for the treatment of horses and other animals. In addition he is holding the position of city veterinarian, and, in connection with this duty, is also the officer in charge of the important duty of looking after the milk supply of the city. With his staff of inspectors, he inspects the sources of milk supply and tests the milk of the dairies supplying the city, including all dairy cattle, the tuberculin test being the main feature of this work, of which he is in charge, and which is rigid and most thorough and which has resulted highly favorable to the health of the city. Doctor Rhea is zealous and conscientious in his work, to which he gives his closest attention, but he has found time to take an interest also in the local business and social life of the city, and is a Knight Templar Mason and a Shriner and a member of the San Antonio Rotary Club.

Doctor Rhea married June 4, 1907, Miss Mary Margaret Bucholz, at Tallahassee, Florida, she being a native of Tampa, that state, and they have one son, Robert Lee, Jr.

John Chupick. The late John Chupick, of Ellinger, was for many years a factor in the agricultural life of Texas, in which state he resided from the time he was seven years of age, in 1856, until his death, December 5, 1905. As is indicated by the name, the family is of Bohemian origin, and John Chupick was born May 8, 1849, at Hostalkov, Moravia. His father was Thomas Chupick, a peasant, who brought little with him to the United States save his family, an honorable name, an eager ambition and an indomitable determination. The family crossed the Atlantic and the Gulf of Mexico, landing at Galveston and crossing Buffalo Bayou to Houston, from which city they went to old Ulm by ox-team, the only means of transit during that day. There the little party settled, bought some land and engaged in farming on the American plan. There the father passed his remaining years as an agriculturist, being buried at Wesley, Washington County, where he had finally removed during the declining years of his life. There were the following children in the family: John, of this notice; Jane, who became the wife of Rev. Adolph Chulumsky and some years ago returned to Moravia, but is now a resident of Svartcuch, Bohemia. The mother of these children prior to her marriage with Mr. Chupick had been united with Mr. Elsik, who died leaving her one son, Steve Elsik, who is now a resident of Cistern, Texas.

John Chupick acquired a fairly good education and among his teachers was the late Judge Teichmueller, of LaGrange. He was a farmer until grown and then moved to Brenham, Texas, and was connected with a mercantile business for a time. When he severed his connection with that concern he moved to Ellinger and purchased the farm which his widow and children now own. This was in 1884, when he had been married but a short time, and the purchase was made from Axel Meerschridt, of San Antonio, in company with his half-brother, Steve

Elsik. Some eight years later he purchased the latter's interest and conducted the property actively and successfully until his death. The farm comprises 800 acres, and when he secured it it was largely covered with timber, but Mr. Chupick, with industry and energy, cleared all but about 250 acres, erected one of the best country homes to be found in Fayette County, and made other improvements of a modern and valuable character. He was a man who employed much labor in the clearing and cultivation of his farm. and among those who worked in his employ, as well as among his associates, he was always known as a man of the strictest integrity and business honor. He was a man of few words and lived rather excluively, save among his family, had little concern about political matters, save as they affected him in his capacity of a good and public-spirited citizen of his community. He was something of a traveler, making a trip to Europe after he had attained years of maturity, and often going to various parts of Texas for both business and pleasure. He was a member of the Lutheran Church and his children were reared in that faith.

Mr. Chupick was married in Washington County, Texas, in 1876, to Miss Frances Sebesta, who was born March 19, 1859, daughter of Paul Sebesta, a farmer of Moravia, who came to the United States prior to the Civil war and settled at Wesley, Texas, where Mrs. Chupick was born. The following children were born to John and Frances Chupick: Mary, who is the wife of J. H. Novosad, of East Bernard, Texas; Frances, who married T. S. Hruska, of West, Texas; Alvina, who married Jo J. Settlemeyer, of Flatonia, this state; Annie, who married Emil J. Sulik, of LaGrange, Texas; John F.; Jo S., born December 19, 1892, and now manager of the Chupick estate and farm; and Rosa and Vlasta, twin sisters, who reside with their mother and brother on the home place.

John F. Chupick, son of John and Frances Chupick, was born March 26, 1889, and received his education in the Ellinger and La Grange schools. After completing his education he was connected for a few years with the Ellinger Mercantile Company, and when he disposed of his interests therein became one of the organizers of the First State Bank of Ellinger and was elected its cashier. He resigned from the bank August 1, 1915, and is engaged in general farming and the live stock business with his brother, J. S. Chupick. In their live stock business they raise thoroughbred Duroc Jersey hogs.

Mr. Chupick is one of the progressive, enterprising young business men of Ellinger, and is also one of his community's boosters and is found connected with every movement for the general welfare of his city and its people. Mr. Chupick is unmarried.

Charles Bittner. Among the old and honored residents of Texas, one who grew up from childhood here was Charles Bittner, of Precinct No. 7, Fayette County, and a farmer on Route No. 2, Weimar Rural Free Delivery. In a hale old age, enjoying the fruits of a busy and well ordered life, he shared the wonderful progress which has been made in this phenomenal state, mostly under his own eyes. Mr. Bittner lived in Texas from 1854 until his death on the 2d of April, 1916, having come hither in the former year with his father, who brought out his family, largely composed of daughters, from Saxony, Germany, in the locality of Warder, where Charles Bittner was born in 1842.

The father of Mr. Bittner was Andrew Bittner, and his mother died when he was a small boy, the children of the family being: Anna, who remained in Saxony, and married there; Mary M., who also remained in her native Saxony and is married; Sophia, who married Frank Wangler and lives at New Ulm, Texas; Christina, who married Herman

Seydler, first, and is now the wife of Kinnie Davis, of Pasadena, California; Caroline, who died in Austin County, Texas, as Mrs. Joseph Seyler; Charles, of this review; and Agnes, who married August Franke, of Industry, Texas.

Andrew Bittner and his children started on their voyage to America from Hamburg, on a sailing vessel, and the journey proved a long and dangerous one, the ship meeting unfavorable weather during much of the trip, while cholera broke out on shipboard and claimed a number of victims, and a small brother of Charles Bittner was stricken, died on board ship and was buried at Queenstown, Ireland. After seven weeks, however, the family arrived at Galveston, Texas, from whence they went to Austin County, and there remained until after the Civil war, when Andrew Bittner removed to the home which is now occupied by his son Charles. He had learned the tailor's trade in his youth, and this he followed in connection with farming until after the Civil war. He died on the farm in Fayette County in 1893, when he had reached the advanced age of ninety-one years, three months and nine days.

Charles Bittner securéd some small amount of education in the public schools of his native land, but did not secure any advantages of this nature in the United States, whence he came as a lad of twelve years. Through his own efforts he learned to read and write the English language, and when a young man secured a position as engineer in a sawmill and cotton gin at High Hill. He was thus engaged at the time of the outbreak of the war between the North and the South, and was conscripted into the Confederate service, being placed in Captain Alexander's Company of La Grange. Mr. Bittner went to Brownsville with this company after passing through a siege of typhoid fever, but he had been opposed to slavery as well as to the secession of the states, had no sympathy with the cause of the South, and could not fight with men with whom he had nothing in common, so that at the first opportunity, at Brownsville, he deserted, crossed the line into Mexico, there took a United States steamboat to New Orleans, and enlisted in the First Texas Cavalry, United States army. The company to which he belonged was C, with Captain Zeller in command, while the regiment was commanded by Col. F. J. Davis, who was to later become governor of Texas. This organization served in Louisiana, Mississippi and Alabama, where Mr. Bittner participated in the work of capturing the City of Mobile, and back to New Orleans, where the command was stationed when the war came to its close. Mr. Bittner saw two years and eight months of service under the Stars and Stripes and participated in many hot engagements, but was never wounded nor made a prisoner by the enemy.

When he resumed the duties of peace Mr. Bittner located on the property on which he was married, but remained there only two years and then came to his late home. He was a farmer throughout the years that followed and was successful in his operations, accumulating a large and valuable property and making many improvements thereon, thus contributing to the upbuilding of Fayette County. Mr. Bittner was plain and unassuming in his conduct, but had the faculty of attaching friends whose esteem, once attained, is never forfeited. He was tolerant of the opinions and careful of the rights of others, recognizing the equal liberty of all. In all the relations which a man bears in life he was most exemplary, fulfilling the obligations of citizen, husband, father and neighbor in the kindliest manner. He was not a politician, but in national matters voted with the republican party, and locally he capably served in the capacity of trustee of the district schools.

Mr. Bittner was married December 2, 1866, to Miss Magdalena Billemek, daughter of Andreas Billemek, who brought his family to the

United States from Mehen, Austria, where Mrs. Bittner was born in April, 1844. To this union there have been born the following children: Rosa, who died unmarried; Emma, who married John Heller and died in 1914; Laura, who became the wife of Harry Meyer, of Schulenburg, Texas; Fred, also a resident of Schulenburg; Charles, who is engaged in farming in Fayette County; Miss Ida, who is unmarried and resides with her parents, and Lillian, who married Lad Stavinoha and died in 1909.

CPSIA information can be obtained
at www.ICGtesting.com
Printed in the USA
BVHW04s1724180918
527821BV00007B/245/P

9 781376 348699